THE
ENCYCLOPEDIA
OF
FICTIONAL
PEOPLE

The Most Important Characters of the 20th Century

Compiled by Seth Godin

BOULEVARD BOOKS, NEW YORK

This book is not authorized by the trademark or copyright owners of the
characters that are included.

THE ENCYCLOPEDIA OF FICTIONAL PEOPLE:
The Most Important Characters of the 20th Century

A Boulevard Book / published by arrangement with
Seth Godin Productions, Inc.

PRINTING HISTORY
Boulevard edition / April 1996

The Putnam Berkley World Wide Web site address is
http://www.berkley.com

ISBN: 1-57297-073-1

BOULEVARD
Boulevard Books are published by The Berkley Publishing Group,
200 Madison Avenue, New York, New York 10016.
BOULEVARD and its logo are trademarks
belonging to Berkley Publishing Corporation.

PRINTED IN THE UNITED STATES OF AMERICA

10 9 8 7 6 5 4 3 2 1

ACKNOWLEDGMENTS

I owe heaps of credit and praise to the many people who made this book possible. The editing staff at Seth Godin Productions kibbutzed from start to finish about the importance of John Travolta's character in *Saturday Night Fever* with respect to his later work in *Pulp Fiction,* as well as the genetic makeup of "people" like Mr. Spock. Thanks to Lisa DiMona, Karen Watts, Megan O'Connor, and Amy Winger for their opinions—and to all of their parents for letting them watch so much TV as children. Thanks to Robin Dellabough and Anthony Schneider for their contributions to our literary list (and to their English professors). Elizabeth Beier and Barry Neville, whom we were fortunate enough to work with at Boulevard, have been nothing less than extremely enthusiastic from the beginning. In-house, Julie Maner commanded the ship that was layout with Karen Engelmann on board for interior design. Frances Small and CJ Anastasio rounded out the crew. Robert Hirschfeld as line editor lent us his astute knowledge of the panoramic world that fictional people inhabit, along with Robin Cook's copyediting expertise. David Bloom generated our index.

Special thanks to Amy Winger, who was instrumental in building this book. Her wit, wisdom, and great sense of humor made this book as much fun to create as it is to read.

And then there are our contributors: Repairing VCRs, rereading college favorites, watching *Nick At Nite,* some of the finest couch potatoes, movie buffs, and writers include:

Jose Arroyo	Don Devich	Paula Hunt	Sharon Rapoport
Cathie Bauer	Lisa Donis	Jodi Ross Kahn	Jennifer Robinson
Arnie Bernstein	Glenn Farrington	Paula Ladenburg	Anthony Schneider
Michael Butzgy	Michael Friedman	Richard Levey	Lee Spratt
Lisa Fields Clark	Judith Gerber	David Maslow	Steven Spratt
Teresa Darkin	Nicole Goldstein	Megan O'Connor	Eric Wilinski
Dan DePrez	Larry Houghteling	Greg Oliver	Mark Wukas

INTRODUCTION

Imagine yourself at a cocktail party where the famous fictional folks of this century are hovering over the same hors d'oeuvres and punch bowl. You see Dorothy Gale breathlessly describing Oz to Dirty Harry in one corner, Holden Caulfield ogling Wonder Woman from across the room, and Hazel trading egg recipes with Rocky Balboa in the kitchen. Arthur Bach is chasing his whiskey with vodka. And the place is mobbed with the likes of Charlie Brown, Princess Leia, Edith Bunker, and the Silver Surfer. Betty Boop is holding court poolside, while Perry Mason and Atticus Finch talk shop nearby.

The comparisons between real people and those who inhabit the fictional realm are endless. People have probably even made a few choice references to who they think you are, flattering or not. Chances are you have worked with a Willy Loman. You probably know Roseanne better than your own mother and wish that your dad could be as understanding as Jim Anderson. You are more afraid of Freddie Krueger than of anything that your own mind could muster.

Our vernacular is saturated with references to Ginger and Maryanne, Mr. Magoo, the Brady kids, and Norman Bates. We all know a Lois Lane, an Alexander Portnoy, a Barney Fife. They are touchstones, they are archetypes, they are vital elements of the scenery that let us know we're safe at home and among friends in this cockamamie century. All of these people loom large in the American consciousness—they inhabit a landscape that's as real and familiar as your own backyard. In fact, it is your own backyard!

WHO'S IN, WHO'S NOT

What makes someone a "fictional person" for the purposes of this book? Do we limit the book to just humans, or can we take a more catholic approach to what we describe as a person? Do we include Spock? He is, of course, only half human. Alice in Wonderland has much in common with the average girl, but unfortunately she has a neck that can stretch out the window. The Terminator acts like a man but is able to withstand a mortar blast. Superman was born on another planet. And once you start including aliens and robots, you open the door to an arkful of creatures, from Flipper to Mr. Ed. And then there are those people who are not really fictional. Kramer's here but not Jerry Seinfeld. Ozzie, Harriet, and Ricky, too—they are too real to be invited to this fictional gala.

We've drawn a line in the sand dividing fictional people who make the cut for the *Encyclopedia of Fictional People* and those who don't. Here are some of the admittedly arbitrary criteria you must

meet if you want to turn up in the book:

- You must be some sort of type. Somewhere, someone is using your name to describe someone else. Rabbit Angstrom is the suburban underachiever. Ann Darrow is the classic damsel in distress.

- You must have been popularized (if not necessarily originated) in the 20th century, and your primary residence must be the good old U.S. of A. Unless, like James Bond or Tarzan or Miss Marple, you have transcended international boundaries and become a part of the collective American psyche.

- You should have a generally human approach to being alive. You must walk on two feet (sorry, Scooby-Doo), not have a snout (sorry, Miss Piggy), and be basically anatomically correct (neither the Simpsons nor the Teenage Mutant Ninja Turtles have five digits on each hand, but the Simpsons don't have snouts, and well, they live in a house, not the sewer. Simpsons in—Turtles out.)

In other words, this book could really be called the *Mostly American, Slightly Xenophobic Encyclopedia of Twentieth-Century Fictional People, Plus a Few Humanoids and Aliens, but No One with a Snout.*

HOW TO USE THIS BOOK

This book is organized alphabetically, by last name, if such information exists. Otherwise, look for fictional people under their first (or only) name. Barbie, for instance, you find in the Bs. Hawkeye Pierce you'll find under P. Like that. The "See" line at the end of each entry directs you to one or two major works where you can see these people in action.

Hey, I don't remember the doctor's name from *Lost in Space*! If this is the case, don't despair—use the index to look up *Lost in Space,* and you'll find the page numbers listed where *Lost in Space* entries appear. (His name is Dr. Zachary Smith.) For readers who might consider themselves more literary than tube-ular, selected authors are also included in the index. Mostly the biggies—the Faulkners and Hemingways of the world. For fictional people who live in the works of any of these authors, you'll find the corresponding page numbers listed here.

So, sidle up to the bar and get yourself a drink. The Partridge Family is playing your favorite song. I think Veronica Lodge just winked in your direction.

Who are you?

ABANDANDO, DONNA

A blond bombshell who works as a secretary at New York City's 15th Precinct, Donna talks with a New York accent and walks with a New York swing. She's very sweet, and somewhat guarded when it comes to men. (She got burned by a married guy she was in love with.) She gets involved with one of the detectives at the precinct, **Gregory Medavoy**.

See *NYPD Blue*

ABBOTT BRADFORD, SANDRA SUE "ABBY"

Supermom. She's active, intelligent, understanding, and career-oriented almost as much as family-devoted. And she's also gorgeous, looking far younger than she actually is. Abby is married to **Tom Bradford**; together, with their children from their previous marriages, they have a total of eight kids.

See *Eight Is Enough*

KING ACHMED

A big, bumbling, mustachioed buffoon, Achmed is king of Warshovia, an itsy-bitsy country in central Europe. When he catches his wife cavorting with the notorious rake **Count Danilo**, he decides to kill two birds with one stone by sending Danilo to Paris to woo and wed the wealthy widow **Sonia**, ensuring that she and her riches stay in Warshovia.

See *The Merry Widow*

ADAMS, EBEN

A starving artist in New York City, who has been unable to endow his paintings with depth of meaning until he meets a young girl in Central Park and paints her portrait. Encouraged when he's able to sell the work, he returns to the park every day to wait for her return. Pleasant and warm, he becomes obsessed with finding more about the girl. His life used to be about painting and now he finds himself in the middle of a mystery that he must solve. He finds himself falling in love with the girl and the portrait that he paints of her contains his feelings for her.

See *Portrait of Jenny*

ADAMS, DR. GALEN

Doc's a curmudgeon. To his way of thinking, there are only two ways to do things in Doc's world: his way or the wrong way. He patches up gunshot wounds and cures diaper rash with the same crusty manner, doling out advice whether you ask for it or not. But under that off-putting facade beats a heart of solid gold. And he makes house calls.

See *Gunsmoke*

ADAMS, KAY

She is a prototypical blond WASP with bouffant hair who's wooed and won by World War II hero **Michael Corleone**, scion of the sinister, powerful Corleone family. She discovers, too late, the nature of the family into which she has married and suffers agonies of contradictory emotions: love for Michael and their children and loathing for the family ethics and profession. Though she's gullible and naive early on, she sheds her illusions and becomes more assertive about her personal morality as the years go by. Unlike earlier generations of submissive Corleone women, Kay isn't about to subordinate her feelings and position and become a docile, deferential housewife.

See *The Godfather,* Mario Puzo

ADAMS, NICK

Nick, a doctor's son, experiences early and throughout his life the random violence and brutality of the world. It might be watching his father operate without anesthesia on an Indian woman in northern Michigan or experiencing firsthand the horrors of World War I. It can happen while he's fishing, or when he nearly falls afoul of two hired killers searching for another man at a restaurant where he's eating. Sensitive, honest, and questioning, Adams comes to learn that life fits Thomas Hobbes's description as being "nasty, brutish and short." Through it all, Nick remains self-reliant and uncomplaining, enduring all of life's misfortunes with a quiet dignity despite the enormous pain.

See *The Nick Adams Stories,* Ernest Hemingway

ADAMS, POOKIE

Pookie is a college-age woman caught between her need for love and her desire for independence. She's prone to eccentric behavior and depressive mood cycles. Pookie also tells elaborate stories, often with only the most ephemeral basis in truth. She's willing to act on her burgeoning sexuality. A creative

Courtesy of Paramount Pictures

Pookie Adams

manipulator of the English language.
See *The Sterile Cuckoo*

ADAMS, RICHARD
Maverick television news camera operator who knows how to get a great shot, no matter what the circumstances. Also handy when it comes to running his camera under clandestine situations. The favorite working partner of television news reporter **Kimberly Wells**.
See *The China Syndrome*

ADAMS, MAJOR SETH
Major Adams, with his trusty crew, leads wagon trains from the East to destinations in the West. His crew—scouts, cook, and the rest—are all first class, and know their jobs well. As a Civil War veteran, he knows when to fight and when to run for cover, without letting his ego get in the way. He's steady and strong, and an ideal leader. Hire Adams to run your wagon train, and you know he'll be there all the way. It's hard to get that kind of help nowadays.
See *Wagon Train*

THE ADDAMS FAMILY
A ghoulish-American family. Gomez is the loving husband and father with a bent for anything self-destructive. The mustachioed paterfamilias favors baggy pin-striped suits and big cigars. He spends much of his day following his fortune on a ticker-tape stock machine. His wife, Morticia, is tall, beautiful and…well, somewhat embalmed-looking. Somber and serene, she likes to hold court in a large rattan chair. She loves horticulture, pampering her rare flesh-eating plants. **Uncle Fester Frump** is Morticia's brother, but Gomez's partner in crime. He's bald and wears monk-like robes. Fester's favorite party trick is to pop a light bulb in his mouth and light it. Pugsley is Gomez and Morticia's spoiled son. Pudgy and mean, he's especially loathsome toward his sister, Wednesday Thursday, who can hold her own in the skullduggery department. Cute on the outside, but macabre on the inside, Wednesday likes to unnerve the Addams's visitors. Grandmama Addams sometimes seems normal, compared to the rest of her family. But she's no sweet little old lady; she's a practicing witch. **Lurch** is a seven-foot-tall butler with a short vocabulary. He greets each visitor with the question "you rang?" While Lurch is possessed of almost superhuman strength, he is a gentle soul by nature. Finally, there's Thing. Thing is there whenever any of the family members need a hand. A disembodied hand, that is, who lives in a black box. Thing is smart and resourceful—for a hand.
See *The Addams Family*

ADDAMS, FRANKIE
Frankie is a skinny, lonely twelve-year-old tomboy on the cusp of adolescence. She wants to be accepted as a grown-up, but still has scrapes on her knees and throws tantrums. When her big brother gets married, she imagines herself a member of the wedding party, and is crushed when not allowed to go along on his honeymoon. Her best friend is her myopic cousin, and she seeks comfort in the arms of her family's black maid, who seems to be the only person who understands her.
See *Member of the Wedding,* Carson McCullers

ADDISON, DAVID
Cocky, handsome detective, and partner in the Blue Moon Detective Agency in Los Angeles. He's very fond of alliterative phrases like "Do bears bear? Do bees bee?" and refers to his lovely partner, **Maddie Hayes,** as "Blondie Blonde." He has a thing for Maddie, which takes a very long time in being consummated. David once got counseling from none other than Ray Charles.
See *Moonlighting*

ADRIAN
Rocky Balboa's mousy, Olive Oylish girl, and sister of Rocky's dumb but loyal assistant, **Paulie.** Frail, slender, and sensitive, she's the greatest possible contrast to her fiancé's muscularity and brutishness. Adrian loves the pets in the shop where she works, and wants nothing more than to convince Rocky to quit his primitive, dangerous career as a fighter. She hangs in there, though, through the remarkable ups and downs of his fistic career. When all is said and done, she believes in standing by her man—whether the man is vertical or horizontal, whole or battered and bruised. "Yo, Adrian," Rocky cries, and Adrian comes running.
See *Rocky*

AGENT 99

Femme fatale secret agent. Crack espionage agent for the U.S. intelligence agency CONTROL in Washington, D.C. She usually and unaccountably defers to slightly more senior (male) Agent 86, **Maxwell Smart**, whom she loves. 99 is often chosen by the **Chief** to work with Max and usually ends up saving the operation he has botched. She has style, wit, intelligence, and the lean beauty of a model. Her poses and disguises often lead powerful bad men to fall in love with her, much to Max's dismay and jealousy. Even KAOS's **Siegfried** finds her attractive. Her knowledge of esoteric cultures and historical events is often the key to discovering the evil plans of Siegfried. She likes to let Max feel he has saved the day. "Oh, Max! Hurry, Max, hurry!"

See *Get Smart*

AGENT X-9

X–9 is so secretive no one knows his name or even the agency he's working for, which happens to be the FBI. Tough-talking but smooth living, X–9's gritty use of street lingo clashes with his penchant for silk smoking jackets and fashionable furniture. On the job he's cool, efficient, and equally quick with a gun or a witty one-liner.

See *Secret Agent X–9*

SISTER AGNES

A hyperemotional, pale, angelic novice whose dreamy flights of spiritual fervor and frightening acts of religious prostration are a cause for concern on the part of her mother superior. The young Agnes's devotion is without question, but her mental state is suspect: she believes that the young baby to whom she gave birth is the son of God.

See *Agnes of God*

ALADDIN

A street urchin who lives from moment to moment and hand to mouth. Quick and nimble, he's deemed a "street rat" by authorities. Often eats on the run (usually without paying). By the way, Aladdin is served by a genie from a magic lamp and travels on a talking flying carpet. He's shy and romantic when it comes to the love of his life, beautiful Princess Jasmine.

See *Aladdin*

ALBRIGHT, SALLY

University of Chicago graduate of 1977, traveling to New York with a ridesharing partner, **Harry Burns**, whom she doesn't like very much. She plans to be a journalist and keeps running into Harry throughout the next decade. Skills: writing a compelling news story, keeping up with the latest hair styles, imitating a woman having an orgasm.

See *When Harry Met Sally*

ALEX

Wearing white from head to toe, he was once the proto-punk, fifteen-year-old leader of an ultra-violent gang of teenage rockers. Alex speaks "nadsat," an argot of Russianized British and American slang, drinks spiked milk, and listens to Beethoven while fantasizing about assault and rape. Has spent considerable time defying the restrictions of his futuristic, repressive society by leading his "droogies"—buddies—in all-night orgies of random violence and destruction. Finally imprisoned, he is subjected to the "Ludovico Technique," a form of aversion therapy that "reconditions" him into a "clockwork orange"—a human being on the outside, but reduced to mechanical reactions within, whom the state holds up as a "model citizen." Not only is Alex now incapable of violence, but the mere sight of it nauseates him. Refers to sex as "the old in-out."

See *A Clockwork Orange,* **Anthony Burgess**

Agent 99

ALFIE

A cynical, womanizing Londoner who aspires to rise to the upper classes, he's held

Sergeant Suzanne Anderson

back by his pronounced Cockney accent. He's amoral and callous with the opposite sex, has a penchant for American cigarettes and trendy clothing. A swinging bachelor of the mod generation.
See *Alfie*

ALLEN, CLARA

Twenty years ago, Clara Allen was a beauty in love with Texas Ranger **Augustus McCrae**. She chose to marry another man (now dead), and the years since have taken a toll on her. But they've strengthened her, too, and in Gus's eyes, she's still as beautiful as the day they met.
See *Lonesome Dove,* Larry McMurtry

ALLNUT, CHARLIE

The scruffy, gin-drinking captain of the leaky, smoke-belching *African Queen*, a supply boat that plies the Congo River. Canadian Allnut loves independence from government, responsibility, and women, all the more reason for his reluctance to allow prim, Bible-toting **Rose Sayer** to ride on his boat after her missionary brother is killed. With his permanent five o'clock shadow, ever-present cigarette, and coarse manner, Allnut is the picture of middle-aged manhood gone to jungle seed. Still, he does try to be on his best behavior when around his ramrod-straight, teetotal passenger, though it's a sore trial. But because he's a good man at heart, his appreciation and attraction toward his remarkable passenger increase with time and proximity.
See *The African Queen,* James Agee

ALPINE, FRANK

A young Italian American whose ambitions far outpace his abilities, Frank arrives in Brooklyn, broke and with no prospects. He robs a Jewish storekeeper, but makes amends and is hired as the man's assistant. When Frank falls in love with the storekeeper's daughter, he becomes intensely interested in Judaism, ultimately converts, and takes over the store after his employer dies.
See *The Assistant,* Bernard Malamud

ALQUIST, PAULA

The meek, gentle niece of a famous opera singer inherits her aunt's home and unknowingly marries her murderer. Paula returns from an idyllic honeymoon with her husband, **Gregory Anton**, but his cool behavior soon has her on edge. Paula's painfully submissive manner puts her at a disadvantage with her sharp-tongued maid, **Nancy Oliver**, whom she suspects of trying to alienate her husband's affections. What she doesn't know is that her husband was initially drawn to her money and jewels, and plans to drive her crazy and immure her forever in a mental institution.
See *Gaslight*

ALTMAN, AARON

A quick-witted, savvy news reporter, he's willing to go on any assignment and is committed to seeing that the broadcast audience is exposed to important stories. Not so secretly craves position as both news anchor and love interest in producer **Jane Craig**'s life. Has difficulty controlling sweat glands at inopportune moments.
See *Broadcast News*

CAPTAIN AMERICA

Freelance artist and crimefighter. Captain America wears red, white, and blue, and never, but NEVER, tries any dirty tricks. He was so frail and skinny as a youth that the Army rejected him. However, his earnest pleas got him into a top-secret program called Operation: Rebirth. Now appropriately reborn, he fights for liberty and justice. Captain America has no superpowers, but is humanly strong as can be; he can press 800 pounds. His only weapons are a Vibranium-Adamantium alloy shield and his expertise at hand-to-hand combat. He keeps a nondescript home base in Brooklyn Heights, New York, and travels the country fighting crime in a custom-built Chevy van that holds his modified Harley. He's currently an active member of the Avengers.
See *Captain America*

THE ANDERSON FAMILY

Family life can't get any better than at the wholesome Anderson home on South Maple Street in Springfield. James, a manager at General Insurance Company, and Margaret, a perfectly cheerful and sincere housewife, spend all their time with their three nicknamed kids, Betty ("Princess"), James Jr. ("Bud"), and Kathy ("Kitten"). Though the siblings have the usual spats and rivalries, no hard feelings ever last, often thanks to James Sr.'s calm wisdom.

James never loses his temper with his kids, but he sometimes is disappointed with their decisions. When giving his wife a driving lesson, though, there was considerable tension in the air. But the well-adjusted kids smooth over the fiasco by pointing out "we should give thanks to heaven each night that we have parents who don't bicker and quarrel." Betty is dark haired and attractive, bearing strong resemblance to her mother. She's unsure of what she wants to do with her life, besides marry the perfect man. She and Bud are always fighting over use of the bathroom. Bud's chief concerns are cars and girls, whom he can't understand. Bud's handsome, and a football player, but not obnoxious. He's a good brother to his little sister, Kitten, whom he calls "Squirt." Kitten fears she's ugly and is frequently jealous of her beautiful and popular older sister. Kitten is really cute as a bug, and a whole lot of fun. The Andersons eat at a meticulously set table, have talks with Dad in his den, and everyone sleeps in separate beds, including James and Margaret.

See *Father Knows Best*

ANDERSON, ARLISS COATES

Arliss is the archetypal frontier boy: trouble on the hoof, with more energy than he knows how to manage. He races from one thing to another, trying to experience everything in his world at the same time. When he gets a dog, Old Yeller, he finds himself a perfect match for mischief.

See *Old Yeller*

ANDERSON, ESTHER

Aunt Esther is the constant bane of brother-in-law **Fred Sanford**'s existence; the two fight like cats and dogs (he's not above calling her ugly; she's not above returning the favor). Esther runs the Sanford Arms, a rooming house next door to Fred's junkyard. She is married to Woody.

See *Sanford and Son*

ANDERSON, RUPERT

Rupert began his career as a southern sheriff and then graduated to the FBI. He's tough, canny, and goal-oriented. He believes that the end justifies the means and will go to any length to get the job done, even if he has to break the law in the process.

See *Mississippi Burning*

ANDERSON, SERGEANT SUZANNE

This tough, athletic, blond, unmarried sergeant of the Los Angeles Police Department is teamed with Sergeant Bill Crowley, but they work regularly with Detectives Joe Styles and Pete Royster. She is usually known by the nickname Pepper.

See *Police Woman*

ANDRE

An enigmatic, once-successful stage director, Andre gives up that career to be a "spiritual seeker," traveling the world in search of "inner truth." A master storyteller, he weaves hypnotic tales of Druid death rituals in Polish forests and Buddhist monks who can balance their bodies on the tips of two fingers. Yet, though he seems to have tried practically everything under the sun, he has seen only small glimpses of "truth," and is as restless as ever. A keen student of life, lanky Andre is insatiably curious about other people's stories, which makes him a good listener. Unlike his timid, pleasure-loving friend, **Wally**, Andre is a risk taker, who has a basic distrust of modern comforts and conveniences. He tells Wally that he would much rather lie in bed shivering with cold than use an electric blanket, since being cold at least reminds you that you're alive.

See *My Dinner with Andre*

ANDREWS, ALEXANDER

Millionaire Andrews spends most of his time looking out for what he perceives to be the welfare of daughter **Ellie**. For instance, he does all he can, including arranging her kidnapping, to stop her from marrying aviator King Wesley. "You're a sucker to go through with this."

See *It Happened One Night*

ANDREWS, ARCHIE

Redheaded Archie, with his preppie outfits and good-times attitude, is the ultimate middle American teenager. His primary occupations are (wholesome) rock 'n' roll, dancing, and hanging out at the local burger joint with his slightly dense but affable buddy Jughead, pert and blond **Betty Cooper**, and slinky, dark-haired Veronica Lodge.

See *Archie*

ANDREWS, ELLIE

She's willful, spoiled, pampered, and beautiful, and the daughter of millionaire **Alexander Andrews.** Ellie admits that she comes from "a long line of stubborn idiots." She jumps a boat in Miami in an attempt to stop her father from meddling in her life and buys a bus ticket to New York. On the bus, she meets up with a whole class of people she's never known, including newspaperman **Peter Warne.** She got on the bus planning to marry pilot King Wesley, primarily as an act of rebellion against Daddy, but by the time she reaches New York, she's had a radical change of heart.

See *It Happened One Night*

ANDY

A quiet, boyish banker sent to prison for murdering his wife and lover. He maintains his innocence and a strange serenity during his years of incarceration. Projects like rebuilding the prison's library and doing taxes for the warden and guards keep him busy, but his real vocation is kept hidden even from his closest friend.

See *The Shawshank Redemption*

ANGSTROM, HARRY "RABBIT"

This Pennsylvanian has his moment of glory as a high school basketball star. Everything after that is anticlimax. He marries girlfriend **Janice Springer** when he gets her pregnant. After tragedy strikes the young family, he runs away from his responsibilities and takes up with another woman, in what begins a repetitive pattern of separation from, and reunion with, Janice (who leaves him for a time, during a rebellious period). He flounders in various enterprises, including fatherhood. He and son Nelson have an ever-strained and difficult relationship. For a long time, Rabbit works in his father's printing business, until automation closes it down. Then he goes to work in his father-in-law's car dealership and manages to achieve a degree of success and relative affluence. Rabbit lives through a lot of history—the Vietnam War, the Apollo space missions, OPEC, the space shuttle—and very slowly comes to terms with the fact that he'll never be eighteen again. This is not to say that he ever attains anything like enlightenment. In his case, age and wisdom don't go together.

See *Rabbit Run*, John Updike

ANNIE

A tough little orphan who picked herself up by the bootstraps and teaches others to do the same, Annie nonetheless depends on the benevolence of Oliver "Daddy" Warbucks, a millionaire industrialist who adopted Annie from a grim city orphanage and protects her from evildoers. Accompanied by a pet dog named Sandy, Annie often ventures from the Warbucks mansion, spending much of her time with ordinary folks and convincing them of the virtues of hard work and frugality. With her trademark mop of red curls, she likes to spend her time working on household chores while delivering sermons on the importance of individual responsibility. Sandy usually agrees: "Arf!"

See *Little Orphan Annie*

ANNIE

Since her driver's license was suspended for speeding, she rides the bus around the greater Los Angeles area. Actually, she once drove the bus around, jumping road construction sites and making unbelievable hairpin turns. Has been held hostage by mad bomber **Howard Payne** and is beginning an intense romance with Lieutenant **Jack Traven.** "It's like driving a really big Pinto."

See *Speed*

ANTHONY, MICHAEL

The executive secretary to **John Beresford Tipton,** a reclusive financier who gives away a million dollars to a different stranger every week. Anthony is very proper and always wears a hat, which he politely doffs when entering someone's home to present him or her with a million-dollar check. He reports the results of what happens to these new millionaires to his boss.

See *The Millionaire*

ANTON, GREGORY

A smooth, suave murderer who kills a famous opera singer for her jewels and then marries the woman's niece, **Paula Alquist,** in order to retrieve them. Anton's postnuptial scheme is to slowly drive her mad, pack her off to an asylum, and live happily ever after on her wealth. Toward this villainous end, he makes full use of the ambience of their dark, gloomy mansion and takes advantage of the attraction he holds for the maid, **Nancy Oliver,** to make

her an ally in his machinations—this even though he cares nothing for the poor, deluded menial. Not only is he a murderer, he's also a cad!
See *Gaslight*

ANTONY, BRUNO
A suave psychopath who likes to pop kids' balloons for fun. The kind of guy who accidentally nearly strangles a fellow cocktail partyer. When he meets professional tennis player **Guy Haines** on a train, he proposes a deal whereby each of them would help the other by committing a murder. The logic is impeccable, if chilling: the two men are strangers, and neither would be a suspect in a murder with which he has no visible connection. The plan shocks and repels Haines, but Antony finds it irresistible and carries out his part of the bargain. When Guy reneges, Bruno is very miffed indeed. And a poorer sport you'd have to go a long way to find.
See *Strangers on a Train,* Patricia Highsmith

MR. APPLEGATE
Devilish deal-maker who can provide what is necessary for someone who offers to swap a soul. Currently working on arrangement with baseball person **Joe Boyd**. Often assisted by **Lola** in his work.
See *Damn Yankees*

APPLETON, JENNY
This cheerful, raven-haired girl has a past which becomes a secret to be unlocked by **Eben Adams**. The daughter of high-wire performers, she's a bubbly, happy girl who likes to sing and grows up to be a beautiful young woman. There is an air of mystery about her, since her dress and manners seem to be from another time. She enjoys having her picture painted and the attention that Eben pays her. Evasive and reluctant to volunteer much information about herself, she nonetheless guides Eben down the road to uncovering the secret that she has been hiding.
See *Portrait of Jenny*

AQUAMAN
This combination of fish and human was happy when he was king of Atlantis and married to the lovely Mera. But the death of their son drove his wife bonkers, and Aquaman left Atlantis to roam around the world's oceans and brood. Then, to top it off, he loses a hand to a piranha. It's replaced initially by a harpoon and later by an ultra-high-tech hook. He talks to fish; they listen up.
See *Aquaman*

ARAGORN
Aragorn, heir to the thrones of Arnor and Gondor, is raised and educated in Rivendell until his noble birth is revealed to him by **Elrond**. His royal lineage makes him leader of the Dúnedain, also known as Rangers, men who live and work in the wilds, quietly protecting the peoples of Middle Earth from evils they scarcely dream exist. Valiant, resourceful, and wise, Aragorn works with **Gandalf**, and his fellow Rangers play an instrumental role during the War of the Ring. He is both a member of the Fellowship of the Ring and a captain of the West, after the fellowship's dissolution. Reclaiming his throne after the war, Aragorn marries Arwen, an elf, the daughter of Elrond, and reestablishes peace in Middle Earth. They have one son, Eldarion, and many daughters.
See *The Lord of the Rings,* J. R. R. Tolkien

ARBUCKLE, JON
He's a loser with women, although he can't stop trying to pick women up, especially Garfield's veterinarian. He's easily entertained and just as easily befuddled by the antics of his cat, Garfield, and his dog, Odie. Has no taste in ties.
See *Garfield*

ARCOLA, CHARLES "CHACHI"
A rough-around-the-edges teenage boy. Chachi's a miniature version of his uncle, the ultra-cool **Fonzie**. He has a raspy voice and wears leather and jeans. Though he looks like a tough, he really isn't. A girl-magnet, but his heart belongs to nice girl **Joanie Cunningham**, much to her parents' chagrin. Mechanic.
See *Happy Days*

ARDEN, DALE
Dale is the sidekick and plucky longtime companion of space warrior **Flash Gordon**. Usually garbed in boots, short skirts, and intergalactic hairstyles. A feminist who has pioneered women's roles in outer-space warfare. Along with Flash and **Dr. Zarkov**,

BAD INSURANCE
RISKS

Inspector Jacques Clouseau
John Rambo
Indiana Jones
Lucy Ricardo
James Bond

she abhors the evil ruler **Ming the Merciless**.
See *Flash Gordon*

ARMITAGE, WILLIE

Willie is a "walk softly and carry a big stick" type of guy. This muscleman, employed by a secret U.S. government agency, does most of the heavy lifting for the ultra-elite, ultra-secret Impossible Mission Force. His job description is actually twofold: he sets up the devices the team is going to need, and, once the mission has been executed, he dismantles them and loads them onto the vehicle. He likes this job because there is no math or deep thinking required.
See *Mission: Impossible*

ARMSTRONG, CHRISTINE

She is a pretty, pert, serious career woman, a TV anchorwoman in Minneapolis, Minnesota, who dates and eventually marries coach **Hayden Fox**. Struggles to enlighten the old-fashioned Hayden on women's issues and deal with his chauvinism. Compassionate, giving, but true to herself. Often wonders why she loves Hayden, who seldom understands her needs.
See *Coach*

ARNOLD, JACK

This grumpy, fatigued father of three works hard and has achieved the American Dream—a house in the suburbs, a lawn mower, and a barbecue. He has as an attractive wife he grumbles at and kids he doesn't really know. Wants his home to be his sanctuary, but he never quite knows what happiness is.
See *The Wonder Years*

ARNOLD, KEVIN

Kevin's an adorable, cherubic, suburban boy-next-door during the Cold War years. He goes through typical adolescent worries about girls, sex, and growing up. Smart and clean-cut, Kevin is nicer and more polite than most teenage boys. He is unusually perceptive about the way people behave, has a constant flow of questions, and is a deep thinker, for a kid. Kevin does have a tendency to worry a lot. He's not a source of grief to his parents and is neither a hugely popular guy nor a social loser, like his best friend, **Paul Pfeiffer**. He has a huge crush on, and an up-and-down relationship

with, his cute neighbor, **Winnie Cooper**. Like most kid brothers, he's tortured by older, obnoxious brother, Wayne.
See *The Wonder Years*

ARNOLD, NORMA

A 1960s housewife, she's cute and chirpy but restless. Norma loves her family but seems disappointed in the way things have turned out. Her three kids and husband **Jack** don't seem to really notice her. She seems more than a little naive for an adult. Her desire for perfection in all things often leads to frustration.
See *The Wonder Years*

ARNOLD, WAYNE

Obnoxious, rude, and loud teenage boy. He's a doofus. Wayne takes sadistic pleasure in torturing younger brother **Kevin**. Wayne thinks he's a laff riot, especially if he's simulating body noises or getting Kevin into trouble. Kind of a whiner. Not too bright and doesn't really care about school. Desperately wants a girlfriend. Good luck to him.
See *The Wonder Years*

ARREGUI, VALENTIN

This tough, macho Marxist writer and fervent revolutionary is imprisoned for antigovernment activities in South America. There, he becomes a "rebellious instigator" of prison hunger strikes. He's initially disgusted by flamboyant homosexual cellmate **Luis Molina**'s intricate plot descriptions of old films: "You gays never face facts. Fantasies are no escape." Arregui reads daily to keep his mind alert. Though his present girlfriend is an unlettered leader in the movement, he guiltily dreams of a prior love, a beautiful bourgeoise who represents everything he is fighting against. An atheist who insists, "Social revolution, that's what's important, and gratifying the senses is only secondary," he nonetheless becomes Molina's lover.
See *Kiss of the Spider Woman*, Manuel Puig

ARTHUR

Hip, funny, smart 1980s Pittsburgh slacker/ Generation Xer. He doesn't get on with his father, an overbearing gangster who doesn't understand or respect his uncommitted, spiritually confused way of life. He's drawn to Cleveland, an anarchic, motorcycling party animal. He flirts with and sleeps with Phlox, a cute girl, but then realizes that his true interest lies in an altogether different direction.

See *The Mysteries of Pittsburgh,* Michael Chabon

ARUJA, DAISY

Portuguese American girl living a blue-collar life in Mystic, Connecticut, where she works in a pizza place with her little sister, **Kat**. A gorgeous, tough-mouthed, big-haired party girl, Daisy would like nothing more than to end up with Charles, a rich preppy with a Porsche and a mean game of darts. Despite class differences and a tempestuous courtship, she and Charles end up building an unlikely but strong love. And despite her resentment of Kat's seemingly bright future, Daisy is there in the crunch for her little sister, helping her learn a tough lesson about the pain of love.

See *Mystic Pizza*

ARUJA, KAT

A cute goody-two-shoes whose wardrobe should be pictured in the dictionary next to the word "preppy"—but in fact she's a blue-collar Portuguese American from Mystic, Connecticut. Kat frowns on her gorgeous older sister **Daisy**'s party-girl antics and awaits the start of her first year at Yale. While babysitting to earn money for school, she meets and falls for an older, married man, an architect with a Yale degree. When she's dumped by the Yalie, Daisy proves there's some intelligence you can't get from books, giving Kat valuable advice about the vagaries of love, not to mention moral support.

See *Mystic Pizza*

ASHBURNHAM, EDWARD

In public, Ashburnham is the model English gentleman with unassailable scruples and a seemingly perfect marriage. In private, he's plagued by uncontrollable sexual aggressiveness, financial irresponsibility, and an utter lack of feeling for his wife. A train of illicit affairs culminates in the suicides of two people, including his own.

See *The Good Soldier,* Ford Madox Ford

ASHLEY, LADY BRETT

A beautiful, emotionally scarred young English-woman who serves as a nurse in the army during World War I. Her innocent love affair with a young soldier ends when he dies, and she embarks on a series of affairs with worthless men. Separated from her husband, a British lord, she lives in Paris and allies herself with a coterie of gay men. "Mannish" and modern, she is an offense to the sensibilities of her age—she smokes, drinks too much, is in the process of a divorce, and is promiscuous. Like **Jake Barnes**, the man she loves (as opposed to the man she is engaged to, the loutish Michael Campbell), she is a hard-boiled realist trying to cope in a world without the moral order once provided by organized religion.

See *The Sun Also Rises,* Ernest Hemingway

AUDREY

This pretty bleached blonde works as a dental assistant to **Orin Scrivello**. She speaks in a high, squeaky voice. Audrey's goal in life is modest: a house in the suburbs with a white picket fence. But she's trapped in the urban environs of Skid Row, where houses and picket fences are scarce. Worse yet, she's often on the receiving end of the sadistic impulses of Scrivello. Her attraction to and involvement with **Seymour Krelboin** lead to her untimely ingestion by Audrey II, a carnivorous plant from outer space.

See *Little Shop of Horrors*

AUNT CLARA

A charming, sweet little old lady, Aunt Clara is also a witch. Aunt to **Samantha Stephens**, her heart is in the right place, but her powers, and memory, are decidedly not. Trying to get an electrician, she once conjured up Ben Franklin instead. Collects doorknobs.

See *Bewitched*

AUSTIN, STEVE

After he survived the crash of an M3F5 test plane, astronaut Steve Austin was "a man barely alive," so the feds rebuilt him with superhuman bionic parts—two legs, an arm, and an eye—to the tune of 6 mil, a nice chunk of change at that time (and still). Now he works for the OSI, a secret government organization, fighting international crime—and the occasional Sasquatch. He can literally jump buildings in a single bound. He jogs 60 mph without breaking a sweat or breathing hard (there's less organic tissue for his heart to send blood to).

See *The Six Million Dollar Man* and *The Bionic Woman*

AVERY, DICK

A famous American fashion photographer with an international reputation, now shooting in Paris. Currently, Dick is working on transforming newcomer **Jo Stockton** into the next superstar model of the fashion industry. In addition to his talents with a camera, Avery also has considerable gifts for singing and dancing, which he uses at the drop of a hat.

See *Funny Face*

AVERY, SHUG

An alcoholic lounge singer in the rural South, she's the mistress of a man named **Mister**, who flaunts Shug in the face of **Celie**, his wife. Shug is world-weary and disillusioned about men and life in general, but eventually forms an intimate bond with Celie, finding for the first time someone who really cares for her.

See *The Color Purple*, Alice Walker

B.C.

He may be a caveman, but he's got an inquiring mind. And there are apparently as many puzzles in his world as there are in ours. He wants nothing more than to understand the world around him. From baseball to the meaning of life, his is an excursion into a world that doesn't necessarily make sense, though it does provide enough diversity to keep it interesting.

See *B.C.*

B.D.

In the 1960s, he was a star quarterback at Yale, but since then, he doesn't have much to do except sit around in his football helmet, parroting the conservative Republican Party line. His main squeeze is blond bimbo **Boopsie**. An army reservist who serves in the Gulf War, he eventually has his helmet surgically removed.

See *Doonesbury*

BABBITT, CHARLIE

A smooth-talking, slightly oily importer of Ferraris that don't exactly conform to EPA standards. Upon the death of his father, he has learned of a brother, **Raymond Babbitt**, who had been sequestered in an institution. Charlie's a hustler who's constantly looking to "beat the system," whether in his automobile dealings or at the Las Vegas blackjack tables. He is also involved in an on-again, off-again relationship with girlfriend Susanna. Charles Babbitt has a long history of attempting to cheat the system—and being thwarted. Style is very important to him—in both dress and presentation. His temper is shorter than it ought to be, which works against him at times, especially when up against adversity.

See *Rain Man*

BABBITT, GEORGE F.

He is a highly representative member of America's keep-up-with-the-Joneses, materialistic bourgeoisie. A real estate agent in suburban Zenith, Babbitt is, on the surface, a true believer in conformity and acquisition. He has a wife, Myra, and three kids—mainly, it seems, for the sake of propriety and appearance, as he rarely seems to think of them when he doesn't have to. He's proud of his taste in art, though it runs to pure kitsch. Somewhere in his mind is an itch of dissatisfaction with his life, an itch that comes out in the form of fantasies involving a fairy child. There's another urge in him, too, and he contemplates having an extramarital fling, an activity that burdens him with considerable guilt. Babbitt feels most free and happy when he's hanging out with his best friend, Paul, with whom he goes camping. He suppresses his true sociopolitical instincts in order to fit in with the consensus of his peers. Though he sympathizes with the workers during a local labor strike, for instance, he loudly proclaims his support of management, to avoid being labeled a socialist. He also caves in to social pressures and joins the racist, antiunion Good Citizens League. But Babbitt does encourage his son to skip college and follow his dream by marrying young and becoming a mechanic. Maybe the boy will escape being trapped in the web of middle-class acquiescence as Babbitt himself has been.

See *Babbitt*, Sinclair Lewis

BABBITT, RAYMOND

A nasal-voiced autistic man with a talent for photographic information recall. His areas of focus include baseball statistics and airline fatality records. It is only Raymond's obsessive study of data that provides him with any continuity in his world. He's capable of grasping astonishing amounts of data very quickly, through unconventional thought processes; he once determined that 246 toothpicks had been spilled on a floor by visually marking them off in three groups of 82. He was institutionalized early by his father, who feared that Raymond might injure others or himself. Essential, unaltered daily routines that provide Raymond with stability include watching *The People's Court,* eating a snack of fifteen cheese balls with a toothpick, and following regularly scheduled meal plans. Once known for his penchant for Kmart underwear but apparently no longer expresses this preference.

See *Rain Man*

BACH, ARTHUR

Fun-loving, alcoholic millionaire playboy who enjoys living life to the hilt and never met a drink he didn't like. Dependent on his imperturbable, efficient, sardonic butler to guide him through life and rescue him from scrapes, often alcohol-produced. Rarely seen in public without being in a state of advanced inebriation. Has penchant for falling for the wrong woman despite seemingly better opportunities set up by his wealthy, domineering father. Loath to make a match for sound business reasons. Not too tall but still looks great in a tuxedo. Enjoys his bubble baths.

See *Arthur*

BADENOV, BORIS

A conniving little spy always out to get Bullwinkle and his buddy Rocky, Boris's favorite trick is to plant a massive amount of dynamite near his unwitting nemeses. Unfortunately for Boris and his menacing partner **Natasha Fatale**, the schemes always backfire. When not in their favorite all-black outfits, the fiendish pair are usually in disguise, even though their thick Russian accents are a dead giveaway.

See *The Rocky and Bullwinkle Show*

BAGGINS, BILBO

Bilbo is a hobbit, residing in the Shire, whose greatest pleasures are tending his garden and enjoying a meal and pipe of tobacco in his cozily furnished home. A student of history, he writes poems on historical topics as well as hiking songs. He is uprooted from his cozy routine by his first great adventure: Bilbo reluctantly accompanies a band of dwarves led by King Thorin II "Oakenshield" to reclaim their kingdom on the Lonely Mountain. During this adventure, he comes to possess the One Ring of Power, over which the War of the Ring is eventually fought. He is smitten by wanderlust and thereafter is regarded as eccentric for his unhobbitlike trait of traveling beyond the boundaries of the Shire and consorting with elves and dwarves. He has further travels and adventures, which involve him with, among others, **Gandalf** and his nephew, **Frodo Baggins**, who become embroiled in the War of the Ring.

See *The Hobbit* and *The Lord of the Rings,* J. R. R. Tolkien

BAGGINS, FRODO

He is a hobbit of the Shire who goes to live at Bag End with his eccentric uncle, **Bilbo Baggins**, after his parents die. Frodo shares with his uncle a couple of very unhobbitlike characteristics: a high degree of moody thoughtfulness and an itch to see more of the great world than the confines of his garden. Frodo eventually inherits all Bilbo's goods, including the One Ring of Power. Along with the Ring come certain duties, which Frodo assumes, not without reluctance. He volunteers to bear the Ring to Mordor in company with the Fellowship of the Ring: **Aragorn**, **Gandalf**, the elf Legolas, the dwarf Gimli, Boromir, the son of the steward of Gondor, and fellow hobbits **Sam Gamgee**, Merry Brandybuck, and Pippin Took. Twice severely wounded during his adventures in the War of the Ring, Frodo never completely recovers, turning distant and melancholy on his return to the Shire. But his having been the Ring Bearer eventually proves to be his salvation and transfigures him.

See *The Lord of the Rings,* J. R. R. Tolkien

BAGLEY, VIVIAN

A loyal best friend. Time and long experience have hardened Viv so that she is no longer surprised at the ridiculous situations her best friend, Lucy Carmichael, gets into, and she's usually willing to

get right in there along with her! Whether it's disguising herself as a maid or just helping Lucy with some harebrained plan, Vivian is a true friend. Though she's there to tell Lucy that her idea is ridiculous, she's also right there to help, and clean up the mess afterward. "Oh, Lucy!"
See *The Lucy Show*

BAILEY, BEETLE
After dropping out of college to enter the U.S. Army, he's stationed at Camp Swampy, where he does his best to resist authority, avoid responsibility, and goof off. His archenemy is Sergeant Orville Snorkle. When on leave, he visits his sister Lois Flagstone and her family. His helmet's too big.
See *Beetle Bailey*

BAILEY, GEORGE
Everything we want to be as people on this earth is embodied in George Bailey. Self-sacrificing, devoted to his family, George is the embodiment of the word "decent." But his apparently inextinguishable faith in goodness and humanity is put to the test when the devious and avaricious **Mr. Potter** plots his downfall. He actually begins to wonder if things are as wonderful as he'd always thought they were. A visitation from a supernatural, if slightly fuddled, being named **Clarence** gives George the opportunity to reexamine the basis on which he's led his entire life.
See *It's a Wonderful Life*

BAILY, STUART
Suave P.I. and globe-trotting man about town. Stu, a Ph.D., an expert in languages, and a former OSS officer, would be teaching college if being a P.I. weren't so much more fun. His partner is **Jeff Spencer**, and the two of them office at the fabulous address of 77 Sunset Strip. A judo expert, Stu gets to use his skills when their action-packed adventures take them to exciting ports of call all over the world. He eventually sets out on his own to crack cases across the globe with only a secretary, Hannah, to help.
See *77 Sunset Strip*

BAKER, FRANK
The older, more enthusiastic half of the lounge duo the Fabulous Baker Boys, a musical partnership with brother **Jack Baker**. He uses a spray cover-up in a not-too-successful effort to hide a growing bald spot. Married with children, he remains devoted to a life as a piano player. Terminally optimistic and can't always comprehend the reality of bad situations.
See *The Fabulous Baker Boys*

BAKER, JACK
The truly talented half of the musical team the Fabulous Baker Boys, which also includes brother **Frank Baker**. Jack lives alone in a mangy apartment, where he dreams of following his own musical inclinations. He's growing tired of the fifteen-year partnership with his brother, which Jack sees as a dead end. Also, he's very intrigued by singer **Susie Diamond**.
See *The Fabulous Baker Boys*

BAKER, OFFICER JON
A pleasant-looking, blond, blue-eyed California Highway Patrol motorcycle cop. Calm and focused—a by-the-book kind of cop—he helps rein in his more fun-loving and exuberant partner, **Ponch Poncherello**.
See *CHiPs*

BAKER, JORDAN
A championship professional golfer, she is a childhood friend of **Daisy Buchanan**. She's selfish and unprincipled and was caught cheating during a golf tournament, from which she was allowed to withdraw to avert scandal. She approaches **Nick Carraway**, with whom she is having an affair, on behalf of **Jay Gatsby** in order to have Nick arrange the meeting between Gatsby and Daisy that leads to a renewal of their romance.
See *The Great Gatsby*, F. Scott Fitzgerald

BAKER, SAMANTHA
A typical American teenager trying to deal with typical teenage problems: oblivious parents, selfish siblings, and unrequited love. When preparations for her older sister's wedding make her family forget her all-important sixteenth birthday, it's way too much. "Grandparents forgetting a birthday? They live for that shit!!"
See *Sixteen Candles*

BALBOA, ROCKY

The quintessential underdog, Rocky is a professional boxer of apparently limited talent but unquenchable grit, living in a rough Philadelphia neighborhood. He's hounded constantly by his girl, **Adrian**, to quit the ring. But Rocky knows that boxing is—for the time being, at least—his life; he doesn't know what else to do, even if he doesn't seem to be going anywhere at first. But fate takes a hand, and Rocky finds himself in the pugilistic spotlight, despite his lack of finesse and polish. His stamina, nerve, refusal to quit, and the tutelage of his crusty veteran trainer, **Mickey**, all serve him well. Win or lose, small-time or big-time, Rocky remains a diamond in the rough and retains such eccentric but endearing training habits as sparring with sides of beef (which can't hit back) and running up and down the steps of Philadelphia's Art Institute. The public likes an underdog, so they love Rocky Balboa. Even when he wins, he's still an underdog, somehow. But he retains his pride and self-respect…and, most of all, he has his woman. "Yo Adrian!"

See *Rocky*

BALDWIN, SAM

He's a talented architect, formerly of Chicago, who has moved to Seattle to try to forget the tragic death of his wife Maggie from cancer. His life issues: he can't sleep; he can't stop grieving over his wife's death; and he can't get used to the fact that he's now a single parent. Career liability: he daydreams frequently, imagining encounters with his dead wife. Luckily for Sam, he's got his son Jonah to take an interest in saving his dad from depression by finding him a new wife. And amazingly, Jonah finds **Anne Reed**, a Baltimore woman who just might be the ticket.

See *Sleepless in Seattle*

BALES, C.D.

A man with a smile on his face but an ache in his heart, C.D. is a small-town fire chief who's popular because he's such a nice guy, but fears he'll never have the love of a woman because of his humongous nose, which is so big it gets in the way when he tries to drink from a glass. He and a handsome, normal-nosed fireman fall instantly in love with a tall, blond newcomer. The handsome fireman is totally tongue-tied with her and turns to C.D., who, despite his own feelings for the woman, helps the flat-faced lout out with some great lines with which to court the gal. But she eventually realizes which of the two men is the real winner, enormous nose or not.

See *Roxanne*

BALESTRERO, CHRISTOPHER EMMANUEL "MANNY"

A jazz musician, Manny is an upstanding citizen, a moral-minded man who's devoted to his family. Then he's arrested for a crime he didn't commit and enters a hellish world—of assumed guilt, of seemingly inaccurate evidence against him—that would seem absurd if it weren't so frightfully real. Throughout the ordeal, Manny manages to hold himself together, but the strain tells much more tragically on his family.

See *The Wrong Man*

BALLANTINE, JOHN "J.B."

He is a powerful, authoritative doctor and chief administrator of a mental hospital—or so it seems. But there are deeper and darker layers to Ballantine. He is in reality something else altogether: an amnesiac who may have murdered the doctor whose identity he has taken, as well as another victim. Consequently, he is suffering from a weighty guilt complex, among his other mental and emotional disturbances. His new lover, **Dr. Constance Peterson**, leads him through Freudian therapy, including the exploration of Daliesque dreamscapes, to get at the truth and to help him conquer his demons. His life gives new meaning to the phrase "living one's dreams." But Dr. Peterson knows that, for this tortured man, knowing who and what he really is, even if he is a murderer, is to be preferred over a life of painful uncertainty and fear of the unknown.

See *Spellbound*

BALLINGER, DREW

Drew is a guitarist with a poet's soul. He's easily led from one adventure to another, never quite suited to the role he's asked to play. Drew is a perfect companion on an adventure, always ready to lighten the night with a song, and always there to say "Aaaah" when you say "Ooooh."

See *Deliverance*

David Bruce Banner

BALLOU, CAT

A schoolmarm in the Old West, she's now a sexy and willful gunslinger with a reputation for trouble. Teamed up with a drunken, former gun-fighting great, Kid Shelleen.

See *Cat Ballou*

BALSER, TINA

Bored Manhattan homemaker, unhappily married to smarmy business executive. Though attempting to spice up her life through marital infidelity, she's still searching for that unknown element that will set her free from a humdrum existence.

See *Diary of a Mad Housewife*

BANDIT

Dashing southern rebel, 1970s style. He lives to speed down the highways and byways in his souped-up car, in the process enraging his nemesis, **Sheriff Buford T. Justice**. He has no problems with the ladies, who are attracted to his oh-so-hip thick mustache and too-tight, chest-hair-exposing attire like bees to honey.

See *Smokey and the Bandit*

BANKS, MRS. ETHEL

The kindly but dull mother of **Corrie Bratter**, who is a bit confused by her daughter's unprepossessing apartment and New York lifestyle. Her attempts to help her daughter are seen as meddling. The modest woman is overwhelmed by the attentions of her daughter's suave neighbor, **Victor Velasco**.

See *Barefoot in the Park*, Neil Simon

BANKS, STANLEY T.

The maniacally overprotective father of an about-to-be-married daughter, he's distrustful of everyone involved with the impending nuptials, including prospective in-laws, caterers, wedding planners, clergy, and even his own wife. Has difficulty accepting the differences in numbers between packaged hot dogs and hot dog buns. Can be extremely stubborn and occasionally selfish in personal matters, though he ultimately means well.

See *Father of the Bride*

BANNER, DAVID BRUCE

This research scientist is ruled by his large, green inner child. Banner is most notable for his research on the effects of stress on physical strength. When his wife died in an auto accident, the distracted and grief-stricken Banner exposed himself to a massive dosage of gamma radiation, which, as it always seems to do, mutated him into a hulking beast. This life change has a devastating effect on his wardrobe and social life, causing Banner to leave his California home and hit the road in search of a cure. He has since held a number of odd jobs, which allows him to buy an inexhaustible supply of blue jeans and flannel shirts.

See *The Incredible Hulk*

BANNON, HUD

Hud's life fits him like a cheap suit. His father, a tough, no-nonsense rancher in control of his life, thinks little of his son, and Hud, for his part, does what he can to justify that low opinion. He sees himself as more clear-sighted than his father, who he believes is weighed down by outmoded beliefs and adherence to a vanishing way of life.

See *Hud,* Larry McMurtry

BANTA, TONY

A young, good-looking, but not very bright boxer who drives for the Sunshine Cab Company in Manhattan while he waits to make it big in the ring—a dim prospect at best. He's an incurable optimist, however, and hopes one day to turn things around as a fighter. But it's a good thing he can drive a cab.

See *Taxi*

BANZAI, BUCKAROO

A terminally hip, ultra-trendy, New Wave, half-Japanese, half-American superhero. He's a quantum physicist, neurosurgeon, rock 'n' roll star, expert in small arms, jet-car driver, and samurai fighter. As security adviser to the U.S. president and leader of the seven-member Team Banzai, Buckaroo saves the universe from the evil plottings of evil extraterrestrial genius Dr. Emilio Lizardo and wins the girl, Penny Priddy. "Always remember that no matter where you go, there you are."

See *The Adventures of Buckaroo Banzai Across the Eighth Dimension*

BARBARINO, VINNIE

Brooklyn born and bred, Vinnie thinks he's the toughest, coolest dude at James Buchanan High

School; actually, he's not quite smart enough to be the coolest, and too sweet to be the toughest. Some street smarts and his good looks (the girls love him) get him by, even with his teacher **Gabe Kotter**, who used to be a would-be delinquent himself. Vinnie's a leading member of the Sweathogs, the unofficial "gang" of guys that crowd the remedial classes. His pals include **Juan Epstein**, Freddie "Boom Boom" Washington, and **Arnold Horshack**. When Vinnie leaves high school, he works as a hospital orderly.

See *Welcome Back, Kotter*

BARBARELLA

Glamour and beauty queen of the galaxy in the forty-first century and ethereal cadet extraordinaire. Has talent for getting involved in scrapes with every known evil outer space has to offer. She has made an art form out of disrobing. Capable of dealing with astonishing eventualities without losing her cool.

See *Barbarella*

BARBIE

The quintessential blond babe. She has a cute little nose and flawless skin and not an ounce of fat on her body. Barbie drives a hot pink Corvette, and the main man in her life is clean-cut Ken. (The speculation on his sexual preference, by the way, is unfounded.) Her flexibility is astounding: she can rotate her legs 180 degrees and do a full 360 with her head. (No, she is not possessed.) On the other hand (so to speak), she can't even bend her fingers. Some might call her skinny, but Barbie is in fact extraordinarily curvaceous; her chest-to-waist measurement ratio is something like four to one. You can easily encircle her waist with the fingers of one hand. She's at the forefront of every new fashion and cultural trend; Barbie has worn everything from miniskirts to ballroom gowns. One would hope she gives her old clothes to Goodwill or the Salvation Army, as she's been known to own thousands of outfits. As outdoorsy as she is urbane and sophisticated, Barbie skates, skis, cycles, and plays volleyball. In addition, she's a real gym junkie. One of her favorite hangouts is ultra-hip Malibu, California, where she lounges in her hot tub. She's got a posh town house as well. When the T-Bird is in the shop, she hits the road in her recreational vehicle. Normally a blonde, sometimes she goes in for weird hair colors and plays in a punk band. She has a preference for high heels. Recently, she's begun having babies. She also has a preteen friend named Skipper, who's essentially a Barbie wannabe.

See *Toys 'R' Us*

BARETTA, DETECTIVE TONY

In jeans and a white t-shirt, a cap cocked over one eye, this tough undercover cop can work the streets by blending in. An inner-city insider, he grew up the son of poor Italian immigrants—just like some of his perps. He knows his way around in the most gritty and grimy sections of the big city. He's an iconoclast with a big heart but prefers to work alone—and live alone, at the musty King Edward Hotel. Friendly with the house detective there—ex-cop Billy Truman—but his best friend is Fred, his pet cockatoo. His car is called the Blue Ghost; his contact in the police department is Lieutenant Brubaker.

See *Baretta*

BARKLEY, CATHERINE

Tall, beautiful, with golden hair and gray eyes, an English nurse serving in Italy during World War I. She's courted by many of the officers but falls in love with American lieutenant **Frederic Henry**, an ambulance driver. Their romance is rocky from the first; she's wracked with fear after premonitions of one of them lying dead in the rain. Simple, brave, selflessly devoted to Henry, Catherine becomes pregnant during the course of their romance. Regulations forbid their marriage. Disillusioned with the war, Henry deserts, and the lovers flee to Switzerland, where they live happily as Catherine approaches term. Misfortune follows, however, and Catherine bravely faces a fate she in no way deserves.

See *A Farewell to Arms,* **Ernest Hemingway**

BARKLEY, VICTORIA

The matriarch of the vastly wealthy Barkley family, whose 30,000-acre ranch is situated in California's San Joaquin Valley in the 1870s. After the death of her husband, Tom, she takes over, running the family's affairs with a stern but always fair hand. Has grown children: lovely Audra, Nick, and Jarrod, who's an attorney. (Young Eugene is away at school.) Virtually adopted Tom's illegitimate son, Heath.

See *The Big Valley*

Barbarella

The Barkleys

BARNES, CLIFF

Blustery good guy tainted by booze, greed, and craving for revenge. Brother-in-law of **Bobby Ewing**, brother of beautiful **Pam Ewing**, and son of Ewing rival **Digger Barnes**, he seeks revenge for the Ewing clan's unfairness to his father. Hates the idea that Pam is a Ewing by marriage. Tries to use position as D.A. to hurt the Ewings but eventually is hurt politically himself. Thwarted desire ultimately leads him to avarice and the bottle.

See *Dallas*

BARNES, JAKE

An American journalist in his midtwenties who expatriates himself to Paris after a stint on the Italian front in World War I. He has suffered a wound that has left him able to experience desire but unable to have sex and, therefore, unable to have a fully consummated relationship with the woman he loves, **Lady Brett Ashley**. Along with his fellow expatriates, Jake holds a disillusioned and unsentimental view of reality and spends his life in Paris going from café to café, drinking too much, and watching the sexual antics of his friends from the viewpoint of an unwilling outsider. Outwardly the quintessential tough-guy hero, Jake is a cynical, clear-sighted realist who hides his feelings but sleeps with a night-light because he's afraid of the dark. He has lost his Catholic faith but struggles to find a way to live in a modern world that is seemingly without meaning or direction. He has passion, courage, pride, and honesty. He doesn't have love, faith, or purpose.

See *The Sun Also Rises,* **Ernest Hemingway**

BARNES, JULIE

A beautiful blond runaway who was rescued from a life on the street as a prostitute when a Los Angeles police detective recruited her to work as an undercover officer. With her partners **Linc Hayes** and **Pete Cochran**, Julie often poses as a hippie to catch similarly attired criminals.

See *The Mod Squad*

BARNES, TEDDY

A divorced mother of two, Teddy is a devoted mom and a brilliant trial lawyer. She was once a prosecuting attorney, working under district attorney **Thomas Krasny**. Her record in prosecution was just about perfect, but she's now switched to corporate law in the private sector. She takes on one noncorporate case: the murder trial of newspaper publisher **John Forrester**, which she wins. She also gets romantically involved with her client—and then begins to have doubts about his innocence.

See *Jagged Edge*

BARNES, WILLARD "DIGGER"

Bitter old Texas wildcatter. Poor, lonely, sad Digger lost his raison d'être when **Miss Ellie** was stolen out from under him by dastardly **Jock Ewing**. Still clings to the feud begun forty years ago when **Jock** cheated him out of his oil partnership and, possibly more important, his girl. Passes the legacy of the feud on to his own children, **Pamela** and **Cliff**, of whom the latter devotes his life to avenging his father's honor.

See *Dallas*

BARRETT, OLIVER, IV

He's from a wealthy blue-blooded family and got a B.A. magna cum laude from Harvard, where he was a hockey star as well as a grind. His great-grandfather, the original Oliver Barrett, built Harvard's Barrett Hall, which Oliver Barrett IV sees as a huge monument to family money, vanity, and Harvard idolatry. He refers to his father, Oliver Barrett III, as "Old Stonyface, walking, sometimes talking Mount Rushmore. Stonyface." He's in love with **Jennifer Cavilleri**, despite the cultural gulf between their families, and marries her, defying his father's wishes. As he says, "I walked out of his life and into my own." He and Jenny start their life together in a cheap North Cambridge apartment as he tackles law school. There, he slips all the way down to third in his class and is editor of *Law Review*. Afterward, he accepts a position with the Jonas and Marsh law firm in New York City. Then Jenny is diagnosed with leukemia.

See *Love Story,* **Erich Segal**

BARRY, FATHER PETE

This crusading Irish Catholic priest gathers his flock among the dockworkers on the New York waterfront. He's a graduate of Fordham University, a heavy smoker, and he knows what it's like to be poor. Father Pete plucks ex-boxer **Terry Malloy** from claws of the waterfront mob and persuades

him to crush the dock racketeers by testifying in front of the Crime Commission.
See *On the Waterfront*, Budd Schulberg

BART, SHERIFF BLACK

Smooth-talking, quick-thinking sheriff of redneck township of Rock Ridge, which doesn't take kindly to the idea of an African American lawman. Overcomes obstacles with Warner-Brothers-cartoon-style antics, including holding a gun to his own head and delivering peppermint-striped dynamite to an adversary. With the **Waco Kid**, **Lili Von Shtupp**, **Mongo**, and a contingent of railroad workers, prevents hostile takeover of Rock Ridge by **Hedley Lamarr**.
See *Blazing Saddles*

BARTLES, FRANK

His sincere small-town charm has helped him stumble into big success with a wine cooler product. Refuses to hire uppity city types for his commercials when he can do them himself just fine, thank you. Loyal to his "silent" partner, **Ed Jaymes**. "Thank you for your support."
See *Bartles & Jaymes Wine Coolers*

BASCOMBE, FRANK

A talented fiction writer who turns to sportswriting because of a persistent writer's block. Fortunately, the simpler truths of the athlete offer Frank a number of useful lessons with which to understand the hardships in his life, in particular the death of his son, the breakup of his marriage, and the suicide of his friend.
See *The Sportswriter*, Richard Ford

BASKIN, JERRY

An independent-minded, grungy, but gruffly charming homeless guy who meets uptight Beverly Hills businessman **Dave Whiteman** and moves in with him and his family. Jerry sleeps with all three women in Dave's life—his wife, daughter, and housekeeper. Something of a natural therapist, he helps Dave's wife overcome frigidity, his daughter overcome anorexia, and his son come to terms with his compulsive cross-dressing. Even the family dog is given a boost in self-esteem. Oh, and he's a dog food connoisseur.
See *Down and Out in Beverly Hills*

BASKIN, JOSH

Thirteen-year-old boy who achieves dream of becoming "big." Unfortunately, while his body becomes that of an adult male, his mind and experience level remain those of a thirteen-year-old. The result is an impish and wide-eyed innocent manchild, happy to be working in dream job as a product tester for a toy manufacturer. Imaginative and open when it comes to expressing his opinion to others regardless of their respective positions. Somewhat confused about his direction in life as he now knows it. Just starting to discover what girls are really all about. Slowly becoming involved with coworker Susan. His best friend is Billy Kopeky.
See *Big*

BASTIAN

A young dreamer who loves to read, Bastian borrows a fantastic book, *The Neverending Story,* from a strange bookstore and enters the world of Fantasia. The story of Atreyu saving Fantasia from The Nothing convinces Bastian of the importance of courage, dreams, and imagination.
See *The Neverending Story*

BATES, DETECTIVE LUCILLE

Hardy, tough policewoman, subsequently promoted to sergeant. She can dish it out and take it. She earns her stripes and the respect of most of the force but feels a constant need to prove herself. Generally one of the guys. Does have a soft spot for hard-luck cases and children.
See *Hill Street Blues*

BATES, NORMAN

He is the proprietor of the eerie old Bates Motel. Gangly and gaunt, Norman's a pathetic creature—thirty-something, still living with his mother. He refers to Mom a lot, but she seems to spend all of her time sitting upstairs in the Gothic Bates residence in her rocking chair, looking at the world outside her window. The motel is not much of a going concern, ever since the new highway bypassed it, and there are often no customers at all. Norman whiles away his many leisure hours with his hobby of taxidermy, and his office walls are full of his macabre work. Mom is something of a trial to Norman, a crotchety old lady who won't leave him alone and plagues him constantly. But, after

Batgirl

all, as he himself observes, "a boy's best friend is his mother," and so he puts up with her and reacts with rage at the suggestion that she be institutionalized. The Bates place is a subject of some conjecture on the part of local people, but they don't really know too much, since the Bateses keep to themselves. Norman sometimes risks his mother's wrath by a little bit of voyeurism—when the rare opportunity comes along and an attractive female customer shows up at the motel. Boys will be boys, after all.

See *Psycho*

BATGIRL

A bit of a bookworm compared to the usual superhero. Batgirl drives a motorcycle and effortlessly fights crime in heels. Her glittery batsuit and pouty lips rarely get in the way of her quick moves. Has strong ties to Gotham's police department. Narrowly escaped marrying the Penguin, who is also her next-door neighbor. Only Alfred knows her true identity.

See *Batman*

BATMAN

The Dark Knight. Muscular crime-fighter who has elected to fight crime while disguised in a chiseled bat suit, mask, and winglike cape. Employs array of special devices, including climbing ropes, boomerangs, and grappling hooks, all stored on utility belt he wears around his waist. Expert driver of customized Batmobile. Also is a skilled pilot at the controls of his futuristic Batplane. Archenemies include Joker, Penguin, Riddler, and Catwoman. Can be called at any time with special Batsignal, an enormous skylight with a bat silhouette that is beamed to the sky. Batman is headquartered in his secretive Batcave, which he has outfitted with a fully functional crime-fighting lab. Unknown to all but Alfred the butler, Batman is the secret identity of Gotham City's well-known millionaire **Bruce Wayne**.

See *Batman*

Batman

BATSON, BILLY

He has the secret life wished for by every boy: by uttering two syllables he can transform himself into a superstrong, superfast superhero. He also gains about fifteen years in age, good looks, a snappy red uniform with a cape, and the name **Captain Marvel**. Not a bad trick for a poor orphan. While peddling his papers one rainy night, Billy was taken to a secret underground lair, where a 3,000-year-old wizard gave the lad the ability to summon the powers of the Greek gods: wisdom, strength, stamina, power, courage, and speed. All he had to do was utter the wizard's name: "Shazam!"

See *Shazam*

BATTY, ROY

In an era when people have developed humanoid creatures called replicants to do their heavy and hazardous labor, Batty is such a being, doomed by genetic engineering to a life span of only four years, and sore about it. In a fit of pique, he breaks the rules and comes to Earth, toward the end of his allotted four years, to pick a bone with the guys who done him wrong.

See *Blade Runner*

BAUER, ALLEN

A successful but romantically unfulfilled guy who finds the void in his life filled suddenly by **Madison**, a gorgeous young woman. Well, not a *woman*, exactly…what she is, is a mermaid (which doesn't make her a bad person). At first his motivation is simple—Madison is a mega-babe, and sex with her is amazing—but as he teaches her the ways of human society, he learns to appreciate her astonishing purity and honesty. But the haunting question remains: can a young modern businessman find true happiness with a being who is half human and half fish and whose table manners leave much to be desired?

See *Splash*

THE BAXTER FAMILY

Scraping out an existence in the Florida scrub just after the Civil War, the Baxter family hovers near the edge of survival. Pa is soft-spoken and kind, with a great fondness for his son, Jody. Ma loves Jody too, but the difficult life that they lead has hardened her, and the boy can't understand why she seems so unforgiving. An only surviving child, Jody is sensitive, lonely, and longs for a pet. When he finds a fawn, he devotes his time and energy to nurturing it. Ma and Pa Baxter are glad for Jody's happiness at having a playmate until the deer grows older and begins eating their crops. Pa and Ma are aware of the tenuousness of their circumstances, so they're forced to make the grim decision to kill their son's beloved pet. Young Jody's maturity, which has evolved as he learned to take care of the deer, enables him to finally understand the necessity of what must be done. The Baxters are a family that sticks together because they love one another and they know that together they will endure.

See *The Yearling*, **Marjorie Kinnan Rawlings**

BAXTER, C. C. "BUD"

Up-and-coming, clean-cut, slightly bashful New York insurance agent desperately trying to climb corporate ladder. Generous to a fault with the lending of his apartment, not too smart when it comes to romances, either those of his colleagues or entanglements of his own.

See *The Apartment*

BAXTER, GEORGE

He is a conservative, solid, middle-aged suburban lawyer, a successful family man with an attractive wife and son and a comfortable home. Despite Baxter's best intentions, his life is run by his outspoken housekeeper, **Hazel Burke**. He's amused by Hazel's antics, even when he has had to get himself (or her) out of one of her scrapes.

See *Hazel*

BAXTER, GEORGETTE FRANKLIN

The sweet but ditzy girlfriend, and then wife, of vain, vacuous Minneapolis TV news anchorman **Ted Baxter**. It takes Ted a long time to reluctantly agree to marry her, even though it's probably the best thing he ever did. They adopt a son, David, and Georgette then gives birth to another child. Though she's hardly assertive, she will not give ground forever and can often get her way with Ted.

See *The Mary Tyler Moore Show*

BAXTER, TED

He is the blowhard, incompetent newscaster at WJM-TV in Minneapolis. He looks the part, with his perfect anchorman hairdo and smile, but he has feet of clay that go right up to the hip. He's constantly butchering copy, making horrible on-air mistakes, and pandering to his own inflated ego. He is the regular butt of newswriter **Murray Slaughter**'s jokes and the bane of producer **Lou Grant**'s existence. His wife is **Georgette Franklin Baxter**, a sweet airhead whom Ted often takes for granted. He has an adopted son, David, as well as a child Georgette bore them. Ted is a tightwad, who pays a high school student five dollars a year to do his taxes. His favorite Disney movie is *Snow White*. His great ambitions in life are to win a Teddy, the local version of the Emmy, and to get a national network job like his idol Walter Cronkite. In Ted's mind, they're in the same league. He'd be hard put

NO FORWARDING ADDRESS

Robert Kincaid
Kwai Chang Caine
Shane

to find anyone to agree with him. Takes six sugars in his coffee.

See *The Mary Tyler Moore Show*

BAXTER, TOM

A gallant adventurer and explorer of ancient Egyptian ruins, he always wears a pith helmet, even in the bathroom. But Tom is actually a "fictional" character in a movie, who steps off the screen one day, straight into "real life," where he romances **Cecilia**, a shy waitress, whose only escape from an abusive relationship is watching romantic movies. By walking out on the movie in which he is starring, Tom earns the enmity of the film's other characters, who can't continue the film without him. Tom's major problem in dealing with the "real" world is that he can only do what he knows how to do in the movies. He can drive a car because he drives a car in his films. But he has no idea how to start a car, since he's never had a scene in which he does that. He has never handled real money, only the prop variety. And so forth. He's better off in the world of celluloid.

See *The Purple Rose of Cairo*

BEALE, HOWARD

An old, boozy, past-his-prime network news anchorman for UBS-TV. Howard could do his job in his sleep—he arrives on the set just seconds before the cameras start rolling. When network management, including ruthless, icy-tough vice-president of programming **Diana Christensen**, informs him they'll be letting him go in favor of a fresher face in the race for higher ratings, he goes nuts. On the air, on his evening national television newscast, he announces his plan to kill himself at the end of his final broadcast. This, along with his on-air obscenities and ranting and raving about the decaying state of society, sends his ratings through the roof. Overnight, having struck a national nerve, he becomes the most popular personality on television—for the moment. Sensing a ratings coup, Diana Christensen gets Beale his own show. For a while it works—his wild gesticulating and passionate diatribes hold the nation spellbound. Across the city, viewers respond to his exhortations to go to their windows and shout out their anger, sending their complaints echoing through the air. But eventually, the fickle, novelty-starved audience tires of his

complaints about American society and television, and the ratings of his show begin to sag. Finally, he's killed on the air—a plot by network management to garner some respectable ratings. "I'm mad as hell, and I'm not going to take it anymore!"

See *Network*

BEANY

A young boy with an adventurous life, Beany lives aboard the boat *Leakin' Lena* with Captain Huffenpuff. The two have exciting encounters all over the world, accompanied by Beany's best pal, Cecil the Seasick Sea Serpent. Beany is extremely good-natured. His trademark is a cap with a propeller on the top.

See *Beany and Cecil* and *Matty's Funday Funnies*

BEAUMONT, JEFFERY

Inquisitive if naive college student, he's an amateur detective who doesn't know when to stay out of potentially murderous situations. Lives in Lumberton with two aunts. Father hospitalized with heart problems, mother deceased. Jeffery has always gravitated to the orthodox, respectable, sunny side of life but becomes fascinated with its dark and even grotesque aspects. He is currently involved with two women: sweet, nice Sandy, a policeman's daughter, and troubled, mysterious chanteuse **Dorothy Valens**, who is under the power of psychopath **Frank Booth**. Drinks Heineken. Prefers to wear black sport jackets and the occasional exterminator's outfit. "It's a strange world."

See *Blue Velvet*

BEAVIS

A ninth-grade boy with a tower of curly blond hair and a deep and abiding love of music videos. Beavis is passionate—the "id" to his best friend **Butthead**'s "ego." He has a weakness for candy bars, and after, like, um, twenty or so, the aftereffects play hell with his digestive tract, and he may go through, like, um, twenty rolls of T.P. He believes that, to be great, a video requires two essential ingredients: chicks and fire. Deepest fear: that he'll grow old without scoring. "GWAR *rules!*"

See *Beavis and Butt-head*

BECH, HENRY

A once successful novelist struggling with chronic writer's block, Bech searches for literary inspiration and a nice Jewish girl to either give him that inspiration or to share its fruits. Hunkered down in a Manhattan hovel, he pounds out articles to make ends meet while his latest novel languishes. Bech bounces from one brief, unsatisfying affair to another, and constantly wonders about his literary and love lives. "What next?"
See *Bech: A Book,* John Updike

BECKER, ARNIE

A rich, handsome, sleazy, playboy lawyer and divorce specialist. Arnie's devilish good looks make him irresistible to his female clients at McKenzie, Brackman, et al., while they're in the process of divorcing their rich husbands. He has little sense of boundaries in legal ethics and would sleep with his best friend's wife if he thought he wouldn't be caught. Eventually, he longs for a commitment with a woman and tries to clean up his act as a lawyer but slides back into his old ways.
See *L.A. Law*

BECKER, DETECTIVE DENNIS

He's a harried, overworked LAPD detective, but he's also solid as a rock. Becker must constantly contend with old pal private investigator **Jim Rockford**'s incessant pleas for help. Becker rolls his eyes and protests, but in the end he always helps the P.I. out, often running afoul of his own superiors in the process.
See *The Rockford Files*

BECKETT, DR. SAM

He's won the Nobel Prize in physics, with his work on the "string" theory of quantum physics, which enables someone to leap (travel) anywhere within his or her own lifetime. Since it's his technology, he uses it, along with Al, his friend and guide, who appears in the form of a hologram. Together, they travel through time correcting injustices. "Oh, boy."
See *Quantum Leap*

BECKETT, ANDREW

A hotshot young lawyer, he's recruited straight out of Penn Law School and quickly rises to a senior partnership in a prestigious Philadelphia firm. He keeps his gay life a secret from his colleagues until he contracts the AIDS virus. He tries to keep that secret, too, but eventually it becomes known, and he's promptly fired, ostensibly for other reasons. He files a wrongful dismissal suit, refusing to believe that his sexual orientation had nothing to do with his firing. He has trouble finding a lawyer willing to take on his former employers until he teams up with **Joe Miller**, a small-time, ambitious attorney, who agrees to represent Beckett, despite his negative feelings about gays. "I bring sorrow to those who love me."
See *Philadelphia*

BECKOFF, ARNOLD

Aka Virginia Hamm, among others. He's a raspy-voiced, hirsute, elfin Jewish drag queen. Born and raised in New York City, Beckoff came of age within the gay community long before the AIDS crisis. A habitué of the backroom scene, involving multiple anonymous partners, he nonetheless develops relationships with Alan, a young muscle boy who is killed in a queer-bashing incident, and Ed, a bisexual with whom he adopts a gay son, David. Beckoff has a caustic wit, which he uses to mask pain and frustration, but he is quite capable of moments of very real passion. Although Beckoff's father is dead, his mother is very much alive and makes no bones of her disapproval of her son's lifestyle.
See *Torch Song Trilogy*

BELKER, DETECTIVE MICK

A scruffy, scrappy, unorthodox police detective. A loner, completely independent, Belker does things in his own way. He's rumpled even at his best moments, and he literally snarls and growls at suspects to shut them up. When Detective Belker is undercover, he's absorbed by his role. Emotionally open only with his girlfriend, Robin.
See *Hill Street Blues*

BELL, VIVIAN

She's a New York schoolteacher who's in Reno to obtain a quickie divorce from an unbearable husband. Vivian likes conservative outfits and wears her hair in a bun. Though she perceives herself as strictly heterosexual, Vivian wavers when confronted by newly aroused feelings after meeting a precocious and aggressive younger woman, **Cay Rivvers**.
See *Desert Hearts*

John Bender

BELLOCQ, E. J.

A sensitive, eccentric photographer whose chief passion is taking arty pictures of prostitutes in a Storytown, New Orleans, brothel. He seems more fascinated with light and shadow than with the women themselves. He falls in love with **Violet**, a child prostitute, and forms a tormented relationship with her.

See *Pretty Baby*

BELLOWS, DR. ALFRED

This NASA psychiatrist is slowly driven crazy by his inability to understand astronauts **Tony Nelson**'s and **Roger Healey**'s strange behavior. He is constantly investigating the strange goings-on around Tony and Roger. Easily foiled, and usually winds up looking like he needs his own shrink. Thinks **Jeannie** is just Tony's fiancée.

See *I Dream of Jeannie*

BELLOWS, DON

A socialite and architect, he's so inspired by actress **Joyce Heath**'s performance one night that it changes his entire life. He opts for what he believes to be a life of the soul over a life of material values. Bellows, handsome, wealthy, engaged to be married, has the world at his feet—and then he takes Joyce from a honky-tonk, ensconces her in his country house, and becomes obsessed with her. His passion is such that he won't heed the warning of his housekeeper (who is very perceptive, in the tradition of housekeepers throughout history) that Joyce is bad for him. *Never* ignore your housekeeper.

See *Dangerous*

BENDER, JOHN

Leather-gloved, earring-wearing high school rebel. He lives with abusive, uncaring father, tends to cause trouble just for the hell of it. Prefers verbal to physical attacks on perceived enemies. Hates upper classes and despises weakness. He does frequent hitches in Saturday A.M. detention. "I want to be an Air Force Ranger, I want to live a life of danger!"

See *The Breakfast Club*

BENES, ELAINE

Once the girlfriend of comic Jerry Seinfeld, Elaine is now just one of his tight coterie of pals. Elaine is beautiful (has particularly lovely hair), smart, funny, and the daughter of a famous writer; but she's not too lucky at work and has a temper that gets her into scrapes. She's dated the head of NBC, former baseball player Keith Hernandez, and a mayoral aide. She's afraid of dogs, her middle name is Marie, and her favorite movie is *Shaft*.

See *Seinfeld*

BEN-HUR, JUDAH

The son of a close-knit Jewish family who is enslaved in a galley ship and saves himself by saving a Roman consul. He is brave, honorable, and proud. He harbors a grudge against his former boyhood friend that develops into a dangerous moral and physical battle. A spiritual awakening gives him the strength to endure his hardships.

See *Ben-Hur*

BENJAMIN, JUDY

A pampered, spoiled Jewish girl, whose second husband dies during sex on their wedding night. She joins the Army to get away, and is horrified to find it…well…dreadfully unchic. But, with the help of tough training officer **Captain Doreen Lewis**, she grows up and toughens up. "What is this, hell week?"

See *Private Benjamin*

BENNEL, DR. MILES

This handsome, commonsensical physician returns from a vacation to his home town of Santa Mira, California, only to find that his friends and neighbors (like **Becky Driscoll** and Dr. Daniel Kaufman) are being systematically replaced in their sleep by alien plant-pod creatures, who look and sound exactly like the originals but have no personalities whatever. He's aghast.

See *The Body Snatchers,* **Jack Finney, and** *Invasion of the Body Snatchers*

BENNETT, BABE

Pulitzer Prize–winning newspaperwoman. She's made herself a success through chutzpah, ingenuity, and tenacity. Her hard-nosed pursuit of the story of **Longfellow Deeds**, however, makes her think twice about the trick she plays on him. Her hardened New York edge is softened by meeting someone who teaches her that being good isn't that bad.

See *Mr. Deeds Goes to Town*

BENTON, DR. PETER

Intense surgical resident in the emergency room at County General Hospital in Chicago. A perfectionist who embodies many of the stereotypical attributes of a surgeon: cool, distant, cocky, hard-edged, brilliant, and technically a master of his work. Has juggled the incredible demands of his job with caring for his sick, aging mother. Dr. Benton is single and could clearly benefit from a little lovin'.

See *ER*

DR. BENWAY

A totalitarian and sadist masquerading as a doctor, Dr. Benway conducts surgery not to heal but as an exercise in perverse aesthetics. Unlike the other residents of the surreal countries of Freeland and Interzone, who all seem addicted to sex and/or drugs, Dr. Benway's addicted to control and committed to spreading Total Demoralization ("T.D.") throughout the population.

See *Naked Lunch,* William S. Burroughs

BERAGON, MONTY

Continental gadabout descended from old Pasadena money. Marty's tall and lanky, with a tiny bald spot. With lots of real estate but little cash, he was born to a way of life that includes "taste, manners and a jaunty aloofness from money." His picture is often plastered across the society pages. Marty, who has never worked a day in his life, is not above accepting handouts from waitress turned restaurateur **Mildred Pierce**. In exchange, he introduces Mildred's capricious daughter, **Veda**, to the Pasadena aristocracy. When his fortunes plummet, he moves into the servant's quarters of his deteriorating mansion. He eventually marries meal-ticket Mildred, which doesn't put a crimp in the affair he's having with Veda. One reason for loving Veda: "She wouldn't pick up a tip."

See *Mildred Pierce,* James M. Cain

BERGER, GEORGE

Hates his name; call him Bananaberger. He thinks of himself as a poor young psychedelic teddy bear. He willfully violates P.S. 183's Personal Appearance Code, knowing people will wonder if he's a boy or a girl. Eighteen years old, bright, funny, wild, he's still serious underneath it all. A rapist, pothead, and neurotic liar who lives by the words "This is 1968, not 1967!" Goals: floating around India, being invisible, staying high forever.

See *Hair,* Gerome Ragni and James Rado and Galt MacDermott

BERLIN, PAUL

A typical young American in the very atypical Vietnam war, Berlin tries to control his fears by daydreaming a fantasy world while he stands guard at an observation post on the South China Sea. After a seventeen-year-old soldier in his unit goes AWOL, Berlin imagines his company pursuing the deserter across the Asian continent and all the way to Europe.

See *Going After Cacciato,* Tim O'Brien

BERNADETTE

A drag queen in the process of going transsexual, who sports well-kept blond hair (running to gray) and an unaugmented bosom. She tends toward overt hostility at the use of her original name, Ralph. Bernadette is at present on an extensive hormonal regimen, pursuant to her upcoming operation. She's capable of incredible alcohol consumption. Careerwise, Bernadette performs in a drag show, where she parades in billowy gowns, elaborate facial makeup, and fright wigs while lip-synching to 1970s disco hits. She possesses a remarkably dry and arch wit. And she's a strong woman, fully capable of staving off a would-be rapist and walking through the desert in search of an automobile repairman while in heels. "I can't sit here crying. My mascara keeps running. I look like a raccoon."

See *The Adventures of Priscilla, Queen of the Desert*

BERNARDO

Leader of the Sharks, the Puerto Rican gang vying for control over the streets of New York City's West Side. Handsome, proud, and sardonic, Bernardo represents the strength of his culture. He hates the rival gang, the Jets, especially when their lieutenant, **Tony**, falls for his sister, **Maria**.

See *West Side Story*, Arthur Laurents, Stephen Sondheim, and Leonard Bernstein

George Berger

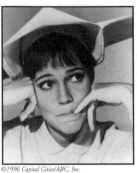

©1996 Capital Cities/ABC, Inc.

Sister Bertrille

BERNBAUM, BERNIE

This small-time swindler is cutting in on the big boys' gambling action. There may be loyalty among some thieves, but Bernie has no loyalty, and most gang types despise him. Eventually, **Tom Regan** is ordered to kill him, and he blubbers, begging not to be shot in the woods "like a dumb animal"; then he blackmails Tom. Not an asset to the gene pool.
See *Miller's Crossing*

BERNECKY, ELDIN

Eccentric house painter on a very extended job at the home of Washington news reporter **Murphy Brown**. He once sold a painting for a million dollars, but that didn't stop him from keeping his day (and night) job at Murphy's place. He's Murphy's Lamaze coach for the birth of her son but has recently left the Brown residence to study painting in Spain.
See *Murphy Brown*

BERNLY, JUDY

She is a newcomer to the corporate world with a lot to learn. She's a by-the-book secretary who's confronted with sexual harassment on the job. Then she discovers aspects to her character she'd never contemplated. Close to coworkers **Doralee Rhodes** and **Violet Newstead**.
See *9 to 5*

SISTER BERTRILLE

She's bubbly, youthful, exuberant, and weighs barely ninety pounds. And she's a nun—with an unusual gift. Inspired by her missionary aunt to join a convent, she is assigned to Convent San Tanco in San Juan, Puerto Rico. When the trade winds are blowing, her cornette (a headgear with wings) lets her soar high above the ground. Sister Bertrille truly wishes to do good but has a knack for finding trouble. She's scolded by **Mother Superior** on a regular basis. She uses her flying powers to benefit her poor community. She's plagued by frequent awkward landings.
See *The Flying Nun*

MISS BERYL

A proper but tough-minded old woman living in upstate New York, Miss Beryl is landlady to **Donald Sullivan**, whom she loves like a son, having

little but disdain for her real son, a smarmy banker. She is forever trying to get Sully to clean up his act, which he's unwilling or unable to do.
See *Nobody's Fool*, Richard Russo

BESS

A disreputable young woman living on the fringes of Catfish Row, South Carolina, Bess's self-destructive traits include alcoholism, drug addiction, and a virtual enslavement to her brutal boyfriend, Crown. When Crown flees the quarter after committing a murder, Bess is shunned by the local women and takes up with a legless street beggar named **Porgy**. She finds comfort and hope in her relationship with Porgy. All that is shattered, however, when she runs into Crown, who tells her he will come to take her from Porgy before cotton season. After Porgy kills Crown and flees Charleston, Bess, unable to bear the loneliness and waiting, wanders off with a group of men, never to return.
See *Porgy and Bess*, DuBose Heyward

BETELGEUSE

Spirited spirit who goes by the nickname Beetlejuice. Assists the newly dead in their often difficult transition process. Not above haunting a house for cheap laughs. Enjoys a good calypso every now and then. Dresses like a jailer, laughs like a banshee, styles hair like a zombie punk-rock star.
See *Beetlejuice*

BETSY

A blond, WASPy campaign worker for the Charles Palatine presidential election campaign, she's characterized by **Travis Bickle** as "an angel" the first time he sees her. A very serious young woman who enjoys the music of Engelbert Humperdinck and does not appreciate pornographic movies.
See *Taxi Driver*

BEULAH

Maid to the Hendersons (Harry, Alice, and Donnie), Beulah is the down-to-earth one, who must constantly come to the aid of her less-than-competent charges. Her boyfriend is named Bill, her best friend is named Oriole. "Somebody bawl fo' Beulah?"
See *Beulah*

BIALYSTOCK, MAX
A down-and-out (but still pompous) theater producer who desperately wants to regain his former glory. He schemes with his accountant, **Leo Bloom**, to win the backing of every spinster in New York for a play that is guaranteed to fail, therefore keeping most of the money for himself. He produces "Springtime for Hitler" written by a Nazi fanatic, directed by an inept transvestite, and starring a mindless, drug-bombed hippie.

See *The Producers*, Mel Brooks

BIBBIT, BILLY
Shy, stammering, virginal, easily shamed young man. He unthinkingly obeys **Nurse Ratched**'s every freedom-stifling order—until **Randle Patrick McMurphy** arrives on the scene. With McMurphy's help, Billy realizes that it's okay to laugh, it's okay to be individualistic—and that lust and sex are a natural part of life. Tragically, he can't overcome feelings of utter shame and worthlessness after enjoying a night of physical pleasure with one of McMurphy's female friends.

See *One Flew over the Cuckoo's Nest*, Ken Kesey

BICEK, BRUNO "LEFTY"
A poor young man living in a Polish neighborhood on Chicago's Near Northwest Side, Bicek is an uneducated street tough who dreams of making it big in the fight game. Basically a good person, Bicek has a limited view of life and its possibilities and is ruled by his animal instincts. His life falls apart after he becomes involved in a gang rape and murder.

See *Never Come Morning*, Nelson Algren

BICKLE, TRAVIS
Aka Krinkle, Henry, he is a sardonic and detached observer of New York City after-hours life, as observed from the front seat of his taxicab. Travis is a scruffily dressed insomniac, with an appetite for pornographic movies, who has been known to sport a Mohawk haircut. Briefly involved with **Betsy**, a worker in the Charles Palatine presidential election campaign. Even more briefly involved in the Palatine campaign. Willing to risk his life to save a young girl from life on the mean streets, Bickle has the occasional habit of conducting dialogues with himself. Even though he sees the nastiest aspects of life, he still has some kind of ideals.

Known to breakfast on white bread and whiskey.
See *Taxi Driver*

BICKLEY, FRANKLIN DELANO
Grouchy downstairs neighbor of **Mindy Beth McConnell**. Lives in Boulder, Colorado, where he is a greeting-card writer. Has a dog named Bickey.
See *Mork & Mindy*

BIGELOW, BILLY
He runs the carnival carousel. Billy is a big, personable, strapping man, but his temper tends to get the best of him, which can cost him things—such as jobs. He is, however, a man true to his word and astounded by his own capacity to care for others. He is devoted to his wife and daughter. He brought the latter a star from heaven.
See *Carousel*, Oscar Hammerstein II and Richard Rodgers

BIGGINS, ROY
Craven, selfish, and stout, Biggins owns a small airline flying out of Nantucket and competes with **Joe** and **Brian Hackett**. He fancies himself very much the ladies' man. He's not. He is very materialistic and often chauvinistic. He's a firm believer in the attracting power of Brylcreem and always wears a tie.
See *Wings*

BILKO, MASTER SERGEANT ERNIE
With little more than ingenuity, bluster, and an ability to think fast on his feet, World War II vet Bilko virtually has the run of Ford Baxter, Kansas, the sleepy military base at which he's stationed. The con man's con man, he runs gambling games, concocts various money-making schemes, and manipulates his immediate superiors, all while running the Company B Motor Pool. He occasionally romances Joan Hogan, a WAC. Stationed in New Guinea during the war, he sold nylons to USO girls at an absurd profit.
See *The Phil Silvers Show*

BILLY
Dope-using, cycle-riding companion to **Wyatt** on the road over the highways and byways of the United States, hoping to find what it's all about, really. Dresses casually and not too concerned about niceties of personal grooming.
See *Easy Rider*

THE OLD GUY IN THE BIG CAR IN FRONT OF YOU GOING 25 MPH

Norman Thayer
Abraham Simpson
Fred Sanford
Benjamin Matlock
Art Selwin

BINGHAMTON, CAPTAIN WALLACE B.

Squirrelly captain in the United States Navy during World War II. He's not without marine experience; before the war, he was the head of the Long Island Yacht Club in New York, where he was born. Despite these credentials, he's not quite up to handling **Lieutenant Commander Quinton McHale** and his crew of unruly misfits, who make a habit of breaking regulations. Behind his back, he is referred to as Old Lead Bottom.

See *McHale's Navy*

BIRDY

Schizophrenic man-child. Passionate bird enthusiast since boyhood days in Philadelphia, now institutionalized in mental hospital with postwar psychological disturbances that have reduced him to behaving in a fowllike manner. Either cannot or will not speak to anyone. Indulges in vivid inner life. Best friend of Vietnam vet **Al Columbato**.

See *Birdy*

BISHOP, CYNTHIA

A tough and cynical—but very sexy—artist, she's so fed up with sister **Ann Millaney**'s naiveté that she doesn't mind sleeping with Ann's husband, **John**. After meeting **Graham Dalton**, who videotapes an interview with her and reawakens her ideals, she ends her sleazy affair.

See *sex, lies, and videotape*

BISHOP, PIKE

The graying, amoral leader of a gang of bandits in the Old West, a land where everyone seems tainted by corruption. He has a fierce loyalty to his men and demands the same in return. Pursued by a gang of toughs employed by the railroad he's made a habit of stealing from, Pike leads his men into Mexico. There, hounded by the railroad men, and running afoul of a local tin-pot tyrant, he faces his final showdown.

See *The Wild Bunch*

BLACKMON, MARS

Short, ambitionless motormouth who woos the beautiful **Nola Darling** in goofy fashion. Loves the New York Knicks and Bernard King in particular. Derides one of Nola's other suitors as a "fake Billy Dee motherfucker."

See *She's Gotta Have It*

BLACKTHORNE, JOHN

An English ship's pilot, who becomes stranded in Japan after a storm blows him off course. Soon he finds himself embroiled in politics as he joins forces with **Toranaga**, who is planning to unify the country under his own rule and become Shogun. Blackthorne (a.k.a. "Anjin-san") adapts quickly to his new life, forgetting his life—and his wife—of the past.

See *Shogun*

BLACKWOOD, CHARLOTTE "CHARLIE"

The target of Pete "Maverick" Mitchell and Nick "Goose" Bradshaw's infamous serenade of "You've Lost That Loving Feeling," Charlie is leery of Maverick's advances. But her dry humor keeps him at bay for only a short while. Sexy, intelligent, and humorous, this WASPy blond bombshell actually brings a sense of stability to Maverick's life. Sophisticated in taste, Charlie wants only the best—she wants Maverick.

See *Top Gun*

BLAINE, RICK

Cynical, hard-boiled owner of successful bistro Rick's Café Américain in World War II–era Casablanca, Morocco. Rick formerly worked as a gunrunner in Ethiopia and mercenary with Spanish Loyalists, though he keeps his past deeply buried. Also deeply buried under his thick hide is a sensitive heart, capable of being wounded. He has a love-hate relationship with many people in this spy-and-intrigue-infested town, including corrupt Inspector Louis Renault, officer of the Vichy government police. Has no respect for Nazi occupiers and openly disdains their rules and pretensions to a "thousand-year reich." Refuses to drink with customers, though when alone he drowns his sorrows in bourbon. Once involved with **Ilsa Lund** during brief whirlwind affair in Paris. Claims he sticks his neck out for no one, though actions often prove otherwise, particularly with regard to Ilsa's husband, **Victor Laszlo**. Wears white tuxedo jacket at work, rumpled trench coat and fedora when traveling through fog, an unexpected but apparently common phenomenon in this desert locale. A cigarette is usually between his fingers or hanging off his lower lip. Has strong aversion to the song "As

Time Goes By." "I'm no good at being noble, but it doesn't take much to see that the problems of three little people don't amount to a hill of beans in this crazy world."
See *Casablanca*

BLAIR, ELIZABETH

Delightful and charming orphan girl. Can sing, dance, and make adults fall in love with her in the blink of an eye. Has a special gift for matchmaking. Devoted to her older sister. "Animal crackers in my soup! Tigers and monkeys loop the loop!"
See *Curly Top*

BLAKE, LIEUTENANT COLONEL HENRY

The commanding officer of the 4077th MASH (Mobile Army Surgical Hospital) unit during the Korean War. Henry's skills are surgical and medical, but not military: he runs an exceedingly loose ship. Decision making and discipline are not his forte, for which lacks his unit loves him. There are two exceptions: by-the-book irritants **Frank Burns** and **Margaret Houlihan**. He is alternately amused and exasperated by the antics of Drs. **Hawkeye Pierce** and **Trapper John McIntyre** and serves as father figure to company clerk **Radar O'Reilly**. His idea of military dress is an old college sweater and a fishing hat with flies attached. He's a cigar smoker and enjoys a drink or three, but only when he can find it. He loves his wife, Lorraine, but isn't a fanatic about marriage vows, especially when there are lots of attractive nurses around.
See *M*A*S*H*

BLAKENEY, SIR PERCY

A foppish and effete English aristocrat by day, Sir Percy is by night the feared Scarlet Pimpernel, who goes to great lengths to rescue French nobility condemned to the guillotine during the French Revolution's Reign of Terror. Resourceful, quick-witted, and daring, Percy dare not show this true self to his wife, who believes him a weak and cowardly man.
See *The Scarlet Pimpernel,* Baroness Orczy

BLAND, MARY

Co-owner with husband **Paul Bland** of eatery Paul and Mary's Country Kitchen. While she's not fond of perversion, immorality, and other things that taint her nice world, she's not above occasional murder and dismemberment, followed by cannibalistic consumption, in order to restore propriety to her country and eliminate repellent individuals.
See *Eating Raoul*

BLAND, PAUL

Boring, mild spouse of **Mary Bland**, living nice, normal, homespun American lifestyle. Okay, he commits murder now and again and also indulges in the cooking and ingestion of the victims. But they deserve it, the perverts. His dream is to open a restaurant with his prim and proper wife. A fairly normal guy, if you overlook a few small peccadilloes.
See *Eating Raoul*

BLANEY, RICHARD

This mild-mannered London resident is believed to be the fiend behind a series of killings dubbed the Necktie Murders. He's a sullen, self-centered type who has little use for most people, one notable exception being his friend **Robert Rusk**. Blaney still resents people not treating him courteously and resents even more being suspected of serial murders.
See *Frenzy*

Rick Blaine

John Bluto Blutarsky

BLOOD, DR. PETER

Irish doctor who has extreme career change. Now travels high seas working as a pirate with rapier replacing scalpel. Handy with sword, swinging from ropes, and other feats of daring physical dexterity not found in many doctors. Also has winning smile and seductive eyes, which no doubt help when he settles into important political career in Jamaica.

See *Captain Blood*

BLOOM, LEO

This timid, neurotic accountant is afraid of loud noises, heights, and just about everything else. For his frequent attacks of nerves, he carries a little square of his blue baby blanket in his pocket to stroke. That piece of cloth is well worn. But it gets an even bigger workout than usual when Leo falls under the spell of shady Broadway producer **Max Bialystock**, with whom he forms the production company Bialystock & Bloom. Together, they're a case of How to Fail in Business While Really Trying.

See *The Producers,* Mel Brooks

BLUE, CHINA

Bored yuppie daytime fashion designer who moonlights nights as sleazy call girl. She lives hard, talks dirty, and has a vicious streak of sadism flowing through her veins. Otherwise, she's okay. Stiletto heels are footwear of choice. Currently engaged in a series of twisted psychosexual games with an unhappily married cop and a deranged street-corner preacher. Just your regular, ordinary young woman.

See *Crimes of Passion*

BLUES, ELWOOD

Harmonica-playing brother to **Jake "Joliet" Blues**, half of the fabulous Blues Brothers team and coleader of their musical revue. Terrific driver, able to leap open drawbridges and unfinished roadways without blinking. Single-handedly can destroy a shopping mall with his automotive skills and can outrun any Illinois law official. Ironically is currently behind the wheel of a reconverted police car. A real ladies' man who knows what he wants and how to get it, no matter what the circumstances. Likes his toasted white bread dry, no butter or jelly.

Like brother Jake, Elwood dresses in black suit, white shirt, skinny black tie, porkpie hat, and ever-present sunglasses. Has his name tattooed on six fingers. "We're on a mission from God."

See *The Blues Brothers*

BLUES, JAKE "JOLIET"

Orphan, ex-con, and dynamite blues singer. Has his name tattooed on the knuckles of one hand. Turns a rather graceful cartwheel despite his girth. Dressed in black suit, white shirt, skinny black tie, porkpie hat, and ever-present sunglasses. With brother **Elwood Blues**, part of the fabulous Blues Brothers and their musical revue. Food of choice is whole fried chicken. Smokes Chesterfields. Hates Illinois Nazis. Once broke the heart of a now-vengeful hairdresser. Given to seeing the occasional vision in church despite his rebellious childhood in a Catholic orphanage. Jake is determined to keep his band together at all costs.

See *The Blues Brothers*

BLUTARSKY, JOHN BLUTO

Frat boy of indeterminate major, inspiration for generations of debauchees at Delta House. Has no use for moderation; enjoys everything to excess, especially beer, food, and sex—but definitely not studying or schoolwork. Not a fan of sensitive guitar-playing folkies or of Young Republican ROTCs. Handy with a ladder down at Sorority Row. Can flatten a beer can against his forehead without flinching. Never a dull moment in the college cafeteria, as his gross-out skills impress the coeds. A devotee of toga parties and role model for underachievers everywhere. Considering a future in politics. "See if you can guess what I am…"

See *Animal House*

BOB

A junkie who leads wife Diane and two cohorts in drugstore-robbing operation up and down Pacific Northwest. He enjoys everything about the drug lifestyle, despite its constant dangers. He also has strong aversions to hats being left on beds and looking at backs of mirrors. A former altar boy in a parish run by **Tom the Priest**. "I'm a junkie. I like drugs, I like the whole lifestyle but it just didn't pay off."

See *Drugstore Cowboy*

BOBBSEY TWINS

Two! Two! Two sets of twins! These rollicking kids live an idyllic life with their perfect parents in Lakeport, a town at the head of beautiful Lake Metoka. Their father is a prosperous lumber merchant. Their mother manages their large, rambling house on a "fashionable" street, while spending her free time shopping. Nan and Bert Bobbsey, the older twins, are tall and slender with dark curly hair, red cheeks, and deep brown eyes. Compassionate Nan likes to bake cakes and make tablecloths out of paper; spirited Bert has endless confrontations with his nemesis, Danny Rugg, the town bully. When Bert and Danny get into a fight at school, Nan pleads for mercy for her twin. Bert's punishment: writing "fighting is wrong" one hundred times on a blackboard every day for a week. Freddie and Flossie Bobbsey, the younger twins, are short, stout, and fair, with round faces, light blue eyes, and fluffy golden hair. Flossie, the little "fat fairy," is the proud mother of five multiracial dolls which she keeps dutifully segregated in a drawer. Freddie, the "fat fireman," loves animals and has a cat (Snoop), a duck (Downy), and a big shaggy dog (Snap). Freddie is a sleepwalker; Bert once mistakes him for a ghost. Sassy Dinah, the plump black cook, presides over the entire household. She's been with the family so long they call her Dinah Bobbsey. She lives with her husband, Sam Johnson, the "man of all work," in "pleasant rooms over the stable."

See *The Bobbsey Twins, Merry Days Indoors and Out,* et al., Laura Lee Hope

BOBER, MORRIS

A Russian Jewish immigrant trapped and embittered in his struggling Brooklyn grocery store. His generous nature compels him to hire a shady young Italian American man over his wife's objections. When the man is caught stealing from the cash register, Morris is forced to fire him. He is finally freed from the store when a competing merchant buys him out.

See *The Assistant,* Bernard Malamud

BODELL, PEGGY SUE

A forty-three-year-old whose 1950s marriage is crumbling in the 1980s. She goes to her twenty-fifth high school reunion, faints, and when she comes to, it's the fifties again! She's got her forty-three-year-old brain, but it's ensconced in her sev-

enteen-year-old body. She can do it all over again and risk making the same mistakes, or she can change everything and risk making a whole set of new ones. Should she keep seeing the guy she eventually married (marries?) or dump him for the brooding, romantic poet-rebel she's always lusted after in her heart? Or neither of the above? "I got pregnant the night of my eighteenth birthday. Peggy Sue got married—end of story!"

See *Peggy Sue Got Married*

BODINE, JETHRO

Muscle-bound and none too bright, country boy Jethro lives with his Uncle **Jed Clampett** in Beverly Hills after Jed strikes oil. Though he only got to sixth grade at his backcountry school, Jethro perseveres to get his grade school diploma in California. Bedazzled by the bright lights of Hollywood, Jethro's always on the lookout for beautiful women and, indeed, fancies himself a playboy. He also dabbles in business, without much success. His twin sister

The Blues Brothers

is named (unfortunately for her) Jethrene; his mother is Pearl Bodine.

See *The Beverly Hillbillies*

BOK, YAKOV

A poor Russian handyman, anxious to conceal his Jewish identity, Yakov leaves the confines of the shtetl to see the world and educate himself. In anti-Semitic Kiev he manages to make a living by passing as a Gentile. Only when falsely accused of murder does he come to terms with the meaning of being a Jew.

See *The Fixer,* Bernard Malamud

BOLLING, BINX

A sensitive, smart, angst-filled southern man, approaching his thirtieth birthday. A broker by trade, he finds no solace in his work and is dismayed by the lack of love in his life. He seeks enduring truths in movies but is turned off by their pat conclusions. Finally, Binx finds a purpose in his life: helping his suicidal relative Kate. This, in turn, allows a deep bond of love to flourish between them.

See *The Moviegoer,* Walker Percy

BOLTON, MICKEY

An expert kisser and pathological liar, who walks out of a mental institution and into Eve's Lounge. Mickey claims to have been a jet pilot, mechanic, spy, and award-winning photographer, and maybe has the magazine covers to prove it. He drinks Smirnoff shooters and Guinness beer chasers with "two inches of head." He asks every woman he kisses to marry him, but only kisses women he'd marry. He also plays a mean hand of poker. Although he sweeps both **Eve** and her roommate, **Dr. Nancy Love,** off their feet, he winds up choosing only one of them.

See *Choose Me*

DR. BOMBAY

Samantha Stephens's physician, this globe-trotting warlock doctor is forever popping in from exotic, romantic sessions with his various nurses. Fancies himself a real lady-killer. His doctoring skills are often second-rate. Darrin refers to him as "the witch doctor." "Calling Dr. Bombay! Emergency, emergency, come right away!"

See *Bewitched*

BONAPARTE, JOE

Concert violinist turned prizefighter. Seduced by his love of material things, Joe abandons a promising career as a musician in the hope of making quick money as a fighter. He loves silk shirts, fast cars, and his manager's girlfriend, Lena. There's also the fact that he killed a man in the ring.

See *Golden Boy,* Clifford Odets

BOND, JAMES

Cool, suave, and debonair, he's a top agent with MI7, Her Britannic Majesty's Secret Service, and contends with the cleverest, most fiendish villains in the world. Bond's code number is 007; the double-0 designation means that he is officially licensed to kill. His favorite cigarette: Senior Service straights. He's tough enough, but he can be gentle when the occasion demands, and he's irresistible to women. Although he'll seduce any attractive lady he can, he genuinely appreciates women and gives as much pleasure as he gets. Of course, in his line of work, he's occasionally obliged to shoot a woman with whom he has only recently been intimate. To his credit, he always regrets this necessity but knows that it's all part of the job. His boss's secretary, leggy **Miss Moneypenny,** has had a massive crush on James for years, but though he flirts with her, he's far too professional to fish off the company pier, so to speak. A masterful driver, Bond loves racing his Aston Martin along twisty mountain roads, especially when chasing (or being chased by) an archvillain. Cars, boats, trains, aircraft, dune buggies, moon buggies: Bond is the master of any means of transportation known to man. One secret of his many successful missions is his total, very British unflappability. No matter how great the danger or how high the stakes, Bond never loses his cool. This calm under fire gets him out of many a tough situation.

See *Dr. No, Moonraker, Goldfinger, Casino Royale,* et al., Ian Fleming

BONDURANT, CAROL KESTER

The snappy, sarcastic secretary and good friend to psychologist **Dr. Robert "Bob" Hartley** and orthodontist **Jerry Robinson.** A single working gal, she finally finds a husband when Larry Bondurant, a travel agent, sweeps her off her feet. Carol is tall and lanky—now that she's lost over a hundred pounds. She is a native of Iowa.

See *The Bob Newhart Show*

BONE, JUDGE HENRY

He's the local judge in Rome, Wisconsin, in his eighties, crusty and impatient, yet always fair-minded. The judge disowns his son, a convicted child molester, then regrets it when his son commits suicide. Attorney **Douglas Wambaugh** is both his chief courtroom nemesis and closest confidant. His usual method of clearing the courtroom: "All right, everybody out!"

See *Picket Fences*

BONE, RICHARD

Beach-bum buddy of **Alex Cutter**, he's aimless and drifting through life, with no real ambition other than just getting by. Against his better judgment, pursuing possible killer at urgings of Alex.

See *Cutter's Way*

BONHAM, JOE

This World War I soldier is horribly wounded in battle. He ends up in a veterans' hospital, limbless, sightless, and deaf, able to communicate only by touch. And so he remains, locked away and abandoned by a society that doesn't want him or his kind around to remind them of the horrors of war.

See *Johnny Got His Gun*, Dalton Trumbo

BONNER, ADAM

A successful D.A. with a doctoral degree and the husband of legal colleague **Amanda Bonner**. He's somewhat old-fashioned in ideas, though committed to the spirit of the law and to seeing justice done in the courtroom. Adam is also capable of being condescendingly paternalistic at times, and an unequivocal chauvinist when dealing with challenges to his deeply rooted, rather conservative beliefs. Being on opposite sides in a notorious murder case (he's the prosecutor, Amanda's the defense attorney), with all the attendant publicity, has brought considerable stress and strain to their marriage.

See *Adam's Rib*

BONNER, AMANDA

Attorney-at-law, married to fellow lawyer **Adam Bonner**. Quick-witted, with a nimble and sarcastic tongue, Amanda is very much a model feminist. Unafraid to say what's really on her mind and willing to do whatever she can to defend a client. Currently, she's defending a murder suspect whom her husband is prosecuting. Despite great differences between Amanda and Adam regarding law, government, philosophy, and the appropriate places for the genders, the Bonners have enjoyed a basically sound and strong marriage.

See *Adam's Rib*

BOOGIE

Rebel, nonconformist, upwardly mobile dude in Baltimore, circa 1959. Fancies himself to be a real ladies' man and smooth talker. He works as a hairdresser while attending law school. Likes taking chances and placing bets on unusual public dares. He's currently attempting to learn to ride a horse.

See *Diner*

BOOK, JOHN

Philadelphia cop who takes the report of a young Amish boy who saw a murder occur in the Philly train station. Smart, incorruptible, and in danger from men on his own force. As the wounded hero who saved the boy and his mother from those who want them dead, Book hides out in Lancaster County Amish country until the day that big city ways clash with the 19th-century values in Book's temporary home.

See *Witness*

BOOPSIE

This ditzy blonde thinks she's a serious actress, even though she gets only bimbo roles. Her guy is ex-jock **B.D.**, who mocks her career choice until he realizes it can earn big bucks. She was last seen trying out for a place on the O. J. Simpson jury.

See *Doonesbury*

BOOTH, FRANK

Psychopath extraordinaire. A sadistic, short-tempered criminal involved in a variety of violent crimes including kidnapping, rape, assault, drug dealing, and possibly murder. He's currently holding the husband and son of **Dorothy Valens** hostage. To keep his energies flowing and his psychotic edge sharp, Booth pops pills, sucks mysterious gases, and drinks Pabst Blue Ribbon beer. Hates imported brew but loves old songs. Occasionally dons makeup and costumes when committing crimes. Carries a police radio so he can stay one step ahead of the law. Knows how to work more profanities into a single sentence than anyone else in town. "Don't you look at me!"

See *Blue Velvet*

BORDEN, HOWARD

The dim-bulb next-door neighbor to **Dr. Robert Hartley** and his wife, **Emily**, in their Chicago high-rise, Howard overcomes severe intellectual challenges to work as an airline navigator and only occasionally gets lost. Divorced and living alone, Howard bursts into the Hartleys' constantly, looking for and always accepting food. He has a son, Howie Jr. Once dated Bob's sister, Ellen. "Hi, Bob. Hi, Emily."

See *The Bob Newhart Show*

BOUDREAUX, OUISER

A tough, mouthy, abrasive resident of a Louisiana small town, whose real name is Louisa. She's one of a group of women who help their friend **M'Lynn Eatonton** through her daughter's illness and eventual death. She's rich, twice divorced, and, by her own account, "mother to three ungrateful children."

See *Steel Magnolias,* **Robert Harling**

BOURNE, JASON

Amnesia victim that somebody wants dead. A chameleon. Has had plastic surgery, enabling him to blend in with the crowd. Pensive. Confrontational. A violent man who usually suppresses his anger, he is a fierce fighter when provoked. Speaks three languages, but most comfortable with English. A nonapologetic person who has an annoying habit of apologizing. Expert with a gun. He races around the world, scrambling for his life and searching for clues to his identity with the words "Cain is for Charlie and Delta is for Cain" running through his head. Learns to trust his instincts. Discovers, to his horror, that he's the only man alive who can identify the world's deadliest assassin, Carlos.

See *The Bourne Identity,* **Robert Ludlum**

BOUVIER, ANTHONY

Good-natured, earnest ex-con. A handyman, he's the black employee of an Atlanta interior design firm run by four white women. Educates **Suzanne** Sugarbaker in the ways of the world outside her own. Banters and gossips with employers **Julia Sugarbaker, Charlene Frazier Stillfield,** and **Mary Jo Shively.** After he gets his college degree, he becomes partner in Sugarbakers.

See *Designing Women*

BOWDEN, DANIELLE

Teenage daughter of troubled lawyer. Trying to come to terms with budding sexuality, family strife, and problems with school. Interested in drama, both onstage and in real life. Finds **Max Cady** a seductive personality and even sexy, despite his dangerous behavior toward Danielle's father.

See *Cape Fear*

BOWERS, ANGELA

Uptight, busy advertising executive and divorced mother. She's much better at her job than at running a home. Therefore, she delegates domestic responsibilities to her housekeeper, **Tony Micelli.** Angela acts older than her mother, **Mona Robinson.** Conservative and a little prudish, she's somewhat in love with Tony but confused about it.

See *Who's the Boss?*

BOWLES, SALLY

Brash, sassy American singer, dancer, and fledgling actress trying to spark career in decadent, exciting 1931 Berlin. Sally is full of sexual energy which often leads her to enormous heartache. Has penchant for green fingernail polish. Can cure a hangover using raw eggs and Worcestershire sauce. Has troubled relationship with father, though she is in constant denial of this.

See *Cabaret*

BOWMAN, DAVID

After the discovery on the moon of a monolith suggesting a previous visit by an extraterrestrial intelligence, this astronaut is sent on a vaguely described mission of exploration. It turns out quite different from what was planned, thanks in large part to the activity of HAL, his spaceship's sophisticated but dysfunctional computer. Still, the epic voyage puts David—and the human race in general—through some fundamental changes.

See *2001: A Space Odyssey,* **Arthur C. Clarke**

BOYD, JOE

Perennially frustrated fan of the Washington Senators baseball team, he makes a desperate bargain and becomes a Senators superstar. Terrific at the plate, in the field, and with a song. He may yield to temptation for a while, but Joe is true-blue down deep.

See *Damn Yankees*

BOYD, PROFESSOR PETER

Likable college professor working on study of relationship between human and simian behavior. Willing to put heredity theories to the ultimate test by bringing chimpanzee subject Bonzo into his heart and home. Handsome and well meaning if a bit on the naive side.

See *Bedtime for Bonzo*

BOYD, WOODY

He's a dim-witted but amiable Boston bartender, and he's very vulnerable, because his sweetness and naiveté make this rural Indiana boy an easy mark in the big city. Respectful of his elders, he addresses his customers as "Mr. Peterson," "Dr. Crane," etc. He especially admires his boss, **Sam Malone**. He wants to be an actor, but he's got little or no talent. He eventually marries extremely rich, equally dim Kelly. Has an entire repertoire of dumb farm life stories. Once wrote and performed a slightly monotonous song for Kelly. Despite the appearance of utter stupidity, Boyd has the unique ability to cut to the heart of any situation. His unvarnished innocence and inability to lie to himself frequently leads to insight.

See *Cheers*

BOYLE, RICHARD

A wiseass, cynical journalist, Boyle leaves a troubled relationship to accompany his friend **Dr. Rock** on a road trip to El Salvador. There, he's shocked to find American interests neck-deep in the corruption and violence that are wracking that country and puts himself in mortal danger by reporting on the events he sees. He also falls in love with a local girl, and to get her to marry him, agrees to confess to a priest for the first time in decades—a rambling, hilarious affair.

See *Salvador*

BRACKMAN, DOUGLAS, JR.

Stuffy, balding, pigheaded, kinky lawyer. He is a senior partner of McKenzie, Brackman, Chaney and Kuzak, the law firm founded by his deceased father, in whose colossal shadow he must live. Douglas has an unstable marriage and a roving eye, coupled with unusual sexual preferences. He runs the business side of the firm with an iron fist, sometimes to the dismay of the other attorneys who rebel. Douglas has few good friends but is closest with **Leland McKenzie**.

See *L.A. Law*

BRADDOCK, BENJAMIN

He is a postgraduate everyman; now that he has graduated from college, he has no idea of what to do next. For now, he's living at home in California, under the comfortable roof of his suburban upper-class socialite parents, who want him to find a job and follow in their conservative footsteps. Awkward, gangly, and shy, Braddock is given a taste of the less conventional aspects of upper-class suburban life by the family's old friend **Mrs. Robinson**, a next-door neighbor. He subsequently gets at least a sense of what he might want out of life when he encounters the Robinsons's daughter, Elaine. His feelings for her catalyze hitherto-untapped reserves of strong will and guts which belie his placid, phlegmatic facade. Is doubtful about his future in plastics.

See *The Graduate*

BRADFORD, OLIVER

Horribly disfigured war veteran with severe facial scars. He is madly in love with **Laura Pennington**, despite all the odds stacked against their romance at the start. Oliver lives in a cottage by the British seaside.

See *The Enchanted Cottage*

BRADFORD, TOM

He is a middle-aged writer and no *Playgirl* pinup; still, he's married to lovely **Abby Abbott Bradford**, his levelheaded second wife. Tom's devoted to her and to their family, comprising children from their previous marriages as well as their one shared biological child, Nicholas—eight kids in all, as diverse in personality as they are in age. With a family of that size, there are plenty of problems for Tom to help deal with—from the childish worries of Nicholas, to the teenage confusion and trouble-making of a couple of older children, to the adult concerns of his oldest kid, a fully independent construction company owner. Staying objective and using the Socratic method, he helps steer his children toward their own solutions to whatever questions or problems they might have.

See *Eight Is Enough*

BRADSHAW, LIEUTENANT NICK "GOOSE"

Tall and thin with nondescript brown hair, Goose looks the part of the sidekick. He's **Pete "Maverick" Mitchell**'s best friend and straight man, both in comedy and action. "I've lost that loving feeling," Maverick warns before serenading **Charlotte "Charlie" Blackwood** in a military bar. "Oh, no," complains Goose, "I hate it when he does that!" Goose tries to keep Maverick from taking too many risks, but dies in a plane accident while at Miramar Naval Air Station as Maverick's wingman. It can be rough for sidekicks sometimes.

See *Top Gun*

BRADY, ALAN

A TV star adored by his fans and feared by his underlings. Brady kicks around brother-in-law **Mel Cooley**, titular producer of *The Alan Brady Show* but, for all practical purposes, Alan's personal punching bag. He's a great comedic talent but has a very large ego and cheats on his wife. He's never hesitant to criticize the work of writers **Rob Petrie**, **Sally Rogers**, and **Buddy Sorrell**. His baldness was a deep, dark secret until it was divulged on national TV by **Laura Petrie**. He was once the subject of a documentary film, *A Day in the Life of Alan Brady*.

See *The Dick Van Dyke Show*

BRADY, BOBBY

The youngest boy in the Brady clan, Bobby is sensitive about his age—and his height. He has an active fantasy life that includes dreams of riding with his hero, Jesse James, and playing football with Joe Namath. (He actually gets to meet the latter.)

See *The Brady Bunch*

BRADY, CAROL

She is a widow with three young daughters who marries architect **Mike Brady**, who has three kids of his own—suddenly making six kids in all. A housewife, she's a member of the PTA and dabbles in photography and sculpting. She once wrote an article about her family that was published in *Tomorrow's Woman* magazine. Mrs. Brady had a moment of fame when she won a twist contest as a teenager.

See *The Brady Bunch*

BRADY, CINDY

Cindy is the smallest of the six Brady kids, wears her blond hair "in curls," and has a bit of a lisp. She constantly complains about being the youngest, attends Clinton Grammar School, and once got onto a quiz show called *Question the Kids*, where she froze up on-camera. Wears braces.

See *The Brady Bunch*

BRADY, GREG

The oldest of six Brady kids, Greg is good-looking and athletic; he pitches in Little League and "letters" when he gets to Westdale High. He loves to surf and works part-time for Sam the Butcher to save up for a surfboard. Eventually, Greg gets his own room in the attic.

See *The Brady Bunch*

BRADY, JAN

She's the middle girl in the Brady clan, as blond and pretty as older sister, **Marcia**, but she's always jealous of her anyway. Something of a tomboy, she's sensitive about her freckles and the glasses that she has to wear. But she's eventually voted most popular girl in her high school class.

See *The Brady Bunch*

BRADY, MARCIA

Blond, perky, popular Marcia is the oldest girl of the six-kid Brady brood. A major burden in her life is having to wear braces. Marcia is active in school clubs, is the editor of her junior high newspaper, and becomes senior class president. She's very competitive with brother **Greg Brady**. Has crushes on Desi Arnez, Jr., Davey Jones, and her dentist.

See *The Brady Bunch*

BRADY, MATTHEW HARRISON

A paunchy, moralistic orator-cum-prosecutor from Weeping Water, Nebraska, married to Sarah Brady. His personal magnetism is matched by his voracious appetite. Brady, once considered a radical firebrand, ran unsuccessfully for the presidency three times. Brady's downfall is his vanity: his public humiliation when cross-examined by **Henry Drummond** on the Bible during an evolutionism vs. creationism trial contributes to his untimely death.

See *Inherit the Wind*

BRADY, MIKE

This widower with three young sons marries widow **Carol**—who has three daughters—and becomes patriarch of the combined brood. An architect, he designed their house on Clinton Avenue in Los Angeles, although clearly not with six kids in mind: it only has four bedrooms. He loves pork chops and applesauce.

See *The Brady Bunch*

BRADY, PETER

Living somewhat in older brother **Greg**'s shadow, Peter is the middle son of **Mike Brady**. He's into girls and sports (he's on the football team) but also makes elaborate science projects, sings in the glee club, and writes a column in his school paper as "Scoop Brady."

See *The Brady Bunch*

BRAINARD, PROFESSOR NED

A well-meaning, disorderly, frequently distracted, and extremely misunderstood science professor. He's always searching for ways to extend the boundaries of human knowledge and capacity through new inventions. But he has difficulty keeping track of the many ideas running through his overcrowded brain. Brainard is loyal to family, friends, and university colleagues, though he concentrates more on the stuff that emerges from his laboratory beakers. Best known invention is "flubber," Brainard's rubbery substance that defies the laws of gravity.

See *The Absent-Minded Professor*

CHIEF BRANDON

Earnest, upright, and devoted to his job, Chief Brandon has the unfortunate tendency to make crucial blunders, sometimes leading to the deaths of innocent people. He encouraged **Dick Tracy** to become a plainclothes police officer, which is a good thing, since Tracy is the one who sets things right after Brandon's mistakes.

See *Dick Tracy*

BRANDT, HELGA

A Tokyo-based SPECTRE agent, a redheaded bombshell with a weakness for British Secret Service agents. Brandt also works for Osata Chemical, a Japanese front for SPECTRE. She's an accomplished pilot, a slightly less able assassin. Ernst Stavro Blofeld has reportedly invited Brandt to help feed his prize fish.

See *You Only Live Twice,* Ian Fleming

BRANGWEN, GUDRUN

A beautiful, self-confident sculptor who returns from London to her small colliery town, even though she is repulsed by its ugliness. For Gudrun, relationships are to be entered into for the sake of experience. She falls in love with mining industrialist Gerald Crich, but their relationship is marred by their destructive, possessive approach to love. Sister of **Ursula Brangwen**.

See *Women in Love,* D. H. Lawrence

BRANGWEN, URSULA

Like sister, **Gudrun Brangwen**, a young woman known for wearing colorful stockings. Also like her sister, she is bored with her limited horizons and longs for excitement and fulfillment. A grammar school teacher in a Midlands colliery town, she marries Rupert Birkin, a school inspector with whom she achieves an ideal sensual union.

See *Women in Love,* D. H. Lawrence

BRASI, LUCA

He's big and strong as an ox but slow and halting of speech. Brasi is the fearsome enforcer for his Godfather, **Vito Corleone**. He follows orders without question or hesitation, filled with the conviction of a true believer in Don Corleone's wisdom and goodness. Once given orders by his master, nothing will deter him from carrying them out, whatever they might be. He is a significant factor in the awe in which the Corleone family is held by

The Brady Bunch

Corrie Bratter

other outfits with which it interacts. The Corleones's enemies fear Luca as the strongest bulwark of the family's defenses.

See *The Godfather,* Mario Puzo

BRATTER, CORRIE

A kooky cut-up, newly wed to **Paul**, who is so square he won't even walk barefoot in the park with her. So what if it's the middle of winter! She romps around hotel rooms in her underwear while he recoils in nervous embarrassment. She bubbles over about their fifth-floor walk-up apartment; he insists it's six floors.

See *Barefoot in the Park,* Neil Simon

BRATTER, PAUL

Good-looking newlywed lawyer who isn't as charmed as his new wife with their modest living arrangements. He tries to use reason with his free-spirited wife, which causes friction. Conservative and unspontaneous, he finally learns to let go and enjoy himself.

See *Barefoot in the Park,* Neil Simon

BRECKINRIDGE, MYRA

The sadistic, movie-mad, transsexual heroine of campy Hollywood misadventures. She's "a dish, and never forget it," and she's bent on getting a share of the wealth of former cowboy star and acting school proprietor Buck Loner, her "late husband" Myron's uncle. She is, in fact, Myron himself, recreated—or, as she would say, "self-created"—as "hot-eyed" Myra. A spiritual child of the Forties, she envisions a new world of Woman Triumphant, a new Eden that will "save the human race from extinction." "Frankly, I can think of no pleasure greater than to approach an open face and swiftly say whatever needs to be said to shut it."

See *Myra Breckinridge,* Gore Vidal

BRENNER, CATHY

Younger sister of attorney **Mitch Brenner,** resident of Bodega Bay, California. Is extremely fond of her two pet lovebirds, which were a gift from her brother. Her teacher at school is Annie Hayworth.

See *The Birds*

BRENNER, MITCH

Young San Francisco–based attorney, older brother of **Cathy Brenner.** Has a tendency to be sarcastic and quick-witted. However, is a sentimentalist at heart. Involved with **Melanie Daniels.** Something of a mama's boy despite his adult successes. Has reservoirs of unknown daring that can be summoned in moments of crises.

See *The Birds*

BREWSTER, ABBY AND MARTHA

Two sweet "little old ladies" in 1940s Brooklyn who have found themselves a fascinating hobby: they take in lonely old men, offer them an arsenic-laden glass of elderberry wine, and, having thereby put an end to their bleak lives, get Martha's son, Teddy (who thinks that he is Teddy Roosevelt), to bury them in the basement. They mean well.

See *Arsenic and Old Lace,* Joseph Kesserling

BREWSTER, CHARLIE

The suspicious teenage neighbor of vampire **Jerry Dandridge** on Oak Street in the all-American small town of Corvallis, Iowa. Charlie is an avid horror fan and believer of the supernatural; so much so that he is able to convince his girlfriend (Amy), his best friend (Evil), and local TV horror show host Peter Vincent to join forces and destroy the vampire before it kills them.

See *Fright Night,* Tom Holland

BREWSTER, PENELOPE "PUNKY"

Cute as a button, this charming little doe-eyed orphan girl can melt the hearts of the crustiest adults—she does just that with building manager Henry Warnimont, who finds her living in an abandoned apartment and ends up adopting her. Punky (it rhymes with spunky; coincidence?) has friends named Cherie and Allen. Her faithful puppy is Brandon.

See *Punky Brewster*

BRIAN, CALLED BRIAN

It's Brian's misfortune to have been born in a particular stable in Bethlehem on a particular day, in the stall next to the one where a much more famous Jewish baby is born. When the Wise Men show up at the wrong stall, they seem a bit confused; after all, a star isn't the most specific landmark. The Wise

Men eventually wander into the historically correct stall, but poor Brian is doomed to spend the rest of his life dodging disciples. He doesn't even know for sure who his father was; according to Brian's mom, who's not too fussy about her customers, he was a nice Roman soldier whose name she can't recall. All Brian knows is his life's been made miserable by hordes of people who don't want to think for themselves, but he does his best anyway, trying to "always look on the bright side of life."
See *Monty Python's Life of Brian*

BRICKER, DR. ADAM

A swinging divorcé. His job as ship's doctor on the cruise ship *Love Boat* provides him with access to a bevy of beautiful women. The doc is seemingly irresistible to female passengers. Divorced numerous times, he worries about alimony payments. Whatever his personal flaws, he's calm, cool, and greatly skilled in medical crises, with the ability to deliver babies and diagnose rare conditions when necessary. Friend and confidant to **Captain Merrill Stubing**.
See *The Love Boat*

BRIDGE, INDIA

Mother and wife, soft-spoken and self-effacing, she always defers to her husband, **Walter**. She lives in Kansas City, and the conservative social values of the Midwest guide her moral compass. She loves her children without completely understanding them; she loves her husband while being overawed by him. He tells her for whom to vote; she wouldn't dare disobey him. Her friends are often frustrated with her lack of confidence. She'd never say a rude or unkind word to anyone, although she does become flustered in awkward situations. Now that she is older and her children are leaving, she is becoming worried what she will do with herself. There is a sadness to her, of a life that is full by some standards and yet empty by others.
See *Mrs. Bridge*, Evan S. Connell

BRIDGE, WALTER

A ramrod-straight Midwest businessman with absolute confidence in himself and assurance that he is always right. Politically and socially conservative, he is unnerved by some of the ideas espoused by his children. He loves his wife, **India Bridge**, but

doesn't see how his dominating personality has crushed her spirit.
See *Mrs. Bridge*, Evan S. Connell

BRITT

You could call him the fastest blade in the West. Britt is one of seven men who have been hired to protect a Mexican village from a gang of thieves, led by one **Calvera**. He's good with a gun as well as a knife. Britt, a tall and angular chap, takes extreme pride in his work. He's also painfully quiet.
See *The Magnificent Seven*

BROCK, DR. JILL

A family physician in Rome, Wisconsin. Dr. Brock constantly struggles to balance her own career with that of her husband, Sheriff **Jimmy Brock**. She is the mother of two of Jimmy's three children, and served a brief, controversial stint as Rome's mayor. Jill was convicted in the "mercy killing" of a terminally ill cancer patient by a deliberate morphine overdose.
See *Picket Fences*

BROCK, SHERIFF JIMMY

The sheriff of Rome, Wisconsin, and husband of Dr. **Jill Brock**. His duties often collide with personal beliefs and family obligations. He has had to arrest friends on more than one occasion, and was at the center of a controversial school busing issue that nearly led to a shootout between Rome police and the National Guard.
See *Picket Fences*

BRODER, HERMAN

Polish-born Holocaust survivor, now residing in Brooklyn. He's a real cad to his Gentile wife, **Yadwiga**, who had hidden him safely during the war, and is now in the midst of an affair with **Masha**, which leads to difficulty in juggling his personal affairs. A true hedonist who is unable to appreciate or consider the possible consequences of his willful lifestyle.
See *Enemies: A Love Story*

BRODIE, JEAN

She's a spinster teacher at Marcia Blaine School for Girls, and she burns with unfulfilled desires. Her select group, the Brodie set, is the *crème de la crème*.

She often asserts that she is in her prime. Her curriculum is unorthodox, filled with fanciful tales of sex, love, and romance. "Give me a girl at an impressionable age, and she is mine for life." But she's forced to resign when one of the Brodie set accuses her of teaching fascism.

See *The Prime of Miss Jean Brodie,* Muriel Spark

BRODY, MARTIN

The newly arrived police chief of seaside resort Amity Island, Brody finds himself up against the commercial interests of the island when a great white shark begins treating their beaches like a gigantic free lunch. He wants to shut the beaches down; they feel that, compared with their livelihood, what's a floating body part or two? Don't make waves, they tell him. But at length, Chief Brody teams up with shark expert **Matt Hooper** and grizzled seaman and shark hunter **Quint** to put out in search of the voracious person-eater—despite Brody's lifelong fear of water. Does Amity Island deserve a police chief with guts like that? Probably not, but they got him.

See *Jaws,* Peter Benchley

CHIEF BROMDEN

The Chief is a towering, powerful, but slow-moving Native American who pretends to be a mute, to escape the world that has so harmed him and his people. His size, if not athletic ability, makes him a natural on the basketball court. He grows to love **Randle Patrick McMurphy**, the new patient who suspects he's faking his muteness, and who exhorts his fellows to defy **Mildred Ratched**, the nurse who oppressively oversees the ward. Finally, he breaks his silence when McMurphy is lobotomized, helps McMurphy to achieve a kind of liberty, and overcomes his personal inertia enough to make his escape from the prisonlike hospital.

See *One Flew over the Cuckoo's Nest,* Ken Kesey

BROOK, JOHN BERNARD "J.B."

J.B. to his friends and enemies alike, he's an aging gunfighter, a shootist, who has contracted cancer. He knows that in the normal course of events, he'll die a painful death from the disease, but he has a better idea. He agrees to one last gunfight, promoted like a sporting event, so he can die quickly and honorably.

See *The Shootist*

BROOKS, CONNIE

The English teacher we all wish we'd had. Connie Brooks is smart, affable, and quick-witted. She teaches at two schools, first Madison High, then Mrs. Nestor's Private Elementary School. One of her students, Walter Denton, likes her enough to drive her to school each day. Connie rents a room from neighborly Mrs. Davis, but hopes to marry—preferably biology teacher Philip Boynton. Is pursued by a gym teacher at Mrs. Nestor's named Gene Talbot; eventually, though, she weds Boynton. She likes purple jelly beans and a "School Teacher's B&B"—bed and a bath.

See *Our Miss Brooks*

BROOM HILDA

Born in 474 A.D., Broom Hilda is a green-hued, warted, vulgar, sex-starved, ineffectual witch. She outlived her last husband, Attila the Hun. Her constant companions are vegetarian Gaylord Buzzard, simple Irwin the Troll, and his beanied nephew Nerwin.

See *Broom Hilda*

BROWN, ANDREW "ANDY" HOGG

Gullible, large, and none-too-bright. Lives in New York City and is a partner in the Fresh Air Taxi Cab Company of America with his friend, **Amos Jones**. A member of the Mystic Knights of the Sea Lodge, he constantly gets suckered by the Lodge's "Kingfish," who always has a new scheme. A forgiving soul, Andy never holds a grudge—even though Kingfish calls him a "big dummy"—and never learns his lesson. Andy's girlfriend is named Madame Queen. Andy is originally from Marietta, Georgia.

See *Amos 'n' Andy*

BROWN, CHARLIE

Chubby, round-faced everyboy who always wears either the same yellow sweater with a black strip zigzagging horizontally across the middle or a whole bunch of identical ones. He's truly inept. Try as he may to excel, Charlie can't seem to do anything quite right. He's perhaps the only utterly winless sandlot pitcher in baseball history. Every autumn, he falls victim to the same prank, perpetrated by **Lucy Van Pelt**: he runs to kick a football, which Lucy pulls away at the last moment, sending poor Charlie sprawling. Seemingly inoffensive trees always devour his kites. His friends include

Schroeder, a Beethoven-worshiping little piano prodigy, always-soiled Pigpen, and freckle-faced tomboy Peppermint Patty—who has a big crush on the boy she calls Chuck. But, for sympathy, Charlie can turn to Snoopy, his floppy-eared dog—and even though Snoopy is a cynical type, ever ready to mock others, he can't help but love his master. Charlie is redeemed from utter nerdishness by his undying optimism—the way he gets right up and tries again, every single time he's knocked down—and his childish willingness to trust others, even those who victimize him repeatedly. Charlie, in his own humble way, says something important about the human spirit.

See *Peanuts,* Charles Schultz

BROWN, DR. EMMETT
Eccentric inventor of generally useless creations. Has ingenious imagination for mechanical engineering and remodeling outdated automobile lines. Pursuing the secret of time travel has been his passion for three decades. Something of a societal outcast, he is considered an oddball. His only close friend is **Marty McFly.**

See *Back to the Future*

BROWN, HANNAH
New partner to song-and-dance man **Don Hewes.** She's young, naive, and determined to make it in showbiz. She can handle a tune and has a romantic heart beating within her. Loves springtime, fancy dresses, and Easter bonnets.

See *Easter Parade*

BROWN, MURPHY
She's the star reporter for the successful Washington D.C., newsmagazine show, *FYI.* Murphy incurred the wrath of the real Dan Quayle when she announced her plans for single motherhood, later giving birth to a son, Avery. A recovering alcoholic (she spent a month at the Betty Ford Clinic), her driven, overbearing personality has made it hard to hold down a secretary. She has a keen news sense and strong ethics, which do not prevent her from terrorizing her interview subjects. Murphy loves Motown music, especially the artistry of Aretha Franklin.

See *Murphy Brown*

BROWN, ODA MAE
Quirky, colorful dreadlock-wearing storefront psychic. A con artist, she's shocked when a spirit—the recently murdered **Sam Wheat**—actually does contact her and reveals that he was murdered by a stock market crook. While she sees nothing wrong with a little scamming here and there, murder and white-collar crime are something else again. With Sam's spirit (visible and audible only to her) advising her, she helps to expose his murderer. Oda Mae also cons a bank manager into writing her a check for the amount the murderer will make from his illegal insider trading. Though the manager has actually met the woman she claims to be, at a cocktail party, he was too drunk then to remember the encounter and therefore doesn't realize that Oda Mae looks nothing like the other woman. Oda Mae reluctantly gives the check to some fund-raising nuns, who think she's crazy when she argues with the invisible ghost. When they see the amount of the check, one of the nuns faints dead away. She also succeeds in bringing Sam's spirit together with the love of his life, **Molly Jensen,** allowing him to occupy Oda Mae's body so the two lovers can make physical contact.

See *Ghost*

BROWN, VELVET
This horse-crazy girl dreams of riding her horse The Pie in England's Grand National steeplechase. She is sweetness mixed with determination. With patience and persistence, she turns an unmanageable animal into a great jumper. She's steadfast in carrying out her plans, which are aided by her mother and a young jockey.

See *National Velvet*

BROWNE, POLLY
Thrust by accident from assistant stage manager to star of a traveling musical show, Polly has to shed her shy and mousy personality and "come back a star." Complicating matters is her overwhelming crush on the leading man. So infatuated is Polly that she spins a fantasy romance in her head, often distracting her from her part in the romance on stage.

See *The Boy Friend*

Velvet Brown

BRUBAKER, HENRY

Southern prison warden with a conscience. Willing to pose as a convict in order to learn more about living conditions of the men he oversees. Tries to maintain his integrity despite corruption that permeates the prison system and is taken for granted by his peers in the business.

See *Brubaker*

BRYANT, DR. FRANK

Alcoholic burnout college professor with reputation for smarts despite his drinking problem. Likes to hide behind facades, though he is being opened up by new pupil **Rita**. Current reading fare is, in no small irony, *The Lost Weekend*.

See *Educating Rita*

BRYANT, JILL

A British diplomat stationed in Indonesia during the upheavals of the 1960s. With two weeks left on her mission, she meets **Guy Hamilton**, a sexy Australian radio reporter with a taste for excitement. As the revolution creeps closer to their Jakarta hangout, and as the stories and dangers get bigger, Guy and Jill become lovers in the midst of a tropical storm.

See *The Year of Living Dangerously*

BUBBA

Mildly retarded resident of small town along a Louisiana bayou. He's a close friend of **Forrest Gump** during military basic training and combat in Vietnam. While he has a pleasant personality, Bubba's mouth and protruding lower lip are constantly hanging open. He dreams of opening up his own shrimping business and knows endless ways to cook shrimp and talk about them.

See *Forrest Gump*

BUCHANAN, DAISY

Impressionable and weak-willed Daisy Fay, a society girl from Louisville, Kentucky, marries **Tom Buchanan** of Chicago. It's done on the rebound after a thwarted wartime love affair with **Jay Gatsby**. Beautiful, vacuous, and selfish, she and Tom have one child, a daughter, Pamela. She appears to tolerate her husband's extramarital affairs and indulges in one of her own with Gatsby, whom she meets again through the combined efforts of her friend **Jordan Baker** and her distant cousin **Nick Carraway**. The greatest attraction of this otherwise unexceptional woman, to both Buchanan and Gatsby, is her position in society. "Her voice is full of money," Gatsby says. The crux of her life is having to choose between her husband and her lover.

See *The Great Gatsby*, F. Scott Fitzgerald

BUCHANAN, LIEUTENANT MITCH

Even though he's forty plus, he looks really good in his regulation L.A. county lifeguard's uniform—a swimsuit. Mitch is in charge of a group of well-toned and well-intentioned lifeguards at Malibu Beach. Divorced, he has won custody of his son, Hobie, from ex-wife Gayle. Has romanced reporter Kay Morgan. A stand-up guy.

See *Baywatch*

BUCHANAN, TOM

Tom is a hulking, fairly gifted athlete and polo player with an animal intensity and drive that he uses to his selfish advantage at every opportunity. He's on the simpleminded side and puts great stock in whatever idea that is *au courant*, no matter how ridiculous, as in his embracing the views espoused in *The Rise of the Colored Empires*. Tom is the scion of an exceptionally wealthy family in Chicago, and he and his wife, **Daisy Buchanan**, live among the idle rich of East Egg on Long Island, across a bay from Daisy's distant cousin **Nick Carraway** and **Jay Gatsby**. Buchanan believes he can make all of his problems disappear by throwing money at them. He preaches family values at the same time that he's having an affair with **Myrtle Wilson**, the wife of the local garage owner, and ends his affair only at the threat of exposure.

See *The Great Gatsby*, F. Scott Fitzgerald

BUCHMAN, IRA

The unmarried cousin of New York filmmaker **Paul Buchman**, he plays the saxophone and has his own band. He's played such blockbuster gigs as a singles dance in a New York state penitentiary and Paul's wedding. Ira recently started dating a friend of Paul's wife (**Jamie Buchman**), but one gets the feeling it won't last. He may not be the brightest, but deep down, he's a really good guy.

See *Mad About You*

BUCHMAN, JAMIE

Jamie is the attractive, thirtyish wife of **Paul Buchman**. The couple lives in a great Manhattan apartment with their dog, Murray. A thinking person's yuppie in the perfect nineties marriage, she has made various career moves and is now trying to operate her own business. Older child who aims to please. She gave up smoking when she got married but still has a puff every now and then. Contemplating having children and told her husband that his nephew was so cute her "uterus hurt."

See *Mad About You*

BUCHMAN, PAUL

Neurotic yet likable New York filmmaker who is married to bubbly, attractive **Jamie Buchman**. They live in an apartment that most New Yorkers would give their right arm to inhabit. Paul's family lives nearby, including his overbearing mother, Sylvia, and his father, Verne. The perfect nineties husband. Adores his less-than-bright dog, Murray, who has a repertory of one trick.

See *Mad About You*

BUCK, JOE

Good-looking but none too bright, this Texan dishwasher gets the bright idea that he can make big money as a male prostitute for rich ladies in New York City. His nasty upbringing at the hands of a single mother and grandmother, both of whom had bizarre sexual habits, has left Joe Buck with warped ideas about love and affection. He soon finds there's a scarcity of wealthy women in need of "servicing" and has to resort to a series of sleazy liaisons of all kinds while he waits to make his big score. All he really wants is unconditional love, and he finds it in the unlikely source of the tubercular, crippled bum **Ratso Rizzo**.

See *Midnight Cowboy*, James Leo Herlihy

BUCK, UNCLE RUSSELL

This gregarious, gambling, fun-seeking bachelor is called upon to pinch-hit in baby-sitting situations. He's fond of turning huge pancakes with a snow shovel and other equally enterprising housekeeping strategies. He's outwardly jolly, but in reality is lonely and enjoys being part of a family, even if only temporarily.

See *Uncle Buck*

BUCKET, CHARLIE

A kind, pure-hearted, poor little British boy whose dream comes true when he finds a winning contest ticket and is permitted to tour **Willy Wonka's** candy factory with his kindly grandfather **Joe Bucket**. Though he once disobeys Wonka's tour rules, the candymaker takes him on as a protégé in the business.

See *Charlie and the Chocolate Factory*, Roald Dahl

BUCKET, GRANDPA JOE

He's poor, but he's kindly, and he's the grandfather of **Charlie Bucket**. In fact, the boy is his main pride and pleasure in life, and he lives to teach him honesty and personal dignity. His teachings bear fruit when he and Charlie tour **Willy Wonka's** candy factory. Charlie is chosen to go to work there, because, despite Charlie's lowly origins, he's far more upright and responsible than other, richer kids.

See *Charlie and the Chocolate Factory*, Roald Dahl

BUD

He is a hard-boiled, hard-smoking, hard-drinking automobile repossessor who takes **Otto**, a new repo man, under his wing, teaching him the tricks of the trade and drumming into him the Repo Man's Code—a list of rules to help the repo man make sense of a fractured, deteriorating world, which he views with cynical detachment.

See *Repo Man*

BUDD, BILLY

A young British sailor of Christlike innocence and good will. An unlettered orphan, Billy looks and acts younger than his twenty-one years. His fatal flaw is a debilitating stutter when under emotional stress. Unable to defend himself against the malicious charges of the ship's master at arms, he lashes out at his accuser with a blow, which results in the man's death. Despite the young man's essential goodness, he must answer to the dictates of naval justice. The penalty for his action is hanging.

See *Billy Budd, Foretopman*, Herman Melville

BUELLER, FERRIS

Self-confident, extraordinarily inventive high school

Ferris Bueller

student in bad need of a day off. Knows how to smooth-talk his way around the adults in his life in order to get the things he needs. He has a distinctive outlook on life and is perfectly willing to share his observations with others. Ferris enjoys the city of Chicago and all that it has to offer. A baseball fan, an art lover, and a true exhibitionist. Very loyal to his friends, he's ready to back them up in bad times.

See *Ferris Bueller's Day Off*

BUFFALO BILL

This eerie serial killer gets the nickname Buffalo Bill because of the way in which he treats his young female victims. He becomes the target of a massive, FBI-led manhunt. One of the hunters is Agent **Clarice Starling**, who gets some off-the-wall counsel from captured serial killer **Hannibal Lecter**.

See *The Silence of the Lambs,* Thomas Harris

BUGGIN' OUT

He is an angry young resident of Brooklyn's Bed-Sty district. Wears distinctive haircut, eye-popping glasses, and prized pair of Air Jordan sneakers. Wants to see justice done—by any means necessary. He's presently organizing a boycott of **Sal**'s pizzeria. Close to both **Mookie** and **Radio Raheem**. "If I wasn't a righteous black man, you'd be in serious trouble."

See *Do the Right Thing*

BUKOWSKI, CLAUDE

He affects a British accent and claims to come from Manchester, England. Claude keeps up with the *London Times*. Human being number 1005963297 dash J, the most beautiful beast in the forest. Actually, he is from Flushing, Queens, New York— a draftee on his way to Vietnam. His fondest wish: "I don't want to be a dentist or a lawyer or a bum…I don't want to be a rock 'n' roll hero or a movie star. I just want to have lots of money."

See *Hair,* Gerome Ragni, James Rado and Galt MacDermott

BULLITT

Bullitt is a single-minded cop who'll do whatever it takes to get his man—except make a bad bust. He has no patience for politics and politicians and is a man of action in every aspect of his life, especially behind the wheel of his muscle car.

See *Bullitt*

BULLOCK, IRENE

A Park Avenue brat who finds her soul in the midst of a scavenger hunt that is part of a gala evening. When she and her sister, Cornelia, go out to find "a forgotten man," they end up at a location near the East River. She befriends **Godfrey Park** after her sister insults him. With Godfrey's help, she wins the scavenger hunt over her sister. She later offers Godfrey a job as the family butler.

See *My Man Godfrey*

THE BUMSTEAD FAMILY

The life of this forever-young married couple is a series of minor domestic misadventures. Blondie, the wife, is a ditzy, curvy, curly-haired blonde, who wears tight sweaters and skirts. Her main function as a wife seems to be to make sure that her husband, Dagwood, has his briefcase as he rushes out the door each morning. He's a sometimes-bumbling businessman who despite his slim physique loves waking in the middle of the night for an oversize sandwich—or any other kind of snack. He's notable for his hair, which resists all attempts at management and sticks out from the sides of his head like a pair of rigid wings. A life of unending disaster seems to be an effective marital bond; in an age of short marriages, Dagwood and Blondie have been together a long, long time.

See *Blondie,* Chic Young

BUNDREN, ADDIE

From the deep South, wife of **Anse**, mother of **Cash**, **Dewey Dell**, **Jewel**, Darl, and Vardaman Bundren. Former schoolteacher taught by her gloomy father that the purpose of life is to prepare for death, she remains a life force who craves passionate encounters. Marries the lazy, selfish Anse in hopes of giving her own life meaning through intense, violent contact with another human. Conceives her favorite son, Jewel, in an affair with the local preacher, Whitfield. Her dying wish is to be buried in her hometown of Jefferson, Mississippi, setting her family off on a long trek with her decomposing body in the back of a mule-drawn wagon.

See *As I Lay Dying,* William Faulkner

BUNDREN, ANSE

A hill farmer who inherits his parents' farm just south of the Yoknapatawpha River in Mississippi. An indolent man who believes that he will die if he sweats and is so ineffectual that his sons wind up making many of his decisions. Though he's mean, simpleminded, and selfish, he nonetheless undertakes the ordeal of returning the corpse of his wife, **Addie**, to be interred in her hometown, Jefferson, Mississippi. That obligation fulfilled, he "borrows" money from **Dewey Dell** for a new set of teeth and promptly finds a new wife. Father of **Cash**, **Jewel**, Dewey Dell, Darl, and Vardaman.

See *As I Lay Dying*, William Faulkner

BUNDREN, CASH

Oldest son of **Anse** and **Addie Bundren**. A wise, good-hearted country type, Cash, short for Cassius, is a carpenter who builds his mother's coffin outside her window as she lies dying. His leg is broken when the wagon containing his mother's coffin is upset during a wild river crossing. He spends the rest of the journey resting on top of the coffin, his leg in a homemade cast that will cripple him for life.

See *As I Lay Dying*, William Faulkner

BUNDREN, DEWEY DELL

Seventeen-year-old daughter of **Anse** and **Addie Bundren**. Unmoved by her mother's death, Dewey Dell is anxious to make the trip to Jefferson only for the sake of buying a "cure" for her pregnancy. Unable to pay for the pills with cash, she gives herself to the drugstore clerk. Earthy, almost animalistic, and vengeful, she betrays her brother Darl because he knows of her pregnancy.

See *As I Lay Dying*, William Faulkner

BUNDREN, JEWEL

Favorite son of **Addie Bundren**, the product of her affair with a local preacher. An eighteen-year-old blend of inarticulateness and action whose most intense relationship is with his beloved horse, which is traded for a pair of mules by his father, **Anse Bundren**, during the journey to Jefferson with Addie's body. He twice rescues his mother's coffin, once from a flooding river and once from a barn fire set by half brother Darl in an attempt to cremate the decomposing corpse. Jewel is badly burned in the fire.

See *As I Lay Dying*, William Faulkner

THE BUNDY FAMILY

"When one Bundy is embarrassed, the rest of us feel good about ourselves." There's not a lot of kindness, caring, money, or food going around the Bundy household in Chicago. Master of the house and the remote is Al, a raunchy, working-class salesman at Gary's Shoes and Accessories for the Beautiful Woman, where he rakes in $12,000 a year. His life is a "catalogue of failure," and Al constantly hearkens back to his moment in the sun, at James K. Polk High School, when he was voted most valuable football player of 1966. He married high school girlfriend Peg Wanker, whom he met at a hangout called Johnny B. Goods, where he still holds the record for the most fries eaten at one sitting. It hasn't been a fairy-tale marriage: Peg thinks Al's job is the pits; Al thinks Peg is a tramp—when he thinks of her at all. Peg doesn't cook or clean and is always ready to jump in the sack, something Al sees as a "marital duty." Peg is often clad in a tight leopard-skin outfit, and nobody can miss her bright red hair and bulging cleavage. Peg's claim to fame is as record-holder for a perfect 300 score at Jim's Bowlarama. Oldest child Kelly shares her mother's affinity for tight clothes and big hair. She's a beautiful blonde who's better off keeping her mouth shut, as she's prone to malapropisms like, "I was born in February. I'm an Aquarium." Bud, the youngest Bundy, has gobs of testosterone raging through his body. He shares his father's attraction to large breasts and babes. Like his dad, he's always getting shot down. Bud calls his pajamas his "love clothes," which is basically wishful thinking. He's got the hots for neighbor **Marcy Rhoades D'Arcy**. Marcy's a loan officer whose first husband, **Steve**, left her after he lost his job, and ran off to become a park ranger. Then she met **Jefferson** while on a drunken binge at a bankers' convention. She and Jefferson have great sex, much to Peggy's dismay. Buck, a big French sheepdog, is often the voice of sanity in the household.

See *Married...with Children*

BUNKER, ARCHIE

A middle-aged, bigoted, blue-collar loudmouth. Balding, gray, and growing a potbelly, Archie is the loading dock foreman at the Pendergast Tool and Die Company. He lives at 704 Houser Street in Corona, Queens, with wife **Edith**, daughter **Gloria**, and son-in-law **Mike Stivic**. He loves his daughter but is appalled at her liberal politics and thoroughly

Archie and Edith Bunker

disgusted with her choice of a husband. Mike, known as Meathead, a Polish American "egghead liberal," is an unemployed sociology student whose presence provides a constant thorn in Archie's side and catalyst for the airing of his ultraconservative and usually biased views. Archie believes society has gone out of control and that the rise of minority groups has led to moral decay. He yearns for the good old days "when girls were girls and men were men." The decline of Archie's America is evidenced by the presence of black neighbors (the **Jeffersons**) and racially mixed coworkers. A perpetuator of every possible negative stereotype and belief about every known racial or sociological group, Archie has a no-holds-barred approach to expressing his opinions. He never saw an ethnic slur he didn't like. Blacks are criminals, Hispanics are lazy, and "England is a fag country." Derogatory nicknames and crude observations are just the beginning for any non-WASP who may find him- or herself in Archie's company. His disdain for others carries over to his wife, whom he loves but treats like a stupid servant and calls "dingbat." Uneducated and unenlightened, he spends much time in his dilapidated easy chair bellowing at those who disagree with his views.

See *All in the Family*

BUNKER, EDITH

Good-hearted wife, superficially mild and dim, but possessing inner strength and common sense. Middle-aged homemaker for husband **Archie Bunker**, grown daughter **Gloria**, and son-in-law **Mike** at 704 Houser Street in Corona, Queens. As Archie's wife, Edith's role in life is to cater to his needs and accept responsibility when she fails to recognize what those needs are. When she errs, she is called "dingbat." She flits around the house bringing Archie what food or drink he requires while listening to his views on society's ills. Much of what is said around her seems to go over her head, but once in a while Edith bests Archie with a zinger straight from the hip. Her voice is high and shrill, and she seems to be in a perpetual nervous state. Though Archie is her lord and master, she does not subscribe to his thoughts on society's ills. She has no prejudices of her own, and her good heart is obvious to those around her. Her best friend is black next-door neighbor **Louise Jefferson**. She

easily shifts from one of her husband's tirades full of racial slurs to a cup of coffee and gossip with Louise. She is a loving and caring mother to Gloria, though can't understand the cultural forces such as feminism and sexual freedom that are shaping the world today. Edith runs interference between Archie and Mike, though seems to favor neither side. She alone sees the cuddly, vulnerable Archie and truly loves him. She's a happy person who prefers to see the best in all people.

See *All in the Family*

BURGER, HAMILTON

This no-nonsense district attorney has a sterling conviction record, except against his archrival, **Perry Mason**. Aided by Lieutenant Tragg, Burger assembles airtight murder cases against Mason's clients, only to be foiled by confessions Mason wrings out of witnesses, passersby, and the occasional gallery member. Don't ever call him Ham.

See *Perry Mason*

BURKE, AMOS

Suave, handsome, and wildly wealthy, he's a detective who drives around L.A. in his chauffeured Rolls Royce and lives in a mansion. Wry, intelligent, and catnip to women, Burke is always dressed to the nines and generally unflappable. When he gets older, his son Peter joins him in fighting crime.

See *Burke's Law*

BURKE, HAZEL

The kooky, irrepressible chatterbox housekeeper of reserved lawyer **George Baxter** and his wife, Dorothy. Hazel is plain-speaking and says whatever comes into her mind, no matter whom she's talking to. Her mouth often gets her in trouble, but people quickly forgive her because she's sincere and endearing, and probably reminds them of their favorite aunt. Though she's devoted to "Mr. B" and "Missy," she frequently gets them into trouble. Hazel pokes her nose into everyone's business. Wears a maid's uniform with a little cap perched on her bright red hair.

See *Hazel*

BURNS, MAJOR FRANK

What a creep. He's part of the 4077th MASH (Mobile Army Surgical Hospital) unit, a mediocre surgeon who blames others for his mistakes. He's a sanctimonious hypocrite who enjoys a torrid liaison with **Major Margaret "Hot Lips" Houlihan**. He's a gutless, chinless, ferret-faced whiner. His roomies are fellow surgeons **Hawkeye Pierce**, **Trapper John McIntyre**, and **B. J. Hunnicut**, for whom he serves as the butt of constant pranks and barbs. Though he's fond of pretending to be a military, macho guy, he's a coward. He's a real McCarthyite flag-waver who refuses to treat prisoners of war. When Hot Lips dumps him, he loses it totally and goes AWOL, to no one's sorrow. The good die young, but Frank gets shipped home early.

See *M*A*S*H*

BURNS, HARRY

Ride-sharing partner with **Sally Albright**, another 1977 University of Chicago graduate. Career choice: labor organizing. Has a tendency to hold forth on his views regarding relations between the sexes. Typical theory: "No man can be friends with a woman he finds attractive. He always wants to have sex with her."

See *When Harry Met Sally*

BURNS, WALTER

He's a crusty, single-minded, hardworking, tough-talking Chicago newspaper editor who lives for the pressure of looming press deadlines. Prefers his job to just about anything else in the world and can't understand why anyone else in the field doesn't have the same attitude. Burns speaks at a rapid clip in order to keep up with his racing thoughts. He'll do anything he has to in order to preserve the sanctity and high quality of his beloved newspaper and secure the continued services of his ace reporter, **Hildy Johnson**.

See *The Front Page*

THE BUTLER

Reticent and proper, he's the personal valet to all those officers designated as Number 2 in this mysterious village and prison compound, ostensibly in England. But beneath that austere and prim facade, there beats a rebellious heart, and the Butler is actually anxious to get out of the Village's gentle but suffocating grasp. "Be seeing you."

See *The Prisoner*

BUTLER, RHETT

The black sheep of a Charleston family, he goes against the grain of the antebellum South, speaking his mind on the subject of the coming Civil War and maintaining that the South is bound to lose. His disinterest in the opinions of others is almost absolute. A gambler at life and at the card table, he makes a fortune running guns and supplies when war breaks out. Tall, dark, and handsome, with a mustache and a cynical smile, he can charm stiff spinsters as easily as giggling young belles. He admires beautiful, spirited **Scarlett O'Hara** and sees the strength underneath her affected gentility. Though he feels no loyalty to any woman or country, as the South falls to the North, pangs of conscience make him join the Confederate Army. His normal objectivity doesn't help in his relationship with Scarlett, and he thinks he can make her love him by catering to her whims. But when she persists in her love of **Ashley Wilkes**, Butler is deeply hurt. He respects **Melanie Wilkes**, even though he thinks her naive in her worship of Scarlett. As he gets older, Rhett becomes tired of pursuing Scarlett as well as the life he has led. Neither has brought him any happiness.

See *Gone with the Wind*, Margaret Mitchell

Hazel Burke
Photo courtesy of CBS

UNORTHODOX SERVANTS OF THE LORD

Rev. Will B. Dunn
Father John Mulcahy
Sister Bertrille
Father Guido Sarducci
Rev. Jim Ignatowski
Father Dowling
Father Merrin

PRINCESS BUTTERCUP

Blond, delicately beautiful young woman who survives separation from her true love, Westley, kidnapping, and a forced marriage. Beneath her demure veneer, she's strong-willed, sharp-tongued, and given to fisticuffs, and poses as great a threat to those who would help her as to those who would harm her.

See *The Princess Bride*

BUTTERMAKER, MORRIS

Failed minor leaguer whose misspent life has left him reduced to coaching a terrible Little League baseball team in Southern California. Not a cheerful, upbeat type at all, his fate has rendered him even more dyspeptic and dour. Encourages dirty play between bouts of berating his hapless, motley squad. Has a love-hate affinity for his star pitcher and the team's hope for respectability, **Amanda Whurlizer**. Coach Buttermaker's other interests and recreation appear to be limited exclusively to beer drinking. His hygiene is questionable. He is occasionally sober.

See *The Bad News Bears*

MRS. BUTTERWORTH

Has devoted herself to brightening the lives of children at the breakfast table. Her methods are transparent. That is, she's made of glass, and she really knows how to pour on the syrup.

See *Mrs. Butterworth*

BUTT-HEAD

He's a heavy-metal-loving, braces-wearing, lispy-voiced ninth-grade boy, with one main goal in life: to score—preferably with local white-trash chicks Lolita and Tanqueray. He worships Todd, a local, hot-rodding, twenty-something punk. Butt-head is obsessed with "thingies." Given the choice, he'd eat a diet consisting solely of convenience-store nachos. He's the dominant partner—uh, huh-huh-huh—in his friendship with **Beavis**. "Shut up, Beavis, before I kick your ass."

See *Beavis and Butt-head*

CADE, JOHNNY

Sure, the local rich kids call him a greaser, but underneath the tough facade, there beats the heart of a sensitive boy who has suffered from being raised in an abusive home. Johnny becomes a wanted man when he knifes a snobbish rich boy who tries to drown his friend **Ponyboy Curtis**. "Picture a little dark puppy that has been kicked too many times and is lost in a crowd of strangers, you'll have Johnny."

See *The Outsiders*, S. E. Hinton

CADELL, RUPERT

A somewhat jaded college professor who's a guest at a dinner party given by two of his former students, **Brandon Shaw** and **Philip**. Cadell, who preaches and teaches some highly intellectualized, elitist philosophies, slowly begins to understand, and be appalled by, the kind of monsters into which his teaching may have turned these young men.

See *Rope*

CADY, MAX

Ex-con now out of prison after serving fourteen years for rape. Well muscled, heavily tattooed, has high native intelligence and a vicious temper. A voracious reader, particularly when it comes to legal books and the Bible. Smooth talker and deceptively charming at times. He can be a pussycat when it suits him, but in the blink of an eye, his psycho- and sociopathic side comes through in frightening fashion. Skilled at manipulating other people and makes only deliberate and well-thought-out moves when it comes to dealing with others. He has a strong revenge motive for cozying up to **Danielle Bowden**. "Come out, come out wherever you are!"

See *Cape Fear*

CAGNEY, CHRISTINE

She's the archetypical New York Irish cop: honest, hardworking, hard drinking, and more than a little bit bullheaded (just like her ex-cop father), except for the fact that she's a woman and she knows she's an alcoholic. Christine is obsessive about her job as a detective, to the point that her personal life has always taken a distant second place. She's a cop without a time clock first, and a human being second—if there's time. She feels that her partner, **Mary Beth Lacey**, should be as committed to the job as she is, despite the fact that Mary Beth has a personal life that includes a family.

See *Cagney & Lacey*

CAINE, KWAI CHANG

Mystical half-Asian man of peace. With his quiet, calm, watchful manner, he completely absorbs his surroundings. Caine was taught the art of kung fu and how to truly live by Chinese masters, and he tries to impart their wisdom to all he meets. Caine seems frail at first glace, but there is steel underneath, in body, mind, and attitude. He is called "grasshopper" by his Chinese masters and "Chinaman" by people he meets in the United States. He'll use kung fu if pushed but prefers to convert his enemies to the peaceful way of life. Wears no shoes and a wide-brimmed straw hat.

See *Kung Fu*

CALL, WOODROW

A former Texas Ranger, Call don't talk much, and when he does, his words seem to leak past his teeth in slow spurts, as if they were pumped from a nearly dry well. But don't think he's slow, because some people who make that mistake have a tendency to wind up dead. This man's so rawhide-tough that he don't shave: he pounds his whiskers through with a hammer and bites them off inside. He's saddened by what he considers to be the loss of freedom caused by the encroachment of settlers and city folk. To escape the congestion, he and his partner, **Augustus McCrae**, decide to drive a big herd of cattle all the way from Texas into Montana, a long journey, with nary a road or a filling station to be found. Augustus is, to him, a lifelong source of aggravation, both when they were Rangers together and ever since. He believes Gus to be in the running for the title of the laziest man alive.

See *Lonesome Dove*, Larry McMurtry

CALLAHAN, HARRY

Rule-breaking, gotta-be-me San Francisco cop with the baddest attitude on the force. Harry is very intense when pursuing criminals, even if it means violating certain constitutional rights and bending, or fracturing, procedural rules. Harry is considered by some to be a crypto-fascist with a badge. Wears raincoat and a permanent sneer. Carries a .44 Magnum, the most powerful handgun ever made. His only humanizing trait is a liking for jazz. Occasionally, he seems unsure about the amount of ammunition remaining in his gun. Known to ask assailants excruciating questions at high-tension moments strictly for laughs. Although a San Franciscan, he never wore flowers in his hair. "Feeling lucky, punk?"

See *Dirty Harry*

CALVERA

The head of a Mexican bandit gang, and a very bad dude. Calvera is wily, imperious, and loves to hear himself talk. He and his men regularly terrorize one small Mexican village, stealing most of the food grown by its farmers, ravishing their womenfolk, kicking their dogs, and making snide comments about the scenery. Calvera was once chased by the U.S. Army for robbing a Texas bank.

See *The Magnificent Seven*

CALVIN

He's a remarkably precocious, towheaded, six-year-old boy. His best friend is Hobbes, a stuffed animal who, to others, is inanimate but with whom Calvin has intense philosophical discussions. Calvin is loaded with pithy observations that point out the foibles and absurdities of the adult world.

See *Calvin and Hobbes*

CAMARERI, JOHNNY

A large, soft-spoken, kindly, levelheaded Italian American man in New York. He gets the pretty, pragmatic **Loretta Castorini** to agree to marry him, but not until the impending death of his beloved mama in Italy, by appealing to her sense of future security. But then mama takes a surprise turn for the better.

See *Moonstruck*

CAMARERI, RONNY

He's a hotheaded, romantic baker. He's lost a hand, for which he blames older brother **Johnny Camareri**. He refuses to relent and forgive, even when Johnny's fiancée, **Loretta Castorini**, comes to invite him to their upcoming wedding. As he explains his reasons, he also falls deeply and completely in love with Loretta and sets out to court her. He is a true believer in fate, romance, and true love. Despite his gruff blue-collar ways, Ronny loves the opera, the art of great, tragic passion and romance. He woos Loretta by taking her to the Metropolitan Opera. His intense feelings are a sharp contrast to his brother's phlegmatic practical-

THE MAID HALL OF FAME

Hazel Burke
Alice Nelson
Nell Carter
Daphne Muldoon
Beulah
Florida Evans
Florence Johnston
Mammy

ity. He also makes a great loaf of bread.
See *Moonstruck*

CAMERON, RACHEL
A sensitive, pretty small-town schoolteacher who, at 35, is at the exact middle of her life, and is thought of, by herself and the world, as a spinster. Still a virgin, she lives to serve her overbearing mother, with whom she lives above the funeral parlor where her now dead father once embalmed corpses. So it goes, until she meets and sleeps with a city man whom she knew as a boy, which awakens her sexuality, and, in turn, makes her see the need to break away from her mother.
See *Rachel, Rachel*

CAMILLE
Self-sacrificing and romantic courtesan who falls in love with wealthy Parisian social figure Armand, which infuriates Armand's stuffy dad. Has nagging cough, the result of tuberculosis, which is slowly killing her. Stoic and somewhat alienated from respectable society due to both illness and reputation. But still, she possesses great beauty, both inside and out, to the very, very bitter end.
See *Camille*

CAMPBELL, BURT
Honest, middle-class Burt is madly in love with his wife, **Mary Campbell**, and tries gamely to understand the many idiosyncrasies of his sons and stepsons. He has an inferiority complex regarding his wealthy in-laws, the **Tates**, and a pathological conviction that he can become invisible by snapping his fingers. Oh, yes, and he also gets abducted by aliens.
See *Soap*

CAMPBELL, MARY
Solidly middle-class, Mary seems a typical American housewife. But that's just on the surface; she's had multiple marriages, her son Danny is a none-too-bright but charming scoundrel; her son Jodie is gay and contemplating a sex change; and then there's Chuck, who carries around a ventriloquist's dummy everywhere he goes, and has earnest dialogues with it/him. Her husband is **Burt Campbell**, and she has a very close relationship with her sister, **Jessica Tate**.
See *Soap*

CAMPBELL, OTIS
He's Mayberry's town drunk. Otis is an unkempt bear of a man whose good heart and harmless alcoholic binges earn him an always-ready jail cell, courtesy of Sheriff **Andy Taylor**. Otis locks himself into the neatly furnished (courtesy of **Aunt Bee**) cell when drunk and sleeps it off. He sings when drunk and is always repentant once he sobers up. He never drives when on a tear but has been known to hijack a bull.
See *The Andy Griffith Show*

CAMPION, ANTHONY
A British vicar sent to Australia by his church to convince artist **Norman Lindsay** to curb his controversially carnal religious paintings. While at Lindsay's estate, Campion's marriage to Estella changes dramatically in the sensually charged atmosphere. "Church-baiting has always been a popular pastime."
See *Sirens*

CAP'N CRUNCH
Lovable pirate captain who leads all sorts of breakfast cereal adventures that often end in mishap. Probably made poor grades in Pirate School. Despite the Cap'n's less than stellar career as a pirate, he was recruited by a leading cereal company to act as their spokespirate. The success of his endorsement opened doors for a wide range of has-been monsters, aliens and animals, including Quisp, Tony the Tiger, Count Chocula and the inimitable Lucky Leprechaun. Crunch is known for posing paradoxes to his fans, including, "stays crunchy, even in milk."
See *Cap'n Crunch Cereal*

CANFIELD, DR. BENJAMIN
Bureaucrat physician. Chief of services at Eastman Medical Center in Los Angeles, he sees great public relations advantage in having teen-genius resident **Doogie Howser** on staff but worries about his lack of experience. Often is at odds with **David Howser** over medical and ethical issues. Tries to run a tight ship.
See *Doogie Howser, M.D.*

CANOVA, LOU

Hard-drinking, two-timing, small-time Italian American crooner desperate to make it in the big time. A big man with a heart of brass. Currently cheating on his wife with Mafia moll **Tina Vitale**. Represented by minor showbiz legend **Danny Rose**, whom Canova wouldn't mind dumping for a better-connected agent.

See *Broadway Danny Rose*

CANYON, LIEUTENANT COLONEL STEVENSON B.

A solid, upstanding pilot for the air force, Steve—as he's known—flies around the country solving problems and finding adventure. Eventually, he becomes the commanding officer of Big Thunder Air Force Base in California.

See *Steve Canyon*

CAPP, ANDY

Snooker, football, a pint of ale, and a lovely lass: these are the things that brighten Andy's life. His mother-in-law, the vicar, and the bill collector: they're the things that cast dark shadows to obscure the brightness—to say nothing of his not-so-understanding wife. Wears a funny cap.

See *Andy Capp*

CAPRICE, BIG BOY

Boss of the criminal underworld. Face permanently contorted, mind always in a state of sheer frenzy. Prefers over-the-top action in every move he makes and every order he gives. Likes wearing big-shouldered suits. Archenemy of good guy Detective Dick Tracy.

See *Dick Tracy*

CARAVELLA, JOHNNY "DR. JOHNNY FEVER"

The doctor is an aging rock 'n' roller. Once he hit the radio heights, but now he works for ailing Cincinnati radio station WKRP. He's been around the rock 'n' roll block but doesn't remember most of it. His personality is droll and dry. He makes out that he's just too cool to really care. There's still some residual hippie in Johnny; even if he's lost the edge, he isn't quite ready to conform. He has little patience for the establishment authority figures at WKRP, his boss, **Arthur Carlson**, newsman **Les**

Nesman, and advertising man **Herb Tarlek**. He lusts after bombshell receptionist **Jennifer Marlowe**.

See *WKRP in Cincinnati*

CARL

Slobbering country club golf groundskeeper whose mind is on permanent vacation. He lives to catch the groundhogs that are digging holes all over the course, coming up with elaborate strategies to flood them out of their tunnels or to blow them up with plastic-explosive models of what he imagines to be sexy female groundhogs. Carl lives in a tiny shack on the country club grounds, where he likes to entertain guests, getting them loaded on "big Bob Marley joints" and cheap wine. He has an active imaginary life—picturing himself making heroically impossible golf shots—and an active libido, picturing himself making it with the club's middle-aged female members. "It's in the hole."

See *Caddyshack*

CARLIN, ELLIOT

This wildly neurotic real estate salesman and entrepreneur thinks everyone dislikes him. Problem is, he's right. A long-term patient of **Dr. Robert Hartley**, he's dour and generally mean-spirited. Mr. Carlin is constantly looking for counsel from Bob—anywhere, anytime—but, dependent though he is, he's still not above calling his therapist a "chump" to his face.

See *The Bob Newhart Show*

CARLSON, ARTHUR "BIG GUY"

He's the owner of floundering Cincinnati radio station WKRP. Well, okay, it's really his mother who owns it, but he's nominally in charge. Well, okay, he's not *really* in charge. The day-to-day operations and most decisions are handled by the receptionist, **Jennifer Marlowe**. Although he's in his fifties, he still fears his redoubtable mother. He's nervous, whiny, and fluttery and tends to spend time hidden in his office, playing with electric trains or other toys. With all his flaws, the Big Guy is essentially a very decent, kind man.

See *WKRP in Cincinnati*

CARLSON, TONY

Glib San Francisco ex-cop and private detective,

©1996 Capital Cities/ABC, Inc

Krystle Carrington

hired for unusual work by **Gloria Mundy**. Working closely with his client on an intriguing case that is leading him toward much bigger things than he's ever been involved with previously. He's also a romantic who violates the Private Eye's First Commandment and falls for his client.

See *Foul Play*

CARLTON "THE DOORMAN"
The doorman in **Rhoda Morgenstern**'s apartment building, he is never seen but often heard over the intercom. He suffers from a chronic identity crisis and is always fearful that people will forget who he is. Thus he seems compelled to reintroduce himself every time he buzzes Rhoda's apartment. "Hi, this is Carlton…your doorman."

See *Rhoda*

CARNEHAN, PEACHEY
As restless ex-soldiers in nineteenth-century India, Carnehan and best friend **Daniel Dravot** have done it all, from smuggling to swindling to blackmail. They set out for greater glory in the isolated, primitive land of Kafiristan, where they plan to become kings. Though things work out even better than they had hoped, Peachey advises Daniel that they take their money and run, but his advice is unheeded, with disastrous results. "We're not little men—so we're going away to be kings!"

See *The Man Who Would Be King*, **Rudyard Kipling**

CAROL
Unhappy with her mediocre grade in class, Carol's even unhappier about how the professor behaves when she talks to him about it. She feels he makes inappropriate advances toward her; he angrily disagrees. But Carol's growing confidence and self-respect allow her to confront him without flinching.

See *Oleanna*, **David Mamet**

CARRAWAY, NICK
This midwesterner went to New York in 1922 to learn the bond business. Carraway takes a small house in West Egg on Long Island next to that of the mysterious and ostentatiously wealthy **Jay Gatsby**. Nick declares himself to be one of the few honest people he has ever known, and possesses the solid midwestern virtues of self-reliance and indus-

triousness, which put him in stark contrast with most of New York society, especially **Tom Buchanan**, a Yale classmate married to his distant cousin **Daisy Buchanan**. He comes to know Gatsby through **Jordan Baker**, whom Nick dates, and arranges a meeting between Gatsby and Daisy, who first met each other during World War I. Nick is capable of great moral outrage and never adapts the pragmatic ethics of the jaded sophisticates of the New York social elite.

See *The Great Gatsby*, F. Scott Fitzgerald

CARRINGTON, BLAKE
Debonair, courtly, silver-haired millionaire oil baron. He's the toast of Denver society and an object of worldwide respect. The loving and devoted husband of **Krystle**, he single-handedly raised daughter **Fallon** and son **Steven**, coping with their myriad problems. He's constantly forced to defend his marriage and business against the plots and attacks of his evil ex-wife, **Alexis**. He has a good moral character.

See *Dynasty*

CARRINGTON, KRYSTLE JENNINGS
Honey-voiced, devoted, sexy wife. Silvery-blond-haired second wife of millionaire oil baron **Blake Carrington**. Sweet disposition masks an inner strength, convictions, and desire to keep her man. Tries to please everyone, but most of all her husband. Drops the sweetness for archenemy **Alexis**. Favors the big-shoulders, small-waist approach to dressing.

See *Dynasty*

CARRINGTON, STEVEN
Sexually confused son. Bouncing from boyfriend to girlfriend, mild-mannered, blond-haired Steven is ever searching for his true self. Not interested in the family business. Though seemingly happy with gay life, he allows himself to be seduced by tarty temptress **Sammy Jo**, the mother of his son, Danny. Son of millionaire **Blake Carrington** and the wrathful **Alexis**, the roots of his problems are deep.

See *Dynasty*

CARTER, CINNAMON
She's a beautiful high-fashion model, but it's just a

cover for her *real* job, as a member of the Impossible Mission Force, an elite covert team put together by the U.S. government to police the world. Like the other team members, she's a specialist, and her specialty is to look beautiful and, on occasion, to flirt with a susceptible bad guy and thereby lull him into a state of lustful distraction.
See *Mission: Impossible*

CARTER, JOHN
Cute medical student doing his emergency room rotation at Chicago's County General Hospital. Aspiring toward surgery, a direction that does not necessarily fit with his sweet manner and relaxed nature. Has a crush on emergency room resident **Dr. Susan Lewis**.
See *ER*

CARTER, VINCE
Paranoid drill sergeant. Short, thick stub of a man with brush-cut hair, bulging eyes, and a booming voice. He's constantly being foiled in his attempts to impress his superiors and get ahead in the Marine Corps, for which he mostly blames **Gomer Pyle**. Carter thinks Pyle is out to get him, but Pyle's sincerity and thoughtfulness leave him not knowing what to think or do. Determined to make a real marine out of Pyle, he becomes Pyle's protector and educator. He has little luck with women, complains a lot to Corporal Boyle, and kisses up to superiors, which fails to produce desired results. "Move it, Pyle! Move it! Move it! Move it!"
See *Gomer Pyle, U.S.M.C.*

CARTWRIGHT, ADAM
The eldest child of wealthy rancher **Ben Cartwright**, he's the sober, intelligent son who's being groomed to one day take charge of the giant Ponderosa Ranch. His mother, Elizabeth Stoddard, died when he was an infant. Adam is virtually a second father figure to his two younger half brothers, **Hoss** and **Little Joe**. Eventually leaves the Ponderosa to strike out on his own.
See *Bonanza*

CARTWRIGHT, BEN
The strong, wealthy patriarch of the Cartwright clan, he came West from New England to find a new life. Finally settled on a claim he calls the *Ponderosa*, a thousand-square-mile ranch on the outskirts of

Virginia City, Nevada. A hard worker, he's honest, diligent, and forthright. Widowed three times, Ben has a son from each marriage, **Adam**, **Eric Hoss**, and **Little Joe**. Ben was a first mate and originally planned to settle in California. He's a loving, if stern, father and pillar of the community.
See *Bonanza*

CARTWRIGHT, ERIC HOSS
The hulking middle son of rancher **Ben Cartwright**, he isn't the brightest cowpoke, but he's got a winningly sweet disposition. Everyone calls him by his middle name, Hoss, which is, aptly, Swedish for "big friendly man." His mother was killed during an Indian attack shortly after Hoss was born. His horse is named Chuck.
See *Bonanza*

CARTWRIGHT, "LITTLE" JOE
The impulsive, handsome youngest son of **Ben Cartwright**, he's most likely to get into scrapes or fall in love with a passing damsel in distress. His mother, Marie DeMarne, died after being thrown from a horse. Little Joe's horse is named Cochise. As an adult, marries and has a son, but dies riding with Teddy Roosevelt's Rough Riders.
See *Bonanza* and *Bonanza: The Next Generation*

CASE, TIFFANY
She's a diamond smuggler for the Mafia and, though she doesn't know it, an employee of villainous mastermind Ernst Stavro Blofeld. The stunning San Francisco redhead arranges shipments of diamonds between Europe and the United States and then gets involved with **James Bond**, a British Secret Service agent.
See *Diamonds Are Forever*, Ian Fleming

CASEY, DR. BEN
A resident surgeon at County General Hospital, Casey is the compassionate, handsome doctor whose bedside manner we'd all like to sample. His mentors include Dr. David Zorba and Chief of Surgery Dr. Daniel Freeland. Casey once fell in love with a patient—Jane Hancock—who had been in a coma for thirteen years. Has an unspoken attraction to fellow doctor Maggie Graham.
See *Ben Casey*

CASEY, JIM

He was an evangelical preacher until he lost his faith. He finds a somewhat different faith when he goes to California with the **Joad**s, a family of Oklahoma tenant farmers looking for work after losing their farm during the Depression. The new message: stand up and fight for your right to survive. "I gotta see them folks that's gone out on the road. They gonna need help no preachin' can give 'em."
See *The Grapes of Wrath,* John Steinbeck

CASEY, MARTIN

Nicknamed Jiggs, he's a Marine Colonel and aide to General **James Mattoon Scott**. Casey stumbles on Scott's planned military coup against the U.S. government and alerts President **Jordan Lyman**. He is torn between his loyalty to and admiration for Scott and his oath to the Constitution. Casey is attracted to Scott's former mistress, Eleanor Holbrook.
See *Seven Days in May*

CASSIDY, AMY

Lovely but zaftig, she's a receptionist at the ad firm where **Kip Wilson** and **Henry Desmond** work; suggests they move into her building—the women-only Susan B. Anthony residence hotel, where they must dress in drag to pass. She's the only woman who knows the girls are really guys. She puts up with it because she's absolutely smitten with Henry, who loves her only as a friend.
See *Bosom Buddies*

CASSIDY, HOPALONG

A plain-talking old cowpoke with intentions as pure and simple as Western dirt, Hopalong got his name from a pronounced limp in his walk. He's a good guy who dresses in black but rides a white horse named Topper. The trail boss at Bar 20 Ranch, the redheaded "Hoppy" is usually accompanied by Mesquite Jenkins, a crusty but reliable trail hand. More gentlemanly and idealistic than most of his leather-skinned counterparts, Hopalong treats women with respect and honors the simple code of justice. Nothing fancy about him, he's content just chewing his tobacco and roaming the plains.
See *Hopalong Cassidy*

CASSIE

A former Broadway chorus dancer who tried her luck as a Hollywood actress, she's now back in Manhattan, starting all over again after being out of work for two years. Her determined nature just won't let her quit dancing or lose sight of her dreams. Once was involved with **Zach** during their younger, leaner days. "I don't want to wait on tables and what I really don't want to do is teach other people to do what I should be doing myself."
See *A Chorus Line*

CASTAVET, MINNIE

A nosy, elderly New York City housewife. Minnie talks a mile a minute in a piercing, accented voice but seems harmless and well intentioned. She takes young new neighbor **Rosemary Woodhouse** under her wing, especially after Rosemary becomes pregnant for the first time. She's a believer in herbal remedies.
See *Rosemary's Baby,* Ira Levin

CASTILLO, LIEUTENANT MARTIN

Latino Miami chief of detectives, he's passionate and ultra-intense. So consumed is he with his job that he seems personally pained by every illegal act committed within his jurisdiction. He struggles to keep his occasionally rambunctious detectives, **Crockett** and **Tubbs**, within the letter of the law, although he's often tempted to look the other way.
See *Miami Vice*

CASTLE, JOHNNY

A smooth operator on the dance floor, Johnny specializes in crotch-grinding numbers, generally referred to as dirty dancing. Enjoys capturing the eyes of numerous women, though now helping reserved, sheltered **Frances "Baby" Houseman** break out of her shell.
See *Dirty Dancing*

CASTLEBERRY, FLORENCE JEAN "FLO"

A waitress at Mel's Diner in Phoenix, southerner Flo is a tough, cynical redhead who'll react to almost any news with "When pigs fly!" A true-blue friend to the people she loves, she can snap with more bite than a rattler—often at her boss, **Mel Sharples**, whom she routinely admonishes to "Kiss my grits!" She's the veteran of the diner's crew of waitresses, is frequently on the prowl for a new man in her life, and seldom holds on to one for long—

possibly because she's simply too hard to handle.

See *Alice* and *Alice Doesn't Live Here Anymore*

CASTORINI, LORETTA

This pretty, pragmatic Greenwich Village woman is aware of the ticking of her biological clock and agrees to marry **Johnny Camareri**, a kindly, somewhat older man who should make a levelheaded marriage partner—but with whom she's not in love. When she goes to give a wedding invitation to Johnny's passionate younger brother, **Ronny Camareri**, she responds negatively at first to his histrionic hostility toward Johnny but agrees to listen to his story of the falling-out between the brothers. After a few glasses of Scotch, she and Ronny discover a powerful and mutual attraction. Loretta is faced with a difficult choice between practicality, as represented by Johnny, and passion, in the form of Ronny. Which way should she turn?

See *Moonstruck*

CASTORP, HANS

A malleable and innocent youth who visits his cousin Joachim in a Swiss sanitorium for the treatment of respiratory diseases, like tuberculosis. His intended three-week stay lengthens to seven years when a problematic spot is detected on his lung. During that period at the isolated spa, far removed from the gathering storms of pre–World War I Europe, Hans grows up in many ways. He develops a mysterious attraction to the Haus Berghof and a less mysterious attraction to one of the young female patients. His exposure to other people with experience and outlooks markedly different from his own helps Hans to become an adult, who has matured in a relatively peaceful and civilized setting, in sharp contrast to the turmoil of the world below.

See *The Magic Mountain,* Thomas Mann

CATES, JACK

The epitome of disheveled undercover big-city cops: large-bodied, lumbering, constantly in need of a shave. His diet consists of fast food, candy bars, and nips of on-the-job whiskey from a silver flask. Rarely without a cigarette, frequently tossed aside in a gesture of his disgust for much of his world. Whiskey and smokes have given Cates's voice a permanent raspy timbre. Despite his contempt for many of his colleagues on the San Francisco Police Department, and the violent criminals he tracks down, Cates is a good, dedicated cop. Though he claims to be in something like love, the job comes first, leaving him little time to attend to his on-again, off-again romance.

See *48 Hrs.*

CATES, JESSIE

A suicidal epileptic. Her husband left her; her son is a drug-addicted thief. Jessie, fortyish and plain, lives with her mother, **Thelma**, to whom she gives Saturday night manicures. It's not too hard to understand her recurrent wish to end it all. "I just want to hang a big sign around my neck, like Daddy's on the barn. 'Gone Fishing.'"

See *'Night, Mother,* Marsha Norman

CATES, THELMA

This middle-aged ostrich is currently living with her depressed daughter, **Jessie**. She's gabby and nosy. She allows that she never loved her deceased husband. But she brews a great cup of cocoa. Though she's an expert cocoa brewer, a fine needleworker, and makes first-rate caramel apples, she's totally unequipped to handle Jessie's severe emotional problems.

See *'Night, Mother,* Marsha Norman

CATHCART, COLONEL

A walking paradox: "Handsome and unattractive, dashing and dejected, poised and chagrined." The colonel smokes cigarettes in an ornate holder. At thirty-six, he's young to be a full colonel with a combat command, but he's still frustrated because he is not yet a general. He keeps raising the number of missions his men have to fly. Willing to try anything to get ahead, he orders the unit's chaplain to "think up some light, snappy prayers that will get me into "The Saturday Evening Post.'"

See *Catch-22,* Joseph Heller

CATHY

A perennially overweight single working girl. She struggles with string bikinis, stringy hair, her mother's purse strings, and her string of lackluster lovers. Cathy is forever on a rollercoaster diet. Her IN basket is always more full than her OUT basket. She loves her puppy and would prefer that her girl-

Jack Cates

Jennifer Cavilleri

friends not date her ex-boyfriends. She's fond of shirts with hearts on them. "Ack!"

See *Cathy,* Cathy Guisewhite

CAULFIELD, HOLDEN

This aimless seventeen-year-old prep school flunk-out, New York born and bred, hates phonies. He wants to puke whenever he hears the word "grand." His older brother, D.B., is prostituting himself in Hollywood, getting rich writing trash. Holden smokes a lot and sees himself as "the most terrific liar you ever saw in your life." Though he reads a great deal, he thinks himself illiterate. At thirteen, he smashed all the garage windows when his younger brother, Allie, died of leukemia. A pacifist, he's been in only two fights his whole life. When he gets presents, he feels sad, and he's often depressed— a "very, very strange boy." After flunking out of Pencey Prep, he holes up in a seedy Manhattan hotel, calling up girls, chatting with strangers, and asking cabbies where Central Park ducks go in the winter. When his beloved little sister, **Phoebe**, demands that he name something he'd like to be, he replies: "I keep picturing these little kids playing some game in this big field of rye and all. And I'm standing on the edge of this crazy cliff. I have to catch everybody if they start to go over the cliff. I'd just be the catcher in the rye and all. I know it's crazy, but that's the only thing I'd really like to be."

See *The Catcher in the Rye,* J. D. Salinger

CAULFIELD, PHOEBE

The adoring younger sister of **Holden Caulfield**, Phoebe is sensitive, precocious, and maintains an innocence as yet untainted by the adult world. Despite this naiveté, Phoebe has no illusions about family politics and knows her brother is deeply troubled as well as in deep trouble. She wants to save Holden from his troubles in much the same way that Holden wants desperately to spare her from becoming corrupted by the adult world when she grows up, in the same fashion as has their older brother, D.B. She hates phonies.

See *The Catcher in the Rye,* J. D. Salinger

CAVALE

A kidnapper and rock 'n' roll wannabe, Cavale is a "deformed woman" (club foot) on a quest to find the true rock 'n' roll savior—not a martyr to save

the music, but a musician who will save mankind *through* the music. "The rock 'n' roll star in his highest state of grace will be the new savior… rockin' to Bethlehem to be born."

See *Cowboy Mouth,* Sam Shepard and Patti Smith

CAVILLERI, JENNIFER

This young woman of Italian descent majors in music at Radcliffe, and graduates magna cum laude. After the death of her mom in a car crash, she was raised by her father, whom she calls Phil. Jenny's a fine keyboard performer and a harpsichord soloist with the Bach Society. Beautiful and brilliant, she loves the Beatles, Mozart, and **Oliver Barrett IV**, who she calls Preppie. Even though she thinks Oliver wants to marry her to get back at his snooty father, she marries him anyway. "Ollie, you're a preppie millionaire and I'm a social zero. In a crazy way, you also love my negative social status." She taught at Shady Lane School and put Oliver through law school. When she's diagnosed with leukemia, she shows herself courageous in the face of death. "Love means never having to say you're sorry."

See *Love Story,* Erich Segal

CECILIA

A waitress in a small diner, Cecilia is romantic and sensitive. Her escape from the harsh reality of an unhappy marriage is the welcoming darkness of a movie theater and the romantic characters in the films she sees. She winds up having a passionate relationship with **Tom Baxter**, a character in a movie who steps right off the screen to romance her. She loves Tom but realizes that the fact that he's fictional may cause some problems. Still, she's determined to try and make it work.

See *The Purple Rose of Cairo*

CELIE

She's an African American woman living in poverty in the rural South during the early twentieth century. Celie dresses in rags. Warmhearted and loving, she's sexually abused by her father, then has the two children she bears him taken from her. Later, she marries **Mister**, a charming but abusive man who cannot see the beauty inside her. Quiet, shy Celie is convinced she's ugly and rarely speaks. Her chief mode of communication is the letters she writes, both to her

sister and to God. Celie adores her sister, whom she hasn't seen since childhood, but Mister keeps her sister's letters from her for many years. Mister even forces Celie to be a virtual servant to his mistress, **Shug Avery**, an alcoholic lounge singer who comes to live with them. Still, Celie's indomitable spirit refuses to be crushed by life, and she grows stronger as the years go by. Eventually, Celie and Shug form an intimate bond, which builds Celie's confidence and gives her someone to care about.
See *The Color Purple,* Alice Walker

CHAMBERS, DIANE
A spectacularly insecure, slender, blond Bostonian who goes abruptly from graduate student to barmaid, a job she considers below her station and destiny. She speaks with a Brahmin accent, tends to be snobbish and egocentric. Diane, who sees herself as a true intellectual, is always citing high-flown authors, philosophers, musicians, and psychoanalysts. She can't stand the fact that a brain like herself is drawn to her handsome but lowbrow boss, **Sam Malone**, a womanizing former baseball player. Her constant combatant in verbal sniping is fellow waitress **Carla Tortelli LeBec**.
See *Cheers*

CHAMBERS, FRANK
This charming drifter lusts after **Cora Smith**, a beautiful restaurant proprietress, from the moment he meets her. Never mind the fact that she's married—the amoral Frank wants Cora so much that he won't let such trivial matters stand in his way. While he isn't ready to die for Cora, he's willing to make someone else die so he can get at her.
See *The Postman Always Rings Twice,* James M. Cain

CHAN, CHARLIE
Part intrepid sleuth, part Confucian philosopher, the pint-sized detective Chan is never in such a hurry tracking criminals that he doesn't have time to dwell on the deeper meanings of his profession. "A man should never hurry except to catch a flea," he likes to say, and whether he's crime-busting in his hometown of Honolulu, or globe-trotting at the request of Scotland Yard, Chan frequently pauses to instruct Barry, his "number-one son" and chief assistant, on the finer points of police work and Chinese philosophy. He is always well-mannered and loathe to show off. "A big head is only a good place for a large headache."
See *Chinese Parrot* or *The New Adventures of Charlie Chan,* Earl Derr Biggers

CHANCE, RICHARD
A determined cop who's become obsessive. Chance works for the Treasury Department as Secret Service agent. He once thwarted a terrorist suicide attack on President Ronald Reagan. Now his life is governed by his need to catch counterfeiter **Rick Masters**. He's been described by fellow agents as a hot dog. A believer that the ends justify the means, Chance will do anything to catch a criminal.
See *To Live and Die in L.A.*

CHANCE "THE GARDENER"
The ultimate naïf. Totally, absurdly absorbed in his profession of gardening, to the point that he knows literally nothing else. But amazingly, people take his simplistic comments as being full of ironic wisdom about the world. Catapulted to national fame, he appears on talk shows and advises the president on issues of the day. "I like to watch."
See *Being There,* Jerzy Kozinsky

CHANDLER, HEATHER
She's the leader of the most powerful clique at Westerburg High until she's killed by her friend **Veronica Sawyer** and school psycho **J.D.** when they give her poison as a hangover cure. They make her death out to be a suicide. "Fuck me gently with a chain saw—do I look like Mother Theresa?"
See *Heathers*

CHANNING, MARGO
She is a great actress and grande dame of the Broadway stage, capable of acts of friendship and of being a hellion of epic dimensions when she feels she's being double-crossed. Margo's bottomless reservoirs of thespian ability can be called up at a moment's notice to serve her in melodramatic scenes both onstage and in her private life. She doesn't believe in moderation in anything, including alcohol. Involved with bon vivant **Addison DeWitt**, she fears she is losing him to her protégée turned rival, **Eve Harrington**. "Fasten your safety belts, it's going to be a bumpy night!"
See *All About Eve*

CHAPPEL, HELEN

Former fat girl turned beauty. She still can't quite believe it. Helen is cute and spunky, but her mouth often gets her in trouble. She's a frustrated cello player who is forced to earn a living by working the lunch counter at the local airport. Helen forsakes her millionaire fiancé for the love of her life, pilot **Joe Hackett.**

See *Wings*

CHARLES

Always a best man, never a groom; Charles, a confirmed "serial monogamist," is caught in wedding bell hell. Through a series of weddings (and one funeral), he pursues a lovely American woman and dodges ex-girlfriends, all the time wondering why everyone but him can handle matrimony.

See *Four Weddings and a Funeral*

CHARLES, NICK

A wisecracking, sophisticated "retired" private eye—"an old Greek fool," originally named "Charalambides." He and his beautiful wife, **Nora,** are a glamorous crime-solving couple, not afraid to get down and dirty with the crooks. Nick has lots of friends from the shadier walks of life, who fascinate the less experienced Nora. Their clever pooch is called Asta. An outrageous flirt, he keeps his whisky glass full, even before breakfast. "This excitement has put us behind in our drinking."

See *The Thin Man,* **Dashiell Hammett**

CHARLES, NORA

A "lanky brunette with a wicked jaw." Her wealthy father died, leaving her a lumber mill and a narrow-gauge railroad. She's married to private detective **Nick Charles**; together they solve cases between and during martinis. Nora's a classy dame with "hair on her chest," and definitely not the jealous type. In fact, she adores her husband: "I love you, Nicky, because you smell nice and know such fascinating people."

See *The Thin Man,* **Dashiell Hammett**

CHARLIE

Successful New York playwright of Irish extraction, now back home in Dublin after burying his father, **Da.** Still maintains strong, sometimes exasperating ties with Da despite the departure of Da's soul from his body. Charlie carries some guilt over his boyhood relationship with Da that the two are still trying to work out.

See *Da*

CHARLIE

A young, mob-connected Little Italy denizen who's trying to carve out a responsible, semistraight life. He wants to take over a restaurant from his gangster uncle, but to do so, he must keep secret his connection with his reckless pal **Johnny Boy**, who's gotten in deep trouble with a loan shark. He also must conceal his affair with Johnny Boy's cousin. Charlie tries to keep all the balls in the air—his loyalty to Johnny Boy, his relationship with his uncle, his love life—but in the corrupt, violent world he lives in, it's not easy.

See *Mean Streets*

CHARLIE

Charlie's a cute, innocent small-town girl whose charming, beloved **Uncle Charlie Oakley** comes to stay with her family. A lengthy period of closer exposure to Uncle Charlie gives her new insights into his character and history and radically changes their relationship as well as posing some very distressing questions for her to deal with, about how to cope with her uncle's actual nature.

See *Shadow of a Doubt*

CHARLOTTE

This mentally and physically frail spinster is haunted by the memory of a crime she believes she committed in her youth. She is reduced to talking to herself and shoots at trespassers on her run-down southern estate. Her pain and confusion make her easy prey for those who would take advantage of her.

See *Hush…Hush, Sweet Charlotte*

CHARNIER, ALAIN

Charming, bearded French business executive, now doing some export-import commerce in New York City. He deals in heroin and can be ruthless when it means getting his job done. Charnier is very sly and knows how to work his way around international laws and deal with police in various nations.

See *The French Connection*

CHASE, ANGELA

A smart underachiever in her sophomore year in

high school who is trying to find her place in life. Torn between her straight, best friend that she grew up with, Sharon, and her new best friend Rayanne, a recovering alcoholic, she regularly offends both of them. During her tormented relationship with Jordan Catalano, a cute but mysterious 17-year-old, she decides that she will not sleep with him.

See *My So-Called Life*

CHATTERLEY, LADY CONSTANCE

After a continental education and a socially and sexually active young womanhood, at twenty-three she marries the robust **Sir Clifford Chatterley**. But by age twenty-six she finds herself the caretaker of a paralyzed and impotent husband on an isolated country estate. Despite her education and social background, she feels increasingly alienated from her husband, whose coldly rational approach to life she does not share. This beautiful, lusty, healthy woman is unfulfilled sexually and has even lost the capacity to respond to the natural world. A woman of intelligence and appetite, she finds little in her life to satisfy her hungers and begins to feel that she is wasting away. She longs for a child but because of her husband's injury, cannot conceive one with him. Unlike her sister and her husband, she does not feel bound by the strictures of her class, a freedom that allows her to embark on a passionate love affair with the gamekeeper, **Oliver Mellors**.

See *Lady Chatterley's Lover*, D. H. Lawrence

CHATTERLEY, SIR CLIFFORD

An English aristocrat, owner of an estate and controller of coal mines. Big, strong, and handsome, he is paralyzed from the hips down as a result of a war injury. Despite his sexual impotence and physical incapacitation, he is determined to make a contribution of some sort and is moderately successful as a fiction writer. Dependent on his young wife, **Constance**, he nonetheless encourages her to become involved with other men, in hopes of having an heir. When writing proves insufficiently fulfilling, he turns his attention to the mines and a study of the means of coal production. His interest in his laborers, however, is that of an intellectual of his social class—he is better at theorizing about their state than getting to know them in reality.

See *Lady Chatterley's Lover*, D. H. Lawrence

CHEECH

Minor crime figure dreaming of greater glory within the Syndicate. Discovers unexpected well of artistic creativity and integrity. Something of a poet, who comes to believe that lack of talent is a capital crime.

See *Bullets over Broadway*

CHEKOV, PAVEL

Ensign Chekov is the Russian member of the starship *Enterprise*'s multiethnic (and multispecies) crew. Young, untried, and often hotheaded, assistant navigator Chekov is nevertheless a good officer in training and he virtually idolizes **Captain Kirk**. His accent is thick and he loves his Russian "wodka."

See *Star Trek*

CHESTNY, JULIAN

A young man in the New South, Julian detests his mother for her unabashed racism and nostalgia for her grandfather's plantation. As he accompanies her on a bus trip to her exercise class, Julian is disgusted when his mother patronizes a black woman by giving her son a nickel. When she suffers the tragic consequences, Julian's disgust turns to guilt and remorse.

See *Everything That Rises Must Converge*, Flannery O'Connor

MRS. CHESTNY

A poor white woman who pines for the lost days of the Old South, when her grandfather owned a regal plantation worked by two hundred slaves. Mrs. Chestny is so comfortable with her racism that she loudly vocalizes her relief that no blacks are on the bus she's taking downtown with her son, **Julian Chestny**. However, it's the New South, and she pays dearly for not recognizing that fact.

See *Everything That Rises Must Converge*, Flannery O'Connor

CHEYENNE

A wanted Old West criminal and gunslinger, Cheyenne finds himself helping widowed **Jill McBain** save her land from evil **Frank**. He's inventive, quick-witted, and vicious, especially in his killing. "When they do you in, pray it's someone who knows where to shoot."

See *Once Upon a Time in the West*

CHICO

An impetuous, arrogant hothead. Chico is one of seven gunslingers hired to protect a Mexican village from the bandits of **Calvera**. Tired of farm life, he's decided to become a gunfighter. While Chico suffers from many of the afflictions of youth, he's also brave and noble. Best of all, he can catch fish with his bare hands.

See *The Magnificent Seven*

CHIGLIAK, ED

This young Native American lives in the small town of Cicely, Alaska. He's a true film aficionado who often uses the wisdom gleaned from the many movies he's watched to make important decisions. His I.Q. is 180, although he often seems simple and naive, which is part of his charm. Ed was recently "chosen" as a shaman, a tribal medicine man, a calling for which he is now in training.

See *Northern Exposure*

CHILTON, DR. FREDERICK

He's the smarmy, lecherous head of the facility holding **Hannibal Lecter**, a renowned and ruthless cannibal serial killer. He hits on FBI agent **Clarice Starling** when she comes to interview Lecter, and tries to intimidate her with lurid tales of Lecter's deeds, failing in both attempts. An unwitting mouse to Lecter's cat in an ongoing struggle for dominance, his fate is sealed when Lecter, who is stalking him on an island, announces that he'll "be having a friend for dinner."

See *The Silence of the Lambs,* Thomas Harris

THE CHINK

This legendary Chinese spiritualist hermit lives near a ranch run by feminist guerrillas and answers all questions with either laughter or poetic prophecies. When he becomes the center of a conflict between the government and the guerrillas, he suggests that society can only be redeemed through poetry and magic. After being shot during the ensuing battle, the Chink convalesces at the ranch, where he counsels and then seduces a beautiful but large-thumbed wanderer named **Sissy Hankshaw**. Sensing that her true desires are for women, he leaves Sissy and the ranch to continue his never-ending spiritual quest.

See *Even Cowgirls Get the Blues,* Tom Robbins

CHIPPING, ARTHUR "MR. CHIPS"

A reserved, bespectacled teacher at a boys' school in England, whose high collars are as stiff as his teaching methods. His rigid manner conceals a shy nature, and, at the outset of his career, he's not popular with students. His taut style is mellowed by marriage to a dance hall singer—a move that takes his fellow scholars by surprise. After learning to love, Mr. Chip's capacity for warmth is revealed and is becomes clear he's a better person and a better teacher than all imagined, in the end beloved by students and peers.

See *Goodbye, Mr. Chips*

CHRIS

Sometimes, good guys wear black hats. Chris recruits an elite cadre of seven men to defend a Mexican village from the depredations of a rapacious gang led by **Calvera**. He's originally from Louisiana, more recently from Dodge City. Chris is the steeliest of the tough guys he leads, and at the same time, serves his own overactive conscience, which makes him take on perilous or impossible tasks. He's also bald. Is this cause and effect? We'll never know.

See *The Magnificent Seven*

CHRISTENSEN, DIANA

A beautiful blonde, Diana is also ruthless, ambitious, and cold-blooded. As vice-president of programming for UBS, a major television network, she's sold her soul for high ratings, indulging in such stunts as funding a black terrorist organization in exchange for exclusive footage of the carnage it wreaks. Ahead of her time, she moves the nightly news from the news division to the entertainment division. She has no problem canning an idealistic, old-school reporter for lack of ratings, after having had an affair with him. Ms. Christensen is about to fire anchorman **Howard Beale** for the same reason, when he goes berserk on the air, threatening to kill himself. Subsequently, she senses that his moment has come and gives him his own show instead. But when he starts criticizing the network and American society, the ratings dive, and Diana plots to have Beale murdered on the air—anything for ratings.

See *Network*

CHRISTIE, ANNA

She's sullen, beautiful, mysterious, and Swedish. Anna's dark moods have roots in her equally shady past. Currently living on her father's barge while reassessing where her life has gone and what—if anything—she has to look forward to in the future. It doesn't appear to be much, or at least nothing good. A natural magnet for broken men and alcohol-soaked women. Speaks in a thick Swedish accent but uses up-to-the-minute thirties slang. "Give me a whiskey with a ginger ale on the side and don't be stingy, baby."
See *Anna Christie*, Eugene O'Neill

CHRISTMAS, JOE

Thought to be part black, Joe is placed in an orphanage by his white grandfather. He is taunted by the other children and then brutalized by the farmer who adopts him. Joe's sexual affair with a philanthropic spinster ends in violence when she tries to force him to assume a black identity. He is captured, castrated, and killed.
See *Light in August*, William Faulkner

CHURCH, MIKE

Devil-may-care private detective working the L.A. beat. Not interested in supernatural, though mind is subject to change if the right circumstances prevail. Drives his convertible like the hotshot he envisions himself to be. Chain-smokes religiously.
See *Dead Again*

CHURCHILL, DANNY, JR.

He's a young, exuberant, female-mad son of a New York newspaper mogul who is sent West to a boys' school to develop restraint regarding women. It doesn't work, and he winds up trying to charm **Ginger Gray**, who lives at the school. She starts off being unresponsive.
See *Girl Crazy*

CLAIBORNE, DOLORES

As rugged and menacing as the Maine island on which she lives, though not nearly as pleasing to the eye, Dolores has no qualms admitting to the police that she pushed her abusive husband down a well thirty years ago, but draws the line at copping to the murder of a dotty old lady who fell down a flight of stairs.
See *Dolores Claiborne*, Stephen King

THE CLAMPETT FAMILY

Once they were a poor Ozark family that could barely be kept fed. Now, thanks to an oil deal on their land in Sibly, they're residents of Crestview Drive in Beverly Hills. Jed, **Granny**, **Jethro**, and Elly May live in a wonderful mansion that's complete with a parlor and a cement pond out back, but is prone to giving off disconcerting bell sounds in the walls. Jed continues to invest with the help of banker and neighbor **Milburn Drysdale**. Since Jed sold his land to the O.K. Oil Company, his net worth has gone from 35 million to 95 million dollars. Granny Moses spends her time being ornery and mixing potent home-brewed potions, including a cure-all called Granny's Spring Tonic. She'd like to find a suitable husband for her bombshell granddaughter Elly May. Elly's interested most in her critters, a rooster named Earl and two monkeys named Beth and Skipper. At different times, she's romanced by movie star Dash Hiprock and Navy frogman Mark Templeton. Cousin Jethro Bodine moved with the Clampetts, leaving his mother Pearl back in Sibly. He thinks of himself as a playboy and, while good-looking, he still hasn't completed grade school. Jethro spent some time in the beatnik scene. He tries to romance Drysdale's assistant, Jane Hathaway, but she's usually just got business on her mind, always needing to tend to the Clampetts's finances and answering her boss, "Yes, Chief." The Clampetts haven't given in to much of Hollywood's glamour as they still drive around in an old beater truck.
See *The Beverly Hillbillies*

CLARENCE

A celestial apprentice, desperate to earn his angel's wings, Clarence gets an assignment as easy as falling down. All he has to do is prevent the suicide of depressed goody-goody **George Bailey**, who can't see the forest for the trees. George actually can't see the good his self-sacrifices have done for the people of Bedford Falls. Weary and a little grouchy, Clarence has to heave himself into the river to get George's attention off himself. With his fumbling and whiny ways, Clarence is Jerry Lewis, Woody Allen, and the Ghost of Christmas Future rolled into one.
See *It's a Wonderful Life*

CLARK, ANDREW

A championship high school wrestler dominated by

Photo courtesy of CBS

Jed and Granny Clampett

GENTLE BENS

Cartwright
Matlock
Casey
Braddock
Franklin Pierce
Stone

controlling father, he's not sure of what he wants in life, though is clearly aware of what he's being programmed to achieve. Alternately likes to tease and protect those who lack his social status. Currently serving Saturday morning detention for locker room antics.

See *The Breakfast Club*

CLARKE, CHUCK "HAWK"

A pathetic schmuck and a terrible singer-songwriter, Clarke considers suicide after his wife leaves him to live his empty life alone. With fellow "musician" **Lyle Rodgers**, "Hawk" accepts a booking in Morocco and, through his ineptitude and credulity, ends up in the middle of a political powderkeg.

See *Ishtar*

CLAVIN, CLIFF

He's a middle-aged mama's boy and mailman. He feels a strong sense of vocation and always wears his uniform. Cliff's off-hours are mostly spent in the Boston bar Cheers with his best buddy, **Norm Peterson**. He likes to be thought of as a guy who knows it all and will launch into lengthy, dull, and usually erroneous lectures on just about anything. What he does know about is postal rates and zip codes.

See *Cheers*

CLAYTON, LEE

Lee Clayton is a bounty hunter, as twisted as the men he hunts. His is a strange, surreal world where murder is done under the sanction of what passes for law. He has a fetish for hats and a more than slightly skewed view of the world. He is a demented Don Quixote, who would make a Sancho Panza storm off in disgust.

See *The Missouri Breaks,* Thomas McGuane

MR. CLEAN

Tall, tan, bald, and built. When it comes to attracting women, he really mops up. Wears a gold earring. Works wonders on kitchen floors.

See *Mr. Clean*

CLEARY, MEGGIE

She grew up as the only female child of Fee and Paddy Cleary, in a house full of boys. "Her hair is not red and not gold but a combination of both and her eyes grey, and they glow like soft, half

opaque jewels, with gold eyelashes." She leads a lonely and laborious life on a vast sheep ranch called Drogheda in the Australian Outback, which she loves deeply. She's been in love with Father Ralph De Bricassart her whole life, but spends her life feeling abandoned by him. She marries Luke O'Neill, a hardworking yet cold man, whose only interest is her money. Meggie doesn't love him, but marries in hopes of getting over Ralph. She and Luke have a daughter, Justine, a fiercely independent actress, to whom Meggie is indifferent because she is too much like Luke. She possesses tremendous self control and pride, and is too proud even to admit to her family that her husband neglects her. Like her mother, she has a son out of wedlock, Dane. "I've always known I could never have Ralph. I've got the part of Ralph the Church can never have; I'll beat God yet." Tragically, she loses Dane when he drowns trying to save a woman while on holiday in Greece.

See *The Thorn Birds,* Colleen McCullough

CLEAVER, JUNE

She is a devoted wife and mother. June is married to accountant **Ward Cleaver** and is the mother of young **Beaver** and **Wally**. A resident of the suburban town of Mayfield, she's tall, slim, attractive—but has no sex appeal. She and her hubby sleep in twin beds. Always wears pearls. Adds an apron to her shirtwaist dress, and she's ready to cook, clean, go to the market, and do the laundry. Sends "the Beaver" and Wally off to school with thoughtfully packed lunch boxes and a kiss on the cheek. Sends Ward off to work with starched shirts, clean underwear, and a peck on the cheek. Plays cards with a group of lady friends. Speaks to Aunt Martha on the telephone. Once taught Wally dance steps. Listens to Beaver's and Wally's problems over cookies and milk, then refers them to Ward. Serves dinner each night in the dining room, making sure the boys eat their vegetables. Discusses thoughts on boys' problems with Ward, but defers to his decisions. Has good intuition. Is treated with great courtesy by her husband and sons. Has no further aspirations. Happy with her life. Concerned about raising good boys. "Ward, I'm worried about the Beaver."

See *Leave It to Beaver*

CLEAVER, THEODORE "BEAVER"

He is a Tom Sawyeresque boy-next-door, a quintessential small-town or suburban American kid of the 1950s, who lives in idyllic Mayfield with flannel-suited dad **Ward Cleaver** and pearls-and-apron mom **June Cleaver**. The Beave plays kick-the-can, roughhouses with his older brother, **Wally**, and has a crush on his teacher, Miss Landers. He tries hard in school, suffers the humiliating taunts of mean-spirited, pigtailed Judy. Beaver's best pals include **Whitey Whitney** and Larry Mondello. His best friend of all is smart, handsome, athletic, popular Wally, but he can't understand Wally's interest in girls. He fears and reveres Wally's friend **Eddie Haskell**. The Beave usually knows right from wrong but is sometimes subject to peer pressure. When he does a bad thing, the Beave usually confesses, "kinda sorta." He thereupon submits to long lectures from Ward while June looks on. Wally and Ward are his founts of wisdom, but he sometimes tries to solve problems on his own. Unconsciously, he poses simple questions of morality and ethics, showing that life is full of human failure and triumph. Always ends his day with a smile and hug from Ward and June and a pillow bomb across the room from Wally. "Ya big oaf!" "Ya little squirt!"

See *Leave It to Beaver*

CLEAVER, WALLY

A big brother. Wally does well in school, is a good athlete, popular, and good-looking. He's considered a real "catch" in the hallways of Mayfield High. Girl problems get tougher for him as he matures. Best girl: Mary Ellen Rogers. Best friends: Lumpy Rutherford and **Eddie Haskell**. Sometimes finds little brother **Beaver Cleaver** a pain, but deep down, loves him. Works after school as a soda jerk. Doesn't like to dance. "Aww, Beave, ya little squirt!"

See *Leave It to Beaver*

CLEAVER, WARD

Everyman. Physically undistinguished and unremarkable in personality. Ward performs solidly as an accountant for boss Fred Rutherford and then suffers in silence when Fred takes credit for his work. With his wife, **June Cleaver**, he lives in suburban Mayfield in a comfortable middle-class house. He is the father of **Wally** and **Beaver**, works nine to five, and returns home to hear reports from his family over dinner about their day. After learning from June the essence of the boys' problems ("What will you do, Ward?"), he decides what action to take. Sometimes he harks back to his days in the service when faced with questions of character. Ward is a strict disciplinarian and punishes bad deeds, sometimes by lectures and the occasional grounding. Treats June with great courtesy and affection but lights no sparks. Tries to counsel the boys about girls. Reads the newspaper in the den. Plays golf or putters around the garage on Saturdays. Likes baseball. "Beaver, your mother and I are very disappointed in you."

See *Leave It to Beaver*

CLIFFORD

As a new kid in a Chicago high school, he makes an enemy of a class bully, **Moody**, with an ill-advised wisecrack on his very first day. Unable to defend himself against Moody and his cronies, Clifford talks the biggest and scariest guy in the class, **Linderman**, into becoming his "bodyguard."

See *My Bodyguard*

CLOUSEAU, INSPECTOR JACQUES

He sees himself as an icy-cool, ace crime-stopper, but that's typical of the way his mind (barely) works, because he's actually a bumbling fool—or, as he himself might say, "fyeeuwell." The inspector's constant flow of nasal, French-accented mispronunciations of English words confuses almost everybody he meets. His Asian houseboy, **Kato**, attacks him whenever he enters his apartment—to keep him on his toes—leading to exhibitions of martial arts technique that would make Bruce Lee roll over in his grave. Somehow, he's brought some master criminals to their knees, but never through competent police work. Caution: prolonged contact with Clouseau can lead to anything from nervous facial tics to full-blown nervous breakdowns—just ask his boss, **Chief Inspector Dreyfus**. But Clouseau always gets his man.

See *The Pink Panther*

COCHRAN, FAYE EVELYN

A spacey, retired flight attendant hired by **Joe Hackett** to work for his airline, Sandpiper Air. She's charming enough but strange and definitely ditzy. Faye scorns the adage about not speaking if you

have nothing nice to say. Married several times, twice to men named George. She sometimes manages to distinguish between them.
See *Wings*

COCHRAN, PETE
A rich kid from Beverly Hills who lived a shady life on the other side of the tracks until he was recruited to work as an undercover Los Angeles police detective. With his partners **Linc Hayes** and **Julie Barnes**, Pete usually poses as a rebellious long-hair to catch criminals operating in the counterculture.
See *The Mod Squad*

COCO
A student at New York City's High School for the Performing Arts. She's a drama major who dreams of great success and glory onstage and in film. Unfortunately, she's been drawn into the tawdry side of movie business. Loyal to both her friends and her ambitions.
See *Fame*

COGBURN, REUBEN J. "ROOSTER"
Reputed to be the toughest deputy marshal around, the one-eyed Cogburn is sought out by fourteen-year-old Mattie Ross to avenge her father's death at the hands of Tom Cheney. Cogburn is fond of drinking, sleeping late, and his horse, Beau. He lives with a philosophical Chinese immigrant and a cat named General Price. Rooster, a Civil War veteran, is undisturbed by the violence of his job and believes, "I never shot nobody I didn't have to." His mission with Ross and Texas Ranger La Boeuf is successful, and proves to Ross that Rooster, like herself, has "true grit."
See *True Grit*, Charles Portis

COHN, ROBERT
A novelist living in Paris during the 1920s and an acquaintance of **Jake Barnes**. Wildly romantic and emotionally needy, the Jewish Cohn seeks love and friendship in an anti-Semitic world that offers him neither. He has an affair with the casually promiscuous **Lady Brett Ashley** and falls hopelessly in love with her, a depth of emotion that is not returned.
See *The Sun Also Rises*, Ernest Hemingway

COLBURN, HOKE
Chauffeur for **Miss Daisy Werthan**, for whom he has great affection, despite her vinegar-laced personality. A pragmatist, he has a way of twisting situations to his advantage. Hoke knows that his role as a black man in pre-civil-rights-era Georgia gives him limited choices in life, though he is not afraid to speak his mind when the situation calls for it.
See *Driving Miss Daisy*

COLBY, ALEXIS CARRINGTON
Glamorous, seductive bitch. Bitter ex-wife of oil baron **Blake Carrington**, always conniving and contriving to win him back. Often haunted by the many constantly emerging secrets of her checkered past, Alexis is the not-too-maternal mother of **Fallon**, **Steven**, and long-lost Adam and Amanda. Archenemy and rival of blond-haired, blue-eyed, big-shouldered **Krystle Carrington**, Blake's current wife. Raven-haired and well endowed, Alexis favors huge shoulder pads and unwieldy hats. Wears outrageous, outlandishly sexy outfits for her business dealings that center around revenge against Blake. Her ruthless, stop-at-nothing tactics sometimes best Blake, forcing him into desperate counterplots. She takes wicked delight when Blake's marriage to Krystle hits the occasional snag. Is not above physically attacking Krystle or plotting harm against her. Has stormy relationships with Fallon and Steven, who felt abandoned as children, and is not above using them as pawns in her maneuvering. Her insatiable sexual appetite requires a constant string of men, including frail-hearted Cecil Colby and the dashing **Dex Dexter**. She will stop at nothing in her goal to destroy Blake, or remarry him. "I'll get you for this! If it's the last thing I do, you'll pay for this, Blake Carrington!"
See *Dynasty*

COLBY, FALLON CARRINGTON
Spoiled rich girl in need of parental guidance. Wild youth gives way to promiscuous young adulthood. Goes from man to man in search of the love she missed as a child. Eventually finds the real thing with rival family's son **Jeff Colby** but has trouble holding on to him. Impetuous, impertinent, and impenitent, Fallon often storms out of the mansion, madly driving away in her red sports car.
See *Dynasty*

COLBY, JEFF

Handsome, solid son-in-law. Good business sense and savoir faire have landed Jeff the keys to Denver-Carrington oil company along with the hand of **Fallon Carrington**. He has the ear and the trust of **Blake Carrington**, who thinks of him as a son, much to the disgust of interloping long-lost brother Adam. Has everything except the ability to hold on to Fallon.

See *Dynasty*

COLE, JOHN GRADY

A sixteen-year-old boy who leaves the family ranch to embark on a picaresque journey to Mexico with his best friend, Lacey Rawlins. On the way, the boys acquire a younger companion, encounter dangers from animals, men, and the terrain, spend time in a Mexican jail, and have their eyes opened to the pleasures and dangers of the world. John's unusual talent for breaking, training, and understanding horses wins him the respect of the wealthy Mexican rancher for whom he works, and the heart of Alejandra, the rancher's daughter.

See *All the Pretty Horses*, **Cormac McCarthy**

COLE, WALTER "TEACH"

An experienced street hood, Teach believes in action and loyalty and himself. He has a quick mind and a temper to match. He knows the streets and expects others to respect and see the wisdom in what he says. "The Past is Past, and this is Now, and so Fuck You."

See *American Buffalo*, **David Mamet**

COLLIER, BARNEY

Barney may look like a geek, but he's actually the hip electronics and computer expert on the ultra-elite, ultra-covert Impossible Mission Force. He owns his own electronics company, where he turns out clever gadgets like noiseless electronic drills and easy-to-assemble helicopters, which help his team out of many scrapes. Still, any twelve-year-old could wipe him out in a game of Doom.

See *Mission: Impossible*

COLLINS, BING

This former professional singer has decided to settle down and devote his time to his family. Now he works as an electrical engineer, although he still sings as a hobby. His wife, Ellie, wishes she could make it in show business in her husband's stead.

Bing has two daughters, Janice and Joyce.

See *The Bing Crosby Show*

COLTON, JACK

An American pilot-for-hire living on the edge of the law of whatever country he finds himself in; in this instance, it's Colombia. Jack finds himself saddled with a hapless romance novelist, **Joan Wilder**, who's been stranded in the jungle and babbling a ridiculous story about her abducted sister, a treasure map, and going to Cartagena. He reluctantly plays the hero while plotting to keep the treasure for himself, but some odd twists of fate and his growing attraction to Joan force him to change his plans.

See *Romancing the Stone*

COLUMBATO, AL

Horribly disfigured Vietnam veteran recuperating from battle scars both physical and psychological. Best friend to **Birdy**, whom he's known since their childhood days in Philadelphia. Lonely for female companionship and somewhat ineffectual in his efforts to recapture his prewar normality.

See *Birdy*

COLUMBO, LIEUTENANT

Rumpled, seemingly bumbling police homicide detective. Often in need of a shave, Lieutenant Columbo dresses in clothes that appear grungy and slept in, including his ancient trademark trench-style raincoat. Drives a geriatric car, always on its last legs. Smokes a cheap cigar, cocks his head and squints when interviewing suspects. He prefers to work alone. The LAPD tolerates his eccentricity because he solves big murder cases for them, often putting away rich and famous murderers. Key to his success is his ability to let the suspect think he's a totally incompetent bumbler, while he is, in fact, shrewd and capable of putting together the most intricate jumble of small clues. His overly gracious, solicitous, and complimentary style lulls suspects into feeling that Columbo is a man to be duped. Slowly but surely, he picks away at the details and inconsistencies of the suspect's story and evidence. Just as slowly, he teases the suspect with the possibility of being exposed, posing questions that merely touch on the key clue. Often uses his never-seen wife as a sounding board, and sometimes her domestic rituals show Columbo inconsistencies in suspects' alibis. Murderers grimace as they see that raincoat and hear the raspy voice say, "So sorry to intrude on you, sir, but there's one tiny thing that bothers me. If I could have just a second of your time…"

See *Columbo*

THE COMPSON FAMILY

A storied Southern family that has run out of time. Compsons of the 19th century include Quentin II, a governor of Mississippi, and Jason Lycurgus II, a Confederate brigadier general. Unable to escape the dinosaurs of its past, the family fades out in the next century. Quentin III is the oldest child, the family's brightest hope. Overly serious and melancholy, he is still a likable fellow. Quentin III is obsessed with the past, especially the self-destruction of another Yoknapatawpha County family, the Sutpens. He's torn by incestuous feelings for his sister, Caddy, equating her virginity with the family's honor. He attends Harvard for a year, and drowns himself following his sister's marriage. Caddy is the lone Compson daughter. Carefree and spontaneous, she mothers her three brothers, especially the retarded Benjy. Her first marriage ends when her husband finds she is pregnant by another man. Caddy gives birth to a daughter, Quentin IV, the last Compson, and later marries and divorces a minor film producer. She's last seen on the arm of a Wehrmacht general in occupied France. Jason IV is practical and cruel, the agent of his family's destruction. He values money and hard work, caring nothing about the past. He blackmails Caddy, has Benjy castrated and institutionalized, and sells the family mansion. Maury, renamed Benjamin, is the retarded youngest child. A big man with fine, pale hair and cornflower-blue eyes, he loves firelight, Caddy, and a pasture once owned by the family. Benjy bellows whenever disorder mars his inflexible world.

See *The Sound and the Fury,* William Faulkner

CONAN

A muscle-bound, broadsword-wielding barbarian on a quest for revenge in a mysterious world of sorcery and mysticism. Conan's childhood was worse than most. First, his parents were brutally murdered by the evil Thulsa Doom; and then he was chained for years to the Wheel of Pain, which is as bad as it sounds. As he grows older, however, Conan devel-ops into a bronze demigod. Finally, he is freed and sets off on a quest to seek and destroy Thulsa Doom. With the help of his friends Subotai the Mongol and Valeria, Queen of Thieves, Conan reaches the warlord's stronghold and beheads him in a satisfying orgy of blood.

See *Conan the Barbarian*

CONANT, JERRY

Jerry is torn between his wife, who's having an affair with his best friend, and his mistress, who's his best friend's wife. An artist, Jerry finds perverse pleasure in the aesthetic symmetry of this love quadrangle, which may explain his indecisiveness. "It's like one of those equations with nothing but variables. I can't solve it."

See *Marry Me,* John Updike

CONKLIN, OSGOOD P.

Cranky, short-tempered, and no match for his best teacher—**Connie Brooks**—Principal Conklin still antagonizes her at every turn. He works as principal of Madison High and then Mrs. Nestor's Private Elementary School.

See *Our Miss Brooks*

THE CONNER FAMILY

A family who teases each other incessantly stays together. In the Conner home, even though mom Roseanne and dad Dan pick on each other and their kids (and their kids do the same), there's no love lost. Roseanne is the queen of the house and everything that goes on inside it. She grew up in Lanford, Illinois, hoping to be a writer, but romance with her high school sweetheart lead to three kids and a sort of domestic bliss instead. Roseanne and Dan have a loving, committed relationship, but there's no doubt that Roseanne's is the mouth that roars. She makes the rules, or tries to for everyone, including her kids Becky, Darlene, and D.J. and even her sister **Jackie Harris**. She even manages to boss around her bosses, whether it be at Wellman Plastics factory, the Lobo Lounge, or Art's Beauty Parlor. She finally becomes the real boss when she and Jackie open up a lunch counter, where they serve up their famous "loose-meat sandwiches." Dan's got a quick wit and a soft heart. He can do battle with Roseanne, but knows that he doesn't have to win every time. A man who works with his hands, Dan's been in construction, owned his own motorcyle shop, and been a mechanic for the city. His prized possession is his Harley; his nickname in high school (when he was a football player) was "Yor." Roseanne and Dan's favorite holiday is Halloween, when they alternately scare and embarrass their children. Becky is usually the most mortified by her mother's behavior (Roseanne once worked at the mall, where she ruined many of Becky's afternoons). She and Darlene fight nonstop until Becky disappears with her boyfriend Mark and gets married. But she's not gone for long: she and Mark move back in with the rest of the family when money runs tight. Darlene is not your usual beaten-up middle child. In fact, she dishes out the sarcasm worthy of a world-hardened woman. As much of an overachiever as she fancies herself an outsider, she attends college on a scholarship and is a talented writer. Her first serious boyfriend, David, lives with the Conners. Youngest sibling D.J. is teased without end by his sisters, particularly Darlene. He is a little weird; he never seems to have many friends (or is hounded by kids he can't stand). He goes through weird stages, including a brief infatuation with religion.

See *Roseanne*

CONNOR, JOHN

A semiretired former police detective, onetime Special Liaison Officer of the LAPD to Japanese VIPs in L.A. There are rumors that Connor is a little too close to the Japanese, who supposedly pay off Americans who are in a position to help their interests. Connor is drawn into active duty to help the current Liaison Officer, **Web Smith**, who's been assigned a sensitive murder case. Connor lived in Japan for several years, is fluent in the language, and is versed in the culture. He understands what Web hasn't learned yet: that things often aren't what they seem. "When something looks too good to be true, then it's not true."

See: *Rising Sun,* Michael Crichton

CONNOR, JOHN

A skate-punk child from late-twentieth-century Los Angeles. Connor is raised by foster parents after his mother, **Sarah Connor**, is institutionalized for paranoid schizophrenia. John is naturally gifted at mechanical manipulation—not only is he adept at

video games, but he obtains money for them by circumventing automated teller machine security systems. Reunited with his mother while still a boy, he's given a full education in military and survival techniques by her and a series of associates, in preparation for his career as a freedom fighter. As an adult, Connor continues his mother's rampage against intelligent machines bent on destroying humankind and is the leader of an insurgent group of humans.

See *Terminator 2: Judgment Day*

CONNOR, MIKE

He's a sharp, seasoned newspaper reporter whose independent spirit can get him into trouble. Mike's breezy, cynical demeanor masks a poetic streak. He prides himself on being smart but sometimes can't tell love when it's right in front of him. An honest guy who wouldn't take advantage of a girl who's had too much champagne.

See *High Society*

CONNOR, SARAH

She's just a perky California waitress until her life changes forever when the **Terminator**, a cyborg assassin from a future ruled by machines, comes to kill her. She learns from **Kyle Reese**, the human soldier sent back in time to protect her, that she's been targeted because she's going to be the mother of **John Connor**, the great antimachine revolutionary leader. The two frantically try to elude the Terminator, keep Sarah alive, and keep the future on course. "Reese, do I look like someone who knows how to fight and organize? I can't even balance my checkbook!"

See *The Terminator*

CONOVAN, MIKE

A fast-talking, semicrooked New York sports promoter-agent who talks "left-handed English," Conovan deals with small-time boxers and horses until he meets **Pat Pemberton**. He promotes her on the square as an all-around woman athlete and in the process falls in love with her. Conovan's "business partners" try to lure him back into fixing sporting events, but he's a changed man and refuses. When thugs try to beat him up, Pemberton saves the day. "Not much meat on 'er, but what's there is cherce."

See *Pat and Mike*

MEN WHO'VE PUT ON WOMEN'S CLOTHING TO GET SOMETHING THEY WANT

Joe/Josephine
Jerry/Daphne
Henry "Hildegarde" Desmond
Kip "Buffy" Wilson
Norman "Mom" Bates
Dr. Robert Elliott
Michael Dorsey
Mrs. Edwina Doubtfire

CONROY, GABRIEL

Schoolteacher, writer, and husband of **Gretta Conroy**, Gabriel is a thoughtful, reserved, self-involved man who does not feel life's passion swirling around him. A Dubliner whose family thinks he married beneath him. Gabriel's discovery that his wife still has feelings for a man who loved her before her marriage shows him how empty his life has been.

See *Dubliners*, James Joyce

CONROY, GRETTA

Wife of **Gabriel Conroy**, the convent-educated Gretta from parochial County Galway is the devoted mother of their two children. While her life with Gabriel is comfortable, she is haunted by a love from her past, who died after catching pneumonia while walking miles to see her on a stormy night.

See *Dubliners*, James Joyce

CONWAY, JAMES

As the leader of a trio of mobsters within the larger mob framework, the smooth, polished Conway is at the same time lethally paranoid and utterly confident. Because he is half Irish, he can never be a "made" man in the Mafia. "What, are you stupid or what?" "What's the matter with you?"

See *Goodfellas*

CONWAY, JAMIE

A would-be writer who spends his days toiling as a fact-checker for a respected magazine and his nights trolling the downtown clubs in the company of his pal Tad Allagash and fueled by "Bolivian marching powder" (cocaine). Deserted by his wife, Amanda, a model, and failing at his job, he eventually comes to see the vacuousness of the club life and comes to terms with the death of his mother.

See *Bright Lights, Big City*, Jay McInerny

COOL HAND LUKE

Witty, sardonic, and irreverent prisoner, currently assigned to a chain gang in the deep South. Enjoys baiting his captors and holds a heroic position among fellow inmates as a symbol of refusal to knuckle under. Has unusual penchant for eating large amounts of hard-boiled eggs. Sometimes has failure to communicate with authority.

See *Cool Hand Luke*

COOLEY, MELVIN

Mel is the archetypal stiff, humorless bureaucrat and the producer of *The Alan Brady Show*, starring brother-in-law **Alan Brady**. He's forever being cowed and bullied by the blustering Brady. While he's definitely a yes-man, Mel does put in a lot of hard work. Tall, large, and completely bald, he's an easy and constant target for writer **Buddy Sorrell**'s barbs and puts up with lots of abuse. His response to Buddy's jokes is a standard "Yech!"

See *The Dick Van Dyke Show*

COOLIDGE, BUTCH

A perennial also-ran boxer, descended from a line of military men, all of whom had a flair for being captured or killed by the enemy. He prizes an heirloom watch above all other possessions. Butch allegedly crossed underworld kingpin **Marsellus Wallace** by not throwing his last fight. His romantic interest is a gamine type named Fabian. He currently resides in the southern United States.

See *Pulp Fiction*

COOMBS, HARRY

An elderly New York man who's kicked out of his apartment when the building is condemned. Harry is never happier than when talking about the old days with Tonto, his beloved cat. Taken in by his son's family, he has too much pride to stay with them, so he embarks on a cross-country journey with Tonto, during which he visits his other children. He realizes that, though he loves them all, he's too independent to live with them.

See *Harry and Tonto*

COONAN, BIRDIE

Ex-vaudevillian and matronly confidante of **Margo Channing**. Dresses sensibly, almost dowdily. Coonan has a sarcastic tongue and doesn't let Channing stampede or intimidate her. As her assistant, she's very protective of Channing.

See *All About Eve*

COOPER, AGENT DALE

He's an FBI agent assigned to a case in Twin Peaks, a seemingly idyllic little town in the Pacific Northwest. With the help of local sheriff **Harry S. Truman**, he investigates the death of local girl **Laura Palmer**. Agent Cooper likes his coffee—

really likes his coffee—which he calls joe in puckish moments. In the course of his investigation, he uncovers a whole lot of seamy, sordid goings-on beneath the serene surface of Twin Peaks: corruption, violence, arson, betrayal, and putting fish in percolators. He's also hounded by a particularly cute, libidinous, bobby-sox-wearing brunette high schooler, who has a big-league crush on him. His dreams occasionally involve a dancing, cheesily dressed midget, who feeds him clues in a voice so weird it requires subtitles.

See *Twin Peaks*

COOPER, BETTY

Archie Andrews's sometime girlfriend. Unlike her friendly rival, Veronica Lodge, blond Betty is down-to-earth, good-natured, and always willing to help. An above-average student at Riverdale High, Betty spends her days doing good deeds and her evenings dreaming of her life as Mrs. Archie Andrews. She despises the always annoying Reggie Mantle.

See *Archie*

COOPER, GWENDOLYN "WINNIE"

A pretty, sweet, and precocious adolescent girl. Winnie is everyone's friend and never has a harsh word for anyone. She's sensitive and somewhat shy. Her brother was killed in the Vietnam War. Shares her first kiss with neighbor **Kevin Arnold**. Though she likes Kevin a lot, she makes him jealous by dating other boys.

See *The Wonder Years*

CORBETT, EDDIE

This deep-thinking seven-year-old is the son of magazine publisher dad **Tom Corbett**, whose wife, Eddie's mom, has passed away. Eddie sorely misses his mother and struggles to understand why she has gone. He spends a lot of time with his dad and offers him advice beyond his years concerning women. His main source of answers to philosophical questions is the Asian housekeeper, Mrs. Livingston. Eddie knows that he can always depend on his dad.

See *The Courtship of Eddie's Father*

CORBETT, TOM

A cute, vulnerable widower father. California magazine publisher Tom lives with young son **Eddie** and housekeeper Mrs. Livingston after the death of his wife. He struggles to give Eddie proper time and attention while working and dating women. His best friend, Norman, lends advice, but it's Eddie who possesses the clear-eyed wisdom. Has his priorities straight. "People, let me tell ya 'bout my best friend…"

See *The Courtship of Eddie's Father*

CORCORAN, EDMUND "BUNNY"

Loud, sloppy, and partial to kitsch, Bunny stands out as the misfit in his group of serious, if somewhat self-important, intellectual friends at Hampden College. He grows increasingly uncomfortable with the clique's secret reenactments of classical Greek rituals and runs afoul of its leader, the foreboding **Henry Winter**. Bunny's lack of discretion hastens his downfall.

See *The Secret History*, Donna Tartt

CORLEONE, FREDO

Nicknamed Freddy by his brothers, who include **Michael Corleone** and **Tom Hagen**, Fredo is the middle son of Godfather **Vito Corleone**. He's pale and thin, lacking the robust health and character of his brothers after suffering from infant pneumonia. He's always seen as the "weak" Corleone brother, which he deeply resents. He accepts the fact that his elder brother, Sonny, comes first in the family hierarchy, but when younger brother Michael, too, is placed

Cool Hand Luke
© 1967 Jalem Productions, Inc. Warner Bros.-Seven Arts

over him, it drives him to despair and unspoken but venomous envy and hostility.

See *The Godfather,* Mario Puzo

CORLEONE, MICHAEL

Youngest son of **Vito Corleone**, destined to step into his father's shoes as head of the Corleone crime family, and be changed forever from an idealistic World War II hero into a cold-blooded murderer. As he follows that path, he will save his father's life, avenge the family honor, woo and marry a beautiful Italian woman, and grieve her death. He'll marry a second time, to the woman he fell in love with as a young Marine captain, **Kay Adams**, who will bear him two children, Mary and Anthony. And, with an icy calm, he'll stand as godfather to his sister's baby while his paid assassins murder a score of his enemies in a single deadly afternoon. Michael's promise to his wife, Kay: "In five years the Corleone family is going to be completely legitimate. Trust me."

See *The Godfather,* Mario Puzo

CORLEONE, VITO

Brilliant and devious, he is a family man, business leader, and murderer. Don Corleone, an immigrant from Italy, reaches a pinnacle of power and wealth, but his greatest pride is his sons, Sonny, **Fredo**, **Michael**, and adopted son **Tom Hagen**. He was born Vito Andolini in the Sicilian town of Corleone. His voice is hoarse, from a childhood bout with smallpox. Vito rises from the lowest ranks of society to assemble a vast crime empire that also defends the interests and desires of the people he regards as his constituency—the humble Italian American population of lower New York City. Even though a wealthy man, he retains some of his humble habits, growing his own tomatoes and shopping for his own fruit. Gambling, prostitution, and the protection racket are the mainstays of the Corleones, but the don draws the line when it comes to drugs—a fateful decision for him and for the family as a whole. He is a criminal, but he regards himself, first and foremost, as a man of honor.

See *The Godfather,* Mario Puzo

COSTANZA, GEORGE

He's the best friend of stand-up comedian Jerry Seinfeld. George is unlucky at pretty much everything, especially with women; he's balding, henpecked by his mother, a bit pudgy, and an accomplished liar. He's different from your average schlub because he knows he's your average schlub. He's been a real estate agent and hand model, only finding success when he decides to do exactly the opposite of what his instincts tell him to do. After that, he lands a dream job with the New York Yankees. George has told women he's a marine biologist and architect to impress them, won't reveal his SAT scores, and was once caught masturbating to a copy of *Glamour* magazine by his mother.

See *Seinfeld*

COSTAS, SYLVIA

This attractive New York City district attorney starts off disliking but eventually becomes smitten by gruff but lovable **Detective Andy Sipowicz**. She comes from a large Greek family and dreams of having a big, traditional wedding. In addition to being a good D.A., she is a supportive mate for Andy, a recovering alcoholic.

See *NYPD Blue*

COUNT CHOCULA

Knew early on that chocolate lust deserved all the respect that blood lust has gotten for centuries. Dedicates his life to chocolate through the breakfast cereal that carries his name. His skin is a rich brown color; Count Dracula pales in comparison.

See *Count Chocula*

MOTHER COURAGE

Businesswoman Anna Fierling drags her canteen behind the armies of the Thirty Years' War, desperately trying to make a profit. Despite her stated goal of keeping her family intact, her trade insures that her two sons and daughter all perish in the general disaster. She moans only when dawning peace threatens to ruin her business. Mother Courage is an ambivalent symbol of both the evil of opportunism and the spirit of survival. "The war's getting along pretty well. More countries are joining in all the time....With a little planning ahead, I can do good business if I'm careful."

See *Mother Courage and Her Children,* Bertolt Brecht

COYLE, EDDIE

A bit player in Boston's branch of the mob, now he's under intense pressure to tell what he knows. Coyle is tired of his life in the underworld and is desperate to make a career break from the organization. He goes by the nickname Fingers in honor of the time his hand was smashed in a drawer.

See *The Friends of Eddie Coyle*

CRABB, JACK

The only survivor of the Battle of the Little Big Horn, from Custer's side, at least. Jack Crabb has led an amazingly full and long life, living at different periods with white settlers and with Native American tribes, and existing uneasily between the two. He's been a gunfighter, a snake oil peddler, and a scout for Custer. The Cheyenne who raised him for years gave him the name Little Big Man.

See *Little Big Man*, Thomas Berger

CRAIG, JANE

Talented, award-winning, and high-strung television news producer. Prefers crying jags to coffee breaks. Loves her job and her colleagues, though she feels an emptiness in her personal life. If there's a man completely and utterly wrong for her, she can find him in the blink of an eye.

See *Broadcast News*

CRAIG, MARK

A brilliant heart surgeon who seems to have no heart of his own, Dr. Mark Craig is pompous, demanding, and cold. Craig, a star doctor at Boston's faltering St. Eligius hospital, is as difficult with his coworkers as he is with his wife, Ellen. He designs an artificial heart called the Craig 9000.

See *St. Elsewhere*

CRANE, DR. FRASIER

He's a successful Boston psychiatrist with ample neuroses of his own. He has been therapist, lover, and, briefly, fiancé to waitress **Diane Chambers**. Even after their relationship goes south, however, Frasier keeps on hanging out with the barflies at Cheers, constantly reminding them that culturally and intellectually they're not in his league. They get along with him, anyway. He rebounds from heartbreak with Diane to marry psychiatrist **Dr. Lilith Sternin**.

See *Cheers*

CRASTER, JULIAN

A passionate, brilliant young composer-conductor, supremely confident in his ability. He has no qualms about calling an entire orchestra to rehearse at dawn. Julian is ecstatic when asked by impresario **Boris Lermontov** to compose a new ballet, *The Red Shoes*. While working on this project, he falls in love with young ballerina **Victoria Page**.

See *The Red Shoes*

CRAWFORD, SONNY

Living in a rooming house in the dusty little Texas town of Thalia, sixteen-year-old Sonny Crawford comes of age through a series of affairs with women young and old. When he's not hanging out at the local movie theater, he's lusting for the beautiful, rich **Jacy Farrow**, or awkwardly succumbing to the advances of **Ruth Popper**, the wife of his basketball coach.

See *The Last Picture Show*, Larry McMurtry

CREED, APOLLO

An extraordinarily gifted boxer, he's the heavyweight champion of the world, a fighter with moves, power, good looks, and a big ego. Apollo loves the limelight and concentrates on charming the press with Muhammad Ali–like wit and smoothness, seeing **Rocky Balboa** as an opponent unlikely to give him much trouble in the ring. But one never knows in boxing, does one?

See *Rocky*

CREED, DR. LOUIS

He is a genteel, droll-mannered, early-middle-age university medic from Ludlow, Maine. Creed is married to Rachel Creed (nee Goldman) and father to two children: daughter Eileen and infant son Gage. He went prematurely gray after the horror of bringing his family back to life via supernatural means.

See *Pet Sematary*, Stephen King

CROCKETT, JAMES "SONNY"

He's an exceedingly handsome cop who manages to maintain a permanent two-day stubble. He wears designer pastel clothing, expensive Italian loafers, but no socks—it gets hot in Miami. He drives a Ferrari and likes tooling around offshore in a supercharged cigarette boat. But, appearances notwithstanding, Sonny's not just a showboat. He's quietly determined to rid Miami of the scum that's making

Vito Corleone

it such a dangerous place. Women dig him, but he's consumed with the memory of his ex-wife, with whom he had an on-again, off-again relationship before she was killed by bad guys. His nemesis is a Cuban gangster who works for mega-powerful Colombian drug lords. Partners with **Tubbs**; together they report to **Lieutenant Castillo**.
See *Miami Vice*

CROFT, SERGEANT SAM

The tough guy par excellence. A lean, unyielding platoon leader who loves combat, and drives his men and himself with tireless intensity. Irked by mundane labor details, he craves the responsibility of leading men into battle, which makes him feel "powerful and certain." He distrusts his emotions. A west Texan who has renounced God, he's a hunter, bar fighter, and bronco buster. The only woman he ever loved cheated on him. Killed his first man, a striker, while serving in the National Guard. "No one you can trust except yourself." He resents the assignment of **Lieutenant Robert Hearn** to lead his platoon on a mission behind Japanese lines, and connives in Hearn's death. "He hungered for the fast, taut pulse he would feel in his throat after he killed a man."
See *The Naked and the Dead,* **Norman Mailer**

CROSBIE, LESLIE

The proud, cool wife of a Malaysian plantation owner, she claims to have shot a man in self-defense. Her refined demeanor is in sharp contrast to her passionate, clandestine love life. Shrewd and imperturbable, she's adept at creating and sustaining lies, but they eventually catch up to her. She manipulates her devoted husband and, unbeknownst to him, spends his entire savings in order to extricate herself from a blackmail plot. Smug in her cleverness, she fails to see who her real enemy is.
See *The Letter*

CROSS, LUCAS

Lucas works as a janitor, but his primary vocation is drinking. He spends all his money on booze, his habits have repelled his son to the point where the son leaves town, his wife has killed herself, and he gets his stepdaughter, **Selena**, pregnant. Aside from that, he's not too bad.
See *Peyton Place,* **Grace Metalious**

CROSS, NOAH

Powerful and murderous Los Angeles business tycoon and political figure of the 1930s. Father to **Evelyn Mulwray**, whom he molested as a child and with whom he ultimately had an incestuous daughter. Has fingers in many pies and is interested in H_2O for more than just drinking purposes. Knows what he wants and usually gets it. "Of course I'm respectable. I'm old. Politicians, ugly buildings and whores all get respectable if they last long enough."
See *Chinatown*

CROSS, SELENA

A pretty, blond high school senior in respectable yet oppressive Peyton Place, Selena enjoys school and her friendship with the smart **Allison MacKenzie**. But there's trouble in her life—in the form of her no-good, drunken stepfather, **Lucas**, who eventually rapes her, resulting in a miscarriage. Finally, Selena's luck changes—she and her boyfriend plan a wedding, and the future looks bright. When Lucas assaults her again, she kills him, but she's so scared of destroying her reputation in the town that she won't reveal the truth about Lucas to clear her name in the eyes of the law— only to have the truth revealed by the brave doctor who treated her.
See *Peyton Place,* **Grace Metalious**

CROW

A rock 'n' roll gypsy killer. Crow has developed a unique playing style, after the models of Roger Daltry and Keith Richards. He is proficient at taking the styles of others and synthesizing them into his own. Crow is a taker, after everything he can scavenge from rock 'n' roll kingpin **Hoss**—including his soul.
See *The Tooth of Crime,* **Sam Shepard**

THE CROW

Late, great rock star returned from the dead to exact revenge. His penchant for black clothing, ghoulish makeup, and memorable entrances serves him well in his after-death excursions. Handy with a hex when there's a need for supernatural backup. Knows how to work over enemies with effective violence.
See *The Crow*

CRUSHER, DR. BEVERLY

The headstrong doctor aboard the starship

Enterprise, Beverly is a staunch advocate of her patients' rights, even if her position seems to conflict with other members of the crew. A widow, she has a precocious son, Wesley, an often unspoken romantic interest in Captain **Jean-Luc Picard**, and an interest in theater.

See *Star Trek: The Next Generation*

CAPTAIN CUMMINGS

Cummings is a goodhearted rescue mission director who is not what he appears to be, i.e., a "nice, modest little fella." He hangs out next door at the bar where luscious **Lady Lou** performs. He follows through on sultry Lou's offer to "come up and see me sometime," but scolds her: "I'm sorry you think more of your diamonds than you do of your soul." He turns out to be a U.S. undercover officer, The Hawk. He doesn't arrest Lou; he marries her.

See *She Done Him Wrong*

CUMMINGS, MAJOR GENERAL EDWARD

His forces invade Anopopei, a Pacific island, and overwhelm Japanese defenders during World War II. Brilliant and tyrannical, he's made himself into a great military leader, but lost his humanity along the way, and part of him regrets this. A proud reactionary, even a fascist, he reveals, in talks with aide **Lieutenant Robert Hearn**, his contempt for ordinary people and their weaknesses, yet he's skilled at talking to his men, who consider him "a swell guy." He is consumed with notions of control and self-control, and uses different kinds of speech for different people, but hardly ever says what he thinks. An excellent chess player, with a mind that works on many levels, he is also a repressed homosexual whose marriage cracked open after his wife realized that in their sex "he fights out battles with himself upon (her) body." Despite paternal and homoerotic feelings for Hearn he sends him off to likely death. He drives his troops to fight the Japanese, the jungle, and the weather, but realizes as victory comes how little all his planning has affected the outcome of the battle. "The trick is to make yourself an instrument of your own policy....(T)hat's the highest effectiveness man has achieved."

See *The Naked and the Dead*, **Norman Mailer**

CUNNINGHAM, HOWARD

This wry, Middle America dad has a gruff exterior but is pretty soft underneath. Even though he complains and whines a lot, like about wanting some peace, he's really basically happy. He loves his wife, **Marion**, and his kids, **Richie** and **Joanie**, and grudgingly tolerates his boarder, **Fonzie**. He's not too strict but doesn't want Joanie to leave the house until she's sixteen.

See *Happy Days*

CUNNINGHAM, JOANIE

A flirtatious 1950s teenager, very perky and upbeat. She is cute as a button. Basically, Joannie is a good kid, but she secretly yearns to be a bad girl like her friend Jenny Piccolo. Likes to hang around her older brother, **Richie**, and his friends. Gets crushes on guys all the time. Joanie loves **Chachi**.

See *Happy Days*

CUNNINGHAM, MARION

The perfect 1950s mom. Everyone loves "Mrs. C." Sure, she seems a little ditzy and a pushover, but she's really strong. Always has time for her kids, **Richie** and **Joanie**, and their friends. Her family is her life. Dotes on her husband, **Howard**, and he can make her blush. "Oh, Howard."

See *Happy Days*

CUNNINGHAM, RICHIE

He is the archetypal Middle America teenager, circa 1957. Earnest, slightly innocent, straight-up, natural. The nicest guy in the world, who'd do anything for a friend. Smart but slightly naive, Richie wishes he were more cool and suave. He tries hard to be hipper, but it usually doesn't wash, because he just can't help being himself. He pals around with **Potsie Weber** and **Ralph Malph** and idolizes his parents' tenant, the rebel **Arthur "Fonzie" Fonzarelli**. Richie is nice to younger sister **Joanie** and is a respectful son who helps out around the house. He favors short hair, letter sweaters, khaki pants, and malts. Girls think he's cute and so nice. Sings "I Found My Thrill on Blueberry Hill" when he gets lucky on a date.

See *Happy Days*

CURLEY

The nasty son of a rancher, Curley is cocky and

Dr. Beverly Crusher

mean. He smears Vaseline in his left glove because he's "keeping that hand soft for his wife." Curley's recently wed to a town girl, **Mae**, who doesn't like him. He's jealous, and she does give him cause. A little guy, with tight, curly hair, he's "pretty handy" with his fists and is a former Golden Glove finalist. He likes to pick fights with big guys, but goes too far when he taunts gentle giant **Lennie Small**, who breaks every bone in his hand. "I'm gonna shoot the guts outa that big bastard myself, even if I only got one hand."
See *Of Mice and Men,* John Steinbeck

CURLY

Curly's a cowhand with everything going for him: a dream job, good friends, and the gal he loves by his side. He's an uncomplicated soul who sees the beauty in a growing cornfield, but doesn't want too many people to know how he feels about **Laurey**…at least not 'til after the wedding.
See *Oklahoma!,* Oscar Hammerstein II and Richard Rodgers

CURLY

Rugged veteran cowpuncher who don't take no sass from soft city boys. Enjoys riding, roping, and hard living. Has an excellent eye when it comes to knife throwing. Works as trail boss for modern-day dude ranch and cattle-driving outfit. Bronzed skin appears to be made of leather.
See *City Slickers*

CURRY, JED "KID"

In an attempt to live the straight and narrow—and be pardoned by the governor—affable outlaw "Kid" Curry takes on the name Thaddeus Jones. It doesn't help much; he and partner **Hannibal Heyes** are still tracked by old pals and new posses.
See *Alias Smith and Jones*

CURTIS, PONYBOY

A fourteen-year-old from the wrong side of the tracks being raised by his brothers. Ponyboy wishes people wouldn't judge him by his lower-class background. But, of course, they do and label him as a greaser. He runs away with best friend **Johnny Cade** after Johnny accidentally murders a rich bully who was on Ponyboy's case. "What kind of world is it where all I have to be proud of is a reputation for being a hood, and greasy hair?"
See *The Outsiders,* S. E. Hinton

CUTTER, ALEX

Disabled Vietnam vet, horribly disfigured by war. Now turned to drink and abuse as a way to work out inner troubles. Belligerent to long-suffering wife **Mo Cutter** and best friend **Richard Bone**. Obsessive in his quest to bring a possible murderer to justice.
See *Cutter's Way*

CUTTER, MO

Long-suffering wife of **Alex Cutter**. Like her husband, she's plagued by her dependence on alcohol to numb personal pain. Caught up in difficult situation because of spouse's obsessive behavior.
See *Cutter's Way*

DA

Late father of **Charlie**, now making a postmortem appearance in his hometown of Dublin, Ireland. Despite his demise, Da has a real knack for showing up at unusual moments. Still harbors a strong desire to be part of his son's earthly existence. Can see through people even though they can't see him.
See *Da*

DAAE, CHRISTINE

This angelic young Swedish opera singer, the daughter of a great violinist, is inspired by a mysterious voice she hears in her dressing room. The love of her life is dashing **Raoul de Chagny**. But she's kidnapped by **Erik, the Phantom of the Opera**, who always wears a mask. She unmasks him, sees his hideously deformed face, and is torn between compassion and horror. She feels compelled to see him again…and again.
See *The Phantom of the Opera,* Gaston Leroux

DAGGETT, LITTLE BILL

He's an amateur carpenter who builds a roof with more holes than a golf course, a professional lawman who is well accustomed to his role of not just enforcing the law but passing judgment and carrying out the sentence to boot. Hard times call for hard men, and Little Bill isn't one to allow his orders to be disobeyed. He rules the town of Big Whiskey, Wyoming, with moral certainty and a bullwhip.

Little Bill doesn't care much for firearms, preferring to let his deputies handle the gunslinging, while he gives the occasional brutal whipping and beating. His idea of justice: when a couple of cowboys slash up the face of a prostitute in Skinny Dubois's brothel, Little Bill decides they'll pay for their crime by giving some of their best ponies to Skinny—but nothing to the disfigured girl. Little Bill has the townspeople cowed, and is unchallenged until the day **William Munny** rides into town to avenge what Little Bill did to his friend Ned.

See *Unforgiven*

DAILEY, HENRY

He is a seemingly washed-up horse trainer who's developed a new zest for living. Feels a spiritual kinship for horses and riders; understands psychology of both beasts. Feels at home only when at the racetrack working with a talented mount. Mentor and companion to **Alec Ramsey**.

See *The Black Stallion*

CAPTAIN DALLAS

Commander of intergalactic cargo ship *Nostromo*. Works closely with crew, including **Lieutenant Ripley** and Mother, a computer that links him to the faceless company for which they work. Competent and, when necessary, tough with the crew, he's brave even in the face of terrifying danger.

See *Alien*

DALLAS, STEPHEN "STEVE"

A swinging bachelor lawyer who lives in a boarding house in Bloom County. Dallas was once crowned Mister America and subsequently appeared on the covers of *Dog World* and *National Geographic*. He's been told by a former lover that he kisses like a squid. Stephen had his chest hair burned off and tried to sue the doctor on *People's Court*.

See *Bloom County*, Berke Breathed

DALLOWAY, CLARISSA

A middle-aged English society woman with an overwhelming sense that her life and love have been somehow misspent or misplaced. Sensitive, emotionally bankrupt, she experiences this crisis most tellingly while, as she prepares for and gives a party, she reflects on her life, family, and friends. As if to prove her point, there arrives on the scene Peter Walsh, the man she had once loved passionately but rejected in favor of order and stability.

See *Mrs. Dalloway,* Virginia Woolf

DALTON, GRAHAM

The confused and sensitive Graham drifts through life, ending up for now in the hometown of his old college buddy **John Millaney** and John's wife, **Ann.** So wounded by a broken heart that he can't be intimate with women, Graham instead videotapes sexually explicit interviews with them, viewing them later to attain satisfaction. Both Ann and sister **Cynthia Bishop** are so excited by Graham's video attention that they tell him all kinds of secrets, and both are spurred to end their relationships with John. In the process, Graham finally rediscovers his desire for physical intimacy and finds the capacity to begin a healing process.

See *sex, lies, and videotape*

DANAHER, MARY KATE

A beautiful Irish lass with flaming red hair and a temper to match, Danaher is courted by and marries American **Sean Thornton**. Her brother Will keeps her dowry from her after the marriage because of his hatred of Thornton. "I'm no woman to be honked at and come a-runnin'."

See *The Quiet Man*

DANDRIDGE, JERRY

This tall, dark, handsome next-door neighbor of teenager **Charlie Brewster** is a vampire. His roomie, Billy Cole, is a ghoul. There goes the neighborhood. They all live on Oak Street, in Corvallis, Iowa. Charlie takes it into his head that Jerry must be destroyed before his antisocial habit of drinking people's blood gets out of hand.

See *Fright Night*, Tom Holland

DANGEROUSLY, JOHNNY

A poor newsboy who grows up to be a successful, self-made crook, all so that he can pay his mom's medical expenses. His archenemy is Danny Vermin. By middle age, Dangerously has settled down and runs a pet store.

See *Johnny Dangerously*

DANIEL, BREE

This bright, successful call girl craves a better life, possibly as an actress, and thinks she's on the way toward getting there. Then an abusive john starts stalking her. Her regular sessions with a motherly psychiatrist, intended to help her leave "the life," can't keep the contradictions in her world from tearing it apart. Detective **John Klute** arrives looking for a missing friend, but stays on to protect, befriend, and finally, love her. She seduces and manipulates him, and finds herself caring for him. Yearning for a return to her old numbness, she tries vainly to drive him away. "What the hell, it's their money; I don't care, I'll swing from a shower rod and whistle 'Maytime.' Except this guy really freaked out on it."

See *Klute*

DANIELS, MELANIE

A wealthy, stuck-up socialite, she enjoys the high life. In an unlikely romance with lawyer **Mitch Brenner**. Not the strong, self-sacrificing type but capable of unique courage in face of extraordinary situations. Has distinct aversion to foul fowl.

See *The Birds*

COUNT DANILO

A handsome, charming soldier living in Warshovia, a tiny Central European country. He's also a womanizer, going so far as to make a move on **King Achmed**'s wife. Achmed sends Danilo to Paris to marry **Sonia**, a mega-rich widow, to keep her money in Warshovia. When she finds out that he's courting her on orders, she spurns his advances—only to relent when he convinces her that he's truly fallen in love with her.

See *The Merry Widow*

DANKO, JILL

The ever-understanding wife of rookie cop **Mike Danko**, Jill is a hardworking nurse who nonetheless always manages to be there for her husband and his two partners/best friends, Terry Webster and Willie Gillis.

See *The Rookies*

DANKO, MIKE

This young California police rookie is committed to his job and tries to find a balance between the tough ways of the old police force and the more humane, socially conscious tactics of modern criminal justice. His loving wife is **Jill Danko**, a nurse. His partners, Terry Webster and Willie Gillis, are equally committed.

See *The Rookies*

DANNY

Hunky, good-hearted country club caddy whose only chance at college is to win the scholarship sponsored by the **Judge**, the VIP of VIPs at the club. He tries, at least at first, to suck up to the Judge, although doing so is a piece of hypocrisy which runs against his grain. What price higher education?

See *Caddyshack*

MRS. DANVERS

Maxim de Winter's beautiful but evil housekeeper who can't stand it when de Winter brings home a new wife. She really knows how to honor the dead: Mrs. Danvers is so devoted to Maxim's deceased wife, Rebecca, that she terrorizes the new Mrs. de Winter. She is also given to a most unfortunate indulgence in playing with fire.

See *Rebecca*, Daphne du Maurier

D'ARCY, JEFFERSON

Pretty-boy neighbor of **Al** and **Peg Bundy**. Married to **Marcy Rhoades D'Arcy**, a loan officer who picked him up at a bankers' convention. He doesn't really work and is supported by his wife. His assets are his great body, good looks, and the fact that he always knows who's on *Oprah*.

See *Married...with Children*

D'ARCY, MARCY RHOADES

Marcy's the next-door neighbor of **Al** and **Peg Bundy**, and a loan officer at a Chicago bank. Her first husband, **Steve Rhoades**, left her after he lost his job and ran off to become a park ranger. Then she met second husband **Jefferson D'Arcy** while on a drunken binge at a bankers' convention. She supports her new husband, with whom she has great sex.

See *Married...with Children*

DAREDEVIL

Matt Murdock, the son of famous boxer "Battling" Jack Murdock, is blinded in his youth by exposure to nasty radioactivity. Consequently, he develops a unique radar sense. When his father is brutally murdered, Matt learns martial arts, fakes his own death, renames himself Jack, puts on a costume, and calls himself Daredevil in order to fight crime and avenge his father's death. Apparently, you can't fight crime without a costume. So acute is his radar that nobody ever suspects him of being blind. Except maybe when he is talking to a mannequin.

See *Daredevil*

DARKMAN

Scientist turned mysterious crime-fighter after being horribly disfigured. His secret potion gives him the ability to restructure his appearance, a handy accomplishment in his second career as a nemesis of crime. Wears hat and cape at all other times to cover his gnarly looks.

See *Darkman*

DARLING, NOLA

A sweet, sexy, African American girl from Brooklyn, who must choose between many suitors, including a smooth philanderer, a nice, humble guy, and the hyperkinetic **Mars Blackmon**. She values her personal freedom, however, above all else, even if her choice results in harm to herself.

See *She's Gotta Have It*

DARLING, WENDY

Wendy, along with her younger brothers, John and Michael, goes on a trip with **Peter Pan** to Never-Never-Land. Pan wants Wendy to be a mother to the Lost Boys and tell them all stories. "Now, Peter, let's stop pretending and be practical."

See *Peter Pan*

DARRELL, LARRY

Scion of a wealthy family in Lake Forest, Illinois, Darrell has his world turned upside down while serving as an ambulance driver in France during World War I. After the war, he renounces his patrician upbringing, leaves the United States, and pursues knowledge for its own sake wherever it may be found. His extensive travels in pursuit of wisdom take him from the coal mines in Germany to the mountains of Tibet.

See *The Razor's Edge,* W. Somerset Maugham

DARROW, ANN

Down on her luck, broke, reduced to theft in order to survive, Darrow is discovered by filmmaker **Carl Denham**, who revives her with coffee and doughnuts and convinces her that she's the actress he needs for his new movie. She's game and winds up on a ship bound for the Pacific. On board, she gets clothes, three meals a day, and falls for handsome crewman Jack Driscoll. They reach a mysterious and uncharted island, and things take a decided turn for the worse when she's kidnapped by natives and offered up as a sacrifice to the fearsome Kong. Kong, a humongous gorilla, finds the young woman strangely appealing, despite the superficial incompatibility, and carts her off into the primeval wilderness, fighting off dinosaurs and the like, who'd like to make her a tasty snack. Driscoll and the sailors save her, knock out Kong with chemicals, and take the big ape back to New York. When the lovesick Kong escapes, and tries to take his beloved somewhere where the two of them can just be together, all hell breaks loose, and she finds herself in Kong's fist, perched on top of the Empire State Building, while a swarm of airplanes shoots machine guns at them. All in all, it's enough to make a girl give up showbiz. Which she subsequently does.

See *King Kong*

DARUWALLA, DR. FARROKH

A middle-aged doctor obsessed with finding the cause of, and a cure for, dwarfism. Born in Bombay, Dr. Daruwalla returns to that city frequently from his home in Toronto to seek out circus dwarves from whom he can draw blood with which to experiment. In his spare time, he pseudonymously writes Western-style gumshoe novels that offend half of Bombay's population.

See *A Son of the Circus,* John Irving

DARYL (1)

Silent brother of **Larry** and **Daryl** who helps out as a handyman at **Dick Louden's** Stratford Inn in Norwich, Vermont. Along with his brothers, runs the Minuteman Cafe in town. Attended Oxford University.

See *Newhart*

DARYL (2)

A brother of **Larry** and **Daryl**, he works as an occa-

Lieutenant Commander Data

sional handyman for **Dick Louden** at the Stratford Inn in Norwich, Vermont. Like brother Daryl, Daryl does not speak. Attended Cambridge University under a rowing scholarship. Runs the Minuteman Cafe in town with his two brothers.

See *Newhart*

DATA

A perfectly sentient android with a complex positronic brain who seems in all ways human except that he lacks emotions; indeed, his driving search is for an emotional life and a better understanding of human nature. He's the operations manager on the starship *Enterprise*, but because of his vast intelligence, he can be called on to do almost anything. He can't use contractions (they're not in his program), was designed by a doctor named Noonien Soong. He paints, and, oddly enough for a mechanism, has a cat named Spot.

See *Star Trek: The Next Generation*

DAVENPORT, JOYCE

She's a tough, good-looking, no-nonsense assistant district attorney in a crime-ridden city. Joyce has strong character and morals as well as an intimidating manner, perhaps developed to discourage unprofessional interest on the part of lustful males. She drives a hard (plea) bargain and is very committed to her job and her lover and then husband, police captain **Frank Furillo**. Tough veneer belies a sensitive and sensual nature.

See *Hill Street Blues*

DAVID, HECTOR

Bad guy in a white hat who shadows and menaces **John J. MacReedy** around the town of Black Rock. He doesn't have a lot to say, but he's never far from his prey. A heavy who takes direction from ringleader **Reno Smith**.

See *Bad Day at Black Rock*

DAVIS, BILL

His demeanor may be gruff, but this New York City bachelor is a softie at heart. He's been saddled with the responsibility of raising his orphaned nieces and nephew, in addition to his demanding career in engineering. Fortunately, his affluence is such that he has the services of an English butler,

Mr. French. Between them, they make a go of it.

See *Family Affair*

DAVIS, BUD

Bud adjusts to big-city life in Aberdeen by adopting Gilley's roadhouse as a second home, filled with his newfound friends, family, and foes. He meets **Sissy** there and they're soon married. Bud rides the mechanical bull at Gilley's to prove his masculinity and to win back Sissy.

See *Urban Cowboy*

DAVIS, BUFFY

An adorable, pigtailed little girl. She's an orphan and lives in a big New York apartment with her beloved Uncle **Bill**, twin brother, **Jody**, and big sister, **Cissy**. She often carries and talks to her bespectacled doll, Mrs. Beasley.

See *Family Affair*

DAVIS, CISSY

This orphaned teenager lives in New York with her much younger twin brother and sister and her Uncle **Bill Davis**. She's pretty and popular but still suffers much adolescent angst over boys. She's at an age that makes her a little self-centered, and she also finds it tough not to have a mom, but Uncle Bill provides support, advice, comfort, and a good deal of engineering skill, should she need any.

See *Family Affair*

DAVIS, CRASH

Nearly washed-up baseball catcher, never quite good enough to make the big leagues. Has bounced around minor-league teams throughout the South during entire career, now working for Raleigh-Durham Bulls. Superb at coaxing the best out of major-league hopefuls. Believes Oswald acted alone at Dallas. Also a fan of slow, deep kisses and the small of a woman's back.

See *Bull Durham*

DAVIS, ISAAC

A wealthy, famous television comedy writer, he longs to get out of the rat race and write a great novel. His greatest dream is to become known as a serious writer. At the age of forty-two he's involved with a seventeen-year-old high school girl. "I'm dating a girl where I can beat up her father. It's the first time that phenomenon ever occurred in my life." He's tiring of that relationship, though, and taking up with **Mary Wilke**, a posturing pseudointellectual who loves to put down Ike's heroes. There's something about her that Ike finds invigorating, despite—or maybe because of—their ongoing bickering and squabbling. In addition to this romantic turmoil, his other current burden is his ex-wife's impending tell-all best-seller about their marriage—including insulting disclosures about Ike's every self-absorbed foible and habit.

See *Manhattan*

DAVIS, JODY

He is an active, raspy-voiced little boy. He's lost his parents and lives with, and adores, his **Uncle Bill**. In fact, he wants to be an engineer just like his uncle. He can be protective of his twin sister, **Buffy**, but is also ready to fight with her at the drop of a hat. Siblings, you know.

See *Family Affair*

DAVISON, SYBIL

An average suburban adolescent girl, just discovering romance and sexuality. Sybil meets a boy and begins a sexual relationship that culminates in declarations that they'll love each other forever. But forever lasts only until that summer, when she goes away to work as a camp counselor and falls for another boy.

See *Forever,* Judy Blume

DAWN, BILLIE

Former chorus girl and now mistress of corrupt wheeler-dealer, she is taken in hand by a journalist tutor hired by her keeper to give her a veneer of respectability. She's blond, perky, and, though uneducated, has a brain and learns more from her tutor than her wheeler-dealer expects—or wants. Killer gin player.

See *Born Yesterday*

DAWN, GAYE

Nee Maggie Mooney, a ruined ex–chorus girl and former consort of **Johnny Rocco**. She smokes and drinks Scotch to excess, but she's also a fair pony handicapper. Given to costume jewelry. Her alto voice was ruined by alcohol and abuse. She's instrumental in the death of Rocco at the hands of **Frank McCloud**.

See *Key Largo*

DAWSON, EB

A gawky, wide-eyed country boy. Flannel shirts, blue jeans, and a baseball cap are the uniform for handyman Eb, who spends his days doing odd jobs for **Lisa** and **Oliver Douglas**. Because he takes everything he hears literally, Eb is in an almost constant state of confusion. He's got a good heart and has a thing for Ralph Monroe.

See *Green Acres*

DAY, CLARENCE

Stalwart Republican and man of business. His temper is short and his demeanor stolid. He keeps his wife on a strict allowance and expects his sons to do as they are told. Though he himself has a great deal to do with it, he cannot understand why his family is incapable of keeping a maid for more than one week at a time. By his reckoning the world has gone to heck in a handbasket ever since Grover Cleveland was elected. His wife calls him Clare.

See *Life with Father,* Howard Lindsay and Russel Crouse

DAY, MAY

This is no shrinking violet or damsel in distress. May Day is the personal assistant and bodyguard to ultra-rich, psycho, computer chip manufacturer **Max Zorin**, and also pinch-hits as an assassin now and then. Once May Day commits to a job, she'll do anything to finish it. Not quite the embodiment of evil, she has a redeeming trait or two.

See *A View to a Kill*

DEAD, MACON "MILKMAN"

He's trying hard to understand himself and his heritage. His father wants Milkman to surrender his identity to white society in exchange for material rewards. But Milkman is drawn to his Aunt Pilate, who hints of a heroic family history, and he eventually sets out to search for the truth about his ancestors. Tracing his roots to Virginia, he finds that his great grandfather was Solomon, a slave who one day rose into the air from the fields and flew back to Africa. Armed with a clearer sense of what he comes from, Milkman is able to cheat death by following Solomon. He's learned that if you surrender to the air, you can ride it.

See *Song of Solomon,* Toni Morrison

KIDS MOST LIKELY TO END UP WITH A TATTOO

Holden Caulfield
Huck Finn
Dennis Mitchell
Ralph
Bart Simpson
Jeff Spicoli
Charles "Chachi" Arcola
John Connor

DeBecque, Emile

A suave, rich French plantation owner living on an island in the South Pacific during World War II, where he spends his time hunting and fishing. He left France as a young man after killing the town bully, married a Polynesian woman, and has raised their two children since her death. M. deBecque believes that life is short and should be lived to the fullest. He becomes a hero when he helps the Allies take control of a neighboring island. He falls in love with American nurse **Nellie Forbush**, and, despite her reluctance, ultimately wins her heart.

See *South Pacific,* Oscar Hammerstein II and Richard Rodgers and *Tales of the South Pacific,* James Michener

de Chagny, Raoul

A virtuous young sailor, the Vicomte de Chagny has loved singer **Christine Daae** ever since he rescued her scarf from the sea as a child. His mother died giving him birth. He is innocent and shy but has steely determination. He's resolved enough to risk everything to free Christine from the haunting power of **Erik, the Phantom of the Opera**.

See *The Phantom of the Opera,* Gaston Leroux

De Fazio, Laverne

She's a wisecracking, guy-hungry, working girl. Laverne works at the Shotz Brewery in Milwaukee with best friend and roommate **Shirley Feeney**. Tall, big-haired, and not gorgeous, Laverne favors tight monogrammed sweaters with her skirts and saddle shoes. Loud and obnoxious, she's really defensive and insecure. She and Shirley fight a lot, but they always make up in the end. Spends her free time bowling and eating pizza. Trying to get ahead and make a life for herself.

See *Laverne and Shirley*

de Marco, Angela

After her husband, Frank "Cucumber" de Marco, is killed by mob boss **Tony Russo**, Angela wants to cut her mob connections, which proves to be a difficult proposition. She moves home to Queens, New York, and gets entangled with the FBI, in the person of special agent **Mike Downey**. She tells FBI agents, "You people work just like the mob. There's no difference."

See *Married to the Mob*

De Palma, Louie

Evolution has passed Louie by. He's a vile, contemptible, stingy, back-stabbing, tyrannical, sneaky little man—and those are his good qualities. He's a cab dispatcher for the Sunshine Cab Company in Manhattan. Louie feels that he is having a good day only when he has left someone emotionally crippled. It's not true, however, that he's a chauvinist; he doesn't respect men, either. What he does respect is money, and he'd trample his grandmother to be the first to grab a dollar bill from the floor. He feels he's surrounded by losers and only trusts **Alex Rieger**, because he knows Alex is too goody-goody to betray his confidence. His version of the Golden Rule is: Do it to them before they do it to you.

See *Taxi*

DeVille, Cruella

A tall, gaunt, flamboyant femme with a mean greedy streak, whose get-rich scheme involves turning Dalmatian puppies into fur coats. A scratchy-voiced diva with shaggy black and white hair, she wears a red dress, matching gloves and a rug-like fur coat. She can berate her two dim-witted henchmen one minute and purringly coax dogs from their owners the next.

See *101 Dalmatians*

de Winter, Maxim

This rich, elegant widower marries the unglamorous **Mrs. de Winter** to the dismay of his housekeeper, **Mrs. Danvers**, who worships the memory of de Winter's late first wife, Rebecca. He seems wistful about his first wife's death, but it gradually becomes evident that he hated Rebecca for her philandering and actually is in danger of being tried for her murder. Though a decent sort at heart, he's unable to see beneath the virtuous facade of the evil Mrs. Danvers, a blindness that proves to be a real problem.

See *Rebecca,* Daphne du Maurier

Mrs. de Winter

A mousy woman who can't believe it when the glamorous **Maxim de Winter** asks her to marry him. She moves into his mansion, where she's terrified by the evil maid, **Mrs. Danvers**, who idolized Maxim's deceased first wife, Rebecca, and resents the new Mrs. de Winter. She's shocked to learn the truth about her husband: that he actually hated his cheating first wife and may have in fact murdered her. She is fated to suffer other unpleasantness in the de Winter home as well.

See *Rebecca*, Daphne du Maurier

DEAN, JASON "J. D."

An apple-cheeked, smiling psychopath, J.D. rides into Westerburg High on his motorbike and starts killing off the most popular students at school, along with girlfriend **Veronica Sawyer**. As one might expect, he has a very dysfunctional home life. "The extreme always seems to make an impression."

See *Heathers*

DEAN, SAMMY JO

Trampy social-climbing poor relation. This white-trash cousin of wealthy **Krystle Carrington** plants herself in the Carrington home. With a goal of getting rich, Sammy Jo uses her very fine body to entice and torment indecisively gay **Steven**, eventually bearing his child. Takes some hard knocks but always comes back swinging.

See *Dynasty*

DECKARD

Tough and laconic, Deckard is a Blade Runner, a member of a special police force whose dangerous assignment is hunting down rogue replicants—humanoid slave-laborers—and "retiring" them, which means killing them. Then he crosses the line and falls in love with the replicant **Rachel**. "Replicants are like any other machine. They're either a benefit or a hazard. If they're a benefit, it's not my problem."

See *Blade Runner*

DEDALUS, STEPHEN

As a sensitive, intelligent, frail child, he is cowed and bullied on the playground; but Stephen is destined to grow into a rebellious young man with the courage and drive to assert his individuality. He feels stifled by the many levels of convention of his society: family, Catholicism, and Irish nationalism. Tormented by his burgeoning adolescent sexuality, he is subjected to a priest's "hellfire" sermon during a school retreat, which exacerbates his moral suffering. He thinks early on that he has a vocation for the priesthood but ultimately rejects the call, having become cynical about religion. He is a young man of contradictory nature: romantic yet realistic; fearful yet bold; lonely yet lacking the warmth to participate in true friendships. The duality of his nature, which creates difficulties in day-to-day life, is an essential and central aspect of the creative artist, which Dedalus is by nature. At university, he embraces the world of literature, philosophy, and aesthetics. Making art his religion, he throws off the shackles of family, religion, and state in order to worship at its altar. He finally resolves to leave Ireland for Paris and "the reality of experience."

See *A Portrait of the Artist as a Young Man*, James Joyce

DEE DEE

A true surfer girl, normally found at the beach clad in a bikini that no one can match. She has a way of often getting into awkward situations but is usually bailed out by ever-loyal boyfriend **Frankie**. Likes to twist, roast weenies, and even sing when the moment is right.

See *Beach Blanket Bingo*

DEEDS, LONGFELLOW

A country poet thrust into the hurly-burly atmosphere of New York City. Originally the unofficial poet laureate of Mandrake Falls, Vermont, Mr. Deeds was also locally well known for his part as the tuba player in the town band. Deeds's simple life is changed forever when a rich uncle dies, leaving his $20 million estate to the Vermont innocent. Once in New York to settle the estate, Mr. Deeds is set upon by all sorts of schemers and manipulators. Finally, fed up with the whole thing, he decides to sink the money into a collective farm colony, for which he is brought before the lunacy commission. Seems appropriate, but he gets off anyway.

See *Mr. Deeds Goes to Town*

DEERING, WILMA

A high-placed officer with the Earth Defense Directorate, she's as competent as she is beautiful. Her mission is to keep Earth safe from various interstellar villains in the complex universe of the twenty-fifth century. Often aiding her is **Buck**

NIGHTMARE DANCE PARTNERS

Robocop
Tattoo
Inspector Jacques Clouseau
Steve Urkel
Herman Munster

Rogers, a twentieth-century astronaut who survived a five-hundred-year suspended animation.

See *Buck Rogers* and *Buck Rogers in the 25th Century*

DELANY, DOC

Failed medical student, now working as a chiropractor in a college town. Has a severe alcohol problem. Married for many years to **Lola Delaney** in what has degenerated into a love-hate relationship. Rents out spare room in his house to university boarders.

See *Come Back, Little Sheba*

DELANY, LOLA

Slovenly, alcoholic homemaker. Desperately worried about missing pooch, Sheba. Is wed to **Doc Delaney**, an ineffectual chiropractor and sot. Shrewish and distrusting, always sticking her nose into other people's business.

See *Come Back, Little Sheba*

DELIGHT, TRIXIE

Trixie is a waitress who takes up with a travelin' man just to get a little excitement into her small-town life. She's got more looks than brains but has a canny streak as wide as the Mississippi River. She knows what she wants and will do whatever, or whomever, it takes, to get it.

See *Paper Moon*

DELLA GUARDIA, NICO

Smooth politician, "shameless in his public conduct." Runs for and wins the office of prosecuting attorney. Always wears a flower in his lapel. Can never complete a brief on time. "Unavoidable Delay Guardia." Red hair, olive skin, light eyes. A "pygmy in his soul." He once shared an office with chief prosecutor **Rusty Sabich**, who later fired him. Wears tailor-made suits. Cocky and confident, his exit line is: "I'll be back." Unsuccessfully prosecutes Sabich for murder.

See *Presumed Innocent*, Scott Turow

DELPINO, VINNIE

Neurotic, sex-crazed teenager, the best friend of **Dr. Doogie Howser**. Vinnie's a budding filmmaker who hates and does badly at school. He wants to be rich and famous. Vinnie uses Doogie's hospital connection as a source for girls. He has a tumultuous relationship with his girlfriend, Janine. Always has an angle. A hanger-on, take-what-you-can-get guy.

See *Doogie Howser, M.D.*

DENHAM, CARL

He's a movie director, best known for jungle adventure films. Denham sets out to make a film on a strange, hitherto-unknown island, where he discovers a hyperthyroid ape known by the natives as Kong. Denham scraps his film idea and succeeds in bringing the great beast back to New York, where he plans to exhibit the creature on Broadway. But his plans go awry when Kong shows that he's no trouper and escapes, only to be hunted down by a swarm of airplanes. Kong had become enamored of a beautiful young woman, and it was this that proved to be his downfall. As Denham says, "'Twasn't the airplanes. It was Beauty killed the Beast."

See *King Kong*

DENNIS, MAME

Flamboyant socialite bursting with energy and unadulterated love for excitement. Doesn't believe in having second best of anything. Mame is constantly attended by fawners, admirers, and a few jealous friends. She takes her timid nephew in hand, determined to put some more spice into his heretofore-tame existence, and succeeds beyond his wildest expectations, even beyond his desires in many cases. Mame has no use for social hypocrisy, stuffiness, bigotry, or orthodoxy. Prefers a wardrobe and vocabulary in keeping with her brash approach to the world. "Life is a banquet and most poor suckers are starving to death!"

See *Auntie Mame*

DERRY, FRED

He is a good-looking young man, a former soda jerk who returns home from World War II as an officer with high hopes for his career and marriage. His confidence is soon eroded when he discovers that his beautiful wife (whose picture he proudly showed off to his men) has been unfaithful and he can't find a good job. Demoralized when he realizes that his wife will never understand his frustration, he turns to the daughter of fellow veteran **Al Stephenson**. After being away from the United States for so long, he feels that

he doesn't fit in. He expected to receive a hero's welcome and his slide into invisibility hurts.
See *The Best Years of Our Lives*

DESMOND, HENRY "HILDEGARDE"
Dresses in drag to get a room at the all-women's Susan B. Anthony Hotel because the rent is so affordable. His female alter ego is Hildy—ostensibly his sister. Works as an ad copywriter but yearns to be a novelist. Eventually forms a commercial production company—called 60 Seconds Street—with best friend **Kip Wilson** and **Amy Cassidy**.
See *Bosom Buddies*

DETROIT, NATHAN
A con man and charismatic gambler, Detroit is also the proprietor of "the oldest established permanent floating crap game in New York," an occupation that takes him to unlikely locales, from the back room at the Salvation Army to the sewers beneath the city. He is engaged to Miss Adelaide, a showgirl at the Hot Box, but doesn't want to make a hasty commitment to marriage. After all, the engagement has only lasted seventeen years!
See *Guys and Dolls,* **Jo Swerling, Abe Burrows, and Frank Loesser**

DEVERAUX, BLANCHE
A lusty, man-hungry, southern belle who never aged, at least in her own mind. A widow dripping with charm, she owns the house in Miami in which she lives with her best friends, Dorothy, Rose, and Sophia. Given to wearing revealing nighties in a house of polyester robes, the other women shrug off Blanche's overt sexiness.
See *The Golden Girls*

DEVITO, TOMMY
A scarily psychotic mob hit man with a homicidal temper, Devito is the loose cannon in a trio of gangsters with **Henry Hill** and **James Conway**. Tommy, who will shoot anyone in a fit of pique, is eventually seen as too uncontrollable by mob superiors.
See *Goodfellas*

DEVLIN
A debonair FBI agent who is ruthless in his pursuit of Nazis in post–World War II Brazil. Loves the beautiful **Alicia Huberman** but is so intent on catching **Alexander Sebastian** that he callously convinces her to marry the evil Nazi. Comes around at the end, though, saving Alicia from her murder-minded husband.
See *Notorious*

DeWITT, ADDISON
Broadway gadabout involved with famed actress and cynic **Margo Channing** but also smitten with lovely newcomer **Eve Harrington**. Addison wants to please all around him, from the theater audiences he depends on to the small circle of people who make up his personal life. Suave, a dapper dresser, the essence of a sophisticated New York male, Broadway variety.
See *All About Eve*

DEXTER, FARNSWORTH "DEX"
Dashing, multitalented, confident playboy. Dark haired, chisel-faced, modellike looks spell success with the ladies for devil-may-care Dex. Disinterested in routine mergers and acquisitions, Dex favors life on the edge and is involved in mysterious commandolike maneuvers all across the world. Steady beau of **Alexis Carrington Colby**.
See *Dynasty*

DEXTER-HAVEN, C. K.
A jazz-loving millionaire who can swing either high or low. His low-key personality and ability not to hold a grudge endear him to his ex-wife's family. Self-assured and happy now that he's on the wagon, he's confident that he can win back his first wife from her humdrum fiancé.
See *High Society*

DIAL, JIM
Stiff, stodgy anchorman on the Washington, D.C., newsmagazine show *FYI*. He's been in the news business for over two decades and was the only correspondent to get an interview with John F. Kennedy when he lost the presidential nomination in 1956. Jim's reserve cracked enough for him to break down and cry during a memorial service for his dog. He

EVIL BUT CHARMING
Lola
Vicomte De Valmont
Michael Corleone
Hannibal Lecter
J. R. Ewing
Alexis Carrington
Fagin

Auntie Mame

and wife Doris go to bed early, and probably *always* wear pajamas, but if they don't, he'd never say.
See *Murphy Brown*

DIAMOND, JOHN THOMAS "LEGS"
Ruthless, brutally violent, and ambitious, Legs is the archetypal Prohibition-era gangster. He rises from petty criminal to a king among bootleggers by crushing his competitors. His taste for power is matched only by his taste for women; he is just as devoted to his showgirl mistress as he is to his adoring wife.
See *Legs*, William Kennedy

DIAMOND, RICHARD
This cop turned private eye uses his NYPD friends and contacts to help him solve cases that might stump other detectives. He then moves to Hollywood, where an answering service operated by the smart, lovely, and leggy Sam is his ace in the hole. He has a phone in his car and a sometime girlfriend named Karen.
See *Richard Diamond, Private Detective*

DIAMOND, SUSIE
Sultry singer with a secretive past. Now she's a chanteuse with the piano-playing lounge duo the Fabulous Baker Boys. Disdains **Frank Baker**, though Susie is tentatively becoming involved with his brother, **Jack Baker**, despite her misgivings. Her piano-top rendition of "Makin' Whoopee" would melt gold fillings.
See *The Fabulous Baker Boys*

DICK "DEADEYE"
A sailor with a dragging limp and a chip on his shoulder, serves under Captain Corcoran of *H.M.S. Pinafore*. A rather jealous fellow, he would like nothing better than to prevent the joyous union of fellow sailor Ralph Rackstraw and his sweetheart Josephine—who is also the captain's daughter. Not surprisingly, Dick is not very popular among his colleagues aboard the ship.
See *H.M.S. Pinafore*

DICKINSON, THELMA
A sexy but dim southern beauty with an enormous smile, she's married to a man who's an oppressive oaf. Life with this goon has left her with a vague feeling of is-that-all-there-is *ennui*, but she isn't quite sure what she wants, or how to find it. With her good friend **Louise Sawyer**, Thelma eventually breaks the ties that bind and goes in search of a life. Having departed from the accepted, orthodox rules of proper wifely submission, she soon becomes an outlaw in earnest and gradually develops a tough hide and sense of self-preservation, though it doesn't happen without mistakes being made. A chance encounter with a handsome drifter makes her aware that sex can be pretty amazing, with the right partner. After a short but intense taste of what life can be like when you're willing to break established rules, Thelma comes to, and acts on, the conclusion that it's better to live and die independent than to merely exist as a man's personal convenience and domestic appliance.
See *Thelma and Louise*

NURSE DIESEL
The hormonally imbalanced, pointy-breasted, psychotic, murderous head nurse of the Psychoneurotic Institute for the Very, Very Nervous. She is the sadomasochistic lover of **Dr. Charles Montague** and falls to her death from the hospital's bell tower.
See *High Anxiety*, Mel Brooks

DIETRICH, ARTHUR
Too smart by half, and always willing to show it. He's the self-appointed "prof" of the 12th Precinct, where he's a detective. Launches into detailed lectures on almost any topic, annoying his colleagues and baffling his perps. He's almost always ready with a sly one-liner for every situation, though.
See *Barney Miller*

DIETRICHSON, PHYLLIS
A serious Southern California femme fatale looking for some way out of her marriage to an extremely wealthy but apathetic husband. Legality is not an issue with Ms. Dietrichson as long as her marriage—and her husband—can be terminated. She's more knowledgeable about the insurance industry than she lets insurance salesman **Walter Neff** realize. When it comes to devising schemes and plotting escapes, she has a real flair. Her greatest asset is the ability to twist people around her fingers in order to get whatever she wants.
See *Double Indemnity*

DIL

An uncommon woman who knows how to keep a secret. Works as a hairdresser by day, lip-synchs to Boy George tunes by night at a local pub. Is still in mourning over death of boyfriend Jody, a British soldier killed in an IRA terrorist incident. Doesn't hold liquor very well. Currently seeing **Fergus**, though they have some difficulties in regard to communication.

See *The Crying Game*

DILLARD, PRESTON

A rising banker in New Orleans, Dillard is the beau of brash southern belle **Julie Morrison** until they fight over the seemliness of a dress she wants to wear. Thereupon, he moves to Philadelphia, takes a wife, and returns to New Orleans three years later, only to have the impetuous Julie try to steal him back.

See *Jezebel*

DILLON, LILLY

She's a hard-shelled, pragmatic survivor who can be motherly, seductive, cunning, unbearable, dispassionate, hysterical, or ruthless, as the circumstances require. Her main employer is a vicious Baltimore bookie, and she drives a Cadillac with a stash of money hidden in the trunk. She's the biological mother of **Roy Dillon** but usually treats him more like a somewhat mentally disadvantaged brother.

See *The Grifters*, Jim Thompson

DILLON, MARSHAL MATT

U.S. Marshal Matt Dillon believes in justice and has dedicated his life to seeing that justice is served in the old Wild West. He patrols the frontier town of Dodge City and the surrounding area with a firm hand and a ready gun. Evildoers and badmen know that, like the Mounties of Canada, Marshal Dillon always gets his man. Marshal Dillon will always give a wanted man a chance to give himself up, or a chance to grab for his gun, if that's what he prefers to do. Matt may be in love with **Kitty Russell**, the woman who owns and runs the Long Branch Saloon, and she may love him, but their worlds are too far apart to make a relationship other than friendship work.

See *Gunsmoke*

DILLON, ROY

A cautious, two-bit crook ("grifter"), Roy holds a sales job but uses confidence tricks to steal small amounts of money. He's not good enough at cons to escape a vicious beating, after which his mother saves him and takes him under her not-very-maternal wing—until he and his girlfriend, **Moira Langtry**, prove to be a hindrance to her.

See *The Grifters*, Jim Thompson

DIPESTO, AGNES

Spacey, wide-eyed, rhyming receptionist at the Blue Moon Detective Agency in Los Angeles. She works for **Maddie Hayes** and **David Addison**, the firm's detective team. Agnes has the hots for Herbert Viola, a scruffy clerk in the office, who is also a fledgling detective.

See *Moonlighting*

DIPESTO, RAYETTE

A sweet-singing, overly-made-up waitress who'd stand by her man, emotionally abusive **Robert Dupea**, if only he'd tell her he loves her. But he can't. She's pregnant, but is too scared to tell him. Rayette is the world's biggest Tammy Wynette fan. "I am not just a piece of crap."

See *Five Easy Pieces*

DIVER, DICK

A brilliant young psychiatrist, Diver is working at a clinic in Switzerland when he meets **Nicole Warren Diver**, the unstable younger daughter of a wealthy family. Rather than stabilizing Nicole, Diver breaks rule number 1 of the psychoanalyst's code, falls in love with her, and is dragged down into corruption and decay by her problems and her family's money. The result: a declining practice and moral erosion, leading to an extramarital affair and the subsequent dissolution of his marriage.

See *Tender Is the Night*, F. Scott Fitzgerald

DIVER, NICOLE WARREN

Nicole, the unbalanced daughter of a wealthy Chicago family, is sent to a sanitarium in Switzerland, where she is treated by Dr. **Dick Diver**. They fall in love and marry, to the approval of her family, who are delighted at the prospect of Nicole getting constant psychiatric care. Although she suffers periodic breakdowns, Nicole eventually

---

TOMBOYS

Jean Louise "Scout" Finch
Velma
Jo March
Jo Polniaczek
Idgie Threadgoode
Peppermint Patty
Amanda Whurlizer

recovers enough to leave her husband after his extramarital affair.

See *Tender Is the Night,* F. Scott Fitzgerald

DIXON, PETE

The teacher everyone always wanted, Pete is committed to his students, smart, understanding, and fair. He teaches history at Walt Whitman High, a large, integrated city school, but his influence goes far beyond the classroom; he's the soul of integrity. He dates Liz McIntyre, a school guidance counselor. His homeroom number is 222.

See *Room 222*

DOBBS, FRED C.

A low, tragic figure, Dobbs is a symbol of the debasing consequences of raw greed. Once, he was the sort of guy who would share his last dime with a friend who needed a cup of coffee. But, while living on the bum in Tampico, Mexico, he and two companions, **Howard** and **Curtin**, go off into the mountains to prospect for gold. Unhappily for him, they find a huge strike, enough to allow them to live in luxury for the remainder of their days, if they just take the gold and split it. But the prospect of all that wealth changes Fred from a nice-enough sort to a paranoid, grasping psychotic. He turns on his associates, who he believes are about to gang up on him, and, consequently, his dreams of ease and a comfortable life are shattered in the Mexican outlands. He's a sort of Everyman, and it might have happened to many others. "Nobody monkeys with Fred C. Dobbs."

See *The Treasure of the Sierra Madre*

DOCTOR WHO

A high-tech deliverer of justice, he travels in time and between worlds in a souped-up police telephone booth (called the Tardis), solving mysteries and righting wrongs. His first clash is with the Daleks, half-crazed machines seeking to "exterminate" him. Dr. Who travels alone or with companions such as Sarah, Leela, or machine dog K-9. He changes shape periodically, sporting a long scarf and mussed brown hair at times, blond hair and a cleaner appearance at others, or one of several other forms.

See *Doctor Who*

DOLLANGANGER, CATHY AND CHRISTOPHER

As young adolescents, they're abandoned by their mother after she's widowed by the tragic death of their father in a car accident. They become charges of their evil grandmother, who imprisons them in the attic of enormous ancestral Foxworth Hall. There they try to make the best of their life, decorating their attic, making a pet of a mouse, and preparing for their chosen future careers of ballerina and doctor. At first they believe that their mother will return to get them, but, with the passage of a great deal of time, they realize that it's not going to happen. Their relationship becomes incestuous in various ways, as they try to figure out how to cope with their dilemma.

See *Flowers in the Attic,* V. C. Andrews

DONIPHON, TOM

Doniphon walks hard-shouldered through the world, taking little notice of the lesser beings around him—unless one of them can be used to further his ambitions, or if one of them should be fool enough to get in his way. Those in the way either move or get stepped on.

See *The Man Who Shot Liberty Valance*

DOOLITTLE, DOCTOR

English veterinarian with great love and empathy for his animal patients. He's a self-taught linguist with a wide repertory of animal languages. Speaks fluently in both mammal and fowl, fairly well in reptile and crustacean. Wears a top hat. Has some female human friends, but his deep love remains Sophie the Seal. Close friends with the parrot Polynesia and human **Matthew Mugg**. "If I could talk to the animals, just imagine it!"

See *Doctor Doolittle*

DOOLITTLE, ELIZA

This poor Cockney flower girl takes elocution lessons from **Professor Henry Higgins**, a grumpy confirmed bachelor and professor of linguistics. Eliza doesn't know Higgins has bet his friend Colonel Pickering that he can pass her off as a duchess in six months ("three if she has a good ear and a quick tongue"); she just wants to learn how to "talk proper—like a lye-dy."

See *Pygmalion,* George Bernard Shaw, *and My Fair Lady,* Alan Jay Lerner and Frederick Loewe

DOONESBURY, MIKE

An intelligent, laid-back liberal who goes to Yale in the late sixties, decries Watergate and Vietnam in the seventies, and eventually becomes a father and sells out, going for the big bucks in advertising. Married to cute J. J. Caucus.

See *Doonesbury*

DOROTHY

This straight-shooting, on-the-level brunette likes her men big and strong. She has a good head on her shoulders and reacts to her friend **Lorelei Lee's** theories of gold-digging with a smile and a shake of the head. She can hold her own as the "straight man" to her blond partner and is a bit protective of her.

See *Gentlemen Prefer Blondes*, Anita Loos

DORRANCE, JERRY D. (JEREMIAH)

He's debonair and handsome with dark brown hair and the knack of being able to light two cigarettes at once without burning his fingers. Jerry is trapped in a loveless marriage to an overdependent wife. He meets and falls in love with **Charlotte Vale** while on a cruise; his pet name for her is Camille. But he can't bring himself to end his marriage, despite his passion for Charlotte. He's either a true romantic or something of a sadist, and he sends her camellias as a constant reminder of their love. "It's stronger than both of us together."

See *Now, Voyager*

DOUBTFIRE, EDWINA

An elderly British widow of dubious origin, now living in San Francisco. A perfect housekeeper and nanny, she has an answer for every problem. Her sympathetic personality gives her instant rapport with just about anyone. However, beneath the lady-like exterior and unflappable composure lurks the ability to let slip some very nasty innuendos. She likes to clean house to good rock 'n' roll tunes and can kick a soccer ball with expertise. Suffers from an unusual case of hot flashes and prefers the "Mediterranean look" for her legs. She's also the alter ego of **Daniel Hillard**.

See *Mrs. Doubtfire*

DOUGHBOY

Gangbanging resident of South-Central Los Angeles. Fully entrenched in street culture and willing to live and die by its unforgiving codes. Drinks Power .45 malt liquor. Enjoys partying and just hanging out with his buddies. Loves his mother and family despite the pain he often causes them.

See *Boyz 'n the Hood*

DOUGLAS, CHIP

Third-oldest son in the Douglas family, which includes brothers **Mike Douglas**, **Robbie Douglas**, and **Ernie Thompson Douglas**, who was one of Chip's best friends before he was adopted by the family. His other childhood pal was Sudsy Pfeiffer. Chip fell in love and eloped with his college girlfriend, Polly Williams.

See *My Three Sons*

DOUGLAS, ERNIE THOMPSON

The bespectacled, adopted son of **Steve Douglas**. He was friends with **Chip Douglas** (now his adoptive brother) before he was brought into the family. Sweet and somewhat goofy, Ernie fits in perfectly as the youngest member of the Douglas clan. Adores the family dog, Tramp.

See *My Three Sons*

DOUGLAS, LISA

Hungarian-born Manhattan socialite. She has been yanked from her luxurious penthouse and plunked down in the middle of Hooterville, which means she's got a great deal of adjusting to do. She's trying to make a go of farm livin' for the sake of her much-loved husband, **Oliver Wendell Douglas**, but is finding it rough going. She dresses in frilly peignoir sets and lots of jewelry and says "darling" quite a bit. Lisa makes a mess of everything she tries in the kitchen.

See *Green Acres*

DOUGLAS, MIKE

Mike is the oldest son of **Steve Douglas**. He dated and married Sally Ann Morrison, his first serious romance since an early crush on Jean Pearson, "the girl next door." After he married, Mike moved away from the family to accept a job teaching psychology at an East Coast college.

See *My Three Sons*

DOUGLAS, OLIVER WENDELL

Successful Manhattan lawyer turned farmer. Fed up with his hoity-toity Manhattan life, Oliver seeks "real" life and "real" people and looks to find both in Hooterville. Eager to make his socialite wife, **Lisa**, happy, he allows her many luxuries never before seen by Hooterville folks. He's an object of suspicion among the townfolk and must constantly show everyone he is no threat but just wants to coexist peacefully. He is always being taken for a ride by salesman Mr. Haney.
See *Green Acres*

DOUGLAS, ROBBIE

The second-oldest son of **Steve Douglas**, Robbie met and fell in love with the lovely Katie Miller, a fellow student at his college, after the Douglas family moved from the Midwest to North Hollywood. After marrying Katie, the couple lived with Robbie's family for a short time. He is now the proud father of triplets Steve Jr., Charley, and Robbie II.
See *My Three Sons*

DOUGLAS, STEVE

An even-tempered, levelheaded aeronautics engineer. Steve moved to North Hollywood from the Midwest, where he had become a widower with three sons to raise: **Mike**, **Robbie**, and **Chip**. His father-in-law, Bub O'Casey, and later Bub's brother, **Charley O'Casey**, lived with the family and helped rear the boys. Steve later adopted another son, **Ernie Thompson Douglas**. He eventually married Barbara Harper, who has a daughter, Dodie.
See *My Three Sons*

DOWD, ELWOOD P.

Elwood is a sweet, ordinary guy, the salt of the earth, whose best friend happens to be an invisible, six-foot-tall rabbit named Harvey. For some reason, the rest of the world seems to have trouble with this concept.
See *Harvey,* Mary Chase

DOWNEY, MIKE

Downey is an FBI special agent on the trail of Long Island gangster **Tony "the Tiger" Russo**. He falls in love with **Angela de Marco**, a widow of another mob man, and puts years of investigation at risk by dating her. Downey is a cat lover and also enjoys going undercover.
See *Married to the Mob*

DOYLE, JIMMY

"Top pain-in-the-ass" tenor sax player who's ahead of his time as a musician. When he meets Wac **Francine Evans** at a V-J Day celebration, he refuses to take no for an answer. "I'm serious. Even though I'm handing you a line, I'm serious." Jimmy is stubborn and volatile, refusing to abandon his kind of jazz, even though it's appreciated only by a very few, mostly at the Harlem Club. Together with Francine, he writes the hit song "New York, New York." A great believer in major chords.
See *New York, New York*

DOYLE, JIMMY "POPEYE"

A nonconforming New York City undercover narc, he has a love-hate relationship with his job, but his effectiveness at police work forces his bosses to give him slack—up to a point. Popeye lives in a seedy apartment with a front door lock that can be easily picked with a credit card. He prefers casual sex to deeper relationships. He's also an excellent driver who can handle himself behind the wheel during high-stress conditions—though he can be rough on a car's bodywork, even if the car isn't his. Constantly wears a crumpled porkpie hat. Doyle is currently investigating a heroin-smuggling operation run by **Alain Charnier**.
See *The French Connection*

DOZIER, JULIE

Julie is a gifted actress, married to untalented actor Steve. Julie's face shows the wear and tear of an eventful life. The couple work on the showboat *Cotton Blossom*, under **Captain Andy Hawks**. There, she becomes a friend and mentor to Hawks's daughter, **Magnolia**. Then comes a thunderbolt: it's revealed that Julie has some Negro blood. Steve, a better husband than actor, agrees to drink some of Julie's blood in order to avoid being charged with miscegenation, and the two flee the showboat. Magnolia eventually finds Julie, years later, a gaunt, gray-haired wraith, working for a notorious Chicago madam. It just goes to show you.
See *Show Boat,* Edna Ferber

DRAKE, JOHN

This dashing international spy works for the British government, righting wrongs and tussling with bad guys and beautiful women. His cases take him all over Europe. Drake may or may not be kidnapped when he leaves government service, and shipped off to a strange island, perhaps run by the Brits (trying to keep him quiet), perhaps by the Russians (trying to find out what he knows). If so, he eventually becomes known only as **Number 6**.

See *Secret Agent* and *The Prisoner*

DRAKE, PAUL

He's a successful private investigator, despite having only one client: ace defense attorney **Perry Mason**. No crook's too sneaky, no clue too well hidden for Paul to track down. Never too busy to flirt with Perry's faithful secretary, **Della Street**, he's always ready to climb into his snazzy convertible and find the vital witness necessary to prove Perry's client innocent. Why doesn't this guy have more customers?

See *Perry Mason*

DRAPER, EVELYN

She calls up a disc jockey every night and asks him to play the song "Misty" for her. Then she gets picked up by him in a bar and soon latches onto him with a passionate jealousy. When the disc jockey's old love shows up, he decides he wants to marry her. But Evelyn begs to differ. And she has a thing for knives.

See *Play Misty for Me*

DRAVOT, DANIEL

After years of soldiering in nineteenth-century India, Dravot and comrade **Peachey Carnehan**, tired of their hand-to-mouth existence, determine to travel to remote, backward Kafiristan, where their expertise and character will enable them to be kings. There, a remarkable set of circumstances results in Danny being recognized not only as a king but as a god. He gets so wrapped up in his new powers and assumed responsibilities that he turns a deaf ear when his friend urges him to leave before he is found to be an imposter. He lives to regret his rashness. "If a king can't sing, it ain't worth being king."

See *The Man Who Would Be King*, Rudyard Kipling

DRAYTON, CHRISTINA

She's a stylish, white, upper-middle-class wife and gallery owner who finds her liberal views put to the test when her daughter declares that she's going to marry an African American scientist. Diplomatic but stubborn, once she decides on something, she can't be swayed from her course. She uses every bit of reason to persuade her husband, **Matt Drayton**, to support their daughter.

See *Guess Who's Coming to Dinner*

DRAYTON, MATT

This prominent San Francisco lawyer has a short fuse but a deep love for his family. He's a longtime liberal whose beliefs are tested by his daughter's decision to marry someone of another race and he's irritated about the fact. His bluster and explosive outbursts betray his advanced age.

See *Guess Who's Coming to Dinner*

DREBIN, LIEUTENANT FRANK

Bumbling police detective from the elite Police Squad. He's a miserable driver and can't detect his way out of a paper bag, but he has dogged determination. Loves his traditional detective raincoat and Police Special .38 revolver. A compulsive narrator, Drebin is so literal-minded it hurts. Showgirl during a raid: "Is this a bust or what?" Drebin: "Yes, it's quite impressive, but that doesn't matter right now."

See *The Naked Gun: From the Files of Police Squad!*

GENERAL DREEDLE

A chunky World War II wing commander with son-in-law problems. "Don't call me Dad!" He has a red nose and bacon-fat eyelids. His young, voluptuous nurse follows him around like a puppy. Dreedle is indignant when he learns he can't execute people at will: "You mean I can't shoot anyone I want to?" He drinks a great deal and frequently declares: "War is hell."

See *Catch-22*, Joseph Heller

DREW, NANCY

Eternally eighteen-year-old titian-haired supersleuth. Her mother died when she was three; she lives with her attorney father and devoted housekeeper, Hannah Gruen, an excellent cook, to whom she confides all her secrets. Her boyfriend, through thick and thin,

is handsome collegian Ned Nickerson. Unable to resist a mystery, she spends her days trying to unravel cases that are dropped in her lap. Nancy has guts, and no qualms whatever about, say, shinnying along the ridgepole of a roof. Taught by her father, she communes with nature to clear her brain and has no known vices. She has a remarkable knack for persuading bad guys to apologize and confess everything at the drop of a hat. Her success rate is roughly one hundred percent. As her tomboy friend, George, sums up: "Nancy Drew, you're the greatest!"
See *The Hidden Staircase,* Carolyn Keene

DREYFUS, CHIEF INSPECTOR CHARLES
The superior of **Inspector Jacques Clouseau** with the unfortunate habit of assigning Clouseau to cases beyond the inspector's very limited abilities. Clouseau's bumbling drives Dreyfus to a breakdown and homicidal rage, although Clouseau avoids death at Dreyfus's hands by "dumb luck."
See *A Shot in the Dark*

DRIFTWOOD, OTIS B.
The oldest and most mischievous of three goofball brothers who make a madcap assault on an opera company and its production of "Il Trovatore." The cigar-chomping, rapid-fire jokester Otis is a phony musical impresario who attaches himself to a dignified lady in the hope of separating her from a generous portion of her $8 million fortune. Once their antics are exposed and the police and opera management are hard on their heels, the trio pop in and out of the opening night production and turn Verdi into an exercise in slapstick buffoonery. Some find it an improvement.
See *A Night at the Opera*

DRISCOLL, BECKY
This beautiful young woman is a resident of Santa Mira, California, and is romantically linked with handsome **Dr. Miles Bennel** of the same town. Their idyllic life is shattered when the town is invaded by extraterrestrials who replace the citizenry by exact replicas, grown from vegetable pods. Becky herself is eventually turned into such a creature. There is little noticeable difference.
See *The Body Snatchers,* Jack Finney, and *Invasion of the Body Snatchers*

DRUMMOND, HENRY
Celebrated, slightly hunched, earthy defense lawyer and civil libertarian from Chicago. He is a brilliant litigator who thinks well on his feet. Although he is not as polished an orator as **Matthew Harrison Brady**, Drummond's tongue-in-cheek style of defense and his homespun manner win jury sympathies.
See *Inherit the Wind*

DRUMMOND, PHILIP
When his housekeeper dies, affable, extremely wealthy businessman Drummond is happy to adopt her two young sons, Willis and **Arnold Jackson**. Seemingly less concerned with work than family, Drummond has nonetheless amassed a fortune with his Trans-Allied, Inc. A widower, his daughter is Kimberly. He remarries a woman named Maggie McKinney, who has a young son, Sam.
See *Diff'rent Strokes*

DRYSDALE, MARGARET
This snobbish wife of bank president **Milburn Drysdale** is a Beverly Hills doyenne who hates the fact that her husband must kowtow to his biggest clients, the country-bumpkin **Clampetts**, not to mention that the Clampetts live next door. She dotes on her poodle, Claude, and is horrified when Claude bears the puppies of **Jed Clampett**'s bloodhound, Duke.
See *The Beverly Hillbillies*

DRYSDALE, MILBURN
The president of the Commerce Bank of Beverly Hills, he dotes on his biggest depositors, **Jed Clampett** and his family, always worried that the country folk will be taken advantage of in the big city (or move their considerable funds to another bank). Obsequious to a fault; married to Margaret.
See *The Beverly Hillbillies*

DuBois, BENSON
As the imperturbable butler for loony **Chester** and **Jessica Tate**, Benson (as everybody calls him) has only his sardonic manner, keen intelligence, and absolute competence to keep him sane. (He also resorts to muttering under his breath a lot.) He eventually goes to work for Jessica's cousin **Governor James Gatling** and proves himself so indispensable in running the governor's household

that he is soon made state budget director and, indeed, ascends to the job of lieutenant governor. Engaged to Diane Hartford, who helps him in his run for the governorship itself, against his old boss, Gatling.

See *Soap* and *Benson*

DuBois, Blanche

A frail and faded southern belle. Blanche grew up on her family's plantation, Belle Reve, in Mississippi, with her sister, Stella. By her own account, Blanche was a popular girl who entertained the most refined "gentlemen callers." Following an ill-fated love affair with "a boy who wrote poetry" and her subsequent breakdown, Blanche became a schoolteacher. Blanche has come to stay with her sister, Stella, and Stella's brutal husband, **Stanley Kowalski**, in their New Orleans apartment, having left Mississippi under some kind of mysterious cloud. Despite her drastically reduced circumstances, she tries to maintain an air of upper-class gentility and clings to her world of gossamer half-truths and idealized memories, making an effort to ignore the more common one of brick-and-steel reality. "I don't want realism. I want magic!…I don't tell the truth, I tell what ought to be the truth. And if that is sinful, then let me be damned for it!"

See *A Streetcar Named Desire,* Tennessee Williams

Dubrovna, Irena

New Orleans resident who suffers from highly unusual sexual dysfunction with feline aspects. She's living with brother who has a similar problem. Irena's involved, logically enough, with a local zookeeper. Tries to keep her romances at a distance; is (understandably) afraid of hurting the men she loves.

See *Cat People*

Duke

He is an aging gonzo journalist who's ready and willing to abuse every possible substance from alcohol to ecstasy, with stops at every point in between. Utterly self-serving, he's always looking for a quick and easy way to line his pockets—never mind if it's legal or not. In Samoa and China, and later in Haiti, where he runs the scam Baby Doc Med School, and Kuwait, where he smuggles arms, Duke keeps an eye out for number one. Assisted by Dean **Honey**, a devoted Chinese girl.

See *Doonesbury*

The Duke Family

This family of good ol' boys and gals hails from Hazzard County, U.S.A, where they act as unofficial Robin Hoods of the county, outwitting the corrupt officials at every turn. Good-natured, handsome cousins Luke and Bo, respectively dark and blonde, drive around in their Dodge Charger (named General Lee) and get into mild scrapes. Their comely and curvaceous cousin—as smart as she is beautiful—is named Daisy (other cousins are Coy and Vance) and their wise old uncle is Jesse. Their enemies are Jefferson Davis "Boss" Hogg—a local politician as corrupt as he is rotund, who fancies white suits—and Sheriff Roscoe P. Coltrane, Hogg's none-too-bright brother-in-law. Luke and Bo try their hand at NASCAR racing when they're not cruising the county.

See *The Dukes of Hazzard*

Duke, Heather

When her friend **Veronica Sawyer** asks Duke why she is "such a mega-bitch," she shoots back, "Because I can be." The death of her friend **Heather Chandler** gives her the chance to become the leader of the most powerful clique at Westerburg High School.

See *Heathers*

Duke, Randolph and Mortimer

Hugely wealthy Philadelphia investment company owners and consummate blue-blooded snobs. They use unwitting human guinea pigs as subjects to carry out a one-dollar wager and see the common run of humanity as little more than insects, born to serve their pleasures and whims. Their employee **Louis Winthorpe** is subjected to harrowing humiliation, and a homeless grifter, **Billy Ray Valentine**, is also dragged into their scheme. But what goes around comes around…some of the time.

See *Trading Places*

Dunbar, Lieutenant John W.

Civil War–era soldier assigned to solo military post in the American West. He keeps a daily journal to record his activities, thoughts, and feelings. He feels torn between the world he came from and the Sioux nation into which he assimilates. He finds the customs of his adopted Native American compatriots superior to the often venal, rapacious white men. Involved with Stands with a Fist, a white woman living with the Sioux. Has adopted the Sioux name Dances with Wolves.

See *Dances with Wolves*

DUNCAN, SABRINA

The cool, intelligent leader of a trio of sexy female undercover detectives working for an unseen boss named Charlie. She's usually the first to ask questions when Charlie relays assignments by telephone, and the one most likely to bail out the other "angels" when things get dicey on the job.

See *Charlie's Angels*

DUNDEE, MICHAEL J. "CROCODILE"

This rugged, charming Australian adventurer has a wry sense of humor. Extremely nonchalant around the dangers of the outback, he knows how to adapt his survival skills to the dangerous expanses of Manhattan. Consequently, Dundee has a knack for disarming both the killer crocodiles who have given him his nickname and New York street thugs. Handy with a variety of implements, including boomerangs and knives. Currently dating an American newspaper reporter. "G'day, mate!"

See *Crocodile Dundee*

DUNLOP, REGGIE

Battle-scarred pro hockey veteran now playing for and coaching the Charlestown Chiefs. Dunlop must deal both with his players—a bunch of has-beens and goons—and with a ruthless management, which wants to sell the team. He's dedicated to winning back his estranged wife, seducing the wife of the team's star, and saving the team, but not necessarily in that order.

See *Slap Shot*

DUNN, THERESA

She leads a schizoid life: a sweet young schoolteacher by day, at night she becomes a bar-cruising party girl. At age eleven she had to spend a year in the hospital in a plaster cast, victimized by scoliosis (curvature of the spine). That, plus the strict Catholicism in which she was raised, has left her torn between respectability and tossing back drinks at Mr. Goodbar's, and a succession of one-night stands, one of which proves her undoing.

See *Looking for Mr. Goodbar,* Judith Rossner

DUNSON, TOM

Single-minded Tom Dunson is as hard and rugged as the land in which he's made a home. He treks west from St. Louis with his friend **Groot Nadine** and ends up in Texas. There, he starts with a single bull and a cow owned by a wagon train friend, **Matthew Garth**, and builds up a ranch with over ten thousand head of cattle. When money grows tight, he decides to drive the huge herd to Missouri to sell. He's ruthless on the trail, going so far as to kill hands who try to oppose his will. But when Dunson attempts to hang two cowboys for "desertion," Garth steps in and announces that he will take the herd the rest of the way. They leave Dunson alone, but he catches up to Garth in Abilene, with a score to settle against his old buddy. The resulting battle is of epic proportions. "Every time you turn around, expect to see me, 'cause one time when you turn around, I'll be there. I'll kill you, Matt."

See *Red River*

DUPEA, ROBERT EROICA

The son of classical musicians, now he's abandoned his own promising career in music for the life of a working-class oil rig laborer. Bears a cynical attitude toward life and is decidedly soured on the idea of the American Dream. He tends to drift though life without making firm commitments to anything and avoids all discussion of his past. Dislikes being given a hard time by anyone and doesn't care whose feelings he might hurt. "You can put it between your knees!"

See *Five Easy Pieces*

DYBINSKI, DAUBER

Dinosaur's incredible hulk, coupled with dinosaur's tiny brain. Plays for the Minnesota State University Screaming Eagles year after year after year. Eventually graduates to become assistant coach under **Hayden Fox**. He shares numskull ideas and thoughts with equally intellectually challenged fellow assistant coach **Luther Van Dam**. Courts and eventually is engaged to basketball coach Judy.

See *Coach*

DYLE, CARSON

He is a cunning and resourceful killer, bent on getting what he believes to be his rightful due; $250,000 in money retrieved from the Nazis at the end of World War II and cached away for many years. Alternately amiable and bloodthirsty, he's quick to share a joke or a liverwurst sandwich. A real wolf in sheep's clothing.

See *Charade*

EARLE, ROY

He used to be a ruthless killer called Mad Dog, but that was then. Now he's a softer, mellower ex-con, recently paroled from the Michigan City, Indiana Penitentiary. Over the years, he's tried straight jobs, but his crazy temper has ensured that most of his adult life has been spent behind bars. Roy is restless, never able to settle for long—unless he's locked up. He had a reasonably happy childhood on an Indiana farm under the wing of his loving grandfather, Earle. More recently he got emotionally involved with a young handicapped girl named Velma. He was startled to realize that he was in love with her: "I thought I was dead inside." Roy wants to marry Velma and gives her the money to surgically repair her club foot. However, he just can't break free of his former life, and ends up with a different kind of woman, dance hall hostess **Marie Garson**. After robbing a desert resort called the Tropico Inn, he's designated America's Public Enemy No. 1, and winds up cornered in the mountains, surrounded by the police. "I just never seemed to fit in no place."

See *High Sierra*

EASTON, CLAY

A 1980s upper-middle-class L.A. kid, presently home on vacation from his college in Vermont. He impassively studies the aimless, self-destructive ways of his too-rich, too-status-conscious peers. It seems they need constant stimulation to fill the emptiness in their lives; the car stereo's always on, blasting vacuous New Wave tunes; drugs are a daily part of life; meaningless sex is used to pass the time.

See *Less Than Zero*, Bret Easton Ellis

EATONTON, M'LYNN

She works at a guidance center in a small town in Louisiana and is also the backbone of her family: husband Drum, daughter Shelby, and sons John and Tom. M'Lynn, with the supportive strength of her four closest women friends, succeeds in coping with her daughter's marriage, baby, illness, and untimely death.

See *Steel Magnolias*, Robert Harling

EBERHART, JOANNA

This newly arrived Stepford wife refuses to become a robot. She plays tennis "whenever I get the chance," and is a semiprofessional photographer. An ex–New Yorker leery about suburbia, she's into politics and big on Women's Lib, as is her husband, **Walter Eberhart**, who doesn't mind that she's not a great housekeeper. When she finds living in Stepford too much like living in Disneyland, she tries to get out. But that proves to be a serious difficulty.

See *The Stepford Wives*, Ira Levin

EBERHART, WALTER

A seemingly liberated middle-class man, who moves with his wife, **Joanna Eberhart**, and their two kids to the suburban town of Stepford. Though he declares he is for women's rights, he joins the misogynistic Men's Association, claiming "the only way to change it is from inside." He goes for boating, football, and collecting Early American legal documents. He gets what he secretly wants when Joanna is diabolically transformed into the perfect hausfrau.

See *The Stepford Wives*, Ira Levin

ECKLAND, WALTER

A refugee from society, now living a solitary but happy life as a beachcomber on a tiny South Seas island. He can be irritable at moments, particularly when forced into situations he wants no part of. However, Walter does have a hidden paternal side that can emerge under the right circumstances.

See *Father Goose*

EDDIE

A huge Baltimore Colts football fan, young Eddie is on the verge of marriage but first determines to make certain that his bride-to-be is qualified, by giv-

E.T. and Elliott

ing her a Colts trivia quiz. After all, marriage is a big step—and it'll mean that he'll spend less time gobbling fries and gravy at the diner with his friends.
See *Diner*

EDGAR, MARNIE

A pretty blonde with big psychological problems. Marnie, a habitual thief, robs her employer, **Mark Rutland**, and runs off. She loves horses and hates the color red. When Rutland tracks her down, she reluctantly agrees to marry him, despite being sexually repulsed by him—and men in general. Behind her sexual problems are long-repressed memories, which she's never brought to the surface or come to terms with.
See *Marnie*

88 KEYS

As adept at tickling the ivories as he is at entrancing naive women, 88 Keys uses his day job as a musician to cover for his other career as a murderer and swindler. He's one of Dick Tracy's most ruthless foes, in part because he comes across as such a smoothie.
See *Dick Tracy*

EL, JOR-

This patrician scientist and elder statesman on the planet Krypton predicts the imminent demise of his planet but is ignored by Krypton's ruling council. He and his wife determine to let his infant son escape the planet's destruction, by sending the baby, Kal-El (later **Clark Kent** and **Superman**), away in a rocket, which eventually makes it to Earth. But that's another story.
See *Superman*

ELEANOR

On a boat trip back to the States from Australia, Eleanor, who is white, falls in love with black boxer **Jack Jefferson**. Their affair and subsequent marriage draw fire from bigots and racists, the more so after Jefferson becomes world heavyweight champion. "I'm not ashamed of wanting Jack as a lover. I wanted him that way."
See *The Great White Hope*

ELIOTT

Second husband of **Hannah**, manages the financial affairs of rock stars for a living. His high sense of morality is at odds with his heathen desire to have carnal relations with one of Hannah's sisters. Eliott's obsession with the sister overpowers his senses, but he's tortured by the thought of committing infidelity against a woman who is so…perfect. Wooing strategy: giving books of romantic poetry as gifts.
See *Hannah and Her Sisters*

ELLIOTT

Lonely boy living in suburban California with mother, older brother, and younger sister. Elliott misses his father tremendously. His inquisitive nature leads him into extraordinary situations. He's freaked out by the establishment and saves a friend by hijacking an ambulance. An expert off-road bicyclist, he gives new meaning to the phrase "getting air." Is close friend and earthly protector of E.T.
See *E.T.: The Extra-Terrestrial*

ELLIOTT, DR. ROBERT

Successful Manhattan psychiatrist, originally from England. He's currently treating **Kate Miller** as well as mysterious patient with blond hair and dark glasses. Interested in dual nature of human personality. Prefers to keep his private life under wraps.
See *Dressed to Kill*

ELROND

Lord of Rivendell, a great refuge of elves in Middle Earth. Long-lived and wise in counsel, Elrond sees firsthand many of the events of the First and Second Ages which lead to the troubles of the Third Age. He raises **Aragorn** at Rivendell, and it is at his council table during the War of the Ring that plans are made to combat **Sauron**, and the Fellowship of the Ring is formed.
See *The Lord of the Rings*, J. R. R. Tolkien

ELSTER, MADELEINE

This frail, elegant, sexy, suicidal blond beauty jumps to her death from a mission church tower—or *does* she? Years later, retired cop **John "Scottie" Ferguson** is astonished to see her again. Is it really her? Does it matter? Scottie resolves to turn this woman into the figure he is so obsessed with. In his growing dementia, Scottie appears ready to do this woman in—if, that is, she isn't already dead.
See *Vertigo*

ENDICOTT, CLAYTON, III

Political aide to **Governor James Gatling**, he's as stuffy and persnickety as he is smart and politically canny. Constantly trying to keep his naive boss from disaster. Often runs afoul of the more commonsensical **Benson DuBois**.

See *Benson*

ENDORA

A full-blooded witch who relishes her powers and her supremacy over "mere mortals," the bane of her existence is her daughter **Samantha**'s marriage to Darrin Stephens—a mortal. Constantly leveling her complaints at Samantha, she acts out at Darrin by (a) never getting his name right (Derwood, Darwin, Dum-Dum); (b) making mischief in his home and office; and (c) putting spells on him that turn him into a goat, chimp, gorilla, mule, goose, etc., even though such mischief is a violation of her "Witch's Honor." No longer married to Samantha's father, Maurice. She's a doting grandmother who lavishes attention on granddaughter **Tabitha Stephens** and grandson Adam, hoping they'll take after "Grandmama." A frequent visitor to the moon.

See *Bewitched*

ENGLISH, JULIAN

He watches himself spiral out of control toward suicide. He is the scion of a prominent pre-Revolutionary family, and member in good standing of its young country-club set—but, as the grandson of a suicide, he's always been beset by feelings of self-doubt. On a whim, he throws a drink in the face of a social-climbing bore to whom he owes money. His drinking and fatalism overwhelm his charm and gallantry.

See *Appointment in Samarra*, John O'Hara

ENGSTROM, DUTCH

A chubby but tough bandit in the Old West. Dutch is loyal to his leader, **Pike Bishop**, and lives to steal gold and go on violent, amoral adventures with his buddies. He travels with Pike to Mexico and his Armageddon.

See *The Wild Bunch*

EPSTEIN, JUAN LUIS PEDRO PHILLIPO

A Puerto Rican Jew and member in good standing of the Sweathogs, a group of low-achieving high school students taught by **Gabe Kotter**. Epstein is stocky and has a lot of curly hair. Because of the hair, he always plays Harpo when the Sweathogs pretend they're the Marx Brothers. Walks strangely. He never does his homework and brings in a note "from Epstein's mother" almost every day to explain why he hasn't.

See *Welcome Back, Kotter*

ERICA

After sixteen years of what she thinks is a happy marriage, Erica is dumped by husband Martin for a woman he met at Bloomingdale's. Alone in New York with daughter Patti, Erica is nervous about, even frightened by, the prospect of having to date again. Her friends rally around her, and their support helps ease the pain of rejection. When she meets Saul, an artist, the pieces of her life slowly begin to reassemble themselves. "Look, all I know is I feel completely and totally alone."

See *An Unmarried Woman*

ERIK, THE PHANTOM

Erik is a vindictive, masked enigma who haunts the opera house and is seldom seen by anyone, except when he chooses to be. But his voice is often heard, though no one knows where it's coming from. He is smitten by young singer **Christine Daae**. He writes threatening letters to the management of the opera house, demanding that "Box Five on the grand tier be placed at the disposal of the Opera ghost for every performance." Among his accomplishments, he is an expert ventriloquist and magician. "The voice" of the Phantom convinces the somewhat gullible Christine that he is the "Angel of Music" of whom her father spoke when she was a child. His ugliness has always been such that his mother made him his first mask. Erik ran away at an early age and grew up among the Gypsies. Now, jealous and miserable, he lives on the shores of an underground lake beneath the opera house, where he sleeps in a coffin under a red-brocaded canopy. For the past twenty years, he's been composing his organ masterwork, "Don Juan Triumphant." He longs to be like everyone else, but this appears to be highly unlikely.

See *The Phantom of the Opera*, Gaston Leroux

MARTIAL ARTISTS

Kato
Mason Storm
Kwai Chang Caine
Daniel LaRusso
Mr. Miyagi

BROTHERS THREE

J.R., Bobby, and Gary Ewing
Michael "Beau," John, and Digby
Geste
Danny, Keith, and Chris Partridge
Chip, Robbie, and Ernie Douglas
Greg, Peter, and Bobby Brady
Larry, Darryl, and Darryl

ERLICH, VICTOR

Tall, blond, bespectacled, and occasionally bumbling, Dr. Erlich would seem the least likely doctor among the residents at Boston's St. Eligius Hospital. But with time and experience, Victor grows into a fine surgeon, a married man, and one of the more stalwart doctors at the hospital labeled "St. Elsewhere" by those who work there.

See *St. Elsewhere*

ESCOBAR, GERARDO

Befuddled attorney spouse of **Paulina Escobar**. Gerardo likes to be helpful but is suggestible and can be easily manipulated. Unsure of how to handle certain situations when they veer out of control.

See *Death and the Maiden*

ESCOBAR, PAULINA

Former South American political activist who has survived physical torture, though psychological scars lurk just below the surface. Married to lawyer **Gerardo Escobar**. She can be unmerciful and obsessively single-minded when faced with a challenge.

See *Death and the Maiden*

ESMERELDA

A sweet-natured witch, she often pops in to help **Samantha Stephens** with baby-sitting and light housekeeping. She's not a very good witch—both timid and forgetful—so her spells often go awry. Once, when asked to make a Caesar salad, she ended up with Julius Caesar. When people admonish her, she gets so flustered she disappears.

See *Bewitched*

ESTERHAUS, SERGEANT PHIL

Crusty, beloved police sergeant. A prince of a guy who loves his job and the men and women he works with. Very paternal personality. Starts each day telling his force, "Let's be careful out there." Leads through humor and patience. Women very attracted to his sensitivity.

See *Hill Street Blues*

ESTRAGON "GOGO"

An archetypal tramp. Always on the lookout for a handout, Estragon (who is always hungry) and his companion **Vladimir** (who thinks too hard) wait for something to happen, for time to pass, for the long-awaited Godot to arrive. Meanwhile, they chat.

See *Waiting for Godot,* **Samuel Beckett**

EVANS, MISS AMELIA

A strapping, fiercely independent woman whose antisocial behavior includes continuous lawsuits against her fellow townspeople. Her nastiness is tempered by the arrival of her amiable cousin Lymon, a hunchbacked dwarf, who helps Miss Amelia open a cafe that serves whiskey and crackers. But Miss Amelia's newfound sociability is shattered forever when Lymon turns against her and leaves town with her vicious ex-husband.

See *Ballad of the Sad Cafe,* **Carson McCullers**

EVANS, FRANCINE

She's a sweet kid with a big-band voice who falls hard for hipster sax player **Jimmy Doyle** against her better judgment. As a newcomer on the scene, she garners great reviews: "A spirited filly…whose musical pace is as smooth as her form." Her marriage is never very secure, and her personal life is less successful than her professional one; she ends up in the movies, starring in the hit film *Happy Endings.*

See *New York, New York*

EVANS, J.J.

The toothpick-shaped eldest son and perpetual center of attention in a black family struggling to get ahead in Chicago. When he's not dogging his sister, Thelma, or trying to pull a fast one on his mother, J.J. is busting rhymes or dancing a long-legged funky chicken. Never one to wrestle with poor self-esteem, J.J. seems to always be on the verge of making it big and has been known to refer to himself as the Ebony Prince. Wardrobe includes what is probably the world's largest collection of platform shoes. Favorite exclamation: "Dyn-o-mite!"

See *Good Times*

EVE

Man magnet and owner of Eve's Lounge. An ex-hooker who "loves men," she's simultaneously involved with three lovers, one of them married. She says she'll never tie the knot because she has "ruined too many marriages to have one of my own." Eve calls radio talk show host **Dr. Nancy Love** for advice. When enigmatic stranger **Mickey**

Bolton asks her to marry him, she hopefully boards the bus to Las Vegas.

See *Choose Me*

THE EVERETT FAMILY

Handsome, brilliant, logical, but occasionally non-plussed Harold is a widower and math professor (at Clinton College in Los Angeles). With three kids to care for, he goes through five nannies before **Phoebe Figallily** arrives to save the day and make life generally wonderful for the three Everett children, Hal, Bentley, and Prudence. Hal, the eldest, is a budding scientist; Bentley—who is called Butch—is the mischievous one; Prudence is musically inclined. Rounding out the frenzied household are Waldo the sheepdog; Myrtle and Mike the guinea pigs; a rooster named Sebastian; and two goats.

See *Nanny and the Professor*

THE EWING FAMILY

The Ewings are modern-day mythic demigods, except they inhabit the Lone Star State instead of Mount Olympus. The family oil empire was founded by wildcatter John Ross "Jock" Ewing. In what becomes the typical underhanded Ewing style, Jock maneuvers partner **Digger Barnes** out of his share of an oil strike, as well as stealing and marrying Barnes's true love, Eleanor, known as "Miss Ellie." Jock and Miss Ellie have three sons. John Ross, Jr., or J.R., is conniving, manipulative, and greedy—and those are his good points. J.R. lives to run his daddy's company, Ewing Oil, and, in that role, often clashes with his little brother, Bobby. J.R. and first wife Sue Ellen have a son, John Ross, III. J.R. is even meaner to women than to men, and goes so far as to try to have Sue Ellen committed. Predictably, he has more enemies than a blue tick hound has fleas. When he's shot and critically wounded, the list of suspects is encyclopedic. Gary is the middle child, confused, weak, and idle. He eschews Southfork for suburban Knots Landing, California, where he lives with on-again, off-again wife, Valene. He's a hunk who attracts mainly manipulative women. Gary's a perpetually unhappy recovering alcoholic, who gets some pleasure out of cars and horses. Bobby, the youngest Ewing, possesses the entire Ewing family stock of morals. He's genuinely nice and is married to Pam Barnes, the beautiful daughter of family rival Digger Barnes.

Bobby was once dead for a whole year, but got better. More and more, he gets sucked into his family's affairs and the battle for control of Ewing Oil.

See *Dallas* and *Knots Landing*

FABER

German spy and loyal Nazi, now working undercover in Britain to learn more about the imminent Allied invasion. He is temporarily living on a rain-swept island off the coast of Scotland. Though seemingly mild-mannered with his new neighbors, Faber is a ruthless killer who lets few things get in his way. Nicknamed the Needle after his predisposition for stilettos.

See *Eye of the Needle*

FABIAN, MAX

Dyspeptic, rumpled Broadway producer, overweight, often overwrought. More concerned about producing an artistic achievement than a financial success. Speaks with an accent and looks, in the words of one actress, "like an unhappy rabbit." Gave **Eve Harrington** her first big stage break.

See *All About Eve*

FAIR, PEGGY

Loyal, hardworking assistant to private investigator **Joe Mannix**. Peggy came to work for Mannix after her husband, a former police officer, was killed in the line of duty. More than just a secretary. Often helps out with the investigative work, leading her boss to key clues that often crack the case.

See *Mannix*

FALCONER, SISTER SHARON

This owner-operator of a traveling religious operation in 1920s American South loves the carnival atmosphere of the evangelistic circuit and professes love for the Lord, too. She can deliver one heck of a sermon, and her power and charisma mesmerize audiences and induce wild bouts of revival-based mania. Works with **Elmer Gantry**.

See *Elmer Gantry*

MR. FANTASTIC

Reed Richards is, or was, a brilliant and enterprising scientist. He was also somewhat rash and decided to try a potentially dangerous experiment, which involved stealing a spaceship, putting not only himself but also wife Sue, her brother, Johnny, and his friend Ben at risk. Science is a cruel mistress. Alas, the best-laid plans of mice and scientists…anyway, there was a glitch. Upon reentering Earth's atmosphere, they found that they'd been *drenched* in nasty gamma rays and turned into mutants. Reed's particular fate was to have a new molecular structure, allowing him to stretch and bend any part of his body in any way he wanted. He now puts this remarkable knack to work in fighting against crime and is probably much in demand for parties.

See *The Fantastic Four*

FANCY, LIEUTENANT ARTHUR

He heads up the detective squad at New York City's 15th Precinct. Tough but fair, he's well liked and respected by the men and women who work for him. He came up through the ranks (he was once a detective himself). A married man, he recently celebrated the birth of his first son (he also has two daughters).

See *NYPD Blue*

FANSHAWE

This brilliant, conniving, elusive writer becomes the main character in his greatest story: the mystery of his own disappearance. Talk about an identity crisis—he calls upon his boyhood friend to take his place. The friend is also a writer, who happens to have known Fanshawe since childhood, and the two look uncannily alike. Fanshawe leaves behind a wife, a child, and a stack of manuscripts. Apparently, he wants his friend to be the executor of his literary estate. His novels sell, and his pal hands over the profits to Sophie, Fanshawe's wife. Soon the new man finds himself lured into the trap Fanshawe built: his life. He marries Sophie and adopts the child, in effect becoming Fanshawe.

See *The Locked Room*, Paul Auster

FARLOW, CLAYTON

Stately, wealthy gentleman. Comes a-courtin' for **Miss Ellie** and eventually snags her. True love and romance are theirs, though the memory of the great **Jock Ewing** is omnipresent. Clayton learns to coexist with Jock's memory as well as with his sons, who do not readily accept him or his marriage to their mother. Wants to take care of Miss Ellie in their twilight years.

See *Dallas*

FARRAGUT, EZEKIEL

Once he was a college professor; now he's a heroin addict, serving a life sentence for murdering his brother. He escapes the tedium of his daily life by roaming outside the walls of Falconer Prison in his mind. Though at first he is alienated from the other convicts, the intellectual and sensitive Farragut finds the active social life of the prison a source of stimulation. Farragut finds redemption when his homosexual feelings are awakened and he falls in love with another prisoner, Jody. He worries that his homosexuality is nothing more than self-love, but after Jody escapes, Farragut's pain convinces him that his feelings were genuine.

See *Falconer*, John Cheever

FARRELL, JOHNNY

A down-and-out gambler and tough guy who is hired by **Ballin Mundson** to watch over his casino and keep tabs on his wife, **Gilda**. Unknown to Mundson, he and Gilda were once lovers, though it remains unclear why they parted. What is very clear is the significant hostility he still harbors for his former paramour. The angry, touchy Johnny isn't reluctant to take a swing at Gilda, or otherwise rough her up, when she annoys him. It's obvious that Gilda's still under his skin and that he's equally infatuated and scornful of her. Johnny is a combination of shrewdness and explosive behavior—a combination that appeals to both men and women. Complicating matters is a threatening undercurrent of homosexual attraction between Johnny and his employer.

See *Gilda*

FARROW, JACY

Because she combines sparkling physical attractiveness, relative wealth, and the cool independence of a modern woman, Jacy Farrow is the object of obsessive desire for all the teenage boys in the sleepy town of Thalia, Texas. Unfortunately for the boys, she's not all that interested in them, but she goes out with them for lack of anything better to do.

See *The Last Picture Show*, Larry McMurtry

FASSBENDER, DR. FRITZ

A Paris-based psychiatrist whose methods include locking his patients in dark closets and flogging them with flower bouquets while singing "Springtime in Vienna." Fritz sports a modified

Prince Valiant haircut and brown velvet suits. In his spare time, he makes crank calls to his attractive female patients, using the name Baby Fritz, and fights with his large blond wife about his infidelities. Dr. Fassbender's diagnostic talents are stretched to the limit when **Michael James**, a fashion magazine editor and compulsive womanizer, comes to him for treatment. "Hello, my little laxative; this is Baby Fritzie here."

See *What's New, Pussycat?*

FAT, WO

This chubby, evil Chinese gangster has a laugh as big as his belly, but his expression can turn deadly serious in tense moments. After being kicked out of Hawaii by his nemesis, **Detective Steve McGarrett**, he runs his villainous operation from China. Though he's no longer resident in Hawaii, he remains McGarrett's chief nemesis, through his multitentacled empire of crime. Perhaps the most cunning, evil criminal to have ever plied his trade on the Big Island, Wo Fat is believed to be an agent of the Communist Chinese government—a theory reinforced by diplomatic intervention after he was captured. Unlike most criminals, Fat feels no remorse—he brings an almost zen-like approach to his nefarious deeds.

See *Hawaii Five-O*

FAT ALBERT

A majorly obese kid with an even bigger heart, Fat Albert lives in a Philadelphia ghetto and is the de facto leader of a friendly neighborhood gang. Other members of this group include young Bill Cosby and Old Weird Harold. For reasons that don't need elaborating, Fat Albert is the undisputed and obvious world champion of buck-buck, a game where players jump on opposing players' backs. "Hey, hey, hey!"

See *Fat Albert and the Cosby Kids*

FAT BROAD

She's the bane of all snakes and the butt of a lot of jokes because of her weight. Sometimes dour, sometimes witty, always determined, she shows her strength best when pushed. She can be kind and gentle when it is appropriate, and she can wield a mean club when kindness isn't the answer.

See *B.C.*

FATALE, NATASHA

A fiendish, mysterious, and seductive spy, Natasha and her partner **Boris Badenov** are usually busy trying to blow up their affable and naive foes Bullwinkle and Rocky with massive amounts of TNT. Funny, but the dastardly schemes always backfire, often to the severe detriment of the black-clad conspirators. Considered by many to be the brains of the operation, Natasha is not afraid to use her feminine wiles to seduce her enemies. "Borees!"

See *The Rocky and Bullwinkle Show*

FAULK, MAXINE

An aging, recently widowed nymphomaniac who operates a run-down resort on the Mexican coast. She likes to run barefoot through the surf and romp with two handsome Mexican youths. Brave and perceptive, her attitude is to grab life and live the way she wants to without apologizing for it. She loves **Reverend T. Shannon** and helps him avoid losing his job as a tour guide.

See *The Night of the Iguana*, Tennessee Williams

FAVOR, GIL

A nineteenth-century trail boss, Favor is the upstanding and trustworthy supervisor of communal cattle drives that crisscross America; working under him is his trusty right-hand man, **Rowdy Yates**.

See *Rawhide*

FEENEY, SHIRLEY

Shy, naive, guy-hungry, 1950s working girl. Shirley's employed on the bottling line at the Shotz Brewery in Milwaukee, along with best friend and roommate **Laverne De Fazio**. Short, perky, and cute, Shirley is always attracting the wrong guy and is easy to take advantage of. She tends to be confused about what she wants in life and in men, especially when it comes to boyfriend Carmine Ragusa. Though she gets into heated arguments with Laverne, they always make up in the end. Wears big poodle skirts and twin sets. Likes to bowl with Laverne and friends and Shotz truck drivers Lenny and **Squiggy**. Falls in love with army medic Walter Meany.

See *Laverne and Shirley*

FELICIA

Nee Adam. A sadistic, manipulative young drag queen. She flaunts her unconventional appearance without regard to local attitudes or self-preservation and wears a genuine "Abba turd" in a vial around her neck. Is both an obvious target for hostile jokes and a source of maliciousness. Performs in drag shows with **Bernadette** and **Mitzi**.

See *The Adventures of Priscilla, Queen of the Desert*

FELIX, ALLAN

He's a nerdy, neurotic San Francisco film critic. After his wife leaves him, he suffers an incredible run of bad luck with the ladies—despite the presence of an imaginary Humphrey Bogart at his shoulder, advising him how to be smooth. It gets so bad that an avowed nymphomaniac is insulted when he makes a pass at her. He might not be Bogie incarnate as a lover, but he does a great selfless renunciation bit in the crunch.

See *Play It Again, Sam*

FELSON, "FAST" EDDIE

Eddie is not only fast, the young pool hustler is brash to the point of arrogance. His attitude gets him into trouble at times, and his lack of sophistication is a sharp contrast to the man he challenges: Minnesota Fats, the reigning, undisputed king of pocket billiards, who hasn't lost in fifteen years. His relationship with girlfriend **Sarah Packard** provides a calming and maturing influence, though Fast Eddie's life is inevitably filled with the kind of turbulence associated with the shady world of pool halls and hustling.

See *The Hustler*

FENWICK

Fenwick is a prototypical slacker, living off his grandfather's trust fund. He's the practical joker in a small group of Baltimore friends. He's got a drinking problem and a very conventional older brother, who disapproves of his aimless lifestyle (mostly hanging out with friends at the diner and watching quiz shows). The brotherly dislike is reciprocal.

See *Diner*

FERGUS

Sensitive, sad-eyed member of IRA hit squadron, he is now doing construction work in London. He's wracked with guilt over past bloody terrorist activities and wants to escape from that life, having had enough of it—which is easier said than done. Currently involved in tentative possible relationship with **Dil**, for whose boyfriend's death Fergus feels responsible. Doesn't care for unexpected surprises and is known to have violent reactions when confronted with shocking revelations. Tolerates drinks with little paper umbrellas sticking out of the glass. "Don't call me 'honey.'"

See *The Crying Game*

FERGUSON, JOHN "SCOTTIE"

A decent fellow who developed a bad case of vertigo, a terrible fear of heights, during his time as a cop, when he nearly died while hanging from a ledge. Retired from the police force as a result, he's hired by an old college chum to tail his wife, **Madeleine Elster**, who is said to be suicidal. He saves Madeleine when she dives into San Francisco Bay, and falls in love with the pale, fragile blond beauty. His life is shattered when she climbs a church tower and jumps to her death. Years later, when the scars have apparently healed, he sees what he thinks is the same woman…except that it isn't, quite. This woman says that she's just a secretary named Judy. But Scottie falls headlong into new obsession with her, never quite certain whether Judy and Madeleine are one and the same, or what their relationship may be, if they're not the same woman. In searching for the painful truth, he must confront all of his old pain and fears.

See *Vertigo*

FEZZIK

He may be seven feet tall and brawny, but this companion to **Inigo Montoya** has a soft-spoken manner that belies his menacing appearance. Still, he's capable of lifting a grown man above his head and spinning him senseless. He joins Westley to defeat Prince Humperdinck and save the **Princess Buttercup**.

See *The Princess Bride*

FIELDS, JENNY

Jenny Fields is a no-nonsense nurse who cares nothing about other people's morals and expectations.

Neither does she care that she puzzles her traditional family by a total lack of interest in marriage and settling down. That doesn't mean, however, that she doesn't want a child, and when the opportunity arises, in the form of a severely wounded ball turret gunner, Jenny proceeds to get herself pregnant, to the shock and distress of the family. She hires on as nurse at a private school for boys to support herself and her son, whom she names after his father, **T. S.** (for Technical Sergeant) **Garp**. When she writes her life story, she becomes a huge success and rallying point for a feminist movement, which really wasn't what she intended at all.

See *The World According to Garp,* John Irving

FIFE, DEPUTY BARNEY

A scrawny, nervous, sometimes inept, but by-the-book deputy sheriff. Barney is the good-hearted, good-humored best friend of his cousin and boss, Sheriff **Andy Taylor**. Tortured by Andy's refusal to allow him a loaded gun, he packs an empty revolver on his hip and stashes one bullet in his breast pocket. He fancies himself a student of the criminal mind and police procedures and is always on the lookout for a caper in progress. Barney loves to go undercover and play detective. His free time is mostly spent in talk and gossip at **Floyd Lawson**'s barbershop. He isn't without romantic interests and in fact has two: serious, proper Thelma Lou and diner waitress Juanita. Barney sings to Juanita over the telephone; on dates with Thelma Lou, he takes her to dinner and they go Dutch. He often double-dates with Andy and Helen Crump. His Sunday best is a "salt 'n' pepper" suit, which he sports when going to hearty Sunday dinners at the Taylors's. Barney can "eat and eat and eat" and not get fat. "It's a mark of us Fifes. Everything we eat goes to muscle."

See *The Andy Griffith Show*

FIGALILLY, PHOEBE

The nanny with the mostest; she's lovely, breezy, English, and possessing of uncanny abilities (ESP? magic?). She arrives unsummoned, because she just knows that the **Everetts** need a new Nanny. She has an Aunt Henrietta—who's as quirky as she is—and likes everyone to just call her Nanny. She's beloved by all.

See *Nanny and the Professor*

FINCH, ATTICUS

A wonderful father and a moral icon. This small-town lawyer in 1930s Alabama is the widowed father of levelheaded **Jem** and scrappy tomboy **Scout**. He's quiet and unassuming, but he's willing to stand by his unusually progressive convictions, especially on matters of race, even if it costs him financially and socially. He agrees to defend an African American man who's been charged with raping a white girl, a brave commitment to make in the deep South of that era. He tries to make his children understand and empathize with their reclusive and dysfunctional neighbor, **Boo Radley**, when other local kids make fun of him and treat him as a Bogey Man. He earns and keeps the love and respect of both his kids—even though Scout, with her hotheaded propensity to get in fights, can be a source of worry in school and in the neighborhood. He is an unassuming hero whose strength of character and strong ethical center make him the most ideal possible role model and parent.

See *To Kill a Mockingbird,* Harper Lee

FINCH, JEAN LOUISE "SCOUT"

This scrappy little tomboy has a propensity for getting into fistfights and consequently gets into constant trouble at school. She's the kid sister of **Jem Finch**, who helps to look after her, and the daughter of lawyer **Atticus Finch**, whose words and actions teach her a great deal about the evils of prejudice and the importance of having an open mind and treating others with respect. Though, like the other local children, she initially fears weird local recluse **Boo Radley**, she ultimately learns better, with her father's help. She also unwittingly defuses a potentially dangerous situation involving a lynch mob. She is still at the point in her life when she's revolted by the prospect of wearing a dress or behaving like a little lady.

See *To Kill a Mockingbird,* Harper Lee

FINCH, JEM

The levelheaded son of **Atticus Finch** and older brother to **Scout Finch**, he admires his father and wants to grow up to be a lawyer just like him. Jem protects and often calms down his hotheaded little tomboy sister.

See *To Kill a Mockingbird,* Harper Lee

PARANOID, AND RIGHTLY SO

Dr. Richard Kimble
Rusty Sabich
Jake Gittes
Winston Smith
J. B. Jeffries
Alec Leamas
Sarah Connor
Danielle Bowden
Tom Sanders
Leona Stevenson

PEOPLE YOU'VE NEVER SEEN

Maris Crane
Wilson
Charlie Townsend
Orson
Vera Peterson

FINCH, J. PIERPOINT

A disarmingly opportunistic young man, Finch can lie more smoothly than most people can tell the truth. Starting as a window-washer, Finch climbs the corporate ladder at World Wide Wickets by knifing or leaping over anyone in his way, buttering up the men on top, and by his unfailing belief in Shepherd Mead's success guide *How to Succeed in Business Without Really Trying* and "the company way." His odyssey takes him from an entry-level position in the mail room, to vice-president of marketing, to chairman of the board.

See *How to Succeed in Business Without Really Trying*

FINDLAY, MAUDE

This is one tough, independent, and extremely outspoken woman. A cousin of **Edith Bunker**, she lives with her fourth husband, **Walter Findlay**, in suburban Tuckahoe, New York. Maude's daughter, Carol (who is divorced), and Carol's son, Phillip, also live with the Findlays. Her liberal politics are often the source of conflict and commotion in the household. She shocked everyone when she got an abortion after discovering her late-in-life pregnancy. She also had a face-lift and recently went through menopause. She's an ardent admirer of FDR, a bone of constant contention with her cousin's husband, **Archie Bunker**, who is politically the polar opposite of left-wing, freethinking Maude. She has had a hard time keeping help around the house and has gone through three maids in the last several years: Florida Evans, Mrs. Nell Naugatuck, and Victoria Butterfield. Maude's next-door neighbor, **Dr. Arthur Harmon**, dated and eventually married Maude's best friend, **Vivian Cavender Harmon**. Though she likes to wear flowing caftans, it's clear that the husky-voiced Maude also wears the pants in the family. When she doesn't get her way, she'll often retort, "God will get you for that!"

See *Maude* and *All in the Family*

FINDLAY, WALTER

Married to outspoken, liberal-minded **Maude Findlay**. He owns Findlay's Friendly Appliances. Walter has his hands full living with Maude, an independent woman who likes to get her own way. They reside in the upper-middle-class suburb of Tuckahoe, New York, next door to his best friend, **Dr. Arthur Harmon**. Walter hit on hard times after battling alcoholism and watching his store fall into bankruptcy. He's been thinking about retiring from the appliance business.

See *Maude*

FINK, BARTON

Newly successful New York playwright lured out to Hollywood to write a wrestling picture. Has difficulties adjusting to the studio life. Although he wants very much to champion nobility of the common man, he doesn't know how to go about it. Dreams of great literary success and exploring the life of the mind. Has serious writer's block.

See *Barton Fink*

FINSECKER, DORIS

Nice Jewish girl with dreams of success in the world of the arts. Doris comes from an overbearing family that doesn't quite understand what she is all about. She studies at New York City's High School for the Performing Arts, where she is close with **Montgomery** and gradually falling for **Raul "Ralph Garcy" Garcia**.

See *Fame*

FIREFLY, RUFUS T.

Newly appointed leader of the country of Freedonia. He has difficulty obtaining transportation, reading official papers, hiring government ministers, and being serious about anything. Firefly is in a long-running feud with Ambassador Trentino of Sylvania, over both affairs of state and the affections of wealthy dowager **Mrs. Teasdale**. "Remember, you're fighting for this woman's honor which is more than she ever did!"

See *Duck Soup*

FIRMIN, GEOFFREY

A charming, cultured British ex-diplomat who's ruined his life through his hopeless alcoholism. He now lives in small-town Mexico, which would be paradise were it not for the constant oppressive presence of death—in the country's poverty and political violence, in the harsh landscape, in the Day of the Dead rituals the peasants use to come to terms with the inevitable cessation of life. He has a chance to redeem his life and do something positive when his wife, **Yvonne Firmin**, a beautiful

American, returns to try to patch things up with him. But so lost is he in despair and jealousy of her prior affairs that he turns away from his wife and loses himself in a haze of tequila. He repeatedly comes across a peasant sign reading, roughly, "You like this garden? Why is it yours? We evict those who destroy it!" This he takes to be a judgment of his life and sins. Maybe he's right.

See *Under the Volcano*, Malcolm Lowry

FIRMIN, YVONNE

The beautiful American wife of **Geoffrey Firmin**, a British ex-consul, Yvonne returns to Mexico to rekindle the relationship with her husband, but fails, because he won't forgive her her affairs with Jacques Laruelle and Geoffrey's own brother Hugh.

See *Under the Volcano*, Malcolm Lowry

FISH, PHIL

A detective at the 12th Precinct, Fish has been a fine cop—he's just been at it too long. Seemingly minutes away from retirement or an imminent demise, Fish does his duties at his speed (slow), in his own way (even slower). Complains constantly in a battered, weary voice—but seems to have cause, what with a wife, Bernice, bound to call at any moment, with long and complex problems, and aging gastrointestinal and urinary systems that send him to the bathroom with alarming frequency. Often seems to envy the quiet time some of his collars will get in jail. After retiring from the force, he and Bernice become foster parents to five unruly teenagers.

See *Barney Miller* and *Fish*

FLAEMMCHEN

An ambitious stenographer on the make at a fancy Berlin hotel is hired by guest **General Director Preysing** but sets her sights on the dying **Otto Kringelein**, who she thinks is rich. She is beautiful and dresses extravagantly for a secretary, but she always has an eye open for the possibility of an advantageous liaison with a wealthy man and doesn't want to be overlooked.

See *Grand Hotel*, Vicki Baum

FLAGSTONE, HI

Comfortably nestled into his suburban home with his loving wife, Lois, Hi's chief concerns are bills and typical domestic problems. Much of the couple's attention is focused on their endearing children: Chip, a rebellious teen, the combative eight-year-old twins Dot and Ditto, and the lovable toddler Trixie, who often speaks in her head to a sunbeam.

See *Hi and Lois*

FLATTOP

Notorious crook with notorious head shape that's perfect for bookshelves. A ruthless character whose criminal mind is unaffected by his crushed cranium.

See *Dick Tracy*

PRINCESS FLAVIA

The blond, beautiful, graceful cousin of Ruritania's Prince Rudolf is committed to a loveless political marriage to the future king. Although Flavia feels bound by a sense of duty to her lot, she still insists on the status of the king's equal and is not afraid to comment on his failings. Her royal obligations ultimately outweigh even her love for **Rudolf Rassendyll**.

See *The Prisoner of Zenda*

FLEISCHMAN, DR. JOEL

A dyed-in-the-wool New Yorker and graduate of Columbia University Medical School, Fleischman was sent to Alaska to work as a doctor, as a means of repaying the state for financing his education. He had expected to be stationed in Anchorage but instead was sent to Cicely, a tiny town, where he is clearly a fish out of water. At first, at least, Cicely's one asset seems to be attractive **Maggie O'Connell**, a pilot, who also owns his house, and with whom he has a curious love-hate relationship. Joel finally asks Maggie to marry him, but she breaks off the engagement. This sends him off into the wilderness, to find himself.

See *Northern Exposure*

FLEMING, HENRY

As an inexperienced young Yankee recruit in the American Civil War, Fleming dreams of performing heroic deeds. The reality of the war, however, turns out to be a nightmare to him. He runs from his first battle at Chancellorsville and lies to his company about where he's been when he catches up with them. But future battles offer him a chance

J. Pierpont Finch

Fletch

Axel Foley

to redeem himself and erase his feelings of failure and cowardice. War is a hard teacher, but Henry learns the true meaning of bravery and grows up on the battlefield. "I've seen all a' that I wanta."

See *The Red Badge of Courage,* **Stephen Crane**

FLETCHER, DR. EUDORA
A pretty, blond psychotherapist who treats **Leonard Zelig**, famed for his extreme Chameleon Complex—he transforms his appearance to fit in with any crowd. Eventually, she falls in love with Zelig.

See *Zelig*

FLETCHER, IRWIN MAURICE "FLETCH"
Fletch is a dedicated, if eccentric, journalist. You could call him independent, or you could call him wayward. He specializes in stumbling into the middle of murder mysteries, which he then must try to solve. He's given to never-quite-ideal romantic entanglements. A master of disguises, he can pass himself off as, say, "Peter Fletcher" to work on a story down in South America, or use the name of a famous politician to hide his true identity from gullible dupes. He does his share of daydreaming; one of his favorites: in blackface and an Afro wig, he becomes an integral part of "Show Time," the 1980s Magic Johnson–led L.A. Lakers basketball juggernaut. He leaves off fantasizing long enough to get the bad guy, though, whether it's a corrupt Beverly Hills rich guy or a presidential candidate's power-hungry son.

See *Fletch,* **Gregory McDonald**

FLETCHER, JESSICA
A lively, lovely widow who achieves local fame late in life through her popular mystery novels and success as an amateur sleuth. She lives in the small town of Cabot Cove on the Maine coast, where she loves to ride her bike around town and fish. She worked as a substitute teacher and PTA volunteer, but her writing career has allowed her to become a seasoned traveler and more than satisfy her love of adventure. Her first book was *The Corpse Danced at Midnight.* Her later books include *All Fall Down Dead, The Corpse Wasn't There,* and *The Killer Called Collect.* When Jessica's not traveling or at her home in Maine, she can be found at her New York

apartment at the Penfield House. Fletcher took the place to be near her publisher and to teach criminology at Manhattan University.

See *Murder, She Wrote*

FLINGUS, BUNNY
She's terrific in the kitchen, but not so hot in the bedroom. Bunny is energetic, a dreamer and hoper who is always willing to ignore unpleasant realities where she can. She is convinced that if she could get her flame, Artie, to divorce his certifiable wife, Bananas, and to marry her, all of her troubles would be over. "I'll sleep with you, Artie…but I won't cook for you, not until we're married."

See *The House of Blue Leaves,* **John Guare**

THE FLINTSTONES
A Stone Age family with modern problems. Fred's the husband, a large, obnoxiously loud, but good-hearted guy with permanent five o'clock shadow. Levelheaded redhead Wilma is the wife, and cute little Pebbles is their infant daughter. Fred works for the demanding Mr. Slate at the quarry, along with his little, lovable best friend, Barney Rubble, who's also the Flintstones' next-door neighbor. While the boys are off getting into trouble, Wilma and Barney's wife, pixieish brunette Betty, stay at home keeping things shipshape. About the only time Wilma and Betty act as childishly as Fred and Barney is when they're admiring hunky Hollyrock film stars like Cary Granite and Rock Quarry. Wilma and Betty certainly have their hands full: when their husbands aren't bumbling their way into trouble that the girls must get them out of, Wilma's cleaning up after the family pet, Dino, and Betty's struggling to calm her superstrong baby boy, Bamm-Bamm.

See *The Flintstones*

FLOTTRIG, ROY
He's a smooth-talking southern charmer and federal prosecutor. He thinks that he can charm **Reggie Love** into handing over her client **Mark Sway** to him, so that Mark can be made to give up some valuable secrets, but he doesn't know Mark—or Reggie. He's not a bad guy, but not an entirely straight one, either. And he does like the limelight. He also has eyes for high elective office someday.

See *The Client,* **John Grisham**

FLYTE, SEBASTIAN

A young English aristocrat with sterling charm and a porcelain, feminine beauty, Sebastian is also deeply eccentric. He carries around a teddy bear, is arrested and imprisoned for drunk driving while at Oxford, travels to Tangier and aids a wounded German soldier, and finally unsuccessfully applies to be a missionary lay brother in a Tunisian monastery.

See *Brideshead Revisited,* Evelyn Waugh

FOLEY, AXEL

Undercover Detroit police officer working in Beverly Hills, California. Harbors powerful and healthy disrespect for authority in all forms. Loves to drive fast, no matter what traffic circumstances allow. Loyal to his partners, though not above employing irreverent policing style in the process, much to chagrin of **Sergeant Taggart** and delight of **Detective Billy Rosewood.** Foley is also something of a con artist, with an ability for impersonation and attitude adjustments that can ease him in and out of all sorts of difficult situations. It also doesn't hurt that he's handy with his gun. Most notable feature: an infectious laugh that sounds like the braying of a happy mule.

See *Beverly Hills Cop*

FOLEY, SERGEANT DENNIS

A sergeant in the police department of Fernwood, Ohio, an average, peaceful small town—until a mass murderer claims the lives of a local family. The sergeant has an affair with local housewife **Mary Hartman.**

See *Mary Hartman, Mary Hartman*

FOLEY, SERGEANT EMIL

A ramrod-straight, by-the-book career military man who believes it is his duty to prevent undeserving candidates from becoming naval officers. He drives his charges mercilessly, so that they'll either achieve their absolute best or drop out of officer training. A man of integrity and honor, he hounds young **Zach Mayo** to determine if he has what it takes to become an officer and a gentleman.

See *An Officer and a Gentleman*

FONTANA, FRANK

A neurotic investigative reporter for *FYI,* the Washington, D.C., newsmagazine show. Frank is single and usually unattached and has been a long-time friend of coworker **Murphy Brown.** The balding Fontana has given in to the demands of TV image priorities and wears a toupee when he appears on-camera.

See *Murphy Brown*

FONZARELLI, ARTHUR "FONZIE"

The epitome of fifties cool. He wears his hair slicked back and full of hair gel and never takes off his leather jacket. He favors Levi's, a white T-shirt, and boots, and rides a motorcycle. He's a rebel, but with a heart. Some of his contemporaries are in awe of him, many envy him, and most of the people who know him think he's pretty nice underneath the facade. The Fonz snaps his fingers and people do what he says. The make-out king. Though he's a high school dropout, he doesn't encourage others to do likewise. He lives in an apartment above the garage at **Howard** and **Marion Cunningham's** house. Howard is a little appalled by him, but Marion calls him Arthur and treats him like one of her kids. He calls them Mr. and Mrs. C. Dispenses advice to the Cunningham kids, **Richie** and **Joanie.** Holds court in his "office"—the bathroom at local hangout Arnold's.

See *Happy Days*

FORBUSH, NELLIE

A U.S. Navy nurse, affectionately known as "Knucklehead Nellie," she's stationed on an island in the South Pacific. She is an attractive strawberry blonde and a "cockeyed optimist." A native of Little Rock, Arkansas, she joined the Navy because she wanted to meet different kinds of people. Nevertheless, it's hard for Nellie to overcome her ingrained prejudice and accept people of different colors. When she falls in love with planter **Emile de Becque,** she must defeat these prejudices to learn to live with him and his two half Polynesian children.

See *South Pacific,* Oscar Hammerstein II and Richard Rodgers and *Tales of the South Pacific,* James Michener

FORD, MARGARET

A famous pop psychologist who specializes in addictive behavior, Dr. Ford's attraction to an underworld of deception and corruption leads her into a new and darker life. One of Dr. Ford's

Photo courtesy of The National Broadcasting Company, Inc.

Sergeant Joe Friday

patients is a gambler who fears he will be murdered over a bad debt. She visits the House of Games, a bar where she thinks she can find the gambler who has terrorized her client. She wants to talk him out of enforcing the debt. He agrees to tear up the marker if she will help him fleece a high-roller Texan in a big-stakes poker game. She complies, but then becomes so entranced by this world of misdirection that she finds herself hopelessly trapped in it.

See *House of Games*

FORREST, ALEX

Beautiful but obsessive-compulsive woman, very upset with **Dan Gallagher** when he terminates their brief sexual fling. She's more than willing to take personal matters to the most extreme ends. Alex dislikes insensitivity in others, enjoys making telephone calls, and hates to lose an argument under any circumstances. She can be extremely Machiavellian if need be. Works in publishing, though has also moonlighted at baby-sitting jobs. Makes a very tasty rabbit stew.

See *Fatal Attraction*

FORRESTER, GENE

Reluctant player in the game of life. Displaced Dixie boy who is an Upper Middler at Devon School in New England. He is goaded into action by his risk-taking best friend, **Phineas**, who has "some kind of hold" over him. Gene is jealous, a "savage underneath." He is a good student who decides to become exceptional so he can compete with Phineas. "A swell guy, except when the chips are down." He deliberately jounces a treacherous tree limb, shattering star athlete Phineas's leg. Haunted by his action the rest of his life, he does not cry when Phineas is buried, because "I could not escape a feeling that this was my own funeral, and you do not cry in that case."

See *A Separate Peace,* John Knowles

FORRESTER, JOHN

Described by a psychiatrist as "manipulative," Forrester marries into money, and uses his high intelligence and ability to guard secrets to become publisher of a major San Francisco daily newspaper. After being with the paper for fifteen years, Forrester is charged with murder after the violent death of his wife, Paige. Despite being cleared and having inherited a fortune as his wife's only beneficiary, Forrester drops plans to run for the U.S. Senate.

See *Jagged Edge*

FORTUNE, LULA PACE

Sexy but loopy blonde who lives for her man, **Sailor Ripley**. When not having sex with him, she oohs and ahs as he leads them on a violent tour of America.

See *Wild at Heart*

FOX, ALLIE

An ingenious and relentlessly driven inventor and pursuer of off-the-wall schemes, Allie sees himself as "the last man" in a corrupt America—"a dope-taking, door-locking, ulcerated danger zone of rabid scavengers and criminal millionaires and moral sneaks." Yet he is in many ways the archetypal American, as his idealistic, optimistic Yankee spirit drives him to take his family to the Mosquito Coast of Honduras, where he plans to make the jungle a cooler place with his ice-making invention. But the plan goes awry and his vision turns into a nightmare. Allie begins to lose his grip on sanity and grows increasingly tyrannical, ultimately destroying himself and almost his family as well.

See *The Mosquito Coast,* Paul Theroux

FOX, COACH HAYDEN

Manly man's man. He's the head coach of the Minnesota State University Screaming Eagles who has brought the team from a depressing losing streak to impressive, championship status. Divorced father of Kelly, a student at the university. Hayden has a longtime relationship with local anchorwoman **Christine Armstrong**, through which he demonstrates both a chronic inability to understand women and profound male chauvinism. Luckily, if unaccountably, Christine loves him anyway.

See *Coach*

FRANCON, DOMINIQUE

An exquisite hellcat with a contemptuous view of the world. Ms. F. writes an interior-design column, along with an occasional architectural critique for *The Banner,* a newspaper for the common man. She's an enchantress who weaves a spell around every man she meets. Unfortunately, she's poisonous as well as passionate. She destroys a priceless statue of a Greek god so she won't have to love it. She has never had a single woman friend. Dominique believes herself incapable of love until she meets her match, **Howard Roark**, but she marries his worst enemy.

See *The Fountainhead*, Ayn Rand

FRANK

A vicious, weathered Old West killer, Frank is the hired gun of the rich Mr. Morton. While Morton slowly dies from tuberculosis, Frank takes more and more power. He's hunted down by the Harmonica Man for the death of his brother. "People scare better when they're dyin'."

See *Once Upon a Time in the West*

FRANKENSTEIN, DR. FREDERICK

Pronounce that name *FRANKH-en-steen*. This scientist and professor tries to distance himself from the work of his late and notorious grandfather, the monster maker. He's so anxious to be his own man that he, too, goes and makes an attempt to create life from inanimate tissue…with results not altogether different from Grandpa's, except that his monster can do a dance routine to "Puttin' on the Ritz."

See *Young Frankenstein*

FRANKIE

Fun-lovin' beach party dude! Enjoys surfing, dancing to the latest rock 'n' roll, surfing, girls (particularly **Dee Dee**), surfing, singing, and—oh, yeah—surfing. Wears unforgettable swim trunks. Squares think Frankie an affront to decent folk, but beach bunnies find him to be absolutely dreamy.

See *Beach Blanket Bingo*

FREELING, CAROL ANNE

This tow-headed tot becomes more intimately involved with television than most people would care to be when her family's home is invaded by poltergeists. She's sucked into the TV by the evil spirits, and becomes a pawn in the battle between her parents and the researchers they bring in to help, and demonic creatures bent on destroying her family.

See *Poltergeist*

FREEMONT, LISA CAROL

Demure but sexy blonde who's dating **J. B. Jeffries**, who's injured and confined to his apartment. At first her sense of propriety makes her disapprove of Jeffries's spying on his neighbors, but soon her curiosity gets her just as excited as he is about peering into the private lives of others. The fun almost backfires, though, when one of the neighbors, a killer, decides that it isn't nice to pry.

See *Rear Window*

FREMONT, KITTY

A Gentile army nurse, she's romantically involved with handsome Jewish freedom fighter **Ari Ben Gannan**. A caring nurturer despite her military background who isn't afraid of showing her femininity when the moment is right. She understands her place in the world and can be a tough-minded worker when pressures build.

See *Exodus*

FRENCH, MR. GILES

A veddy proper English butler now working in America for **Bill Davis** and Davis's orphaned nieces and nephew. He's a jack-of-all-trades who keeps the house spotless and everyone well fed. Though he seems stiff at first, he's very sensitive to the kids' needs and can be said to function as another surrogate parent for them. Mr. Davis relies heavily on French's child-rearing advice, and the children love him.

See *Family Affair*

FRENGER, JUNIOR "FRANK JR."

This extremely likable psychopath was known for a short time as Herman Gottlieb. Officially, his most recent occupation was as an "investment counselor," but the greater part of his time has been spent acting as a kind of modern-day Robin Hood, except that, in his words, "I don't give the money to anybody." After a stretch in prison, he shares his life with **Suzi "Pepper" Waggoner**.

See *Miami Blues*

FRIDAY, SERGEANT JOE

Terse, matter-of-fact, stone-faced police sergeant dedicated to fighting crime in Los Angeles. "This is the city," says "just a cop" Sergeant Friday as he narrates his own dramatic criminal investigations and pursuits. He acts as straight man to wisecracking partner **Bill Gannon**. Single and single-minded. Has short bulletlike body and walks without moving his arms, as though in a full body cast. Sometimes gets discouraged by criminals' lack of remorse, especially youthful offenders. Has seen it all. "Just the facts, ma'am."

See *Dragnet*

FRIENDLY, TOD

A man for whom, paradoxically, time flows backward. As an old doctor in Chicago, he's haunted by guilt-filled nightmares. Later, these nightmares turn out to have their genesis in what he does as a doctor in a World War II Nazi concentration camp. Strangely, though, everything in the concentration camp is beautiful. Clouds of souls funnel down into furnace chimneys, animating Jewish corpses. Operations put gold-filled teeth into gums, bloody organs into bodies, making the dead come to life and the sick healthy. The Holocaust, it seems, has turned standard conceptions of life and humanity upside down.

See *Time's Arrow,* Martin Amis

FRUMP, UNCLE FESTER

He is egg-bald, bulging-eyed, and vegetally dim. Though blood-related to **Morticia Addams**, Fester has eyes and a behavior pattern more reminiscent of his brother-in-law, **Gomez**. He lives with the Addams family in their large, dark, musty Victorian house. He dresses in monklike robes and often appears seemingly out of nowhere.

See *The Addams Family*

FU, DR. MANCHU

A brilliant, diabolical scientist with a long, pointy mustache, he has only one use for his mad genius—the destruction of the West. From Asia, he sends various agents on elaborate schemes, with plans to devalue U.S. currency, spread germ warfare, and the like. (He also dabbles in more mundane evil deeds, like smuggling.) His nemesis—and the man always on his trail—is Scotland Yard inspector Sir Dennis Nayland-Smith.

See *The Adventures of Fu Manchu,* Sax Rohmer

FUDD, ELMER

This little man is easily outsmarted and often confused. An avid hunter, particularly of rabbit, he never makes a good shot. Elmer once tried to lure a rabbit to his house by putting up "Welcome Easter Bunny" signs. He has an unlikely affinity for opera, sometimes doning tights and a full Viking costume. His speech impediment is unforgettable. "You wascawwy wabbit!"

See *Merrie Melodies*

FUNN, MEL

This dapper film director with a glorious future behind him tends to abuse alcohol when the industry turns against him but has a support network that includes cronies Marty Eggs and Dom Bell. He's willing to go to extreme lengths to ensure participation on his movies, like trapping prospective actors in their showers. Linked romantically with Vilma Kaplan.

See *Silent Movie*

FURILLO, FAYE

A crusading social worker and defender of lost causes, Faye is a frequent visitor to her ex-husband **Frank Furillo's** police station. Whines incessantly to him about their son and her causes. Probably still a little in love with him, despite her affair with Furillo's underling **Henry Goldblume**.

See *Hill Street Blues*

FURILLO, CAPTAIN FRANK

Captain Furillo is a stoic, honest, competent police captain who forcefully commands the Hill Street Precinct. He has a very controlled personality, though his emotions are right under the surface. Furillo can suddenly erupt in anger. He's gritty and tough like the city he serves, and his characteristic posture is standing with his arms crossed tightly over his chest. Frank is fair-minded and very loyal to his men. He will not tolerate unethical actions but is willing to push the envelope if it means getting the bad guys. Not afraid of getting his hands dirty even though he's now got a desk job. He is even nice to ex-wife **Faye Furillo**, who barges into his office frequently to discuss his son or her work and her problems. While he does take his job home, he's helped there by his beautiful second wife, Assistant District Attorney **Joyce Davenport**. They generate a lot of heat. Sometimes talk shop in bed, but usually they quickly become distracted by each other.

See *Hill Street Blues*

FURTER, FRANK N.

He's "just a sweet transvestite, from Transsexual, Transylvania." Well, actually, he's more like an alien from another planet. Furter is a mad scientist, an inventor who is demented, perverted, and oversexed. He's got great powers of persuasion and virtually no morals at all. He takes great pleasure in seducing innocent victims like **Brad Majors** and **Janet Weiss**, when they wander within reach. Frank lives in a dark, old castle with a staff of eccentric and oversexed servants. He wears six-inch platform shoes, a garter belt, bright red lipstick, black gloves and a cape, and has beautifully manicured fingernails. He's built himself a man, a technological hunk with blond hair and a tan, called **Rocky Horror**, who is "good for relieving my tension." Frank is intelligent and sharp-tongued. His entire body is an erogenous zone. Frank is also given to killing people who annoy him. The facts that he's power-mad and has discovered the secret to life itself make him very dangerous. "There's no crime in giving yourself over to pleasure."

See *The Rocky Horror Picture Show*

FURY, NICK

The hard-bitten and crusty director of SHIELD (Supreme Headquarters, International Espionage Law Enforcement Division). A World War II veteran now a little older and lot wiser, Nick Fury wears an eye patch from a war wound and runs his super-scientific spy agency tighter than a drum. Greatest source of personal pain: his brother Scorpio is the agency's chief nemesis.

See *Nick Fury, Agent of SHIELD*

GAILEY, FRED

A handsome young man deeply in love with **Doris Walker**, whom he hopes to make his wife. Her sometimes steely demeanor doesn't scare him, and he knows that the way to her heart lies through winning over her daughter, **Susan**. Then he can pop the question. In his efforts, he enlists the help of store Santa (and more) **Kris Kringle**.

See *Miracle on 34th Street*

GALE, DOROTHY

Dorothy is a simple Kansas farmgirl—with Broadway-quality pipes. She loves her cute little dog, Toto. A tornado which uproots her house takes her and Toto to the magical land of Oz. Despite a certain shock of displacement, she must admit that Oz is a lot more colorful than drab, dreary, corny Kansas. In Oz she's lionized as a heroine, which she actually is, though through no fault of her own. She not only makes a lot of grateful friends, she also makes a few nasty and powerful enemies. Dorothy's a down-to-earth young lady, and unearthly phenomena such as talking trees, dancing scarecrows, and winged monkeys, which might permanently unhinge many youngsters, hardly faze her. But she soon grows homesick for colorless, comfortable Kansas, and travels through Oz in search of a way back home. In her travels, she teams up with a scarecrow, a tin woodman, and a cowardly lion, who agree to join her in seeking out the fabled and powerful **Wizard** of Oz, who rules over all, and who, it is hoped, can provide her with a one-way ticket back to her beloved fields. Dorothy has many adventures, some

Dorothy Gale

Dan Gallagher

fun and some frightening, and meets a lot of fascinating people and other creatures, certainly a much greater variety than Kansas has to offer. But, in the end, she learns a very important lesson: you can take the girl out of Kansas, but you can't take Kansas out of the girl. Or, as she herself puts it, over and over again: "There's no place like home!"

See *The Wizard of Oz,* L. Frank Baum

GALLAGHER, DAN

Happily married New York City attorney, though not above the occasional departure from his wedding vows. He recently had a brief fling with **Alex Forrest**. Once, Dan bought a pet rabbit for his kid. He tries to keep his wife out of his business—and some personal—affairs, though situations may arise that make this impossible.

See *Fatal Attraction*

GALORE, PUSSY

The tough leader of a female crime syndicate, Pussy is good-looking, aggressive and a lesbian. She initially supports **Auric Goldfinger** in his plot to rob Fort Knox, but then changes her mind and helps British Secret Service agent **James Bond** thwart Goldfinger's plans.

See *Goldfinger,* Ian Fleming

GALVIN, FRANK

Galvin's a down-on-his-luck lawyer who's crawled into a bottle and pulled the cork in after him. A laughingstock of his profession, he stays drunk enough to not have to hear the snickers. Then, he's presented with a medical malpractice case that's his last chance to prove to himself that he's worth saving.

See *The Verdict*

GAMGEE, SAMWISE "SAM"

A hobbit of the Shire and a gardener by trade, Sam is honest, guileless, and fiercely devoted to his friend **Frodo Baggins**. After selflessly aiding Frodo and serving briefly as bearer of the One Ring during the War of the Ring, he returns to the Shire, where he serves seven terms as mayor. He marries Rose Cotton, with whom he has thirteen children.

See *The Lord of the Rings,* J. R. R. Tolkien

GANDALF

Gandalf the White, formerly the Grey, is a member of the Istari, a group of wise and powerful beings sent to help the peoples of Middle Earth combat the power of **Sauron**. Gandalf's personality and appearance range from genial and avuncular to powerful and threatening. Fearless, tireless, and wise in counsel, Gandalf actively involves himself in the affairs of all races of Middle Earth, who call him many names, not all of them flattering. His given name, however, is Olórin. Gandalf the Grey ultimately becomes Gandalf the White; in both roles, he plays an instrumental role in the War of the Ring, the struggle to overcome the oppressive and evil regime of Sauron.

See *The Lord of the Rings,* J. R. R. Tolkien

GANNAN, ARI BEN

Handsome Jewish leader of Zionist freedom fighters during the violent birth spasms of the state of Israel. Known for bravery, authority, and more than a little daring, he's willing to do anything necessary to see his cause emerge victorious. Involved in an unlikely romance with army nurse **Kitty Fremont**.

See *Exodus*

GANNON, OFFICER BILL

A working-stiff police officer, he's just an ordinary guy who happens to be a cop. Gannon solves crimes with partner **Sergeant Joe Friday**, often working out of bunco squad. He has definite likes and dislikes to air to his partner and confides in Joe about problems with Mildred, his longtime wife. Especially incensed at the morals of today's teens. Slightly intimidated by Friday. Not above cracking the odd joke now and then.

See *Dragnet*

GANNON, DR. JOE

Young, handsome, caring, and single, this Los Angeles doctor can cure what ails you. Extremely accomplished, he works as an associate professor of surgery and heads his hospital's adjoining student health service. He also has very shiny brown hair.

See *Medical Center*

GANT, EUGENE

This sensitive young southern scholar finds poetic beauty in all of life, including its more sordid levels. Obsessed with girls, he contracts a venereal disease after sleeping with a hooker and later has an affair with Laura James, an engaged older woman. After the death of beloved brother Ben, Gant ends up leaving the South and going to Harvard.

See *Look Homeward, Angel,* Thomas Wolfe

GANTRY, ELMER
A smart, ambitious, Bible-thumping evangelist whose rousing sermons are calculated more to fill his pockets than to save souls. Gantry is a master salesman who has found in religion a marvelous way of preying upon people's guilt, fear, and loneliness, in order to reap fistfuls of cash. The greedy, libidinous, liquor-loving preacher criticizes from the pulpit the very behavior he engages in on the side. Gantry woos fellow evangelist **Sharon Falconer**, whose spiritual healing act he admires for its monetary potential. Together, they build a ministry that makes them rich and famous, but Gantry is not satisfied with one woman or one business. Under his charming veneer, Gantry is a cynical opportunist who believes that ethics are for suckers only.

See *Elmer Gantry,* Sinclair Lewis

GARCIA, RAUL "RALPH GARCY"
An acting student at New York City's High School for the Performing Arts. Though Puerto Rican by birth, he has adopted an Anglo stage name. Plans to be a comedian, though his obnoxious antics sometimes leave his friend **Montgomery** fuming. A big fan of the movie *The Rocky Horror Picture Show*. Beneath his overbearing personality, Raul is hiding some deep psychological trauma. He is gradually falling for **Doris Finsecker**.

See *Fame*

GARFIELD, ELLIOT
He is an aspiring actor from Chicago who's been thrown together unwillingly with jilted dancer **Paula McFadden** and her ten-year-old daughter, Lucy, in a too-small Manhattan apartment. He is, in many ways, a stereotypical actor, with his insatiable ego, his insecurities, and his need for approval and admiration—all of which make him a less-than-ideal roommate for Paula, who has troubles enough of her own. He likes romantic moonlit dinners under the stars and dislikes pantyhose hanging from the shower rod.

See *The Goodbye Girl,* Neil Simon

GARNER, PAUL D.
Paul, a fugitive slave, copes with his painful memories by shutting down his feelings. His vulnerability makes him attractive to women, however, and he eventually moves in with **Sethe,** also a fugitive slave. But to win her over, he has to do battle with the ghost of Sethe's dead daughter.

See *Beloved,* Toni Morrison

GARP, T. S.
Son of **Jenny Fields**, who wanted to have a child but not a husband. Garp goes through life regretting that he has no father. His life's goal is to become a writer, and naturally he seeks many experiences so he'll have fodder for his novels. Sexual experiences interest him particularly, but the coed Garp chooses to woo—won't. Hobbies: wrestling, sex.

See *The World According to Garp,* John Irving

GARRETT, KELLY
This former Las Vegas showgirl gave up her fast lifestyle for an even faster one; she decided to become a cop. But after graduating from the police academy, she was hired by a mysterious, unseen figure named Charlie to work as an undercover detective with two other sexy-but-tough "angels."

See *Charlie's Angels*

GARSON, MARIE
A Los Angeles dime-a-dance girl who hooks up with **Babe Kozak**, only to learn that he's in on a jewel heist. She's smart and can keep her head in the middle of trouble. She recognizes that she's better for **Roy Earle** than the goody-goody girl he holds a torch for.

See *High Sierra*

GARTH, MATTHEW
After his wagon train is attacked by Indians, young Garth is taken in by cattle rancher **Tom Dunson**. He comes to love Dunson as a father. On his return from the Civil War, Garth agrees to go with Dunson on a cattle drive to Missouri. But Garth is shocked by Dunson's brutality toward his men and finally leads a successful rebellion against him. The older man threatens to kill Garth, who finishes the drive and gets the cattle to their destination. But he figures that Dunson will show up one day and demand satisfac-

Elmer Gantry

tion. And, in Abilene, the two finally come face-to-face and engage in a monumental brawl. "I'll take your orders about work, but not about what to think."

See *Red River*

GATLING, GOVERNOR JAMES

Extremely affable and well intentioned, Governor Gatling is nonetheless not terribly bright and certainly is lacking in the cutthroat skills that would seem necessary for political office. As a result, often looks to his staff for council, particularly butler and then Lieutenant Governor **Benson DuBois**. Dumped by his political party, he becomes an independent. A widower, has a young daughter, **Katie**. Cousin of **Jessica Tate**.

See *Benson*

GATLING, KATIE

Daughter of **Governor James Gatling**, she has the run of the executive mansion. Blond and cute, she is beloved by her father, and although her mother is dead, finds many parental figures in the various staff, particularly lovable **Benson DuBois**, housekeeper **Gretchen Kraus**, and her father's secretary, Marcy Hill.

See *Benson*

GATSBY, JAY

Originally from the Midwest, he was born Jay Gatz, in humble circumstances. Driven by his rejection, some ten years ago, by **Daisy Buchanan**, an old-money southern belle, he has changed his name and devoted himself to joining the wealthy classes. He's been fabulously successful as a result of crooked, bootleg-liquor business dealings in the Prohibition 1920s, and now he has moved East, to Long Island. Here he lives in an enormous mansion in West Egg—across the bay from the ultra-elite enclave of East Egg, where his old flame, Daisy, lives with her rich scoundrel of a husband, **Tom Buchanan**. Gatsby, the quintessential romantic, is devoting his whole life to winning Daisy back, and he spends evenings peering longfully out across the bay at the green light on Daisy's dock. Though Gatsby gives enormous lawn parties, he doesn't really have fun at them; he throws them solely in the hope of seeing Daisy. As a possible entree to Daisy, he puts up an old midwestern acquaintance, **Nick Carraway**, Daisy's cousin, who helps get

Gatsby access to her. But Gatsby can't understand that there's a gulf between what he represents—new money, criminally obtained—and the situation into which Daisy has married—old money, made respectable by intervening generations since the robber barons that created the wealth. The past is the past, and it can't be relived, as he finds out, to his sorrow.

See *The Great Gatsby,* F. Scott Fitzgerald

GEORGE

George, referred to as the Time Traveler, is a late-nineteenth-century inventor and scientist who builds a time machine to help him satisfy his thirst for knowledge. George is one of those men who are too clever to be believed, and his friends think him mad when he tells them about traveling in time. He falls in love with Weena, a woman he meets in the year 802,701. He finally vanishes, never to be heard from again.

See *The Time Machine,* H. G. Wells

GEORGE

This jungle denizen is long on brawn but short on brains. He loves to save people in distress, whether they need help or not. His preferred mode of jungle transport is the vines with which he swings from tree to tree. Or he does so, that is, when he doesn't swing smack *into* a tree, further scrambling the few marbles he had to begin with. Always on hand is his trusty pet elephant, Shep, who thinks he's a dog.

See *George of the Jungle*

GEORGE

This jaded college history professor's life is one long sparring session with **Martha**, his domineering wife. Like Martha, he's disappointed at missed opportunities, such as his failure to succeed as a novelist and his present powerlessness to change things. Martha's hold over him stems in part from the fact that her father is George's boss, the college president. When Martha invites **Nick** and **Honey**, a young professor and his wife, over for a few too many drinks, George, seeing in them a reflection of himself and Martha at a younger, more promising age, and resenting them for it, tries to draw them into the elaborate, hateful mind games he and Martha play to spice up their lives. He goads Nick into revealing his contemptuous attitude toward

Honey and thereby drives an emotional wedge between the young couple. When booze-fueled Martha ups the mind-game ante by making overtures to Nick, the games become nastier, and more lacerating to all four participants. A pivotal, though never-seen figure in this game session is George and Martha's son, who is more frequently referred to as the evening drags itself onward. In the last analysis, it seems that George does still need, and even love, Martha, although their relationship is burdened with an incredible amount of unpleasant baggage. "Martha? Rubbing alcohol for you?"

See *Who's Afraid of Virginia Woolf?*, Edward Albee

GEORGY

A tall, considerably overweight girl whose goofy charm and low self-esteem endear her to wealthy **James Leamington**. The gawky girl is embarrassed by the man's advances and then finds herself admired by her narcissistic roommate's handsome boyfriend. As her life becomes more complicated, she rises to the challenge of accepting responsibility and recognizing that she deserves the good things that happen to her.

See *Georgy Girl*

GEPPETTO

This kindly old woodcarver finishes painting a new marionette, Pinocchio, and wishes upon the Wishing Star for his own son to love and raise. His wish comes true: Pinocchio becomes flesh and blood after his selfless act of heroism in saving Geppetto from the belly of Monstro the whale.

See *Pinocchio*

GERARD, LIEUTENANT PHILIP

A relentless lawman, obsessed with recapturing **Dr. Richard Kimble**, an accused murderer who has escaped him on more than one occasion. Gerard is a fundamentally honorable man, and though he will bend heaven and earth to catch Kimble, he's troubled by the possibility that the man he wants to bring to justice may actually be innocent.

See *The Fugitive*

THE GESTE FAMILY

Three orphaned brothers are brought up in wealth by a kind benefactress and vow to always stick together. The eldest, Michael "Beau" Geste, is a confident and generous leader. The middle brother, John Geste, is kind and romantic. The youngest, Digby Geste, is more rash than his older brothers, but a good sport. The three brothers rarely fight or argue. They love acting out adventure stories of Vikings and knights in shining armor. When they grow up, they turn their love of adventure into a reality by joining the French Foreign Legion. Michael becomes a tall, soft-spoken, but valiant soldier. Although John appears more genteel than his older brother, he is no less brave. Digby has matured also, but he still retains a boyish enthusiasm and a hint of roguishness. In the Foreign Legion, the brothers meet the martinet Sergeant Markoff, who is hated by his men for his joy in inflicting punishment. Markoff is abetted by the sniveling, hyena-like Rasinoff, who has returned to the Foreign Legion after being kicked out for stealing. John and Digby have always looked up to Michael, but it isn't until after their elder brother dies that they learn about his noble deed that saved a woman's honor and their own fortunes.

See *Beau Geste*

GIDDENS, REGINA

A tigress in the guise of a southern belle, willful and greedy, Regina is married to businessman Horace Giddens and has a daughter, Alexandra. She is constantly on the lookout for new territory to conquer and has no scruples about getting what she wants. Not a woman you'd want to turn your back on.

See *The Little Foxes*, Lillian Hellman

GIDEON, JOE

Chain-smoking, workaholic, goateed director of Hollywood pictures and Broadway spectacles. Self-centered, egotistical, Joe can be difficult, yet is respected by his peers—like the ex-wife with whom he still has a professional relationship. Romantically, Joe goes for young dancers half his age. Has a vivid, Felliniesque fantasy life and a critical heart condition.

See *All That Jazz*

GIGI

A bright little Parisian tomboy with a winning smile and charm to spare, Gigi is highly resistant to her grandmother's notion that she should grow up. She ultimately gives in to her grandmother's plan for her to learn all the graces of a lady so that she may become a professional mistress. It just so happens that the first bachelor she is set up with turns out to be the man of her dreams, and, inspired by her first experience with love, Gigi blossoms into a graceful, sophisticated woman and wife.

See *Gigi*

GILBERT

This college freshman might as well have NERD tattooed on his forehead, what with his too-short slacks and other nerdy trademarks. He and his nerd buddy, **Lewis**, form a fraternity to fight back against the football players who persecute them. Gilbert falls in love with a nerd babe while helping her learn how to use a computer. He proves to be a skillful and impassioned speaker on behalf of nerds everywhere.

See *Revenge of the Nerds*

GILBERT, WHITLEY

Whitley is a pampered southern belle, now at the primarily black Hillman College. A product of a broken home, she grew up showered with material things but little love. She uses caustic, catty wit to hide her own vulnerabilities and show others their place. Found offensive by some, her style, insight, and foibles are admired by sometimes boyfriend **Dwayne Wayne**. Her accent is drawly, her clothes emphasize her slender, fit figure. Loves Chanel perfume and spending money—not necessarily in that order.

See *A Different World*

GILDA

A tall, alluring woman married to Buenos Aires casino owner **Ballin Mundson**, for whom she has more fear than love. In tight gowns, tossing her long hair, she performs sultry song-and-dance routines for the casino's patrons. Gilda is sexuality personified. When her husband hires destitute gambler **Johnny Farrell**, she finds herself reunited with her former lover, who nurtures a deep-seated grudge against her. We don't know what Gilda did to Johnny, but, whatever it was, she isn't driving herself crazy with remorse. Though she's selfish, spoiled, and willing to compromise herself for a soft life, there is something likable about her. She can make jokes about herself and doesn't take life as

seriously as those around her. Gilda is an enigma— a woman with a past who lives for the moment. She enjoys teasing Johnny, and when he reacts by roughing her up, it doesn't come as an unpleasant shock; in fact, it's quite the contrary.

See *Gilda*

GILLESPIE, DR. LEONARD

Stern but caring supervising doctor on the staff at Blair General Hospital. He oversees the work of intern **James Kildare**, among others, offering guidance with a firm hand. He has great instincts and gentle wisdom and encourages learning by doing. Grapples daily with limits of medical science. Thinks of young Dr. Kildare as a son.

See *Dr. Kildare*

GILLIAN

This pretty, innocent, upper crust Chicago girl has psychokinetic powers. She's enlisted to help secret agents who plan to use her abilities for nefarious purposes, all unbeknownst to her. Only when **Peter** comes on the scene, looking for his missing son— another psychic teen—does she realize what's up. Eventually, she faces up to the wicked agent who had been manipulating her and uses her powers to give him the ultimate migraine.

See *The Fury*

GILLIGAN

Simpleton crewman. As the sole deck hand of the SS *Minnow*, a sight-seeing charter boat, he's been stranded on an uncharted South Pacific island with the **Skipper** and five passengers for over three years. Gilligan wears a red shirt, white pants, and hat, the same clothes, every day (the clothes he was shipwrecked in, which wear incredibly well). He has half-witted schemes for getting rescued, while at the same time often ruining the rescue schemes of others. He's capable of hard work and is still occasionally bossed, bullied, and blamed by the Skipper, his best friend. Kind, gentle, and well meaning, he is frequently thwarted by his own ineptitude. He kind of likes farmgirl **Mary Ann Summers** and sort of fears sexpot **Ginger Grant**. Looks to the **Professor** as a fount of wisdom. He's the eternal, wide-eyed, innocent, incurable optimist. "Gee whiz, Professor!"

See *Gilligan's Island*

GILLIS, DOBIE

An early '60s college student, his main passions are beautiful girls and pondering life's meaning. One of his favorite hangouts is a park bench beneath a statue of "The Thinker," where he sits and worries about the future. He wears a crewcut and striped polo shirts. He's tired of telling people that his name is "Dobie," not "Dopey." To earn extra money, he works for his father, Herbert T. Gillis, who owns a neighborhood grocery store. The senior Gillis constantly nags Dobie and gripes about how much tougher life was when he was Dobie's age. Much of Dobie's so-called "love life" consists of fruitlessly pursuing gorgeous but mercenary Thalia Menninger and avoiding brilliant but homely **Zelda Gilroy**, who is determined to marry him. His best friend and closest confidant is **Maynard G. Krebs**, a jazz-loving, goateed beatnik.

See *The Many Loves of Dobie Gillis*

GILROY, ZELDA

Brilliant but plain, Zelda pursues **Dobie Gillis** with single-minded determination. She feels that, with her brain and Dobie's sweetness, their child would be just about perfect. Even though Dobie constantly resists her advances, Zelda knows she'll eventually wear him down, simply because she's so much smarter than he is. In fact, she often tells Dobie that he may as well save himself the trouble and give in to her now, a sentiment echoed by **Maynard G. Krebs**, Dobie's best friend, who sees Zelda as a force of nature that cannot be denied. She has a strange mannerism of wrinkling her nose and squinting in such a way that Dobie is somehow compelled to imitate her, which drives him crazy. Zelda uses this to demonstrate to Dobie that he's totally in her power.

See *The Many Loves of Dobie Gillis*

THE GIRL

She's a perky, buxom, not-too-bright blond model, originally from Denver, Colorado, and now living in a sublet apartment in New York City. Among the many things of which she's ignorant are the ways of lustful males and music, except that she allows as how she has "the biggest thing about Eddie Fisher." She hates hot weather and keeps cool by putting her undies in the ice box. An undraped "artistic photo" of her appeared in *U.S. Camera*. She's

moved up from modeling to being the spokesperson for Dazzle Dent Toothpaste with her own commercial: "I had onions at lunch; I had garlic dressing at dinner; but he'll never know, because I stay kissing sweet the new Dazzle Dent way!" She becomes friends with **Richard Sherman**, whose wife is out of town for the summer, and stays in his apartment because he has air conditioning, causing poor Richard no end of lascivious thoughts. "I just have no imagination at all; I just have lots of other things." "Isn't it delicious?"

See *The Seven Year Itch*

GITTES, J. J.

Cynical 1930s Los Angeles private detective and ex-cop, specializing in marital strife. Though he has a clever mind and has been around the block, he has a knack for getting into situations beyond his control. He was forced to leave the police department in disgrace. Has a nose for trouble, which is liable to get his nose in trouble. Currently, he is investigating a domestic problem for **Evelyn Mulwray**, though he suspects (with reason) that there's more to the situation than meets the eye. "I tried to help someone and all I ended up doing was hurting them."

See *Chinatown*

GLADNEY, JACK

College professor and family man. He heads the Hitler Studies Department at a nameless liberal arts college. He associates with the New York Intellectuals, a group of professors who are totally unable to find real meaning in the world they look at so ironically from the ivory towers. The TV's always on in his house, usually tuned to the latest disaster coverage. Gladney tries to whisk his family away from a nebulous but threatening airborne toxic event, such as might happen anywhere and everywhere these days. He's amazed by his toddler son's lack of technophobia, as he steers his tricycle nonchalantly across a crowded highway.

See *White Noise*, Don DeLillo

THE GLASS FAMILY

Former vaudevillians Les and Bessie Gallagher Glass are the parents of the intellectually gifted seven Glass children: Seymour, Webb "Buddy," Boo Boo, twins Walt and Waker, Zachary "Zooey,"

J. J. Gittes

and Franny. They grew up in New York, and each of them appears on the radio quiz show *It's a Wise Child.* The eldest were veterans of World War II, although Waker was a conscientious objector who later became a Roman Catholic priest. Boo Boo served as an ensign in the Waves, and Walt was in a U.S. Army artillery in the Pacific, where he was killed in an accident.

See *Nine Stories, Franny and Zooey, Raise High the Roof-Beam, Carpenters,* and *Seymour: An Introduction,* J. D. Salinger

GLICK, SAMMY

A heel-hero who will lie, cheat, and step on anyone on his way up the ladder of success. A slickly affable Johnny-one-note (it's "mi mi mi"), his story brilliantly demonstrates the idea that greed promotes misery. He's a human ferret, sharp and quick, always running, but "agile without grace." He matures without mellowing. Though he thinks his associates hate his guts, he's right. He can cry when it suits him, but has no tears for genuine tragedy. He can't bear being alone. His disastrous marriage to a haughty heiress reveals his hollowness and insecurity. "No fair! For Christ's sake, grow up, this isn't kindergarten any more, this is the world."

See *What Makes Sammy Run?,* Budd Schulberg

GLINDA

A pale, frail beauty with a flutteringly light voice, she's a good witch in the land of Oz. When **Dorothy Gale** and her house land on top of the Wicked Witch of the East, it is Glinda who points her down the Yellow Brick Road.

See *The Wizard of Oz,* L. Frank Baum

GLOSSOP, MIMI

She's a modern woman who wants a divorce and hires the services of a professional corespondent to get it on the grounds of infidelity. She sees professional dancer **Guy Holden** as her ticket to freedom, but he sees her as the object of his affection and seeks to ensnare her in another marital entanglement. Fast with a quip, with a charming cynical chip on her shoulder, she's initially disdainful of Guy but finds that he grows on her and makes a fantastic dancing partner.

See *The Gay Divorcée*

GODELL, JACK

Weary company man working at close-knit nuclear power plant in California. Loyal to his coworkers and the business, though his firm faith in his industry can be shaken under the right circumstances. Ultimately, an ethical man willing to risk career and possibly his life if it means doing the right thing.

See *The China Syndrome*

GOLDBERG, MOLLY

The matriarch of a middle-class Jewish family. Molly is warm, motherly, and stout, wears an apron, and keeps her hair in a bun. Much of her time is spent in the kitchen, preparing traditional dishes for her family, or gossiping from the rear window with neighbors across the courtyard. To get her attention, just lean out your window and yell, "Yoo hoo!…Mrs. Goldberg!"

See *The Goldbergs*

GOLDBLUME, LIEUTENANT HENRY

Competent, smart, soft-spoken, and sweet detective lieutenant at Hill Street police station. Reports dutifully to **Captain Frank Furillo,** to whom he is something of a right-hand man. Goldblume's trustworthy and stable, but not a natural-born leader, though he tries hard. He itches for more responsibility and a harder image. He has an affair with Furillo's ex-wife, **Faye.**

See *Hill Street Blues*

GOLDFINGER, AURIC

A brilliant criminal with a shining obsession. Goldfinger is a millionaire always looking to increase his gold supply. Short, heavy, and usually sunburned, he likes to make love to women covered in gold paint, although it has a disastrous effect on their complexion and respiration. Goldfinger masterminds Operation Grand Slam, the planned robbery of Fort Knox. He's almost always accompanied by his powerful Korean manservant, Oddjob.

See *Goldfinger,* Ian Fleming

GOLDMAN, OSCAR

An operative with the OSI—the Office of Scientific Intelligence—Oscar is the contact for **Steve Austin** and **Jaime Sommers,** his two bionic agents. He operates out of Washington, D.C., where his pretty secretary, Peggy Callahan, takes care of day-to-day business. He's probably more emotionally involved in the lives of Steve and Jaime than he should be.

See *The Six Million Dollar Man* and *The Bionic Woman*

GOLIGHTLY, HOLLY

"A real phony." She has calling cards from Tiffany's inscribed, "Miss Holiday Golightly, Traveling." Independent and unattainable, she lives in an apartment full of suitcases and unpacked crates. She calls her writer neighbor, **Paul Varjak**, "Fred," because he reminds her of her brother. Her red cat has no name because "I haven't a right to give him one: he'll have to wait until he belongs to somebody." Holly supports herself by getting fifty-dollar bills for the powder room from older men, and visiting racketeer, Sally Tomato, at Sing Sing every Thursday. She thinks it's "tacky to wear diamonds before you're forty." When a Texas horse doctor shows up on the doorstep claiming to be her husband, Paul discovers that her real name is Lulamae Barnes, and that she once had a shot a being a movie star, but decided that "you've got to want it to be good and I don't want it." Holly wears prescription dark glasses, even indoors. She suffers from what she calls "the mean reds": "You're afraid and you sweat like hell, but you don't know what you're afraid of." Her passions include riding horses in Central Park and the movie *Wuthering Heights*, which she's seen ten times. She keeps her enormous Christmas tree up until March. After becoming an unwitting victim and being arrested for narcotics smuggling, she abruptly abandons her cat and heads for South America.

See *Breakfast at Tiffany's,* **Truman Capote**

GONDORFF, HENRY

Aka Mr. Shaw, this seemingly ineffectual drunken slob is actually an old master of the confidence game. His style of swindle is much more thought out and premeditated than that of his protégé, **Johnny Hooker**. He lives in Chicago in a merry-go-round-cum-bordello with his girlfriend, Billie, an excellent pickpocket in her own right. Gondorff understands the need to properly set the stage of any swindle. "Always drink gin with a mark" is one of his sage pieces of advice. "They can't tell if you cut it." Drinking has not, by and large, affected his facile card manipulation. In addition to a fondness for liquor, Gondorff smokes cigars. Gondorff's expertise is the "big con"—an elaborate and carefully plotted setup that requires a large initial outlay but can net a very large gain. When he decides to take hard-boiled money man **Doyle Lonnegan** by means of an intricate scam, he counsels his coworkers to take a purely intellectual, and not an emotional, approach to their work. "Revenge is for suckers. I been griftin' thirty years and never got any."

See *The Sting*

GOODE, CHESTER

Chester lives in the Old West town of Dodge City, where he's the deputy to **Marshal Matt Dillon**. Saddled with a bum leg, Chester is limited somewhat in what he can actually do in the rough-and-tumble world of the frontier, but he gamely does all that he can to help his hero and friend, Marshal Dillon.

See *Gunsmoke*

GOODLOVE, ADRIAN

Shrewd and vilely manipulative psychoanalyst who persuades **Isadora Wing** to abandon her husband, **Bennett Wing**, at a psychoanalysts' convention in Vienna for an "existential" drive through Europe. Although he claims to be the best thing that could happen to Isadora, Goodlove does not live up to his name either emotionally or physically.

See *Fear of Flying,* **Erica Jong**

GOODSEN, JOEL

Horny, hunky high school senior; self-trained entrepreneur. Initially, he's an innocent, in matters sexual and otherwise, till his folks leave him in charge of their suburban Chicago home while on vacation. Then he cuts loose, dancing in his underwear to the music of Bob Seger. But that's only the beginning of his education about parts of the *real* world way beyond his prior experience. He finds himself up to his neck in a world of often alluring call girls, menacing pimps, thievery, brothel management, car chases, car sinkings(!), and other shady dealings and scary aspects of life's seamier underside. Not only must he grapple with all of this, but he is expecting to be interviewed by a representative of Princeton University, which his parents devoutly hope he will attend the following

Holly Golightly

year. He handles his complex dilemma in a way that restores our faith in the indomitability and resourcefulness of American youth. Not that his parents fully appreciate his gifts, of course.

See *Risky Business*

GOOGLE, BARNEY

A little rogue with big, bubble eyes and little respect for law, order, property, or marriage. He often associates with hillbilly Snuffy Smith and the knocked-kneed racehorse Spark Plug. He lives in Chicago but travels the world.

See *Barney Google* and *Spark Plug,* Billy De Beck

GORDON, ARTEMUS

A United States Secret Service agent during the Ulysses S. Grant administration and, more important, a man of a thousand faces. Artemus was once a stage actor and utilizes the makeup techniques and dialects he learned in his old profession to come up with countless disguises. One moment he's an Indian, and the next—presto!—he's President Grant. It helps being a man of a thousand faces when your best friend and fellow agent, **James West**, is constantly getting into jams. Jim's life span would certainly be shorter if it weren't for Artemus saving his butt on many occasions. He is also very proficient with guns (all his guns have his initials on them) and some very special smoke bombs that he carries at all times in his vest pockets. He's a scientific genius, loves a good cognac, and the presence of a beautiful lady brings great satisfaction to both parties.

See *The Wild, Wild West*

GORDON, BERT

The oily bagman for Minnesota Fats. He's got slicked-back hair and slippery morals. Bert has a knack for sensing championship qualities in people—and knows how to separate the winners from the losers. He drinks only milk while gambling so as not to dull his wits. Bert is the one who initially backs the rise to pool prominence of **"Fast" Eddie Felson**, as he once did for Minnesota Fats.

See *The Hustler*

GORDON, BARBARA

This police commissioner's daughter does far more

than her civic duty in Gotham. She was once nearly duped into marriage by the villianous Penguin. Thankfully, her apartment doubles as her hideout for the crime-fighting **Batgirl**.

See *Batman*

GORDON, CHARLY

A poignant victim of scientific curiosity, Charly is a retarded man who takes part in a medical experiment that triples his intelligence level—and then, at the peak of his intellect, he discovers that to continue the treatment is likely to be fatal. But to stop will mean reverting back to his original I.Q.

See *Flowers for Algernon*

GORDON, FLASH

Hero of the universe. Blond-haired, square-jawed, tights-wearing interplanetary good guy. He's handy at the controls of a spaceship and can hold his own against anyone in a ray gun shoot-out. Flash is a quick thinker who doesn't know the meaning of fear. His main foe is cruel, despotic **Ming the Merciless**. Flash, as he is known to his friends, is often assisted in his heroic deeds by **Dr. Zarkov** and **Dale Arden**.

See *Flash Gordon*

GORMAN, VERA LOUISE

A timid little slip of a thing and the dimmest bulb among the lights of Mel's Diner in Phoenix. She's not much of a waitress, but she's sweet, and survives the spilled coffee and other mishaps that always appear on her watch. Her pets are a cat (named Mel) and hamsters Mitzi and Harold.

See *Alice* and *Alice Doesn't Live Here Anymore*

GRACE

Crime dolly who's outlived both her era and her looks, though she refuses to admit departure of either. Now living meager existence in Atlantic City. Unlikely but determined courier for cocaine dealers. Involved with retired bottom-level organized crime member **Lou**, who worked for Grace's husband years before.

See *Atlantic City*

GRACE

She is a modern woman of Los Angeles, currently suffering from severe memory problems, who has hired private eye **Mike Church** to help her out.

Unwittingly connected with notorious 1940s Hollywood murder case.
See *Dead Again*

GRAHAM, BARBARA

A flaming redhead and good-time girl who burns the candle at both ends and winds up getting badly burned herself. A voracious reader who quotes the *Rubaiyat*, Barbara is also a pathological liar. She obeys the thieves' code and does time rather than roll over on her bad-guy buddies. Tough-talking and gutsy, when asked, "What do you do?" she replies, "The best I can." She earns a good deal of her money gambling and driving getaway cars. When she decides to have a baby and go straight, she winds up married to a hopeless junkie but still proves to be a devoted mother. Ironically, it's only after she straightens out that she's arrested for a murder—one crime she didn't commit. But even though she's been legit for a while, she still won't squeal, even when her life is at stake. She snarls, "No dice." One cop calls her "the hardest cookie I've ever run up against." She wears flaming-red pajamas the night before her execution and paints her nails to match. Still proclaiming her innocence, she goes to the gas chamber with her head held high.
See *I Want to Live*

THE GRANDMOTHER

An elderly southern woman whose professed belief in goodness is put to an extreme test when she and her family are set upon by escaped convicts, led by one called the Misfit; she persists in believing that the Misfit will not harm them because he comes from "good people." She realizes her error—that good and evil don't necessarily have any relationship with one's roots—only at the point of death. As the Misfit says of her, "She would of been a good woman, if it had been somebody there to shoot her every minute of her life."
See *A Good Man Is Hard to Find,* Flannery O'Connor

GRANT, ALAN

A world-famous paleontologist. He's an early proponent of the theory that some dinosaurs were warm-blooded, lived in herds, and had maternal instincts. His favored dig sites are in the badlands of Montana. A widower, he's romantically involved with paleobotanist **Ellie Sattler** and has something of an aversion to children. Grant is part of a team of scientists assembled by **John Hammond** to examine Jurassic Park, a theme park containing live, cloned dinosaurs.
See *Jurassic Park,* Michael Crichton

GRANT, GINGER

She's a sexpot starlet. The glamorous element among the SS *Minnow* passengers stranded on an uncharted desert island. She seems to have brought along lots of luggage for a three-hour cruise. Wears slinky gowns and practices acting roles, even though casting opportunities are scarce. Uses **Gilligan** as stand-in actor in love scenes. Finds little in common with Nebraskan farmgirl **Mary Ann Summers**.
See *Gilligan's Island*

GRANT, LOU

He learned journalism as a tough reporter in Detroit and then became producer of the *Six O'Clock News* at WJM-TV in Minneapolis. Lou comes off as cantankerous, but his bark is worse than his bite. Married and divorced, he has three daughters and four grandchildren. His colleagues at WJM-TV include associate producer **Mary Richards**, whom he hires and looks out for like a daughter (Mary always refers to him as Mr. Grant); **Murray Slaughter**, the newswriter on the show; and **Ted Baxter**, the station's incompetent newscaster. Lou is briefly the unwilling object of desire for another one of the station's regulars, **Sue Ann Nivens**, the host of WJM's *Happy Homemaker Show*. No teetotaler, he likes to hang out at the Happy Hour Bar (his bar tab regularly comes to the station on the fifteenth of each month) and keeps a bottle of booze in his bottom desk drawer. After he's fired by new ownership at WJM, he moves to Los Angeles and works as city editor of the *Los Angeles Tribune*. There, no mellower than ever, he often clashes with the paper's powerful and autocratic publisher and owner, **Margaret Pynchon**. Favorite actor: John Wayne.
See *The Mary Tyler Moore Show* and *Lou Grant*

GRANT, VICTORIA

British would-be nightclub singer living in Paris. Desperate for work, Grant assumes a male alter

Flash Gordon

PUBLIC TRANSPORTATION OPERATORS

Travis Bickle
Otto, the School Bus Driver
Ralph Kramden
Alex Reiger

ego—Victor—under the direction of her friend Toddy, in order to obtain nightclub bookings as a transvestite male-to-female impersonator. She once had a romantic assignation with a Chicago gang lord.

See *Victor/Victoria*

GRANTHAM, GRAY

This brave reporter for the *Washington Herald* risks his career and even his life helping **Darby Shaw** prove her theory that a government-business plot is behind the assassination of two Supreme Court justices. Only his investigative skills and his connections—even inside the White House itself—will enable Darby to solve the mystery.

See *The Pelican Brief*, John Grisham

GRAPE, GILBERT

He's a dreamer and the middle son of the Grape family, but he's forced into the father role in his dysfunctional clan. His mother is a chair-bound "porker," his brother is a "retard," and his sisters are pains in the butt. Gilbert works at Lamson Grocery in Endora, Iowa, stocking shelves and delivering groceries to a sex-starved housewife. Pretty young Becky comes to town, lights up his life, and he learns that "regret is the ugliest word."

See *What's Eating Gilbert Grape?*, Peter Hedges

GRAVAS, LATKA

This otherworldly garage mechanic works for New York's Sunshine Cab Company, having emigrated to the United States from a small country somewhere in eastern or middle Europe. He sometimes finds it hard to understand American customs but is always willing to give them a try. He is madly in love with his wife and compatriot, Simka, and considers **Alex Rieger** to be one of his closest friends. He seems to have a number of personalities, one of which is oily playboy Vic Ferrari. "Tank you veddy much."

See *Taxi*

GRAY, DORIAN

A beautifully handsome young man in late-nineteenth-century London who arrives like a thunderbolt on the high-society scene. **Lord Wotton**, an aging libertine, takes an almost obsessive interest in him. While having his portrait painted, Gray wish-

es aloud that he could keep his looks forever—not realizing that a nearby Egyptian statue immediately grants his wish. He falls totally under Wotton's influence and becomes an amoral fixture in London's decadent, partying set. As he sheds his inhibitions, he also sheds his ethics, causing no small amount of distress to others, including his onetime mentor, Lord Wotton. And, just as he had once wished, with all of his excesses and overindulgence, his outward appearance remains completely unchanged. That's more than can be said of that portrait, which grows more ugly and grotesque with the passage of time and Gray's accumulation of immoral deeds. Gray eventually learns that one should beware of making a wish; it might come true…not necessarily a good thing.

See *The Picture of Dorian Gray*, Oscar Wilde

GRAY, GINGER

This pretty, resourceful girl lives at a boys' school in Arizona, but though she's surrounded by males, she can't seem to find love. The students see her as a buddy rather than a potential girlfriend. Along comes young **Danny Churchill, Jr.**, who is interested in her as a possible romantic subject, and she's turned off by his attentions—at first.

See *Girl Crazy*

GRAYLE, VELMA

Nightclub singer of some distinction, though she's apparently been missing for some time now. Young, naive, and easily manipulated, Velma may not be all that everyone thinks she is. The object of **Moose Malloy's** affections.

See *Farewell, My Lovely*

GREEN GIANT

Found life in juvenile fairy tales and opted for a more challenging career in marketing canned and frozen vegetables. Large, green, and muscular. Is often seen with his sidekick L'il Sprout, a Brussels sprout. "Ho Ho Ho!"

See *Green Giant*

GREEN HORNET

By day the dashing and wealthy young publisher Brit Reid, by night a masked avenger who matches wits with those lurking in the depths of the criminal underworld. With his faithful valet Kato at the wheel, the Green Hornet zooms around the city in the sleek automobile known as Black Beauty, seeking out evildoers and righting wrongs with inimitable flair. He may be a vigilante bent on seeking justice, but he also thinks there should be a limit on vengeance. The hornet's sting is a gas gun that puts criminals and racketeers to sleep rather than killing them.

See *The Green Hornet*

GREEN LANTERN

With a special ring given to him by an alien, jet test pilot Hal Jordan is endowed with a broad array of superpowers that transform him into Green Lantern, masked crusader and member in good standing of the Justice League of America. Not only does it allow him to fly, the ring also projects a malleable force field, which Green Lantern shapes into giant scissors, flying fists, or whatever else the situation calls for. When he's not hanging out at Justice League headquarters he can be found roaming city streets with his part-time partner in crimefighting, the ace bowman Green Arrow.

See *Green Lantern*

GREEN, NATALIE

Plump but smart, popular, and wry, Natalie is a student at Eastland School for Girls in Peekskill, New York. She works on the school paper and aspires to be a writer. Of her tight-knit group of girlfriends, she's the first to lose her virginity, to her boyfriend, Snake. Her best friend is **Dorothy "Tootie" Ramsey**.

See *The Facts of Life*

GREENE, DR. MARK

Even-tempered, extremely competent chief resident in the emergency room at Chicago's County General Hospital. Should have a bright career ahead of him. Married to Jennifer, an attorney, and father of young daughter, Rachel. The family has sacrificed a lot for Mark's career, and Jennifer recently told Mark that she had given up too much and was planning to leave him.

See *ER*

GREENER, FAYE

A tall, long-legged platinum blonde, Faye wants to be a leading actress but has to settle for bit parts such as a dancing girl in harem movies. Though **Tod Hackett** loves her, the vapid, ambitious, and scheming Faye does not return his ardent affections. Instead, she'll date anyone who she thinks can advance her career.

See *The Day of the Locust*, Nathanael West

GREENER, HARRY

Past-his-prime vaudeville performer trying to survive in 1930s Hollywood. Hawks homemade silver polish to eke out a living for himself and daughter **Faye Greener**, who has a dim notion of following in her father's unsuccessful showbiz footsteps. A clown by profession, he rarely goes out of character, even when suffering heart attacks.

See *The Day of the Locust*, Nathanael West

GREENWAY, AURORA

Controlling, domineering, always certain she's absolutely correct in all things. Aurora's the widow of Rudyard and the mother of **Emma Greenway-Horton**. She is desperately lonely but afraid to admit any sort of need to anyone. Her fears come out as meanness. It's typical of Aurora to remark to her daughter on Emma's wedding day: "You are not special enough to overcome a bad marriage." Aurora's never remarried, but has no lack of suitors—just none special enough to meet her high standards. But two will stay with her until the end: Vernon Dahlart, the sweet but silly man who adores a woman who feels only fondness for him, and Garrett Breedlove, the suave astronaut who grimaces when Aurora says, "I love you." To this he smiles and drawls, "I was just inches from a clean getaway."

See *Terms of Endearment*, Larry McMurtry

GREENWAY-HORTON, EMMA

Smothered emotionally by her mother, **Aurora Greenway**, Emma has turned out remarkably well-balanced. Okay, so she smokes pot with her friend Patsy behind her mother's back, and is engaged to a man named Flap—the young English teacher Aurora can't stand, who will give her three kids and be consistently unfaithful to her. Still, Emma loves her mother and overlooks her more nagging characteristics—like constantly telling her how to lead her life. Emma's time for a little excitement comes when she meets Sam Burns, the banker, and learns

Faye Greener

she's not as unappealing as she thinks she is. But Emma dutifully follows Flap wherever his itinerant scholar's career takes him, until one day she must take a journey on her own.

See *Terms of Endearment,* **Larry McMurtry**

GREENWOOD, ESTHER

A gifted young writer trapped in 1950s America, a society that is blind to her talent and scoffs at her ambition to use it. Esther wants to write poetry, travel, and expand her mind but feels unremitting pressure to marry and become a mother and house-wife. The conflict between her desire for self-fulfill-ment and the demands of the patriarchal world eventually drive her insane. She becomes increas-ingly depressed and gradually descends into suicidal obsessions. Esther feels as though she is trapped beneath a glass bell jar, able to see a freer world but unable to breathe its air.

See *The Bell Jar,* **Sylvia Plath**

GREGG, CAPTAIN DANIEL

He's an old salty sea captain, now deceased. His ghost inhabits Gull Cottage on Schooner Bay, coexisting, against his wishes, with the Muir fami-ly. He sometimes communicates with **Mrs. Muir** through an oil painting of himself. Despite his iras-cible personality and desire to have the cottage to himself, the late captain has a good deal of fondness for Mrs. Muir.

See *The Ghost and Mrs. Muir*

GREGORY, BRIDGET

Selfish and self-absorbed, she's the ultimate bitch. But Bridget is still a joy to observe—her smoky voice and lithe limbs make her smolderingly sexy, and the obvious glee she takes in screwing over everyone she meets makes her astoundingly enter-taining. She's well versed in state-of-the-art obscen-ity and enjoys having steamy sex in public places. Ultimately, she betrays all the men in her life: she absconds with the money that husband **Mike Gregory** steals, she practices blackmail, she suborns murder, and she runs rings around a detective. She's totally amoral, but give credit where it's due: she bakes a great batch of cookies.

See *The Last Seduction*

GREGORY, MIKE

A man who'll do anything for his wife, **Bridget Gregory**, including stealing large amounts of cash. Unfortunately, his love isn't requited as he would wish it to be. The knowledge of being shafted turns him from a tenderhearted, if slightly criminal, lover into a hard-shelled, cynical avenger, who will stop at nothing to give his betrayer what she deserves.

See *The Last Seduction*

LORD GREYSTOKE

Lost in the jungle as an infant, John Clayton, the seventh Earl of Greystoke, is raised by apes and is given the name **Tarzan**. As a young man, he is dis-covered by an explorer and returned to Scotland, where he begins a difficult transition into the world of men.

See *Greystoke, The Legend of Tarzan, Lord of the Apes* and *Tarzan of the Apes,* **Edgar Rice Burroughs**

GRIFFIN, GLENN

Escaped convict and desperate individual, with very poor social skills. Likes to wave gun around in an irresponsible fashion and won't hesitate to use violence to get what he demands from others. Currently located amidst a suburban household.

See *The Desperate Hours*

GRIFFIN, JACK

Griffin is almost an albino, with a pink and white face and red eyes. After dropping medicine in favor of physics at University College, he found that "light fascinated me." He discovers that by chang-ing his body chemistry so as not to reflect, refract, or absorb light, he becomes invisible. As the Invisible Man, he is driven mad, forced to live in the world outside men. A reign of terror follows and he is betrayed and killed by confidant and classmate Dr. Kemp. "The more I thought it over, Kemp, the more I realised what a helpless absurdi-ty an invisible man was."

See *The Invisible Man,* **H. G. Wells**

GRIFFITH, DEL

A huge, bumbling, well-meaning oaf. Del's a trav-eling salesman—he sells shower curtain rings—whose Christmas Eve flight to Chicago is canceled due to snow. He hooks up with a snooty, fastidious advertising man who's also trying to get home to Chicago. The adman doesn't like Del, who first steals his cab to the airport and then takes off his shoes on the plane to air his smelly "dogs," but together they endure a series of harrowing misadventures before finally making it to the Windy City. By then, the adman has grown to love Del, whose goofy overfriendliness is really a cover for the sadness he feels at having lost his beloved wife.

See *Planes, Trains and Automobiles*

GRIFFITHS, CLYDE
A small-timer with big dreams. Suffocated by his parents' provincial evangelism, he longs for fancy clothes, pretty women, and the heady air of high society. Finally, he meets a rich girl who can make his wishes come true. Mixing love with materialism proves to be Clyde's undoing, however, as his effort to break from his old life results in two deaths, including his own.

See *An American Tragedy*, Theodore Dreiser

GRUBER, HANS
Sneering, foreign born terrorist, currently headquartered in high-tech Los Angeles office building. Interested in safecracking, money, and—when he can find a chance—sadism. Has a definite lack of holiday spirit. Not overly fond of **John McClane**.

See *Die Hard*

GRUMBY, JONAS "THE SKIPPER"
Well-meaning, oafish ship's skipper. Carries the burden of not having saved the SS *Minnow* from a wreck but retains a good sense of humor. His perennial outfit consists of white pants and blue shirt. While best pals with crewman **Gilligan**, or "little buddy," he can get bossy. The Skipper hopes to rebuild the ship and get off the island. He reveres the **Professor**, has a lust-fear relationship with **Ginger**, and has a liking for **Mary Ann**. Bunks with Gilligan. Constantly disappointed with Gilligan's antics. "Oh, Gilligan, not again!"

See *Gilligan's Island*

GRUNICK, TOM
Good-looking television news anchor who's as shallow and dumb as he is handsome. Irresistible to broadcast executives for his telegenic appeal and producer **Jane Craig** for his sex appeal. Grunick

knows only one thing in life—how to look good on-camera. His intelligent appearance is belied by almost anything he says that isn't scripted. If need be, can command tears at will.

See *Broadcast News*

GRUSSINSKAYA
This unhappy, world-weary ballerina checks into the Grand Hotel to escape fate and fans. In her loneliness, she finds companionship in fellow hotel guest **Baron Felix von Gaigern**, who breaks through her remote exterior to discover the sadness and restlessness that are masked by her glamorous clothes and circumstances.

See *Grand Hotel*, Vicki Baum

GUILDENSTERN
A dapper Elizabethan courtier, Guildenstern senses that he and his companion, **Rosencrantz**, serve a function in the play *Hamlet*, but he can't figure out what it is. Not willing to accept this existential dilemma, Guildenstern seeks to solve it, initially through clever word games, and later, with increasing agitation, by way of soul-searching soliloquies. Guildenstern is so perplexed that at one point he mistakes himself for Rosencrantz. As the pair drift in and out of *Hamlet*, Guildenstern's depression deepens, and he's unable to find solace in Rosencrantz's optimism. He is proven the wiser when the two are executed for reasons beyond their control or understanding.

See *Rosencrantz and Guildenstern Are Dead*, Tom Stoppard

GUISHAR, LARISA FEODOROVNA
A beautiful survivor who can't outrun her past. Lara's life is dominated by three men: Moscow lawyer Victor Komarovsky, **Yurii Zhivago**, and her husband, Pavel Antipov, also known as Strelnikov. The inspiration for Yurii Zhivago's greatest poetry, Lara is smart, resourceful, and independent. She has two daughters, Katenka and Tania. Lara disappears in 1929; she probably dies in a Soviet labor camp.

See *Doctor Zhivago*, Boris Pasternak

GUITAR, JOHNNY
This thoughtful, quiet ex-gunslinger has traded in his gun for a guitar. There is still an element of dan-

ger in the handsome cowboy as he strums his instrument and watches his old flame, Vienna, try to fight off the railroad barons who've come to take her land. Will he put the guitar down and pick up a gun again? Or will he make music and not war?
See *Johnny Guitar*

GUMP, FORREST

Unlikely everyman from Alabama. He's devoted to his mother and the down-home wisdom she doles out. Despite a low I.Q., Forrest is, by turns, a college football star, Vietnam War hero, resourceful business entrepreneur, and folk hero to several generations. He has met with presidents, celebrities, and other historical figures. Founder and CEO of the Bubba Gump Shrimp Company. Gump enjoys running and once took off a few years for an epic cross-country marathon. He usually wears his hair in a crew cut. Enjoys telling his life story to anyone who cares to listen for a few minutes. Has lifelong affection for his grade school girlfriend, **Jenny**. His best friend in the army was **Bubba**, and he also tries to remain close to his wounded former commander, Captain Dan. A determined, caring individual whose quiet, mild-mannered ways offer an inspiration all their own. "Mama always said life is like a box of chocolates: you never know what you're going to get."
See *Forrest Gump*

GUNN, PETER

A hip, smooth, jazz-loving private investigator. Works the right side of the law, but isn't afraid to get into a scrape if he has to—even if he gets more than his share of bumps and bruises in the process. This tough guy has a soft spot for a girl named Edie—his girlfriend, who's the torch singer at his favorite nightclub, Mother's. His police contact is Lt. Jacoby.
See *Peter Gunn*

HACKENBUSH, DR. HUGO Z.

A horse doctor with a distinctive bedside manner, he's currently working at a health sanitarium despite his dubious credentials. Though others try to expose his true identity, Hackenbush's quick wit and forceful personality keep him one step ahead of his adversaries. "Either this man is dead or my watch has stopped."
See *A Day at the Races*

HACKETT, BRIAN

After washing out of NASA, Brian turned small-time Nantucket pilot. The washout didn't damage his cosmic-sized ego. He's brash, aggressive, spoiled, overconfident, and a dedicated womanizer. He's exactly the kind of guy who would steal his brother's fiancée, marry her, and then ask him for a job when she dumps him. Kind of a lovable jerk, though.
See *Wings*

HACKETT, JOE

This straight-arrow, nice-guy pilot is somewhat luckless. Sensitive Joe can't forgive his mother for leaving the family when he was a kid. His onetime fiancée was stolen away by his brother, **Brian**. He's compulsively neat, and kind of compulsive in general; in fact, his first rash act ever was proposing to his former girlfriend, **Helen Chappel**, on the eve of her wedding.
See *Wings*

HACKETT, TOD

Tod works as a set and costume designer for National Films, while he dreams of being an artist and painting a surreal masterpiece titled *The Burning of Los Angeles*. Sensitive and complicated, he is in love with **Faye Greener**, an aspiring actress who considers him "good-hearted" but sees such men of modest means "only as friends."
See *The Day of the Locust,* Nathanael West

HAGEN, TOM

Tom is the adopted son of Godfather **Vito Corleone** and *consigliere*, or counselor on matters legal and not quite legal, to the Corleone Mafia family. He's German Irish by birth, highly competent, and totally devoted to his Godfather. With his law school training (provided courtesy of Don Corleone), the thoughtful, reflective Hagen is the voice of reason and moderation when the Corleone family faces its greatest challenge. And he also serves as an effective buffer between the Corleones and other families in the ongoing strategic maneuvering for power and wealth among the members of the mob. But despite his devotion and hard work, he's never fully accepted by many in the Corleone clan, because they feel that nobody of German Irish descent can be truly Machiavellian.
See *The Godfather,* Mario Puzo

HAGAR THE HORRIBLE

A disheveled, overweight Viking who works hard at conquering and pillaging and is darn proud of it. Even though he's living and working in the ninth century, Hagar still has to deal with the taxman every year, his wife Helga is a constant nag, and he has to listen to his neighbors prattle on about their dull lives. Sort of a barbarian everyman, Hagar dreads his yearly bath, eats whatever he can find, and generally lives his life as fully and lustily as he can. He worries about his kids following in his footsteps and his simpleminded lieutenant Lucky Eddie never understands his orders. Oh, to be sacking Europe!

See *Hagar the Horrible*

HAGGEN, FESTUS

Festus comes from a long line of hill-country feuding stock, a clan who can carry on a gun-shootin' vendetta for generations. He serves as deputy to **Marshal Matt Dillon**. At one point, Festus asks Dillon to give him time off to deal with a man who's come to town to shoot his ear off: "not the whole thing, just the little hangy-down part."

See *Gunsmoke*

HAINES, GUY

He's a professional tennis player who'd love to get rid of his wife—by legal process, that is. Then he meets **Bruno Antony** on a train, who offers him a chance to realize his dream, although the means would be murder. All Guy would have to do in exchange would be to kill Bruno's dad, and both their problems would be solved. Guy has second thoughts, but Bruno goes ahead with his part of the deal. Then, when Bruno learns that Guy won't go along, Guy finds himself with a nasty-tempered psychopath on his trail.

See *Strangers on a Train*, Patricia Highsmith

HAINES, MARY

Mary is a Park Avenue wife by way of vocation. Charming and elegant, she is a step above her gossipy friends until a manicurist drops the bomb: Mary's husband is cheating on her with a perfume salesgirl. After her divorce, Mary decides to get catty and fight for the man she loves. Her explanation for her success: "I've had two years to sharpen my claws."

See *The Women*, Clare Booth Luce

HALL, ANNIE

Chippewa Falls, Wisconsin, native turned hopeful New York actress. Enjoys tennis, photography, calls them "neat." Worried she's not cerebrally equal to comedian boyfriend **Alvy Singer**. Disturbed brother Dwayne still lives with Annie's parents. Dabbles in singing; considering making it her next career move. Has an eclectic, mix-and-match attitude toward fashion. Drives beat-up convertible VW Bug like a maniac. Likes parties, meeting new people, trying new things. Not very political, easily swayed by the men in her life. "Well, la-dee-dah, Annie, la-dee-dah."

See *Annie Hall*

HALLIDAY, MARK

Successful novelist and very dear friend of **Margot Wendice**. His fiction-writing skills can prove to be useful in determining the outcome of unorthodox real-life situations.

See *Dial M for Murder*

HAMILTON, GUY

A foreign correspondent for an Australian radio network, Guy is sent to Indonesia in the midst of its revolution. He is a lanky, chain-smoking hunk with a noble bearing and an attraction to danger. Guy learns the ropes from **Billy Kwan**, a native dwarf who seems to know everybody, and falls in love with a nervy British diplomat, **Jill Bryant**.

See *The Year of Living Dangerously*

HAMMER, MIKE

He's as hard-boiled as a thirty-minute egg. The softest part of him is his front teeth. This private detective sees the world in black and white, in absolutes of right and wrong. Hammer lives and works in the zone between the forces of law and order and the denizens of the underworld. He is sometimes hailed and sometimes hated by the police for his freedom to act outside the system. He's uniformly hated and feared by those who prey on the soft underbelly of society, who know that Mike Hammer's delivery of justice is often accompanied by a dose of lead poisoning from his .45, a decision that allows no appeal. Hammer's as much at home in the city night as any of the other predators who dwell there, but he's even more deadly, because he knows how to get away with killing bad guys. With

Annie Hall

123

trusty Velda, his beautiful raven-haired secretary, he prowls the mean streets in the name of a justice that can't be bought in a crooked court of law or on the pad of a crooked cop. There are no lawyers in search of loopholes in Mike Hammer's world, at least no successful ones, because there are no loopholes in Hammer's law. There is only right and wrong. Right means you live. Wrong means you die.

See *I, the Jury,* et al., Mickey Spillane

HAMMOND, JOHN

Either a megalomaniac plutocrat or a grandfatherly old man with an interest in dinosaurs, take your pick. Either way, he's bought a little island off the coast of Costa Rica and turned it into Jurassic Park, a theme park that is home to whole herds of genetically re-created dinosaurs. Hammond, originally from Great Britain, is aware that some see the project as inherently hazardous, but he's too single-minded to pay any heed. The apples of his eye are his two bright grandchildren, Tim and Alexis.

See *Jurassic Park,* Michael Crichton

HAMMOND, REGGIE

A wisecracking, egotistical convict and—ironically—a fan of the rock group the Police. Has a knack for talking his way into and out of tight spots, though he's not above using hard words or even fists if soft words won't work. A phenomenal ladies' man in his own eyes, Hammond doesn't believe in subtlety in seduction attempts. Style-wise, prefers foreign automobiles and $500 suits. Thrown together as a temporary partner with San Francisco cop **Jack Cates**, he resents the other's personality and attacks on his character, replying, "Yeah, but I look good."

See *48 Hrs.*

HAND, LAUREL McKELVA

This daughter of the South has made a life as a successful fabric designer in Chicago. Her father's operation, and eventual death, bring her back home to New Orleans, where she comes to terms with her past and the deaths of her mother, her husband, and now her father.

See *The Optimist's Daughter,* Eudora Welty

HAND, ROLLIN

He's the ultimate master of disguise, who can look more like you than you do. He's part of an elite covert group sponsored by the U.S. government, with the not-very-impenetrable code name of Impossible Mission Force. He loves to slather his face with liquid latex and look exactly like someone else, usually a bad guy. By the way, don't try that at home. Leave it to the professionals.

See *Mission: Impossible*

HANDELMAN, IRWIN "SKIPPY"

Geek without brains. A frequent visitor to his next-door neighbors the **Keatons**, because his own family constantly rejects him. The Keatons find him incredibly stupid but put up with him because he's good-hearted. He suffers from totally unrequited love for Mallory Keaton, who would no more date Skippy than she would read a book or wear thrift-shop clothes.

See *Family Ties*

MR. HANEY

Haney is a fast-talking, con-artist salesman who travels the environs of Hooterville selling junk and phony goods out of a wooden truck to unsuspecting victims such as **Oliver Wendell Douglas**, who bought Green Acres. Has an uncanny knack for knowing when someone needs something he has. Travels with his wooden Indian, Irving Two Smokes.

See *Green Acres*

HANKSHAW, SISSY

A perfect beauty except for her monstrously oversized thumbs, Sissy Hankshaw uses her deformity to hitchhike out of her depressing hometown of Richmond, Virginia. During her hitchhiking adventures, she's hired as a model for a female deodorant spray, falls in love with **Bonanza Jellybean**, the leader of a ranch of feminist guerrillas, and learns the importance of personal freedom from a Chinese spiritualist known as **The Chink**. After Bonanza is assassinated by a government agent, she settles down on the ranch but pines for the freedom of her wayward youth: "When I was younger, I hitchhiked 127 hours without stopping—across the continent twice in six days, and cooled my thumbs in both oceans."

See *Even Cowgirls Get the Blues,* Tom Robbins

HANNAH

The consummate earth-mother, former wife of **Mickey Sachs**, and current wife of **Eliott**, the two men who've both managed to disappoint her in life. But she's seen as the stable one, the strong one, in comparison with her two sisters. Nothing pleases her more than staying home with her husband and seven children. A former stage actress and daughter of an acting couple who need as much care as Hannah's sisters.

See *Hannah and Her Sisters*

HANS AND FRITZ

These two little, wildly mischievous German brothers live with a boat captain and his wife on Dogfish Island. They run amok not only there but also on neighboring islands and even on the high seas. They are called the Katzenjammer Kids because *Katzenjammer* is German slang for "hangover."

See *The Katzenjammer Kids,* Rudolph Dirks

HARDY, FRANK AND JOE

When not aiding their father Fenton Hardy, an internationally renowned detective, or solving local mysteries of their own, the dark-haired Frank and his blond younger brother Joe attend high school in the small town of Bayport where they live with their mother and aunt Gertrude. Operating out of a home-made crime lab in their barn, the Hardy Boys solve case after case with a winning mixture of wry wit, laserlike intelligence, and unshakable poise. With the aid of their ever-faithful friend Chet Morton, the boys outwit, ensnare, and foil every assortment of evildoer, from international jewel thieves holed up in Bayport to Panamanian terrorists running guns out of Paris.

See *The Tower Treasure* and *Evil Inc.,* Franklin W. Dixon

HARDY, JOE "SHOELESS"

Out-of-nowhere phenom ballplayer for the eternal doormats of baseball, the Washington Senators, whom he takes to the top—for a brief moment. Has an unusual connection with fan **Joe Boyd**.

See *Damn Yankees*

HARMON, DR. ARTHUR

New York gynecologist who lives next door to his best friend, **Walter Findlay**, and Findlay's wife, **Maude**, in Tuckahoe, New York. Arthur was a rather hapless widower until he started dating Maude's best friend, **Vivian Cavender**, whom he later married.

See *Maude*

HARMON, VIVIAN CAVENDER

Known as Viv by those close to her, she's the bubbly, kooky best friend of **Maude Findlay** and the wife of **Dr. Arthur Harmon**. Viv lives next to the Findlays in Tuckahoe, New York, a well-to-do suburb. A frisky lover who probably wears lacy undergarments.

See *Maude*

HAROLD

A dark, brooding young man obsessed with dying and the best way to commit suicide. Harold is the scion of a wealthy family, and wealth bores him. Everything bores him in life, except for devising ever more ingenious ways to end it. Before he can actually do the deed, he meets **Maude**, an elderly woman who is full of life and shows him how to enjoy living.

See *Harold and Maude*

HAROLD

A tough, florid, snappily dressed Chicago gangster with a thick Irish brogue. While drunk, he meets **Treat**, a street punk he calls a Dead-end Kid. Harold foils Treat's attempt to rob him, and instead, befriends him and his little brother **Philip**. Together, they renovate Treat's and Philip's ramshackle old Newark house, becoming a family in the process. Harold teaches the boys a lot about life before his gangland life catches up with him.

See *Orphans*

HARRINGTON, EVE

Nee Gertrude Slochinski, the fast-rising, popular, talented, cherubic stage and movie actress left her native city of Milwaukee after being caught in an affair with a brewery manager. She came to New York City, assumed the Harrington persona, and ingratiated herself with reigning star actress **Margo Channing**. Using guile and contacts made while living with Channing, Eve becomes Channing's understudy in *Aged in Wood* and gets her big break the only time Channing fails to appear for a per-

Harold

formance. Publicly charming, Harrington is an adept manipulator who uses a combination of passive aggression and outright scheming to get what she wants, which is, eventually, to replace Channing at the pinnacle of Broadway success. Wears her hair cut short and upswept. Met her match for deviousness in her paramour, **Addison DeWitt.**

See *All About Eve*

HARRINGTON, JEAN

She's a sultry, seductive brunette, a professional card shark and gold digger, and a gifted but amateur actress. She travels with her father, conning unsuspecting millionaire bachelors out of their money. She seems coldhearted and incapable of love until she meets and falls in love with **Charles Pike.** But even in loving him she resorts to trickery and deception to get him. "Don't you know it's dangerous to trust people you don't know?"

See *The Lady Eve*

HARRINGTON, RODNEY

The handsome, stuck-up son of Peyton Place's dominating figure, the mill owner whose business keeps the town thriving. Even though he kisses **Allison MacKenzie** during her birthday party, he lusts after and loves his girlfriend, Betty. He finally stands up to his father, giving up the opportunity to go to Harvard in order to marry the girl he loves. But he comes to a tragic death in World War II.

See *Peyton Place,* **Grace Metalious**

HARRIS, JACKIE

She may be neurotic, but she means well; Jackie's life is often a mess, but that never stops her from telling everyone else how to run theirs. Still, it's her sister, **Roseanne Conner,** who thinks she knows what's right for Jackie, and the two subsequently have a very close but occasionally exasperating relationship. Jackie has run through almost as many careers as she has men, working in a factory, as a cop, and finally with Roseanne in their own restaurant. She settles down after getting pregnant and marries her son's father, not without reluctance to commit herself. She has even more problems with her mother, Bev, than Roseanne does.

See *Roseanne*

HARRIS, RON

This upwardly mobile New York City detective maintains an expensive lifestyle by turning his measly salary from the 12th Precinct into stocks and bonds. (He's constantly on the phone to his broker.) Always looking to make extra money, Harris finally capitalizes on his intelligence and erudition by writing a potboiler cop thriller called *Blood on the Badge.*

See *Barney Miller*

HARRIS, ZONKER

This burned-out, pot-smoking ex-hippie has devoted his life to hedonism. At one time he was among the foremost professional tanners in the world, rivaling even the legendary George Hamilton. Later, Zonker tries to upgrade his image by buying a British lordship.

See *Doonesbury*

HART, JENNIFER

This glamorous, witty, intelligent woman lives with her rich, devoted husband, **Jonathan Hart**—to whom she's equally devoted—in a posh Southern California mansion. With the help of their chauffeur, **Max,** they uncover and fight corruption for the government.

See *Hart to Hart*

HART, JONATHAN

Whatta guy! He's handsome, charming, sophisticated, and rich. Not only that, he's devoted to his gorgeous wife, **Jennifer Hart.** With all his wealth, he could just retire and clip coupons, but *no.* Instead, he and Jennifer work for the government, uprooting corruption in high places.

See *Hart to Hart*

HARTLEY, EMILY

Attractive and savvy, she's the better half to psychologist **Dr. Robert "Bob" Hartley.** They share a swank apartment in a tony high-rise in Chicago. Emily teaches third grade and then becomes vice-principal at Tracy Grammar School. Her maiden name is Harrison and she was born in Seattle.

See *The Bob Newhart Show*

HARTLEY, DR. ROBERT

This successful Chicago psychologist wanted to be

a professional drummer but went into psychology instead. Now he works in private practice at the Rampo Medical Arts Building, where he treats individuals as well as groups. He is married to **Emily**; they have no children. He's smart, straight-laced, humorous, and utterly unflappable—and everyone calls him Bob.

See *The Bob Newhart Show*

HARTMAN, GUNNERY SERGEANT

Hard-nosed, leather-lunged marine drill instructor stationed on Parris Island. He disdains weakness in any form. He doesn't consider himself a bigot because he abuses recruits of all races, creeds, and colors equally. He seems to take pleasure in humiliating his charges, particularly **Leonard "Private Pyle" Lawrence**. In spite of his tough-minded attitudes toward maintaining discipline, Hartman does have a rather dark sense of humor.

See *Full Metal Jacket*

HARTMAN, MARY

Sweet but slow-witted stereotypical American housewife who lives in Fernwood, Ohio. She married **Tom Hartman** when she was seventeen years old. A true naïf, she believes everything she sees on television and is obsessed with the prospect of "waxy yellow buildup" on her kitchen floor. Something is always going wrong in Mary's life: her father, George Shumway, disappears; her somewhat senile grandfather Raymond Larkin is known as the Fernwood Flasher; her daughter, Heather, is kidnapped by the town's mass murderer; her husband, Tom, is impotent but cheats on her anyway; and her best friend, Loretta, is paralyzed. She also has an affair with local cop **Dennis Foley**. She eventually suffers a nervous breakdown.

See *Mary Hartman, Mary Hartman*

HARTMAN, TOM

He is an assembly-line factory worker at an automobile plant in Fernwood, Ohio, married to **Mary Hartman**, a housewife, and the father of Heather Hartman. Tom has had a problem with impotence but has managed to rise above that complaint in order to cheat on his wife. His coworkers include his father-in-law, George Shumway, and Charlie Haggers, the husband of his wife's best friend.

See *Mary Hartman, Mary Hartman*

HARWOOD, JOYCE

Delicate blonde who is the wife of a man implicated in the murder of **Johnny Morrison**'s wife. She knows she's courting danger by falling in love with Morrison, but she senses a sensitive soul under his hard emotional armor. She is a moll with class.

See *The Blue Dahlia*

HASKELL, EDDIE

Potential used-car salesman. Goofs off at school, lies, cheats, and bullies little kids. ("Ya hear me? Now scram!") Tries to get **Wally Cleaver** to go along with his schemes, to no avail. Jealous of Wally's popularity with girls. Tries to score. Obsequious to adults, especially **Ward** and **June Cleaver**. "My, Mrs. Cleaver, might I say you look especially lovely today?"

See *Leave It to Beaver*

HATCH, MARY

The patient, long-suffering wife of **George Bailey**. If George hadn't been born, she'd have spent her life as a spinster librarian. She isn't actually aware of this fact, and she means it sincerely when she says, "George Bailey, I'll love you for the rest of my life."

See *It's a Wonderful Life*

HATHAWAY, JANE

The long-suffering, competent secretary to bank president **Milburn Drysdale**, she's the all-around gal Friday to Drysdale's biggest depositors, **Jed Clampett** and his family. Businesslike and efficient, she sports glasses and seems to live for her job. "Yes, Chief."

See *The Beverly Hillbillies*

HATHAWAY, NURSE CAROL

Lovely nurse in the emergency room at County General Hospital in Chicago. Attempted suicide by overdosing and was treated in the E.R., where she normally works. Recovered from the suicide attempt and returned to her job as charge nurse. Once dated pediatric resident **Dr. Douglas Ross**. Now engaged to Dr. John Taglieri, an orthopedic surgeon at the hospital.

See *ER*

HATTIE

A prostitute living with her twelve-year-old daugh-

OLDER BROTHERS

Wayne Arnold
Bart Simpson
Wally Cleaver
Willis Jackson
Jack Baker
Adam Trask
J. R. Ewing
Frasier Crane
Ira Buchman

ter, **Violet**, in a New Orleans brothel. Hattie hates her life and dreams of escaping but still allows her daughter to be auctioned off to the highest bidder. Hattie finally escapes by marrying a wealthy man from St. Louis, but her daughter prefers to stay where she is.

See *Pretty Baby*

HAWK

Tall, bald as a cueball, and foreboding, Hawk is a very tough, very serious dude who packs an enormous Magnum and often comes to the aid of his best pal, Boston private eye **Spenser**. Hawk knows the streets and is enough of a mercenary to play both sides; in the end, though, he'll usually side with Spenser and the underdog.

See *Spenser*

HAWKINS

Former circus clown now working undercover as court jester in hopes of overthrowing evil king. Has unusual romantic problems and amazing knack for getting into escalating intrigues. Somehow a winner despite his own worst efforts. "The pellet with the poison's in the vessel with the pestle!"

See *The Court Jester*

HAWKINS, CYNTHIA

African American operatic soprano living and working in Paris. Despite singular success in her chosen field, Cynthia refuses to let her voice be recorded for posterity. She is also missing a favorite dress. Has unusual connection with young French letter carrier **Jules**.

See *Diva*

HAWKINS, JIM

Young Jim sets out on an adventure on the ship *Hispañola* to find buried treasure on Skeleton Island. While on the cruise, he discovers his great love for the sea as well as a high level of courage. Perhaps his ability to judge character is wanting, inasmuch as he befriends the untrustworthy "Long" John Silver.

See *Treasure Island*, Robert Louis Stevenson

HAWKS, CAPTAIN ANDY

A lifelong sailor, Cap'n Andy finds his true calling as the owner of the Cotton Blossom Floating Palace Theatre—a showboat plying the Mississippi. He and his wife, Parthenia, raise their daughter, **Magnolia**, on the boat. "At night. That's when it's like a fairy tale. When the lamps are lighted; and all the people; and the band playing."

See *Show Boat*, Edna Ferber

HAWKS, MAGNOLIA

She's grown up on a showboat on the Mississippi, and she's gotten her education there. She's learned acting from the resident troupe, and cooking and spirituals from employees Queenie and Jo. Maggie's best friend is actress **Julie Dozier**. Her charm and vivacity attract the attentions of gambler-actor Gaylord Ravenal, who woos and weds her. Her daughter, Kim, follows her mother into the theater. "I love it. The rivers. And the people. And the show boat. And the life. I don't know why. It's bred in me, I suppose."

See *Show Boat*, Edna Ferber

HAYES, LINCOLN "LINC"

A ghetto kid with a criminal background pressed into service as an undercover detective on the Los Angeles police force. Like his partners **Julie Barnes** and **Pete Cochran**, Linc always feels conflicted between his new duties and being true to his "people." Usually ends up spouting black nationalist rhetoric while working to send his "soul brothers" to jail.

See *The Mod Squad*

HAYES, MADDIE

This glamorous former fashion model now runs the Blue Moon Detective Agency in Los Angeles. Her modeling career came to an end after her manager embezzled her fortune. One of the few assets left was a failed detective agency, which she was talked into saving by its principal employee, **David Addison**, now her business partner. The sexual tension between Maddie and David is always palpable, and the two finally consummate their relationship after several years of untraditional courtship. Maddie becomes pregnant with David's child but later has a miscarriage.

See *Moonlighting*

HAYWOOD, JUDGE DAN

An American judge overseeing a post-war trial of Nazi judges accused of crimes against humanity.

Seen as the symbol of fair play and the just arbiter of the rights of man, Judge Haywood bears the weight of the world with unflinching dedication to the power of reason over human deficiencies.

See *Judgment at Nuremberg*

HE-MAN

The strongest man in the universe. Well, not always. He is Adam, Prince of Eternia, but he turns into He-Man when he holds his magic sword above his head and says, "By the power of Greyskull!" He is obligated to protect the secrets of his home, Castle Greyskull, from the evil Skeletor, who has vowed to destroy him. Being the strongest man in the universe definitely helps.

See *He-Man*, Lou Scheimer and Arthur H. Nadel

HEALEY, ROGER

Bumbling astronaut. Not a brain surgeon, but very sweet and needy. Only person except **Tony Nelson** who knows who **Jeannie** really is. Loyal and true friend to both. Will conspire with Jeannie to help Tony. Bachelor who can't find a girlfriend. Wishes he could have his own genie.

See *I Dream of Jeannie*

HEARN, LIEUTENANT ROBERT

An aide and confidant to **Major General Edward Cummings**, he both admires and fears the general, and challenges his fascistic views about American society and world history. After angering his boss, he's sent off to lead **Sergeant Sam Croft**'s platoon on an impossible (and, it turns out, unnecessary) mission behind Japanese lines. A large man with an immobile face, cold eyes, and a thin, contemptuous voice, he is attractive to women, but likes few people, and can barely conceal his disgust for most of his fellow officers. Born into a wealthy midwestern family, he insisted on working his way through Harvard after a quarrel over Marxism with his father. Dismissed by college Communist friends as a bourgeois intellectual and by the general as a liberal, Hearn's dirty secret is that he, too, possesses the same desire to control others that he hates in Cummings and in Croft. He struggles—mostly unsuccessfully—against it. "He was above all the kind of man other men love to see humiliated."

See *The Naked and the Dead*, Norman Mailer

HEATH, GORDON

The wimpy estranged husband of actress **Joyce Heath**. He's suffered a fall in life and now works as a bookkeeper in a company he used to own. It has made him masochistic and whiny. He refuses to grant Joyce a divorce because he wants no one else to have her. He insists that being her husband is the only thing he'll have "'till the day I die." She's not happy.

See *Dangerous*

HEATH, JOYCE

She's a brilliantly talented actress whose career has ended because of her reputation as a jinx. Self-destructive and hard-drinking, she's taken in by **Don Bellows**, an up-and-coming architect, while he is out slumming. Joyce warns him off: "Helping Joyce Heath is like shaking hands with the devil." Joyce is tough, and changes her moods to suit her purposes. When Don's housekeeper makes her breakfast, she is surly: "I don't want any of your greasy food; give me a drink." When she chooses, she can turn on the charm and be angelic. A complex personality, she's capable of violently destructive acts as well as an occasional noble gesture.

See *Dangerous*

HEDLEY, ROLAND, JR.

A globe-trotting television news correspondent. He has filed reports from everywhere, from Washington to Beijing. But his most famous—and risky—job was a bold venture deep inside the vast and dangerous void of Ronald Reagan's brain.

See *Doonesbury*

HELPER, JERRY

A genial dentist, Jerry lives next door to **Rob Petrie** and shares his passion for Broadway plays. He's a good friend and neighbor who operates his dental practice from his house. He's married to **Millie Helper** and is the father of Janey and Freddie. Goes skiing, boating, golfing, and fishing with Rob. Once in a while, their friendship is strained when Jerry's ribbing goes too far. "Just kidding!"

See *The Dick Van Dyke Show*

HELPER, MILLIE

Screwball neighbor, nervous, worried, and disaster-prone, Millie's problems often become those of

good friend and neighbor **Laura Petrie**. She is married to dentist **Jerry Helper** ("that Jerry!") and mother of Janey and Freddie. Millie is fast-talking and well meaning. She's forever borrowing or lending something. Plain-Jane Millie is sometimes jealous of Laura's looks and glamorous friends, to say nothing of Laura's superior avocado dip. Still, she considers Laura a dear friend and thinks of her as deep. "So deep."
See *The Dick Van Dyke Show*

HENDRIX, SUSY
Attractive, blind housewife. Susy lives in a basement apartment in Greenwich Village. She's a bit timid and jumpy, and her photographer husband encourages her to be more independent, to which she replies: "Do I have to be the world's champion blind woman?" She's forced to tap her real inner resources when, left alone in her apartment, she's terrorized by a gang of criminals looking for heroin.
See *Wait until Dark*

HENKEL, AUDREY
A sexy, mysterious, bohemian downtown New York girl who seduces proper investment banker **Ray Sinclair** into road tripping with her to her hometown in Pennsylvania. There, with his help, she tries to pass herself off at a high school reunion as a conservative family woman. Unfortunately, a violent ex-boyfriend gets jealous of her new man and puts Audrey and Ray through hell. She eventually finds that yuppieism is infectious.
See *Something Wild*

HENRY
A taciturn young man whose calm, even behavior hides a casual and frequent killer. Henry's neat, clean, and works for a pest control company. He holds his crude, slovenly roommate (with whom he shares an apartment in a run-down area of Chicago) in low regard, but doesn't complain. When his roommate's sister moves in with them, Henry shows a surprising interest in her, which she interprets as sympathy. Henry's low-key demeanor and reserve are easily misread as a kind of compassionate nature, but it is this very attitude that allows him to deceive his victims. Henry is coldhearted and shows no emotion or empathy when he murders. When Henry viciously kills his roommate

after the man attempts to rape his own sister, she believes that he does it for her. Henry's complete lack of guilt or acknowledgment of the immorality of his crimes are his most frightening qualities.
See *Henry: Portrait of a Serial Killer*

HENRY, FREDERIC
American lieutenant who's a volunteer driver in the Italian Ambulance Corps during World War I. Sincere and dedicated officer who likes Italy and Italians, especially his friend Rinaldi. He falls in love with **Catherine Barkley**, a beautiful hospital nurse, and she returns his affection. Never one to shirk duty, Henry leaves Catherine, who has become pregnant, and returns to the front after recovering from a wound. Grows disillusioned with the war as the Italian Army retreats following a major defeat at the hands of Austrians and Germans. When he sees Italian enlisted men shooting officers who are separated from their troops, he senses that all the noble things in which he once believed—honor, truth, and loyalty—are lies. He and Catherine flee to Switzerland to have their baby. Misfortune follows, and Henry learns more about how cruel the world can be in its impersonality.
See *A Farewell to Arms,* Ernest Hemingway

HERMAN, PEE WEE
An adult who's definitely in touch with his inner child. A surreal combination of fastidious and funky, straitlaced and androgynous. Highlights of his daily uniform include black high-top sneakers, too-tight gray suit, and red bow tie. Noted for his nervous, high-pitched voice and his exaggeratedly girlish gait. Pee Wee loves his bicycle, a mint-condition antique accessorized with all kinds of buzzers, lights, and bells, and will travel across the country to retrieve it when it is stolen. What makes him so funny is that he's in on the joke—he knows he's a nerd, and he's not afraid to share a "wink-wink, nudge-nudge" to that effect with the audience. "I'm a loner. A rebel."
See *Pee Wee's Big Adventure*

HERZOG, MOSES
Intellectual king, emotional pawn. Cranky, brilliant, meditative adult education professor who can't get his life in order. Compulsively cerebral, he

loses himself while tying his tie in the morning and runs through a swift mental journey of the history of Western philosophy. Unfortunately, his mental prowess only serves to render him totally ineffectual. He intellectualizes too much, then acts rashly. The result: he confuses and frustrates himself. He can't get over his ex-wife and can't seem to date anyone else for very long. He just doesn't understand women: "They eat green salad and drink human blood," he complains. He's perplexed and angry about what he sees going on in the world around him and writes letters to everyone from the Governor of New York to a zoologist he met only once. He puts all the letters in his overstuffed pockets and invariably forgets to mail them. On the way to see his lawyer about gaining custody of his daughter, he hears about a child abuse case. Obsession soon gets the better of him, and he catches a train to Chicago armed with an old revolver. He doesn't shoot anyone, and he doesn't get his daughter back; he gets arrested for possessing a gun. Back in New York, Herzog heads out of town where he resolves to live a saner, better managed life and not drive himself so crazy. "If I am out of my mind, it's all right with me."
See *Herzog*, Saul Bellow

HEWES, DON
Hardworking entertainer now working with **Hannah Brown** after personal complications have forced him to find a new stage partner. He wants to make it to the top and won't stand for anything blocking his road to stardom. Good with a soft-shoe and a song.
See *Easter Parade*

HEYES, HANNIBAL
A lovable rogue with a criminal past—he was a leader of the Devil Hole Gang—he attempts to go straight with his partner, **Jed "Kid" Curry**, in 1880s Kansas; he even takes on a new name—Joshua Smith. A promised pardon by the governor never comes through.
See *Alias Smith and Jones*

HICKEY, JAMES
A fast-talking, hard-drinking traveling salesman, who could sell iceboxes to Eskimos, who seems to have undergone a sudden character change. Now he's intent on exhorting his drinking buddies, the motley, sodden crowd at Harry Hope's Saloon (where Hickey usually comes for an annual bender), to reject their comforting fantasies and embrace reality, no matter how harsh. This, he believes, will bring them true freedom. "Forget your pipe-dreams, and face the world."
See *The Iceman Cometh*, Eugene O'Neill

HICKS, DANTE
Dumpy, goateed Generation Xer working in a dumpy, suburban New Jersey convenience store. A sensitive guy, he's bothered by the fact that before she met him, his current girlfriend gave blowjobs like other girls give out sticks of gum. Wonders if he should go back to his old girlfriend, a more popular (but bitchier) girl. Loves hockey and doesn't hesitate to close the store to play roller hockey on the roof. He tries his best to ignore the drug-dealing kids hanging out in the parking lot. His best friend is **Randal**, who works in the video shop next door and who tells him he's crazy to think of leaving his current girlfriend—who else would skip an opportunity to go away to college to be near Dante? Who else willingly brings him trays of lasagna? The decision is made easier when his old girlfriend shows up at the store and has sex in the darkened bathroom with a man she believes is Dante but is in fact the recently deceased **Mr. Smith**.
See *Clerks*

HIGGINS, HENRY
An aristocratic Englishman, Higgins is a confirmed, middle-aged bachelor and an authority on the many forms and varieties of the English language. He's also the creator of Higgins' Universal Alphabet. He makes a bet with his friend Colonel Pickering that he can get slatternly Cockney flower girl **Eliza Doolittle** to speak like, and pass for, a lady of the upper classes. Thereafter, he browbeats Eliza into a total makeover, all the while remaining oblivious to her feelings. "The question is not whether I treat you rudely, but whether you ever heard me treat anyone else better."
See *Pygmalion*, George Bernard Shaw and *My Fair Lady*, Alan Jay Lerner and Frederick Loewe

HIGGINS, JONATHAN QUAYLE, III
Higgins is an enigma. English by birth, he's the

scion of a wealthy family, and yet he works as care-taker and business manager on a wealthy novelist's Hawaiian estate. Most of the time he seems stodgy, but then he suddenly shows flashes of a highly trained military mind, which suggests that his history isn't as stodgy as one might have thought.

See *Magnum, P.I.*

HILL, HAROLD

Harold Hill poses as a traveling salesman, but he's really a gifted con artist who specializes in intuiting people's deepest desires and fulfilling them. He can also make them believe they have desires they never knew about! The people of River City, Iowa, are the latest to receive his attention, and they fall for "Professor" Hill's warnings about the danger of snooker and the virtues of a student band, which will play instruments and wear uniforms he'll be happy to procure—at a price. He has a novel theory of music education, called the Think System (think of a tune and you can play it). Salesmanship strategies: talk fast, prey on fears, distract, be a moving target. And the oldest move in the book: seduce the woman who doubts your bona fides. In this case, mousy librarian **Marian Paroo**.

See *The Music Man*, Meredith Willson

HILL, HENRY

From a very early age, Hill's only ambition is to become a member of the Outfit—the Mafia. He lives out his dream, becoming a true mob dandy, with all the best cars and women. But then cocaine comes into his life, and the dream turns very sour.

See *Goodfellas*

HILLARD, DANIEL

Out-of-work actor (specialty: cartoon voices) living in San Francisco. His irreverent and playful personality gets him through life, though it can be too much for others to bear with on occasion. He's going through a painful divorce and is engaged in a bitter custody fight with his ex-wife over their three children. He has a gay older brother and a love-hate relationship with his out-of-town mother. Daniel has a day job as a television station maintenance man, though he dreams of bigger things. He moonlights in the role of a character of his own creation, **Edwina Doubtfire**.

See *Mrs. Doubtfire*

HILLYER, DADDY

A tradition-minded southern patriarch, he takes in **Rose**, a simple, sexy girl without a home. At his repressed wife's urging, he tries to discipline the girl after her overt displays of sexuality threaten the family's respectability. But he can't help but love her for her honesty and for the way she reminds him that humans are sexual animals.

See *Rambling Rose*

HILTS, "THE COOLER KING"

The coolest member of a group of Allied prisoners of war developing an ingenious plan to break out of a German maximum-security concentration camp. Smooth and cunning, Hilts passes his time in solitary confinement whacking a baseball into a glove while a tunnel to freedom is being built under his feet.

See *The Great Escape*

HINKLEY, ROY "THE PROFESSOR"

Fount of wisdom. He wears tweed jackets and button-down collars. Among his areas of expertise are engineering, meteorology, oceanography, botany, mathematics, history (including ancient civilizations), anthropology, and shipbuilding. A castaway on a desert island, his challenge is to devise a viable plan for getting off the island. Often he's thwarted by **Gilligan**.

See *Gilligan's Island*

HIX, BILLY

He's the mussed-hair sexpot in a group of seven college friends whose hangout is St. Elmo's Bar in Washington, D.C. After graduation, Billy finds it hard to grow up and accept responsibilities, even though he's married with child. Plays the sax at parties and can't forget his frat party days. When he saves his friend Jules, a cocaine addict, by telling her a little story about St. Elmo's fire, he gets a little focus in his own life. After his wife annuls their marriage, he moves to New York to pursue his music career.

See *St. Elmo's Fire*

HOBBS, ROY

This handsome midwesterner possesses quiet confidence; while his demeanor is humble and unassuming, he has complete faith in his extraordinary baseball skills. He owns a good-luck bat called

Wonderboy, made from the wood of a lightning-struck tree near where his beloved father (and baseball mentor) died. As a teenager, he goes to Chicago to try out with the Cubs, leaving behind his wonderful girl, Iris. He gets his first taste of major-league success when he strikes out the **Whammer**, a Babe Ruth–like superslugger, on three pitches. But things take a sudden, tragic turn when he gets mixed up with a crazed, star-struck woman, who shoots him in the gut before jumping out a hotel window. Twenty years go by before he gets another shot at the majors, this time with the lowly New York Knights. Hobbs quickly makes his mark—once literally tearing the cover off a ball with a hit—and leads the team to first place. But the team management has secretly bet against the Knights and hires a sultry blond siren to distract Roy and hurt his play. At the critical moment, Iris comes back into his life, setting the stage for a climactic play-off battle between good and evil.
See *The Natural*, Bernard Malamud

HOBSON, HENRY HORATIO
A boozy, belching old curmudgeon who runs his family shoemaking shop with patriarchal authoritarianism, Hobson's only ambitions are to keep the business afloat and maintain his three daughters in a state of peonage as his workers. His biggest problem is eldest daughter, **Maggie**, whose aspirations to control the shop are at odds with her father's dictatorial impulses.
See *Hobson's Choice*, Harold Brighouse

HOBSON, MAGGIE
Spirited and sharp as a boot tack, Maggie works in her father's shoemaking shop. Despite being labeled an old maid at the age of thirty, she selects slavish and timid shoemaker **Willie Mossop** to be her husband. Once married, she attempts to take over the family business, presenting her curmudgeonly and disapproving father with a "Hobson's choice."
See *Hobson's Choice*, Harold Brighouse

HOENIKKER, FELIX
Nobel Prize winner and one of the fathers of the atom bomb. He is coldly scientific—people aren't his "specialty." His conscience and humanity have been stifled by a desire to pigeonhole all of life in quantifiable classifications. He is the inventor of

"ice-nine," a form of water that freezes at 114.4 degrees Fahrenheit and eventually leads to the destruction of mankind.
See *Cat's Cradle*, Kurt Vonnegut Jr.

HOGAN, COLONEL ROBERT
A U.S. soldier held prisoner in Stalag 13, a Nazi camp headed by comically ineffectual **Colonel Klink**. A charming wisecracker on the surface, Hogan actually works at a serious, and even dangerous, business: leading his fellow prisoners in running a spying and POW-freeing network from Stalag 13, deep inside enemy lines. This doesn't mean they can't have a few laughs along the way.
See *Hogan's Heroes*

HOLDEN, GUY
A professional dancer who falls in love with the soon-to-be-divorcée **Mimi Glossop**. He tries his best to charm the prickly young woman, and his self-deprecating manner deflects her barbs. With a combination of persistence, grace, and fancy footwork, he finally woos the reluctant object of his affections.
See *The Gay Divorcée*

HOLLY
Middle America high school cheerleader who enjoys baton twirling and devouring movie magazines. Involved in passionate romance with **Kit**, even though he's murdered her father. Has a naive, wide-eyed innocence that cannot be shaken by murder or living life one step ahead of the law.
See *Badlands*

HOLM, HELEN
At Steering School, where her father is the wrestling coach, Holm meets future husband **T. S. Garp**. With Garp she has three children and becomes a college professor. She has an affair with graduate student Michael Milton that ends disastrously and tragically. "If I marry anybody, I'll marry a writer."
See *The World According to Garp*, John Irving

HOLMES, CAPTAIN DANA
This overbearing but insecure army captain wants a promotion to major at any cost and tries to exploit a new recruit in order to get it. Holmes wants **Robert E. Lee Prewitt** to join the company's box-

Johnny Hooker

ing team, the success of which will reflect creditably on him. When the young man refuses, Holmes humiliates him by ordering him to complete a series of petty, degrading details. Although he's the titular commander of his unit, it is really **Sergeant Milton Warden** whom the men respect.

See *From Here to Eternity*, James Jones

HOLMES, KAREN

The unhappy wife of **Captain Dana Holmes** conducts herself with a ladylike demeanor that hides her dissatisfaction with her unpopular husband. Icy on the outside, underneath she burns with passion and is in the midst of a torrid clandestine affair with **Sergeant Milton Warden**. There's an air of sadness and fatalism to this woman with a past, who knows that her brief spell of happiness is fated to end all too soon.

See *From Here to Eternity*, James Jones

HOLSTROM, KATRIN

The determined daughter of Swedish immigrants. Katrin brings a positive attitude to everything she undertakes and doesn't understand the meaning of the word "no." She's currently running for a congressional seat, though her political ambitions are definitely playing havoc with her personal life.

See *The Farmer's Daughter*

HOLT, LAURA

Extremely smart and competent, this Stanford grad opens her own detective agency, only to find no one trusts a woman as a gumshoe. So she invents **Remington Steele** and—lo and behold—he turns up and becomes her partner. She never loses all her skepticism about Remington, but he's a good detective and she's vaguely in love with him. She also loves chocolate.

See *Remington Steele*

HONEY

Cute, not-too-bright wife of **Nick**, a hotshot young science professor. She finds her life turned upside down when she and Nick go for drinks to **Martha** and **George**'s, where alcohol loosens far too many inhibitions and bares more ugly truths than most relationships could withstand.

See *Who's Afraid of Virginia Woolf?*, Edward Albee

HONEY

An innocent girl from Communist China who comes to America and is forever corrupted by decadent Western culture. She becomes enthralled by the drug-and-drink-soaked **Duke** and takes the position of dean of his Baby Doc Med School. She always addresses him as "sir," even while pointing out the self-serving nature of all his actions and attempting to show him the path of righteousness (to no avail). Upon her return to Communist China, her knowledge of the ways of the decadent West make her something of a love goddess.

See *Doonesbury*

CAPTAIN HOOK

A scourge of the sea, reputed to be a friend of Blackbeard the Pirate, Hook becomes obsessed with doing away with **Peter Pan** after Pan cuts off his hand and feeds it to a crocodile. The croc, for its part, would love to make a meal of the remaining parts of Hook. But Hook can always hear the beast coming, on account of the ticking of a clock it once swallowed (must be a Timex). Presumably, he's called Hook because of the hardware he wears instead of the missing hand, and what he was called when he was two-handed is not known. His right...er, left...only-hand man is his trusty bos'n, Mr. Smee. "This is no mere boy. 'Tis a fiend fighting me. A flying devil!"

See *Peter Pan*

HOOKER, JOHNNY

Aka Kelly, Johnny's a good-looking penny-ante grifter who got his start in Joliet, Illinois, under the tutelage of old-timer Luther Coburn. His perpetual adversary is Lieutenant William Snyder of the bunco squad. He has the tools of a confidence man—charm, a quick mind, a love of easy money, and a lack of morals—but the refinement that separates a two-bit operator from the elite seems to be missing in him. The extra gloss that a manicure, for example, might provide is outside his experience. He's also too much of a sucker for a pretty face, which isn't smart in his trade. Nevertheless, he is quick on his feet, and with the right training could be an excellent "big con" swindler.

See *The Sting*

HOOLIGAN, HAPPY

This pleasant, simple, prickly-headed, Irish

American tramp always wears a plaid coat and a can on his head in place of a hat. He is often in the company of his friend Professor Jones.

See *Happy Hooligan*, Fred Opper

HOOPER, MATT

Matt Hooper, enthusiastic marine biologist, has a particular passion for sharks, and comes to Amity Island at the behest of police chief **Martin Brody** after a few locals get ingested by a mysterious predator. After clashing with Amity's avaricious tradespeople, who don't like the notion that shark panic might cut into their tourist trade, Hooper allies himself with Brody and leathery veteran shark catcher **Quint** to hunt down the monstrous carnivore. Though he loves sharks in general, he's willing to make an exception of this one. He brings with him a whole arsenal of state-of-the-art shark-catching gear…but he's never seen a shark quite like this one. Live and learn…if you live to profit by the learning.

See *Jaws*, Peter Benchley

HOP SING

Houseboy and general aide-de-camp of wealthy **Ben Cartwright**, he is an indispensable member of the family. Of Chinese birth, he speaks in pidgin English but is helpful, courteous, and always available to Ben and his three sons, **Adam**, **Eric**, and **Little Joe**.

See *Bonanza*

HOPEWELL, HULGA

A highly educated, deeply embittered young woman with a wooden leg, who lives with her mother on their farm. A self-proclaimed nihilist, she believes herself morally and intellectually superior to common humanity, particularly her mother, but, without any moral or philosophical grounding, she is actually living in a spiritual void.

See *Good Country People*, Flannery O'Connor

HOPKINS, RALPH

The lonely workaholic president of the United Broadcasting Company. He's tremendously wealthy but doesn't get to enjoy it; he's estranged from his wife and daughter. His life goal is to head a committee on mental health, "a truly holy cause." He hires family man **Tom Roth**, because he

reminds him of his dead son, who knew there was "only one way to play it—straight." He has sacrificed everything, since "big successful businesses are built by men like me." His one mistake: "being one of those men."

See *The Man in the Gray Flannel Suit*, Sloan Wilson

HORNBECK, E. K.

A sardonic star newspaper columnist for the *Baltimore Herald*, he's a good reporter—and knows it. Hornbeck, in his midthirties, is a city sophisticate who sneers at all things rural and has little use or respect for orthodox religion. He can be quietly humane—when it suits his journalistic needs. "I do hateful things for which people love me, and lovable things for which people hate me."

See *Inherit the Wind*

HORRIGAN, FRANK

A tough, case-hardened Secret Service agent, he's tired and nearing retirement. His job has cost him his family life, and he spends his evening hours playing jazz piano in a bar. These days, he runs down counterfeiters and the like, but on a dark day in 1963 he failed to take a bullet for his president, and the memory haunts him still. Now the grizzled veteran has to shake off the cobwebs and remember every lost skill, because once again a madman has targeted the president for assassination! And, even more chilling, he knows all about Frank's past: "I see you standing over the grave of another dead president." Horrigan snarls back, "That's not gonna happen!"

See *In the Line of Fire*

HORROR, ROCKY

The well-developed, biologically engineered blond boy toy of **Dr. Frank N. Furter**. He reaches full sexual maturity at the age of seven hours, but her emotional development severely lags behind his/her (take your pick) physical development. Birth date: August 8, 1974. Killed during second day of life by **Riff Raff**.

See *The Rocky Horror Picture Show*

HORSHACK, ARNOLD

Idiotic but sweet Brooklyn high school student of **Gabe Kotter**. Horshack is a member of a group of

Matt Hooper

academically challenged students named the Sweathogs. He's very thin but not wiry; in fact, he hardly seems to have muscles at all. Often raises his hand in class and shouts, "Ooh, ooh, Mr. Kotter, Mr. Kotter," while squirming in his seat, which does *not* mean that he has a correct answer. He has trouble with any question, with the possible exception of "Who are you?" His laugh can clear a room. No one calls him by his first name except Mr. and Mrs. Kotter. In the old country, *horshack* means "the cattle are dying." Not very successful with girls, he wishes he were as smooth as classmate **Vinnie Barbarino**.

See *Welcome Back, Kotter*

HOSS

He's a gangster, cowboy, and rock 'n' roll star. Hoss developed his craft in the very old schools of Doo Wop, Elvis, and Orbison. Over the years he has developed a close-knit cadre of "people," including his own cosmic interpreter, Galactic Jack. Hoss is the man, the main man, rollin' over cities and makin' clean kills. Until he meets **Crow**…

See *The Tooth of Crime*, Sam Shepard

HOULIHAN, MARGARET "HOT LIPS"

She's blond and gorgeous, and there's a cauldron of sexuality simmering under her no-nonsense military facade. She's the chief nurse of the 4077th MASH (Mobile Army Surgical Hospital) unit in Korea, and she adores the army. Despite having her pick of men in the unit, she takes up with reviled **Frank Burns**, because he puts on a military front. She, like Frank, is constantly harassed by Drs. **Hawkeye Pierce**, **Trapper John McIntyre**, and **B. J. Hunnicut**. Despite her idiosyncrasies, she's a fine nurse, in every respect. The other nurses under her command respect her but also find her personally off-putting, which occasionally bothers her. She eventually marries Major Donald Penobscott but is shattered when he cheats on her.

See *M*A*S*H*

HOUSEMAN, FRANCES "BABY"

Nice Jewish girl living an overprotected life. She's rarely wanted for anything. Vacationing with family in the Catskills while preparing for college. Baby is intrigued by "forbidden" aspects of life, sexuality, and dance, which she sees personified in **Johnny Castle**.

See *Dirty Dancing*

HOUSTON, MATLOCK "MATT"

A handsome, independently wealthy private eye and the son of a millionaire oil baron. Matt moves from Texas to California to handle the family's off-shore drilling operations, but he spends most of his time doing what he really loves: detective work. He spends his leisure time as a playboy, always surrounded by beautiful babes. One of these is C. J. Parsons, a knockout attorney who helps Matt with his work. The license plate on his car reads COW-BOY1. Has a computer named Baby.

See *Matt Houston*

HOWARD, DAVID

A young, fast-talking, hotshot corporate executive who's a bit full of himself, and neurotic to boot. When passed over for a promotion that he feels he deserves, Howard confronts his boss and goes ballistic, forcing a totally unnecessary and unlooked-for reaction—his firing. He convinces himself that he's glad to be out of the corporate food chain and that it's time to take a journey, both geographical and spiritual. Together with his shy, demure wife, he sets out in a mobile home on a tour of the United States, wanting to "touch an Indian." But the plans go awry almost immediately, amidst the glitz and bright lights of their very first stop—Las Vegas, which releases hitherto-unknown destructive impulses in his wife. The hapless couple go into a tailspin, and David learns to regret the impulse that cost him his once-despised but now much-missed niche in the corporate world he'd left behind.

See *Lost in America*

HOWE, REBECCA

You'd never believe that this gorgeous woman has serious man problems. Now in her thirties, she's always falling for the wrong guy and suffering the consequences. She becomes manager of the Boston bar Cheers, where she fends off constant passes by bartender **Sam Malone**. Eventually, she warms to him. She's an easy crier and a quick drunk.

See *Cheers*

HOWELL, THURSTON, III

A millionaire, he's a shipwrecked passenger of SS *Minnow*, now stranded with the other passengers and crew on an isolated Pacific island. He speaks in a haughty Newport accent and knows little about the life of the common man. Married to Lovey, whom he couldn't live without. Dresses in casually elegant clothes, of which he has trunks full. He's been able to find a means of following the stock market and continues to live the life of privilege.

See *Gilligan's Island*

HOWLAND, PERCE

A sleepy-eyed bronco rider with mother problems and an old friend of cowhand **Gay Langland**. He's a "resident of nowhere who most often sleeps in his clothes." Perce has been rich and broke in the course of an afternoon. He rebelliously sets free the wild mustangs he rounded up with Gay at brokenhearted **Rosyln Taber**'s request. He's purty sensitive.

See *The Misfits*, Arthur Miller

HOWSER, DR. DAVID

Respected doctor, thoughtful father. Married to **Katherine Howser** and father of only child **Doogie Howser**, child prodigy. Suffered through his son's bout with childhood leukemia. Now he worries that Doogie underemphasizes the human element of medicine. Tries to show "Douglas" that, while he may be smart, he doesn't have all the answers.

See *Doogie Howser, M.D.*

HOWSER, DR. DOUGLAS "DOOGIE"

Teenage genius doctor and frustrated man-child. He graduated from Princeton at age ten, finished med school at fourteen, and is currently a resident at a Los Angeles hospital. Seems normal other than his I.Q. He has regular teenage friends, like **Vinnie Delpino**, and even a girlfriend, Wanda Plenn. Doogie likes to watch TV, see movies, and look for girls. He lives with his father, **David Howser**, also a doctor, and his mother, **Katherine Howser**. All three work at the same hospital. He occasionally develops a crush on a nurse or older woman he meets (including Nurse Curly Spaulding), which sometimes is reciprocated. Though he loves Wanda, their timing is off. Thwarted when maturity, experience, and skills don't match aspirations. Keeps a computer

journal of hopes, thoughts, and fears.

See *Doogie Howser, M.D.*

HOWSER, KATHERINE

Concerned mother and loving wife. Mother of genius teenage doctor **Doogie Howser**. Lives in comfortable suburban Los Angeles home with Doogie and husband **Dr. David Howser**. Works alongside husband and son at the hospital, to Doogie's embarrassment. Often catches Doogie in humiliating situations.

See *Doogie Howser, M.D.*

HUBERMAN, ALICIA

The beautiful, idealistic blond daughter of an imprisoned Nazi in post–World War II Brazil. Alicia falls for the conniving but suave FBI agent **Devlin** and is convinced by him to marry evil **Alexander Sebastian** to uncover Nazi secrets. She nearly dies at her husband's hands but is rescued by Devlin.

See *Notorious*

HUDSON, BLANCHE

Blanche was a movie star but suffered a crippling auto accident at the height of her career. Now she's confined to a wheelchair and totally at the mercy of her deranged sister, ex–child star Baby Jane Hudson. The two share a decrepit mansion in Los Angeles. She's always let Baby Jane think the car accident was Jane's fault, when in reality she herself was to blame.

See *Whatever Happened to Baby Jane?*, Henry Farrell

HUDSON, JANE

A spoiled-rotten child star trapped in a spinster's body. She dyes the ringlets of her hair cherry-red and wears too much make-up. Fantasizing about when she was a famous tyke, she likes to play dress-up and sing kiddie songs. Jane has a bad drinking problem, and, savagely jealous of her invalid ex-movie-star sister, **Blanche**, enjoys dreaming up new methods of torture: "What are you now, you old cripple? Let's see you dance around and show off how pretty you are. Let's see you do it now!" She's apt to serve Blanche dead animals on a lacquered lunch tray. She's become an expert at forging her sister's signature and mimicking her voice over the telephone, and has methodically cut wheelchair-bound Blanche off from the rest of the world. She

CONFIRMED BACHELORS

Archie Andrews
Bruce Wayne
Gilligan
Jack Tripper
Major Roger Healey

drives her sister's old gray coupe, heavy on the pedal. Guilt-ridden and moody, with "a fever in the eyes," she's mean and deadly with a hammer on occasion. She likes to recall what her beloved Daddy told her: "You can't ever lose your talent. Once you're born with it, you have it all your life long."

See *Whatever Happened to Baby Jane?*, Henry Farrell

THE HUMAN TORCH

Johnny was his name, until flame became his game. He's the brother of Sue Richards, the wife of brilliant but irresponsible scientist Reed Richards. This guy experimented on his friends and family and got them squirted by a bunch of gamma rays, so they all mutated. With friends like this, you don't need enemies. In Johnny's case, the rays gave him the power to set himself on fire whenever he wants. Somehow, he's turned this power into a weapon in the never-ending fight against crime. In this crusade, he works along with his sister, now known as **The Invisible Woman**, **Mr. Fantastic**, and **the Thing**. "Flame on!"

See *The Fantastic Four*

HUMBERT, HUMBERT

A middle-aged intellectual whose quest for eternal innocence manifests itself as a passion for young girls between the ages of nine and fourteen, particularly twelve-year-old Dolores Haze. He marries her mother as a way to be near her; when her mother dies, Humbert takes the girl, now renamed **Lolita**, on a journey across America. Betrayed by Lolita when she leaves him, Humbert murders his successor, Clare Quilty.

See *Lolita*, Vladimir Nabokov

HUME, CHARLIE

This experienced newspaperman is the managing editor of the *Los Angeles Tribune,* under owner-publisher **Margaret Pynchon**, and boss of city editor and old friend **Lou Grant**. He does his work professionally and is often called upon to be a buffer between Mrs. Pynchon and the outspoken Grant.

See *Lou Grant*

HUNNICUT, CAPTAIN B. J.

He replaces **Trapper John McIntyre** as a surgeon in the 4077th MASH (Mobile Army Surgical Hospital) unit and also as **Dr. Hawkeye Pierce's** best friend and chief coconspirator. B.J. is a low-key personality but also a gleeful practical joker. He joins happily in torture of tentmate **Frank Burns**. "Beej" is a devoted husband and father and is well liked in the unit. He has a true heart of gold and has "adopted" a Korean family. He is, however, a little competitive with Hawkeye.

See *M*A*S*H*

HUNT, LAURA

This classy young "bachelor girl" evolves from a gawky Colorado Springs kid into a gracious, sophisticated New Yorker. Shunning Park Avenue, she keeps a brownstone on East 62nd Street. Laura works in advertising, "a man's job, with a man's worries," and roots for the Brooklyn Dodgers. She's kind, generous, and values her privacy. When she's found dead in her home, Detective **Mark McPherson** investigates her murder. The more he learns about her, the more fascinated with her he becomes. But there's a big surprise in store for him as far as Laura is concerned—something remarkable enough to stun a case-hardened New York cop.

See *Laura,* Vera Caspary

HUTCHINSON, KEN

A plainclothes police detective in Southern California, Hutch—as everyone calls him—is a tough cop with a tender heart. He is absolutely devoted to his rougher partner, **Dave Starsky**, a bachelor, and once acted as a disadvantaged youth's Big Brother.

See *Starsky and Hutch*

HUTCHINSON, TESSIE

A model wife and mother, Tessie is a well-known and popular woman who participates fully in the community life of her tradition-bound village. However, she shows a different, and less cooperative, side on the occasion of the traditional lottery the town holds each year on June 27.

See *The Lottery,* Shirley Jackson

HUXLEY, DAVID

Shy, bookish, hopelessly buttoned-down paleontologist engaged for the moment to demure though controlling Miss Swallow. Through circumstances beyond his control, now trying desperately to cope with chaotic changes brought on by **Susan Vance**, which have upset his usual decorous existence.

See *Bringing Up Baby*

THE HUXTABLE FAMILY

The Huxtables live in a comfortable New York brownstone. They're a large African American family with enough fun and love and money to go around. Heathcliff is a loving husband, a fair but firm-handed father, and a caring obstetrician. Claire is a lawyer who spends a great deal of time happily taking care of their five kids and working. Fortunately for her, Heathcliff loves to cook and loves to romance his wife. His office is also in the basement, which means he has more time to be at home with the kids. The Huxtables raise their kids to look for the good, be fair, and be honest. Though all the relationships in the Huxtable house are good, problems arise now and then. Claire and Heathcliff try to let their children learn for themselves. Eldest **Sondra** is gentle and quite smart. She studies at Princeton and follows a predictable track toward success until she meets and marries somewhat goofy **Elvin Tibideaux**. **Denise** is fiery and unpredictable, beautiful like all the Huxtable women. After a year of college, she drops out and goes to Africa, only to return with husband and step child. She gets along best with her younger brother Theo, who dislikes school and looks for girls. His parents keep their eyes on him. Like her sister Sondra, Vanessa is a serious student and a high achiever. She likes Theo's friends a lot (they're boys), and does a good job of managing the sibling rivalry between Denise and Theo. The littlest child, Rudy, is the sweetheart of the family. She and her dad spend time together cracking jokes.

See *The Cosby Show*

HYATT, ALICE

A recent widow, Alice moves from New Jersey to Phoenix, Arizona, with young son Tommy in tow, dreaming of a new life. Her ambition is to make a living as a singer, but instead, Alice ends up waitressing at Mel's Diner for the minimum wage of $2.90 an hour, plus tips. Alice does the best she can to juggle a job and a precocious twelve-year-old, and still sings now and then (usually in a piano bar, with all her friends in the audience) and dates (usu-ally men who come into the diner). Her fellow waitresses, **Flo Castleberry** and **Vera Gorman**, are also her closest friends, and their nemesis (and occasional buddy) is diner owner **Mel Sharples**.

See *Alice* and *Alice Doesn't Live Here Anymore*

HYDE, CAPTAIN BOB

Tightly wound American soldier fighting in Vietnam. Grows insanely jealous of wife **Sally Hyde** and does not want her to so much as talk with other men while he's gone. Disapproves of her working in disabled-vets' hospital. Known to go completely berserk when things don't go his way.

See *Coming Home*

MR. HYDE

Snarling beast of a man, currently terrorizing London by night. Rather hirsute, with long, unmanicured fingernails and unusually sharp canine teeth. Definitely a hothead, he can be extremely bad-tempered and doesn't give a hoot about social skills. Is the alter ego of **Dr. Jekyll**.

See *Dr. Jekyll and Mr. Hyde*, Robert Louis Stevenson

HYDE, SALLY

Mousy, well meaning, and initially naive, she's the wife of Vietnam hero **Captain Bob Hyde**. Likes maintaining a calm status quo, though she's interested in expanding her limited horizons. A volunteer at the local veterans' hospital. Despite loyalty and love for her husband, Sally is involved with embittered disabled war veteran **Luke Martin**.

See *Coming Home*

I

A truth-seeker and a truck driver. He's an unmarried man whose last two relationships "degenerated into power struggles." I is a former idealist who failed in his approach to working with abused children. He lives reclusively in his grandfather's cabin on a lake until, restless and disenchanted, he feels the urge to move on. After dining with an old friend, he hops on a plane to Peru to search for a prophetic 600 B.C. manuscript containing insights into the mysteries of life. There, he discovers the Ninth Insight at the Celestine ruins and learns how to raise his rate of vibration. I believes in spiritual evolution and wonders "how human culture will change as the overall energy level rises."

See *The Celestine Prophecy,* James Redfield

IGNATOWSKI, "REVEREND" JIM

A poster boy for the antidrug movement, Jim is a burnout who took massive quantities of drugs in the sixties, with the result that the seventies, eighties, and nineties have become a blur. During flashes of consciousness, he works as a cabdriver for the Sunshine Cab Company in Manhattan. He lives in a condemned building downtown until a wrecking ball crashes through his wall and suggests that it might be time to move on. But he's capable of an occasional intuition of great insight, which, when decoded, proves to be valuable. He's got a unique palate; his favorite lunch is Spaghettios and herring. He's a sweet and loyal friend and one of the few people in the world that can handle being around **Louie De Palma.** "Ho-o-okey doke."

See *Taxi*

IGOR

The pop-eyed hunchbacked assistant to **Dr. Frederick Frankenstein** insists that his name be pronounced *EYE-gore.* He has a hump—of which he is apparently unaware—that shifts from one side of his back to the other. His lack of attention to his work leads to catastrophic results and demonstrates that sometimes a brain would have been a good thing to waste.

See *Young Frankenstein*

THE INCREDIBLE HULK

Mean, green, and not too bright. The alter ego of **Bruce Banner** is given to violent rages when the sun goes down or simply whenever the urge hits him. Wears a ripped verson of whatever Bruce had on.

See *The Incredible Hulk*

INVISIBLE MAN

This invisible man is a talented young black man in twentieth-century America, and thus, while he's quite visible physically, he lives beneath the social vision of white people. He tells the story of his life from the brightly lit rooms he inhabits in the abandoned basement of a "whites only" building on the edge of Harlem. His life is a string of disjointed, slightly surrealistic experiences—as valedictorian of his high school class in the South, as a disoriented student in a "Negro" college from which he is eventually expelled, as a factory worker in New York City, and as a rising figure in Harlem left-wing politics. His life is marked by various crises of racial and individual identity, but through these experiences he eventually achieves self-awareness, summed up in his self-description: he realizes that black skin in American society makes one "invisible" to white eyes. What finally forces him to give up on politics is a climactic race riot in Harlem, in which he observes the destructiveness and futility of black nationalism and the failure of doctrinaire Communist attempts to reform society. He retreats to utter invisibility in an underground sewer, which he furnishes and lives in while writing his memoirs. While his life in the sewer is severely limited, he ultimately achieves one thing he could not in the outside world: his consciousness of the social phenomenon of "invisibility" has provided him with the possibility for freedom of personal action.

See *Invisible Man,* Ralph Ellison

INVISIBLE WOMAN

Sue Richards is the beautiful and intelligent wife of scientist Reed Richards. This lucky woman's husband decided to make her one of his experimental guinea pigs (along with himself, it should be noted). As a result, she was utterly slathered with dangerous gamma radiation. Consequently, she now has the power to make herself invisible whenever she wishes. Whenever Reed (**Mr. Fantastic)** has an idea for a new experiment, she is nowhere to be found.

See *The Fantastic Four*

IRONSIDE, ROBERT

A bullet from a hit man's gun has left this powerful man confined to a wheelchair. However, though he's had to give up his post as chief of detectives of the San Francisco Police Department, Ironside has remained attached to the force as a special consultant. As such, he's still a scourge of evildoers, using his formidable intellect to find and bring to justice any number of menaces to society.

See *Ironside*

IRONSON, LOUIS

Opinionated, overly analytical, angst-ridden boyfriend of **Prior Walter,** who leaves him for Joe,

an uptight law clerk and confidant of Roy Cohn. Louis works as a word processor in the appeals court and drives his friends crazy with his never-ending moral suffering and discourses on history.
See *Angels in America,* Tony **Kushner**

MRS. ISELIN

She may be the ultimate nightmare mom. Coldly, she manipulates and uses her son, Sergeant **Raymond Shaw**, Korean war hero and Medal of Honor winner, as well as her doltish second husband, rabid, Red-baiting Senator John Iselin. She herself appears to be a superpatriot of the farthest right wing, but she's got an agenda that others are unaware of. With a mother or wife like this, you'd need decades of analysis, and it still probably wouldn't be enough. "When I take power, I will grind them into the dirt for what they've done to you, Raymond."
See *The Manchurian Candidate*

ISUZU, JOE

Also known as the Liar. Prone to gross exaggeration. Once told his teacher that a dinosaur ate his homework and hasn't been able to stop since. Landed a great job as a spokesperson for a Japanese car company by—what else—lying.
See *Isuzu*

IVERS, MARTHA

A wealthy, corrupt, and greedy heiress who controls an entire town. She is a murderess who saw an innocent man executed for her crime, and she lives in fear that her secret will surface. Always beautifully coiffed and dressed, she marries a weak man whom she bullies and ridicules. Her paranoia and fear of losing her wealth steadily chip away at her reasoning.
See *The Strange Love of Martha Ivers*

JACK

A harried househusband who stays home to tend to the house and family while his wife commutes every day to her high-powered business job. In the process of leading a domestic life, he undergoes a series of brutal lessons about just how accurate the phrase "slaving over a hot stove" really is.
See *Mr. Mom*

THE JACKAL

An expert international assassin who almost always gets his man. Little is known about him by any police authority. He is blond, impeccably groomed, and probably British. The Jackal is rumored to have hastened the demise of Trujillo, dictator of the Dominican Republic, in 1961. He'll go to any lengths to finish a job, assuming new identities and killing people who get in his way. The Jackal reportedly receives $500,000 per hit. Tax free.
See *The Day of the Jackal,* Frederick **Forsyth**

JACKSON, ARNOLD

Cute and energetic, but with his share of street-smarts and mischievousness, chubby-cheeked, pint-sized Arnold moves from Harlem to Park Avenue with his older brother, Willis, when his mother dies and her employer, **Philip Drummond**, adopts him. His hobbies include model railroads and a video game named Space Sucker. Pets are a goldfish named Abraham and a cricket named Lucky. He likes to hang out at Hamburger Heaven. "What you talkin' about!"
See *Diff'rent Strokes*

JAMES, MICHAEL

A charming British magazine editor living in 1960s Paris who can't commit to his girlfriend and bounces from one farcical seduction to another. James seeks the help of **Dr. Fritz Fassbender** to overcome his compulsion for seduction. "You know, in a certain light, I'm almost handsome."
See *What's New, Pussycat?*

JAMISON, RUTH

A "sweet-to-the-bone" girl from Valdosta, Georgia, and co-owner of the Whistle Stop Cafe. Everyone falls in love with her at first sight, especially wild girl **Idgie Threadgoode**. Soft-spoken and shy, Ruth has light auburn hair and brown eyes with long lashes. A born nurturer, she takes care of folks, and is given to prayer. In an effort to get Idgie off her mind, she marries wife-beater Frank Bennett. But, after one black eye too many, she finds the strength to leave Frank for Idgie. She bears a son, blond Buddy, Jr., (named after Idgie's beloved dead brother), known as "Stump" after he loses an arm in an accident. She's diagnosed with cancer, and doesn't linger long, because she "knows when to leave the party."
See *Fried Green Tomatoes at the Whistle Stop Cafe,* Fannie **Flagg**

JANSEN, IRENE

Trial-watcher with more than a passing interest in the **Vincent Parry** case. She's having an affair with **Madge Rapf's** husband, Bob, though at the same time, she's falling hard for Vincent. Irene has a good eye for intrigue and knows her way around the law when it really counts.

See *Dark Passage*

JARRETT, BETH

A wife and mother whose drive for perfection in herself and her family won't let her acknowledge that anything is wrong when her eldest son dies and her younger son attempts suicide. Her flawless attire, spotless house, and unflappable, unbreakable veneer are the outward marks of a cold woman who views sympathy and tragedy as weaknesses.

See *Ordinary People*

JARRETT, CODY

A psychopathic gangster driven to a life of crime by his mother, on whom he develops an unhealthy fixation. An epileptic, homicidal maniac, he avoids being sent to prison for murder by taking the rap for a lesser crime. He abuses his unfaithful wife, who can never live up to his mom. He's tough, smart, and perceptive but wildly unpredictable. Being betrayed by one of his gang members and deceived by his cellmate in jail fuels Jarrett's sense of paranoia and hostility. When he hears of his mother's death, he goes crazy, and his subsequent hysterical rampage ends in an apocalyptic finale.

See *White Heat*

JARRETT, CONRAD

A sensitive young man tortured by the death of his beloved older brother.

Jeannie

Conrad always lived in the shadow of his brother, and now his life is ruled by guilt, low self-esteem, and the fact that his mother doesn't love him. Unable to cope with the pain of his therapy, Conrad finally learns to confront himself and the truth about his family.

See *Ordinary People*

JARRETT, MA

She's the ringleader of a group of gangsters and leads her son **Cody** into a life of crime. There's an oddly close relationship between the two that suggests something deeper than mother and son. She's old, but she's sharp and her death sends Cody over the edge into madness.

See *White Heat*

JASON

This teen-killing psychopath hides his identity behind an ever-present white hockey mask. Jason is apparently unstoppable by anything thrown in his way. He has a knack for staying hidden until just the right moment. His true passion is for chain saws, though other sharp implements such as knives, hatchets, and axes also satisfy his need for means to his grisly ends. Reports of his death have often turned out to be exaggerated.

See *Friday the 13th*

JAWS

A burly enforcer who has made a career out of working for enemies of **James Bond.** As if being seven-foot-two, massive, and seemingly impervious to pain weren't enough, Jaws is equipped with a gleaming permanent set of razor-sharp steel dentures capable of biting through a thirty-cent steak. In addition to allowing him to slash his meat budget, the choppers provide him with a formidable weapon.

See *The Spy Who Loved Me,* Ian Fleming

JAYMES, ED

Has discovered that if he lets his friend Frank do all the talking, things work out just fine. Rumored to be the brains behind the successful wine cooler product he co-owns with **Frank Bartles.** Wears a baseball cap.

See *Bartles & Jaymes Wine Coolers*

JEANNE

Fleshy twenty-year-old Parisian heiress. Her sensuality affirms her sexual nature: she views sex with a stranger more as an intriguing proposition than a risky endeavor. Engaged to Tom, a documentary-film maker. Instrumental in the death of **Paul**, an American she allowed to sodomize her.

See *Last Tango in Paris*

JEANNIE

Innocent, trusting, remarkably well preserved ancient genie from Baghdad. Born in 64 B.C., she doesn't look her age. An energetic, ebullient blond who dresses in pink and magenta belly-dancer garb but never exposes her belly button. Ample cleavage. Can perform magic with a cross of her arms and a blink of her eyes. She's the only genie in Cocoa Beach, Florida. Jeannie tries to help her adored master, astronaut **Tony Nelson**, and his friend **Roger Healey**. But her "help" usually leads to trouble for them, from which she generally manages to extricate them. Sleeps in a small, jeweled bottle, into which she disappears when she's mad. Also, she doesn't photograph. At all.

See *I Dream of Jeannie*

JEEVES

Jeeves is the epitome of the imperturbable, impeccably mannered, resourceful gentleman's gentleman, or valet, to featherbrained **Bertram Wooster**. He's loyal, discreet, and understands fully his employer's mental shortcomings. He carefully, if unsuccessfully, tries to steer his master away from what he correctly perceives as pitfalls, whether it's baby-sitting a distant cousin or merely choosing the right suit for the evening. When Wooster gets into a bit of a sticky wicket, Jeeves exhibits his behind-the-scenes ability to rescue Wooster from these scrapes. He is especially aghast at his employer's occasional notions to marry, for Jeeves knows that, should Wooster ever take a wife, Jeeves's position as the *de facto* head of the household will be forfeit, and with it will go Bertie's comfortable life. He is a member of the Junior Ganymede Club for gentlemen's personal gentlemen, where he is able to keep abreast of gossip from other households, which he often puts to good use in the service of his employer.

See *The World of Jeeves*, P. G. Wodehouse

JEFFERSON, GEORGE

This loudmouthed, self-made millionaire is something of a legend in his own mind. A black man from humble beginnings, he turns a small dry-cleaning business into a small empire. Newly wealthy, he's able to move his family "on up" from Queens to the East Side of Manhattan, into a "deluxe apartment in the sky." Maybe his pompousness is a defense mechanism for sensitivity about his short stature, for which he tries to compensate by being as loud and noticeable as possible. He's very excitable and distrusts whites (at the top of his voice) and prefers not to deal with them. Deal with them he must, however; his son Lionel's fiancée is the child of an interracial marriage. George is always giving her white father, Tom Willis, grief. He tolerates Tom's wife, Helen, but can't imagine why she married him. He's vain about his money and will brag about it to anyone in earshot. George has come to equate wealth with importance and even wisdom. He loves his wife, "Weezy," but his boasting and tantrums drive her up the wall.

See *The Jeffersons*

JEFFERSON, JACK

While on his way to becoming the first black heavyweight boxing champion of the world, Jefferson always smiles. But after he wins the title, his smile disappears. He becomes a target for bigots in both the white and black communities, who want him to end his relationship with his white lover, **Eleanor**. The law and boxing promoters conspire to wrest his title from him. Jefferson leaves America to avoid imprisonment on a trumped-up charge but can find little happiness anywhere else. "I ain't fightin' for no race. I ain't redeemin' nobody. My mama told me Mr. Lincoln done that. Ain't that why they shot him?"

See *The Great White Hope*

JEFFERSON, LOUISE "WEEZY"

Wife of millionaire **George Jefferson**. Thanks to George's success in business, she's lived an upwardly mobile life, but she hasn't forgotten her roots or her down-to-earth values. Sure, she likes having money, and the good things in life aren't too hard to take, but Weezy still hasn't lost touch with her sense of proportion or her common sense.

See *The Jeffersons*

TRADEMARK SAYING

I'll be back!—The Terminator

Jenny

JEFFRIES, J. B. "JEFF"

A hotshot, globe-trotting photographer who gets a major case of cabin fever when confined to his Manhattan apartment with a broken leg. He dates the gorgeous and sexy **Lisa Carol Freemont** but is still keeping her at arm's length, despite her desire for a real commitment. To relieve his boredom while bedridden, he begins studying the occupants of the apartments across the courtyard, using his reliable telephoto lenses. Jeff isn't much bothered by the ethics of his spying, which in effect makes him nothing more than a Peeping Tom. After a time, he begins to suspect that one of the neighbors has committed a murder, and his little pastime takes on sinister, and even dangerous, overtones, as he and Lisa try to pursue an investigation. It turns out that life can have its share of excitement even when one is wearing a cast from toe to hip.

See *Rear Window*

DR. JEKYLL

A repressed Victorian doctor interested in duality of the human mind, he's sexually frustrated over the delay of his upcoming marriage. While he has lofty intellectual ideas, he's willing to take unprofessional risks to test his theories in a less-than-safe, and less conventional, fashion. A budding chemist with an interest in mood-altering mixtures, Jekyll has a close bond with **Mr. Hyde**.

See *Dr. Jekyll and Mr. Hyde*, Robert Louis Stevenson

JELLYBEAN, BONANZA

The uncompromising but romantic leader of a band of feminist rebels which has taken over a western cattle ranch. Along comes a hitchhiking wanderer named **Sissy Hankshaw**, whose astonishing beauty and quest for personal freedom make Bonanza fall head over heels in love. Bonanza preaches to her naive new lover and her followers on the ranch that every woman should be free to realize her fantasies and avoid the trap of heterosexual marriage. When the last remaining flock of whooping cranes appears at the ranch, an armed conflict develops between the feminists and the federal government, which culminates in the assassination of Bonanza.

See *Even Cowgirls Get the Blues*, Tom Robbins

AUNT JEMIMA

A throwback to the Old South, her dignity is still intact thanks to her impressive talents in the kitchen. Wears kerchief on her head. Has a beautiful smile. Loves pancakes.

See *Aunt Jemima*

JENNY

Lifelong friend of **Forrest Gump**. She was sexually molested by her father, which haunts her throughout her life. She has some college education and is involved with the anti–Vietnam War movement. She's also had problems with substance abuse and has considered suicide, though she's been able to work through these problems. Jenny, who dreams of becoming a singer, floats in and out of Forrest's life, though she is always at her happiest when she's with him.

See *Forrest Gump*

JENNY

Young, enigmatic, and extremely attractive—so attractive that one obsessed man rates her an 11 on a 10-point beauty scale. She's prone to wearing revealing clothing and knockout swimwear, and her hairstyle features cornrows and lots of beads. Ravel's Bolero is Jenny's musical aphrodisiac of choice.

See *10*

JENSEN, MOLLY

A faithful woman who loves her man, **Sam Wheat**, and mourns when he is killed way before his time. She transforms vase-making into an erotic act. With the help of psychic **Oda Mae Brown**, she contacts Sam in the afterlife. Finally, through Oda Mae, Sam speaks the words she's always wanted to hear: "I love you"—proof that there is such a thing as undying love.

See *Ghost*

JEROME, EUGENE

Jerome is suffering from an extreme case of puberty. All of his time is spent either in school, where he cannot bring himself to talk to girls, on the beach, where he can look at girls (but still can't talk to them), or at home, trying to get his older brother, Stanley, to tell him about girls. His beautiful cousin Nora is living with them. He thinks he's in love.

See *Brighton Beach Memoirs*, Neil Simon

JEROME, EUGENE

Nice Jewish boy from Depression-era Brooklyn. Keenly aware of ethnicity, whether in fights with family, serving his country in Biloxi, Mississippi, or working on his fledgling comic theatrics. Razor-sharp tongue, occasionally kept in cheek. Also possesses wry sense of self when situations get out of hand.

See *Broadway Bound*

JERRY

Boyish, clean-cut, nervous 1920s bass fiddler. He agrees to assume a female persona (Daphne) in order not to be deprived of the further use of his life by a hit man. But the job that comes along with it, of playing in an all-girl band, proves to have a downside as well as a few positive features, especially for a man who has an eye for a good-looking young lady. His bass fiddle has four bullet holes in it. A confidant of **Sugar Kane**.

See *Some Like It Hot*

JESSUP, COLONEL

Marine commander of the American base at Guantánamo Bay, Cuba. The colonel is a loyal military man who will not tolerate weakness in the troops or assaults on the corps by outsiders. Enjoys his cigars and his liquor. A smooth talker who tends to play his cards close to the vest when he feels it necessary. He can be quite amusing, though he often uses his charm to veil more sinister aspects of his personality. When forced to the wall, he can be downright brutal. "You can't handle the truth!"

See *A Few Good Men*

JETSON, ELROY

This futuristic kid is obsessed with technology. He likes to invent gadgets, but his inventions are seldom successful, and often messy. He wears a strange beanie on his head and likes to play with his dog, Astro. Elroy admires and respects his dad, **George Jetson**, and wishes he could spend more time with him.

See *The Jetsons*

JETSON, GEORGE

Good-hearted patriarch of a retro-style Space Age family. He's devoted to "his boy **Elroy**, daughter **Judy**, and **Jane**, his wife." Work pressure doesn't seem to have lessened any in the future, however, and he's often torn between his job and his family. If he could choose (which he can't always), he'd prefer to make his family happy. But his domineering boss, **Cosmo G. Spacely**, is very hard to please, and equally hard for George to stand up to. George tries to please everyone and often succeeds, though not without a struggle.

See *The Jetsons*

JETSON, JANE

Jane is the attractive and supportive wife of **George Jetson**. She's basically a space hausfrau, though her load is lightened by her maid, Rosie the Robot. She's usually upbeat and happy and is given to giggling. She's also a good and attentive mom, who really listens to her teenage daughter, **Judy**, and small son, **Elroy**. She is a stylish dresser.

See *The Jetsons*

JETSON, JUDY

Okay, she's a cool space chick, but Judy is also a fairly typical teenage girl. She's interested in boys, her looks, popularity, and makeup and spends a lot of time in front of her mirror. Judy basically gets along with her family, but she's at that age when they don't always understand her. She finds her young brother, **Elroy**, a pest but loves him anyway.

See *The Jetsons*

JIM

He is the quintessential troubled youth, whose sideburns and short, brushed-back hair are emblems of his 1950s cool. A sullen, confused teenager, his troublemaking forces his family to make frequent moves. Though handsome and sexy in a vulnerable way, he lacks the words to describe his pain. So what's wrong with him, exactly? It seems to be the standard my-parents-just-don't-understand-me angst. New to L.A., he befriends **Judy** and **Plato**, two other rebellious teens. Attracted to the pretty Judy, he impresses her by the way in which he establishes that he's cool among his new peers: by standing up to Judy's boyfriend, agreeing to play a version of chicken involving jumping out of speeding automobiles as close as possible to the edge of a cliff. The game has tragic results for the boyfriend, but Jim inherits Judy as his girl, and they team to protect the fragile Plato—

The Jetsons

it's the three of them in a doomed fight against the adult world.

See *Rebel Without a Cause*

THE JOAD FAMILY

They're Okies—folks who leave the drought-stricken midwestern Dust Bowl in search of a better life in milk-and-honey California during the Depression. Tom, the son, is recently out of jail after serving time for killing someone in self-defense. He returns to the family's Oklahoma farm to find they've picked up and headed West. With kind, upright, ex-preacher **Jim Casey**, he heads after them. They hook up with the rest of the family, who are traveling in a ramshackle old truck with all their belongings. It's a tough, dangerous trip—the Joad grandparents fail to survive it—and when they get to California, there's no pot of gold at the end of that particular rainbow. There are the haves and the have-nots, and the haves don't want to part with what they've got. Tom's family suffers more losses and disaster, and Tom is witness to countless examples of man's inhumanity to man, as well as the occasional redemptive act of kindness. Preacher Casey decides that the only moral response to what is going on is to preach a new text: unionize and fight for your rights. Tom then follows his lead.

See *The Grapes of Wrath,* **John Steinbeck**

JOE

Alcoholic executive married to **Kristen**. Usually drunk, though he doesn't think he has a problem with the stuff; booze, he believes, makes him happier. He's starting to show significant physical and emotional effects from a lifetime of drinking.

See *Days of Wine and Roses*

JOE

During the Civil War, the mysterious, cheroot-smoking Man with No Name (whose name is Joe) finds himself entangled in a dubious relationship with Mexican bandit **Tuco**, searching for a Confederate treasure chest full of gold. As he and Tuco get more drawn into the war, Blondie (another name for the Man with No Name, who actually has two names) remarks, "I've never seen so many men wasted so badly." Joe, a terrific shot, is the only one who knows in which grave the gold is buried, and both Tuco and another ugly character, bounty

hunter **Setenza**, must keep him alive to learn his secret. "I'll keep the money. You can have the rope."

See *The Good, the Bad and the Ugly, A Fistful of Dollars,* **and** *For a Few Dollars More*

JOE

Happy-go-lucky Prohibition-era saxophonist who doesn't shrink from betting the rent money at the dog track. Joe's willing and able to assume a variety of identities to suit his aims, including a playboy and a lady jazz musician (Josephine). Joe has shapely ankles and type O blood. Linked romantically with **Sugar Kane**.

See *Some Like It Hot*

JOHN

Pedantic university professor. John is the walking embodiment of the contradictions of progressive academia. In his classes and written work he professes that the entire U.S. system of education is flawed to the point of uselessness, while at the same time he is in the process of receiving tenure and being made a full professor. He has just recently been accused of sexual harassment.

See *Oleanna,* **David Mamet**

JOHN "THE SAVAGE"

Illegitimate son of two residents of Utopia, a grim, high-tech, futuristic society, John "the Savage" grows up an outcast on a reservation in New Mexico. Educates himself by reading Shakespeare and develops a moral sensibility based on Christianity, Native American beliefs, and the ethics he finds in Shakespeare. The exemplar of the "noble savage" ideal, John is imported into Utopia as an experiment, but the contradiction between his beliefs and the prevailing ethos of the "brave new world" is too much for him.

See *Brave New World,* **Aldous Huxley**

JOHNNY

An amoral young man living in an ethical and cultural wasteland that blights much of modern-day England. He flees Manchester after raping a girl in an alleyway and winds up in London, where he mooches off old friends. A truly uplifting fellow, Johnny justifies his aimless life by pointing to the decrepitude of society. At the same time, he entertains with his extreme intelligence, black charm,

and devastatingly sharp sense of humor.
See *Naked*

JOHNNY BOY

Off-the-wall, aimless young punk in New York City's Little Italy who gets through life on recklessness and dumb charm. But when he gets in over his head with a loan shark, his problems become more serious than he can appreciate or deal with. Despite his connected pal **Charlie's** efforts to help him, to spirit him out of town, Johnny Boy continues on his obnoxious, self-destructive way, under the apparent impression that he can't be hurt by the dangerous people whom he flouts.
See *Mean Streets*

JOHNSON, ALICE

She seems slightly ditzy and barely older than her students, but student teacher Alice Johnson makes it through her first year to become an English teacher at Walt Whitman High School. Full of energy—maybe a bit too much for her own good—Alice is not above getting into a scrape now and then. She finds wisdom from **Pete Dixon**, a history teacher who's one of the best.
See *Room 222*

JOHNSON, BRIAN

A nerd with a gun. Lonely geek who desperately wants to be liked, though an easy target for others in his high school, particularly **Andrew Clark** and **John Bender**. Socially inept, never quite knows the right thing to say. Nicknamed the Brain by his peers in Saturday morning detention.
See *The Breakfast Club*

JOHNSON, FRANCESCA

A transplanted Italian turned Iowa farm wife. This daughter of traditional parents grew up in Naples during World War II. She's pretty and bright with long, black hair. Suppressing her girlhood dreams, she marries a kind but unexciting American soldier for the promise of a new life in the States, and they have two children. She likes to celebrate her birthdays alone with a glass of brandy and a single cigarette. Her degree in comparative literature has never been put to good use. When "magician" photographer **Robert Kincaid** drives into her life, he awakens old "poetry and music feelings" inside her.

After deciding to do the rational thing and stay with her family, she lives out the rest of her days "loving him desperately."
See *The Bridges of Madison County,* Robert James Waller

JOHNSON, FRED

A basically despicable guy with only one arm (people refer to him as "the one-armed man"). He attempts to burglarize **Dr. Richard Kimble's** home and is surprised by Kimble's wife, Helen, who he kills with a lamp base. When Kimble is convicted of the crime and escapes, he spends four years chasing Johnson down. Johnson is killed by the cop tailing Kimble, **Lt. Philip Gerard.**
See *The Fugitive*

JOHNSON, HILDY

A crack Chicago newspaper reporter, but now on his way out of journalism and into wedded bliss—in that order. Once considered an ace in his field, with a real nose for scooping all the other journalists in town, he is consequently the favorite staffman of his boss, manic, workaholic editor **Walter Burns.** Though eager to get on with his new life, Hildy does feel growing pangs of regret over his upcoming retirement from the newspaper business.
See *The Front Page*

JOHNSON, RON

An easygoing, goof-off student at mostly black Hillman College. Can't match the academic performance and style of best buddy **Dwayne Wayne.** Eternally searching for girls, mostly without success, and in lust with **Whitley Gilbert.** Wants to make big bucks—but not by taking over Daddy's car dealership.
See *A Different World*

JOHNSTON, FLORENCE

The wisecracking, streetwise maid to **George** and **Louise Jefferson,** Florence is always outsmarting and conspiring against Mr. Jefferson in her support of Louise. As a maid, she's inadequate and incompetent, preferring to talk and boss others around. Full of pride, she takes nothing from anybody. When the doorbell rings, she doesn't move. Instead, she says sarcastically, "You want me to get that?"
See *The Jeffersons*

JOKER, PRIVATE

This smart-mouthed marine recruit is now in training at Parris Island for eventual duty in Vietnam. He tries to take unit scapegoat **Leonard "Private Pyle" Lawrence** in hand and becomes his only friend. While he professes not to believe in the Virgin Mary, he is interested in Jungian theories on duality of human condition. Hopes to become a field reporter for the military newspaper *Stars and Stripes.*

See *Full Metal Jacket*

JONES, AMOS

Co-owner with his friend **Andrew Hogg Brown** of the Fresh Air Taxi-Cab Company in Harlem. He's hard-working, mild-mannered, sensible, and gentle, a family man devoted to his wife and daughter. Amos is the down-to-earth half of the company, who wants to make his way by patience, honesty, and hard work.

See *Amos 'n' Andy*

JONES, BARNABY

Gentle, grandfatherly Barnaby may seem like an aging yokel, but he can catch criminals with the best of them. Actually retired, he returns to the gumshoe biz after his son Hal—to whom he left his L.A. investigations firm—is murdered. (Part of his motivation is to find his son's killer.) His trusty secretary is Betty, Hal's widow; an eventual partner is young cousin J. R. Jones. Barnaby is an amateur forensics expert who examines evidence in his basement lab.

See *Barnaby Jones*

JONES, BRUTUS

The self-styled emperor of a poor, "undiscovered" West Indian island. Jones was born in the U.S., worked as a Pullman porter, and, in all likelihood, murdered a man. This last most probably prompted his sudden departure from this country. He is a man who rules by fear, intimidation, and, impressively, the ability to exploit the superstitions of the locals. Most notably, the residents of this dirt-poor island believe that Jones can only be killed by a silver bullet.

See *The Emperor Jones,* Eugene O'Neill

JONES, GERALDINE

Sassy, bigmouthed 1970s black woman with a blond wig and high heels and a body that looks surprisingly like a man's—a linebacker's, even. "The Devil made me do it!"

See *The Flip Wilson Show*

JONES, JOHNNY

As ace reporter for the *New York Globe,* he works as a foreign correspondent assigned to cover the upcoming war in Europe, using the name Huntly Haverstock. He's inquisitive, extremely perceptive, suspicious, and brave. Johnny will stop at nothing to get his story: "I do know a story when I see one, and I'll keep after it until I get it or it gets me." Though counterespionage is not his forte, he matches wits with a sinister spy ring in an effort to not only get the story, but to serve the cause of good. Jones is in love with Carol Fisher and plans to marry her.

See *Foreign Correspondent*

JONES, NORVAL

A shy bank clerk, Norval's in love with beautiful **Trudy Kockenlocker**, hopelessly—he thinks. World War II is raging, but he can't serve because of a nervous stutter. He's presssed into a different kind of service, that of marrying Trudy when she's made pregnant by an anonymous soldier or sailor. Earnest, well-meaning, and genuinely in love, he ends up being accused of impersonating an officer, forgery, and kidnapping.

See *The Miracle of Morgan's Creek*

JONES, PROFESSOR HENRY "INDIANA," JR.

A renaissance action man: Indy is an ace archaeologist and adventurer, university professor (his classroom tends to be full of adoring coeds), and daredevil. He can survive fire, poison, gunfire, and explosions, without losing his hat. He's totally focused on his goals and lets nothing stand in his way. Though he'd do it for the sheer love of it, his worldwide search for ancient relics is in fact extremely lucrative. At least, it would be, if he kept the relics instead of bringing them back to the university. He's constantly at odds with those who covet those same objects for profit or a base political motive. He has contacts all over the world. In addition to his razor-sharp intellect, Indy's developed the physical skills he needs. He's a crack shot and an expert with a bullwhip. He fears nothing and no one, not even the wrath of an angry God… well, there *is* one thing: he can't stand snakes. Ugly, squirmy creatures. Indy has a soft spot for pretty girls and little kids. He explains his aches and pains: "It's not the years, it's the mileage."

See *Raiders of the Lost Ark*

JORDACHE, RUDY

Handsome, intelligent, and ambitious, Rudy manages to overcome working-class roots and an abusive father to go to college, succeed in business, and eventually become a U.S. senator—a second-generation immigrant's American Dream. He has a complex love-hate relationship with his less polished brother, **Tom Jordache**; his first and only true love is Julie Prescott.

See *Rich Man, Poor Man*

JORDACHE, TOM

Born of poor immigrants, rebellious and headstrong Tom uses brute strength and street cunning to survive; he becomes a boxer, while his brother, **Rudy Jordache**, succeeds in business and politics. Boyish charm mixed with a raw masculinity makes him a magnet for women; one of them gives him a son, Wesley. Tom has a lifelong enemy in Arthur Falconetti.

See *Rich Man, Poor Man*

MR. JORDAN

The suave manager of the Way Station, where the dead board a Concorde en route to their final destination. Mr. Jordan has to intervene personally when **Joe Pendleton**, quarterback for the Los Angeles Rams, is accidentally removed from the living before his time has actually come. "There's a reason for everything. There's always a plan."

See *Heaven Can Wait*

JORDAN, ROBERT

An idealistic, macho American, a demolition expert, who goes to 1930s Spain to help the Loyalists fight the Fascists. He hooks up with **Pilar**'s band of soldiers in a rugged mountain region, where he's supposed to blow up a key Fascist bridge. Jordan is deeply committed to these people and their struggle for freedom. He falls in love with Maria, a silent waif who's been raped by evil Falangists. When he and Maria make love, in Jordan's mind it's as if the earth moves—which is a good thing, in this case. He manages to help Pilar and her partisans, becoming more and more emotionally involved as he does so. Emotional involvement of this sort is not a wise thing when one is in the midst of a war, as Robert Jordan finds out—to his cost.

See *For Whom the Bell Tolls,* **Ernest Hemingway**

JUDGE

He's an anal, hypocritical, corrupt, silver-haired, deep-voiced leader of the country club set. As the sponsor of a college scholarship for caddies, he's ready to hand it to **Danny**, a caddy, until the boy starts hanging around with some of those he regards as the club's questionable element. Since he who touches pitch gets defiled, such associations remove Danny from among the chosen few, in the Judge's narrow mind.

See *Caddyshack*

JUDSON, SERGEANT FATSO

This sadistic NCO runs a brutal army stockade in Hawaii before World War II. He enjoys doling out physical punishment with a heavy hand and takes particular pleasure in dealing with Private **Angelo Maggio** during his stockade residencies. A heavy, greasy, leering bully, Judson uses his position of authority to intimidate and humiliate the unfortunate men who end up in his detail.

See *From Here to Eternity,* **James Jones**

JUDY

A pretty girl who's got a bone to pick with the world. It doesn't matter that she comes from a good home—she's a teenager, and teenagers don't need any reason to be angry. She likes to stay out past her curfew and is attracted to equally troubled boys, like the sexy, dangerous **Jim**.

See *Rebel Without a Cause*

JULES

Opera-loving teenager living alone in a Parisian loft. He drives a moped around town in his job as mail carrier. Jules is handy with a covert tape recorder, though this talent sometimes gets him into extreme difficulties. Jules is known to pilfer items now and then. Has undying obsession for talented soprano **Cynthia Hawkins**.

See *Diva*

JULIA

This simple, sexually open young woman initiates a relationship with **Winston Smith** in defiance of the totalitarian laws of Oceania, the dystopia in which they live. She neither embraces nor rejects the prevailing party line, but accepts history as rewritten by Big Brother, the symbolic head of government. Smart, funny, attractive, and loves her man—but when their illicit liaison is discovered, she betrays him.

See *1984,* George Orwell

JOSHUA, PETER

Call him that for the moment; he's used many names. Whatever he's going by at the time—Peter Joshua, Alexander Dyle, Adam Canfield, or Brian Cruikshank, to name a few possibilities—he's witty, charming, and hard to pin down. Beautiful **Reggie Lambert** is greatly attracted to him, but he has one potential flaw: he might be trying to kill her.

See *Charade*

JUSTICE, SHERIFF BUFORD T.

He's the archetypal backwoods-cop-as-buffoon. The great burden of his existence, the thorn in his side, is a roguish hot-rodder and hell-raiser, whom he lives to bust, some sweet day. But this is one cop who's doomed to a life of frustration—as a man and as a driver, he just can't keep up with that dol-garned **Bandit.**

See *Smokey and the Bandit*

KAFFEE, LIEUTENANT J. G.

Flip, seemingly callow navy attorney who rarely takes his job seriously. He enjoys a good game of softball. He's something of a sexist, though willing to work with women. Has few problems tackling authority. Ready to do the right thing when necessary and the opportunity presents itself.

See *A Few Good Men*

KANE, AMY

A beautiful, soft-spoken Quaker who marries the sheriff of a small western town. Morally opposed to violence, she decides to leave her husband when he feels he must protect the town from a dangerous killer, who is returning from prison with the intention of killing the sheriff who sent him away. At the last moment, she has second thoughts.

See *High Noon*

KANE, BARRY

When accused of being a Nazi saboteur of U.S. aircraft production, he is forced to flee both the police and some genuine saboteurs. Barry has a moment of truth while on a visit to the Statue of Liberty, an experience that we wouldn't want to share.

See *Saboteur*

KANE, CHARLES FOSTER

As a child, he grew up in an idyllic rural setting, though they were poor (thanks largely to his feckless dad). His life turns around when he inherits a fortune, and he ultimately winds up as a hugely wealthy but lonely newspaper tycoon. Brash and opinionated, backed with excellent education and riches, he thinks running a newspaper is fun, and is even willing to lose money at it, if need be. He starts with high principles, but somehow they don't stay with him for very long. Married and divorced twice, first to refined Emily Norton, whom he left for uncouth singer Susan Alexander, whom he tried unsuccessfully to make into a star opera singer. Lives at enormous estate he names Xanadu. Though in his public image Kane tries to maintain a sense of integrity, he is rather unscrupulous in his professional career and personal dealings. He is an obsessive collector of exotic statues, paintings, and many other objects, many of which lie moldering in crates in the enormous cellars of Xanadu. A failed political candidate who doesn't realize that elections can't be bought. Troubled by lifelong and unrequited yearning for an innocent youth that really never was. Despite enormous successes and failures throughout life, can't quite forget loss of his favorite childhood toy, a sled named Rosebud. "If I hadn't been very rich I might have been a really great man."

See *Citizen Kane*

KANE, ERICA

Gorgeous, glamorous, and totally self-involved, Erica is the biggest star living in suburban Pine Valley—and she'll never let you forget it. Model, actress, cosmetics executive, talk show host, whatever Erica does she does big. (Her autobiography is called "Raising Kane.") Daughter of motherly

Mona and jet-setting film director Eric—who abandoned her—Erica is always looking for love, hence her full name: Erica Kane Martin Brent Cudahy Chadler Montgomery Montgomery Marick Marick. And those are only the ones she married; other "great loves" include Nick Davis, Jeremy Hunter, and one of her husband's brothers, Jackson Montgomery. She has two daughters, beloved Bianca and devilish Kendall, whom she gave up for adoption as a teen. "I'm Erica Kane!"

See *All My Children*

KANE, MARTIN

A smooth, wisecracking private detective who solves murders. His base of operation is New York where he regularly worked with Lieutenant Bender to solve the case. His hangout, Happy McMann's Tobacco Shop, is where he seeks his information.

See *Martin Kane, Private Detective*

KANE, SUGAR

She's curvaceous, naive, ditzy—a spun-sugar blond twenty-five-year-old ukulele player in an all-girl band, nee Sugar Kowalczyk. Changing her name was probably the last sensible thing she did. In true 1920s style, she keeps a silver flask filled with bourbon in her garter. Sugar just can't help drawing attention to herself, mostly from lusting males. She is always, as she puts it, getting the fuzzy end of the lollipop; she gets into troubles not entirely of her own making. As she says, "All the girls drink. I'm just the one who gets caught." Her fondness for alcohol has contributed to a lowered resistance to disease. Sugar's ideal mate would be a wealthy man who plays the tenor sax. Known to be romantically involved with **Joe**, a tenor saxophonist of doubtful intentions and questionable financial worth.

See *Some Like It Hot*

KANE, WILL

This tall, stoical western sheriff is respected for his integrity and beloved by the townspeople whom he has served for years. After marrying **Amy Kane** (a much younger woman), he decides to leave his old life and become a rancher. When it's learned that killer **Frank Miller**, whom Kane sent to prison, has been released, the townspeople beg him to stay and protect them. Although Kane

has promised his new wife that he won't go back to the law, his sense of duty compels him to stick around, despite her protestations. Commitment to the law outweighs, for the moment, commitment to marriage, but he's dismayed when, at the crisis, the townspeople abandon him to fight the killer and his gang by himself. He's not a superhero, but he's tough and smart, and needs all of his wiles and strength to meet the four men who want him dead.

See *High Noon*

KAPLAN, GEORGE

He is an elusive U.S. government agent who is on the trail of a gang of international spies. They, in turn, are on *his* trail, but having a hard time; Kaplan is very adept at covering his tracks, and they aren't even certain what he looks like. He goes from place to place, checking in and out of hotels across the country, baffling and frustrating his increasingly edgy adversaries. Finally, they think they have him in their sights…and the game's afoot.

See *North by Northwest*

KATO

He's the Asian manservant to **Inspector Jacques Clouseau**. Other than normal household duties, Kato keeps Clouseau's fighting reflexes honed by unexpectedly attacking him. Speaks with a stereotypical **Fu Manchu** accent and shows remarkable durability, once waiting for his employer in a refrigerator.

See *A Shot in the Dark*

KAUFFMAN, SEYMOUR

He may seem dour, but Seymour is a good guy at heart; it's just that his job—principal of Walt Whitman High School, with some three thousand students—is nothing if not draining. His slightly sarcastic streak may keep him sane. He's friends with **Pete Dixon**, one of his best teachers.

See *Room 222*

KAVAKOV

Wily Israeli, member of the Mossad. A sly thinker with consistently probing mind. Determined in his combative efforts against Black September and other Mideast terrorist groups. Unafraid of heights and willing to go to anywhere, no matter how imminent or potentially explosive the danger, if it means completing his mission.

See *Black Sunday*

KEATING, PETER

Mediocre architect and schoolmate of the brilliant **Howard Roark**. As a student at Stanton Institute of Technology, he cut a wide swath, being voted Most Popular Man on Campus, etc. He's a gorgeous hunk of man. His overbearing, ambitious mother pushes him to dump the woman he loves for the chance to marry his boss's statuesque daughter, **Dominique Francon**, and become a partner in the firm.

See *The Fountainhead,* Ayn Rand

THE KEATON FAMILY

Children of the sixties, parents of the eighties and beyond, Steven and Elyse Keaton drove a Volkswagen minivan while they were at Berkeley. But now they're a full-fledged family with three kids in Columbus, Ohio. Steven didn't sell out like so many of his friends, and manages a public television station. He's slightly goofy, but endearing. Beautiful and strong, Elyse is an architect, not to mention a community activist in her spare time. Their kids haven't really bought into any of their wacky flower-child ideals. Oldest son Alex reveres Dick Nixon, Milton Friedman, and money. He even sleeps under a poster of William F. Buckley, Jr. A lifetime subscriber to *The National Review,* Alex carries a briefcase and wears a tie to high school, and believes that he is more intelligent than anyone he meets. He's fond of torturing the younger Mallory, who is a scatter-brained mall rat. Mallory is obsessed with her looks, clothes, and her popularity. The nerdy neighbor boy **Irwin "Skippy"**

The Keaton Family

Photo courtesy of The National Broadcasting Company, Inc.

Handelman is in love with Mallory, and the rest of the good-hearted Keaton household. Mallory, however, is in love with high school dropout and garbage artist, Nick, whose language skills are largely limited to saying "Ayyy." The youngest Keatons, Jennifer and Andy, are often pulled around by their family members to choose either a politically conservative or liberal lifestyle, even though they're way too young to vote. There's a lot of love in the Keaton household, and they have many family talks in the kitchen.

See *Family Ties*

KEEBLER ELVES

A family of animated elves who live in a tree and bake cookies and crackers. Always wear green. Frustrated because people don't believe they exist.

See *Keebler*

KELLER, JOE

He's an American businessman whose firm has thrived during World War II. But he is a man of sorrow, too: one of his sons is missing in the war and believed (by everyone except his wife) to have been killed; and his company allowed some faulty airplane parts to be shipped overseas, resulting in fatalities, a situation for which his former partner has gone to jail. Joe believes that everything he has done has been done in the best interests of his family.

See *All My Sons*, Arthur Miller

KELLER, STEVE

Smart and literate Steve is a college-educated detective on the San Francisco police force and paired with an older partner, **Mike Stone**. Steve is handsome, young, and a man of his time, using up-to-the-minute police procedure to solve cases and maintaining a liberal attitude in contrast to that of his partner. Steve does, however, have great respect for Mike.

See *The Streets of San Francisco*

KELLY, DETECTIVE CHIN HO

An Asian American cop in Hawaii. Because of his racial background, he can sometimes elicit trust from native islanders faster than his white colleagues, **Steve McGarrett** and **Danny Williams**.

See *Hawaii Five-O*

KELLY, ELOISE Y.

A sultry, earthy showgirl stranded in an African big game camp. Sarcastic, funny, and sure of herself, she's not easily frightened by snakes or wild animals. She's got her eye on big game hunter **Victor Marswell**, and bides her time until his attraction to Linda Nordley wears off. Pride and decency underlie her gaudy exterior.

See *Mogambo*

KELLY, JOHN

A New York City police detective who works at the 15th Precinct until he turns in his badge after becoming embroiled in a controversy involving his ex-girlfriend, police officer **Janice Licalsi**. John's father was also a cop and was killed in the line of duty. Kelly was married to, and then divorced from, Laurie, who worked for a short time in the D.A.'s office. He's an ace interrogator, known for his ability to "reach out" to people.

See *NYPD Blue*

KELP, PROFESSOR JULIUS

This shy college chemist brews a miracle potion and transforms himself into a Casanova-type alter ego called Buddy Love. The scholarly mouse and the egotistical lady-killer vie for the same body, but the professor finally reverts to his original personality—and wins the girl anyway.

See *The Nutty Professor*

KELSEY, ANN

Intense, capable, idealistic, sometimes moody lawyer. She seeks a partnership at McKenzie, Brackman, Chaney and Kuzak and finds an unlikely love mate in fellow lawyer **Stuart Markowitz**. She constantly feels put upon by the male establishment at her firm. Ann tries to "have it all" by taking care of her baby while practicing law. Most of the time, she enjoys a great sex life with Stuart. Loves that "Venus Butterfly."

See *L.A. Law*

KENDALL, DENISE HUXTABLE

The fiery, offbeat, unpredictable, outgoing, second daughter, Denise lives at first with parents **Cliff** and **Clair Huxtable** in a New York brownstone with her three sisters and brother Theo, with whom she gets along best. After a year of college, she drops out and

Professor Kelp

goes to Africa, from where she returns with a husband and stepdaughter, to the delight of her parents. She's always searching for her true self but never quite finds it.

See *The Cosby Show*

KENDALL, EVE

This beautiful, sexy blonde gets entangled in an ugly, messy world of spies and counterspies and chiefly with a suave but dangerous gentleman named **Phillip Vandamm**. She subsequently meets handsome **Roger Thornhill**, and a welter of confusing emotions confuses her life still further. She desperately tries to extricate herself from this sticky web and find true love in the process, but the process is both long and very dangerous. In the course of her adventures, Eve gets to see the famous Mount Rushmore monuments in a way that very few tourists ever manage.

See *North by Northwest*

KENICKIE

A 1950s greaser, self-centered Kenickie leads the T-Birds gang at Rydell High in California. Chicks and restoring a battered car for racing are far more important than schooling. He grows up quickly after finding out **Rizzo** might be pregnant. "A hickey from Kenickie is like a Hallmark card."

See *Grease*

KENOBI, BEN "OBI-WAN"

A kindly, white-haired old man, Ben Kenobi lives on a world far from ours, where he functions as a mentor to young orphan **Luke Skywalker**, to the distress of his ultra-conventional foster parents. But Ben, as he is generally known, has had a remarkable history, as Obi-Wan Kenobi, one of the greatest and most redoubtable figures among the mystical order called the Jedi Knights. He aids Luke in his attempt to become one of these powerful and virtuous figures and to help in the battle to liberate the known universe from the iron grip of the oppressive and evil Empire, which has stamped out freedom in all but a few pockets of the galaxy. He instructs Luke in the Way of the Jedi, including the use of the Force, a Zen-like discipline that involves tapping into one's deep inner strengths and enables an adept to perform extraordinary feats. His tutelage starts Luke off on a long journey of personal discovery and adventure in the cause of freedom and virtue. "May the Force be with you."

See *Star Wars*

KENT, CLARK

Shy, bumbling reporter for the *Daily Planet* with a secret past and present. Pines away for reporter **Lois Lane**, but is slow to admit his crush, partly out of fear that she'll discover his true identity. Has a chiseled jaw; wears large black glasses as a sort of disguise.

See *Superman*

KERSEY, PAUL

Once a mild-mannered liberal, this architect becomes a self-styled vigilante after his wife is murdered and his daughter brutally raped by thugs. He entraps would-be muggers and thieves, whom he then guns down, always staying one step ahead of the police and one silent step behind the criminal element. His weapons of choice are handguns. Paul is definitely not given to long-winded speeches.

See *Death Wish*

KETTLE, MA

A rambunctious and outspoken middle aged hillbilly, with a brood of children and a husband, **Pa Kettle**, who never brings in any money. Ma is kindhearted and wants people to know that "we don't stand on no ceremony here." She's a terrible housekeeper because, she says, "she used to fight with Pa about being clean, and since he wouldn't change, she changed into being dirty." She wears outrageous hats when she dresses up to go somewhere nice. A great instinctive cook, she says it's all a matter of "a drop of this and a drop of that and mix it together and then stick it in the oven." She makes a new quilt every year and is saving them for her children so she'll have something nice to leave the "younguns" when she dies.

See *The Egg and I* and *Ma and Pa Kettle*

KETTLE, PA

This scruffy hillbilly wears tattered clothes and a battered hat. He's married to **Ma Kettle** and has a house full of children. He drives a beat-up pickup truck, in which he goes from neighbor to neighbor, borrowing things that he never returns. He is a scavenger and kind of a dim bulb. Pa is forever coming up with get-rich-quick schemes, like the time he bought two minks that he was going to breed and make lots of money, but they died on him. He tries to be a handyman, but he's hapless, clumsy, and incompetent. His wife calls him "an awful lazy so-and-so," and says he ain't much for working or bringing in any money to his household. He isn't even much of a moonshiner; the still in his barn is always blowing up.

See *The Egg and I* and *Ma and Pa Kettle*

KICKING BIRD

Sioux warrior and highly evolved person. Strong and skilled as hunter, he's wary at first, though ultimately a friend of **John W. Dunbar.**

See *Dances with Wolves*

KID

A plucky, waiflike orphan living in a Dickensian underworld, Kid is trapped under the thumb of a mean, nasty, selfish, and exploitive street dweller named Steve the Tramp. Strapped with poverty, but endowed with great physical strength and a courage well beyond his eleven years, Kid earns his way into **Dick Tracy's** care.

See *Dick Tracy*

KILBOURNE, LORELEI

She's the crusading star reporter on the *Illustrated Press,* the large cosmopolitan daily in Big Town. Is romantically interested in her boss, good guy editor Steve Wilson.

See *Big Town*

KILDARE, DR. JAMES

Handsome young doctor. Intern, then resident, at Blair General Hospital under the tutelage of **Dr. Leonard Gillespie.** He struggles with the rigors of internship and the emotional stresses of medicine, works hard to impress Gillespie, and gets deeply involved in patients' lives. His cure rate is high. An object of great romantic interest around the hospital, Dr. Kildare occasionally falls in love.

See *Dr. Kildare*

KILEY, DR. STEVEN

A young, handsome doctor who works with general practitioner **Marcus Welby.** He originally trained to be a neurologist and contracted to work with Dr. Welby for only one year, but ended up staying. Dr. Kiley fell in love with, and married, Janet Black, public relations director of Hope Memorial Hospital. This groovy doc makes house calls on his motorcycle.

See *Marcus Welby, M.D.*

KILGORE, LIEUTENANT COLONEL

Macho, gung-ho leader of U.S. Marines in Vietnam. Favorite composer: Wagner. Takes **Captain Willard** on a detour to a killer surf break before finally sending him on his mission upriver to kill **Colonel Kurtz.** "I love the smell of napalm in the morning. Smells like…victory."

See *Apocalypse Now*

KIMBLE, DR. RICHARD

A man who knows he's innocent of the murder of which he's been convicted and sets out to prove it. Kimble, a respected Chicago surgeon, returns home one night to find his wife fatally beaten by a one-armed man who flees after a struggle. His story of the intruder is given short shrift in the courtroom, and Kimble is sentenced to death, but escapes during a collision between his prison bus and a train. He's pursued in a manhunt directed by a top-notch, relentless lawman. Evading capture through many close calls, Kimble is brave and stoical through his ordeal as a fugitive.

See *The Fugitive*

KINBOTE, CHARLES

A demented literary scholar who claims to have been king of the country of Zembla, Kinbote is presently preparing a critical edition of *Pale Fire,* a long, autobiographical poem by **John Shade,** a murdered poet, who, like Kinbote, came to America from Zembla. The consummate pedant, Kinbote gradually turns what starts off as a tribute to his countryman into a personal history—either real or imagined.

See *Pale Fire,* **Vladimir Nabokov**

KINCAID, CHET

The coach and phys ed teacher at a lower-middle-class school in Los Angeles, Chet is a warm, good-hearted guy with a keen sense of humor and a real interest in his students. Single, Chet has a

Dr. Richard Kimble

close relationship with his mother, Rose, brother Brian, and sister-in-law Verna.

See *The Bill Cosby Show*

KINCAID, REUBEN

The curmudgeonly manager of the singing Partridge Family pretends he doesn't like kids very much, but—guess what?—he's a softie underneath! Reuben plays the role of Dad in these fatherless kids' lives, which makes up for the fact that he's not the world's best manager and often books the group into bad locations. He seems to have a big crush on Mom, **Shirley Partridge**, and is frequently tormented by precocious young **Danny Partridge**.

See *The Partridge Family*

KINCAID, ROBERT

At fifty-two, he's a *National Geographic* photographer "still watching the light." Kincaid likes his work and wittily observes, "I like the road, and I like making pictures." He lives in the state of Washington, eats no meat, and writes poetry, "just for himself." Divorced because his long absences were hard on the marriage, he never hears from his ex-wife. He wears faded Levi's, lights his Camels with a Zippo, and opens bottles of Bud with his trusty Swiss Army knife. He'd like a dog, and calls his old Chevy pickup Harry. He hops in Harry to hunt for covered bridges, and discovers lonely housewife **Francesca Johnson**. After an intense, four-day love affair, he wants to whisk her away from her farm. He rhapsodizes, "We'll make love in desert sand and drink brandy on balconies in Mombasa...." When Francesca whispers that she feels overwhelmed, he replies: "I am the highway and a peregrine and all the sails that ever went to sea." No wonder he generally keeps his poetry to himself.

See *The Bridges of Madison County,* Robert James Waller

THE KING

Big-nosed monarch. How short is he? He's so short his feet don't reach the ground when he sits on the throne from which he makes pithy pronouncements. He reacts to the absurd situations of his subjects' lives with a look of half-bemused, half-disgusted disbelief.

See *The Wizard of Id*

KING BRIAN

He's the leader of an underground leprechaun network in rural Ireland. Small of body but big of heart. When caught off guard, he's willing to grant three wishes. Currently holding **Darby O'Gill** hostage.

See *Darby O'Gill and the Little People*

KING, AMANDA

A bored divorcée and mother of two (Philip and Jamie), Amanda finds her true calling in undercover spy work, when she accidentally crosses paths with dashing government agent **Lee Stetson**. The two become partners, working for "the Agency," although Amanda keeps her job a secret from her family and friends. Eventually, she and Lee marry (and keep that a secret, too).

See *Scarecrow and Mrs. King*

KING, ROCKY

He's a New York homicide detective. Neither flashy nor violence-prone, he uses sheer hard work and perseverance to solve his cases. Married to Mabel, he has a son—Junior—and a partner named Hart.

See *Rocky King, Inside Detective*

KING, SKY

As owner of Arizona's Flying Crown Ranch, King is one cowboy who adapts to the modern world—as a pilot, with his twin-engine Cessna, *The Songbird,* as his trusty steed. When not righting wrongs or tending to his ranch, King is stand-in father to his niece Penny and nephew Clipper.

See *Sky King*

KINSELLA, RAY

He is a former 1960s campus activist, now living

Captain James T. Kirk

quiet life as an Iowa farmer. Married with one daughter. Ray's a huge fan of baseball and exhaustively knowledgeable about the history of the game. Still feels pangs of regret over untimely death of his distant father. Ray has the ability to hear and see things no one else can. Though his actions seem impulsive to outsiders, there is a real method to his apparent madness. A voracious reader and student of life, he drives a beat-up van. Has his own private baseball diamond built in a plowed cornfield. A good friend of fallen baseball player "Shoeless" Joe Jackson and other sports legends, deceased and otherwise.

See *Field of Dreams*

KIRK, CAPTAIN JAMES T.

As the bold, dashing captain of the USS *Enterprise*—a powerful starship of the United Federation of Planets, circa the twenty-third century—Kirk is an intergalactic gladiator, a stellar swashbuckler, a cosmos-hopping cowboy, going where "no man has gone before" to "search out new life and new civilizations." A man of action, Kirk is quick with a phaser, but he's also a man of ideals, who believes in the Federation's "Prime Directive" (noninterference in the ordinary development of other cultures), even though he'll bend rules every now and then to get the job done. (To a man of passion like Kirk, blind adherence to the rules is somewhat less important than doing what he feels is right.) He's bold, he's heroic, he's cute, and he's got an uncanny ability to bag intergalactic babes—blue ones, shape-shifter ones, android ones, it hardly seems to matter. Bottom line, though, Kirk's first and only true love is the *Enterprise,* and he's been known to stroke her lovingly. He's also deeply committed to his crew, particularly First Officer **Spock**, ship's physician **Dr. Leonard "Bones" McCoy**, and chief engineer **Montgomery "Scotty" Scott**. Kirk is eventually promoted to the rank of admiral, a desk job. He finds that he sorely misses being in the thick of the action. He has a son, a brother named Sam (who dies on the planet Deneva), and his middle name is Tiberius.

See *Star Trek*

KIT

Rural South Dakota garbage collector with major homicidal streak. Maintains an indifferent attitude toward murder. Wields a shotgun with ease and deadly expertise. Dresses mainly in tight-fitting T-shirts and dirty blue jeans; walks with a deliberate James Dean–like swagger. In love with fourteen-year-old **Holly** despite their age difference.

See *Badlands*

KITTREDGE, FLANDERS

This soulful Manhattan art dealer is the proud owner of a double-sided Kandinsky. He has no gallery but deals in private sales. He thinks he's happy in his marriage to talkative **Ouisa** and with his life in general; his kids go to Harvard; he wears English shoes and drives a Mercedes. But he feels betrayed when smooth-talking **Paul Poitier** cons him and then turns out to be a fraud. His life isn't the same thereafter.

See *Six Degrees of Separation,* John Guare

KITTREDGE, OUISA

Her life certainly seems to be dandy. She lives in *soigné* surroundings with her wealthy art dealer husband, **Flan Kittredge**, she dines out every night, her life is a mad social whirl. Then she's charmed by a young black man, **Paul Poitier**, who claims to be Sidney Poitier's son. When his story is revealed as bogus, she sees that, under the glossy veneer, her life has been a big lie and that she is a "collage of unaccounted-for brush strokes."

See *Six Degrees of Separation,* John Guare

KLAATU

Peace-loving, highly evolved humanoid from another world with important warning for all earthlings. Close friends with destructive robot Gort. Klaatu has the ability to stop time when circumstances call for it. "Klaatu barada nikto!"

See *The Day the Earth Stood Still*

KLINGER, CORPORAL MAXWELL

A native of Toledo, this Lebanese American wears dresses in an unavailing effort to get a Section 8 (mental incapacity) discharge from the Korean War and his duty with the 4077th MASH (Mobile Army Surgical Hospital) unit. He's not a cross-dresser at heart, just a would-be dischargee. He does, however, collect a remarkably large wardrobe (for someone of his build) and a formidable collection of accessories. He will try anything to get back

Lieutenant Theo Kojak

to Toledo; he'll set himself on fire or try to put on a huge amount of weight. But it never works, because his urge to get out of Korea makes it clear that he's sane. He roots for the minor-league Toledo Mud Hens, pals around with company clerk **Radar O'Reilly**, and takes over as clerk when Radar gets shipped home.

See *M*A*S*H*

KLINK, COLONEL WILHELM

This self-absorbed, self-important Nazi officer is too easily swayed by compliments for the good of the Reich. He heads up Stalag 13, which, as he points out with pride, is the most secure prison camp in the nation. But that's only because American prisoner **Robert Hogan** and his men want it that way; with Klink free from worry about his prisoners, and free to spend all his time sucking up to his superiors, Hogan and his gang can freely run their elaborate behind-the-German-lines spy ring.

See *Hogan's Heroes*

KLUGMAN, NEIL

He is a sensitive, reasonably horny twenty-three-year-old living with his overbearing aunt in 1950s Newark, New Jersey, since his parents' move to Arizona. A graduate of Rutgers and an army veteran, he works at the Newark Public Library, where he helps a little kid find a Gaugin book in the "heart" section. Neil falls hard for **Brenda Patimkin**, whom he loves and hates for the new, more wealthy lifestyle to which she introduces him.

See *Goodbye, Columbus*, Philip Roth

KLUTE, JOHN

The squarest and most honest of small-town private detectives, he comes to big bad New York City looking for a missing friend, and finds call girl **Bree Daniel** instead. He moves in near her, spies on her, then starts protecting and taking care of her as she disintegrates and her life appears threatened. Ignoring her efforts to drive him away, he gradually wins her trust and love.

See *Klute*

KNIGHT, MICHAEL

Black-clad dude who cruises around in his black sports car, solving crimes and breaking chicks' hearts. His is no ordinary car, though—it's called KITT, and it's a technological marvel with a state-of-the-art computer mind of its own, and a cultured voice to boot.

See *Knight Rider*

KNOX, MALLORY WILSON

Thin, eighteen-year-old sexpot endowed with a wicked style of dancing and devastating kickboxing skills that'll put a man down in seconds. She'll use weapons in a pinch, but leaves the heavy-duty killing to her beloved, **Mickey Knox**. Career highlight: featured on the top-rated TV show *American Maniacs*.

See *Natural Born Killers*

KNOX, MICKEY

Tall, handsome, attended Lansing High School. Owns a cherry-red 1970 Dodge Challenger 383 convertible. Forever in love with **Mallory Wilson Knox**, who loves him too, despite the fact that he drowned Mallory's dad, Ed Wilson, in the family aquarium. Likes: Mallory, his car, his ten-inch hunting knife. Dislikes: people.

See *Natural Born Killers*

KOCKENLOCKER, TRUDY

She is an effervescent blonde whose one night of revelry with a soldier ends disastrously. She'd had a drink or six, and can't remember the name of the man she apparently married—and she's pregnant. Desperate, she asks sometime boyfriend **Norval Jones** to marry her and make her respectable. After he agrees, she realizes what a swell fellow Norval really is.

See *The Miracle of Morgan's Creek*

KOJAK, LIEUTENANT THEO

"Who loves ya, baby?" A bald sex symbol. Kojak is a smooth, suave New York City police detective who, with coolness and patience, wears down his suspects. Orally fixated, he either smokes or sucks on a lollipop. Kojak is a born leader who demands and gets the respect of his men. He calls them by their last names, barking out "Crocker," "Stavros," and "Saperstein" with a New York accent. Often zings his troops with sarcastic comments. Kojak can be openly affectionate, kissing women's hands or hugging close friends.

See *Kojak*

KOLOSKI, KAREN CHARLENE "K.C."

This jaded wartime prostitute and heroin addict lives and works near Da Nang at China Beach during the Vietnam conflict. Walks in two worlds—the grim drug and prostitution scene, and the office of base supervisor Major Lila Garreau. Feels morally inferior but superior in worldly wisdom and experience to Nurse **Colleen McMurphy**, with whom she eventually reaches some common ground. Suffered through childhood in Kansas City at the hands of sexually abusive father. She fell into prostitution partly to make money and came to drugs as an escape. Maintains business goals and has aspirations for the future. Has a daughter back in the States. Wounded psyche helps her identify with and comfort the psychologically, emotionally, and physically crippled who pass through China Beach on their way to and from the battlefields of 'Nam.

See *China Beach*

KOOKSON, "KOOKIE" GERALD LLOYD

Tragically hip—or at least he thinks so. As a parking lot attendant at a Hollywood restaurant named Dino's, Kookie wants nothing more than to work for the swell detective firm next door at 77 Sunset Strip, run by **Stu Baily** and **Jeff Spencer**; it would be "the ginchiest." With his inventive lexicon and wild enthusiasm—he helps out as often as he can, even if it means performing a composition called "Kookie, Kookie, Lend Me Your Comb"—it's not long before he's made a partner.

See *77 Sunset Strip*

KOTTER, GABE

Wisecracking but caring teacher of intellectually limited Brooklyn high school students known as the Sweathogs. He teaches at the same high school he went to and totally identifies with the kids. His teaching methods are unorthodox; they have to be, to have a chance of working. He believes he can make a difference in their lives.

See *Welcome Back, Kotter*

KOWALSKI, STANLEY

A modern Neanderthal, Stanley is aggressive, possessive, and territorial. He's a machinist in a New Orleans factory; he works hard, drinks beer, and plays poker regularly. He is a creature of raw male sexuality, which is a primary attraction for his wife, Stella. But his new (and possibly permanent) houseguest/sister-in-law, **Blanche DuBois** thinks of him as an unrefined, uncouth, and mean-spirited savage. Neither sister is altogether wrong. "In this state we have what is known as the Napoleonic code...."

See *A Streetcar Named Desire,* Tennessee Williams

KOZAK, BABE

This hot-headed neophyte bad guy gets involved in a jewel robbery with legendary gangster **Roy Earle**, which makes him think he's hot stuff. He's not. He talks big and blusters, but he's not too sharp. He doesn't like dogs and he beats his girlfriend **Marie Garson**.

See *High Sierra*

KRALIK, ALFRED

A clerk in Matuschek & Co., a quaint little store in Budapest, Alfred is accused by his boss of having an affair with Madame Matuschek. But Alfred has been doing nothing worse than conducting an anonymous lonelyheart correspondence with a dream girl who happens to be working in the shop—although neither of them realizes it, and they don't get along at all.

See *The Shop Around the Corner*

KRAMDEN, ALICE

A smart, sensible, practical woman. These are useful qualities when you're the wife of **Ralph Kramden**, bus driver and general screwup. Unaccountably, she loves the guy, and manages their limited budget, and patiently endures Ralph's constant inept scheming, with frequent support and backup being provided by her best friend, **Trixie Norton**. Even as dim a bulb as Ralph knows what a gem he's married to, even if he forgets now and then (like every hour on the hour).

See *The Honeymooners*

KRAMDEN, RALPH

He's a big man with a big mouth and an inflated opinion of himself, which frequently gets him into hot water. Ralph is a bus driver for New York City

Kookie Kookson

Stanley Kowalski

Photo courtesy of CBS

Ralph Kramden

Transit and lives at 358 Chauncey Street in the Bensonhurst district of Brooklyn. He feels that he is destined for better in life and is forever trying to prove it. His primary aider and abettor in his hare-brained get-rich-quick schemes is his best buddy and fellow member of the Raccoon Lodge, **Ed Norton**, sewer worker extraordinaire. Norton is roughly Ralph's equal in intelligence, which is to say that the brainpower of the two combined equals that of a fairly bright tree stump. Ralph is often frustrated and takes out his frustrations on those closest to him, especially his long-suffering wife, **Alice**. ("One of these days, Alice, one of these days…Pow! Right in the kisser!") But he is, as Alice is aware, more bark than bite, and deep down, he knows that he'd be lost without her. His fits of temper end as quickly as they begin, and he usually has the grace to be embarrassed by them. He loves bowling, Raccoon Lodge meetings, shooting pool, and eating Alice's home cooking. Most of all, after all the shouting dies down and the latest disaster has been worked out, he loves his wife. "Baby, you're the greatest!"

See *The Honeymooners*

KRAMER, COSMO

The wildly eccentric neighbor of stand-up comedian Jerry Seinfeld, he barrels through Jerry's front door and into his life constantly. His hair is high, his ideas seem insane, his manner is crazed, but somehow, he's catnip to women (including nuns). How Kramer supports himself is anybody's guess, but he's managed to get jobs as a Calvin Klein underwear model, a stand-in on *All My Children,* one of Murphy Brown's secretaries, and an actor in a Woody Allen movie, with the line "These pretzels are making me thirsty." He also came up with a cologne that smells like the beach and a book called the *Coffee Table Book of Coffee Tables,* which was shaped like a coffee table (after which he appeared on *Live with Regis and Kathie Lee*). He eats apples whole, core and all, and his mother's name is Babs.

See *Seinfeld*

KRAMER, JOANNA

An attractive, well-educated, and sophisticated woman living on the Upper East Side of Manhattan, Joanna seems to have it all but wants out of her marriage. With little overt warning, she leaves her husband and young son and moves to California, where she spends a year and a half "finding" herself with the help of a therapist. Returning to New York a newly self-assertive woman, she's fiercely determined to gain legal custody of the child she walked out on. Not surprisingly, Joanna faces stiff resistance from her husband, who has since learned to be not only a responsible father but also a surrogate mother. She begins to suspect that her mission may have to end in compromise.

See *Kramer vs. Kramer*

KRAMER, TED

A wry advertising executive whose divorce from his wife, **Joanna Kramer**, and subsequent custody fight for their son, Billy, prove to be something of an exception to traditional mother-gets-custody divorce settlements. While Kramer is not inherently domestic, he is able to adapt to the rigors of homemaking put upon him by his divorce. Ted is comfortable dating after his divorce and does not have the traditional Puritan reluctance about having dates stay overnight with him in the same home as his son. Although his son is inevitably injured during the initial separation period, Kramer is a dedicated and caring father. Custody of Billy is lost in a court challenge, but Joanna ultimately gives custody back to Ted.

See *Kramer vs. Kramer*

KRAPP

A bitter old writer. Krapp is a sentimental alcoholic who methodically keeps an extensive and personal tape journal. He uses this to evaluate the choices he has made with his life.

See *Krapp's Last Tape,* Samuel Beckett

KRASNY, THOMAS

Possessed of cool cunning and tremendous ambition, Krasny is never without two expensive cigars in his suit breast pocket. D.A. Krasny, a former superior of **Teddy Barnes**, would like to move up the political ladder, and knows that he needs convictions on high-profile cases. He needs all his considerable skills to try to salvage his career after Barnes divulges Krasny's breach of ethics in case #26022, the People vs. Henry Styles.

See *Jagged Edge*

KRAUS, GRETCHEN

Housekeeper in the governor's mansion of **James Gatling**, she is German through and through: blond, tough, and humorless. She is often at odds with **Benson DuBois**, whose more easygoing manner and close relationship with the governor is a constant annoyance. On rare occasions, she displays humanity, usually to the governor's daughter, young **Katie Gatling**.

See *Benson*

KRAVITZ, ABNER

His nose always stuck in a newspaper, the low-key husband of the meddlesome **Gladys** doesn't believe one word of her outrageous stories about their neighbors the **Stephenses**. Can barely get up to even look across the street; when he finally does, whatever bizarre phenomenon that Gladys reported is always gone. Consequently, thinks Gladys's "curlers are wound too tight."

See *Bewitched*

KRAVITZ, GLADYS

The meddling neighbor of Darrin and **Samantha Stephens**, she always seems to be watching their house or "dropping by" unexpectedly. Manages to see just enough weird stuff—unlikely animals in the living room, George Washington driving their car—to be sure that something funny is going on, but can never prove it. **Abner Kravitz**—"Abner!"—is her husband.

See *Bewitched*

KREBS, MAYNARD G.

The best friend of **Dobie Gillis**. A classic beatnik, Maynard has shaggy hair and a little goatee. He loves modern jazz, and worships the great musicians as gods. Charles Mingus is an oft-mentioned icon. Maynard's usual attire consists of raggedy sweatshirts, patched jeans, and sandals. A favorite activity is to "go downtown and watch them tear down the old Endicott building." Maynard loves to show how the building is being demolished by pretending his head is a wrecking ball and bashing it into Dobie's arm, while uttering appropriate sound effects. Another pet pastime is mooching food at the grocery store owned by Dobie's father, who constantly rides herd on Maynard to keep from being eaten out of business. Maynard worries about "the bomb," and is certain that the human race is about to blow itself up.

See *The Many Loves of Dobie Gillis*

KRELBOIN, SEYMOUR

An amiable schlemiel and amateur botanist who works in Gravis Mushnik's Skid Row flower shop. He either discovers or creates (we aren't certain of this) a carnivorous plant that thrives on human blood. Seymour names the plant Audrey II after the love of his life, dental hygienist **Audrey**, assistant to sadistic dentist **Orin Scrivello**. Starved for love and attention, Krelboin is easily manipulated by evil forces, to his great cost. If he has one true passion aside from botany, it is his unconsummated love for the human Audrey. Krelboin's wishy-washiness, though, results in inner conflict over whether he can honorably act as the supplier of the human blood needed for Audrey II's survival and growth. The upshot is a Hamlet-like episode of self-doubt and resultant inertia, leading in turn to some deaths. Krelboin's creation proves not only to be his claim to fame and obsession but, quite literally, the death of him, which should serve as a warning to amateur botanists the world over.

See *Little Shop of Horrors*

KRINGELEIN, OTTO

A lowly, terminally ill bookkeeper who decides to spend his final days pretending to be a wealthy man and living in luxury at the Grand Hotel. After living a life of humility, Otto wants to taste a little respect and luxury before dying. Kind and goodhearted despite his ruse, he is the only person who treats **Flaemmchen** with kindness.

See *Grand Hotel*, Vicki Baum

KRINGLE, KRIS

The retirement community hasn't been invented yet, so he lives in an old-folks home. Kris is a kindly looking old man with a white beard, so it's natural that he's brought in by Macy's executive **Doris Walker** to replace a drunken Santa Claus in the store's Christmas float. Hired as their Santa for the holidays, he charms the customers, if not the management, with advice to shop at other stores for their gifts. He loves children and can speak to them in any language. With patience and good humor, he convinces Doris's unbelieving daughter, **Susan**

Lady Lou

Walker, of the existence of Santa Claus. Upbeat, friendly, and unflappable, he's calm even when one of the store's executives thinks that he is insane and takes the issue of Santa Claus's reality to be settled in court. Clearly, Kris thinks that he's the genuine article, and in any case, he is able to win many over and impart the true meaning of Christmas.

See *Miracle on 34th Street*

KRISTEN

Spouse to **Joe**, she has joined her husband in a downward life slide via alcohol abuse. Given to crying jags at times, she believes booze can take away all pain. Has difficulty dealing with reality.

See *Days of Wine and Roses*

KRUEGER, FREDDY

The ruthless child-murderer of Elm Street, who, after being acquitted on a technicality, was hunted down and burned to death by neighborhood parents. Now, with his dirty brown fedora, red-striped sweater, and weapon of choice—a leather glove with razor-sharp steel blades attached to the fingers—he's returned from the dead. He hasn't come back to life but can be found in the nightmares of children and others among the residents of Elm Street.

See *A Nightmare on Elm Street*, Wes Craven

KURTZ, COLONEL

Enigmatic soldier, brilliant but now insane. After years in the jungle, has taken to agreeing with remote natives, who believe that, with his superior technology, he's a god come to lead them. Gives voice to his madness before being assassinated: "The horror…the horror."

See *Heart of Darkness*, Joseph Conrad, and *Apocalypse Now*

KURYAKIN, ILLYA

The blond, boyish Russian superagent who worked for UNCLE (the United Network Command for Law Enforcement). Working out of the secret American headquarters in New York, he was teamed with **Napoleon Solo** to fight the international crime syndicate THRUSH.

See *The Man from UNCLE*

KUZAK, MICHAEL

He's a sexy, handsome, successful lawyer, the chief litigator for the firm of McKenzie, Brackman, Chaney and Kuzak. Has principles and a true sense of decency but also likes to win in court. Kuzak loves fellow jurist **Grace Van Owen**, but theirs is a tumultuous union. He can be temperamental when it comes to getting what he thinks he deserves.

See *L.A. Law*

KWAN, BILLY

A half-Asian, half-European dwarf living in Indonesia during the revolution of the 1960s, Billy is easy to spot in his gaudy tropical shirts. He befriends an Australian radio reporter, **Guy Hamilton**, and shows him the ropes. Billy knows just about everyone of importance in and around Jakarta.

See *The Year of Living Dangerously*

LACEY, MARY BETH

Mary Beth is a cop because she wants to make a difference in the world and because it's something she does well. But for her, it's still just a job, albeit a job she does with an unswerving dedication to her own integrity. She realizes, though, that she must balance, like plates spinning on sticks, her job and her marriage and two children. She provides a steadying influence on her headstrong partner, **Christine Cagney**, both personally and professionally, by counteracting Cagney's obsessions and adding a dose of reality to the mix.

See *Cagney & Lacey*

LADY LOU

Bawdy, lusty barroom singer dripping with diamonds. "I wasn't always rich. Why, there was a time I didn't know where my next husband was coming from." Men are crazy about her; women respect (and envy) her. A brash, buxom platinum blonde poured into skin-hugging dresses, she lives, surrounded by Paris imports, above the Bowery saloon where she performs sultry songs. She is kept by the saloon owner, Gus Jordan, who plies her with the jewels she adores. "Diamonds is my career." A friend to conmen and damsels in distress, she tells a distraught young girl not to worry: "When women go wrong, men go right after them." Lou has a maid named Pearl who loves working for her. Unable to resist a good-looking man, she invites all the men she meets "to come up and see me sometime." She's always ready with a quip, and can more than hold her own in a fight. When a rescue mission opens up next door, she falls for its innocent-appearing young captain, **Captain Cummings**, "a new kind of man" who wants to save her soul. She explains her life's choice to him: "It was either diamonds or the choir. I chose diamonds."

See *She Done Him Wrong*

LaForge, Geordi

Born into a Starfleet family (his mother was a ship's captain), LaForge becomes the brilliant engineer on the starship *Enterprise,* despite being born blind. He wears a specially designed device called a VISOR that gives him better-than-standard vision. Is very good friends with **Data** and has problems asserting himself with women.

See *Star Trek: The Next Generation*

Lake, Peter

A turn-of-the-century street person who's fated to play a role in the ongoing battle between good and evil, beauty and destruction. He teams up with a huge white horse, Athansor, who can fly and even travel through time. He's the lover of beautiful, dying Beverly Penn. After being set adrift in New York Harbor by parents who weren't allowed into the country, he grew up with the Baymen, a tribe of Hudson River marsh dwellers. He is the nemesis of evil gangster Pearly Soames.

See *Winter's Tale*, Mark Helprin

LaLoosh, Ebby Calvin "Nuke"

He is a raw but talented minor-league pitcher determined to make it to the "show." Extremely dim-witted, though baseball talents are good enough to attract the attention of baseball groupie **Annie Savoy**. A member of the Raleigh-Durham Bulls, LaLoosh is mentored by catcher **Crash Davis**.

See *Bull Durham*

Lamarr, Hedley

Avaricious right-hand man of Governor William J. Lepetomane. A ruthless opportunist and double-dealer. He hates it when his name was confused with that of actress Hedy Lamarr. Known to associate with Nazis, Ku Klux Klansmen, desperadoes, and other assorted no-goodniks. Killed by **Sheriff Black Bart**.

See *Blazing Saddles*

Lambert, Reggie

Beautiful Reggie infuriates female friends and baffles males by eating voraciously and never gaining weight. Ms. Lambert's husband, Charles, was murdered before she could finish filing the divorce papers. But Reggie still hasn't learned her lesson about falling in love with men about whom she knows little; her latest spontaneous flame is charming, witty, possibly murderous **Peter Joshua**—if that is, in fact, his name.

See *Charade*

Lana

She is a sexy Chicago call girl. After sleeping with him, Lana gets **Joel Goodsen** into money trouble with her pimp; then she helps Joel in a mad scramble to restore order and sanity to his suburban existence—before his parents get back from their vacation. She proves to be a friend, indeed.

See *Risky Business*

Landau, Nathan

Manipulative, unbalanced, highly intellectual lover to **Sophie Zawistowska**, and friend of **Stingo**. He torments Sophie for surviving Auschwitz and Stingo for being a southerner. Eventually, he loses what little sanity he had.

See *Sophie's Choice*, William Styron

Lander

A dangerously unbalanced Vietnam vet, he was tortured by captors when held as a POW. Now flying Goodyear blimps for television crews to capture sporting events for nationwide audiences. Easily manipulated, politically naive. Fascinated by explosives, arching light patterns, and the ultimate in public mass murder. Despite serious mental instability, manages to keep his dual life in some semblance of order.

See *Black Sunday*

Lane, Hondo

Hondo is as much at home in the wild desert country of the Southwest as are the Apaches who were there first. He sometimes works as a scout for the U.S. Cavalry and sometimes just roams around, savoring the freedom he can enjoy in the vast untracked expanse of the desert.

See *Hondo*, Louis L'Amour

Geordi LaForge

LANE, LOIS

Beautiful and brash reporter at the *Daily Planet*. She is in love with **Superman** (he granted her an exclusive interview) by night and works beside **Clark Kent** by day. Lois doesn't realize just how strange that relationship may turn out to be. Superman once turned back time in order to bring her back to life.

See *Superman*

LANE, PATTY AND CATHY

A pair of physically identical, bubbly blond teenage cousins living with Patty's family in Brooklyn Heights, but the resemblance ends there. Cathy is a sophisticated world traveler who has lived on six continents, attends the ballet, and adores crepes suzette. Patty, on the other hand, is the classic all-American girl. She's never lived outside her neighborhood, goes crazy over rock and roll, and loves a good hot dog. The pair is often shadowed by Patty's nerdy brother Ross. "One pair of matching bookends as different as night and day."

See *The Patty Duke Show*

LANGLAND, GAY

He's a modern-day cowboy as well as a "wondrous listener." He won't be a follower, and he won't be a leader either. He makes no promises so he won't be held to any. Gay keeps an unfinished house outside of Las Vegas in memory of his wife, who died in childbirth. He falls for unstable **Roslyn Taber** and hunts wild horses for dog food despite her protests. "I never bothered to battle a woman before. And it was peaceful, but a lot like huggin' air."

See *The Misfits,* Arthur Miller

LANGTRY, MOIRA

She's a sexy, self-assured con artist who reckons her body is her greatest asset. She tries to convince lover **Roy Dillon** to team up with her, but his mother, **Lilly**, sees her as a threat. Then it becomes a question of which of the two women will survive.

See *The Grifters,* Jim Thompson

LAPP, RACHEL

Amish widow with a young son, Samuel, who sees a brutal murder in the Philadelphia train station during a rare trip outside their Lancaster County, Pennsylvania home. Sweet, graceful, and beautiful, Rachel captures the heart of a big city detective, **John Book**. Samuel and Book become close, somewhat to Rachel's horror: "I just don't like my son spending all this time with a man who carries a gun and goes around whacking people."

See *Witness*

LARRY

Eccentric local character who occasionally helps out as a handyman at **Dick Louden**'s Stratford Inn in Norwich, Vermont. Along with his brothers, **Daryl** and **Daryl**, runs the Minuteman Cafe. Is the only one of the three siblings who talks. Attended Mount Pilard Technical School. For some reason, his gas bill is paid by Johnny Carson.

See *Newhart*

LaRUE

A loyal, best girlfriend. As **Gidget**'s closest friend, LaRue feels obliged to show her a life beyond boyfriend Moondoggie. That means plenty of hours of fun and sun at the beach, where the boys are. Though she loves her dearly, she thinks Gidget's a little too "good." LaRue is less restrained and sometimes has ideas that lead to trouble.

See *Gidget*

LaRUE, DETECTIVE JOHNNY "J.D."

This scheming, fairly sleazy police detective cuts more than his share of procedural corners in catching bad guys. He's a habitual abuser of alcohol and police regulations and is more often than not in deep water, financially and personally. He's subjected to frequent reprimands by his boss, **Captain Frank Furillo**.

See *Hill Street Blues*

LaRUSSO, DANIEL

After this boy has spent his whole life in New Jersey, Mom drags him clear across the country to the San Fernando Valley outside L.A. Daniel soon finds that his New Jersey style and sense of independence come across as cocky and brash to kids in the Valley, especially the local boys who study karate under a sadistic and nasty bully. He finds aid and comfort from an unlikely source: the mild and kindly **Mr. Miyagi**, the manager of the apartment building where Daniel and his mom live. Mr.

Miyagi not only teaches Daniel martial arts techniques but proves to be a mentor who educates the boy in the philosophy behind karate. That and a little romance eventually brighten his perspective on Southern California living.

See *The Karate Kid*

Lassiter

Despised and feared by the Mormons of Utah, this notorious gunslinger is actually a champion of the poor and the helpless. He rides from town to town battling his Mormon persecutors and aiding women in distress. Pursued by the sinister Elder Tull, Lassiter and his true love Jane Withersteen escape into the back country, discover an Edenic, isolated valley, and live there happily ever after.

See *Riders of the Purple Sage,* **Zane Grey**

Laszlo, Mike

A U.S. citizen for thirty-seven years, Laszlo is proud of the life he has built in his adopted homeland through years of hard work and determination. The steel-worker from Hungary met his wife (now deceased) in a refugee camp in Hungary. Laszlo is proud of his son (who also works in the steel mill) and his daughter, lawyer **Ann Talbot**, and is a fond grandfather, as well. Mike can still do more pushups than the average young man, and has regular trysts with a widow in town. His past as a clerk in the police department in his native Budapest during WWII has gotten him into trouble with federal authorities, who believe him to be a war criminal.

See *The Music Box*

Laszlo, Victor

Legendary Czechoslovakian partisan leader, married to **Ilsa Lund**. An escapee of a Nazi concentration camp, often rumored to have been killed. Drinks gallons of champagne cocktails, though never appears inebriated. An unshakable believer in his cause. His continued existence is a thumb in the Nazi eye. Sees a side of **Rick Blaine** that few perceive. "Welcome back to the fight. This time I know our side will win."

See *Casablanca*

Laurie

"Guys think I'm too smart." That's how Laurie explains her dateless Saturday nights, which she usually spends baby-sitting. Although she's been known to share a joint with one of her best friends (Annie and Lynda, both of whom were killed October 31, 1978), Laurie tends to spend a lot of time studying. Bright and resourceful, Laurie gets along well with children and is trusted to take care of errands for her father, a real estate salesman. When nervous or thoughtful, Laurie has a habit of twirling a strand of hair around her left index finger. Never the right, and never any other finger.

See *Halloween*

Laurey

A pretty girl who turns many a head, Laurey only has eyes for one feller, a handsome cowboy named **Curly**. But Curly's not quite ready to settle down, and this is the Oklahoma Territory, just after the turn of the twentieth century, where not even a feisty woman like Laurey can make the first move.

See *Oklahoma!,* Oscar Hammerstein II and Richard Rodgers

The Lawrence Family

A conventional-looking family with too many problems. The Lawrence clan is well-off financially, but they manage somehow to stumble on to nearly all of life's crises. Like when the father, Doug, was temporarily blinded, or when the mother, Nancy, discovered that she had breast cancer. Doug and Nancy have made a comfortable home on Milan Avenue in South Pasadena for their three children, Nancy, Willie, and Buddy, complete with a guest house in the front yard. The oldest daughter Nancy's own ill-fated marriage to Jeff Maitland produced one child, Timmy, and a lot of angst. Nancy often uses her blonde hair and body to get what she wants, often at the expense of other people's feelings. Middle son Willie doesn't share his father's traditional work ethic, and has dropped out of college to try and make it as a writer. This lifestyle causes no end of turmoil between the two men of the family. Buddy, or Letitia, as her mother sometimes calls her, is the youngest of the clan. She ran away once during a particularly stressful time. The family tomboy, Buddy tears around Pasadena on her skateboard, and prefers jeans and sneakers over dresses. Born well after her sister and brother, she is adored by her family, especially her brother, who calls her "Peaches." As if this isn't enough action for one household, the Lawrences adopt Annie, a young girl whose parents died in a car accident.

See *Family*

LAWRENCE, FRANCINE "GIDGET"

She's a fun-loving, beach-going teenager. Surfing, sunbathing, drinking milk shakes, and talking about boys are the chief activities in a typical day for perky Californian Gidget and her friends. The daughter of widower **Professor Russ Lawrence**, Gidget must answer to him as well as older married sister Anne. She's always getting into trouble with schemes and plans—usually revolving around boys—concocted with the help of her best friend, **LaRue**. Her best boyfriend, Jeff, is away at college, but Gidget doesn't stay home pining away for him. There's too much fun to be had!

See *Gidget*

LAWRENCE, LEONARD "PRIVATE PYLE"

Overweight, immature, mentally slow marine recruit, failing miserably in his attempt to get through basic training. Nicknamed Private Pyle by drill instructor **Gunnery Sergeant Hartman**. Befriended by **Private Joker**, Lawrence is cold-shouldered by everyone else in his unit, who think he's a disgrace to their outfit. He once concealed a doughnut in his footlocker. Despite his many failings in the military, he scores high on the rifle range. He also harbors deeply hidden and dangerous psychological problems.

See *Full Metal Jacket*

LAWRENCE, PROFESSOR RUSS

Exasperated, well-meaning dad. What a tough job it is to raise a teenager in California as a single father! Luckily, Professor Lawrence has plenty of good sense and experience from raising his older daughter, Anne. But **Gidget** is a high-spirited handful who requires every ounce of patience and parenting skills he can muster. "That Gidget!"

See *Gidget*

LAWSON, FLOYD

This philosophical, talky barber operates Floyd's Barber Shop, the town center for news, gossip, and innuendo. There, Floyd dispenses advice, and gathers and passes on news, while cutting hair. He fantasizes about expanding to a two-chair operation. His great creative achievement is "Hail to Thee, Lady Mayberry," written for the Founders Day ceremonies. Floyd is not only a habitual embroiderer of the truth, he's a ready listener to tall tales. The gullible barber is often duped by charlatans who visit Mayberry with remarkable frequency.

See *The Andy Griffith Show*

LAWSON, COLONEL TAD

An American officer in postwar Germany who's given the task of prosecuting a quartet of Nazi judges accused of war crimes. With a hammering style, Colonel Lawson strikes boldly at the character of the men on trial but is foiled at nearly every turn by the steely German lawyer for the defense.

See *Judgment at Nuremberg*

LEAMINGTON, JAMES

He's a wealthy middle-aged Englishman with a sickly, annoying wife. He employs **Georgy**'s parents in his household. The childless Leamington starts off treating Georgy like a daughter, but his feelings toward her take a decidedly amorous turn and he asks her to be his mistress.

See *Georgy Girl*

LEARY, MACON

Methodical to a fault, bubbling with suppressed emotions, he is the reluctant author of the *Accidental Tourist* book series, a collection of travel guides written for businesspeople who hate to travel. Wracked with guilt over death of young son and the resulting breakup of his marriage, Macon has withdrawn into an isolated lifestyle and wants nothing out of the ordinary to disturb his uneasy solitude. Because of a broken leg, Macon is temporarily living with his eccentric family. He owns a Welsh corgi, which creates problems of both canine and human varieties.

See *The Accidental Tourist*

LECTER, HANNIBAL "THE CANNIBAL"

A serial killer known for eating his victims, he's charming, eerily intense, and exceptionally intelligent. His eloquence and fastidious diction give him

a certain elegance. He's enlisted for his peculiar expertise by **Clarice Starling**, an FBI agent, to help track down another serial killer. Over a period of time, he and Starling find a strange rapport, and he actually favors her with some of the fruits of his intellect. Though he's not horrific to look at, he does project an incredible sense of menace, especially for someone securely incarcerated in what would appear to be an escape-proof situation. He's not without a kind of ghoulish humor and he relishes the fear he puts into people and the opportunity to shock their pedestrian sensibilities. Though, as a practicing psychiatrist he has very little use for the Hippocratic Oath. "A census taker tried to test me once. I ate her liver with some fava beans and a nice Chianti."
See *The Silence of the Lambs,* Thomas Harris

LEE
This sartorially elegant gunslinger is haunted by his past and obsessed by the difficulties inherent in finding good dry cleaning on the Western frontier. He's hired as one of a seven-man army to protect a Mexican village from pillage by a gang led by a Señor **Calvera**. On the run from a lifetime's worth of enemies and his own conscience, Lee usually hides when there's a fight. He can talk the talk, but he's lost his nerve.
See *The Magnificent Seven*

LEE, BASIL DUKE
As noble as his middle name suggests, Lee learns the hard way that rewards in life come only from hard work and sincere effort. Though he's tempted by women, in the end Lee successfully resists entrapment by feminine wiles and instead follows his credo of "ambition, struggle and glory."
See *The Basil and Josephine Stories,* F. Scott Fitzgerald

LEE, LINDA
It's an alias, used by **Supergirl** after she is hurled to Earth from a settlement of survivors of the catastrophe that destroyed the planet Krypton. Once settled in the USA, she attends Midvale High, a girls' private school. Ironically enough, her roommate there is Lucy Lane, the little sister of Lois Lane, reporter at the *Daily Planet*.
See *Supergirl,* Mort Weisinger and Otto Binder

LEE, LORELEI
Like her fabulous namesake who vamped men on the Rhine, this beautiful blonde is always on the lookout for a man, preferably with a well-filled wallet and a big diamond in his pocket. Lorelei is no dummy when it comes to hunting down the richest man in a crowd, and her exploits can be a cause of concern for her best friend, **Dorothy**.
See *Gentlemen Prefer Blondes,* Anita Loos

LEE, WILLIAM
A junkie living from one fix to the next, Lee lives on the streets of various American cities and does whatever it takes to satisfy his nine dollar-a-day heroin habit, including stealing from drunks and hoboes. His mind is awash with paranoid fantasies of totalitarian police states exerting control over the populace with drugs, thought control, and degradation. Or are they fantasies?
See *Naked Lunch,* William S. Burroughs

LEECH, ARCHIE
Mild-mannered British barrister who likes to live life in an orderly fashion. Currently, he is defending a diamond thief. Archie finds himself perplexed by **Wanda**, though definitely attracted to her. Somewhat fearful of **Otto**. A man who just hates to be caught with his pants down—or off.
See *A Fish Called Wanda*

LEEDS, JAMES
Sensitive, lonely teacher at school for the hearing impaired. Does not have a hearing problem himself. Leeds has an inquisitive mind and likes to take a creative approach to problem solving both in the classroom and in his personal life. Single, but romantically involved with **Sarah Norman**.
See *Children of a Lesser God*

LEEP, JACQUES
French-Canadian handyman, hired to supply firewood to the Grand Hotel in northern Canada. Implicated by the Royal Canadian Mounted Police in no less than five gruesome murders—all of which took place at night and involved small children—Jacques continues to elude the Mounties, and is frequently seen paddling his canoe throughout the national parks of Canada.
See *The Mad Trapper*

365 BAD HAIR DAYS A YEAR

Clubber Lang
Alfalfa
Kramer
Polyester
Mr. Spock
Henry Spencer

LEITER, FELIX

American CIA agent. Leiter, who lost his right arm and leg to a shark, has also worked for Pinkerton's Detective Agency. The Texan has developed an excellent working relationship with Commander **James Bond** of the British Secret Service. The two have joined forces on several missions vital to both Washington and London.

See *Live and Let Die,* Ian Fleming

LELAINA

Pretty, brunette twenty-something, she's filled with angst. Lelaina is instinctively creative; her outlet for her creative impulses is making a video documentary of her friends' lives. Like those friends, she makes light of her generation's bleak prospects through the extensive use of irony. She fills her life with kitschy knick-knacks from the seventies, jokingly fetishizing the useless products and cultural icons she's grown up with. She wants romance with her longtime friend **Troy**, but his aimlessness convinces her that she'd be better off with **Michael**, an upwardly mobile type. But when Michael compromises her work, editing her documentary into a snappy, empty-souled, MTV-like production, she realizes that staying with him would mean selling out her vague but apparently very real ideals. Likes 7-Eleven Big Gulps and dancing to the Knack's "My Sharona."

See *Reality Bites*

LENNY

He's a neurotic Jewish New Yorker, honeymooning in Miami with his whiny new wife. There, Lenny meets and falls head over heels for a drop-dead-gorgeous, blond midwestern college girl—a classic WASP. Smitten, he goes to ridiculous lengths to evade his wife and pursue his dream girl, despite the presence of many obstacles, not the least of which is the girl's domineering, disapproving father.

See *The Heartbreak Kid*

LEO

The formidable top dog of the Irish gang in town. Leo's sentimental and trusting, though his trust is sometimes misplaced. He is "an artist with the Thompson" submachine gun. Leo is nuts about **Verna**, a ballsy young broad who's had a thing with his number two man, **Tom Regan**. So smitten is he

that he risks all-out gang war to protect Verna's mealymouthed brother, **Bernie Bernbaum**. He tells rivals: "You're exactly as big as I let you be, and don't forget it, ever."

See *Miller's Crossing*

LEON

A pre-op transsexual with a permanent two-day growth of beard, he's involved in an off-again, on-again relationship with **Sonny**, whom he has married in a homosexual ceremony. Prone to suicide attempts, fainting spells, and enormous feelings of anxiety. Wears a ratty bathrobe.

See *Dog Day Afternoon*

LEONARD

This villanous thug works as a "secretary" to **Phillip Vandamm**, trader in state secrets. Leonard's steely blue eyes, slicked-back hair, and cool manner make a civilized mask for a stone killer. His ability is tested to the limit when he tries to get rid of supposed superspy George Kaplan, aka **Roger Thornhill**.

See *North by Northwest*

LERMONTOV, BORIS

Boris is a megalomaniac ballet impresario who "can't bear amateurs." He's a workaholic and a recluse who has little liking for the common run of humanity. When **Julian Craster**, a young composer, tells him that his music professor stole his composition for a new ballet, he hires him on the spot and enlightens him: "It is much more disheartening to have to steal than to be stolen from." He makes a star of young ballerina **Victoria Page** and crushes his creation when she falls in love with Craster.

See *The Red Shoes*

LEROY

He is a dance major at New York City's High School for the Performing Arts. Originally from a poor family in Harlem, he wants to use his dancing to move up in life. Involved in secretive romance with a ballet dancer from wealthy Manhattan family. Hopes to audition for the Dance Theater of Harlem or Alvin Ailey.

See *Fame*

LESTER

Obnoxious, egotistical television producer, he's a

womanizer who's totally brazen when it comes to using his professional power as an element of his seductions. Likes to quote W. C. Fields's theories on comedy. Currently the subject of an unflattering documentary by filmmaker and despised brother-in-law **Cliff Stern**.

See *Crimes and Misdemeanors*

LESTER, JEETER

A dirt-poor, white southern farmer with a peasant's attachment to the soil. City life isn't meant for a man with the love of the land in him. Jeeter is unabashedly selfish and would just as soon steal from a family member as from a stranger. He thinks of his wife and children as sources of food, labor, and money.

See *Tobacco Road,* **Erskine Caldwell**

LESTER, VICKI

Young Esther Blodgett is discovered by fading, dissolute movie star **Norman Maine**, who convinces her that she has what it takes to become a megastar and marries her. Maine gets his studio to give Blodgett a shot, and she excels as both a singer and an actress. Seeing potential in her, the studio changes her name to Vicki Lester and she fulfills Maine's prophecy of stardom. Although he spends a lot of time drunk and acting embarrassing in public, Vicki never stops loving her husband. "Hello, everybody. This is Mrs. Norman Maine."

See *A Star Is Born*

LEVENE, SHELLEY

A pathetic old loser swimming in a sea of sharks, Levene is the least talented member of a cutthroat band of Chicago real estate agents. It is his profound misfortune that a contest has commenced in which the agent who sells the most lucrative piece of property gets a brand-new Cadillac, the runner-up a set of steak knives, and the losers get fired. Knowing his chances are slim to none, Levene piteously and unsuccessfully begs the office manager for a list of the firm's best customers. His relationship with **Ricky Roma**, the eventual winner, seems to be Levene's saving grace, until Roma reveals that business always comes before friendship in the real estate game.

See *Glengarry Glen Ross,* **David Mamet**

LEVI, DOLLY

She is not only a matchmaker, but a veritable mistress of all trades, handing out her business card to all: "Just leave everything to me." "Call on Dolly for social introductions arranged in an atmosphere of elegance and refinement." She lives in 1890s New York City, and is the widow of Mr. Ephraim Levi. Dolly believes in her late husband's adage: "Money should circulate like rainwater and should be flowing in and out of people's lives." She is in love with "half a millionaire" **Horace Vandergelder** and is conniving to get him to marry her. While she's bossy and prone to meddling, Dolly has a heart of gold and only wants to make people happy—herself included. She loves the Harmonia Gardens Restaurant, fine clothes, jewelry, and champagne. As superstitious as she is flamboyant, she's waiting for her late husband to give her a sign that it's okay to go on with her life without him and marry Horace. "I've got to feel my heart come alive again before the parade passes by."

See *Hello Dolly* and *The Matchmaker,* **Thornton Wilder**

LEVY, LARRY

Hard-driven movie executive out to take over the job of the studio vice president. Joins Alcoholics Anonymous because that's where the best deals are being made. Can make up a movie scenario out of any news story, pointing out that screenwriters are superfluous.

See *The Player,* **Michael Tolkin**

LEVY, THOMAS BABINGTON "BABE"

A studious Columbia University graduate student and distance runner, awkward with women. His father committed suicide after personal humiliation at the hands of Joe McCarthy and his minions, inspiring Babe's Ph.D. research into American tyranny. After his brother dies suddenly, at the hands of **Christian Szell**, a former (and present-day) Nazi, Levy is involuntarily mixed up in a diamond-smuggling plot.

See *Marathon Man*

LEWIS

Like father, like son—they're both nerds. Lewis is a pocket-protector-wearing, bespectacled young man

Thomas Levy

who goes away to college, only to find himself persecuted by the boorish members of the football fraternity. With his best friend and fellow nerd, **Gilbert**, he forms his own fraternity, fighting back against the jocks. It is his superior lovemaking skills that help him win a babe cheerleader away from the all-American quarterback.

See *Revenge of the Nerds*

LEWIS, CAPTAIN DOREEN

Stationed at Fort Biloxi, Lewis is a tough, mean commander to female Army recruits. She meets her match in **Private Judy Benjamin** and her life disintegrates. Lewis rebuilds her career in Europe, only to have another run-in with Benjamin. "Don't push me, punk."

See *Private Benjamin*

LEWIS, EDWARD

Inside this hard-shelled, wealthy specialist in corporate takeovers, there's rumored to be a nice guy. But he thinks he can buy people, as well as companies, for money. Among those he buys (or rents out, anyway) is a beautiful hooker, **Vivian Ward**. Supposedly, he doesn't want to buy her for her body, but merely for companionship. It stands to reason that he needs to buy attractive female companionship, as he is only devastatingly good-looking, almost an American gigolo with an MBA. He keeps the inner good guy hidden away and treats his business life as guerrilla warfare, in which no holds are barred. He shows little or no feeling for anyone, not his New York girlfriend, and not those who work in the businesses he buys and then guts. "People have nothing to do with it," he explains. "It's strictly business."

See *Pretty Woman*

LEWIS, DR. SUSAN

A resident in the Emergency Room at County General Hospital in Chicago, she has not yet decided on her field of specialization. She's a good doctor, who sometimes has a hard time being as tough as the men with whom she works. Dr. Lewis has a dysfunctional sister who drops in on her without warning and is always in some kind of trouble. Pals with ER coworker **Dr. Mark Greene**.

See *ER*

LICALSI, JANICE

A former New York City police officer, Licalsi is a real beauty with a great body. Her father, also a police officer, is "mobbed up" and on the take. In order to protect her dad, Janice reluctantly starts doing favors for the mob. She gets turned around by the cops and eventually kills two mobsters. Unable to live with herself thereafter, she turns herself in—even though she could have gotten away with it. Her old flame is **Detective John Kelly**.

See *NYPD Blue*

LIDENBROCK, PROFESSOR OTTO

After following the route of Icelandic explorer **Arne Saknussemm** into the center of the Earth, Lidenbrock, "the Columbus of these subterranean regions," returns to new-found fame. He's an impatient, excitable man but very determined. His faith in science never wavers amidst the wonders of the underground.

See *Journey to the Center of the Earth,* Jules Verne

LIGGETT, WESTON

Trapped in a marriage to a socially prominent woman and in her family's business as "vice-president in charge of nonsense," Liggett has energy to burn. He finds happiness and love in the arms of high-society call girl **Gloria Wandrous**. "I'm going out to look for my pride. Alone."

See *Butterfield 8,* John O'Hara

LICHTMAN, DAVID

A nerdy high schooler, he's into computer hacking and sometimes uses his knowledge in an effort to impress girls. When not changing grades in the high school computer data banks, David likes to work his way into forbidden territory—like U.S. Defense Department computers. There, he learns that a little knowledge can be a very dangerous thing. It can even mean the destruction of the world, a high price to pay for impressing a girl.

See *WarGames*

LIME, HARRY

This witty, clever American lived in chaotic postwar Vienna, until his untimely accidental death. Or so it would appear. Then his old American friend shows up in Vienna, and unpleasant past and pre-

sent truths about Harry begin to surface. Harry is fond of Ferris wheels.
See *The Third Man*

LINDERMAN
Regarded as a "psycho" by his high school classmates, Linderman's really just a misunderstood teen with tragedy in his past. He's hired as a "bodyguard" by a new kid in school, **Clifford**, to protect him from the class bully, and, as might be expected, they develop a genuine friendship.
See *My Bodyguard*

LINDSAY, NORMAN
A provocative Australian artist, Lindsay uses his imagination, his family, and a trio of beautiful models to create paintings and sculptures that put sexuality back into spirituality. "I am an artist, and I refuse to be compromised by the feeble scruples of the public."
See *Sirens*

LINDSTROM, PHYLLIS
Neighbor and landlord of **Mary Richards** and **Rhoda Morgenstern**, who live in Phyllis's Minneapolis apartment house. She is given to butting into other people's business and is often oblivious to others' feelings, though she considers herself a highly evolved, modern woman. Phyllis is the mother of Bess Lindstrom and the wife of Lars Lindstrom, a terminally dull dermatologist who owns the apartment building. Kooky? Yes. Flaky? That, too. But she means well, as a rule (except where Rhoda is concerned).
See *The Mary Tyler Moore Show* and *Phyllis*

LITTLE NEMO
A little boy who passes into the magical world known as Slumberland when he falls asleep each night, Nemo braves fearful perils and encounters fantastic, exotic creatures in his alternate universe, only to be awakened just when things are getting good. Among the inhabitants of Slumberland are King Morpheus, ruler of the dream world, Flip, an ugly dwarf who gets in the way of Nemo's fun, and Impy, a young cannibal. His parents and grandparents explain his nightly adventures as merely bad dreams caused by his strange eating habits before bedtime. His nocturnal diet can include anything from sardines to raw onions and ice cream.
See *Little Nemo in Slumberland*

LOBO, SHERIFF ELROY P.
Underhanded and mildly corrupt, good-ol'-boy Sheriff Lobo of Orly County, Georgia, who considers trucker **B. J. McKay** his principal nemesis, but continually pursues him to no avail. With dim-witted brother-in-law Deputy Perkins, he somehow manages to nab crooks. Eventually works for special police task force in Atlanta, due to massive bureaucratic oversight.
See *B.J. and the Bear* and *Lobo*

LOGAN, TED THEODORE
A truly awesome dude and half of the heavy-metal rock group Wyld Stallyns. Constant companion to **Bill S. Preston** through thick and thin. Likes to travel via continuum-bending phone booth. Has knack for getting out of difficult situations which belies overtly dazed demeanor. Along with Bill, is worshiped as unheralded genius in futuristic society centuries removed from present-day Southern California. Involved with one bitchin' medieval babe.
See *Bill and Ted's Excellent Adventure*

LOGAN, TOM
Logan is a horse thief and scoundrel in the waning days of the Old West. He knows that the time has come for men like him to leave their wicked ways and accept the coming of civilization, but he just can't resist one more golden opportunity when it's presented.
See *The Missouri Breaks*

LOLA
Sultry siren of the baseball diamond. She believes in living for the moment and having it all, no matter what the cost (to someone). Close associate of **Mr. Applegate**. Has her eyes fixed on **Joe Hardy**. Singing and dancing talents are second to none and have been known to hold audiences captive. "Whatever Lola wants, Lola gets!"
See *Damn Yankees*

LOLITA
Born Dolores Haze, this twelve-year-old nymphet is an object of desire for her middle-aged stepfather

Humbert Humbert. Old beyond her years, she turns out to be far more than he is able to deal with, and after she has had her way with him, she leaves him for another man, Clare Quilty, driving Humbert to the point of murder.

See *Lolita,* Vladimir Nabokov

LOMAN, BIFF

The tortured older son of salesman **Willy Loman**, Biff never got over finding out that his father cheated on his mother while on the road. In high school, he was a football star and had a "lotta dreams and plans," but he abandoned all of them, never made anything of himself, and has never been able to hold a job. He and Willy have a thorny relationship.

See *Death of a Salesman,* Arthur Miller

LOMAN, HAPPY (HAROLD)

Happy, the shallow younger son of **Willy Loman**, has had success in bedding women, yet he is lonely for love. He thinks there's a higher destiny waiting for him but can't seem to locate it. "I can outbox, outrun, and outlift anybody in that store, and I have to take orders from those common, petty sons-of-bitches till I can't stand it anymore."

See *Death of a Salesman,* Arthur Miller

LOMAN, WILLY

He is a tired, aging traveling salesman, who believes devoutly in the notion that success comes to him who is "well liked." Acceptance, however, is only part of Willy's list of desires. After a lifetime on the road, he wants the company for which he has toiled to give him a nontraveling position. He wants to be out from under the weight of debt. He wants his sons, Happy and Biff, to respect the enormous effort he has made to make himself a success. And he wants Happy and Biff to be successful in their own right. Since none of these dreams are anywhere close to fruition, Willy is a frustrated and unhappy man still looking for a way to leave behind something tangible for his family, wanting to believe in a pot of gold at the end of the rainbow, but beginning to realize that he might not find it. "A man is not a piece of fruit."

See *Death of a Salesman,* Arthur Miller

THE LONE RANGER

Cleaner and more wholesome than your average trail hand, the Lone Ranger is the quintessential cowboy hero. He and his trusty sidekick, **Tonto**, use ingenious and daring ploys to defeat the bad guys in black hats at every turn, but are so good-hearted they never kill anyone. With his trademark white hat and black mask, the mysterious avenger prefers to use his gunslinging expertise to shoot the weapon out of an outlaw's grasp. Astride his trusty horse, he gallops off to another adventure with the cry "Heigh-ho, Silver!" leaving the outlaws to rub their hand and wonder aloud, "Who was that masked man?"

See *The Lone Ranger*

LONGSTOCKING, PIPPI

The freest spirit and self-proclaimed "strongest girl in the world." A freckled nine-year-old with carrot-colored hair worn in tight braids, Pippi gets her last name from wearing one black and one brown stocking with black shoes that are twice as long as her feet. Her mother died when she was very young, and so Pippi has had to learn to fend for herself. Living alone in her little ramshackle house called Villa Villekulla, Pippi's only companions are a horse who lives on her porch and a monkey named Mr. Nilsson. "Don't you worry about me. I'll always come out on top."

See *Pippi Longstocking*

LONIGAN, WILLIAM "STUDS"

The son of Patrick and Mary Lonigan, Studs Lonigan is a street-smart tough with a good heart. But Studs gets mixed up with some low-life types from his Irish and Jewish neighborhood on Chicago's South Side, during the summer after his graduation from grammar school. The eldest of four children (Frances, Martin, and Loretta) in a middle-class Irish Catholic family, Studs wants to skip high school and join his father, a painting contractor, in the family business. His mother, a fanatically devout Roman Catholic, hopes Studs will stay in school and study for the priesthood.

The Lone Ranger

Beneath the tough exterior, Studs has a soft heart which he shows only to Lucy Scanlan, with whom he shares what he considers the greatest moments of his life before alienating her. She nevertheless remains his greatest love.

See *Young Lonigan, The Young Manhood of Studs Lonigan,* and *Judgment Day,* James T. Farrell

LONNEGAN, DOYLE

Lonnegan is a New York City–based banker-gangster, who regularly plays a high-stakes poker game on the luxury train running between New York and Chicago. Lonnegan walks with a slight limp in his right leg and speaks with a heavy brogue. A humorless, touchy fellow, he'd readily kill anyone he senses as a threat to his operations, or who makes him look foolish. He was born in the New York slum called Five Points but claims Forest Hills as his turf; it's a more upscale area. Lonnegan cares a lot about status and has worked hard to make himself a pillar of respectable society—he has even become a grand knight in the Knights of Columbus. He doesn't drink, smoke, or chase women, but he has some vices. For instance, he cheats at poker. He is usually accompanied by two goons.

See *The Sting*

DR. LOOMIS

A dedicated and determined psychiatrist, Dr. Loomis has made patient **Michael Myers** his primary focus since the boy was admitted to the institution at which he works in 1963. After the young man gets free, the doctor's sense of responsibility causes him to make extraordinary efforts to bring his patient back to the state hospital at Smith's Grove, Illinois—or, if that's not possible, to make certain that he's not allowed to live. "I spent eight years trying to reach him and then another seven years trying to keep him locked up because I realized that what was living behind that boy's eyes was purely and simply evil."

See *Halloween*

LOOMIS, GEORGE

A cynical, socially inept man with a shaky mental health history, he has a tendency to break into violence. He grows obsessed with jealousy at the thought of being cheated on by his va-va-voom wife, **Rose Loomis.** Loomis foils Rose's lover's attempt to murder him, then chases after Rose, strangling her for betraying him. Distraught and wanted by the law, he flees on a boat that's low on gas. A crisis on the boat presents him with an opportunity for one last heroic and redeeming act.

See *Niagara*

LOOMIS, ROSE

Beautiful, curvaceous, sexy, soft-voiced blond who left behind an "easy" reputation to marry **George Loomis.** But she's had enough, and is tired of her husband's tempestous nature; she's taken a dark, handsome lover, with whom she's plotting George's murder during their vacation at scenic Niagara Falls. When the murder goes sour, she's chased and confronted by her husband in the very same tower whose chimes once rang out what was for Rose and her lover "their" song—and is strangled to death by him there.

See *Niagara*

LORD JIM

A parson's son and an essentially decent young man, Jim faces a court of inquiry for his role in the *Patna* affair, having abandoned a ship full of refugees during a storm. Jim loses his certification, after which he befriends **Marlow** and takes a job as an agent for **Stein** at a trading post at Patusan. He succeeds as a trader, finds love, and regains his lost honor through the utmost sacrifice.

See *Lord Jim*, Joseph Conrad

LORD, TRACY SAMANTHA

The spoiled and uppity daughter of a rich Philadelphia family, Lord is a schemer who can't decide what she wants out of life. She's forced to choose between three would-be suitors: her fiancé, her ex-husband, and a charming reporter. "I don't want to be worshipped; I want to be loved."

See *The Philadelphia Story*

LOU

Former gangster, now in his declining years. Maintains dapper wardrobe and stylish appearance. Desperately wants to do something important with his remaining time, though only knows crime and hustling as means to that end. Involved in off-and-on relationship with aging moll **Grace.** Has protec-

Lou

tive crush on his neighbor **Sally**, whom he secretly watches from his apartment window. Despondent over what he sees as inevitable decay of his beloved Atlantic City. Prone to exaggerate his importance in the old days.

See *Atlantic City*

LOUDEN, DICK

Former New York writer of how-to books who decided to renovate and reopen the Stratford Inn (built in 1774) in Norwich, Vermont. Also hosts *Vermont Today*, a local television talk show on station WPIV. Married to **Joanna Louden**, a real estate broker and Dick's partner at the inn. (Dick met Joanna when they worked together at an ad agency in New York.) Dick's how-to books include *Installation and Care of Your Low-Maintenance Lawn Sprinkler, How to Make Your Dream Bathroom,* and *Pillow Talk* (a book on how to make pillows). Also wrote a novel called *Murder at the Stratley* (a takeoff on the Stratford Inn). A history buff whose favorite sport is diving. Accidentally burned down a French restaurant, Maison Hubert, when he tossed a lit cigarette in the trash can in the men's room.

See *Newhart*

LOUDEN, JOANNA

Lovely former New Yorker who, with her husband, **Dick Louden**, headed to Norwich, Vermont, to renovate and run the Stratford Inn. Born in Gainesville, Ohio, and met Dick when they worked together at an ad agency in New York. Joanna's a real estate broker who also hosts a TV show called *Your House Is My House*. (To boost ratings and reflect Joanna's "hot" sex appeal, the name of the show was changed to *Hot Houses*.) Holds the town record for renting out the video *60 Days to a Tighter Tummy.*

See *Newhart*

LOVE, DR. NANCY

This neurotic, uptight radio psychologist dispenses advice to the lovelorn but has never been in love herself. "Men fantasize about her; women trust her." Her preferred drink is scotch, neat. Using an assumed name, she decides to research ordinary folks and moves in with bar owner **Eve** to gather material. Her repressed sexuality bursts to the sur-

face after a romantic interlude with mysterious **Mickey Bolton**.

See *Choose Me*

LOVE, REGGIE

A defense attorney with a fighting spirit and bull-dog tenacity. She was an alcoholic and was forced to relinquish custody of her child, so now she feels an intense need to protect her young client, **Mark Sway**, from the grasp of ambitious prosecutor **Roy Flottrig** and, more important, some heavies who'd like to get rid of Mark permanently. The deck seems stacked against her, but Reggie, as she insists on being called, is deceptively resourceful.

See *The Client*, John Grisham

LOVELESS, DR. MIGUELITO

This little man always has huge plans—usually ideas such as threatening to poison all the water on Earth or to blow up the planet unless he is made the supreme ruler. You have to hand it to him; he thinks big, and he's quite an inventor. Among the things he's come up with in his quest to rule the world are laser guns and LSD. This is remarkable, considering it's only the nineteenth century. But he has worthy adversaries in the persons of U.S. agents **Jim West** and **Artemus Gordon**. So far, they've managed to keep him from world domination, but the rascal always manages to escape their clutches.

See *The Wild, Wild West*

MRS. LOVETT

Maker of meat pies and infamous accomplice to famed Victorian serial killer **Sweeney Todd**. Lovett, a shrewd and wily woman whose pie shop is below Todd's barbershop, convinces him to send down the bodies of his victims so that she can use them in her pies. "What with the price of meat what it is."

See *Sweeney Todd*, Stephen Sondheim and James Lapine

LOWELL, ALLIE

She was a Connecticut stay-at-home mom and housewife until she was left by her husband of twenty years, Charles Lowell. She often professes to hate him now but secretly thinks she might get back together with him if he asked—a debatable point. She turns out to be tougher than she thought she'd be and is brave enough to leave suburbia for the wilds of New York and move in with her college roommate, **Kate McArdle**. Allie is totally unprepared for single and city life. Very conservative, she looks like she stepped out of a Talbot's catalog. Allie is devoted to her two children, Jennie and Chip, and sometimes appalled by Kate, whom she loves regardless. Very maternal, she's at her best when she's able to help someone.

See *Kate & Allie*

LOWENSTEIN, SUSAN

"Go-to-hell" New York woman psychiatrist, tall, black-haired, expensively dressed. She likes listening to Vivaldi, going to her favorite restaurant, Petite Marmite, and sipping Macon Blanc. When a patient, poet Savannah Wingo, attempts suicide, she sees her cynical Southern brother, **Tom Wingo**, hoping for a clue as to why. Though she's slender and beautiful, her violinist husband thinks she's fat and unattractive. She's the mother of a petulant son, the daughter of a disapproving mother and a father who worshipped, then abandoned her. She dreams of dancing with Tom in the Rainbow Room above a snow-drenched city. She tends to be paranoid about her Jewishness. After she falls in love with Tom, and he decides to go back to his wife, she implores him: "When you get back to South Carolina, dream one for me. Dream one for Lowenstein."

See *The Prince of Tides*, **Pat Conroy**

LOWRY, SAM

Humble office worker at Ministry of Information in decaying England of the future, turned unlikely hero thanks to glitch caused by randomly placed insect remains. Surrounded at work and home by endless miles of ducts, cables, and governmental red tape gone mad, as well as constant terrorist bombing. When promoted to ostensibly higher position, he finds that he shares the desk in his closet-sized cubicle through the wall with a coworker and engages in tug-of-war to keep his workspace. Escapes from drab, hideous, repressive reality into romantic fantasies; develops sudden, irresistible fixation on young woman who draws him into underground revolutionary movement. Has brief but satisfying revolt from the norm.

See *Brazil*

LUCAS, JACK

Former radio shock jock, now working in a video store. Carries deeply buried guilt over a long-ago radio stunt gone bad. Trying to get his career back on track, though these moves are tentative to date. Wears his hair in a ponytail, tends to walk like he's in pain. Alternately fascinated and repelled by slightly off-kilter homeless Manhattan resident and his various eccentric friends.

See *The Fisher King*

LUCK, HARRY

He's fast with his mouth, likewise with a gun. Luck is one-seventh of a team hired to repel the unwelcome attentions of Señor **Calvera** and his banditos, when they return to rampage yet again through a helpless Mexican village. He's a pragmatist, always looking for a hidden angle, with an eye for possible caches of gold, silver, or jewels. Luck is also something of a gambler, although he doesn't exactly have a poker face.

See *The Magnificent Seven*

LUGER, FRANK

A veteran cop, now an inspector from "downtown," Luger's become a bureaucrat, although he occasionally longs for the old days and the action of the street. Or he claims to, at any rate. Seems to have found a home away from home on the crusty, aging couch in Captain **Barney Miller**'s office at the 12th Precinct, where he comes to air his many complaints and lay his usually insoluble problems and insecurities at Barney's feet. Possesses an alarming lack of understanding of the most mundane details of life, combined with a seeming inability to actually listen to what anyone is saying. (Which might be why he now has a desk job.) A constant annoyance to Barney and the detectives at the 12th. Totally politically incorrect, and probably was forty years ago as well.

See *Barney Miller*

LUMET, SONNY

Blond and curvaceous, she's adored by **Kip Wilson**—when he's not dressed as "Buffy" to pass at the women-only residence they share. Is finally successfully wooed by Kip, who ultimately tells her of his charade. A registered nurse, roommates with **Amy Cassidy**.

See *Bosom Buddies*

LUMLEY, GEORGE

Blue-collar, attentive, garrulous cabdriver who enjoys talking with his fares and listening carefully to their stories. He's involved with fraudulent medium **Blanche Tyler** in both romance and scams. Currently, George is caught up in difficulties well beyond his usual petty scheming and is seriously out of his depth.

See *Family Plot*

LUND, ILSA

An almost ethereal presence whose courage, beauty, and romantic allure capture the hearts of many men. Loyal wife to freedom fighter **Victor Laszlo**, though she was once involved with **Rick Blaine**. Had orthodontic work done as a teenager. Wore blue dress when Nazis invaded Paris. "Kiss me as if it were for the last time."

See *Casablanca*

LUNG, WANG

A poor, simple Chinese farmer who weds the gentle **O-Lan** in an arranged marriage. Even though he is honest and hardworking, it is his wife who pulls the family through drought and hardship. His easygoing ways often jeopardize the good fortune that sometimes comes his way. After he becomes rich and successful, he leaves his farm and takes a second, younger wife. His greed blinds him to the sacrifices O-Lan made for him and the struggles they endured together. It isn't until O-Lan dies and he returns to his farm that he remembers too late the goodness of his wife.

See *The Good Earth*, Pearl S. Buck

LURCH

This extremely tall, taciturn butler has the appearance and vocabulary of a particularly dim movie monster. "You rang?" is almost the extent of Lurch's vocabulary—which is really all he ever needs, or wants, to say. As the family manservant, Lurch answers the door and telephone and performs other domestic chores. Over seven feet tall, he towers over all family members and has the strength to crush any of them, which, of course, he would never do. In his black tie and tails, Lurch cuts a compelling figure, and it is *so* hard to get good servants these days.

See *The Addams Family*

LYMAN, JORDAN

A visionary but controversial U.S. president. Lyman becomes very unpopular after negotiating a nuclear disarmament treaty with the Soviet Union. This leads to an attempted military coup masterminded by **General James Mattoon Scott**, Chairman of the Joint Chiefs of Staff. The result is a toe-to-toe confrontation between Lyman and Scott over the future of the country.

See *Seven Days in May*

M

Thoroughly professional, unquestionably upright, highly enigmatic director of MI5, Her Majesty's Secret Service. M acknowledges that **James Bond** is among the best of his agents, although he disapproves of the man's proclivity for girls, fast cars, and good times. M's censorious attitude can leave Bond feeling like a chastened schoolboy, even when he's being sent on a mission to investigate the murder of another agent—or to commit a necessary homicide or two himself. M doesn't believe in mixing business with pleasure, tolerates no funny business, and more closely resembles in style and attitude a conservative businessman than what we generally envision as the head of a top-secret agency dealing with danger and espionage.

See *Dr. No, Goldfinger, You Only Live Twice*, et al., Ian Fleming

MAAS, OEDIPA

Oedipa is a California woman, the ex-lover of recently deceased Pierce Inverarity and the wife of Mucho Maas. Intrigued by a mysterious bequest to her in Pierce's will, she embarks on a bizarre search for the truth about it. Gradually, she learns—or thinks she learns—about an immense but shadowy communications network, Tristero, through which those in the know trade secret information. Or maybe she's just very paranoid.

See *The Crying of Lot 49*, Thomas Pynchon

MacKAY, KATE

The madcap mom in a house full of even zanier kids, Kate and her drama critic husband, Lawrence, fight to make themselves heard above the constant din created by their brood of hellions. Trouble develops when Kate notices that Lawrence is opting for easy and nasty jabs in his

work, where fair criticism would be more appropriate.
See *Please Don't Eat the Daisies*

MacKenzie, Allison

She's a willowy high school senior, an aspiring writer who worships her dead father's memory. Sensitive and thoughtful, she befriends town oddballs like her semiboyfriend, Norman, and yearns to break free from the stifling conventions of Peyton Place—conventions rigidly adhered to by her mother, **Constance**. Eventually, she learns the truth about her past: she's an illegitimate child, borne of Constance's scandalous relationship with a married man. Allison leaves town, disgusted with her mother's hypocrisy. But when she returns for the trial of her friend, **Selena Cross**, mother and daughter finally come to a loving understanding.
See *Peyton Place*, Grace Metalious

MacKenzie, Constance

A single mother living in ultrarespectable 1940s Peyton Place, a small New England town. She constantly tries to shield her daughter, **Allison**, from any activity that might be construed as being at all improper. She spurns the advances of the handsome, upright new school principal, even though she's attracted to him. Eventually, the reason for her oddly fearful behavior becomes clear: Allison is the illegitimate offspring of a nonmarital liaison, and Constance wants to protect herself and her daughter from a bad reputation. She briefly loses Allison to the big city, only to reconcile with her at last.
See *Peyton Place*, Grace Metalious

MacKenzie, Karen Fairgate

Stalwart. The most stable (and only brunette) female resident of Knots Landing, California. Karen is the perfect confidante and hostess. She is a caring friend, mother, and wife who listens to everyone's problems. Survives the untimely death of her beloved husband and rises to love again. Hair always looks good.
See *Knots Landing*

MacNeil, Regan

A sweet-faced youngster turned foulmouthed fiend after being possessed by hellish demon. She'll spew vulgarities and pea-green vomit at a moment's notice. She also has the ability to levitate and turn her head completely around. Regan has been known to show extreme disrespect for religious trappings or clerics. Despite her current personality problems, she's looking for a return to her former peaceful existence. "Mother, make it stop!"
See *The Exorcist*

MacReedy, John J.

A one-armed stranger who gets off the train one day in post–World War II Black Rock, a small, nearly abandoned town in the middle of the desert. A prematurely white-haired veteran in a baggy, dark suit, his reserve and unwillingness to tell the curious inhabitants his reason for visiting incite a paranoid reaction. MacReedy takes the spying and menacing curiosity of his hosts with a smile, but he is perceptive enough to realize the danger that surrounds him. As he searches for a certain Japanese farmer, he also learns about the terrible secret that the town has been keeping. He realizes that the more he knows, the more dangerous it becomes for him to stay. But his mission has a moral purpose that he refuses to abandon.
See *Bad Day at Black Rock*

Madge

Friendly, no-nonsense manicurist. Has a great knack for gaining people's trust. Known to use a certain dishwashing detergent on her customers because it's so mild. Sneaky. "You're soaking in it."
See *Palmolive*

Madigan, Elvira

A circus tightrope walker with a romantic soul. Madly in love with a soldier, she won't let anything stop their affair. She always looks like an oil painting rendered by Disney, even under stress. A Mozart fan.
See *Elvira Madigan*

Madison

The ultimate male fantasy, with only a single flaw from a typical man's viewpoint. She's lovely, sensual, intelligent, open, honest, faithful, and pure, but she's a mermaid. She's willing to sacrifice her life in the sea, if necessary, to be with her sweetheart, **Allen Bauer**. Over lobster in a fancy restaurant, it becomes apparent that she likes seafood—really likes seafood.
See *Splash*

MADISON, FRANKLYN "FRANKIE"

Decertified psychiatrist, currently working as a grocery store box boy. Foulmouthed with a manic personality, a factor that ultimately led to his professional downfall. Still interested in the workings of the mind, and friends with **Mike Church**.

See *Dead Again*

MADISON, OSCAR

Look up the word "slob" in the dictionary, and you'll find a picture of Oscar. Pigs keep their sties more neat and clean than his apartment. He washes his clothes yearly, whether they need it or not, and has had neckties condemned by the Board of Health. Oscar is a sportswriter for the *New York Herald*. While he loves all sports, his favorite is horse racing. His supposed expertise never helps him at the betting window, but he won't stop trying. He's perennially behind with alimony payments to his ex-wife, Blanche, even though one would think he'd save thousands on dry cleaning and laundry alone. Oscar has an unlikely roommate in his Park Avenue apartment: his old friend the recently divorced neat-freak and compulsive cleaner, **Felix Unger**. While they share a few enthusiasms, such as their regular poker games, they also find infinite ways to drive each other crazy, in addition to basic lifestyle incompatibility. Oscar loves sports and putting moves on women, while Felix loves opera and is still hung up on his ex, Gloria. But despite the fact that they're polar opposites, they somehow remain friends. Call it a tribute to the strength of the basic human instinct to socialize. "Are you still living here?"

See *The Odd Couple*

MAE

The flirty wife of jealous rancher **Curley**, she's "got the eye." She gets talked of a lot by the ranch hands, who call her a "tart." Left alone in the main house, she shows up nightly at the men's quarters, saying "I'm lookin' for Curley." Mae goes for heavy make-up, red fingernails, and red ostrich-feather mules on her feet. A "lulu," she wants to be a movie star: "A guy tol' me he could put me in pitchers." She fancies herself something special and wears her hair in tiny sausage curls, brushing it a lot to keep it soft. When dimwitted big guy **Lennie Small** confesses he likes to pet soft things, she replies, "Well, who

don't," and invites him to stroke her hair, which turns out to be a bad idea.

See *Of Mice and Men,* John Steinbeck

MAGGIO, ANGELO

A likable but trouble-loving enlisted man whose repeated run-ins with army policy land him in **Sergeant Fatso Judson**'s stockade on a regular basis. Maggio is a mercurial Italian American who likes women, alcohol, and fighting, often all at once. Although they're temperamentally very different, he has a good friend in **Robert E. Lee Prewitt**.

See *From Here to Eternity,* James Jones

MAGOO, QUINCY

A myopic old man with a fleet of guardian angels. Mr. Magoo is a crusty old gent with a lot of money and a terrible case of nearsightedness. This problem, which he refuses to acknowledge, is forever leading him to the brink of disaster, but somehow he never quite tumbles over the edge. Often, he's rescued by his manservant, Charlie. Magoo is a veteran of stage and screen, once playing Ebenezer Scrooge in *A Christmas Carol*.

See *Famous Adventures of Mr. Magoo*

MAHONEY, BREATHLESS

Sexy singer extraordinaire. Known to make grown men quiver like jelly. Dresses only in form-fitting outfits that reveal her femininity fatale. Despite her bad-girl image, Breathless can't help herself when she falls for square-jawed, square-shooting detective **Dick Tracy**.

See *Dick Tracy*

MAINE, NORMAN

Once he was among the top stars in showbiz, but his time is quickly passing. He tries to drown his sorrow in alcohol and then meets pretty, talented young Esther Blodgett, whom he takes under his wing. He marries her and helps her rocket to the top as a singer-actress (her name is changed in the process to **Vicki Lester**), but as she rises, the increasingly sodden Maine plummets. His contract is bought out by the studio, whereupon he drinks even more, behaving scandalously and causing his loving wife agony and embarrassment. He can't cope with failure, and she won't let him go.

See *A Star Is Born*

MAJOR, MAJOR

Reluctant major with a strong resemblance to Henry Fonda. Born "too late and too mediocre," he impresses people with how unimpressive he is. His father is a farmer with a warped sense of humor who waited fourteen years for a son he could name "Major Major Major." M.M.M. is obedient and polite, until he goes to war. A squadron commander who has never flown a plane, he longs to be an ordinary enlisted man and play basketball with the boys. He wears dark glasses and an organ grinder's mustache as a disguise. Major Major refuses to see anyone while he is in his office, but will see them when he is not there, frequently escaping his office via the window. After determined **Captain Yossarian** tackles him and begs to get out of the war, Major Major forlornly tells him "there's nothing I can do." An unhappy victim of practical jokes, he insists he is "just a guy trying to do his job."

See *Catch-22,* Joseph Heller

MAJORS, BRAD

A four-eyed weenie—shy, awkward, and oh so virginal. He's a classmate of **Janet Weiss**, who later becomes his fiancée. The fact that he's seduced by **Dr. Frank N. Furter** *does not* necessarily mean that he's a practicing bisexual. Confrontation with expanding sexual horizons drives him back to infantilism.

See *The Rocky Horror Picture Show*

MALCOLM, IAN

This brilliant mathematician and iconoclast is a chaos theorist and creator of the so-called Malcolm Effect, which dictates that an inherently unstable system may suddenly collapse at any time. He is a member of an elite team of scientists picked by **John Hammond** to check out his new facility, Jurassic Park, a theme park full of live, cloned dinosaurs. His attitude toward the possibility of breakdowns makes Malcolm see trouble ahead. "When 'The Pirates of the Caribbean' breaks down, the pirates don't eat the tourists!"

See *Jurassic Park,* Michael Crichton

CAPTAIN MALLORY

Mallory isn't a soldier by nature, but he's dynamic, active, and a man who gets things done. A world-class mountain climber, Mallory is pressed into service in World War II to lead a team up a sheer cliff face to destroy a battery of Nazi guns threatening Allied ships from the Mediterranean island of Navarone, thus clearing the way for an Allied invasion of Greece.

See *Guns of Navarone,* Alistair MacLean

MALLOY, MOOSE

Brutish, hulking ex-con, now back on the streets of Los Angeles after spending a few years in the can. Tends to walk on the seamier side of life, perfectly at home amidst society's lowest crust. He's mad for **Velma Grayle**, even though he hasn't seen her in a long, long time.

See *Farewell, My Lovely*

MALLOY, OFFICER PETE

Competent beat cop, senior patrol officer of Los Angeles Police Department, teamed with rookie **Jim Reed**. Robberies, homicides, and assaults are routine for the team. Malloy tries to teach Reed what it is to be a cop. Dedicated to the job, he hasn't yet taken the time to find the right woman. "One Adam-12, One Adam-12. See the man…"

See *Adam-12*

MALLOY, TERRY

A has-been at age twenty-eight, "the kid" is an ex-prizefighter. Despite having been on the receiving end of a lot of punches, Terry's good-looking; despite having grown up in the mean streets, he's rather naive. His pride and joy are the pigeons he keeps in a coop on the roof. He still simmers at older brother Charlie "the Gent," who ordered him to take a dive in a critical fight. He tells Charlie, "I coulda been a contender! I coulda been somebody, instead of a bum, which is what I am!" Terry falls hard for sweet, innocent Katie Doyle, whose brother, Terry's friend, was murdered by the waterfront mob.

See *On the Waterfront,* Budd Schulberg

MALONE, SAM

As a relief pitcher for the Boston Red Sox, he had a few moments in the sun before succumbing to the lure of the bottle. Now he's a recovering alcoholic who runs a pleasant Boston bar called Cheers, where he confines himself to coffee and chases women, many of whom he catches (but always

Tony Manero

throws them back). His black book is encyclopedic. Sam is obsessed with his perfect hair and his Corvette. He seems shallow, and is, but is not without some sensitivity. He's a true friend, both mother hen and psychotherapist to the bar regulars, who call him Sammy. Waitress **Carla Tortelli** worships him. His initial ambivalence about barmaid **Diane Chambers** is always with him; her pretentiousness and snobbery turn him off, but her body turns him on. He can't make up his mind about her, and neither can she about him. Eventually, he lets her go her way, but not before a great deal of agonizing for both parties. He subsequently gets the hots for new bar manager **Rebecca Howe**.

See *Cheers*

MALPH, RALPH

A would-be class clown who laughs uproariously at his own jokes and then says, "I've still got it." His favorite gag is to wrap his arms around himself and pretend he's making out with a girl. A bit obnoxious but harmless. Hangs around with **Richie Cunningham** and **Potsie Weber**. His dad's a dentist.

See *Happy Days*

MAMA

She's a Norwegian immigrant in San Francisco who manages the affairs of her husband and four children with kindness and reason. Mama is a paragon of resourcefulness and frugality who keeps the family "bank" and parcels out funds with an eye on the bottom line. She is the diplomat of her extended family and is slow to judge others. Mama keeps her promises and works hard to give her children what they want, even if it means sacrificing a family heirloom. When she's frustrated, she finds that cleaning house helps her to think. She's an inveterate worrier but a problem solver who likes to take matters into her own hands.

See *I Remember Mama*

MAMMY

A tough, honest slave woman who raised **Scarlett O'Hara** and her mother before her. In her white kerchief and voluminous dresses that conceal a vast bulk, she rules the plantation house with a hand of iron, and no one dares to question her. She is an intimate part of Scarlett's life, accompanying her throughout her marriages and adventures. Mammy

is the one person who Scarlett cannot fool; she sees through Scarlett's duplicity and schemes and Scarlett knows it. She shows compassion and understanding for **Rhett Butler** when he refuses to leave the body of his dead daughter. She asks sweet-natured **Melanie Wilkes** to console him. A noble, honest woman. It is not her place to disobey, but she lets her feelings be known.

See *Gone with the Wind,* Margaret **Mitchell**

MARLBORO MAN

The strong, silent type. Weathered by life on the range, he's a classic cowboy with rugged good looks. A brooder. Really likes his cigarettes.

See *Marlboro*

MANDRAKE THE MAGICIAN

A suave magician garbed in the customary top hat, cape, and tails, Mandrake relies on his quick wit, moral superiority, and uncanny skill as a hypnotist to right the wrongs of the world. Usually accompanied by his companion Lothar, an African strongman, and his knockout girlfriend Narda.

See *Mandrake the Magician*

MANERO, TONY

A chain-smoking, smooth-dancing, narcissistic habitué of the finest discos in Bensonhurst, Brooklyn, New York. Tony is a man with no concerns in the world except his desire to move to that disco beat and astonish the world with his style and grace on the dance floor. He works in a hardware store, has a brother in the clergy, and still lives at home, where he is upbraided for having no direction in life. Though he has a relationship with Annette, a dance partner with whom he captures several contests, he ultimately throws her over in favor of an upwardly mobile woman named Stephanie. Manero is not totally devoid of character: he once publicly gave a dance trophy he won in a rigged dance contest to a couple that outdanced him and his partner but were denied the prize due to their ethnicity. Tony takes a great deal of pride in his polyester wardrobe and appearance. "Don' hit my hair. I work hard on my hair an' you hit it."

See *Saturday Night Fever*

MANN, DORIS

She's a showbiz veteran from the old school of

Hollywood. A hard worker, Doris has achieved fame and fortune. She's also tried to be a good mom, but, between the long absences from home and the divorces, that hasn't worked as well as her career. She tries to help daughter Suzanne Vale in the struggle to get her career off the ground and to conquer her substance-abuse problems, but the history of tension and problems between the two is hard to overcome. Maybe it's a generation gap problem, and maybe it's a daughter trying to get out from under her mother's shadow, but whatever it is, it's no storybook relationship.

See *Postcards from the Edge*, Carrie Fisher

MANNIX, JOE

Handsome, gutsy, Los Angeles–based private detective. Was employed by Intertect, a sophisticated detective firm which used elaborate computers and other scientific detection aids. Mannix often relies on his instincts and bare hands to solve a case. Left Intertect to start his own firm, aided by his loyal assistant, **Peggy Fair**. Has a tendency to get into fistfights.

See *Mannix*

MANTEE, DUKE

The leader of a criminal gang, he's a vicious and desperate killer on his way to Mexico to try and make a new life. He holes up in an Arizona cafe and takes hostages while waiting for the rest of his gang, so they can head for the border. Though he's a killer, he still has a romantic side; he won't go to Mexico without his girlfriend. He says that he "spent most of my life in jail and it looks like I'll spend the rest of my life dead." As with so many hardened vicious killers, it is the love of a woman that proves to be his undoing.

See *The Petrified Forest*, Robert E. Sherwood

MANTLE, BEVERLY

A good-looking Canadian gynecologist, he's very close to his (physically) identical twin brother, **Elliot Mantle**. Likes to share everything with his twin, including women. Displays an occasional streak of unfraternal self-interest, not always with the best results.

See *Dead Ringers*

MANTLE, ELLIOT

Twin brother of **Beverly Mantle**. A practicing gynecologist who shares thriving practice with his sibling. Emotionally unstable and very dependent on Beverly. He has designed some highly unusual medical equipment.

See *Dead Ringers*

MAPLE, GABRIELLE

She's a waitress at her dad's small roadside cafe in the Arizona desert, where the dull life is a source of frustration to her. Gabby, as folks call her, is a romantic who dreams of going to France to study painting, because she thinks she belongs where people and things are more aesthetically inclined than where she is. She paints her beautiful yet disturbing desert scenes, waits on tables, keeps the books, reads poetry (especially Francois Villon), and copes with the unwelcome romantic attentions of Boze Hertzlinger, the gas station attendant. One day she meets and falls for romantic loser–writer **Alan Squier**, and also encounters vicious murderer **Duke Mantee**. All in all, it's a more than usually eventful day for Gabby.

See *The Petrified Forest*, Robert E. Sherwood

THE MARCH FAMILY

Four lively sisters, economically poor but rich in love, live with their adored mother, Marmee, in Massachusetts while their father fights in the Civil War. They do plays together, form a "Pickwick Club," and adopt Laurie, the lonely rich boy next door, as a friend and member of their inner circle. The oldest girl, Meg, beautiful and pious, secretly longs for wealth. When she goes to a party dressed in borrowed finery and later regrets it, Marmee educates her: "Poverty seldom daunts a serious lover." She does marry a poor man, John Brook, Laurie's tutor. Jo, the next daughter, is an effervescent youngster who longs to be a writer. She doesn't care for girlish things and declares: "I am the man of the family now papa away." Spontaneous and headstrong, she sells her hair, "her one beauty," to help her wounded father. She rejects the marriage proposal of Laurie, who loves her, and moves to New York City to write. She marries her mentor, bearing "a wilderness of sons," and settling down on her old aunt's estate. The third daughter, Beth, called Little Tranquility by the others, is fragile and courageous, and delights most in playing the piano. Tragically, disease claims her and she dies young, after telling

©1996 Capital Cities/ABC, Inc

Anne Marie

Jo that "love is the only thing we can carry with us when we go." Elegant, blond Amy, the youngest, dabbles in drawing, determined to cultivate aristocratic tastes. She has a lifelong crush on Jo's castoff, Laurie, whom she finally marries, becoming the gentlewoman she'd always hoped to be.

See *Little Women,* **Louisa May Alcott**

MARCH, AUGIE

The big-city Jewish dead-end kid and wisenheimer as picaresque antihero. Born a bastard into grinding Chicago poverty, self-educated, he's clever and charming enough that a succession of wealthy patrons offers him access to their worlds. Time and again, though, he spurns the easy path to success and avoids commitment, moving on to another occupation, another adventure. His women try to mold him and he resists them too. A "listener by upbringing," he refuses to believe in anything, himself included, yet is the archetypal survivor. Like the eagle he trains to hunt iguanas but which refuses to kill them, Augie is too independent and perverse to settle on one belief, one goal, one life. Sometimes pathetic, but mostly full of curiosity and good humor, he celebrates "the laughing creature in me, forever rising up."

See *The Adventures of Augie March,* **Saul Bellow**

MARCO, MAJOR BENNETT

This Korean war veteran, once the superior officer of Sergeant **Raymond Shaw**, has recurring nightmares in which Shaw murders two members of the company in cold blood, at the command of Russian and Red Chinese generals. He's ambivalent about Shaw, who is ostensibly a war hero. "It's not that Raymond Shaw is hard to like. He's impossible to like!"

See *The Manchurian Candidate*

MARDUKAS, JONATHAN

As a mob accountant, Mardukas manages to embezzle $15 million, most of which he gives to charity. He runs from the mob but is captured by bounty hunter **Jack Walsh**, who intends to bring him back alive and redeem a bail bond Jonathan has forfeited by running. "I didn't think I'd get caught."

See *Midnight Run*

MARIA

She's a beautiful young dressmaker and seamstress, a wide-eyed, innocent *puertorriqueña* in 1950s Manhattan. When she falls in love with **Tony**, who's not Latino, and is a gangleader of the Jets, it means trouble for everyone, and especially for her. "I love a boy, and that's all that I need, right or wrong, and I know he needs me too."

See *West Side Story,* **Arthur Laurents, Stephen Sondheim,** and **Leonard Bernstein**

MARIE, ANN

She's a fashionable actress with an equally fashionable flip hairdo, struggling to be an independent woman and conquer Broadway. Originally from Brewster, New York, she now lives in a small apartment on the Upper West Side. Despite her insistence on independence, she still wants to keep house and cook and clean for boyfriend Don Hollinger. So far, she's acted only in a few TV commercials and bit parts in plays. She supports herself with odd jobs, usually in department stores, but she's also been a less-than-outstanding waitress. In her TV debut, she played a bank teller who got killed. Ann studies at the Benedict Workshop of the Dramatic Arts. Like most actors, she has a bad case of optimism.

See *That Girl*

MARJORIE

This quiet working woman is transformed into vengeful hellion after being brutally raped. She's handy with insect repellent and can be inspired to sadistic invention when the spirit moves her. Lives with two very surprised roommates.

See *Extremities*

MARKOWITZ, STUART

An affable, rotund, charming tax lawyer, Stuart seeks a partnership at McKenzie, Brackman, Chaney and Kuzak. A man of hidden talents and hidden wealth. He thinks himself lucky to snare **Ann Kelsey**, the woman of his dreams. Together they have an uneasy marriage, though they love each other. Stewart occasionally yearns to be involved in the more exciting aspects of lawyering but is usually confined to tax matters.

See *L.A. Law*

MARLOW

A thoughtful, introspective man who has spent his entire life observing the ways of the world and man. Marlow is a superb storyteller who regales those around him with tales of his travels from the Far East to the depths of the Congo River. Marlow befriends **Lord Jim** after his disgrace in the *Patna* affair and helps the young seaman find a job and keeps in contact with Jim through the years. At another time in his life, Marlow treks by boat to a remote upriver outpost, surrounded by jungle, in search of **Kurtz**, a once-valued company asset, who is rumored to have "gone native" and is now ill. In all these adventures, Marlow is able to stand back and observe his surroundings, and he sees the struggles of men with their world, their fellowmen, and their own hearts.

See *Heart of Darkness* and *Lord Jim,* Joseph Conrad

MARLOWE, JENNIFER

The extremely well endowed receptionist for Cincinnati radio station WKRP. Though some might take her for a dumb blonde, she fits that role only in hair color—and that, only through artificial means. She sits decoratively at the front desk but doesn't appear to do much actual work. Despite this, it's clear she actually runs the radio station. Men are intimidated by her looks, and she uses this often to help rescue WKRP from the brink of disaster. Her boss, **Arthur Carlson**, is especially awed by her, and she plays him like a violin.

See *WKRP in Cincinnati*

MARLOWE, PHILIP

Very few things surprise this cynical, tough, middle-aged private detective who loathes violence and is not above bending a law when it gets in his way. He's a loner who has learned the hard way to be sparing with his trust, and uses sarcasm as a shield. His props are a fedora, a dark suit, a drink in one hand and a cigarette in the other. Marlowe may operate on the fringes of mainstream society, but he maintains a personal code of ethics which makes him a basically good guy.

See *The Big Sleep, The Long Goodbye, The Lady in the Lake, Farewell, My Lovely,* et al., Raymond Chandler

MARPLE, MISS JANE

Miss Marple is the stereotypical nosy old spinster next door, with one little difference: when she gets wind of a murder, this elderly British lady with the blue-tinted hair is apt to sniff out the killer. When not knitting mufflers for her many nieces and nephews (and grandnieces and grandnephews) or writing a chatty letter, she's watching her neighbors' comings and goings, asking a question here and making a seemingly innocent comment there. She may seem vague and distracted, but with her keen observations, innate curiosity, and encyclopedic memory for things that aren't really any of her business, she misses little and figures out much. She can ramble on at length about the latest doings of her favorite nephew, Raymond (who writes those "very modern books all about rather unpleasant young men and women"), or her second neighbor down the lane, who just may have murdered his sweet young wife. With a twinkle and a "Won't you stay for tea?" she can lull a culprit into carelessness and trip him or her up. And then, though she'd blush to say it, she's quite likely to feel "just a teeny weeny bit pleased" with herself.

See *A Pocket Full of Rye,* Agatha Christie

MARRIOTT, LINDSAY

He's a man who gets off on contacts with the underworld—until it proves to be more than he can handle. Suave, good-looking, but not much substance. Women see him as a decorative escort, and he sees them as occasionally useful. He proves to be a real pain to private eye **Phil Marlowe**. A denizen of both sides of the tracks in 1940s Los Angeles.

See *Farewell, My Lovely*

MARSWELL, VICTOR

A virile, seasoned big game hunter who leads African hunting expeditions and falls in love with two kinds of women: his kind and the wrong kind. He's rough with women, which seems to be fine with them, but he feels guilty about making some guy a cuckold. A straight-shooter with no patience for games or foolishness.

See *Mogambo*

MARTELLI, BRUNO

Cocksure music student at New York City's High School for the Performing Arts. Handsome, with dark eyes and hair, and a sensitive force at the school. He plans to be a musician and is very skilled at his craft. Creative and driven, but prone to occasional musings or broodings.

See *Fame*

MARTHA

Martha's a domineering, alcoholic faculty wife who's bitter to think that her best days have passed her by. She is married to **George**, a mordant-witted history professor whom she considers emotionally impotent. She is also the daughter of George's boss, the college president, a fact she relishes holding over her husband. The terminally jaded Martha invites **Nick** and **Honey**, a hunky young professor and his dim-bulb wife, for a boozy get-together at her house. There, she and George slowly draw Nick and Honey into the sick mind games they play with one another to give their disappointing lives meaning and variety: games like Humiliate the Host, Get the Guests, and Hump the Hostess. The evening becomes an escalating series of attacks, sexual encounters, and unpleasant revelations, which Martha and George are used to but which devastate their young guests, who have never come across anything as potent and destructive as what Martha and her husband dish out. Under the bravado and the leathery hide, there's a wounded, unhappy woman in Martha, and George knows this. In fact, the two are actually supportive of each other, in a strange and unlikely way, and prop each other up, even though it seems they spend their time knocking each other down.

See *Who's Afraid of Virginia Woolf?*, Edward Albee

MARTIN, DONNA

Pretty, blond Southern California native somehow lives in the shadow of her prettier (**Brenda Walsh**) and blonder (**Kelly Taylor**) best friends at West Beverly Hills High. When she dates **David Silver**, she doesn't sleep with him—the last holdout among her crowd—although they share an apartment (with Kelly). Romances a construction worker, although she's wildly wealthy.

See *Beverly Hills 90210*

MARTIN, DORIS

She is the perfect, perky, widowed mother of two. Doris is blond-haired and blue-eyed and favors coatdresses and color-coordinated ensembles. She moves from city to country and back again in search of herself, after losing her husband. She works for *Today's World* magazine as a secretary and later becomes a writer. She always smiles through her problems and always looks nice. "*Que sera, sera*. Whatever will be, will be."

See *The Doris Day Show*

MARTIN, EVELYN "ANGEL"

A sleazy ex-con, Angel is never without some get-rich scheme/scam or other, often embroiling his old cellmate, **Jim Rockford**, much to Jim's distress. Jim gets him back by using Angel's seedy contacts and flair for invention on cases. Angel is a devoutly nonviolent person (read "chicken").

See *The Rockford Files*

MARTIN, LUKE

Paraplegic veteran of Vietnam War. Armed with a sardonic wit and sarcastic nature in an attempt to protect his psyche from inner pain. Faithful to friends and sympathetic to their needs above and beyond his own. Tentatively romancing **Sally Hyde**, despite fears of sexual inadequacy and hurting her husband, **Captain Bob Hyde**, a fellow soldier. "Pee-wee, I can crawl again."

See *Coming Home*

MARTINEZ, JAMES

A Latino, he is an energetic young New York City police officer who was recently made a detective at the 15th Precinct. Shy and sweet. Martinez is a little insecure when it comes to women. He was mentored by Detective John Kelly, when he first came to the station, and got his gold badge. He often works with Detective Gregory Medavoy.

See *NYPD Blue*

CAPTAIN MARVEL

Billy Batson's crime-fighting, superstrong, red-caped alter ego. When Billy uttered "Shazam!" he became Captain Marvel, endowed with all the qualities of the Greek gods: wisdom, strength, stamina, power, courage, and speed. He also aged about fifteen years and picked up a sharp red costume with a lightning bolt on the chest.

See *Shazam*

MASON, PERRY

Defender of the innocent, fearless supporter of law and order, Perry Mason is a trial attorney who takes only murder cases, and he's never lost one yet—at least not when his client is truly honest with him. With the able assistance of only his devoted secretary, **Della Street,** and his trusted private eye, **Paul Drake,** Perry assembles thousands of hours of work in a few weeks' time, building rock-solid defenses guaranteed to focus blame on someone other than his client. With the tiniest lift of one eyebrow in disbelief, Mason has crushed many an eyewitness, reducing them to tears and uncertainty. No matter how obscure the connection to the deed or how airtight the alibi, Mason will ferret out the evildoer. And pity the poor villain who takes the witness stand on behalf of the prosecution! Perry's sarcastic objections and scathing cross-examinations have hammered more than one witness into confessing on the stand, or even forced some guilt-ridden soul into admitting his or her sin from the gallery. Not even District Attorney **Hamilton Burger** can hope to get a conviction against a Mason client, no matter how much of the taxpayers' money he spends in the effort. Yet somehow, through it all, Mason manages to stay on friendly terms with Burger and the police. After all, he needs them to stand ready to arrest the real culprit.
See *Perry Mason*

MASHA

Married survivor of Nazi death camps who lives in the Bronx. She's also lover of **Herman Broder,** whom she knew in Europe before the war. Though her experiences have embittered her, she remains a sensualist who enjoys physical relationships.
See *Enemies: A Love Story*

MASTER OF CEREMONIES

Decadent host of smoky Berlin nightclub, circa 1931. He's energetic, insinuating, and graceful, while maintaining a somewhat ambiguous sexual persona onstage. His songs and satire reflect and comment on the turmoil that is quickly enveloping Germany. Friend of **Sally Bowles,** with whom he sings a duet. His face is always obscured beneath friendly/sinister makeup. "Ladies and gentlemen, *mesdames et monsieurs, Damen und Herren,* I am your host!"
See *Cabaret*

MASTERS, RICK

Masters is a criminal genius with a flair for design. While serving time in prison, he became an accomplished painter, but his first love remains counterfeiting. He's very particular about his creations, sometimes burning his paintings or his currency when they don't meet his high standards. Definitely anal retentive, Masters tends to act out his pique toward people who upset his sense of order by killing them.
See *To Live and Die in L.A.*

MATHER, LOWELL

This ancient airplane mechanic may have known the Wright Brothers up close and personal. Lowell always speaks in a very deep monotone, and his expression never changes. His ex-wife, Bunny, was a nymphomaniac. Lowell would probably score in double digits in an I.Q. test. He once had a lot of money but blew it when he decided to build a wax museum.
See *Wings*

MATHESON, PAIGE

This conniving, power-hungry young woman uses her considerable looks to get what she wants. She battles her father, Mac MacKenzie, over her choice in men and is frequently at odds with her stepmother, **Karen MacKenzie.** Desperately in love with old-enough-to-be-her-father **Gregory Sumner** and will do anything to get him.
See *Knots Landing*

MATLOCK, BENJAMIN L.

He is a successful, canny, Harvard-educated defense attorney based in Atlanta. Matlock has an uncanny ability to consistently prove his clients' innocence. His unassuming rumpled manner and southern drawl serve to conceal a shrewd, calculating, and clever lawyer who commands upwards of $100,000 a case. He is also adamant about his no-smoking policy, even with his best-paying clients.
See *Matlock*

MAUDE

Though she's elderly, she's still full of life and love, and is spiritual and fun-loving. Maude can always see the good in everybody. She lives in a funky home which she's converted from an old school bus. When

Zach Mayo

she meets terminally bored, suicidal **Harold**, Maude teaches him how to love and how to enjoy life.

See *Harold and Maude*

MAVERICK, BRET

When word gets around about a high-stakes poker game, Bret Maverick will hear the call—no matter where, no matter when. Maverick'll drop what he's doing and hit the trail like a knight searching for the Holy Grail. He's a fast-thinking man with a slow southern drawl, easy to get along with, unless you push him too hard. Even then, he'd rather avoid trouble than fight. But when he's cornered and has no choice, he's able to defend himself. The ladies (shady and otherwise) love him, 'cause he's every inch a gentleman, treating each and every one of them with dignity and respect. Men, aside from other professional gamblers, are generally suspicious of him because he isn't like them. He dresses better than they do, and the only work he does with his hands is shuffle and deal cards. He's an honest gambler, but he still knows every way there is to trim a deck, mark cards, or just plain cheat at poker. This knowledge is a professional necessity, without which he'd be just another sucker to be bilked by the skilled hands of a card mechanic—and whatever else he is, Bret Maverick is no sucker at the card table.

See *Maverick*

Bret Maverick
©1996 Capital Cities/ABC, Inc.

MAX

Wrinkle-faced, gravel-voiced old chauffeur. Max, an earthily charming fellow, is devoted to his wealthy socialite employers, **Jennifer** and **Jonathan Hart**. He helps them fight against corruption and crime, often showing up at just the right moment to save them from sure death. And when one thinks how hard it is to get good servants these days…

See *Hart to Hart*

MAXSON, TROY

A natural baseball player, a skill he developed while doing time in prison for killing a man. He is a proud patriarch, a great talker and storyteller, but is unwilling to listen to anyone but himself. "You've got to take the crooked with the straight."

See *Fences,* August Wilson

MAYO, ZACH

Zach grew up on the sleazy side of the tracks and has a single dream: to be a naval officer. But to survice officer training, he must learn new skills: a lifelong loner, he must become part of a team; instead of cheating his way through, he must take pride in doing his personal best. Trying to see that he measures up is tough, honorable, training sergeant Emil Foley.

See *An Officer and a Gentleman*

MAYPO, MARKY

Sassy little boy who knows what he wants and how to get it. Has his parents wrapped around his little finger. Just add milk, and he's a heavy drinker. "I want my Maypo!"

See *Maypo*

MAYTAG REPAIRMAN

Very lonely middle-aged man who's job has rendered him useless. Longs to fix appliances. Relates well to **Willie Loman**. Wears perfectly pressed uniform and sighs a lot.

See *Maytag*

McARDLE, KATE

The individualistic, free-spirited, divorced mom of a teenager. She is very urban and fairly hip, having grown up, and had her consciousness raised, in the 1960s. Kate remains idealistic and acts young. She lives in New York City and would never dream of living anywhere else. Open and liberal with her daughter, Emma, Kate is not a strict mother and is trying her best to raise Emma to be a strong and independent woman. An easygoing woman, Kate takes in best friend **Allie Lowell**, along with Allie's two children, and tries to loosen Allie up. Enjoys men and almost always has a boyfriend but is invariably disappointed.

See *Kate & Allie*

McBAIN, JILL

After her husband is killed by **Frank** for his land, the beautiful McBain decides to sell it. Two unlikely rogues, **Cheyenne** and the Harmonica Man, come to the aid of the former New Orleans prostitute after they realize the value of the land once the railroad arrives.

See *Once Upon a Time in the West*

McCABE, JOHN Q.

He's an ambitious man who doesn't know when to leave the poker table. McCabe, whose past is shrouded in mystery, uses some poker winnings to open the first whorehouse in the northwestern frontier town of Presbyterian Church. Now he wants to sell his house of ill repute, but only for a price he considers right.

See *McCabe and Mrs. Miller*

McCAIN, LUCAS

This taciturn widower and his young son, Mark, live outside of North Fork, New Mexico, on a 4,100-acre ranch. Besides tending to his property and raising Mark, Lucas helps the local law enforcement deal with a variety of scoundrels, always with the help of his trusty customized rifle, a .44-40 Winchester that's been specially outfitted to fire off as many as eight shots in two and a half seconds.

See *The Rifleman*

McCALLISTER, KEVIN

This cute, towheaded kid is seemingly helpless when his parents unwittingly leave him at home while they fly off to Europe on a Christmas vacation. But when his house is targeted by determined thieves, he proves he's old enough and smart enough to be on his own. Again and again, using techniques reminiscent of the Road Runner with Wile E. Coyote, he thwarts the thieves' attempts to get into the house or get their hands on him: by heating the front door's brass handle to skin-scorching temperatures; by using an old gangster-movie video to convince the thieves there are tough guys with machine guns waiting to ambush them; by acting like Tarzan and swinging on a rope out to his tree house, then cutting the line when the thieves try to follow him. He also learns compassion through his trials; instead of mocking a lonely, sad neighbor, as he would have done previously, he now offers the neighbor his Christmas company. When his worried parents finally get home, they have no idea what their little, ostensibly vulnerable son has been through.

See *Home Alone*

McCARTHY, LEO

Rapscallion police officer with a good cop instinct and a nose for trouble. His cynical sense of humor and hardened attitude toward his job get him through life. Currently, he is investigating a notorious murder case that is not what it appears to be. Big-bellied, with close-cropped hair. In an unusual friendship with **Rollie Tyler**.

See *F/X*

McCLANE, JOHN

Resourceful New York police detective with an affinity for high-tech action, currently vacationing in L.A. Handy with guns, grenades, and always willing to make a smashing entry into a dangerous situation. Estranged from wife, of whom he's still very fond. Usually dressed in an artistically torn undershirt that accentuates his pumped-up biceps. "Yippie tie-yi yay!"

See *Die Hard*

McCLOUD, DEPUTY SAM

Sam's a slow-talking, laid-back deputy sheriff from Taos, New Mexico, a character straight out of the Old West. But an exchange program sets him smack-dab in the middle of Manhattan instead, where he works with the somewhat bemused

NYPD. And he learns that tracking bad buys in the big city just takes slightly different tools and a longer rope.

See *McCloud*

McCLENNAN, CLARISSE

In a world where the typical person's goal is to have four wall-TVs and thus be able to totally anesthetize oneself, Clarisse stands out as a curious, inquisitive teenager who likes to take walks in the rain, talk, and watch other people on the subway. She meets **Guy Montag** and inspires him to change his life. "So I've lots of time for crazy thoughts, I guess."

See *Fahrenheit 451*, Ray Bradbury

McCLOUD, MAJOR FRANK

This levelheaded World War II veteran with a sense of duty has gone to Key Largo to visit the father of George Temple, a soldier killed while under his command. When McCloud entered the service, it was with the intention of ridding the world of evil. The horrors of war have left him with an "every man for himself" attitude, but he's never wholly lost his earlier ideals. McCloud is believed responsible for the death of gangster **Johnny Rocco**. He rarely uses alcohol, even when under pressure. His prewar professional experience included a stint as a newspaper circulation director. Has knowledge of seaborne craft. Frank had romantic involvement with Temple's widow, **Nora Temple**.

See *Key Largo*

McCONNELL, FREDRICK

The conductor of the Boulder City Orchestra and father of Boulder newscaster **Mindy Beth McConnell**, he previously owned and ran McConnell's Music Store. He is presently married to his second wife, Cathy, who plays the flute in the orchestra. (Fred's first wife, Beth, died.) Conservative by nature, Fred was shocked to learn that **Mork**, an alien from the planet Ork, was living in his daughter's attic.

See *Mork & Mindy*

McCONNELL, MINDY BETH

Sweet, pretty earthling, married to **Mork**, an alien from the planet Ork. She attended Boulder High School and studied journalism at the University of Colorado. After working for a time in her father's music shop, Mindy became a newscaster at KTNS-TV, where she also hosts a show called *Wake Up, Boulder*. Mother of a son, Mearth. Known on planet Ork as the Soft-Lapped One.

See *Mork & Mindy*

McCOVEY, BILLIE NEWMAN

An ambitious young girl reporter. Charming, dedicated, and very late-seventies, Billie works hard to bring in a good story for the *Los Angeles Tribune*. She has to overcome gender bias out on the beat and at the paper, but not from fair but tough boss **Lou Grant**. She's best buddies and best competitor with **Joe Rossi**. She likes stories with a good political bite and isn't above meeting men on the job.

See *Lou Grant*

THE McCOY FAMILY

You can take the West Virginians out of West Virginia, but you can't take the West Virginia out of the West Virginians. The McCoys picked up stakes from their mountain home and moved to the San Fernando Valley in California when Amos, the patriarch of the McCoy clan, inherited his brother's ranch. Amos was born in Smokey Corners, West Virginia. He calls his beloved Model-T Ford "Gertrude." Gruff but lovable, Amos is a widower. He's always got his nose in everybody else's business, especially that of his grandson, Luke. Luke's little brother Little Luke and little sister Hassie are cared for by Kate, Luke's wife, whom he calls "sugar babe." When Kate dies, Amos spends a great deal of his time trying to find a new wife for Luke. Eventually Luke is romanced by widow Louise, who moved into the farm next door.

See *The Real McCoys*

McCOY, JULIE

Think of her as a perky, updated Doris Day, with a Dorothy Hamill haircut and cutesy uniform to add to her schoolgirl charm. Julie's job as cruise director of the *Love Boat* means keeping all the guests occupied and happy, and seeing that all problems are solved. She helps squabbling lovers make up and occasionally plays matchmaker. She also falls in love now and then herself. Julie favors halter-top gowns of unnatural fibers and shares some sexual tension with **Gopher Smith**.

See *The Love Boat*

McCoy, Dr. Leonard

As ship's doctor on the starship *Enterprise*, Dr. Bones McCoy is a twenty-third-century healer, with all kinds of superior technology at his fingertips, but he claims he's just "an old country doctor" at heart. A man being pulled into his century, Bones hates the transporter that "beams" the *Enterprise* crew down to planets and is constantly irascible about having to "cure" all manner of alien life-forms; he'll often tell **Captain Kirk** that he's "a doctor, not an escalator/bricklayer/miracle worker." He also spends a lot of time pronouncing that "he/she/it's dead, Jim" to Kirk and coming up with eleventh-hour cures to strange, hitherto-unknown space ailments. Steadfastly human, Bones has a genuinely genial relationship with Kirk (he calls him Jim, which very few others get away with) and a bickering love-hate one with **Spock**, whose adherence to logic the emotional Bones finds exasperating.

See *Star Trek*

McCoy, Sherman

A self-proclaimed "Master of the Universe" at age thirty eight, Sherman is the number one bond salesman at Pierce and Pierce, one of Wall Street's hottest investment houses. He's got it all: a $2.6-million co-op on Park Avenue; Judy, his interior-decorator wife, whose work is regularly featured in *W* and *Architectural Digest;* Campbell, his cherished only daughter, who goes to an exclusive private school; and Maria, his sexy socialite mistress. However, a series of chance mishaps—calling his wife when he meant to call his mistress; taking a wrong turn from the airport and winding up in the worst part of the Bronx; accidentally hitting a black youth with his car (during what may or may not be a robbery attempt)—spirals into a cruel comeuppance for the old-school WASP. In a city boiling over with racial tension, his case is seized on by a black activist minister with political ambitions, an anxious Bronx D.A. up for reelection, and a drunken tabloid reporter on the verge of being fired—all with their own reasons for raking "Mr. Park Avenue" over the coals—and Sherman is turned into a live target for the public's resentment of Wall Street's excesses. "It's damned sobering, how fast it goes when it goes. All these ties you have, all these people you went to school with and to college with, the people who are in your clubs, the people you go out to dinner with—it's all a thread, all these ties that make up your life, and when it breaks...that's it!"

See *Bonfire of the Vanities,* Tom Wolfe

McCrae, Augustus

A very laid-back ex–Texas Ranger, Gus ain't actually lazy, at least not the way he sees it. No, he's just got his priorities straight, he'd as soon sit in the shade drinking whiskey and watching his two pet pigs kill rattlesnakes as run around in an unseemly fashion in the hot sun. Then when the sun goes down and it starts to cool off a little bit, it's time to head for Lonesome Dove for a game of cards and a poke at his favorite whore, and not necessarily in that order. This seems like pure fecklessness to his longtime partner, **Woodrow Call**. But Gus can jump into action fast, when the need arises, and has a lurking hair-trigger temper, which, when it busts loose, surprises even Woodrow by its depth and dangerousness.

See *Lonesome Dove,* Larry McMurtry

McDeere, Mitchell

Brimming with sincerity and ambition, Mitch McDeere is a poor boy making good. After rising from humble origins to finish fifth in his Harvard Law School class, Mitch takes a job with a Memphis firm that he then he begins to suspect of operating outside the law. Soon, Mitch finds himself outrunning killers and outthinking lawyers to save his career, his marriage, and his life.

See *The Firm,* John Grisham

McDonald, Belinda

A deaf and mute young woman living in Nova Scotia, Belinda is raped by the town bully but experiences a spiritual flowering under the tutelage of a young doctor. Her bleak life is brightened during instruction sessions with the doctor, who teaches her to express herself through sign language. Belinda is forced to shoot the rapist when he tries to take her baby away. Acquitted of murder, she suddenly gains the power of speech upon being reunited with her child, and is paroled in the custody of the doctor, who confesses to having loved her all along.

See *Johnny Belinda*

McDonald, Ronald

A friendly clown who loves children and lives at a well-known hamburger restaurant. Guards the hamburgers and fries from evil. Red hair, red nose, red and white striped socks.

See *McDonald's*

McEwen, Axel

As nephew and lab assistant to **Otto Lidenbrock**, Axel accompanies his uncle on a journey to the center of the Earth as a fellow mineralogist and the log keeper. He's always questioning his uncle's wild plans. McEwen is betrothed to Grauben, a ward of Prof. Lidenbrock.

See *Journey to the Center of the Earth,* Jules Verne

McFadden, Paula

She's a dumped-on divorcée and devoted mom who fights like a lioness protecting her den when her latest boyfriend leaves town to do a movie and sublets their apartment. Paula has an affinity for actors who leave her. An ex-dancer, she limbers up and leaps, cautiously, once more into the breach with her new actor roommate, **Elliot**. "It's my third time as a cheerleader."

See *The Goodbye Girl,* Neil Simon

McFly, George

George is (a) a nerdy, put-upon adult/teenager involved in unusual father-son/admiring friend relationship with **Marty McFly** or (b) a confident, successful writer of fantasy fiction—depending on which time continuum you pick. Haircuts are rarely grease-free. Wears thick, black-framed glasses, flood pants, plastic pocket protectors. Lives in fear of **Biff Tannen**. Has romantic aspirations that he longs for Marty to help him out with.

See *Back to the Future*

McFly, Marty

Ultra-cool skateboarding high schooler unhappily stuck with nerdy **George McFly** for a father. Talented guitarist who can play a mean Chuck Berry cover. Partial to Calvin Klein underwear and Nike sports shoes, Marty wants bigger and better things from life but feels burdened by very limited finances, largely the result of Dad's lack of hustle, spine, and initiative. Develops the most horrendous girl problem since *Oedipus Rex*. A good friend and occasional assistant to **Dr. Emmett Brown**.

See *Back to the Future*

McGarrett, Detective Steve

He's the utterly dedicated chief of the elite Five-O unit of the Honolulu Police Department. With his assistant, **Danny Williams**, and fellow detectives like **Chin Ho Kelly**, he works at keeping the islands the peaceful paradise that tourists think they are. He's into long sideburns. His archenemy is the ruthless gangster **Wo Fat**, a true mastermind of villainy. He seems straight, but McGarrett is hip enough to talk to kids in their own language, the language of narcotics and rock 'n' roll. He drives a big old black Dodge V-8—a gas-guzzling muscle machine. Steve is simply too dedicated to his work to have a romantic relationship—even though there are plenty of ladies who'd be glad to have him in their lives. "Book 'im, Dan-O."

See *Hawaii Five-O*

McGee, Fibber

A somewhat lazy but breezy and charming suburban husband, Fibber is forever hatching one harebrained scheme after another to get rich quick. A former vaudeville performer, Fibber uses his acting abilities to convince and cajole his always-skeptical wife, Molly. Bald and usually seen wearing the trademark cardigan sweater of the 1950s suburban man.

See *Fibber McGee and Molly*

McGee, Travis

A self-described "salvage consultant," tall, lanky McGee is a free spirit often mistaken for a beach bum. By his own admission, he has been "taking my retirement in installments," working only when necessary. Since the early 1960s, his permanent residence has been an oceangoing houseboat named *The Busted Flush* (for the hand that won him the boat in a poker game). McGee retrieves lost goods and money for his clients, who have usually given up hope of ever retrieving it otherwise, taking half for his efforts. He is often aided by his only known regular associate, a large bearded economist named Meyer. His retirement seems to have become permanent since 1979, when he was contacted by a daughter he never knew he had. He has had a series of relationships with different women, never very long, but never superficial either…at least, that's his opinion.

See *The Deep Blue Good-by,* et al., John D. MacDonald

McGill, Tess

This ambitious secretary can't get her ideas taken seriously by her superiors. When her new boss, **Katherine Parker**, proves to be yet another snake in the grass, Tess takes matters into her own hands—along with her boss's lover, **Jack Trainer**. "I've got a head for business and a body for sin."

See *Working Girl*

McGinty, Dan

A shrewd drifter who uses his gift for gab and fisticuffs to hustle his way to the top of the political heap, rising from alderman to mayor to governor. As he moves up he becomes more honest, a change that angers the hoods that helped him get where he is, and have raked in graft during McGinty's amoral years.

See *The Great McGinty,* Preston Sturges

McHale, Lieutenant Commander Quinton

He's the commander of PT boat 73 during World War II. McHale is based on the island of Taratupa in the South Pacific, where he resides with his crew, Squadron 19, a motley band of piratelike seamen. He's forever butting heads with his commanding officer, **Captain Wallace B. Binghamton**. One of the many ways in which he departs from navy regulations is in secretly housing an unreported prisoner of war, Fuji, who serves as his personal cook.

See *McHale's Navy*

McIntyre, John "Trapper John"

Best friend and drinking buddy of Dr. **Hawkeye Pierce** in the 4077th MASH (Mobile Army Surgical Hospital) unit during the Korean War. With his dry sense of humor, the irreverent Trapper teams with Hawkeye in making bootleg hooch, stunts, jokes, nurse-violating, and the torture of tentmate **Frank Burns**. He's a fine surgeon, and, though he's married, he isn't above playing around.

See *M*A*S*H*

McIntyre, Liz

A guidance counselor at the large, integrated Walt Whitman High School, Liz is committed to her job and often comes to the aid of troubled kids. She dates **Pete Dixon**, a beloved history teacher.

See *Room 222*

McKay, B. J. "Billie Joe"

This handsome, freewheeling trucker—former Vietnam chopper pilot—works the South in his red and white eighteen-wheeler; his pet chimp, Bear, rides shotgun. Is pursued relentlessly by corrupt southern sheriff **Elroy P. Lobo**. His C.B. handle, "Milwaukee Kid," refers to his hometown. Eventually forms a trucking company called Bear Enterprises in California, employing seven shapely women.

See *B.J. and the Bear*

McKay, Dylan

Brooding and good-looking, this Beverly Hills teen lives on his own, off the estate of his wealthy parents. He is best friends with **Brandon Walsh** and dates his sister **Brenda**, but both those relationships end with jealousy and recrimination, the latter when Dylan starts dating Brenda's friend **Kelly Taylor**. Dylan is bright but opts out of college. Loves poetry and surfing. Spoiled by wealth and lonely, he battles alcoholism and a tendency to live way too fast. Co-owns the Peach Pit.

See *Beverly Hills 90210*

McKenzie, Leland

A dignified, venerable lawyer and the sole surviving founding partner of the law firm of McKenzie, Brackman, Chaney and Kuzak, primarily responsible for maintaining its character. Bespectacled, balding, and carrying a spare tire, Leland commands respect through his dignified manner and fairness. Occasionally, Leland goes head-to-head with his deceased partner's son, **Douglas Brackman**, over firm policies. Still has an eye for the ladies and a good head for the law.

See *L.A. Law*

McLaughlin, Ken

An earnest and romantic teenager living and working on his father's Montana ranch, Ken's one wish is to have a horse of his own. His father is dubious when Ken brings home a wild, seemingly untamable colt. But Ken pours love and kindness upon "Flicka," who is not only tamed, but saves the ranch from destruction. Really.

See *My Friend Flicka*

McLEOD, JUSTIN

From one angle, he's a handsome teacher; from another, he's a burned-up freak. From either side, he's a reclusive New England scholar with half his face full of scar tissue. Angry and bitter at the hand life has dealt him, his only companion is a fierce German shepherd named Mickey, the "Hound from Hell." He keeps an attic full of dress-store dummies, and supports himself by drawing covers for *Harpers, Time,* and *Newsweek.* A topic of discussion among local townspeople, he muses: "I've become a proper fairy tale troll." He reluctantly agrees to tutor young upstart **Chuck Norstadt**, who becomes his friend. His philosophy: "People spend too much time thinking of the past. Whatever else it is, it's gone."

See *The Man Without a Face*

McMURPHY, NURSE COLLEEN

Complex "good girl" army nurse. Stationed at Vietnam evacuation hospital near army vacation center at China Beach, outside Da Nang on the South China Sea. Treats mortally wounded soldiers as well as those on R&R. "Good Catholic girl" Colleen from the Midwest gets an education and battles culture shock amidst war horrors and realities of wartime living. Aloof, alone, and sometimes afraid, McMurphy pretends nothing bothers her. Overcomes some differences and develops odd friendship with **K. C. Koloski**, American prostitute and heroin addict. Learns from love affairs while carrying a quiet torch for married Dr. Dick. Occasionally returns home to the farm to find she no longer fits into "real life."

See *China Beach*

McMURPHY, RANDLE PATRICK

A fun-loving, libidinous drifter. In jail for sleeping with an underage girl, he escapes work detail by feigning mental illness. But there's no fun to be had in the mental ward—**Nurse Ratched** runs too tight a ship, and her patients have been cowed into submissive obedience by her powerful presence.

McMurphy can't stand to see this oppression, this waste of life, and sets about shaking up the ward, getting the men to question Nurse Ratched's authority for the very first time. McMurphy takes his fellow patients on an unauthorized field trip—breaks them out of the hospital and takes them fishing. He grows to love his fellow patients and treats them as adult men, despite their mental handicaps—unlike Nurse Ratched, who wants to stifle their power and individuality. He sets the ashamed, virginal **Billy Bibbit** up for a night of sex with a female friend. Because of him, the ward becomes a place of life, humor, and enthusiasm—just what Nurse Ratched doesn't want. In the end, he's sent by Ratched to be lobotomized; he's rescued from life as a vegetable by **Chief Bromden**.

See *One Flew over the Cuckoo's Nest,* Ken Kesey

McNAMARA, HEATHER

Never a leader, always a follower, cheerleader McNamara is a member of the most popular clique at Westerburg High. "God has cursed me," she says when calling a radio talk show, because her friend **Heather Chandler** and an old lover have both apparently committed suicide.

See *Heathers*

McNAMARA, JIGGS

A redheaded, Irish American bricklayer whose life changes drastically when he unexpectedly acquires great wealth by winning the Irish Sweepstakes. His everyday escapades and shenanigans are generally focused on his attempt to maintain his old lifestyle and blue-collar friends, despite the demands of his nagging, socially ambitious wife, Maggie.

See *Bringing Up Father,* George McManus

McNUTT, BOOB

A classic stooge and ignorant clown whose innocent blunders and adventures run a wide gamut. His associations include Pearl (his girlfriend), Major Gumbo (a rival), Bertha (his Siberian Cheesehound), Olga (the singing lizard), **Mike** and **Ike** (identical twins), and Professor Linoleum (an inventor who uses Boob as his guinea pig).

See *Boob McNutt,* Rube Goldberg

McPHERSON, MARK

Chain-smoking, hard-talking, seen-it-all lieutenant

of police in love with a corpse. Has a "silver shin-bone from a gun battle with a gangster." When asked, "Have you ever been in love?" he replies, "A doll in Washington Heights once got a fox fur outta me." A trenchcoat detective who doesn't pass up a drink before noon. He is fixated on beautiful alleged murder victim **Laura Hunt**, reading her diaries and sleeping at her apartment. "Murder victims have no claim to privacy." Not above using drastic measures to get what he wants. "I suspect nobody and everybody. I'm merely trying to get at the truth."

See *Laura,* Vera Caspary

McSwain, Remy

Corrupt New Orleans undercover cop. Though not totally corrupt, he's inclined to run red lights, eat free at restaurants, and find other little ways to fracture the law when it's in McSwain's own interest. He's also on the take. Partial to cuddling stuffed alligators at bedtime. Involved with New Orleans D.A. **Anne Osborne**.

See *The Big Easy*

Meany, Owen

He's brilliant, he's preposterous, but is he God's anointed one? Born in Gravesend, New Hampshire in 1942, Owen has an unnerving voice and an unshakable belief that he's the instrument of God. His underdeveloped vocal cords give his voice a sound like gravel grating. Owen is so small that his legs don't touch the floor when he sits in a chair. He is mortally cute, and a little doll to the girls. Owen's skin is translucent, the color of gravestone, a fitting complexion for the son of the owner of the Meany Granite Quarry. His mother is a recluse. Both his parents and Owen himself believe that he is the result of a virgin birth. An avid collector of baseball cards, the Little Leaguer stoically and philosophically deals with the fact that his foul ball struck and killed Tabitha Wheelwright, his best friend's mother. Owen's sense of predestination and martyrdom would shame John Calvin.

See *A Prayer For Owen Meany,* John Irving

Medavoy, Gregory

Ultra-nervous, hypochondriacal New York City detective who works at the 15th Precinct. After getting out of an unhappy marriage, Medavoy becomes involved with **Donna Abandando**, a striking blonde who works at the station. He's basically sweet but has more than his share of problems and hang-ups (he's got asthma, food allergies, and breaks out in a lot of rashes). He has been accused (with some justification) of not letting himself enjoy life.

See *NYPD Blue*

Medford, Alexandra

A frustrated witch and mother of four, Lexa keeps the multicolored dust of her former husband in a jar on a kitchen shelf. She owns a black Lab named Coal. Alexandra, slightly plump, sculpts chunky figurines of female bodies which she sells at local gift shops. Together with her witch buddies, **Sukie Ridgemont** and **Jane Smart**, she conjures up the perfect man—the devil.

See *The Witches of Eastwick,* John Updike

Meeber, Caroline "Carrie"

A poor girl from a small town in Wisconsin, Carrie moves to Chicago to live with her sister and her husband in hopes of a better life. Self-interested but not totally selfish, Carrie finds that the drudgery of work in a shoe factory is more than she can bear. A young woman of modest intellect, she is vain and materialistic, with a certain charm which she carefully nurtures. She uses her unerring instinct to guide her in all life decisions. Beautiful and shapely, Carrie is courted by two men, Charles Drouet and George Hurstwood, a well-to-do married man. Each man wants her to become his mistress, and Carrie is willing to become a kept woman if it means an escape from hard work. Her ultimate decision, like all her others, is made for her material betterment, even if it's costly to others.

See *Sister Carrie,* Theodore Dreiser

Meechum, Bull

An unbending martinet of a military officer in 1960s South Carolina. Meechum is as strict a disciplinarian with his son as with his troops, and drives the boy, a sensitive kid, mercilessly. In a climactic struggle, he goads his son into playing him in one-on-one basketball. The result has to be a no-win situation for Bull: either he wins, and further humiliates his son, or he loses, a prospect that is intolerable to him.

See *The Great Santini,* Pat Conroy

Photo courtesy of CBS

Fred Mertz

MELLISH, FIELDING

He is a neurotic, Jewish, New York product tester turned Latin American revolutionary hero. Has an overwhelming interest in sexual fulfillment, though admittedly doesn't like to beg and plead on first dates. Enjoys wide variety of reading material, though somewhat shy about taste in magazines. Mother and father are both surgeons and disappointed that Fielding hasn't gone into family business.

See *Bananas*

MELLORS, OLIVER

Gamekeeper on the estate of **Sir Clifford Chatterley**, a man of both another social class and another life philosophy from that of his employer. The son of a miner, trained as a blacksmith, he enters the army to get away from his wife and ultimately achieves the rank of lieutenant. Back in England, he puts his affinity for the natural world to work when he takes the position of gamekeeper. His education and manner make it possible for him to pass as a member of the upper classes, but he despises authority and prefers his solitary existence. Mellors is a tall, strong man with dark hair and blue eyes, his vigor in sharp contrast with Sir Clifford's incapacitation. It is his willingness to be emotionally open to love that draws **Lady Constance Chatterley** to his arms.

See *Lady Chatterley's Lover*, D. H. Lawrence

MELMAN, ROXANNE

A buxom, competent secretary, Roxanne holds the key to **Arnie Becker's** success by handling all the details and affairs of his daily life. She also happens to be deeply in love with him, of which he takes full advantage. She lives a difficult life, which gets even worse after her disastrous marriage. Eventually, she enters into a love relationship with Arnie, but that doesn't provide true happiness, either. She fights for the rights of the secretarial staff at McKenzie, Brackman, Chaney and Kuzak, and wins.

See *L.A. Law*

MELNITZ, JANINE

Sardonic, bespectacled, smart-aleck receptionist for the Ghostbusters firm. She likes to read *People Weekly* and worries that people find her too intellectual. She has a secret crush on Ghostbuster **Egon**

Spengler, who's oblivious to her interest in him. Hobby: racquetball.

See *Ghostbusters* and *Ghostbusters II*

MERRILL, NEDDY

This slender, middle-aged prepster decides, one boozy afternoon in the waning days of summer, to leave the Westerhazys' cocktail party and *swim* across the county, to his home in South Bullet, using the pools of all the wealthy socialites in between as his route. And so he does, walking from pool to pool, swimming a length in each, covering miles of ground and years of personal history in the process. Some of those he encounters treat him with pity, and others, with disdain—like the Biswangers, whom he and his wife have snubbed repeatedly, and Shirley Adams, his old mistress. When he finally reaches his house, he makes a shocking discovery, not only about his home but about the entirety of his life to date.

See *The Swimmer*, John Cheever

MERRIN, FATHER

He is a troubled priest working to free **Regan MacNeil** from the demon that possesses her. His worries about his own inner turmoil and troubled psyche have left him doubting his vocation ability to serve God. Despite his many questions and inner turmoil, he truly wants to do good in this world.

See *The Exorcist*

MERTZ, ETHEL

Easygoing, sweet, and often exasperated best friend of wacky **Lucy Ricardo**. Ethel is always dragged into one of Lucy's "plans." She's willing to go along, especially if there's a chance for her and husband **Fred** to dust off their old vaudeville act. Loves Fred even though he's grouchy and cheap.

See *I Love Lucy*

MERTZ, FRED

Beneath his crusty and crotchety exterior, Fred's a lovable pussycat. Throws nickels around like manhole covers. This old vaudevillian still has the theater bug. He's also **Lucy** and **Ricky Ricardo's** landlord and the grouchy but loving husband of **Ethel**. He's willing to take part in Lucy's outrageous schemes if it means a chance to perform—and it won't cost money.

See *I Love Lucy*

MICELLI, TONY

Spirited, confident, cute, happy-go-lucky Brooklyn guy working as a housekeeper in Connecticut to give his daughter a better life. He turns out to be an excellent housewife. Manly enough to vacuum and wear an apron without flinching. Warm and affectionate. Protective of his boss, **Angela Bower**, he's also in love with her.

See *Who's the Boss?*

MICHAEL

This BMW-driving, Armani-clad yuppie dates and apparently loves **Lelaina**, but loses her to **Troy** when he overedits her documentary on the Generation X lives of her friends, in an effort to make it more commercial for the MTV-like company for which he works.

See *Reality Bites*

BLACK MICHAEL

Officious, monocled, sneering, and bug-eyed. He is the older half brother of Prince Rudolf of Ruritania. Michael, the Duke of Strelsau, feels cheated out of the Ruritanian throne; although he's actually the king's firstborn, his mother "wasn't exactly acceptable in court circles." His bitterness turns to vengeful acts against his brother.

See *The Prisoner of Zenda*

MICHAELS, DOROTHY

Okay, she has a little bit of five o'clock shadow. And that southern accent hides a voice that's just a mite too husky. Oh, and don't stare at the prominent Adam's apple. Dorothy Michaels is the hottest star of *Southwest General*. The soap opera was buried in the ratings until the brash new hospital administrator, Ms. Emily Kimberly, arrived on the scene. Dorothy plays Emily with the abandon of an actress immersed in her role. She's given to ad libs that leave the other actors (and the crew) dumbfounded. Dorothy falls in love with Julie Nichols, the sexpot nurse on the soap. It takes four hours of makeup to hide the fact that she's really struggling actor Michael Dorsey. Michael's confession to Julie: "I was a better man with you, as a woman, than I ever was with a woman as a man...I've just got to learn to do it without the dress."

See *Tootsie*

THE MICHELIN MAN, BIP

Large, imposing male figure made up entirely of tires. Thanks to his friendly face, he's not as frightening as he could be. Hard to miss on a billboard.

See *Michelin tires*

MICKEY

The quintessential grizzled small-time boxing trainer. An old man, he sees in **Rocky Balboa** a final chance to train a potential champion and, as a result, drives the boxer to new heights of physical and mental preparedness.

See *Rocky*

MIKE

Vietnam vet, loyal to his old friends from small Pennsylvania town. Enjoys beer drinking and pool playing with his buddies. Although he is deeply disturbed by what he has seen in the war in Vietnam, he's nevertheless willing to return there for the sake of best friend **Nick**. Enjoys male bonding experiences but finds greatest rewards, spiritual and physical, in solo tracking of deer.

See *The Deer Hunter*

MIKE AND IKE

Identical, derby-clad twins previously named Tom and Jerry and referred to as "the Look-alike Boys." They're the long-lost sons of a local farmer and his wife whom **Boob McNutt** finds working at a circus as acrobats. The boys have previously been panhandlers who'd lost dozens of jobs and been kicked out of both the army and the navy. They remain tramps but continue their association with Boob.

See *Boob McNutt,* **Rube Goldberg**

MIKEY

All-American little boy whose cheeks have probably been squeezed more often than he likes. Sometimes used as a guinea pig by his older brother to try things of suspect, like a "healthy" breakfast cereal. "He likes it! Hey, Mikey!"

See *Life cereal*

MIKEY

The illegitimate child of a neurotic New York yuppie mother, he's a precocious baby with a surprising command of the English language, despite being too young to talk yet. He can use his sophisticated

Mike

vocabulary and high-powered brain only in internal monologues, which go on more or less continuously. He helps his mom and babysitter, a guy who drives a cab, to acknowledge that they love each other.

See *Look Who's Talking*

MILL, GRIFFIN

A sleek, well-dressed, and ice-cold vice president at a Hollywood studio, Griffin Mill has never really worked for a living and doesn't really care. He makes enormous sums of money by listening to people hawk movie ideas. One rejected pitch man sends anonymous hate mail to him, so Griffin kills him.

See *The Player*

MILLANEY, ANN

This gorgeous, naive, somewhat sexually frozen woman doesn't understand why there's no passion in her marriage to **John** and wonders why folks make such a big deal about sex. Upon exposure to newcomer **Graham Dalton** and his hobby of video interviews, a new awareness dawns in Ann—about life in general, and about her life in particular, especially her relationships with husband **John** and sister **Cynthia Bishop**.

See *sex, lies, and videotape*

MILLANEY, JOHN

An amoral yuppie lawyer who's so sleazy he's sleeping with **Cynthia Bishop**, the sister of his sweet wife, **Ann**. His old college buddy **Graham Dalton** comes to town, but John's too wrapped up in his world of deceit and material goods to understand his friend's spiritual confusion. He's about as good a friend as he is a husband. Maybe he's a good lawyer.

See *sex, lies, and videotape*

MILLER, BARNEY

Captain of the 12th Precinct in New York's Greenwich Village, he's a voice of reason in his very colorful and frequently chaotic world, where the cops and civilians are almost as bizarre as the perps. Being a cop has had its personal cost; he's divorced from the understanding-and-tolerant-up-to-a-point Elizabeth. He's well served by his unflappability, an ever-present sense of gentle humor, and a sardonic, world-weary attitude, as he copes with the madness, most particularly a squad of detectives who are at times as unruly as children, and a police bureaucracy that always seems to operate by regulations running directly counter to common sense.

See *Barney Miller*

MILLER, CONSTANCE

A frontier prostitute who dreams of a better life. Miller is the madam at **John McCabe**'s whorehouse in the northwestern town of Presbyterian Church. She's tough-talking, cynical, and beautiful. While Miller is a supreme realist, she frequently loses herself in a haze of opium smoke. The London native wants to leave Presbyterian Church and return to San Francisco, where there's more money to be had and more to spend it on.

See *McCabe and Mrs. Miller*

MILLER, FRANK

This vicious killer was caught by **Sheriff Will Kane**, but he's now been freed from confinement on a technicality, and is bent on getting even with Kane by killing him. He rounds up his former henchmen to help him do the job. If ever a guy deserved to wear a black hat, it's this one.

See *High Noon*

MILLER, JOE

A small-time Philadelphia personal-injury lawyer who rises to fame by defending AIDS victim **Andrew Beckett** in a landmark wrongful-dismissal suit. During the course of the trial, he slowly sheds his antigay bias and forms a strong bond of respect and friendship with his client. "We don't live in this courtroom, do we?"

See *Philadelphia*

MILLER, KATE

Frustrated and bored homemaker trying to relieve psychological pressures through therapy sessions with **Dr. Robert Elliott**. She enjoys touring museums and anonymous flirtations. Kate can be forgetful at awkward moments and sometimes has problems in elevators.

See *Dressed to Kill*

MILLER, PETER

A determined, steel-nerved German reporter obsessed with tracking down and exposing a sadistic Nazi war criminal, Miller stumbles upon a secret society of former Gestapo officers conspiring to produce rockets that will destroy Israel. To foil the conspiracy he masquerades as an S.S. man, only to find his identity exposed and his life threatened.

See *The Odessa File,* Frederick Forsyth

MILLER, RUTH-ANNE

Wise seventy-something shopkeeper in the small town of Cicely, Alaska. She owns the town's only emporium, a one-stop shop that serves as local market, library, post office, and video store. Dispenses psychological insights with her customers' purchases.

See *Northern Exposure*

MILLHONE, KINSEY

This witty, intelligent private investigator lives and works on the California coast, in the city of Santa Teresa. She was orphaned in her youth and reared by her tough, independent aunt in a trailer park in the same area. Now in her thirties and twice divorced, she lives in a studio garage apartment located on the property of her landlord and best friend, eighty-something retired baker Henry Pitts. Kinsey will carry and even use a gun but would rather not. Her bouts with marriage have left her with a strong need for independence.

See *"A" Is for Alibi,* et al., Sue Grafton

MILO

This bored but intelligent schoolboy never knows quite what to do with himself and considers everything "a waste of time." Milo, who's adept at following instructions when he puts his mind to it, assembles a mysterious tollbooth and sets off in his electric automobile, hoping for adventure. He enjoys himself tooling around the Kingdom of Wisdom countryside (which he accesses via the tollbooth) with a watchdog named Tock. Milo's other great skill is the ability to count to one thousand. He's an excellent dinner guest, gracing the table of cranky King Azaz the Unabridged, and he especially likes half-baked ideas for dessert. He develops a crush on the Princesses Rhyme and Reason. On returning home, he discovers he doesn't have enough time to take another trip. "There's just so much to do right here."

See *The Phantom Tollbooth,* Norton Juster

MILTON, GEORGE

A pragmatic dreamer. A cattle ranch hand linked by loneliness to big palooka **Lennie Small** because "you get used to goin' around with a guy an' you can't get rid of him." George does the talking for both of them. He's small, but wiry. The two work the ranches in the Salinas Valley of California. He doesn't want trouble, but Lennie drags him into it wherever they go. He likes to tell Lennie that they are not like the other ranch workers: "They got no family. They don't belong no place. They ain't got nothing to look ahead to. With us it ain't like that." He wants to build up a stake and some day buy a ranch of their own, with rabbits for Lennie to tend. George, tough but compassionate, takes an immediate dislike to the boss's son, **Curley:** "I don't like mean little guys." After Lennie unwittingly kills Curley's provocative wife, **Mae,** he knows that there's only one solution left for Lennie: a quick, compassionate death. "Everybody gonna be nice to you. Ain't gonna be no more trouble. Nobody gonna hurt nobody nor steal from 'em. Look acrost the river, Lennie, and I'll tell you like you can almost see it."

See *Of Mice and Men,* John Steinbeck

MINDERBINDER, MILO

The ultimate black-market entrepreneur and mess officer for the 256th Squadron who knows where to get a fresh egg. Milo makes a profit by acting as his own middleman. Cunning and enterprising, he is elected mayor of Palermo because he brings Scotch whiskey to Sicily. Every serviceman has a share of his syndicate. Milo steals any supplies he needs to trade, leaving notes that say, "What's good for M&M Enterprises is good for the country." After he can't unload a shipment of Egyptian cotton, he tries to pass it off as chocolate-covered cotton candy. He bombs his own airfield when the Germans make him a reasonable offer: cost plus six percent. His motto: "I only lie when necessary."

See *Catch-22* and *Closing Time,* Joseph Heller

MING THE MERCILESS

Bald-headed libertine tyrant from another world, and the force behind many a nefarious plot to destroy peace lovers throughout the universe. Ming, as his enemies call him, wears a distinctive **Fu Manchu** beard and mustache; he's also into

Ming the Merciless

metallic clothing and the occasional odd-looking collar. Enjoys giving orders, doling out cruelty, and making evil plans. The archenemy of **Flash Gordon**.

See *Flash Gordon*

MINIVER, MRS. KAY

This upper-middle-class English wife and mother is gentle, courageous, and strong. She enjoys the simple things in life: gardening and flowers, her home, and her husband and children. She finds pleasure in such ostensibly insignificant things as buying a new engagement book, or a bunch of chrysanthemums. Accustomed to a certain degree of comfort in her life, which is divided between her London flat and Starlings, her country home, Mrs. Miniver must adapt when World War II begins to touch and change her way of life.

See *Mrs. Miniver,* Jan Struther

MINNIFIELD, MAURICE

A former astronaut and current president of the Chamber of Commerce in tiny, isolated Cicely, Alaska. As a wealthy local real estate mogul, Minnifield views Cicely as having limitless potential and wants to turn it into the "Alaskan Riviera." He is egotistical, a bit of a blowhard, and extremely judgmental, but he does seem to mean well and shows potential for learning a thing or two.

See *Northern Exposure*

MIRANDA, ROBERTO

Music lover. Also, possibly, a onetime torturer of political prisoners, including **Paulina Escobar**. He likes to play out difficult situations with a deliberate, thoughtful approach. A lover of drink and conversation, prone to giving wry and mysterious remarks when occasions warrant.

See *Death and the Maiden*

MIRIAM

A sweet-talking, middle-aged southern belle whose ostentatious concern for her cousin **Charlotte** veils her greed for the fragile woman's wealth. She's sweet and patient with her cousin, while severe and blunt to others. Cold-hearted and confident, she plots Charlotte's downfall with a frightening single-mindedness.

See *Hush…Hush, Sweet Charlotte*

MISS LONELYHEARTS

The "agony aunt" for the *New York Post-Dispatch,* Miss Lonelyhearts started his (that's right—his) career as a reporter. After spending months as Miss Lonelyhearts, he suffers daily as he reads the private griefs of those seeking his advice. He takes his job too seriously, for which he is ridiculed by Shrike, the feature editor.

See *Miss Lonelyhearts,* Nathanael West

MISTER

His real name is Albert. Handsome, charming, physically powerful, he's the abusive husband of **Celie**, a sensitive young African American woman coming of age in the rural South. Mister is away from home for long periods and likes to flaunt his mistress, **Shug Avery**, in front of his wife. Perhaps more ignorant than evil, he cannot recognize Celie's real inner beauty.

See *The Color Purple,* Alice Walker

MITCHELL, DENNIS

The world's most dangerous five-year-old. Dennis is a pint-sized blond sociopath in red overalls who delights in breaking rules and testing limits. He's such a handful that his parents don't dare have another child. When Dennis isn't playing with friends like Joey and Gina, he's matching wits with frumpy Margaret or terrorizing next-door neighbor Mr. Wilson.

See *Dennis the Menace,* Hank Ketchum

MITCHELL, LIEUTENANT PETE "MAVERICK"

Maverick is an eighties' sex symbol incarnate, complete with leather jacket, sunglasses, and motorcycle. When **Charlotte "Charlie" Blackwood** tells him that the floor is cold and hard for love, he quickly insists, "Actually, I had this counter in mind …" Not too tall, but still dark, built, and handsome, Maverick lives up to his name, wreaking havoc in flight towers and a general's life with forbidden flybys and passes at the general's daughter. He seduces Charlie, a teacher at elite Miramar Naval Air Station. After losing best friend, **Nick "Goose" Bradshaw** in a flight accident, Maverick learns the meaning of life, love, and forgiveness.

See *Top Gun*

MITTY, WALTER

He's just an average middle-aged man living in suburban Connecticut, where he manages to escape from his dreary quotidian life by retreating into a world of exciting daydreams. In body, he may be in town on errands with his oh-so-practical, somewhat overwhelming wife, but in spirit, he's not shopping for overshoes and puppy biscuits; he's a whole series of pulp-fiction heroes: a world-renowned surgeon with billion-dollar hands; a seasoned daredevil navy commander who flies his hydroplane with nerves of steel and ice water for blood; the insouciant Captain Mitty, tossing down brandy after brandy, with no apparent effect on his faculties, and flying a solo bombing run through dense flak barrages; and so on, and so forth, on and on…until reality bursts in, in the shape of his wife, demanding to know *why* he forgot the dog treats, or the overshoes, or whatever forgettable thing it may have been. Then, for a little while, he becomes plain old inoffensive Walter Mitty again until he spots some everyday object that sends him back to his world of make-believe, so much more satisfying than that other world his body occupies. "Ta-pocketa-pocketa-pocketa…"

See *The Secret Life of Walter Mitty,* James Thurber

MITZI

She was born Anthony and is sometimes called Tick. A butch drag queen who choreographs and appears in lip-synching shows. Solidly muscular, with a compact frame. She frequently performs in drag shows with **Bernadette** and **Felicia**. Formerly married—although emphatically not a switch-hitter—with one son, Benjamin. Mitzi sews her own gowns and drinks Long Island Iced Teas.

See *The Adventures of Priscilla, Queen of the Desert*

MR. MIYAGI

He is a gentle man who came to live in America from Japan. He seems unremarkable on the surface, just a quiet apartment building manager, but proves to be a lot more than that when he takes young **Daniel LaRusso** under his wing. He teaches the boy, newly arrived in California from New Jersey, some important life lessons, not to mention a good deal of high-octane karate. He turns out to be a lot more impressive, both in his history and in his accomplishments, and helps Daniel grow up. His likes include gardening, bonsai trees, vintage automobiles, and occasionally getting weepy after too much saki. He has no use for bullies and lazy teenage boys. Words to live by: "Wipe on….Wipe off."

See *The Karate Kid*

MNEMONIC, JOHNNY

This guy's a real chiphead. Specialized neurosurgery has given him the capacity to store any complex computer data in his brain. And, unlike his electronic equivalent, he won't go down in a power outage. Clients store software in him and use a password to put Johnny into a trance, during which he reels off the information. Consciously, he retains no knowledge or memory of the programs. He lives in "the Sprawl," also known as the Boston-Atlanta Metropolitan Axis. Someone has stashed a stolen program in his head, and Johnny is now on the bad side of the Yakuza, the Japanese Mafia. He's hiding out, and, with the help of Molly Millions, Johnny is trying to blackmail the Yakuza into leaving him alone. "I'm a very technical boy."

See *Johnny Mnemonic,* William Gibson

MOLINA, LUIS

A gay window dresser condemned to eight years imprisonment in a Buenos Aires penitentiary for fooling around with minors. Molina escapes the horrors of prison life by regaling his cellmate, political prisoner **Valentin Arregui**, with fanciful narratives of old Hollywood movies. He always relates to the heroines, and believes "if men acted like women there wouldn't be any more torturers." At age thirty-seven, he's still tied to his mother's apron strings, waiting for a "real man" to come along. After he falls in love with Valentin and is released from prison, Luis is swept into a web of political intrigue, and risks his life for the cause of the man he loves.

See *Kiss of the Spider Woman,* Manuel Puig

MOND, MUSTAPHA

The Controller, one of the ten-member ruling cabal of the futuristic World State. An educated man, trained as a scientist, Mond uses his unassailable position to read of forbidden books such as the works of Shakespeare and the Bible. He has there-

Tony Montana

by gained a uniquely broad perspective on the world, with an understanding of concepts and ideas outside the mandated state philosophy. Such exceptional awareness has given him a virtually unique power—that of Freedom of Choice. But Mond's response to this opportunity has not been to turn into a rebellious dissident, but instead, to become part of the tyrannical clique; rather than use his insights for moral purposes, he employs them to shore up and further the immoral goals of the state.

See *Brave New World,* **Aldous Huxley**

MISS MONEYPENNY

Secretary to the mysterious **M,** chief of operations of MI5. The lovely Moneypenny has always been smitten by master spy **James Bond,** and it seems that she'd be delighted for a chance to climb into bed with him, if such liaisons weren't strictly against company policy. So she is forced, by the call of patriotic duty, to confine herself to periodic flirtations. So it goes.

See *Dr. No, Goldfinger, From Russia with Love,* et. al., **Ian Fleming**

MONGO

Itinerant railroad worker capable of coldcocking a horse with one punch. Extremely poor eating habits and hygiene. Assists **Sheriff Black Bart** in saving the township of Rock Ridge from Hedley Lamarr's land-snatching scheme. Occasionally prone to statements beyond his limited intellect: "Mongo only pawn in game of life."

See *Blazing Saddles*

MONROE, MILES

This nerdy health food store operator undergoes a routine surgical procedure, only to wake up two hundred years later as a ward of a totalitarian state. Miles overcomes his initial shock and the unwillingness to believe that such a fate could befall him (he discounts the notion of karmic retribution for the occasional customer of his health food store coming down with botulism). Monroe has a penchant for understatement—his comment on seeing a twenty-foot genetically engineered chicken was "That's a big chicken." When scholars try to mine him for information about his era, he's perfectly capable of lying to tickle his sense of whimsy: a videotape of Howard Cosell was, he confirms, used

as a means of torture. But, horrified by what he sees as the ethical and aesthetic decay of this new world, he eventually tries to do something to change it. He is also profoundly unimpressed by the futuristic attempt to mechanize sex—and has no use for robot pets.

See *Sleeper*

MONTAG, GUY

He works as a futuristic fireman, which is to say that he goes around setting fire to books, since the printed word is now forbidden. He's content with life until he meets a nonconformist named **Clarisse McClennan;** then he realizes how empty his life is and begins to wonder what is in the books he burns. He subsequently becomes a closet reader, and his life changes forever. He becomes a fugitive and joins the book vagrants, who each keep one book in their head and share it as they travel. "This fire'll last me the rest of my life. God! I've been trying to put it out, in my mind, all night. I'm crazy with trying."

See *Fahrenheit 451,* **Ray Bradbury**

MONTAGUE, DR. CHARLES

Known to use the alias Mr. McGuffin, he is an ambitious, scheming, ruthless psychiatrist at the Psychoneurotic Institute for the Very, Very Nervous. He conspired with **Nurse Diesel,** his sadomasochistic lover and colleague, to kill Dr. Ashley, the institute's chief of staff, in hopes that, as second-in-command, Charles would be his replacement. But often, crime doesn't pay.

See *High Anxiety,* **Mel Brooks**

MONTANA, TONY

"This country, first you gotta get the money, then you get the power, and when you got the power, then you get the women." Anthony Montana is Cuban, one of the criminals Fidel Castro has taken from his jails and sent as émigrés to Florida. Endowed with street smarts and a crazy temper that makes him a menace under pressure, he has simple goals: to get a green card and achieve the American Dream. Not, in his case, by hard work, however; he will be a big-time drug dealer, providing the cocaine that Americans are so in love with. That's the key to the money, the power, and the women. Tony's mother thinks he's a bum, but his nine-teen-year-old sister worships him. He's totally amoral and won't hesitate to murder when it serves his purpose. While he has no ethics, he has honor: honor among partners, that is. He is actually well on the way to achieving his goals when he develops too great a liking for the stuff he peddles, and things start to go downhill. Motto: The World Is Yours.

See *Scarface*

MONTGOMERY

He's an acting student at New York City's High School for the Performing Arts, with a huge mop of hair and major personal insecurities. Is very close to **Doris Finsecker** and disdains **Raul "Ralph Garcy" Garcia**. Unsure of his own sexuality and is painfully struggling with this inner conflict.

See *Fame*

MONTOYA, INIGO

A swashbuckling, mustachioed adventurer and sometime criminal with the heart of a softie. With **Fezzik** and Westley, he rescues **Buttercup, the Princess Bride**. He speaks in a Spanish accent as thick as Heinz ketchup. Inigo is obsessed with his father's murder and is constantly rehearsing lines that he longs to say one day for real: "My name is Inigo Montoya. You keel my father. Prepare to die."

See *The Princess Bride*

MOODY

This sadistic high school bully shakes down his classmates for their lunch money. And that's on his friendly days. But he gets more than he bargains for when he starts picking on the newest kid at school, **Clifford**. Clifford knows how to delegate responsibility and hires even bigger, tougher **Linderman**, the one guy at school Moody's afraid of, to protect him.

See *My Bodyguard*

MOOKIE

Mookie is employed by **Sal** as a pizza deliverer and appears to have little ambition beyond collecting his paycheck. He's a fixture in his Bedford-Stuyvesant neighborhood, with distinctive skinny legs jutting out of his short pants. Involved with Tina, by whom he has fathered a child, though marriage isn't in his plans. He lives with his younger sister, Jade. His friends include **Buggin' Out** and **Radio Raheem**, though Mookie is sometimes at odds with his buddies over his place of employment. Capable of extreme rage when emotions reach a boiling point. "Make that money. Get paid."

See *Do the Right Thing*

MOONEY, THEODORE J.

A perennially exasperated boss. The proper, dignified, strict "Mr. Mooney" depends on "Mrs. Carmichael" to do her job but must constantly cope with her enormous personal problems and complications. He tries to keep a steady hand while acting as vice-president at Westland Bank (or president of the Danfield First National Bank in Danfield, Connecticut) but is constantly thwarted by the outrageous antics of Lucy Carmichael. He is forever throwing up his hands and insisting he can't take any more of it. However, he really has a soft spot for Lucy.

See *The Lucy Show*

MORALES

A graduate of New York City's famed High School for the Performing Arts. Originally envisioned herself as a serious actress but eventually realized that the "method" was not part of her own private madness. Now a chorus dancer and loves the life, despite the harsh realities of the business. "Won't regret, can't forget what I did for love."

See *A Chorus Line*

MORBIUS, ALTAIRA

The daughter of philologist Edward Morbius; she and her father are the only survivors of an expedition to the planet Altair. She hasn't seen a human, other than her dad, for many years and is something of an innocent. She's also beautiful and mischievous. Her best friend and guardian is a massive robot named Robby, and she's chummy with ferocious local animals who would gobble you for a quick snack if they saw you. With no one but Robby and the animals to peek, she's given to wearing scanty clothing and to skinny-dipping in forest pools. This is no big deal to Robby and the animals, but when some Earth males show up in this extraterrestrial paradise, things get a bit complicated.

See *Forbidden Planet*

DR. MORBIUS

A world-weary scientist who is now living on a planet far from Earth. He's making a desperate effort to carve out a new version of paradise for himself and his daughter—one untainted by other humans, if possible. Often assisted in his work by mechanical creation Robby the Robot.

See *Forbidden Planet*

MORGAN, HUW

Youngest son in an impoverished Welsh mining family. With a shy and stalwart manner, Huw seeks to escape the crushing tragedy of life in a coal town. Luckily, the local pastor perceives talent and yearning for better things in the boy, and inspires Huw with spiritual zeal and a thirst for knowledge that ultimately deliver him from "the pit."

See *How Green Was My Valley*, Richard Llewellyn

MORGAN, REX

Handsome, dark-haired, unmarried doctor up to his ears in love, lust, and murder. Almost immediately after arriving in the small town of Glenbrook, Dr. Morgan gets tangled up with a spoiled, reckless heiress, her rich, doting father, and his lovely dark-haired nurse June Gale. Oh, and he tends to the sick and injured.

See *Rex Morgan, M.D.*

MORGENSTERN, BRENDA

The younger sister of **Rhoda Morgenstern**, Brenda grew up in the Bronx, then moved to Manhattan, where she works as a bank teller at First Security Bank. Smart and funny, but insecure, Brenda is always on the lookout for the right guy and fighting a bit of a weight problem. She's somewhat in awe of her slimmed-down older sister, and often follows in Rhoda's footsteps, including having a similarly complex relationship with their controlling mother, **Ida Morgenstern**. One of Brenda's long-standing boyfriends is Benny Goodwin, a bespectacled, good-hearted fellow.

See *Rhoda*

MORGENSTERN, IDA

Overly involved in the lives of her two daughters, **Rhoda** and **Brenda Morgenstern**, Ida enjoys guilt trips, especially when she makes her daughters take them. She's meddlesome and controlling, with a biting sense of humor, and while she's petite, barely topping five feet, she's got a steel core at her center. She does occasionally melt, usually in the company of her long-suffering and far more relaxed husband, **Martin**. She treats being a mother—and marrying off her two single daughters—like a military campaign. Her headquarters is her Bronx apartment on the Grand Concourse; once, she spent a year traveling around the country in an RV with Martin. Even though he can put up with a lot, Martin eventually leaves her.

See *Rhoda*

MORGENSTERN, MARTIN

Funny, dashing, handsome, and yet down-to-earth, Martin Morgenstern is almost instantly beloved by anyone who meets him. Invariably, they wonder why he stays married to the tight and controlling **Ida Morgenstern**. He's absolutely worshiped by his two adult daughters, **Rhoda** and **Brenda**. A resident of the Bronx, Martin himself ultimately comes to wonder why he's married to Ida. When he can't come up with a satisfactory answer, he separates from her.

See *Rhoda* and *The Mary Tyler Moore Show*

MORGENSTERN, RHODA

A deep-dyed New Yorker from the Bronx, Rhoda moved to Minneapolis to look for a job and an apartment and a life. She is a neighbor and best friend of **Mary Richards**, who lives downstairs in Rhoda's building. Their friendship didn't start out well, since Rhoda had wanted to take over the apartment Mary occupied. She works as a window dresser at Hempel's Department Store. Rhoda, like Mary, is still single in her thirties, but unlike Mary, she's dying to find a man. Ultimately, she moves back to New York, where she takes a place with her kid sister, **Brenda Morgenstern**, in a building on 46th Street. The doorman there is named **Carlton**. In New York she marries and divorces Joe Gerard, who owns a wrecking company. When first back in the Apple, she starts her own window design business but later goes to work for the Doyle Costume Company. The major burden in her life, what she moved to Minneapolis to escape: her meddling, aggressive mother, **Ida**.

See *The Mary Tyler Moore Show* and *Rhoda*

MORK

An alien from the planet Ork. A misfit on his own planet because he has a sense of humor, he was sent away by the Orkans to study earthlings. When he first landed on Earth, he tried to kidnap **Richie Cunningham**. He later returned in a giant eggshell and touched down near Boulder, Colorado. Now Mork is married to kind and pretty **Mindy Beth McConnell**, who was the first person to befriend him when he came to this planet. Mork gave birth to the couple's son, Mearth, who weighed 225 pounds. (Orkan children are born old and become young with time.) He tends to wear his suit backward, and although he can speak English, says good-bye in Orkan: "Na Nu, Na Nu."

See *Mork & Mindy*

MORNINGSTAR, MARJORIE

A young, raven-haired Jewish girl who grows up with ambitions to be an actress. When she goes away to summer stock, she changes her name and puts aside the moral strictures her mother tried to instill in her. She has an affair with a director, and naively believes that he takes it as seriously as she does. Her enthusiasm and hope eventually turn into resignation and disappointment.

See *Marjorie Morningstar*, Herman Wouk

MORRISON, JOHNNY

Ex–navy fighter pilot whose excitement at returning home to his wife from the Pacific changes into cool fury when he discovers that she has been unfaithful. When he's wrongly implicated in her murder, he goes into hiding and looks for her killer. Calm, reserved, and determined, he displays a virtually emotionless demeanor until he meets **Joyce Harwood**.

See *The Blue Dahlia*

MORRISON, JULIE

A brash, beautiful New Orleans belle, Morrison is an egocentric schemer who pouts when she doesn't get her way. She tries to wrap banker **Preston Dillard** around her finger but fails because he is obsessed with his work. He leaves for Philadelphia, and when he returns three years later, she's devastated to learn that he is married. She's resilient, though, and plans to win him back. When Dillard takes sick during the yellow jack epidemic Morrison commits the first unselfish act of her life by nursing him back to health. "I've got to think, to plan, to fight."

See *Jezebel*

MORSE, JOE

A once-idealistic attorney-at-law, Joe is slowly losing his moral foundation. He's presently working for a mob outfit that runs a numbers racket. He tends to be tormented by an internal conflict over his work versus his ideals. Has a hard time with staircases.

See *Force of Evil*

CAPTAIN MORTON

He's the hated commanding officer of the USS *Reluctant,* a cargo vessel plying the South Pacific during World War II. "The old man" hates the crew and officers back, especially **Lieutenant Roberts**. His prized possession is a potted palm tree he keeps on deck.

See *Mister Roberts*

MOSELEY, SERGEANT HAKE

Sergeant Moseley is a member of the Miami Police Department, a bachelor, living in scruffy digs at a residential hotel. Mosely is cagy, but when he crosses paths with psycho killer **Junior Frenger**, he winds up losing his badge, his gun—even his teeth. He sets out to bring Frenger to justice, but the man proves to be a dangerous and wily adversary. But Mosely lives to chew again.

See *Miami Blues*

MOSES, DAISY "GRANNY"

Uprooted from the Ozarks to Beverly Hills, Granny—mother-in-law of **Jed Clampett**—brings her mountain-woman ways with her. She remains ornery and fussy, and spends her time mixing potent home-brewed potions, including a cure-all called Granny's Spring Tonic. She wants badly to find a suitable husband for granddaughter **Elly May Clampett**. She's got a mean hand with a broom.

See *The Beverly Hillbillies*

MOSS, GRIFFIN

He is a British artist and postcard designer who's given to depression and loneliness. Into his rather dreary life, amazingly, comes **Sabine Strohem,** a woman halfway around the globe, who sees his artworks in her mind's eye as he creates them. Through their correspondence, he grows to love Sabine and wants nothing more than to get together with her—but seems doomed not to find her.

See *Griffin and Sabine,* Nick Bantock

MOSSOP, WILLIE

A talented shoemaker whose shyness prevents him from aspiring to greater prestige or remuneration, Willie is employed by the Hobson family shoe-making business and is chosen by kind but aggressive **Maggie Hobson** to be her husband. Willie accedes to Maggie's wishes and slavishly follows her in a plan to take over the business, despite the protestations of Maggie's father.

See *Hobson's Choice,* Harold Brighouse

MOTES, HAZEL "HAZE"

A child of the fundamentalist South, Haze turns against his upbringing after leaving the Army. He becomes the sole spokesman and antiprophet of his "Church of Christ Without Christ." He seeks to disprove the possibility of redemption in a world where "the blind don't see and the lame don't walk and what's dead stays that way."

See *Wise Blood,* Flannery O'Connor

MOTHER SUPERIOR

The stern but compassionate head of the order of nuns at Convent San Tanco in Puerto Rico. She likes to use the front of her habit as a hand muff. While she's secretly amused by **Sister Bertrille,** she tries to keep the flying nun's feet planted on the ground. She's pragmatic enough to accept assistance from **Carlos Ramirez,** handsome man-about-the-island. She's cool enough to drive a woody station wagon.

See *The Flying Nun*

MOWGLI THE MAN CUB

After being separated from his parents in the jungle, little Mowgli is taken in by a pack of wolves. Mowgli, "the Frog," learns the ways of the jungle from his teachers, the bear Baloo, and the black panther Bagheera. As he grows older, Mowgli has to deal with a dual existence—he is both a man and a wolf, but not fully a part of either world.

See *The Jungle Book,* Rudyard Kipling

MUGG, MATTHEW

This rascally, Victorian-era Englishman lives in Puddledy-on-the-Marsh and is a good friend of the eccentric **Doctor Doolittle.** Sings, dances, and enjoys a good flirtation when one happens along.

See *Doctor Doolittle*

MUIR, MRS. CAROLYN

A cute, gutsy, purposeful widowed mother. Mrs. Muir lives in charming Gull Cottage on Schooner Bay in New England, with her two children and dog Scruffy—and a ghost! The spirit of **Daniel Gregg,** a nineteenth-century sea captain, shares the house with the Muirs and sometimes even helps Carolyn cope with her life as a widow. She's very good-natured and fearless, often letting Captain Gregg know that she's in charge.

See *The Ghost and Mrs. Muir*

MULCAHY, FATHER JOHN

He starts his service as a chaplain with the 4077th MASH (Mobile Army Surgical Hospital) unit in Korea as a sensitive, naive, type and finishes it little changed, although the ugly aspects of war have toughened him. He's well meaning but out of his element in the relatively depraved environment of the MASH unit. He's always ready with an appropriate citation from the Bible and is often helpful in the O.R. when things get frantic.

See *M*A*S*H*

MULDER, FOX

Calm, polite, intense, dark-suited FBI agent who's derided by his unimaginative colleagues for his obsession with "X" files—cases involving unexplainable phenomena, everything from half-animal, half-human creatures to time travelers. He has a quiet, dry sense of humor. Under that calm, polite exterior, he feels more for his pretty partner, **Dana Scully,** than he'd ever admit.

See *The X-Files*

MULWRAY, EVELYN

Elusive femme fatale of 1930s Los Angeles. The most important thing in Evelyn's life is her mentally retarded younger "sister," whom she'll do anything to protect. She's the daughter of **Noah Cross,** who sexually abused her as a child and subsequently fathered her "sister." Married to possible philanderer Hollis Mulwray, head of L.A. Water and Power department. Also having an affair with detective **J. J. Gittes**.

See *Chinatown*

MUMBLES

Ferret-faced underworld figure. He speaks incomprehensibly, hence his nickname. Known to drive everyone around him just a little crazy due to poor articulation, even by the standards of undereducated underworld types.

See *Dick Tracy*

MUNCHAUSEN, BARON

He is a devil-may-care traveler of known worlds and then some. The baron prefers unconventional craft to more traditional vessels—like an aircraft made from ladies' undergarments. Love for adventure characterizes everything he undertakes. Baron Munchausen is by no means a shy type and will go out of his way (way out of his way!) to hobnob and rub elbows with the famous, the infamous, and those somewhere in between. He loves to tell long accounts of his many exploits. He's also more than willing to embellish them, or even make up new ones out of whole cloth. Though not exactly addicted to the truth, he has some admirable traits, such as a totally open mind when it comes to dealing with unusual life-forms.

See *The Adventures of Baron Munchausen*

MUNDSON, BALLIN

Mysterious Buenos Aires casino owner who inexplicably hires down-and-out gambler **Johnny Farrell** as an enforcer at his ritzy establishment. In addition to gambling, the creepy Mundson is involved with the Nazis in a mineral cartel. Mundson has no love for his beautiful wife, **Gilda**, although he is nevertheless jealous of attentions paid her by others. Nattily dressed, sporting a cane, Mundson abhors violence, but likes it when Johnny explodes with anger. He plays a psychological cat-and-mouse game with Johnny that insinuates a sexual attraction between the two. For all his smooth, polished ways, Mundson is a dangerous man whom people fear.

See *Gilda*

MUNDY, GLORIA

Quiet San Francisco librarian, the last one you'd expect to have to run for her life from a motley but nasty group of thugs and assassins who are plotting to kill the pope. She's resourceful when she has to be and can tap inner strengths not previously explored. Teamed up with gumshoe **Tony Carlson**.

See *Foul Play*

MUNNY, WILLIAM

The dark forces live inside all men, some more than others. William Munny is a murderer, and some say he's one of the best gunmen there ever was. But he got caught up in the love of a Christian woman, who made him stop drinking whiskey and gave him two children before she died. He promised her on her deathbed that he'd continue to refrain from drinking and killing. And he's kept his promise all through these hard years of farming inhospitable land. But righting an injustice and making some sorely needed bounty money bring Munny back to the gunman's trade one last time, against his better judgment. When Munny wipes out the corrupt Sheriff **Little Bill Daggett** and his cronies, he explains the success of his one-man vendetta with a simple phrase: "I've always been lucky when it comes to killing folks."

See *Unforgiven*

THE MUNSTER FAMILY

Just your ordinary, pale-faced family living at 1313 Mockingbird Lane. Father Herman looks like a lab creation, complete with bolts in his neck. He's seven-foot-three, but only dangerous because he's kind of goofy. He works at the Fateman, Goodbury, and Grave funeral home and writes poetry for *Mortician's Monthly* magazine. He and Lily keep a happy home. Lily tends to housewifely duties, staying active in a charity, Bundles for Transylvania. She's coy about her age, which is somewhere between 150 and 306. Lily has the complexion and jet-black hair common in her family, the Draculas. The boy of the house is Eddie. He has a severe widow's peak stabbing into the middle of his forehead, almost down to his eyebrow. Unlike other boys his age, Eddie always wears a formal black jacket with short pants. The weirdo of the family is blond-haired Marilyn, the neice. They all love her and worry on account of her abnormally normal looks. Marilyn attends State University. Grandpa Munster turns into a bat when the mood

Kathryn Murphy

strikes him. The family's motley assortment of pets includes Spot, a fire-eating dragon; Kitty Kat, who roars like a lion; and Eddie's pet snake Elmer. Herman drives the family around in a hot rod.

See *The Munsters*

MURDOCK, BUZ

After growing up an orphan in Hell's Kitchen, New York City, Murdock works for **Tod Stiles**'s father, who dies suddenly, leaving his son nothing and Buz out of a job. Buz then hooks up with Tod, a 1960 Chevy Corvette, and some wanderlust to get his kicks on Route 66.

See *Route 66*

MURGATROYD, MUGSY-AMBROSE

The rough-and-tumble, cigar-smoking, card-playing, loyal "bodyguard, governess, and valet" to **Charles Pike**. He is very protective of his innocent boss, and once saved his life in a brawl. As cynical as Pike is green, he's suspicious of everyone and everything. He once suspected a bishop of being a pickpocket. He'll go to any length to protect Charles. "That's the same dame, she looks the same, she walks the same, it's the same dame."

See *The Lady Eve*

MURPHY, ALEX J. (ROBOCOP)

He's a doomed man brought back to life, almost like Frankenstein, but with his brain partly intact and law enforcement his new mission. Murphy's a Detroit cop, and a good one, but he's caught by a wicked gang of desperadoes and shot to bits. But the power of OCP, the conglomerate that now runs the police department, can revive Murphy with artificial parts, thunderous weaponry, and a helmet that masks his head and eyes. Holy bionics, Robocop! Though not as graceful or swift as the Caped Crusader, Robocop's lust for stopping criminals is no less vivid. One human weakness remains: memories of his wife and family flash across his consciousness, drawn from some deep reservoir of his surviving brain cells.

See *Robocop*

MURPHY, KATHRYN

By-the-book public prosecutor who prefers plea bargains to the risk of long-drawn-out court proceedings. Cool, calm, and collected despite burden of being a woman working in a sexist judicial system. Despite her own feelings, ready to stand behind her client **Sarah Tobias** to push a controversial rape case to the legal limits.

See *The Accused*

MURTAUGH, ROGER

This veteran Los Angeles police detective has just turned fifty and worries about the gray hairs that are starting to show up on his head. He's a family man cruising toward retirement, with a lot to lose through his dangerous job. Above all else, Murtaugh loves his wife, his kids, and the boat that he's building in his driveway. The last thing he needs is to be partnered with a dangerous, suicidal cop named **Martin Riggs**. So what do you think happens to him?

See *Lethal Weapon*

MUTT AND JEFF

The tall one, Archibald J. Mutt, is married and has a son named Cicero. His wife hates his short, single, prankster friend Edgar Horace (Jeff). Regardless, the two friends are generally together, and they have lost in countless business ventures and suffered through innumerable scrapes.

See *Mutt and Jeff*, H. C. "Bud" Fisher

MYERS, MICHAEL

Tight-lipped, determined, and homicidally psychotic, Myers was born in 1957 in Haddonfield, Illinois, where he was raised until October 31, 1963. At that time, he took a large kitchen knife and stabbed sister Judith to death. He was a resident of a mental health facility from that day on until October 30, 1978, when he received an unintentional early release. Extremely intelligent and physically fit, he avoids contact with others whenever possible. When last seen, he was walking around with six bullets inside him, courtesy of his primary caregiver, psychiatrist **Dr. Loomis**.

See *Halloween*

NADINE, GROOT

Nadine travels to Texas with his good friend **Tom Dunson**, whom he helps to start and build a cattle ranch. When Dunson decides to drive his herd to Missouri, Groot goes along as cook and provider of comic relief.

See *Red River*

NANCY

This little girl, about eight or nine years old, always wears a dress and a bow in her black, prickly, tightly curled, football-helmet-shaped hair. Her best friend is a tough kid from the poor side of town named Sluggo. She sometimes lives with her Aunt Fritzi.

See *Nancy and Sluggo*, **Ernie Bushmiller**

NARDO, ELAINE

This beautiful young single mom wants one day to run her own art gallery. However, until then, she must drive a cab for the Sunshine Cab Company in Manhattan. She figures things could be worse—she could be married to **Louie De Palma**. Gross.

See *Taxi*

NARDO, MICHELLE

Insecure and a bit overweight, she's one of **Dr. Bob Hartley**'s patients and a member of his overeaters' therapy group. Sweet-natured but a bit of a whiner.

See *The Bob Newhart Show*

NASH, JOAN

Blonde, energetic, smart, and fun, she's a mom to four growing boys, but doesn't seem like a mom—she's the really cool mom next door that you wish was your mom. She hates housework and cooking (best left to trustworthy maid Martha) and works as a newspaper columnist (when she's not chasing down the boys—or the giant sheepdog, Ladadog). She met her husband, the slightly more staid Jim, when she was his student at Ridgemont College, where he still teaches English. She looks great in peddle pushers.

See *Please Don't Eat the Daisies*

NAT

The owner of a diner called the Peach Pit, located near West Beverly Hills High. He listens to all the kids' woes, particularly **Dylan McKay**'s, since he co-owns the restaurant. The Peach Pit is an unofficial hangout and frequent party site. Employs **Brandon Walsh**. Once had a heart attack.

See *Beverly Hills 90210*

NEARY, ROY

An ordinary family guy and power company lineman, a freak encounter suddenly transforms him into an obsessive visionary with a fixation on Devil's Tower, Wyoming. Enjoys sculpting his fixation in a variety of mediums, including pillows, mashed potatoes, and indoor mud and brush. Has unique one-sided sunburn. His growing eccentricity drives his very conventional wife half-crazy. Knows how to quickly make new friends who share similar passions. Enjoys travel, particularly to places he's never seen before. He's willing to make quick decisions, even when the consequences are very, very, very far-reaching.

See *Close Encounters of the Third Kind*

NEFF, WALTER

Cynical, brooding California insurance salesman who suddenly realizes he's been leading a very dull life. Walter appears to be, and in fact is, a trustworthy and decent employee who is highly respected within his firm. He makes a point of selling the most appropriate policies and takes satisfaction in dotting all the i's and crossing all the t's—until he runs into **Phyllis Dietrichson**, kicks over the traces, and wants to start sowing wild oats with Ms. D. Somewhat naive, Walter is easily manipulated and doesn't always realize it. Sows wild oats galore during his steamy affair with Phyllis.

See *Double Indemnity*

NELL

A "wild child" who has grown up in a forest wilderness in North Carolina and speaks a language no one has heard before. When first discovered, she has been living alone in an isolated cabin, where first her twin and then her mother had died. It's speculated that the twins developed a private language, based on English, before one died. Once thrust into the crass and noisy modern world, Nell seeks only to impart the message that the natural is better than the civilized. "You are hungry for silence," she tells her new friends.

See *Nell*

NELSON, ALICE

Working as **Mike Brady**'s live-in housekeeper, Alice continues to run the household when Mike marries **Carol**, who brings her three daughters into the ménage. Alice is devoted to all the Bradys but would happily settle down with a husband, should the chance come along. Her main target is Sam

Franklin, owner of Sam's Butcher Shop, but there is a man from her past named Mark Millard. Her virtually identical twin cousin is named Emma. Alice's self-effacing good humor and charm keep her from getting flustered by six rambunctious kids. She doles out advice, along with homemade cookies.

See *The Brady Bunch*

NELSON, TONY

An astronaut and handsome all-American hero, he is the reluctant master of a genie named **Jeannie**. He had it all together—till Jeannie came along. Now his life is complicated by the fact that his every wish is granted, which has made him very nervous. He tries unsuccessfully to stop Jeannie from using her powers, and loves her, despite the jams she gets him into.

See *I Dream of Jeannie*

NESMAN, LES

A mega-nerdy newsman, Les fancies himself as another Walter Cronkite. But he's fated to toil away unrecognized at a Cincinnati rock 'n' roll station, WKRP, where news rates low in the order of things. A small man with large complaints, Les hates the notion that he doesn't have a private office. So he's taped a line around his desk and makes people "knock" before coming in.

See *WKRP in Cincinnati*

NEWSTEAD, VIOLET

This prim, no-nonsense office veteran is, in her own quiet way, a true feminist. She easily bonds with her female colleagues, especially **Judy Bernly** and **Doralee Rhodes**. When push comes to shove, Violet can be a real take-charge personality without fear of consequences.

See *9 to 5*

NICK

American POW left behind in Vietnam, now a heroin-addicted participant on the Southeast Asian professional Russian roulette circuit. Once close friends with **Mike**, still maintains a vestigial connection with wounded pal **Steven** by sending him gifts. "One shot?"

See *The Deer Hunter*

NICK

A young, hunky science professor who goes with his wife, **Honey**, for drinks at middle-aged **Martha** and **George**'s house. Full of confidence in himself and his logic, in the idea that he and his wife are bound to have a happy future, Nick initially resists the cruel mind games George and Martha try to draw him into, but eventually takes part, getting so involved as to seriously compromise his marriage. He says things about Honey that should never have been said, and does things with Martha that not even alcohol can really excuse. He is shaken to the core to see in George and Martha a possible preview of his life with Honey—if they can still have a life, after what has passed.

See *Who's Afraid of Virginia Woolf?,* Edward Albee

NIVENS, SUE ANN

Single, sex-crazed, forty-something host of WJM-TV's *Happy Homemaker Show*. She conveys domestic tips and cooking advice to her viewers. Her saccharin-sweet manner thinly disguises a manipulative and aggressive nature, and her desire to succeed at her career and find a man (not necessarily in that order). For a time, station news producer **Lou Grant** is the object of her lustful stares, to his great discomfort.

See *The Mary Tyler Moore Show*

DR. NO

A smoothly sinister Chinese scientist with aspirations to world dominance. His scheme involves controlling nuclear missiles taking off from Cape Canaveral via a device on his private Jamaican island. He's confident of success, but then British superagent **James Bond** crosses his path, and the result is a battle of wits and weapons, which brings out the evil doctor's sadistic side when he gets Bond in his clutches.

See *Dr. No,* Ian Fleming

NOLAN, FRANCIE

The daughter of **Katie Nolan** and **Johnny Nolan**. A romantic loner not conscious of being alone, she's a book lover and storyteller. Born into poverty, Francie considers it—and the privilege of growing up in Brooklyn—ennobling, but is active in her quest to climb from it. Finds strength in the form of a small sapling.

See *A Tree Grows in Brooklyn*

NOLAN, JOHNNY

A handsome, alcoholic singing waiter, this first-generation Irish American is the only one of four brothers to live past thirty. He is married to **Katie Nolan** and is the father of three children, including **Francie Nolan**. He is a proud man who never allows himself to go out without a clean paper shirtfront. His hopes tragically exceed his ability to realize them, and in the family tradition, he dies young of alcohol-related pneumonia.

See *A Tree Grows in Brooklyn*

NOLAN, KATIE

Born Rommely, she's the forthright, strong-willed pillar of the Nolan household in the Williamsburg section of Brooklyn. Katie supplements her husband's meager income by doing chores for other local residents. Mother of Cornelius (Neely), Annie Laurie, and **Francie Nolan**. After her husband, **Johnny Nolan**, dies, marries police sergeant Michael McShane.

See *A Tree Grows in Brooklyn*

NORDLEY, LINDA

This blond sophisticate turns up her nose at the idea of roughing it on an African safari, but she tries to stick it out because she has the hots for big game hunter **Victor Marswell**. Unlike her rival in love, **Eloise Y. Kelly**, she is elegant and cultured, but her tempestuous behavior threatens to upset the entire camp.

See *Mogambo*

NORMAN

He's an effeminate theatrical dresser and the devoted servant to **Sir**. While he's well meaning, he can be nagging and annoying at times. Still, he is handy in a crisis. He loves being part of the theater, no matter how obscure or thankless his role is in the grand scheme of things.

See *The Dresser*

NORMAN, SARAH

Alienated hearing-impaired young woman. She works in the maintenance department of the school for the deaf from which she graduated. Fiercely independent and also deeply angry at the world. She uses sex as a means to release her hostility, but refuses to entertain the prospect of love. Her romance with new instructor **James Leeds** is slowly bringing her out of her shell and easing her bitterness.

See *Children of a Lesser God*

NORSTADT, CHUCK

A troubled boy vacationing in New England with his oft-married mom and bitchy older sister, he wants nothing more than to attend the military academy which graduated his father, who died when Chuck was two. He befriends a mysterious, horribly disfigured **Justin McLeod**—a surrogate father figure—who was once a teacher and who tutors him for the upcoming academy entrance exam. But their relationship is cut short when the authorities incorrectly assume that the man is sexually abusing Chuck.

See *The Man Without a Face*

NORTON, ED

You have to look on the bright side if you spend your life working in the New York sewer system like Ed. He's eternally upbeat and basically innocent. He lives in the Bensonhurst section of Brooklyn with his wife, **Trixie Norton**, and loves to hang out with **Ralph Kramden** for whom Ed serves as best friend and foil. Both he and Ralph are members of the Raccoon Lodge, and Ed never misses an episode of *Captain Video*. "Hiya there, Ralphic boy." "As we say in the sewer."

See *The Honeymooners*

NORTON, TRIXIE

An efficient and pragmatic housewife, she's married to **Ed Norton**, who works in the sewer system of New York City. She is a good soul but apparently, she also has no sense of smell. Her best friend in the world is **Alice Kramden**, and she hopes that someday they will all be able to move out of Brooklyn.

See *The Honeymooners*

NOVAK, KLARA

A lovely young clerk working in Matuschek & Co., a Budapest store filled with charming bric-a-brac, Klara reserves the warmest place in her heart for "Dear Friend," the recipient of her anonymous lonelyheart correspondence. Little does she know that her pen lover is another clerk in the store with whom she scarcely gets along.

See *The Shop Around the Corner*

NUMBER 6

Once he was a shrewd, cunning British spy. Then he resigned, for personal reasons, but that made him a liability, a man who knew too much. So now he's been kidnapped and is a prisoner on a remote island, where he is confined to a comfortable but strange place known only as the Village. It seems that everyone else in this Village either was brought here for the same reason he was or is a government plant sent to keep tabs on the others. Unfortunately, it's hard to distinguish between prisoners and the keepers. Residents of the Village have lost their names and are known only by numbers. It becomes apparent that the lower one's number, the higher one's rank in the local hierarchy. But the identity, and even the existence, of Number 1 remains an unsolved mystery. Again and again Number 6 tries to escape the island but is always brought back by a nasty little piece of technology named Rover, which somehow tracks him down, sucks him up, and returns him.

See *The Prisoner*

O-LAN

The gentle, patient sacrificing wife of farmer **Wang Lung** was an abused kitchen servant before her marriage. Although quiet and humble, she uses her strength and resourcefulness to pull her family through many hardships. A lucky turn of events enables her to provide for their family, but Wang's greed soon jeopardizes their happiness. She recognizes her husband's weaknesses but always stands by him. When her husband takes a second wife, she calmly accepts his decision, even though it is painful. She puts on a brave face in all situations because she knows that her husband will eventually recognize his mistakes and she will forgive him for them.

See *The Good Earth,* Pearl S. Buck

OAKES, WALTER

Dorm manager and supervisor of a community center who doesn't get the respect he merits. Tall and good-looking, but with a troublesome love life, centering on Jaleesa Vinson. A Hillman college grad, tries to help **Whitley Gilbert, Dwayne Wayne,** and **Ron Johnson** with their problems. Has an endless supply of throwaway lines.

See *A Different World*

OAKLEY, UNCLE CHARLIE

A handsome, charming, affable man with a kind word for everyone, he comes to stay with the family of his sister in their small-town home. His apparent special favorite is his niece and namesake, **Charlie.** He succeeds in creating a wonderful impression with almost everyone he meets, but eventually he reveals hitherto-unsuspected depths to his character. He has a particular affinity for women of means and advanced age.

See *Shadow of a Doubt*

O'CASEY, CHARLEY

Charley is a crusty, retired sailor with a good heart. He lives with his widowed nephew by marriage, **Steve Douglas,** and Steve's sons. To the family, he's just Uncle Charley. He cooks meals for the family and runs the house like a tight ship.

See *My Three Sons*

O'CONNELL, MAGGIE

This adorable, highly independent bush pilot (she once built her own plane from a kit) is also a landlady in the small town of Cicely, Alaska. She has the reputation of being a "love curse," since five of her last boyfriends have met with untimely deaths. Maggie has an intense chemical attraction to **Dr. Joel Fleischman,** who can also drive her crazy. The couple seems to be on the verge of a future together when Joel proposes, but Maggie breaks it off. A real frontier type, she likes guns and is not afraid to use them.

See *Northern Exposure*

O'GILL, DARBY

Irish caretaker with big heart, big imagination, and big problems. A sublime storyteller, though he often has difficulty getting listeners to accept his yarns as the utter truth. Has problems with wee little people and their leader, **King Brian.**

See *Darby O'Gill and the Little People*

O'HARA, SCARLETT

A dark-haired, green-eyed southern belle who is proud of her seventeen-inch waist and her string of admiring beaux. But while she loves to flirt and toy with men's affections, her heart belongs to childhood sweetheart **Ashley Wilkes**. Having been coddled and adored by her daddy since birth, she's spoiled, petulant, and calculating. He has passed along to her a great and abiding love for their plantation, Tara. When Ashley Wilkes dashes her hopes and marries his cousin **Melanie**, Scarlett marries Melanie's brother in a fit of pique, even though she doesn't love him. Luckily for her, her groom dies early on during the war, and she can deck herself out in mourning. During this period, she scandalizes Atlanta by accepting **Rhett Butler**'s bid for her at a dance auction, beginning a tangled relationship with the handsome, saturnine gambler. War toughens her, and she's forced to fight for her life and her land. She'll do practically anything to save her beloved Tara, including stealing her sister's fiancé. She becomes a shrewd businesswoman, though in the process, she alienates friends and family. But she can't forget her lifelong love for Ashley Wilkes, and by the time she realizes that he is a broken man, Rhett has given up on her and gone his own way. But Scarlett's unquenchable spirit will prevail, and she'll rise above it all, somehow.

See *Gone with the Wind*, Margaret Mitchell

O'HARA, TIM

This young, handsome reporter for a Los Angeles newspaper witnesses the crash of a UFO and befriends the craft's pilot, Exagitious $12\frac{1}{2}$, an anthropologist from Mars. He decides to help the Martian maintain a cover and invites him to move in with him at his home on 21 Elm Street (a place he rents from a widowed landlady, Lorelei Brown). Tim poses as the nephew of the Martian, who adopts the earth alias **Uncle Martin**.

See *My Favorite Martian*

OLD LODGE SKINS

A Cheyenne chief and stoic observer of the American Indians' loss of the West. Old Lodge Skins adopts **Jack Crabb**, an orphaned white settler, as his grandson. He is blind as the result of a U.S. Cavalry attack on his village. "It is a good day to die."

See *Little Big Man*, Thomas Berger

OLD MAN

Beleaguered father trying to do his best for his family in 1940s midwestern America. Loves entering contests, is convinced someday his mania will bring him great rewards. Not particularly handy around the house. Has ongoing battle with next-door neighbor and his dogs. Married with two sons, **Randy** and **Ralphie**. Though gruff on the outside, is really a soft touch when it comes to Christmas giving.

See *A Christmas Story*

OLIVER, NANCY

Sharp-tongued Cockney maid who schemes to lure **Gregory Anton** away from his wife, **Paula Alquist**. The bold, impertinent girl acts far above her lowly station and treats poor Paula with contempt and disrespect. Her behavior helps to erode Paula's fragile self-esteem and furthers Anton's attempt to drive her insane.

See *Gaslight*

O'MALLEY, FATHER CHUCK

A low-key young priest whose easygoing ways and notions don't sit well with strait-laced Sister Benedict, who runs the church he's been sent to rescue from financial disaster. Father O'Malley is helpful in financial, spiritual, and family matters and enjoys a good song. His charm eventually thaws Sister Benedict and brings her around to his side.

See *The Bells of St. Mary's*

O'NEILL, DANNY

Bookish and baseball-loving, Danny lives in the same South Side Irish and Jewish neighborhood as **Studs Lonigan**, who is a few years older. Unlike Studs, Danny works hard for an education in order to escape the conservative

Scarlett O'Hara

"Radar" O'Reilly

provincial squalor of his Irish Catholic upbringing. His intellectual curiosity makes him something of a misfit among his peers, and the neighborhood toughs like Lonigan tease him about his studious ways. Growing increasingly liberal as he grows older, Danny comes to reject his neighborhood, its bigotry, its bourgeois values, the Roman Catholic Church, and everything of his youth. He turns to writing as a means of self-expression and hopes to "destroy the old world with his pen" and help create a new one in which men will live as brothers.

See *The Face of Time, A World I Never Made, No Star Is Lost, Father and Son, My Days of Anger,* and *The Studs Lonigan Trilogy,* James T. Farrell

OOP, ALLEY
A good-hearted if somewhat dumb caveman who fights himself into and out of adventures with limitless energy and unswerving morality, Alley Oop is the people's Neanderthal. With the help of Professor Wonmug's time machine, Alley Oop and his glamorous but romantically frustrated girlfriend Oola jet through time and space, ever in search of fresh challenges. The couple get involved with American cowboys, medieval crusaders, Roman legionaries, and World War I soldiers. Alley Oop feels most comfortable in a fur loincloth, naturally, but he tries to accommodate to the styles of other places and times, particularly when he's flying to the moon on an Apollo mission.

See *Alley Oop*

OPHELIA
A shapely, gum-snapping hooker with a heart of gold. She takes in **Louis Winthorpe**, a snobbish banker turned crazed criminal, nursing him back to health and sanity, teaching him that goodness comes from compassion, not wealth. Having transformed Louis, she falls in love with her creation.

See *Trading Places*

O'REILLY, BERNARDO
A sardonic gunfighter with a soft spot for children. O'Reilly is one of seven men hired to protect a Mexican village from **Calvera** and his banditos. Half Irish and half Mexican, he was once a high-priced hired gun. But his conscience seems to have caught up with him, and he's trying the path of goodness and morality, for the moment.

See *The Magnificent Seven*

O'REILLY, WALTER "RADAR"
You can take the boy out of Iowa, but you can't take Iowa out of the boy. He's an adorable perpetual preadolescent, a total innocent, who sleeps with a teddy bear. Despite his youth and naiveté, he basically runs the 4077th MASH (Mobile Army Surgical Hospital) unit, near the front lines of the Korean War. Radar prides himself in his work as company clerk. He got his nickname from his uncanny ability to anticipate what's about to happen. He deeply admires the doctors he works with, especially **Hawkeye Pierce**. While everyone else around drinks whatever alcohol they can find, Radar prefers grape Nehi soda. He's devoted to his mother and Uncle Ed back home on the farm in Ottumwah. Girls interest but frighten him. He has a very tender heart where animals are concerned and keeps rabbits and guinea pigs. He sees the commanding officers of the unit as father figures.

See *M*A*S*H*

ORGANA, PRINCESS LEIA
Fiery, witty, tomboyish member of interstellar royalty. The princess is a leader of the rebellion against the evil Empire that controls the galaxy and its chief enforcer, the emperor's right hand, **Darth Vader**. A symbol of resistance to tyranny, she is sought after by the emperor's forces, who want to make her their prisoner. Her allies include young **Luke Skywalker**, with whom she has a strange affinity, Jedi knight **Ben Kenobi**, and ne'er-do-well space roamer **Han Solo**, with whom she has a stormy relationship.

See *Star Wars*

ORSON
Overweight, humorless leader of the planet Ork, which is far, far from Earth. He supervises the work of **Mork**, an Orkan sent to Earth to study its inhabitants. Mork often refers to Orson as "cosmic breath." Orson communicates with Mork via mind transference. In this way he is able to receive Mork's Scorpio Reports (the information Mork gathers for his job as an Earth observer).

See *Mork & Mindy*

ORWELL, HARRY

A laid-back private eye. He lives in a beach front bungalow in Southern California and takes on cases when the spirit moves him. A former Marine turned cop, Harry was pensioned from the force after taking a bullet in the back. His police contacts are Lieutenant Quinlan and Lieutenant Trench.

See *Harry O*

OSBORNE, ANNE

Straight-arrow district attorney working in New Orleans. Sick of corruption she finds rampant in the police department, particularly the ubiquitous and overtly praetorian Widows and Orphans Fund. Not so smart when it comes to romance, she is involved with libertine law officer **Remy McSwain**.

See *The Big Easy*

OSBORNE, JOHN

A rich American furrier, his scheme to break the Soviet sable monopoly leads to murder. Identified by Moscow detective **Arkady Renko** as a prime suspect, he toys with the investigator. Osborne speaks perfect Russian and is possessed of a "physical smoothness" that Renko has seen only in Western magazine ads. "Set on his silver hair was a black sable hat that must have cost more than Arkady earned in a year."

See *Gorky Park,* Martin Cruz Smith

OTTO

Hyperkinetic, dim-bulb boyfriend of **Wanda**. He may be involved with the CIA. Otto believes that the London Underground is a radical political movement. He enjoys eating fish, is turned on by sniffing bodily aromas and verbally assaulting those he considers inferior.

See *A Fish Called Wanda*

OTTO

Early 1980s L.A. punk who goes straight, getting a job as a repo man—an automobile repossessor. Repo men are seemingly the only sane people in a city full of adults who are brainwashed by generic consumer products and TV evangelists, and aimless young punks who live to eat sushi and "do" crime. Otto finds himself on the trail of a mysterious Chevy that's also wanted by top-secret government agents, because of the strange and (possibly) unearthly contents of its trunk.

See *Repo Man*

OWENS, ALEX

She's a Pittsburgh laborer who dreams of becoming a ballet dancer. Her days are spent working in the steel mills, but she also has an evening job performing exotic disco dances in a popular nightclub. Alex takes dance lessons from a great ballet star in preparation for an audition with a major company. She is never wanting for energy and diligently practices her dance routines at her loft apartment when her job shifts end. In her spare time, she's currently having an affair with her boss at the steel plant.

See *Flashdance*

OYL, OLIVE

An old-fashioned girl torn between two sailors. Ostensibly, she's the girlfriend of **Popeye** the Sailor, but she also seems to be drawn to the brutish and hirsute Bluto. Olive, who's as thin as a pipe cleaner, has a brother, Castor Oyl. Olive also cares for an infant, Swee'Pea, who just happens to live with her. Draw your own conclusions.

See *Popeye*

PACKARD, DAN

This parvenu was loud and coarse before hitting the big time, and he still is; only now he wears fancy clothes and lives in a garishly decorated apartment. The shady business deals that landed him in his comfortable spot are about to unravel and he's desperate to get his hands on some money—unless his brash, hotheaded attitude doesn't scare everyone away. His relationship with his wife, **Kitty Packard**, a tough ex-chorine who isn't afraid of his bluster, is marked by mutual antagonism.

See *Dinner at Eight*

PACKARD, KITTY

A platinum-blond gold digger who hit the jackpot when she married millionaire **Dan Packard**. Kitty likes to sit in her huge bed all day, reading movie magazines and eating chocolates. She wears tight silk gowns adorned with feathers and diamonds and loves the way in which her outrageous spending drives her husband crazy. Although she's no brain trust, Kitty is shrewd enough to know that her position is secure as long as she has the

Alex Owens

Godfrey Park

goods on her husband's fishy business deals.
See *Dinner at Eight*

PACKARD, SARAH
Sarah is **"Fast" Eddie Felson**'s alcoholic girlfriend. Though she has a somewhat atrophied left leg, she's pretty as well as witty and literate. She somehow manages to combine her steady drinking with part-time college studies, living off a stipend from her absentee father. Her liaison with Fast Eddie fundamentally alters her life.
See *The Hustler*

PAGE, VICTORIA
Exquisite red-haired, red-shoed ballerina, the aristocratic niece of Isabel, Countess of Neston. Victoria is a raw, passionate talent who won't be cowed by demanding ballet impresario **Boris Lermontov**. When he asks, "Why do you want to dance?" she replies, "Why do you want to live?" She gets a first break in a matinee of the "Lac des Cygnes" at the tiny Mercury Theatre on a rainy afternoon. After she's cast in the principal role of the new ballet, "The Red Shoes," she falls in love with its brilliant composer, **Julian Craster**. Stubborn and hardworking, she doesn't give in when she feels she's in the right. Her peers call her "an inspiration" and "a miracle." Ambitious and sometimes calculating, she's still willing to take the challenge and stand by the man she loves. When Lermontov demands: "What do you want from life?" she answers: "To dance." When she's forced to choose between her love for Craster and her compulsion for ballet, she opts for dance, with fatal results.
See *The Red Shoes*

PAINE, JOSEPH
A once-honest senator who's been sucked into the corrupt world of Washington politics. Dubbed the Silver Fox, he's eloquent and distinguished on the outside, scheming and manipulative underneath. He was good friends with the father of junior senator **Jefferson Smith**, whom he tries to intimidate into being a "yes" man. When Smith protests, he tells him: "This is a man's world and you have to check your ideals outside the door, like you do your rubbers."
See *Mr. Smith Goes to Washington*

PALADIN
Paladin, as his name suggests, is a fellow who champions causes—in his case, for a price. This doesn't make him a bad person; far from it, in fact. Even though his services are for hire, he chooses his clients carefully and will work only for those he deems to be good people. Between jobs, he lives in a posh hotel in San Francisco and is looked after by his Chinese cook, **Heyboy**.
See *Have Gun Will Travel*

PALEY, DOLORES
Flight attendant having rather one-sided love affair with **Judah Rosenthal**. Seemingly normal on the outside, she has an obsessive streak that can dominate her entire personality. Lives alone and longs for permanent companionship.
See *Crimes and Misdemeanors*

PALMER, LAURA
This popular, seemingly respectable blond high school girl is found murdered by the side of a river in the town of Twin Peaks, in the Pacific Northwest. Her murder and the subsequent investigation by FBI agent **Dale Cooper** and local sheriff **Harry S. Truman** lead to the exposure of a seamy underbelly to the town that would do a big city proud, with some wrinkles that even New York or Los Angeles would never have come up with.
See *Twin Peaks*

PALMER, LELAND
A respected but corrupt Twin Peaks businessman. He misses his murdered daughter, **Laura Palmer**, more than seems natural. He'll weep copiously at the mere mention of her; he jumps into the grave as she's being buried.
See *Twin Peaks*

PALOOKA, JOE
A kind, naive, all-American country bumpkin turned heavyweight boxer. His career is managed by cynical, mean Knobby Walsh. After a very long engagement with his equally kind, naive, all-American girlfriend, Anne Howe, they marry in 1949.
See *Joe Palooka,* Ham Fisher

PAN, PETER
The mischievous and daring leader of the Lost Boys

in magical Never-Never-Land, Pan is a boy who doesn't want to grow up. Never-Never-Land, located at the second star to the right and straight on until morning, is a playground for young boys, full of pirates, Indians, and mermaids. Pan's best friend is the pixielike Tinker Bell, who speaks in bells that only he can understand. One night, he seeks out **Wendy Darling** to come to Never-Never-Land and be a mother for the Lost Boys—boys who have all run away from home. "Once you're grown up, you can never come back. Never."

See *Peter Pan*

PANCHO

Good-natured, trustworthy, corpulent, as fast with a bullwhip as he is with a quip, Pancho's the sidekick to The Cisco Kid, a Southwestern Robin Hood. Pancho's English isn't too good, but his bravery and friendship are unequaled.

See *The Cisco Kid*

PANTUSSO, "COACH" ERNIE

He's a good-natured ex–baseball player and coach who now tends bar at the Boston hangout Cheers, but he may have been beaned once or twice too often. Among the players he coached is the owner of Cheers, **Sam Malone**. He's dumb but sweet, and he can remember how to mix drinks. Jilted by fiancée after she wins the lottery.

See *Cheers*

PARADISE, SAL

A young man who strikes out from Paterson, New Jersey, in search of experience and Life. He meets a wildly exciting, charismatic guy named Dean Moriarty and becomes his disciple, in New York. Alone, Sal heads cross-country, living a hobolike "beat" existence, bumming rides, meals, and accomodations, rapping about the universe with other drifters, falling in and out of love, and finding inspiration in wine, women, and song—especially jazz. Leaving his job as a security guard in San Francisco, he hooks back up with Dean, and together they go back out on the road in search of "It"—transcendence above the everyday into an inspired, poetically aware plane of existence. Together they hit Denver, San Francisco, and points in between, before heading down to Mexico. While on the road, Sal admires Dean's passion for experiencing as much as possible of life, as well as his wild flights of poetic fancy. But he learns that Dean has a dark, selfish side as well, when his mentor dumps him and leaves him stranded.

See *On the Road,* Jack Kerouac

PARK, GODFREY

He was a Harvard man, but now he's a handsome gentleman bum, living in a nest of shacks near the East River in Depression-era New York City. When he encounters flighty, selfish young socialite **Irene Bullock**, he's sufficiently drawn to her to agree to serve as the Bullock family butler. He hides his origins as the spoiled son of a family of Boston Brahmins, who walked away from that life because of bitterness when a woman dumped him. While serving in the wildly dysfunctional Bullock household, he uses his innate grace and common sense to straighten them all out, not least of all Irene, with whom he falls in love. With the help of his unfailing gentility, erudition, and dry sense of humor, he tries to pass on the life lessons he's learned to the Bullocks, and, to a surprising degree, he succeeds. "The only difference between a derelict and a man is a job."

See *My Man Godfrey*

PARKER, KATHERINE

A corporate barracuda who pretends to encourage her secretary **Tess McGill**'s ideas, then steals them and takes the credit herself. When a skiing accident forces her to take a vacation, Katherine is blissfully unaware that Tess is using her office and home to put the deal together herself.

See *Working Girl*

PARKER, PETER

When his Uncle Ben is killed by criminals, partly due to his own selfishness, Peter decides to use his abilities to fight injustice and evil-doing wherever he finds them, in the dark corners and on the rooftops of New York City. Like everyone else, Peter forgets appointments and gets sick. Unlike other people, he has spiderlike superpowers.

See *Spider-Man*

PARMENTER, CAPTAIN WILTON

The bumbling but endearing captain of F Troop at Fort Courage, a Union Army outpost on the fron-

BUS RIDE SEATMATES FROM HELL

Dell Griffith
Bill S. Preston and Ted Logan
Radio Raheem
Jethro Bodine
Cliff Clavin
Herb Tarleck
Michael Myers
Dante Hicks
Jeff Spicoli
Forrest Gump

tier. From a long line of stalwart military men, Wilton is by far the shortest and least competent of the great Parmenters. Assisted at every turn by his chief aide Sergeant Morgan O'Rourke. "I fall down a lot."
See *F Troop*

PAROO, MARIAN
The River City librarian, Marian Paroo also teaches piano to the town's young 'uns. She lives at home with her mom and younger brother. She's smart and commonsensical, and she sees right through "Professor" **Harold Hill** when he shows up in town claiming to be a music scholar. But she witholds judgment, because he has a way about him that's quite different from the nice, dull local swains. Soon she's in love with a man she's deep down sure is a swindler, and she blooms like a rose.
See *The Music Man,* Meredith Willson

PARRISH, HOMER
Due to an accident, the friendly sailor who always looked out for others returns from World War II without arms and little hope for the future. He snubs the girlfriend who waited for him because he doesn't want to be a burden. His combat injury makes him feel like an outsider rather than a hero.
See *The Best Years of Our Lives*

PARRY
He is a New York City homeless man whose frenetic energy and mental free associations are tools to cope with the horrors of life on the streets. Faced with an immense, impersonal city, peopled with cold, ugly rat-racers, he retreats into a world of romance and fantasy. Parry lives in a subterranean labyrinth of trash beneath a bridge. Considers himself and his fellow homeless people to be knights in search of the Holy Grail. The Red Knight relentlessly chases Parry. Befriends **Jack Lucas**, former king of the radio shock jocks. Likes being naked in Central Park.
See *The Fisher King*

PARRY, VINCENT
Escaped convict, falsely convicted of killing his first wife because of **Madge Rapf**'s trial testimony. He is currently undergoing plastic surgery to improve his chances of making a clean getaway. Has unfortu-nate knack for being in the wrong place at the wrong time. Involved with **Irene Jansen**.
See *Dark Passage*

PARTANNA, CHARLEY
A hitman with a heart. "Straight-arrow Charley, the all-American Hood." Don Corrado Prizzi, Godfather of the Brooklyn Mafia, pledges to be his second father on the day he is born. As a child, he gets brass knuckles for his birthday. An excellent chef, his father praises him: "When I close my eyes and eat your cooking, Charley, I think your mother's still with us." He breaks off his engagement to the Don's wilful, wily granddaughter, Maerose, causing her disgrace. Charley spots his future wife, **Irene Walker**, at a Prizzi wedding, the strains of "Ave Maria" playing in the background, and it's love at first sight. When he finds out Irene is a hitter too, he ponders: "Do I ice her? Do I marry her?" But eventually, he must choose between the Prizzi family, to whom he has sworn loyalty, and his thieving wife.
See *Prizzi's Honor*

PARTRIDGE, DANNY
The precocious preteen member of the singing Partridge Family, who also plays bass. His family often call him a "midget," because he seems old beyond his years. Danny bosses people around, has a love of money, and a head for business (he reads the *Wall Street Journal*). He often leads to clashes with the band's manager, **Reuben Kincaid**, and he tends to play Hardy to Reuben's Laurel. Danny has bright red hair, a sharp tongue, and a quick wit, which helps him to get the better of older brother **Keith Partridge**. Danny charges interest on the money Keith borrows and teases sister **Laurie** about her boyfriends. He once followed her on a date. His best friend is Punky Lazaar.
See *The Partridge Family*

PARTRIDGE, KEITH
With his long brown hair, big green eyes, and skinny body, he's a teenage heartthrob and is the lead singer and lead guitarist of the group the Partridge Family. He also writes their songs, usually about girls: "I Think I Love You," "I Woke Up in Love This Morning." Keith is cool and cute, and girls flock to him, which he loves. He's not super bright,

and even though he is the oldest male Partridge, sometimes it seems that his younger brother **Danny** is in charge. But he is serious about his music. He's on the leading edge of fashion, with his bell bottoms, pukka shell necklaces, and velvet vests. Even though girls hang on him, he gets crushes easily. Protective of his mother and his sister, **Laurie**. Laurie loves to make fun of his attempts to get girls, but he is most often ridiculed by Danny. Sensitive for a teenage guy and sweetly insecure for a pop "star."

See *The Partridge Family*

PARTRIDGE, LAURIE

This pretty, sensitive, smart teenager plays keyboards for her family group, the Partridge Family. She never has trouble getting dates and probably never had a pimple in her life. She has the typical family look: slender, with long brown hair and green eyes. She gets off on teasing older brother **Keith** about girls and his lack of brains. She is a protofeminist.

See *The Partridge Family*

PARTRIDGE, SHIRLEY

She's the mother and piano player of the pop group the Partridge Family. Widowed, she raises the kids on her own with some help from band manager **Reuben Kincaid**. Ms. P. is warm, loving, wise—the perfect mother. And she's pretty, too. Her kids truly like her and (mostly) listen to her advice, which is usually good.

See *The Partridge Family*

PATIMKIN, BRENDA

Brenda's an attractive, bespectacled Radcliffe girl home for the summer in Short Hills, New Jersey. Her family are country-clubbers with an overwhelming sense of entitlement and privilege. Her father spoils her, but her mother's jealous of her youth. At the club, she's wooed by and falls for **Neil Klugman**, an older guy with whom she soon starts sleeping. She even gets a diaphragm at Neil's suggestion.

See *Goodbye, Columbus,* Philip Roth

PAUL

A paunchy, brooding expatriate American living in Paris. His wife's suicide causes him to conclude that relationships are inherently ephemeral. He has a fling based in anonymity with **Jeanne**, who is open to his kinky sexual behavior. At the time of his death, Paul realizes his need to leave some trace of himself in the world.

See *Last Tango in Paris*

PAULIE

This born loser is **Rocky Balboa**'s pal and assistant. Paulie does experience jealousy of and anger at Rocky, both for the boxer's success and for his occasional mistreatment of the love of Rocky's life, Paulie's sister **Adrian**. At the same time, though, he never stops worshiping the tough boxer.

See *Rocky*

PAYNE, HOWARD

Howard is psychotically angry at the world and at the LAPD bomb squad in particular. He was originally an officer in Atlanta but was forced into retirement when an explosive device blew up on him and he lost a thumb. He did get a gold watch out of the deal. Has a bit of an obsession with Lieutenant **Jack Traven** and bus #2525.

See *Speed*

PEACHUM

Believing greed and ruthlessness to be virtues, Peachum heads London's network of thieves and is also a booking agent for fake cripples and beggars. A true businessman, he concentrates on amassing power and money in the underworld and marrying off daughter Polly to someone of high social rank (and wealth). Peachum and his wife will go to any lengths to keep Polly from becoming wed to the despicable MacHeath.

See *Threepenny Opera,* Bertolt Brecht

PEEL, MRS. EMMA

Lovely, athletic secret agent. Daring, sophisticated, and mysterious, Emma Peel is a major asset of the nameless British intelligence agency that employs her, along with her partner, agent **John Steed**. She's slender and wears jumpsuits, usually black, which effectively set off her great legs and lithe body. Her shiny, thick hair is worn straight. Her charm and way with men are often the secret to her success as an agent. Her husband, "Mr. Peel," is spoken of but never seen. Occasionally, Mrs. Peel extracts Steed

Photo courtesy of CBS

Rob Petrie

from a dangerous situation, but more often than not it is she who is tied up with rope in a room that's about to explode. Steed rescues her at the last moment, often making her suffer his quirky sense of humor. Sexual tension looms now and then, but she's a married lady, and they *are* British, after all.

See *The Avengers*

PEMBERTON, PAT

She's a phys ed teacher at Pacific Tech, engaged to college administrator Collier Ward and happy (she thinks) in her contemplated marriage. But after she realizes how good she really is at golf, at an amateur tournament, Pemberton joins sports agent **Mike Conovan**'s stable of athletes to prove her real talent, to herself and others. As a pro on the tennis and golf circuits, she makes a pot of money for herself and Conovan. Whenever fiancé Ward shows up, however, she is jinxed. Well, which guy would *you* choose?

See *Pat and Mike*

PENDLETON, JOE

He's a quarterback for the Los Angeles Rams who dies prematurely when a heavenly "escort" takes his soul from his body after an auto accident that he was fated to survive. The escort and his boss, **Mr. Jordan**, temporarily house Joe's spirit in the body of a newly deceased multimillionaire, until they can sort out the whole unfortunate business.

See *Heaven Can Wait*

PENNINGTON, LAURA

English woman of the World War II era in inspiring romantic relationship with **Oliver Bradford**. She is chock-full of human kindness, and her incessant good cheer would drive some mad. A friend to all who is carried through life by her enthusiastic emotional responses. She also has a knack for styling her hair in ways that deemphasize her basically plain features.

See *The Enchanted Cottage*

PEPPER, WALDO

Waldo Pepper lost a piece of himself in World War I, a piece he's desperately trying to retrieve by doing the only thing he knows how to do, now that the war is over: barnstorming. He's a great pilot searching for meaning in his life. He's at home only when he's flying, and flying is his only joy.

See *The Great Waldo Pepper*

PERRY, JOSEPHINE

The flirtatious, vain, and irresponsible Josephine comes from a wealthy Chicago family. She's arrestingly beautiful and a highly popular girl at Ivy League dances, a quintessential young flapper who lets nothing stand in the way once she decides what she wants. This doesn't mean that she always gets it.

See *The Basil and Josephine Stories*, F. Scott Fitzgerald

PETER

Ex–secret agent whose son possesses extraordinary psychic powers. The boy is taken by another agent, supposedly a friend, but actually a man looking to use the son's powers for evil ends. Presumed dead after an assassination attempt in the Middle East, the superdetermined Peter makes his way back to the United States, where, with the help of **Gillian**, another psychic, he tracks down his son.

See *The Fury*

PETERSON, DR. CONSTANCE

This beautiful doctor works at a mental hospital, where she's all business. But she has a passionate side as well and falls in love with **J.B. Ballantine**, the hospital's new chief doctor. But she learns that there is more to him than meets the eye, and that he is in need not only of her love but of her professional services as well. She takes him in hand and, through psychotherapeutic techniques, tries to aid him to plumb his own depths and learn who and what he really is.

See *Spellbound*

PETERSON, ELLA

This vivacious, blond answering service employee gets overly involved in the problems of her charges. Her devotion to her job is such that her own life—and love life—suffer. But even love can sometimes be found on the other end of the telephone line, even if it isn't listed in the Yellow Pages.

See *The Bells Are Ringing*

MR. PETERSON

A short, piping-voiced nebbish of a man, he's one

of **Dr. Bob Hartley**'s patients. He wears glasses and flunked shop in high school.

See *The Bob Newhart Show*

PETERSON, NORM

This corpulent, beer-loving accountant has his own permanent barstool at Cheers. When he walks into the bar, everybody in the place yells, "Norm," in greeting. He could keep the place solvent by himself…if he'd pay his tab regularly. He's willing to take a free "brewski," and you don't have to twist his arm. He's married to the long-suffering Vera, whose main contact with him seems to be by phone, from the bar. He's handy with a wisecrack, most of them at the expense of his sidekick, **Cliff Clavin**.

See *Cheers*

PETRIE, LAURA

The sexy, perfect wife and mother, Laura is everyman's dream wife incarnate. She dances, sings, cooks, cleans, sews, throws dinner parties, and goes to PTA meetings. She has fabulous woman's intuition and usually knows what's best for husband **Rob Petrie**. Laura is an inspiration for Rob, often providing the seeds for his comedy sketches. She dresses stylishly, often sporting capri pants. Her best friend is next-door neighbor **Millie Helper**. Her string of ex-boyfriends includes a priest and a corporate magnate, and is remarkably long, for a woman who had to lie about her age to marry Rob at seventeen. Laura broke her foot on the occasion of her first meeting with Rob, while performing for the USO at Camp Crowder, Missouri. Her maiden name is Meehan, or maybe Meeker. She loves to eat Moo Goo Gai Pan and sleeps in a twin bed, wearing two-piece pajamas. She also has a secret bank account. Favorite refrain: "Oh Rob!"

See *The Dick Van Dyke Show*

PETRIE, RITCHIE

Cute, obedient son. He lives in New Rochelle, New York, with father **Rob Petrie** and mother **Laura Petrie**. Ritchie is always on the lookout for trinkets his daddy might have brought him, and he has a fondness for hiding in cabinets. His best friend is neighbor Freddy Helper. He loves animals and once kept a duck in the kitchen sink for over a week. He has big birthday parties and is old enough to know not to hit girls. Middle name: Rosebud.

See *The Dick Van Dyke Show*

PETRIE, ROB

He is a debonair version of the boy-next-door grown up. A successful comedy writer, Rob balances suburban life as husband of attractive, attentive **Laura** and father of **Ritchie** with his job as head writer of *The Alan Brady Show*. He commutes from 448 Bonny Meadow Road in New Rochelle, New York to Manhattan. At home Rob worries about crabgrass, the PTA, and the city council, on which he has a seat. He is best friends with neighbor **Jerry Helper**. Tall, handsome, witty, and charming, Rob will perform at the drop of a hat. He often hosts or attends dinner parties where he, his wife, and coworkers **Sally Rogers** and **Buddy Sorrell** showcase their talents in song, dance, and stand-up comedy. His arm needn't be twisted for him to sing "Mountain Greenery" or "You Wonderful You" while doing a soft-shoe duet with Laura. He was raised with brother Stacey in Danville, Illinois, and met Laura while in the army at Camp Crowder, Missouri. Worked as radio D.J. in Ohio before landing his head writing job. Rob fantasizes about writing a novel someday.

See *The Dick Van Dyke Show*

PFEIFFER, PAUL

Gawky, awkward teenage boy who might never grow out of it. A classic geek, Paul wears thick glasses and uncool clothes. Though socially immature, he is sweet, and aware of his shortcomings. Paul tends to be a little neurotic, getting nervous and worrying about everything. His best friend, **Kevin Arnold**, often has to calm him down.

See *The Wonder Years*

THE PHANTOM

Also called **Kit Walker** and Sir Christopher Standish and known as "the ghost who walks." His crime-fighting commitment has been handed down from father to son since the sixteenth century. His trademark logo, a skull, makes criminals all over the world quake like jellyfish. His companion is his faithful gray wolf, Devil. He started the crime-fighter fad of wearing a costume that covers him from head to toe.

See *The Phantom,* Ray Moore

PHELAN, FRANCIS

After accidentally killing his infant son, Francis

Jean-Luc Picard

embarks on a life of voluntary exile and a career as a perpetual loser. He tries to start over and make something of his talent as a baseball player, but it's no use; it seems that there's a powerful self-destructive urge governing all his actions. He gets swept up in a violent labor dispute and is responsible for another death, though such hadn't been his intention. His instinct to survive is strong, but he is determined to punish himself. Francis seeks some kind of redemption through communion with the spirits of those he killed.

See *Ironweed,* William Kennedy

PHELPS, JIM

A natural-born leader with a **Clark Kent** demeanor. He had been in the military and then ran a fishing business with his father, before the U.S. government called him back into active service. Now he heads a covert operating team called the Impossible Mission Force, working for a top-secret government agency. His job, "should you decide to accept it," is to carry out whatever extremely risky mission the government wants him to do—always knowing that, if he's caught, the government will claim never to have heard of him. Anything's better than forever smelling of fish.

See *Mission: Impossible*

PHIL

Phil is the owner of Phil's, a fabled Capitol Hill watering hole and the hangout for the staff of newsmagazine show *FYI.* Raspy-voiced, overweight Phil mans the tap as he chats with presidents, senators, and other Washington bigwigs. The men's room at Phil's is a hot spot where the town's power brokers often meet. Phil knows where many bodies are buried.

See *Murphy Brown*

PHILIP

This panicky bachelor, the roommate of **Brandon Shaw,** is goaded by Brandon into trying some desperate deeds, just for the sake of the experience. Unable to rationalize away the impact of what he's done, like his companion, Philip begins to go to pieces. He proves to be a great disappointment to Brandon, who claims to be actuated by the philosophy of Nietzsche.

See *Rope*

PHILIP CAREY

A shy young painter in Paris who recognizes his limited artistic talent and decides to become a surgeon in London instead. He also nurses a bitter, martyr-like streak because he has a club foot. As a medical student, he becomes obsessed with slutty waitress **Mildred Rogers,** who humiliates him by ridiculing his physical and mental shortcomings. A dreamy romantic, he nonetheless hates himself for his deformity and destructive relationship with Mildred. Because of his weakness for a bad woman, he feels himself to be spiritually crippled, as well. Sensitive and kind, his goodness makes him a martyr to those who would take advantage of him.

See *Of Human Bondage,* Somerset Maugham

PHINEAS "FINNY"

Charismatic daredevil at Devon School during the summer of 1942. An inspiration to fellow classmates, he always "moves in groups the size of a hockey team." Pure of heart. Relishes finding new rules to break. He coaxes his competitive but admiring best friend, **Gene Forrester,** into jumping off a dangerous tree limb and into the river, founding the Super Suicide Society of the Summer Session. Shockingly self-accepting. Can get away with anything. Never afraid. Never hates anyone. The best athlete in the entire school, he breaks the school swimming record and doesn't tell a soul except Gene. Believes "you always win at sports." Skips chapel and misses meals. When Gene fatefully jounces the perilous tree limb and Finny shatters his leg, he refuses to believe it wasn't an accident. Becomes convinced that World War II is a fake, cooked up by "fat old men who don't want us crowding them out of their jobs." Destined for tragedy.

See *A Separate Peace,* John Knowles

PICARD, JEAN-LUC

In the twenty-fourth century, Parisian-born Jean-Luc Picard joins Starfleet as a young man (where his mentor at the Academy is the gardener) and rises to the rank of captain, first spending twenty-two years as the commander of the USS *Stargazer,* then helming the Federation's flagship, the USS *Enterprise.* Picard is absolutely respected by his crew, for he's a thoughtful, determined, brilliant leader who is more comfortable with diplomacy than violence (although he'll use force when called for; one fight as a youth resulted in his being fitted with an artificial heart). A true man of letters, Picard reads classics in his spare time and has an abiding love of archaeology. His idealism is genuine and he believes fiercely that all sentient beings—whether microscopic, invisible, or just plain nasty—have an absolute right to self-determination; Picard will only circumvent the Prime Directive (noninterference in alien cultures) after much soul-searching and when absolutely necessary. Passionate about his family (his brother, Robert, owns a vineyard; he has a nephew, Rene) and his crew, Picard nevertheless keeps his own council and will rarely share his deep emotions with others. He's also more a cerebral adventurer than a swashbuckler and, as is logical, will let his crew do planetary reconnaissance. A few women have greatly touched him in his life, including an archaeologist-adventurer named Vash, and the *Enterprise*'s doctor, **Beverly Crusher**, whom later in life he marries.

See *Star Trek: The Next Generation*

PIERCE, DR. BENJAMIN FRANKLIN "HAWKEYE"

Drafted as a surgeon to serve in the Korean War, he hates war and the military mind-set, but is dedicated to his patients. He is attached to the 4077th MASH (Mobile Army Surgical Hospital) unit, where he delights in flouting rules. Hawkeye is a wise guy and a natural wit who delights in tormenting his hypocritical tentmate, **Frank Burns**. He also runs a fine little still out of his tent, along with his friends **Trapper John McIntyre** and, later, **B. J. Hunnicutt**. He sometimes indulges in self-righteous preachiness, but nobody's perfect. He remains almost universally admired at the 4077, the exceptions to the cult being Burns and head nurse **Margaret Houlihan**. He tries constantly to catch Burns and Houlihan in compromising positions and to get various nurses in compromising positions. He's a pacifist, but he has plenty of guts and will stand up to army brass when his principles are at stake. He's devoted to his father back home in Crab Apple Cove, Maine. Hawkeye's uniform of choice is a faded old bathrobe. He makes and drinks a good moonshine martini.

See *M*A*S*H*

PIERCE, MILDRED

A rags-to-riches-to-rags restaurateur, doting mother, and baker extraordinaire from Southern California. When her first marriage to Bert Pierce turns sour, she slaves as a waitress and sells pies on the side to keep her two daughters in good schools and fine clothes. Obsessed with her haughty elder daughter, **Veda**, Mildred tries to buy her love with money and music lessons. She starts keeping company with breakfast customer and socially prominent playboy **Monty Beragon**. When her younger daughter, Kay, dies suddenly, she's secretly thankful it wasn't Veda. Mildred has a pair of fabulous "immoral" legs and is apparently great in the sack. Through tenacious hard work, she opens a successful chicken place in Glendale, derogatorily nicknamed the Pie Wagon by Monty and Veda. With her new money, Mildred tries to control others and marries Monty in order to appear "good enough" in Veda's eyes. She's shattered to discover Veda in Monty's bed, tries to strangle her daughter, and then tries to put the pieces of her life together again—without Monty and Veda. "To hell with her!"

See *Mildred Pierce*, James M. Cain

PIERCE, VEDA

Arrogant she-devil created by her fawning mother, **Mildred Pierce**. Spoiled and conceited, she has coppery red hair, light blue eyes, and a "scramble of freckles" across her face. She forces the maid to wear her mother's waitress uniform and walk two paces behind her: "If she was going to take my things to the pool, I naturally wanted her decently dressed." Though she's not a great piano player, she's a brilliant sight-reader, and quits school at sixteen to devote herself to music. A blatant social climber, she is infatuated with Mildred's socialite boyfriend, **Monty Beragon**. Veda drives a dark green Packard 120 that Mildred bought her "to go with her hair." She'll do anything for money, even attempt to blackmail a rich boy into marriage. After becoming estranged from her mother, she discovers her true talent lies in singing, and becomes a famous coloratura soprano "worse than all the snakes in all the world."

See *Mildred Pierce*, James M. Cain

PIGGY

A smart British schoolboy who's stranded on a trop-

Photo courtesy of CBS

Hawkeye Pierce

ical island with his classmates, without any adults. As the right-hand man to early leader **Ralph**, he's obsessed with maintaining civilized order, and tries, for instance, to catalog the names of all the survivors. But order is doomed to perish here; as the boys devolve into a cruel, primitive state, they lose both names and their individual moral centers, becoming mere pieces of a bloodthirsty amoral horde. Identical twins Sam and Eric, for example, collectively become Samneric, while another boy forgets his name altogether. Like all the others, Piggy succumbs to the powerful appeal of the most bloodthirsty boy of all, as the children give themselves over to the most atavistic urges.

See *The Lord of the Flies,* William Golding

PIKE, CHARLES

A naive millionaire naturalist, who loves snakes and travels around the world to study them. He is heir to Pike's Pale, "The Ale That Won for Yale." Despite his travels, he is naive with women and too trusting of them. He falls in love with **Jean Harrington**, a glamorous gold digger, while on an ocean cruise. Despite being "suckered" by her, he ends up forgiving and marrying her. "They look too much alike to be the same."

See *The Lady Eve*

PILAR

This fiercely proud, down-to-earth woman heads up a band of 1930s Spanish Loyalists battling the Fascists. She's married to Pablo, a weak-willed, heavy-drinking soldier, whom she simultaneously loves and hates. Pilar is also an unofficial protector to Maria, a young girl who has been brutally raped by the Fascists. She and her partisans aid American **Robert Jordan** in his effort to blow up a key Fascist bridge.

See *For Whom the Bell Tolls,* Ernest Hemingway

PILETTI, MARTY

This lonely, overweight bachelor lives with his possessive Italian immigrant mother in the Bronx. Marty is good-hearted and sensitive, but directionless. He became a butcher by default when he got out of the army at age twenty-five; now he contemplates buying the butcher shop from his boss. He usually ends up spending his Saturday nights with his best friend, Angie, drinking beer and watching television. "So, what do you wanna do tonight, Marty?" "I dunno, Angie. What do you wanna do?" Tired of having his bachelor status thrown up at him by friends and family, he longs for the love of a woman, but he's shy, self-conscious, and believes that women find him ugly. Marty is a churchgoing Catholic who feels his world shrinking and paling as he gets older; then he meets Clara, a homely schoolteacher, and suddenly there's a ray of bright sunshine pouring through a crack in the walls that immure him. "We ain't such dogs as we think we are."

See *Marty,* Paddy Chayevsky

PILGRIM, BILLY

A mild-mannered, Middle American, World War II veteran. His astrological sign: Cancer. His favorite activity: curling up on the sofa with a nudie magazine. Billy is married and the father of two grown children. He's passive, kindhearted, and getting bald. His wife constantly promises that she will lose weight for him, and a mysterious enemy he made during the war has been trying to kill him for over twenty years. But his real problem is that he is "unstuck in time." He's forever flipping in and out of different periods of his life, from his youth as a German prisoner of war, to his present in a dull, lifeless marriage, to his future as a pampered prisoner on the planet Tralfamador, where he shares a glass cage with the beautiful porn star Montana Wildhack.

See *Slaughterhouse Five,* Kurt Vonnegut Jr.

PILLSBURY DOUGH BOY

Cheerful boy made out of dough who familiarizes the nation with baking products and recipes. Wears large chef hat. Giggles when poked.

See *Pillsbury*

PLATO

A dark, deeply disturbed teenage son of rich, divorced—and thus emotionally distant—parents. Proof that man is not dog's best friend—arrested for senselessly killing puppies. A helpless puppy himself, he goes nuts when **Jim** and **Judy** can't give him the impossibly large amount of emotional support he needs.

See *Rebel Without a Cause*

PNIN, TIMOFEY PAVLOVICH

An escapee from Lenin's Russia who, after completing his college education in Prague and living for a time in Paris, moves to America and becomes a professor of Russian at an American college. The bumbling professor undergoes a series of mishaps, beginning with getting on the wrong train on his way to deliver a lecture in English, a language of which his knowledge is extremely incomplete.

See *Pnin,* Vladimir Nabokov

MASTER PO

Chinese kung fu master and teacher of **Kwai Chang Caine**. Despite his blindness, he sees all. He is a wise older man, always ready with sage advice, and a patient teacher, who calls his student "grasshopper." He teaches Caine the martial art of kung fu, but, most important, he instructs his young charge to live a peaceful and meaningful life.

See *Kung Fu*

POIROT, HERCULE

Heroic, semiretired Belgian detective. He's not much to look at, and his heavy accent and neatly manicured moustache seem to suit him better for the Parliament than for the police force. His large ego makes up for his small stature, and he's put hundreds of criminals behind bars.

See, e.g., *One, Two, Buckle My Shoe,* Agatha Christie

POITIER, PAUL

That's not his real name, but since he claims to be Sidney Poitier's son, it's the name he's taken. After being groomed by his educated gay lover, he transforms himself from a rough street punk to an elegant Harvard student in only three months. He then seduces wealthy Manhattan families into letting him spend the night. Fascinating and eloquent, Paul drops clues about his true motives when giving a dissertation on the meaning of *The Catcher in the Rye* to art lovers **Flan** and **Ouisa Kittredge**. Among his many assets, he is a wizard in the kitchen: "Cooking calms me." He challenges everyone he encounters in a wealthy and socially prominent clique to scrutinize his or her reason for existing. "The imagination is God's gift to make the act of self-examination bearable."

See *Six Degrees of Separation,* John Guare

POLHEMUS, CAROLYN

"A smart, sexy gal," not bright enough to keep walking the earth. Wears jangling jewelry, silk blouses, red lipstick, and painted nails. A "helluva lawyer" who sleeps with whomever she needs to, including her superior, **Rusty Sabich**. Not your typical big-chested blond babe, she takes pleasure in breaking the rules. Tough. Magnetic. A prosecutor who asks to be assigned to the Rape Section, she ends up hog-tied with a cracked skull.

See *Presumed Innocent,* Scott Turow

POLLIT, BIG DADDY

The wealthy patriarch of an old southern family. He's a large man possessing a large voice, large ideas, and a large bank account. His family is well aware of both his wallet size and the fact that he is dying of cancer.

See *Cat on a Hot Tin Roof,* Tennessee Williams

POLLITT, BRICK

The handsome eldest son of the powerful, wealthy **Big Daddy** is nonetheless filled with self-loathing, because of his unfulfilled life and sexual frustration. A former star high school athlete and the apple of his father's eye, Brick is nursing a broken leg suffered while trying to jump hurdles while drunk. His stubborn, self-destructive nature and loathing of his grasping, conniving family spur his drinking. While most blame his alcoholic intake on unhappy marriage and despondency after the death of his best friend, Brick's beautiful, frustrated wife, **Maggie**, knows that the roots of his problems run deeper. The true nature of Brick's relationship with his late friend reflects the ambiguity of his sexuality. He senses that, to survive, he must escape his family and the hypocrisy they personify.

See *Cat on a Hot Tin Roof,* Tennessee Williams

POLLITT, MAGGIE

A doe-eyed southern belle with a soft voice and silky manner, Maggie turns out to be a tough adversary in siding with her husband, **Brick Pollitt**, in the battle over the estate of his not-yet-dead father, **Big Daddy**. She loves her husband, but his remoteness since the death of his best friend has damaged their relationship and she can't break through his icy rejection of her advances. Though she has no children of her own, Maggie is con-

Hercule Poirot

temptuous of her sister-in-law's perpetual state of pregnancy. Maggie uses her considerable charm to woo Big Daddy into leaving control of his wealth to her husband and isn't above lying to get his sympathy. More than the money itself, her actions are motivated by her love for her husband and the desire to do something to get him back.

See *Cat on a Hot Tin Roof,* Tennessee Williams

POLNIACZEK, JO

From her first days at Eastland School for Girls, Bronx-born Jo has always been tougher and rougher than her wealthy roommates. While at Langley College, she works part-time at Edna's Edibles in Peekskill, N.Y. After college, she leaves her old friends **Blair**, **Natalie**, and **Tootie** to embark on a business career and marry a musician named Rick.

See *The Facts of Life*

PONCHERELLO, FRANK "PONCH"

Ponch is a hunky Hispanic California Highway Patrol cop. He's effervescent and even flirtatious, but in the crunch, he can get serious and do the job. He's devoted to his partner, **Jon Baker**, and together, they ride the freeways on their motorcycles, solving problems and stopping crimes.

See *CHiPs*

POPEYE

This mumbling, squint-eyed sailor has the biggest forearms you'll ever see. He sports a tattoo of a ship's anchor, smokes a pipe constantly, and chugalugs a can of spinach whenever he needs superhuman strength. The light of his life is mousy, squeaky-voiced **Olive Oyl**—recognizable by her shiny, pulled-back black hair—and he battles for her affections against his archrival, big, obnoxious Bluto. Popeye is a plain old salt, and his lack of savoir faire puts him at a disadvantage in comparison with Bluto, who's surprisingly suave and slick. Popeye is a good friend and protector to his mooching loser of a friend Wimpy, who will "gladly pay you on Tuesday for a hamburger today." He also possesses the ability to get his pipe to emit a ship's "toot-toot!"

See *Popeye*

POPPER, RUTH

Stuck in a marriage with a fat, loutish high school sports coach in a nowhere Texas town, Ruth Popper seeks relief in the arms of sweet teenage boys like **Sonny Crawford**, a player on her husband's basketball team. Unfortunately for Ruth, the affection the orphaned Sonny seeks is maternal, and her quest for conjugal love goes unfulfilled.

See *The Last Picture Show,* Larry McMurtry

POPPINS, MARY

An angel disguised as a British nanny. Perky, pretty, and almost always smiling, she arrives out of nowhere in pre-automobile London. There, she goes to work for a family whose kids have run a series of nannies out of town with their shenanigans. Quickly, she institutes a regime combining discipline and fun. Without resorting to preaching or lectures, she helps her charges learn about proper conduct and responsibility and gives them the resources they need to get through life's trials. She has a magical black umbrella, which enables her to fly. Mary is magical herself, speeding up household chores with a mere touch and an incantation. She has a particularly warm relationship with the bumbling but good-hearted local chimney sweep. While educating the children, she also helps their father, a buttoned-up banker, get in touch with his inner child and let his hair down now and again. Then she's off on her umbrella to find more dysfunctional families to work on. "Supercalifragilistic!"

See *Mary Poppins*

PORGY

Enigmatic and lonely, Porgy is a legless street beggar in turn-of-the-century Charleston, South Carolina. He is a fixture in the Catfish Row section of the city, where the residents and passersby sense his alienation but treat him with kindness and pity. Porgy's life is transformed by **Bess**, a heroin addict and the girlfriend of a fugitive murderer, who appears in the quarter and moves in with Porgy. Porgy's newfound happiness is short-lived, however, when he murders Bess's former boyfriend in a bid to save her from his clutches. Haunted by guilt and superstitious fears, Porgy, suddenly an old man, flees downriver to Savannah.

See *Porgy and Bess,* DuBose Heyward

PORTER, JANE

A beautiful damsel always in distress, Jane is lucky

to have **Tarzan** there to bail her out. Marooned with her father on a teeming African coast, Jane is immediately imperiled by numerous tropical dangers, most notably a killer ape who wants to make her into his lunch. When Tarzan swings in from the trees and saves Jane and her father, she gets a serious case of jungle fever and falls in love with the wild man. Finally, Jane and her father are bailed out by the French navy and return to Wisconsin. When Tarzan finally tracks her down in his quest to civilize himself, Jane's attraction for him ebbs. Must have been the heat.

See *Tarzan of the Apes,* Edgar Rice Burroughs

PORTER, JIMMY

Living in London, Jimmy is the quintessential 1950s, alienated, "angry young man." University-educated but working at a street market, Jimmy seethes with resentment and rage. His anger makes its way home to his wife, Alison, his mistress, Helena, and back to Alison.

See *Look Back in Anger,* John Osborne

PORTNOY, ALEXANDER

A highly intelligent, mother-dominated, guilt-ridden, sex-obsessed Jewish boy from New Jersey. He becomes assistant commissioner for Human Opportunities in New York City, but his rise in station doesn't free him from his afflictions. He tries to exorcise his angst in hilarious stories told to his psychiatrist.

See *Portnoy's Complaint,* Philip Roth

PORTNOY, SOPHIE

The Jewish mother to end all Jewish mothers. She alternates between smothering her son **Alexander** with concern and threatening him with doom. Naturally, she doesn't understand him.

See *Portnoy's Complaint,* Philip Roth

POTTER, COLONEL SHERMAN

He's the gruff, no-nonsense commanding officer of the 4077th MASH (Mobile Army Surgical Hospital) unit during the Korean War. A career army man, he's also a caring and skilled surgeon. He knows when to bend the rules out of consideration for his troops, whose loyalty he commands. He's an old cavalry man and loves his horse, Sophie. He also loves his wife, Mildred, and enjoys—up to a point—the antics of unit surgeons Hawkeye Pierce and B. J. Hunnicut.

See *M*A*S*H*

MR. POTTER

Wizened, bitter, cigar-chomping Potter, confined to his wheelchair, greedily plots the material and spiritual domination of Bedford Falls. He's a financial mastermind for whom the word "enough" doesn't compute, and, anyway, power is the name of the game. The focus of his evil machinations is kindly, generous, forthright, warm, honest, saintly **George Bailey**. When Potter seems to have Bailey's Building & Loan firm on the ropes, it looks like evil will triumph over good. Mr. Potter is a poke in the eye for advocates of wheelchair occupants everywhere.

See *It's a Wonderful Life*

POWELL, HARRY

He's a charming but vicious ex-con turned preacher. He has the word "LOVE" tattooed on the knuckles of one hand and "HATE" tattooed on the knuckles of the other. Having killed an indeterminate but large number of wealthy widows, Harry marries and kills another in an attempt to get the cash her recently executed first husband stole and hid. After her death, the only one aware of where the cash stash is, is the late widow's young son, who knows it's in his little sister's doll. He pursues the two kids in a nightmarish chase, singing righteous hymns as he goes.

See *Night of the Hunter*

Popeye

Tom Powers

POWERS, TOM

An audacious policeman's son from the South Side of Chicago, who begins his life of crime by pestering girls and selling stolen goods to a local fence. He encourages his best friend to join him in his illegal pursuits, and when they grow older, they become deliverymen by day and rob by night. During their biggest heist, Powers kills a cop before escaping. With the advent of Prohibition, the resourceful Powers starts robbing liquor warehouses for a local mob. As he rises up the criminal ladder, Powers demonstrates invincibility, confidence, brutality, and ruthlessness. He even shoots the horse who killed his boss when the man accidentally fell from it. With his new-found wealth, he becomes a snazzy dresser who still wields a mean hook and a gun. He has no respect for women other than his widowed mother, to whom he tries to give money, but she would rather continue to take in laundry than accept her son's ill-earned cash. Powers's unquenchable thirst for violence instills audacity in him rather than fear.
See *Public Enemy*

PRAY, ADDIE

Addie is too smart for her own good, as well as being an accomplished grifter at the age of eleven. Having been well taught by her con man dad, **Moses**, she's a master of the glib half-truth that is too close to the truth to be disbelieved. Give her half a chance, and she'll have you thanking her for stealing you blind.
See *Paper Moon*

PRAY, MOSES

He'd rather lie than tell the truth. He'd rather steal from the public and con his marks than earn his money honestly. Too slick to ever stick to one place, he drifts across the country with daughter **Addie**, looking for that one big break, his one chance at big bucks and the good life.
See *Paper Moon*

PRENTICE, JOHN

A calm, mature research scientist of African American descent, with a streak of stubbornness that sometimes gets the best of him. His whirlwind romance with the white daughter of **Matt Drayton** and **Christina Drayton** seems out of character for his studied nature. Although gentle, he is also defensive. Erring on the side of caution, he makes his decision to marry their daughter contingent upon their approval.
See *Guess Who's Coming to Dinner*

PRESTON, BILL S.

A most excellent dude, one-half of the heavy-metal rock group Wyld Stallyns. Best friend and loyal bud to **Ted Logan**. Ranks in the top 99 percent of his class at San Dimas High School. As inadvertent time traveler, gets up close and personal with Socrates, Freud, Lincoln, and Joan of Arc, among others. Looked after by futuristic friend Rufus.
See *Bill and Ted's Excellent Adventure*

PRESTON, LAWRENCE

Accomplished long-time defense attorney, he gives fatherly counsel to his junior partner, who happens to be his son, Kenneth, just out of law school. Preston and Preston are unafraid to take on the tough cases.
See *The Defenders*

PREWITT, ROBERT E. LEE

A soldier in the pre–World War II army, Prewitt is both a gifted bugler and a talented boxer. But he refuses to fight again after he inadvertently kills a man in the ring. When he transfers to a new unit, he puts up with interminable abuse and humiliation rather than agree to fight for his commanding officer **Captain Dana Holmes**'s boxing squad. A compassionate, sensitive man, he is also tough and stubborn. Prewitt forms an unlikely friendship with the scrappy **Angelo Maggio**, and the two outsiders look out for each other. He also seeks comfort in the arms of a sympathetic canteen "hostess."
See *From Here to Eternity*, James Jones

PREYSING, GENERAL DIRECTOR

An avaricious business magnate whose industrial empire is on the verge of collapse. He's full of pomp and swagger, but his ruthless demeanor is meant to hide anxiety about his dire financial straits. He tries for a sophisticated image but hasn't outgrown his lowly beginnings and coarse manner, which he demonstrates by bullying busboys and clerks.
See *Grand Hotel*, Vicki Baum

PRITCHETT, MURIEL

A dog and people lover, outspoken and offbeat. Muriel runs her own canine obedience school and kennel business. She never hesitates to say whatever's on her mind, regardless of consequences, and has an unusual sense of fashion—anything goes with Muriel and somehow manages to work. Her instinct for the personalities of both humans and animals is excellent. She doesn't let convention or other people's opinions stand in her way when it comes to romance. Muriel is a well-rounded combination of dreamer and doer as well as a devoted mother to her boy, willing to do anything to see him through his illness.

See *The Accidental Tourist*

PROCTOR, JOHN

Farmer. A God-fearing and upstanding citizen of Salem, Massachusetts. Proctor follows his conscience, even when the cost may be personally devastating. He has been accused of being a witch by his former lover, Abigail Williams. "I speak my own sins; I cannot judge another."

See *The Crucible,* Arthur Miller

PROFANE, BENNY

This drifter likes to ride New York subways all night—when he's not in the sewer system, hunting all those alligators flushed down the city's toilets. He hangs around with the Whole Sick Crew, a band of anarchic party animals. Benny gets temporary employment as a night watchman in a robot factory. He also has occasion to visit Malta. He's a hard fellow to pin down: either his whole life is random or it's subject to some mysterious plan instituted by some mysterious conspiracy.

See *V.,* Thomas Pynchon

PROTAGONIST, HIRO

Samurai-cybersurfer-hacker, best known for creating the most realistic avatars in the metaverse. He lives in a storage facility outside Los Angeles, and spends most of his spare time on-line. Occasionally, he takes part-time work, usually as a delivery specialist for a pizzeria.

See *Snow Crash*

PRUFROCK, J. ALFRED

Conventional, timid, even cowardly, Prufrock is self-reflective to the point of paralysis. Middle-aged and balding, Prufrock clearly has let his life slip away as he ponders where to part his hair or whether he dare eat a peach. Although he mourns his life's passing, he will do nothing to reverse his descent into *ennui* and old age. Prufrock maintains the trappings of civilization by dressing carefully and abiding by society's rules and rituals, but the grime that pervades the unnamed industrial city in which he lives is a reflection of his own psyche. He is not without his dreams—"I have heard the mermaids singing, each to each"—but he also knows their song is not for him.

See *The Love Song of J. Alfred Prufrock,* T. S. Eliot

PULVER, ENSIGN FRANK

The laundry and morale officer of the USS *Reluctant,* Pulver spends most of his time avoiding responsibility, grousing about the skipper, **Captain Morton,** and talking to his best friend and mentor, **Lieutenant Roberts.** Pulver is big on talk and short on action, but the crew likes him.

See *Mister Roberts*

THE PUNISHER

His name is Frank Castle. This ruthless, vengeful, violent ex-soldier is a crime-fighter, but, for a wonder, he possesses no superpowers. His wife and children are killed when they accidentally witness a gang murder, after which he vows revenge and executes every criminal he can get his gun sight on. He may not have superpowers, but he wears a costume—black, with a giant white skull across his chest.

See *The Punisher,* Gerry Conway and John Romita

PUPKIN, RUPERT

A middle-aged nerd who fantasizes himself as a television star. He practices in his basement, holding mock talk shows with cardboard cutouts of celebrities. His dream is to get a stand-up comedy slot on the country's biggest late-night talk show. When the host brushes him off, Rupert won't take no for an answer, and kidnaps the host to force the show to give him air time.

See *The King of Comedy*

Gomer Pyle

PYLE, GOMER

Innocent country bumpkin turned soldier. Tall and gangly, Gomer has a goofy grin and an aim to please. He quit his job at Mayberry's fillin' station to join the marines. Now he is stationed at Camp Henderson, California. Gomer really does strive to be the best possible marine for **Sergeant Vince Carter,** who mistakes his naiveté for insolence. He brings kindness, thoughtfulness, and music to the Marine Corps. Seeing through his innocent wide eyes, others learn to appreciate things they often took for granted. He unwittingly disobeys orders and can't resist helping others. Enjoys getting to know the other "fellers" in the barracks. Misses the folks back in Mayberry. Professional-caliber singer. Women want to mother him. "Shazaam!"

See *Gomer Pyle, U.S.M.C.*

PYNCHON, MRS. MARGARET

Powerful, multimillionaire newspaper owner. Looks like a typical old rich lady, with luxurious clothing and an expensive little heel-nipping dog. Underneath is a tough old broad with fair ideals and a good conscience. She often goes head-to-head with city editor **Lou Grant,** and doesn't always win. She wants what's best for the *Los Angeles Tribune* but will forsake profit for honor.

See *Lou Grant*

Q

A brilliant, if socially inept, inventor who creates ingenious gadgets for the British Secret Service, many of which are employed by agent **James Bond** in his various missions. Staying within the safe walls of MI5's labs, Q may be a bit jealous of his more dashing colleague and definitely disapproves of Bond's whimsical attitude toward his brainchildren. Bond always gets the glory and never shows much appreciation for the numerous ways in which Q has saved his bacon in tight spots.

See *Dr. No, You Only Live Twice, Goldfinger,* et al., Ian Fleming

QUAID, DOUG

Quaid may be a victim of mind-tampering. He believes that he's a construction worker living on Earth with his wife, Lori, but that may be an implanted figment. He may be a secret agent on Mars, unless that's an illusion, and he really *is* a construction worker. Or maybe both are illusions, and he's actually an Austrian bodybuilder who thinks he's none of the above.

See *Total Recall*

QUEEG, CAPTAIN

He's the commander of the ancient, rusty World War II minesweeper *Caine.* Tough to the point of sadism on his charges. Nicknamed Old Yellowstain by his crew, who know that he is apt to crack under pressure—such as might be caused by coming under hostile fire or being menaced by a typhoon. Plays obsessively with three steel balls he rolls around in his palm. "I kid you not."

See *The Caine Mutiny*

QUEEN, ELLERY

The author of a series of books detailing his own adventures as a master sleuth in New York City, Queen is tall and gangly with the look of a young professor. A match for even Sherlock Holmes in the art of "ratiocination," his dazzling powers of deductive reasoning can solve seemingly unsolvable murder mysteries. With his quick wit, breezy charm, and boyish good looks, Queen has his share of female admirers, but prefers to remain a bachelor. He shares an apartment with his father, **Richard Queen,** a New York police detective.

See *The Roman Hat Mystery,* Ellery Queen (Frederick Dannay and Manfred B. Lee)

QUEEN, INSPECTOR RICHARD

An inspector with the New York Police Department who regularly calls in his son Ellery, a slightly absentminded mystery writer, to help him solve murder investigations. He marvels at his son's ability to reach the proper conclusion by finding the most obscure clues and piecing them together.

See *The Adventures of Ellery Queen*

QUINCY, DR. R.

Quincy is a Medical Examiner (coroner) with a compulsion to find and bare the truth. Nothing is ever what it seems to Quincy, a gifted medical detective. Tireless in his quest, he expects no less from his staff, who respond to his passion with their own commitment. Having found the cause of death, he'll usually track down the killer as well, at no extra charge.

See *Quincy*

QUINLAN, HARRY

American border-town lawman whose exterior appearance mirrors his inner corruption. Bloated and leaning heavily on his cane, he will stoop to anything to get his man, or find a man who can be made to look the part. When a rich man turns up dead, he doesn't hesitate to frame the man's son-in-law. His passion for nailing bad guys may stem from the fact that, years ago, his wife was murdered and the killer escaped. But this time, he's up against a righteous cop: **Mike Vargas**, who's determined to expose Quinlan's corruption.

See *Touch of Evil*

QUINT

Grizzled, ex-Marine shark killer—that is, when he's not running charters on his boat, the *Orca,* to make ends meet. Has had a passion for killing sharks ever since the devastating experience of waiting for rescue in the ocean for 110 hours after the sinking of the U.S.S. *Indianapolis* during World War II. "Eleven hundred men went into the water, three hundred sixteen come out, and the sharks took the rest," he tells **Martin Brody** and **Matt Hooper** while the three men wait for dawn. Favorite weapon against the Great White: number 12 piano wire attached to harpoons at one end and 50-gallon floating barrels at the other—just to get the beast close enough to blast with his Marine's M1 rifle. He's covered with scars that he'll be delighted to show you when he's had enough rum.

See *Jaws,* Peter Benchley

QUOYLE

A third-rate journalist, a shambling, clumsy man with a monstrous chin and "a great damp loaf of a body." He returns to his ancestral home in Killick-Claw, Newfoundland, with his two young daughters. There, he takes a job writing the shipping news for the local newspaper and progresses from being a bumbling outsider to a respected journalist.

See *The Shipping News,* E. Annie Proulx

RACHEL

This lovely young woman thinks she's a normal human being, with a normal past, until she's tested by a "Blade Runner"—a specialist police officer—named **Deckard**. It turns out that she's a replicant, a half-human, half-machine being, who's got an inbuilt life expectancy of just four years. She and Deckard fall in love, and she tries to deal with the numerous problems she never knew she had, until recently. Has a fondness for pompadour hair and high collars. "Is this testing whether I'm a replicant or a lesbian, Mr. Deckard?"

See *Blade Runner*

RACINE, NED

Small-time Florida lawyer. Prefers meaningless sex and easy pickups, which can lead to awkward entanglements. Has reputation among colleagues for representing lowlifes, though current legal work for wealthy **Matty Walker** is a killer career move. Racine prefers to smoke cigarettes immediately after jogging. His uncouth manners and pathetic case of tunnel vision make Racine his own worst enemy.

See *Body Heat*

RADLEY, BOO

Boo is an emotionally wounded recluse. For most of his life, his religious-fanatic father has kept him imprisoned in their house, denying him contact with other people. Over the years, a scary and bizarre reputation has grown up around him, and local children, like **Jem** and **Scout Finch**, fear him, looking on him as a spooky freak. But their father, **Atticus Finch**, helps them to see the pitiful truth behind the frightening facade. Boo develops a strange, but not unfriendly relationship with the Finch children.

See *To Kill a Mockingbird,* Harper Lee

RAFF, RIFF

Ostensibly, he's the lanky manservant of **Dr. Frank N. Furter**; in reality, he's an invasion project overseer from planet Transsexual, located in the Transylvanian galaxy. Riff affects a long fringe of blond hair surrounding a bald pate. He has an incestuous relationship with his sister, Magenta, which isn't such a terrible thing where he comes from. He's a killer when it comes down to the clutch.

See *The Rocky Horror Picture Show*

RAHEEM, RADIO

Brooklyn homeboy who rules the streets of Bed-

Sty. His prized possession is an enormous boom box, which he carries on his shoulders around the neighborhood, music blaring loudly. He wears a lettered set of brass knuckles on each hand, one reading "LOVE," the other reading "HATE." Good friends with **Mookie** and **Buggin' Out**; has intense dislike for **Sal**. "If I love you, I love you, but if I hate you…"
See *Do the Right Thing*

RALPH
He is a natural leader among boys, self-assured and charismatic. When he and his schoolmates are stranded on a tropical island without any adults, he becomes head of their little society and with the help of his right-hand man, **Piggy**, tries to maintain some kind of civilization. But he can't keep the others from gravitating toward the lusty, violent lure of the boy who leads the hunting parties. Eventually, the group degenerates into a primitive tribe, complete with a bloodthirsty religion, an idol to be worshiped, and—in the end—human sacrifice.
See *The Lord of the Flies,* William Golding

RALPHIE
1940s grade schooler with one true burning desire in life: to own an authentic Red Ryder BB gun. He spends much of his time in a colorful world of fantasy, often envisioning how neat life will be once he has that Red Ryder air rifle in hand. In real life, he must contend with contest-mad **Old Man**, well-meaning mother, and bratty younger brother **Randy**. Also a frequent target of neighborhood bullies.
See *A Christmas Story*

RAMBO, JOHN
A former Vietnam War Green Beret, now he's a one-man army capable of just about anything in the way of violence. An expert in weapons, explosives, booby traps, and survival techniques. Extremely well muscled and in amazing shape, Rambo's been trained to take all sorts of punishment and still remain in control of his faculties. A fierce patriot, he has difficulty understanding the attitudes of some of his fellow Americans. Rambo isn't much of a talker and tends to speak in monosyllables.
See *First Blood*

RAMIREZ, CARLOS
This good-looking Puerto Rican playboy is a friend to the local wing-hatted nuns. He's charming and suave and owns a San Juan disco, Casino Carlos. He usually has a beautiful woman on his arm. Carlos is endlessly bemused by the antics of flying nun **Sister Bertrille**, but he's always there to bail her out of a jam.
See *The Flying Nun*

RAMIUS, MARKO
He's devious, brilliant, and deadly. In the mid-1980s, Ramius is the most respected sub driver in the Soviet Navy, entrusted with the most advanced technology his country can devise. But what is he doing with his priceless boat? Tall for a submarine commander, Ramius commands respect. His very bearing inspires confidence in the truth of his lies. And that's what makes him so dangerous, to the U.S. and to the Soviet Union as well. Is there anyone who can get inside his head? Perhaps **Jack Ryan** can.
See *The Hunt for Red October,* Tom Clancy

RAMSEY, ALEC
Young adventurer capable of holding his own on a deserted island or at the racetrack. Beloved owner and rider of mystical black stallion. Eager to learn and filled with a sense of wonder, no matter what his surroundings.
See *The Black Stallion*

RAMSEY, DOROTHY "TOOTIE"
The youngest and most enthusiastic of a group of girls who attend Eastland School for Girls. She wears braces, gets around on roller skates, and has a cat named Jeffrey. An aspiring actress, she's the first black girl at Eastland to play Juliet. Grows up to get engaged and attend the Royal Academy of Dramatic Arts in London. Her best friend is **Natalie Green**.
See *The Facts of Life*

RAND, YEOMAN JANICE
A yeoman on the starship *Enterprise,* Rand is blond, lovely, and all dewy-eyed in the presence of **Captain Kirk**; he gives her the occasional seductive glance, but nothing much develops between them. She does look good in her twenty-third-century regula-

tion Federation miniskirt, however.
See *Star Trek*

RANDAL

Twenty-something convenience-store philosopher and video shop clerk. Has a quirky way of looking at the world, including a taste for watching hermaphrodite porn videos. Gets his best friend, **Dante Hicks**, in trouble, first by selling cigarettes to a four-year-old girl, later by giving an elderly man, **Mr. Smith**, a lethally stimulating porn magazine to read in the bathroom. Advises Dante to forget about his popular-bitch old girlfriend and appreciate his loving, if slightly shopworn, current girl.
See *Clerks*

RANDY

Younger brother of **Ralphie**, whom Randy constantly tags along after. Basically a good kid, he can be trouble when he wants to be. Dislikes wearing layers of winter clothing, particularly when it interferes with lowering his arms to his sides. Somehow he survives, though he eats hardly anything, ever.
See *A Christmas Story*

RAPF, MADGE

Shrewish wife of Bob Rapf. She's not above twisting the facts to suit her needs, particularly when it comes to the murder of **Vincent Parry**'s dead wife. Lets few things or people get in the way of what she wants. Has problems when standing near open windows.
See *Dark Passage*

RASSENDYLL, RUDOLF

He's an English-born major, recently retired from Her Majesty's service. He's also a distant cousin of and, but for his goatee, a doppelgänger for Ruritania's Prince Rudolf. The lithe Rassendyll is deft with a sword and, unlike his look-alike, is charismatic, romantic, and personable. Rassendyll is by no means a monarchist—in his own words, he "was born with a natural distaste for crowns." Despite this, he agrees to impersonate Prince Rudolf to save the future king from **Black Michael**. The courtly, chivalrous, witty Rassendyll dislikes coronations (he'd rather be fishing) but finds himself the central character in one. He also falls in love with the king's future queen, **Princess Flavia**. A true

officer and gentleman, he is willing to risk his life for his love.
See *The Prisoner of Zenda*

RATCHED, MILDRED "BIG NURSE"

A quintessential ice queen, the tyrannical nurse that everyone loves to hate. With her perfectly clean, perfectly starched and pressed uniform and unwaveringly stern face, she's the picture of someone who believes in doing things by the book. Seemingly without a sense of humor or a personal life, she lives to exert control over her charges—which seems exceedingly unfair, since her charges consist of a wardful of mental patients who are too childlike or afraid to make it in the world outside the hospital walls. In the name of giving their lives order, she keeps an iron hand on the men under her "care," refusing to allow any individuality or freedom of expression. She even oppresses the black men who work as orderlies under her, who'd like to joke around and sympathize with the patients but are too afraid of Nurse Ratched to do so. When her patients try anything that she can't utterly control, she's very quick to hand out punishment—anything from a reminder of painful events in the patient's life, to a forced, painfully cold shower, to electroshock therapy. Her primary nemesis in the ward is new patient **Randle Patrick McMurphy**, whom she (correctly) suspects of feigning his mental problems. She grows infuriated by the way in which McMurphy triggers feelings of confidence, freedom, and personal creativity in the other patients—the way he helps them stand on their own two feet and become better prepared to leave the hospital and go out on their own in the world. She's particularly upset when, late one night, the patients invade her inner sanctum—the nurse's office, from which she dispenses mind-numbing drugs and makes P.A. announcements. Finally, in her rage at the threat McMurphy poses to her domain, she sends him to be lobotomized. In all, she is a symbol of the depersonalizing coldness and oppression inherent in large institutions and bureaucracies—the superego to McMurphy's id.
See *One Flew over the Cuckoo's Nest*, Ken Kesey

RAVENAL, GAYLORD

As skilled in card games as he is in winning the hearts of women, Gaylord uses his good looks and charm to get a job as the leading man on a Mississippi showboat when his luck as a gambler runs out. Soon after joining the company of the Cotton Blossom Floating Palace, Gaylord woos and secretly weds **Magnolia Hawks Ravenal**, the leading lady and daughter of the showboat's owners. Unable to persuade Magnolia's mother that he has left behind his seamy past, Gaylord convinces his wife to move to Chicago, where he turns once again to the uncertain and ultimately self-destructive life at the roulette table.

See *Showboat,* Edna Ferber

RAVENAL, MAGNOLIA HAWKS

Born and raised on a Mississippi showboat, Magnolia is a child of the river whose destiny is on the stage. Kind and open-hearted, Magnolia befriends the crew of the Cotton Blossom Floating Palace and the black river men who work along its route. As Magnolia blossoms into young womanhood, the opportunity opens for her to become an actress. Over her mother's never-ending objections, Magnolia becomes a star, weds **Gaylord Ravenal**, the leading man, and moves to Chicago. But perhaps Magnolia's mother is proved right in the end, when Gaylord abandons her and she returns to the Mississippi to take her mother's place as queen of the Cotton Blossom.

See *Showboat,* Edna Ferber

RAWLINS, EZEKIEL "EASY"

Down the mean streets of Watts he goes, wary, wisecracking, and usually up to his neck in trouble. Like his spiritual progenitor, **Philip Marlowe**, he's too cagey to believe in much of anything, but too smart and honorable to believe in nothing at all. He keeps an eye on several apartment buildings he secretly owns by working as their janitor. Easy has a reputation for fairness and integrity among the poor, hard-pressed African Americans of 1950s Los Angeles, for whom he often does unpaid favors, asking only that they return the favor when they can—"a real country way of doing business." His mistrust of authority was confirmed by his time in the army. "Somewhere along the line I had slipped into the role of a confidential agent who represented people when the law broke down. And the law broke down often enough to keep me busy."

See, e.g., *Devil in a Blue Dress,* Walter Mosley

REED, ANNE

Even an attractive reporter for the *Baltimore Sun,* who is engaged to be married to an ideal man and is seemingly poised for career and personal success, can find herself touched by a poignant story about a lonely man thousands of miles away. Annie is not quite sure what's lacking in her life. Maybe it's the kind of romance and love seen in her favorite movie, *An Affair to Remember.* Maybe her fiancé isn't quite exciting enough for her. Maybe, just maybe, Cupid's arrow will strike atop the Empire State Building on the evening of St. Valentine's Day, and **Sam Baldwin** will be there.

See *Sleepless in Seattle*

REED, OFFICER JIM

Young rookie cop, partnered with veteran Los Angeles Police Department officer **Pete Malloy**. Eager to impress Malloy, sometimes missing the other's quirky humor, respectful of and grateful for the on-the-job training. Married to a young wife, Jean, shows signs of becoming a fine officer. "One Adam-12, One Adam-12. See the woman…"

See *Adam-12*

THE REED SISTERS

Brought together to help their mother, Beatrice, after their father's death, the Reed sisters now care for each other. Life in Winnetka, Illinois, isn't as peaceful as it sounds for these four sisters, whose names make them sound more like brothers. Elegant and sophisticated Alex is at times happy just to be a rich surgeon's wife, but she's also compassionate and tough, and she'd do anything for her family. Her grown daughter is Reed; after divorcing the surgeon, Alex marries a local Winnetka businessman named "Big Al." Georgie is the one to whom everyone turns. But when she breaks, she really shatters, contemplating suicide, having an affair with her therapist. She battles leukemia and rebellion in her two sons, Evan and Trevor, as well as a shaky marriage to her husband, John Whitsig. Stunning, funny and warm, iconoclast Teddy is a glamorous fashion designer who nevertheless spends most of her time in jeans and a baseball jacket. A rebellious spirit, she's a handful for her daughter Cat, often because of their continuing battles with alcoholism. Once married to Mitch, she finds true love with a cop, until he's murdered.

Frankie is the baby of the family, and has survived them calling her "Stinkerbelle" to grow up an accomplished, beautiful businesswoman. She marries and has a child with Teddy's ex, Mitch. After creating a children's character named "Cowlotta" that's purchased by a Japanese conglomerate, she moves to Tokyo with her small son. The Reed sisters often have flashbacks to their collective childhood that help them deal with the present.

See *Sisters*

REESE, KYLE

Resourceful soldier from the early twenty-first century. Reese has been dispatched on a crucial mission back to the twentieth century, where he shows extraordinary familiarity with its technology. Among his military assets is a rudimentary knowledge of chemistry, allowing him to improvise explosives from household items. The grimness of the world from which he comes has left him without any apparent sense of irony or humor.

See *The Terminator*

REGAN, TOM

A principled Irish gangster with an acerbic wit, Tom's the right-hand man to head honcho **Leo**. "The man who walks behind. The man who whispers in his ear." He's a compulsive gambler and drunk. He's also been sleeping with **Verna**, a "twist" that Leo wants to marry. Smart and loyal in his fashion, he engineers an elaborate double cross against the Italians trying to take over town by offering them sniveling **Bernie Bernbaum**, Verna's brother. He believes "Nobody knows anybody. Not that well."

See *Miller's Crossing*

REILLY, IGNATIUS J.

Hugely obese, decked out in a green hunting cap, tweed trousers, and plaid flannel shirt, Ignatius is the self-appointed moral critic of New Orleans. Ignatius, with his dysfunctional pyloric valve, and the denizens of the Quarter exert a strange mutual fascination on each other. He lives with his mother, watches TV all day, and goes to movies at night. He keeps a diary, inspired by Boethius, indicting the twentieth century's lack of theology and geometry. After a series of misadventures, his mother is ready to have him committed. Instead, Ignatius

heads to New York with "girlfriend" Myrna. "Oh, good heavens! What degenerate produced this abortion?"

See *A Confederacy of Dunces,* **John Kennedy Toole**

REINHART, CARLO

A lumbering, strong-armed young American soldier stationed in post–World War II Berlin, Carlo is an innocent in a world perverted by war, depression, and political upheaval. Surrounded by intrigue both high and low, Carlo feels disoriented amid the circus atmosphere of the German capital in flux.

See *Crazy in Berlin* or *Reinhart's Women,* **Thomas Berger**

REISMAN, MAJOR

He is the rugged commander of an outlaw World War II American army special unit fighting Nazis in Europe. Nihilistic personality, despises just about everything that life has to offer. His only real interests are violence, destruction, and male bonding. "We got enough here to blow up the whole world!"

See *The Dirty Dozen*

REMUS, UNCLE

A dignified, and even respected, slave on a Georgia plantation, Remus loves retelling the African American myths and legends of the deep South. His favorite stories feature Brer Rabbit, Brer Fox, Brer B'ar, Brer Wolf, Brer Coon, and friends. He is tall, gray-haired, wears glasses, smokes a pipe, and uses a cane. Remus, over seventy, is superstitious and rheumatic. He considers that he has a personal interest in the welfare of the plantation run by "Miss Sally," whom he raised as a child. For her part, Miss Sally looks to Remus to keep order about the house. He drives the carriage when needed and does many chores—from tanning leather to making shoes to feeding the livestock. At times, he can be overbearing and quarrelsome, both with other slaves and with Miss Sally. But Remus is never grim. He comes to life when telling stories, to the children on the plantation or to reporters from the *Atlanta Constitution*. Remus also loves to sing.

See *Uncle Remus: His Songs and His Sayings,* **Joel Chandler Harris,** and *Song of the South*

Photo courtesy of CBS

Lucy and Ricky Ricardo

RENAULT, LARRY

Larry, a handsome, has-been matinee idol, suffers debilitating depression at the collapse of his life, work, and health. Now middle-aged, he has little left to show for his fame except his name and an abiding bitterness. Alone in a hotel room, he contemplates his life and, through soul-searching, reaches a kind of acceptance of what he must do with what is left of it.

See *Dinner at Eight*

RENKO, ARKADY

The chief homicide investigator for the Moscow police, who's given the case of three bodies found defaced and frozen in Gorky Park. A decent man trapped in an inhuman system, he ignores forces that would rather drop the investigation, which implicates **John Osborne**, a well-connected American fur merchant. He is the son of a heroic Stalinist Soviet general, but a skeptic about Communism. The tall, slovenly, out-of-shape Renko claims—ironically—that he uses "Marxist dialectic" to find answers. He links up with a New York police detective who is looking for his missing brother. Renko's wife, who wants the good things in life ("a television, a washing machine, even new clothes I can wear"), is leaving him for an ambitious party official. Above all a Russian, he finds love but not a new life abroad with the beautiful Irina Asanova.

See *Gorky Park,* Martin Cruz Smith

RENKO, OFFICER ANDY

A hick in the big city, Renko is a country boy turned hardened cop. Sports a southern accent. He's usually struggling to keep his weight down. Rather aggressive, he can take out job and personal frustrations on suspects. His partner, Officer Bobby Hill, must often rein him in. A big motorcycle fan.

See *Hill Street Blues*

REYNOLDS, ALLISON

She's a weird silent type, a complete social outcast among her fellow high school students, living in her own strange world. Out and out rejected by family, she seems to prefer having no friends. Has a bad case of dandruff, though her artistic winter landscape drawings help to compensate for her scalp problems. Dresses in basic black.

See *The Breakfast Club*

RHOADES, STEVE

He used to live next door to **Al** and **Peg Bundy**, when he was married to, and rapturously in love with, **Marcy Rhoades D'Arcy** (he called her Angel Cups; she called him Sugar Tush), until the Bundys destroyed their newlywed bliss. Steve lost his job as a bank loan officer after lending Al $50,000, which he could never repay. After months of unemployment, he left Marcie to become a park ranger at Yosemite. His last known job was as a chauffeur.

See *Married …with Children*

RHODES, DORALEE

A cute, sassy secretary from the South. Sharp wit tends to mask a naive, country-girl heart. Wears figure-hugging short skirts and tight dresses. She has a vivid fantasy life and is tough in the crunch. "I'll turn you from a rooster into a hen!"

See *9 to 5*

RHODES, LONESOME

A vagabond soul with homespun wit and natural charm, now he's vaulted to household-name status by TV masterminds. Doesn't care for corporate politics and manages to swim amidst executive sharks with unlikely aplomb. A shy romantic on the surface with a shark's soul beneath, his earthy appeal makes him an improbable hit with women.

See *A Face in the Crowd*

RICARDO, LUCY

This zany redhead has a knack for getting into mischief. She's a housewife who longs for a career in show business but is forever thwarted by her Cuban-born bandleader husband, **Ricky**. They rent a modest New York apartment at 623 East 68th Street from their good friends and eavesdropping landlords, **Fred** and **Ethel Mertz**. Lucy's always concocting harebrained schemes while Ricky works at the Tropicana nightclub, playing the conga and singing "Babalu." She enlists Ethel to help her carry out these madcap ideas. She's not great with money and pays bills by tossing them into the air and seeing which ones land faceup. Consequently, she's usually short of cash and has to connive to get more money. ("Dear Teller. Be a lamb and don't put this check through until next month.") Her favored alias when she needs one—which happens surprisingly often—is her maiden name, Lucy MacGillicuddy. She's certain in her own mind that the only thing keeping her from stardom is Ricky's intervention, and she's forever crashing his auditions. (Lucy: "What's Ricky got that I haven't got, except a band, a reputation?" Ethel: "Talent!") Though her antics are often a trial and make Ricky burst out in rapid-fire Spanish expostulations, they're a loving couple and are delighted when, after eleven years of marriage, she gives birth to a son, Little Ricky. Motherhood does not stifle her theatrical ambitions, however; she manages to appear in her husband's new Indian show, with the baby strapped to her back, like a papoose.

See *I Love Lucy*

RICARDO, RICKY

Ricky's the long-suffering husband of **Lucy Ricardo**, who often wonders why he married "that crazy redhead." A Cuban-born bandleader who headlines at the Tropicana nightclub, where he plays the bongo drums and sings "Babalu." He's handsome, with sultry looks, a velvety voice, and a heavy accent. Pronounces his wife's name *Looo-cy* and frequently tells her she has a lot of "splainin'" to do. A constant target of Lucy's schemes to get into showbiz, he often discovers these schemes and designs plans to thwart them. His mother-in-law, Mrs. MacGillicuddy, calls him Mickey. Despite all, he really loves Lucy.

See *I Love Lucy*

RICE, ARCHIE

A down-and-out, two-bit British music hall performer, the son of a much-loved old-time song-and-dance man, Archie is now working the circuit along British seaside resorts. Though he has some talent, he lacks what it takes to make the big time. He's abusive in his relationships—especially with regard to his wife—and prone to temper tantrums. He's got a tendency to blight the lives of those close to him but doesn't have a clue as to why he is so unloved. A truly difficult yet oddly compelling person. His signature tune is the ironically titled "Thank God We're Normal."

See *The Entertainer*

RICH, RICHIE

The Richest Kid in the World is Richie Rich, with a weekly allowance of $100,000. He uses his wealth for good causes and for adventures with his dog Dollar, his girlfriend Gloria, and his nasty cousin Reggie Van Dough. Irona the robot maid and Cadbury the Perfect Butler take good care of him.

See *Richie Rich*

RICHARDS, MARY

The ideal single career woman, who works as an associate producer, and later producer, for the Channel 12 "Six O'Clock News" at WJM-TV in Minneapolis. Mary could "turn the world on with her smile." Independent and ambitious, she's also warm, vulnerable, and well-liked by all her colleagues. She moves to Minneapolis after breaking up with a man she had dated for years. Mary never lacks for a date, but is in no hurry to settle down unless the right guy happens along. She's not averse to serious physical relationships in the meantime. Her first place in Minneapolis is a studio apartment in a building owned by her friend **Phyllis "Phyl" Lindstrom**. Her boss is cantankerous **Lou Grant**, who hired Mary as associate producer when the secretarial job she had hoped for turned out to be filled. Mary's best friend is upstairs neighbor **Rhoda Morgenstern**. Mary and most of her coworkers eventually lose their jobs when new management takes over the station. In an effort to raise ratings, the new management fires everyone except for bumbling anchorman **Ted Baxter**, the single biggest reason for the news broadcast's sagging popularity.

See *The Mary Tyler Moore Show*

RIDGEMONT, SUKIE

Monkey-faced, redheaded gossip columnist for the local Eastwick paper, who uses her witchy powers to cast love spells and turn milk into cream. Sukie's pet weimaraner is named Hank. With cauldron colleagues **Jane Smart** and **Alexandra Medford**, she falls under the spell of demonic, dark, wealthy stranger Darryl Van Horne.

See *The Witches of Eastwick,* John Updike

RIEGER, ALEX

What makes him different from all the other cab-drivers who work for New York's Sunshine Cab

Photo courtesy of CBS
Mary Richards

Company is that he's a cabdriver, period. He isn't marking time until he succeeds as an actor, curator, boxer, physicist, or whatever; he's in for the haul. Alex has problems that he has trouble solving, but he's very good at solving the problems of others. The man is one of the all-time great listeners and has a good heart. He'll help out anyone in need, even a creep like **Louie De Palma**.

See *Taxi*

RIGGS, MARTIN

This burned-out L.A. cop has been left neurotic and suicidal after the death of his wife in an auto accident. But Riggs can't bring himself to end his life, and so he channels his rage and self-destructive impulses into his cases. That makes him dangerous, not only to himself but to other cops, like his partner, **Roger Murtaugh**, but a nightmare to criminals! Loves his beach-parked mobile home and his dog. A Vietnam vet, angry, tough, relentless.

See *Lethal Weapon*

RIKER, WILLIAM T.

Iconoclastic and strong-willed, with a deep sense of fun and a strong libido, Will Riker is the first officer (or "Number One") aboard the starship *Enterprise* under **Captain Jean-Luc Picard**. Raised in Alaska, Will had an affair with **Deanna Troi** previous to their serving together on the *Enterprise*. Will likes cooking and jazz and plays the trombone.

See *Star Trek: The Next Generation*

RILEY, CHESTER A.

A great big blundering blowhard with a heart (if you can find it) of low-grade gold, Riley's charm is derived from unremitting stupidity. Working as a riveter, Riley is always broke and offers little material or intellectual satisfaction to his long-suffering wife or their offbeat children. "What a revoltin' development this is!"

See *The Life of Riley*

THE RINGO KID

Under arrest as an escaped convict, he vows that he won't go back to prison until he does a job in Lordsburg. The men who have killed his father and his brother are waiting for him so that they can kill him as well. So, he joins the fated band of travelers on a stagecoach journey. During the journey, he falls in love with Dallas, a prostitute who is escaping her gossip-mongering town and who ultimately causes his demise.

See *Stagecoach*

RINGO, JIMMY

The Fastest Gun in the West, even faster than Wyatt Earp. But he's grown sick of his reputation, sick of the challenges to his manhood he receives in every two-bit town he visits. Now he'd like nothing more than to take off his black hat and live in peaceful anonymity with his wife and son, whom he left years before, in order to protect them. But up-and-coming young guns, eager to make a quick reputation, won't let him be, and it's only a matter of time before he's only the Second Fastest Gun in the West. Or even Third.

See *The Gunfighter*

RINK, JETT

A young ranch hand who flies in the face of the Texas cattle-ranching tradition by drilling for oil on a small plot of inherited land. As money from his oil wells rolls in, rivalry with a powerful rancher intensifies; meanwhile, Jett falls hard for the rancher's wife, who doesn't return the favor. All his money cannot buy him happiness; it only increases his bitterness and feelings of inferiority in the Texas society that has only reluctantly admitted him into its sphere. Prematurely aged by drink, he relishes his role of outsider while bemoaning the fact that he is alone.

See *Giant*, Edna Ferber

LIEUTENANT RIPLEY

Tough, dedicated officer on an intergalactic freighter, *Nostromo*, owned by a gigantic, anonymous industrial complex. She can cope with monstrous crises with whatever is at her disposal: blowtorches, explosives, and imaginative uses of emergency air locks. Has an affinity for cats, protecting innocent victims, and flimsy sleeveless T-shirts.

See *Alien*

RIPLEY, SAILOR

He is a quirky, violent ex-convict with sideburns

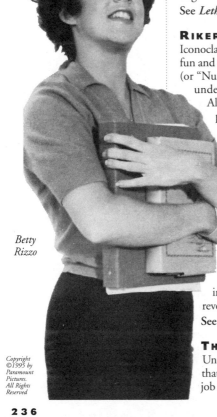

Betty Rizzo

who likes cruising the country in a convertible and having torrid sex with his girl, **Lula Pace Fortune**. He is subject to visions; when he's in trouble, he is visited by the good witch from the Wizard of Oz.

See *Wild at Heart*

RIPPER, GENERAL JACK D.

An unhinged U.S. Air Force general, he's responsible for initiating a preemptive nuclear strike against the USSR. Though he knows military secrets, he's a true-blue patriot and won't reveal them. He thinks that war is too important to be left to politicians. Despises communism with every cell of his being. "I can no longer allow Communist infiltration, Communist indoctrination, Communist subversions and the international Communist conspiracy to sap and impurify all of our precious bodily fluids."

See *Dr. Strangelove: or, How I Learned to Stop Worrying and Love the Bomb*

RITA

Determined, commonsensical British working-class woman of Britain, trying to better herself through education. She knows what she wants once she finds it, and won't let anything stand in the way of getting it. Her current mentor is alcoholic professor **Dr. Frank Bryant**.

See *Educating Rita*

RIVVERS, CAY

A young resident of Reno, Nevada, she has a lusty appetite for life and a definite interest in reserved, about-to-be-divorced eastern schoolteacher **Vivian Bell**. Prefers pants to skirts and is open-minded with regard to her sexuality and relationships.

See *Desert Hearts*

RIZZO, BETTY

As the rebellious leader of the Pink Ladies, Rizzo is one cynical, tough bitch. She's out to rule Rydell High and have all the men at her feet. She takes aim at destroying goody-two-shoes newcomer **Sandy** and her relationship with **Danny Zucco**. "Listen fella, if this is a line, I'm not biting."

See *Grease*

RIZZO, RATSO

A scruffy New York bottom-dweller, he lives in an abandoned, broken-down warehouse so drafty that it aggravates his tuberculosis. Rizzo's given name is Enrico, but everyone calls him Ratso, because of his thin frame and hollowed, pinched face. Ratso, a small-time thief, meets naive country boy **Joe Buck** in a coffee shop and sees the wannabe gigolo as a meal ticket. He offers to become Joe Buck's "manager" and find him clients who'll pay to have sex. His secret dream is to retire to Miami, where it's warm and he can breathe without the racking coughs—anything to get out of the bleak cold that also symbolizes his life.

See *Midnight Cowboy*, James Leo Herlihy

ROARK, HOWARD

This genius architect would rather starve than compromise his ideals. He's always been a boat-rocker, having been expelled from Stanton Institute of Technology because his projects were judged insane. He's always been sure of himself, and he's willing to pay the price of originality, stating, "A building has its own integrity, just like a man." When a housing project he designed anonymously is altered, he blows it up with the assistance of the equally principled **Dominique Francon**. His crowning achievement is the Wynand Building, the tallest structure in the world.

See *The Fountainhead*, Ayn Rand

MR. ROARKE

A suave, sophisticated man, darkly handsome, with more than a touch of mystery about him. Helped by **Tattoo**, he runs Fantasy Island, a place where people come to live out their dreams. Mr. Roarke invariably manages to send his clients home with an important lesson about ethics and life under their belts. "Welcome to Fantasy Island."

See *Fantasy Island*

ROBERTS, LIEUTENANT DOUG

It's World War II, and despite being loved and admired by the crew of the USS *Reluctant*, Roberts wants to get off the cargo vessel and into some real fighting. "The Bucket" has become a cage to him, and he's constantly at war with the authoritarian **Captain Morton** over the latter's harsh treatment of the crew. "Take it out on me but not on the men." He is the first (and only) winner of the Order of the Palm by the crew of

Photo courtesy of The National Broadcasting Company, Inc.

Chester A. Riley

the *Reluctant* for throwing the captain's beloved palm tree overboard.
See *Mister Roberts*

ROBIN, CHRISTOPHER
A blond young boy in a sailor suit whose animal toys provide fun and adventure. Christopher Robin is mature beyond his years and is always getting his stuffed friends—especially Winnie the Pooh—out of trouble. He is patient, kind, thoughtful, and better behaved than most boys his age.
See *Winnie the Pooh*, A. A. Milne

ROBINSON, JERRY
This swinging-single orthodontist shares a secretary with **Dr. Robert Hartley** in the Rampo Medical Arts Building in Chicago. He fancies himself a real smoothie, but, in his geeky dentist's smock, he doesn't quite come off in the role. He maintains a playful love-hate banter with his secretary, **Carol Kester**. His middle name is Merle.
See *The Bob Newhart Show*

ROBINSON, JUDY
She is a pretty eldest daughter, who finds that being lost in space is made bearable by the presence of dreamy **Major Donald West**, the object of her lust. Still in her teens, she's a little young to begin anything serious, especially under the watchful eyes of her parents. But the Alpha Centauri star system seems to mature people quickly, and there's a future ahead for her and Don, as long as they're both lost in space.
See *Lost in Space*

ROBINSON, MAUREEN
A devoted space-age mother and wife. She's just doing the best she can to keep peace in her family and among *Jupiter II*'s crew members as they all drift aimlessly from one planet to another. Maureen tries to guide daughter **Judy** through her teenage years and her younger kids through adolescence. She's responsible for day-to-day details, including laundering their one-piece outfits and cooking their space-age meals.
See *Lost in Space*

ROBINSON, MONA
Energetic, hip grandmother. Mona's unconvention-al, a bit promiscuous, and enjoys displaying her still-good body. She is much more outgoing and loose than her daughter, **Angela Bower**, and often attempts to get Angela to be more uninhibited. She enjoys flirting with Angela's housekeeper, **Tony Micelli**, but would love to see Angela and Tony get together.
See *Who's the Boss?*

MRS. ROBINSON
An alcoholic woman trapped in a sexless marriage, she turns to her neighbors' college-age son, **Benjamin Braddock**, for comfort. She is a forceful woman and doesn't believe in subtlety as a technique in seduction. Rather, Mrs. R. is very aware of her sexuality and can radiate it at will. She is a very sexy woman—she favors heavily mascaraed eyes and has a full, sensuous mouth. Although she is self-assured and determined, she is not in search of a soulmate or a meaningful relationship, but only a sex partner. When she's crossed or thwarted, she can be mean and vindictive, even if it costs the happiness of her daughter, Elaine.
See *The Graduate*

ROBINSON, PENNY
This precocious little girl is often the first member of her family to recognize the hard truths of their daily lives, as they drift through outer space. She alone can and will ask the big questions the others avoid. Occasionally, she wanders off and is imperiled by some outlandish monster but is always saved by brother **Will** or one of the adults. She looks cute in the junior version of the women's one-piece space outfit. Has as big a crush on **Don West** as does sister **Judy**.
See *Lost in Space*

ROBINSON, PROFESSOR JOHN
A concerned, frustrated father and scientist. When his whole family is lost in space, he does all he can to try and find his way back home. That has become the primary occupation of John Robinson, a calm, cool, and brilliant man who has brought his family to the brink of the unknown, where they seem to be stuck. He tries not to lose his self-control when push comes to shove with **Dr. Zachary Smith**. Solves disputes and monitors activities of three kids, a robot, and

crew members aboard the spaceship *Jupiter II*.
See *Lost in Space*

ROBINSON, WILL

An inquisitive, intelligent boy, lonely Will spends his days exploring whatever planet *Jupiter II* has landed on in its quest for a way back home from chartless outer space. His exploration often leads to dangerous meetings with monsters and human-eating plants. Often Will is saved by the group's trusty robot and occasionally even by the evil **Dr. Smith**.
See *Lost in Space*

ROCCO, JOHNNY

Stocky, belligerent crime figure, who operated a considerable underworld fiefdom until being deported to Cuba. Crude, lewd, and ultimately cowardly, he refers to himself in both first and third persons. Rocco is brash and impetuous and can be manipulated by playing to his vanity. Wears a pinky ring on his left hand. Ultimately, he's killed by **Frank McCloud**.
See *Key Largo*

DR. ROCK

Big, friendly guy, always looking for a good time—a party on wheels. The doc convinces his buddy **Richard Boyle**, a journalist, to take a trip with him to El Salvador—in Rock's book, a land of dirt-cheap booze and exotically beautiful women. What they find is a whole other story.
See *Salvador*

ROCKFORD, JIM

He's an ex-con, and he's a private investigator, and he's very sharp. While he may not be the youngest or fastest P.I., Jim is nonetheless one of the smartest and wryest, with a world-weary "seen it all" outlook and cunning and humor enough to get him out of most tight spots. Although he'll stretch the truth on a job (using false IDs, for instance), he's actually got integrity to spare, is loyal to the end, and champions the underdog. (He has a healthy disrespect for authority.) Working out of a mobile home near Malibu beach, he charges $200 a day, plus expenses, often solving cases that have been officially "closed"; he knows the value of new evidence, since that's what got him out of jail, when he did time on a bum rap. He loves to fish with his dad, **Rocky**,

and one of his best friends is **Dennis Becker** of the LAPD. Some people call him Jimbo.
See *The Rockford Files*

ROCKFORD, JOSEPH "ROCKY"

This aging, retired trucker has got an unabashed affection for his middle-aged son, P.I. **Jim Rockford**. He lives near Jim in L.A., loves to go fishing off the piers, and is forever urging Jim to find a good woman, settle down, and get out of the investigation business. He's down-to-earth and loved by his son, even though he has a tendency to meddle.
See *The Rockford Files*

RODEATANSKY, MAX

After seeing his partner, the Goose, burned beyond recognition by a ruthless gang of motorcyclists, Max quits the Bronze, the police force that patrols Australia's highways. He tries to escape from the prevailing violence with his wife and child but is hunted down by the same gang. Following the murder of his baby and wife, he is reborn as "Mad" Max. In that role, he roams about in a souped-up police car, hunting the thugs down, one at a time. "I'm scared. It's a rat circus out there and I'm beginning to enjoy it."
See *Mad Max*

RODGERS, LYLE

An amazingly bad singer-songwriter, Rodgers, with equally inept partner **Chuck Clarke,** accepts a gig in Morocco at the urging of their down-and-out agent. The team soon ends up the target of both sides of a political war. "It takes a lot of nerve to have nothing at your age."
See *Ishtar*

ROGERS, BOND

Bond Rogers is a young idealist with a penchant for hero worship. Every time daydreams catch him up, his mother is there to prick his balloon. Rogers jumps from one hero to another, like a frog jumps from one lily pad to another, until he finally learns that heroes are just men, too.
See *The Shootist*

ROGERS, BUCK

A NASA astronaut, Captain Buck Rogers is thrown

into suspended animation when a freak accident befalls his deep-space probe in 1987. Awakening in 2491, Buck finds the world a wholly different place, and he must acclimate to it while working to save it from various evil factions. Buck is classically American, honest and trustworthy and brave. He is often aided by **Wilma Deering** and the Earth Defense Directorate for which she works.

See *Buck Rogers* and *Buck Rogers in the 25th Century*

ROGERS, MILDRED

This tarty, foul-mouthed London waitress flirts with all of the men, but takes particular pleasure in humiliating and taking advantage of sensitive medical student **Philip Carey**. She makes public fun of him and cruelly mocks his compassionate nature. His obsession with her amuses her. She makes a date to go out with him and breaks it to go out with a crude salesman. It gives her pleasure to manipulate people in general and Philip in particular. With her slouched posture and flimsy, clinging dresses, she looks like someone who works the street rather than in a restaurant. Mildred's loose behavior eventually backfires when she becomes pregnant and must go to Philip and ask for his help. Her situation, however, doesn't mitigate her cruel manner, and she continues to betray him without compunction. Until her very unpleasant end, Mildred is a hard-hearted, remorseless woman whose unkind and selfish nature continue to fascinate Philip.

See *Of Human Bondage,* **Somerset Maugham**

ROGERS, SALLY

Man-hunting, aging spinster, Sally is a solidly built, aggressive career woman who's "the best in the business" of comedy writing. She cowrites *The Alan Brady Show* with **Rob Petrie** and **Buddy Sorrell** and also types the scripts. Though she complains about her love life, she has a steady relationship with dull Herman Glimpshire. Sally lives with her cat, Mr. Henderson. Often quotes her dear Aunt Agnes. Has stand-up comic routine with partner Buddy and sings solos in a voice like Durante.

See *The Dick Van Dyke Show*

ROJACK, STEPHEN

Plagued with self-doubts, this onetime war hero and current TV personality strangles his taunting, estranged wife and fakes her suicide. He sees this murder, as well as other lurid adventures, as steps not toward punishment but toward regeneration. "I was weary with a most honorable fatigue, and my flesh seemed new. I had not felt so nice since I was twelve….She was dead, indeed she was dead."

See *An American Dream,* **Norman Mailer**

ROLFE, HANS

A German lawyer drafted to defend four Nazi judges accused of war crimes. With flinty firmness, Rolfe deflects the American prosecutor's bludgeoning attacks on his clients' character. To win this battle, he must remain stubbornly resistant to moral influence, but, in the end, the contest is decided by even less moral politics outside the courtroom.

See *Judgment at Nuremberg*

ROMA, RICKY

The sharpest, saltiest, and most ruthless salesman in a Chicago real-estate office, Roma treats you like an old buddy while he's selling you worthless swamp land. So it's no wonder he wins an office contest in which the agent who sells the most lucrative land gets a Cadillac, the runner-up a set of steak knives, and the losers get fired. To win the contest he induces a naive client into buying land at Glengarry Glen Ross, a dubious Florida property. Despite maintaining a warm relationship with **Shelley Levene**, the underachiever in the office, his aggressiveness and ambition ultimately produce in him a profound moral bankruptcy. Motto: "Do those things which seem correct to one today."

See *Glengarry Glen Ross,* **David Mamet**

THE ROMANO FAMILY

Spunky, redheaded, dungaree-clad Ann is the young mom of two girls, Julie and Barbara. After divorcing their father, Ed Cooper, Ann takes back her maiden name—Romano—and strikes out for liberated women everywhere. She gets a job at Conners and Davenport advertising, moves with the girls to an apartment in Indianapolis (where the building super, Dwayne Schneider, becomes their unofficial guardian), and begins dating her divorce lawyer, a younger man named David Kane. After she and David break up, Ann is happily single for years, until she meets and for a while romances her partner in an ad firm, Nick Handris. Julie is the rebel of the two girls; she runs away, tells people she's on the pill, and basically acts out. As she gets older, she marries quirky Max Horvath—who calls Ann "Shortie"—and they have a daughter, Annie. Julie can't shoulder the responsibility, though, and leaves the family. Barbara, a basketball-playing tomboy, grows up to be the apple of her mother's eye: beautiful, charming, and fun. She goes to college for a while but then works at a travel agency. She marries Mark Royer, a handsome young dentist. His father, Sam, a smart, charming architect, is the one who finally gets Ann to remarry.

See *One Day at a Time*

ROMMELY, SISSY

Promiscuous Brooklyn woman who believes in the power of happiness through sexual satisfaction. Sister to **Katie Nolan**. Married to Steve and mother to two children—a son and adopted daughter. Freely offers domestic advice, even though the stability of her own situation leaves something to be desired.

See *A Tree Grows in Brooklyn*

ROSE

She is a lithe, libidinous blonde who's taken in by the Hillyers, a traditional southern family. Rose is unable to repress her sexuality: she flirts with **Daddy Hillyer** without even realizing it; she invites Daddy Hillyer's on-the-cusp-of-adolescence son into her bed, introducing him to his first sexual excitement; and she has an affair with a local boy. As a result, she threatens the family's respectability, especially outraging the middle-aged, seemingly postmenopausal Mrs. Hillyer. But her guileless sexiness charms the family's male members, including Daddy Hillyer; they can't help but love her, even as they lust after her.

See *Rambling Rose*

ROSE, DANNY

Legendary figure at Carnegie Delicatessen, where a sandwich is named in his honor. Former Catskills comic, now agent to a number of two-bit novelty performers including a one-legged tap dancer, a stuttering ventriloquist, and a horde of bird acts, balloon folders, singers, jugglers, and other minor, though unusual entertainers. Biggest name in his fold is singer **Lou Canova**. Has a knack for bringing protégés to the brink of fame, whereupon they dump him for better management. Believes sincerely (and often erroneously) in the talents of each and every one of his clients and treats them like family. Invented hand-to-hand microphone toss used by nightclub comics everywhere.

See *Broadway Danny Rose*

ROSE OF SHARON

The newly married and pregnant oldest daughter of the **Joad** family. "Rosaharn's" husband deserts her after the family reaches California, and the hardships she's lived with result in the baby's being stillborn. She then saves a starving man with her breast milk.

See *The Grapes of Wrath*, John Steinbeck

ROSENCRANTZ

All duded up as elegant Elizabethan gentlemen, but seemingly with no place to go, Rosencrantz and his sidekick **Guildenstern** are constantly confused as to their roles in the play *Hamlet*. They wait for someone to tell them what to do, and pass the time with witty word games. Unlike his comrade, Rosencrantz is content with having no past and an uncertain future. He attempts to comfort Guildenstern, who grows increasingly anxious about their lack of identity and purpose. But Rosencrantz's naiveté prevents him from understanding the reason for Guildenstern's gloom or his own sense of impending doom.

See *Rosencrantz and Guildenstern Are Dead*, Tom Stoppard

ROSENTHAL, JACK

He's a low-level mob enforcer, doubling as an occasional hit man if the situation calls for it. Not wholly without scruples and efficient at his work. Loyal to brother **Judah Rosenthal** despite Jack's reputation as the black sheep of the Rosenthal family.

See *Crimes and Misdemeanors*

ROSENTHAL, JUDAH

Philandering optometrist, cheating on wife with unstable flight attendant **Dolores Paley**. Excellent at profession and regarded as a pillar of the community. Troubled by disgraceful direction his private life is going, willing to do anything—or have it done, at least—to get out of his sticky situation. Brother of **Jack Rosenthal**.

See Crimes and Misdemeanors

ROSEWOOD, DETECTIVE BILLY
Nice-guy undercover cop on Beverly Hills police force. Loves his job but hates the official stuffy demeanor maintained throughout the department. Known to rebel in quiet, subtle ways after arrival of renegade Detroit cop **Axel Foley**.

See Beverly Hills Cop

ROSIE
Learned early in life that it pays to be prepared. Became a waitress in a diner and earns the respect of all her customers by always having an absorbent paper towel around just when it's needed. "Bounty—the quicker picker-upper!"

See Bounty

ROSS, DR. DOUGLAS
Dr. Ross, a handsome pediatric resident at County General Hospital in Chicago, is known for his womanizing and drinking binges, but lately, he is showing signs of yearning for monogamy and sobriety. He used to date **Carol Hathaway**, the hospital's lovely head nurse. Has a young son he's never met. A champion of children, Dr. Ross has a wonderful bedside manner and puppy-dog brown eyes.

See ER

ROSSI, JOE
He's an aggressive, hustling investigative reporter who works under **Lou Grant** at the *Los Angeles Tribune*. Zealous in pursuit of a story, Rossi sometimes has to convince boss **Lou Grant** that his methods are acceptable or that the story is worth pursuing. Sometimes sees eye-to-eye, sometimes just competes with fellow reporter **Billie Newman**. Looks a little like Carl Bernstein.

See Lou Grant

ROTH, GABE
Although thoughtful and sensitive, Gabe's weakness is, as he puts it, "kamikaze women." He recently broke this pattern when he and his wife **Judy Roth** divorced, and he gave up on the idea of a tryst with one of his students. An acclaimed novelist, Roth teaches fiction writing at a New York university and is presently working on his first new novel in years. He describes his social circumstances: "I'm out of the race. I don't want to get involved with anyone, I don't want to hurt anyone, I don't want to get hurt."

See Husbands and Wives

ROTH, JUDY
She has a black belt in passive/aggressive behavior, and claims she's "never angry." She left her husband of five years for **Gabe Roth**, taking with her the daughter from that marriage, and hoping to have another child with Gabe. Judy's marriage to Gabe falls apart about the same time that her good friend Sally gets back together with her husband, Jack. "Am I cold in bed? But I am inhibited, right?"

See Husbands and Wives

ROTH, TOM
A nine-to-five commuter—with a smoldering secret. His daily uniform is a gray flannel suit. He lives with his ambitious wife, Betsy, and three kids in a dumpy little house in Connecticut; on the wall is a crack in the shape of a question mark. Tom served in World War II as a paratrooper, reaching the rank of captain. During the war, he killed seventeen men he "was actually looking at," cut a German soldier's throat for his coat, and blew up his best friend with a hand grenade (accidentally). Unbeknownst to Betsy, he also fathered a child with a beautiful Italian girl, Maria. This mild-mannered fellow attempts to boost his modest income by applying for a job with a Madison Avenue public relations firm; but he refuses to write his autobiography and finishes the sentence "The most significant thing about me is…" with the words "I would probably do a good job." Tempted to play it safe with his new boss, millionaire **Ralph Hopkins**, he is conflicted when Betsy pushes him not to become just another yes-man. He sums up his generation's life experience: "One day a man is catching the 8:26 and then suddenly he's killing people. Then a few weeks later he's catching the 8:26 again."

See The Man in the Gray Flannel Suit, Sloan Wilson

ROUNDY, GEORGE
A top Beverly Hills hairdresser, he's trying to focus

on his career. George is very popular with wealthy female customers because of his sensuous hair-styling method and good looks. This means that what starts in the salon often ends in the bedroom. Now he plans to put all that fun behind him, open his own shop, and settle down with his girlfriend, Jill. "Want me to do your hair?"
See *Shampoo*

RUDKUS, JURGIS
A Lithuanian immigrant in Chicago. He's thankful to be working for peanuts in the stockyards, but his luck turns, and he undergoes a terrible series of hardships. His wife becomes a prostitute; he drinks too much; he loses jobs because of injury; he spends time in jail after attacking evil capitalists; his relatives die; he ends up on the streets, begging. Finally, when he's hit rock bottom, he finds new hope in the promise of socialism.
See *The Jungle,* Upton Sinclair

RUSK, ROBERT
A likable man-about-town type—a real people person. He's flirtatious with women and good in business. He remains friendly to **Richard Blaney**, despite Blaney's possible involvement in murder. Though he wears classy neckties, he has a habit of misplacing them in unlikely spots. Has the same trouble with stickpins. "Lovely! Lovely!"
See *Frenzy*

RUSSELL, KITTY
She calls the Long Branch Saloon her home, and she runs her business with grace and style. She's as honest as she is beautiful, and many a cowboy just off the range falls in love with her flashing eyes and beauty spot. But her heart seems to belong to the one man she can't have, **Marshal Matt Dillon**. Neither of them ever gets around to talking of how they feel about each other, but it's pretty darn obvious.
See *Gunsmoke*

RUSSO, BLOSSOM
With her colorful, offbeat wardrobe—think lots of floppy hats—Blossom is hardly a typical teenager, although that's surely what she longs to be. Awfully smart and extremely mature for her age, she's often the most adult member of her household, which includes her divorced dad and two brothers,

Anthony and **Joey**. A terrific dancer, Blossom has energy to spare. Somewhat resents her mother, a singer who travels the world. Her best friend and frequent partner in crime is named **Six**; longtime boyfriend is Vinnie.
See *Blossom*

RUSSO, CONNIE
The obsessively jealous wife of one of Long Island's Mafia clans, she'll do whatever it takes to cling to her privileged status and control her womanizing husband, **Tony Russo**. "You can call me a ball-buster, but it's just the way I am."
See *Married to the Mob*

RUSSO, JOEY
Not exactly the brightest light on the block, Joey is the good-natured brother of **Blossom** and Anthony Russo. Considering himself great with women, he must avoid the longing looks of Blossom's best friend, **Six**. Hopes to play professional baseball. "Whoa."
See *Blossom*

RUSSO, TONY "THE TIGER"
Russo is the boss of one of Long Island's leading mob syndicates, intimidating, suave, and a terrific shot. He's also a womanizer who pursues **Angela de Marco**, the widow of former mob hit man Frank de Marco. The only person in the world that he's scared of is his wife, **Connie Russo**. He loves to eat at Burger World. "Some clown just tried to kill me!"
See *Married to the Mob*

RUTLAND, MARK
This suave young businessman is fascinated by a gorgeous blond employee, **Marnie Edgar**. When she robs him and bolts, he tracks her down and persuades her to marry him. But it's not exactly a marriage made in heaven; Marnie suffers from industrial-strength sexual repression and feels repulsion toward men, rooted in past experiences which she's managed to repress for many years. Rutland sets out to help her conquer her problem.
See *Marnie*

RYAN, JACK
A CIA agent who is right when everyone else is

wrong, Jack Ryan is a handsome but down-to-earth intelligence hack suddenly caught in a cat-and-mouse game of nuclear brinkmanship. Jack's job is to convince the entire United States military that a renegade Soviet submarine captain is trying to defect, not launch a one-man nuclear assault on New York and Washington. Time is of the essence, however, because the Pentagon is itching to blow the Red October out of the water. A desk-bound bureaucrat until now, Jack can't believe he's in the middle of a massive field exercise in which the fate of the entire world is at stake.

See *The Hunt for Red October,* Tom Clancy

SABICH, BARBARA
Jealous housewife and eternal doctoral candidate who's handy with a crowbar. A whiz at math, she has a general aversion to most human beings. Cynical. Suspicious. While waiting for inspiration on her dissertation, she reads library books on arcane subjects. A "ferocious intellect." Known to throw things when angry. Mother of one. Miserably married to cheating husband **Rusty Sabich**, she cleverly frames him for his mistress **Carolyn Polhemus**'s murder.

See *Presumed Innocent,* Scott Turow

SABICH, RUSTY
Innocent chief deputy prosecutor accused of murder. "A nonpolitical guy." Stable. Mature. Somebody everyone can depend on. His best friend is a cop with whom he has nothing in common. Feels an "unspeakable sorrow" when his beautiful mistress and colleague, **Carolyn Polhemus**, is raped and murdered. Brooding, passionate, and madly obsessed with the dead woman, he gets a perverse pleasure when he is assigned to head the investigation. Born an only child. Lonely and alone. Sympathetic to his frustrated wife, **Barbara Sabich**'s, disappointment, he feels powerless to do anything about it. "In me, some human commodity is lacking. And we can only be who we can be." Remarkably understanding when he discovers Barbara is one who framed him and committed the perfect crime.

See *Presumed Innocent,* Scott Turow

SACHS, MICKEY
First husband of **Hannah,** manic Jewish producer of a Saturday late-night comedy sketch show. Though highly successful in his stressful life, Mickey nevertheless feels there's something desperately wrong. Symptoms: hypochondria, loss of faith. Remedies: brain scan, Catholicism. "I want to believe in God. I'm willing to do anything. I'll dye Easter eggs if it helps."

See *Hannah and Her Sisters*

SAKNUSSEMM, ARNE
A 16th-century Icelandic savant, naturalist, alchemist, and traveler whose courage matches his genius. Saknussemm is the first to discover a route to the center of the Earth. Following his discovery, he is persecuted for heresy. His name is cleared when **Otto Lidenbrock** successfully follows his path into the Earth.

See *Journey to the Center of the Earth,* Jules Verne

SAL
Italian American resident of Bensonhurst, Brooklyn. He hangs on to Sal's Famous Pizzeria in Bed-Sty, despite misgivings of his sons about the neighborhood. Has love-hate relationship with his pizza deliverer **Mookie,** complicated by a secret crush on Mookie's sister, Jade. Sal is proud of his heritage and has pictures of famous Italian Americans on the walls of his establishment. Though Sal has certain prejudices toward his African American clientele, he still enjoys working in the Bed-Sty area. "Extra cheese is two dollars!"

See *Do the Right Thing*

SAL
Silent, moody criminal partner of bank robber **Sonny.** Not very bright, he believes Montana is overseas. He's never been on an airplane and does not relish the idea of his first flight. Heterosexual and doesn't like being labeled gay by association. There's a dangerous psychotic edge bubbling beneath his quiet exterior.

See *Dog Day Afternoon*

SALLY
Divorced Atlantic City resident trying to better her position in life. Studying to become a casino card dealer. Bathes her skin with fresh lemon juice every night to cover the fishy smells that envelop her at

work (at a shellfish bar). Tries to help disturbed sister and punk brother-in-law, though this is a difficult task. Lives in same apartment complex as **Lou**. Enjoys listening to opera.

See *Atlantic City*

SAM THE LION

A legendary figure in the sleepy little town of Thalia on the dirt plains of north central Texas, Sam the Lion owns and operates the only forms of public entertainment in town: the pool hall and the movie theater. He also serves as the surrogate father for love-starved teenagers, including **Sonny Crawford** and Billy, a retarded boy to whom he bequeaths the theater.

See *The Last Picture Show*, Larry McMurtry

SAMMLER, ARTUR

An elderly Polish Jewish refugee of intellectual inclination who spends his time observing with bewilderment and disdain his adopted hometown New York City and its oddball residents. When not reading in the library, Sammler ruminates on the horrible events of his life during World War II or wanders the streets, astonished by the nihilism and hypersexuality of modern America.

See *Mr. Sammler's Planet*, Saul Bellow

SANDERS, STEVE

Blond and athletic, any of Steve's actual positive qualities are overshadowed by his egotism. Always chasing after girls, he used to date **Kelly Taylor**. Thinks of himself as a real ladies' man but is actually kind of a dork. Pledges a fraternity at California University with far too much enthusiasm. He's adopted.

See *Beverly Hills 90210*

SANDY

A sweet, blond, bland transfer student to Rydell High from Australia, Sandy puts singing, dancing, and boys far ahead of school. Her romantic relationship with **Danny Zucco** is constantly strained until she decides to change into the type of woman he is used to.

See *Grease*

SANFORD, FRED

Crotchety and misanthropic senior citizen Fred Sanford runs a Los Angeles junkyard with his beloved son, **Lamont Sanford**. Fred can be quick-witted and amusing, but that's only on occasion. His usual demeanor is ornery and nasty to everyone around him, including his son. His particular target is sister-in-law Esther, with whom he has a continually fractious relationship. He does seem to like Donna Harris, a nurse, although he never makes good on his promise to marry her. A widower, Fred has a controlling hold on his pride and joy, Lamont; whenever Lamont threatens to move on, Fred fakes a heart attack and screams for his dead wife: "I'm coming, Elizabeth, I'm coming!"

See *Sanford and Son*

SANFORD, LAMONT

Smart and energetic, he dreams of a better career—and could surely find one—but the upstanding son of **Fred Sanford** stays on at the family-run junkyard for the love of his crotchety dad. He gets engaged to Janet, a single mother.

See *Sanford and Son*

SANTIAGO

He is an elderly Cuban fisherman and widower. Santiago loves the New York Yankees and, above all, the great DiMaggio. With advancing age, he feels his life and energy slipping away and yearns for the virile potency he felt as a younger man. Even though he hasn't landed a fish in more than eighty days, he puts to sea at the urging of the little boy who is his only real friend. This time, in an effort to change his fortune, he goes far out at sea, where, to his delight, he hooks the biggest marlin he's ever seen. There ensues an epic battle, as Santiago desperately wants one last great triumph over the forces of age and time. First, he must fight the great fish, and then he must fight hordes of ravenous sharks for possession of his catch, as he tries to get the marlin back to shore intact. But nature has no respect for age.

See *The Old Man and the Sea*, Ernest Hemingway

SARUMAN THE WHITE

Greatest of the Istari, a council of wizards, Saruman is corrupted by *hubris* and seduced by his own ambition into an alliance with **Sauron**. He is thereupon succeeded as leader of the Istari by **Gandalf**.

Sandy

Fred Sanford

His fortress is the tower of Orthanc, in the fortress of Isengard.
See *The Lord of the Rings*, J. R. R. Tolkien

SATTLER, ELLIE

She's a paleobotanist and studies prehistoric flora. Men tend to underestimate her intellect, fooled by her good looks, but they soon get set straight. She works in the badlands of Montana with **Alan Grant**, noted paleontologist, with whom she's also romantically involved. Sattler is a member of a team of scientists gathered by **John Hammond** to examine Jurassic Park, a new theme park that contains living, cloned dinosaurs.
See *Jurassic Park,* Michael Crichton

SAUNDERS, CLARISSA

The feisty, Washington-wise secretary to corrupt senator **Joseph Paine**. Clarissa is jaded and cynical and also fed up with being a "secretary to a leader of little squirts." When new young senator **Jefferson Smith** comes to town, she's amazed, then charmed by his naiveté. She's attractive and sharp-tongued and will take a drink or two. Clarissa winds up shedding some cynicism and falling in love with Smith, and masterminding his one-man filibuster.
See *Mr. Smith Goes to Washington*

SAUNDERS, DANNY

The brilliant son of a Hasidic rabbi, Danny is expected to take his father's place as spiritual leader of their sect in Brooklyn. Tall and chiseled, he wears the beard, earlocks, and dark suit of the Hasidim, but Danny's penchant for a different kind of study leads him to pursue a Ph.D. in psychology rather than accede to his father's wishes.
See *The Chosen,* Chaim Potok

SAURON

An age-old being whose evil spirit seeks to enslave Middle-earth in the Third Age. The key to his success is possession of the One Ring of Power, for which he puts forth all his efforts from his seat of power in Mordor. His desire to find and obtain the One Ring precipitates the War of the Ring.
See *The Lord of the Rings,* J. R. R. Tolkien

SAVOY, ANNIE

Worshiper at the Church of Baseball. Known for choosing one player per season for coaching in field athletics and bedroom gymnastics. This year, her choice is young pitcher **Ebby Calvin "Nuke" LaLoosh**, though she's also intrigued by veteran catcher **Crash Davis**. Has candle-encrusted shrine in her home dedicated to late Yankee catcher Thurman Munson. "Oh my…"
See *Bull Durham*

SAWYER, LOUISE

A woman who's been around the block a few times. Tough and cynical, she still possesses a smoldering sexiness. In a relationship with a guy who doesn't want to commit. When her friend **Thelma Dickinson** is attacked in a small town bar's parking lot, she shoots the would-be rapist, making her and Thelma criminals. Fleeing west in a convertible, they discover that they love the freedom of the open road, that they never want to go back to their old, dead-end lives. It's a blast: they rob convenience stores, booze it up, and lock a macho highway patrolman in his own trunk. But while Thelma has nothing but fun as a fugitive, the jaded Louise is too smart for that—she knows their adventure will come to a painful end. Ultimately, she and Thelma choose to go out on their own terms, driving off a cliff rather than going to jail.
See *Thelma and Louise*

SAWYER, VERONICA

When her dream of killing off her self-centered, bitchy high school friends starts becoming a reality, thanks to boyfriend **J.D.**, Sawyer begins to have second thoughts. Maybe mass murder isn't all it's cracked up to be. "Dear Diary, I need to kill and you have to believe it's for more than just selfish reasons."
See *Heathers*

SAYER, ROSE

The sister of missionary Reverend Samuel Sayer, Rose is a prim, deeply moralistic woman who is dead set against the consumption of alcohol and tobacco as well as vice in every other form. But she's tough and clever; when faced with difficulties that would faze ordinary individuals, Rose has no problem devising schemes to meet crises and doesn't hesitate to place herself (and any companions) into potentially dangerous situations. Indeed, despite her proper exterior, Rose is a rugged individual whose adamant belief in life and her God ultimately affects those who have the opportunity to cross paths with her. She has a real knack for turning the intellectual tables on anyone who disagrees with her uncompromising moral strictures.

See *The African Queen*

SCARAMANGA

The world's highest-paid assassin, Scaramanga turned to crime as a boy after shooting a policeman who killed a pet elephant. Now he commands a fee of a million dollars per killing. His weapon of choice is a golden pistol, which he assembles from a cigarette case, a lighter, a pen, and a cuff link. He also possesses a unique anatomical feature: a third nipple. But that didn't make him turn bad; it was that elephant.

See *The Man with the Golden Gun*

SCHEARL, DAVID

The only child in a Jewish immigrant family, David dreads his father's violent outbursts and clings to his protective mother. But the dominant neurosis in his life is a disabling fear of the dark, engendered and fostered by the cloistered confines of grim New York tenements. David's resulting attraction to light leads him to a near deadly encounter with the third rail of a train track.

See *Call It Sleep*, Henry Roth

SCHULTZ, SERGEANT HANS

He's a bumbling, overweight World War II German soldier—with a heart of gold. Schultz likes **Colonel Hogan** and the other prisoners he's supposed to guard at Stalag 13, so much so that he repeatedly allows himself to be charmed into doing things that help Hogan's secret spy ring. Protects himself—and Hogan—from his boss, **Colonel Klink**, by saying, "I know nussink!"

See *Hogan's Heroes*

SCISSORHANDS, EDWARD

Delicate, sensitive, leather-clad artificial boy created by an ingenious but all-too-mortal professor. Sadly, Edward is left unfinished, with scissors where the great majority of people have fingers. Often pokes himself with these razor-sharp items, which leave many cuts and scars on his pale, sensitive features. Striving to overcome his limitations, he's become an ace at creating ice sculptures and trimming bushes. Currently living with friendly Avon Lady and her family.

See *Edward Scissorhands*

SCOTT, JAMES MATTOON

This messianic Air Force general and Chairman of the Joint Chiefs of Staff reacts to the ratification of an unpopular nuclear disarmament treaty with the USSR by attempting the military takeover of the U.S. government, in order to unseat President **Jordan Lyman** and take his place as the Man in Control. Scott's arrogance is not quite balanced by his bravery; he has received the Congressional Medal of Honor. But that doesn't mean he's a great guy.

See *Seven Days in May*

SCOTT, MONTGOMERY

As chief engineer aboard the starship *Enterprise,* "Scotty" keeps the Federation's flagship running during the fiercest galactic battles, during encounters with awesome aliens, even an entity that takes over the soul of the woman he loves. Forever pushing the ship beyond its capabilities, Scotty's an invaluable member of the crew, and his Scottish brogue makes even his engineer's technobabble sound dramatic.

See *Star Trek*

MR. SCRATCH

Ever-smiling, crafty Beelzebub. Deals in souls, preferring the seven-year plan when inking a contract. Owns **Jabez Stone** for eternity in bargain-basement agreement. Also has knack for rigging juries. Not overly fond of attorney Daniel Webster.

See *The Devil and Daniel Webster*

SCRIVELLO, ORIN

Sadistic psychopath who finds his true calling as a dentist. He is able to attract a clientele that finds his psychopathic tendencies highly stimulating. Scrivello is a believer in laughing gas—used primarily on himself, to spur his dental depravity. He has a long history of cruelty to animals as well as humans. Scrivello is not entirely blameless for his temperament—his mother steered him away from teaching and the clergy toward dentistry, a profession in which, she felt,

TOO YOUNG TO DIE

his proclivities would be best fulfilled. Involved with his oral hygienist, **Audrey**, whom he physically abuses, he prefers the title of "Dr." to any other name. Mechanically adept, Scrivello builds a special gas-dispensing helmet, which eventually proves to be his downfall. He who lives by nitrous oxide…

See *Little Shop of Horrors*

SCULLY, DANA

Dedicated young FBI agent with soft red hair, creamy-soft skin, and a closetful of tight sweaters that J. Edgar Hoover would have envied. She partners with agent **Fox Mulder** to investigate "X" files—unexplainable phenomena—and for whom she has something of an unprofessional yen. But she'd never let on about that. In their partnership, she's the one with a rational explanation for every weird phenomenon, from space aliens to ghosts.

See *The X-Files*

SEBASTIAN, ALEXANDER

An evil but strangely charming Nazi living in post–World War II Brazil. Sebastian marries the beautiful **Alicia Huberman**, only to learn that she's spying on him for G-man **Devlin**, the man she truly loves. He tries to strike back at his wife by giving her poisoned coffee, but she's rescued by Devlin, leaving Sebastian in the angry hands of the fellow Nazis, who see him as a traitor.

See *Notorious*

SEFTON

Enterprising, confident German POW camp entrepreneur whose trade is contraband and telescopic peeks into the ladies' showers. His free enterprise success incurs the jealousy of his fellow prisoners. A cynic and a loner, he is interested in making a profit, not in being a pal. His antisocial ways, however, arouse the suspicions of others when an informer is believed to be housed in their midst. He's tough and takes the abuse, but is clever enough to plan a scheme to find out who the real villain is.

See *Stalag 17*

SENORITA CHIQUITA

Stands out in a crowd not just because of her exotic good looks, but because she carries tropical fruit, mainly bananas, on top of her head.

See *Chiquita bananas*

SERENA

Cousin to **Samantha Stephens**, this dark-haired vixen is a comely young witch, who uses her powers as consistently as Samantha refuses to use hers. For some reason, always has her eye on Darrin and flirts with him—indeed with any man—shamelessly. Often pretends to be Samantha—though quite badly because she can't be that normal.

See *Bewitched*

SETENZA

This vicious bounty hunter is searching for one Bill Carson, who is said to possess a map that will lead to hidden treasure. He becomes a sergeant in the Union Army as a means of pursuing his goal. Angel Eyes, as he is also known, lucks out when desperadoes **Joe** and **Tuco** arrive as prisoners with the information he needs.

See *The Good, the Bad, and the Ugly*

SETHE

Sethe is a fugitive slave whose love for her children is so great that she chooses to kill them rather than see them return to slavery when they're tracked down by her owner. Sethe is haunted by the past, manifested in the ghost of her dead daughter, who battles for Sethe's affection with **Paul D. Garner**, a fellow fugitive slave.

See *Beloved,* Toni Morrison

SHADE, JOHN

A reclusive genius, author of *Pale Fire,* an autobiographical poem in narrative couplets which, after his death, is seized upon by his neighbor, the nutty scholar **Charles Kinbote**, who idolizes him and monopolizes his masterwork to the consternation of his saner colleagues.

See *Pale Fire,* Vladimir Nabokov

THE SHADOW

Keep this under your hat, but his real name is Lamont Cranston. He's a potent crime-fighter who uses secrets learned in the Orient to cloud men's minds and render himself invisible, which makes it easier to catch bad guys. He knows what evil lurks in the hearts of men. He also knows that the weed of crime bears bitter fruit. And he has a truly nasty laugh.

See *The Shadow*

SHAFT, JOHN

A dashing New York City private eye, Shaft is tough, streetwise, and very cool. He'll help almost anyone out if they need it, and he's not afraid to use deadly force. When official information is required, he goes to Lieutenant Al Rossi of the NYPD.

See *Shaft*

SHAGGY

He is the least sophisticated of a four-member teenage crime-fighting club. Shaggy is also the owner of a cowardly Great Dane named Scooby-Doo. His taste in clothes runs to T-shirts, jeans, and sneakers, and his bushy hair has seldom felt the touch of a comb. His best friends and fellow crime-fighters are Velma, Freddy, and Daphne. The crimes that they solve often have a supernatural aspect.

See *Scooby-Doo, Where Are You?*

SHAKAPOPULIS, VICTOR

An American nebbish in Paris, Victor divides his time between ineffectual pursuit of Carol, the long-suffering girlfriend of **Michael James**, and his job: helping strippers dress between acts. His pay? "Twenty francs a week—it's all I can afford."

See *What's New, Pussycat?*

SHANE

This mysterious stranger rides into the lives of the close-knit Starret family. He's slight of build but has a quiet power. Joe Starret, father and homesteader, admires him. Feisty mother Marian Starret falls in love with him. Young Bob Starret idolizes him and wants Shane to teach him how to shoot. Shane doesn't wear a gun but keeps a "beautiful and deadly" single-action Colt under his bunk. Things have happened in his life that have left him with an aversion to sitting by windows. When a brutal old cattleman summons a two-gun killer to run local farmers off their land, Shane puts his gun back on to defend the defenseless. "A man is what he is, and there's no breaking the mold. I've tried that and I've lost. There's no going back from a killing."

See *Shane*, Jack Schaefer

SHANGHAI LILY

Immaculately groomed, her shellacked blond hair hidden by ostrich feathers, her face shaded by a veil, she's China's most infamous shady lady. She is a seductress who is confident about her power over men and can beat any woman at her own game. She moves slowly but with a purpose and is willing to put her body on the line for the man that she loves.

See *Shanghai Express*

SHANNON, REVEREND T.

This defrocked Episcopalian priest now works as a tour guide in Mexico. His once-handsome face is a map of pain and suffering. He is filled with self-loathing and on the verge of a mental breakdown. Despite his emotional instability, he's pursued by **Maxine Faulk** and an underage member of his tour group. His relationship with a poor artist helps him to regain his confidence in others, but he still walks on broken glass to punish himself. There is a poignancy to his condition that makes him sympathetic, even though the root of his pain remains ambiguous.

See *The Night of the Iguana*, Tennessee Williams

SHARPLES, MEL

The owner of grubby Mel's Diner in Phoenix, Mel is almost as famous for his dirty white T-shirt as he is for his chili. Gruff, balding, and cheap, deep down he's got a heart of gold—very deep down. Has a paternal love-hate relationship with all of his waitresses, **Alice Hyatt**, **Flo Castleberry**, and **Vera Gorman**. Middle name is Emory.

See *Alice* and *Alice Doesn't Live Here Anymore*

SHAW, BRANDON

He is a chillingly amoral young bachelor who takes the teachings of **Rupert Cadell**, an elitist professor, and warps them into a Nazi-like justification of his superiority. This superiority he goes to quite extreme lengths to demonstrate, with the reluctant help of his roommate, **Philip**. He is a less-than-ideal dinner host.

See *Rope*

SHAW, DARBY

Darby's a young New Orleans law student having an affair with her law professor, an admirer of a Supreme Court justice who's just been assassinated. She's beautiful, true, but also smart as a whip—and

John Shaft

Shanghai Lily

she knows who's behind the plot. Now all she has to do is stay alive long enough to prove it, with the help of investigative reporter **Gray Grantham.** Those who know that she knows don't want her to ever tell the tale.

See *The Pelican Brief,* John Grisham

SHAW, RAYMOND

A Korean war veteran who spent time as a prisoner of war and was subjected to procedures by his Communist captors that go against the rules and against any concept of individual decency. He receives the Congressional Medal of Honor and tries to take up a normal civilian life, though, with a stepfather like flag-waving jingoist Senator John Iselin, and a mother like nasty **Mrs. Iselin,** his chances of achieving normality are slim to none. And his mom has big plans for him…

See *The Manchurian Candidate*

SHAYNE, DAVID

Nervous fledgling author feverishly working on his first theatrical production. Less talented than he believes he is, Shayne is nevertheless terribly determined. However, he's not above selling out his dreams of higher artistic ideals to the notion of quick success, if the chance arises. Apt to lose his moral compass when faced with temptation.

See *Bullets over Broadway*

SHEENA, QUEEN OF THE JUNGLE

Sheena is the daughter of an American husband and wife team of archaeologists, who met an untimely death in a cave-in at their dig site in Africa. An infant at the time, Sheena was adopted by the Zambuli tribe and reared by the tribe's shaman, who taught her to communicate with animals telepathically. She lives in the jungle and chats with her feathered and four-legged friends.

See *Sheena, Queen of the Jungle,* W. Morgan Thomas

SHELDON, PAUL

A famous romance novelist who celebrates the completion of each book by trekking to the isolated Colorado cabin where he completed his first novel. His heroine, Misery Chastain, is his pot of gold but also the ball and chain that prevents him from using his gifts to complete a serious work that

will give him a real literary reputation. To rid himself of his now-superfluous meal ticket, Paul decides to kill off Misery in what will be the final volume in the series. Then he'll finish off his new book, an unflinching look at the lives of kids who live on the streets, packed with realistic dialogue and profanities galore. But the idea of killing off Misery doesn't sit at all well with **Annie Wilkes,** his "Number One Fan!" And she gets the chance to let him know about it.

See *Misery,* Stephen King

SHEPARD, GIL

This handsome, young matinee idol plays the movie role of explorer Tom Baxter. But when Tom takes on a real life of his own, stepping out of the screen into the real world, it means that there are two Gil Shepards walking around, which is one too many for his taste. Gil must persuade Tom to leave the real world and go back into the movie, where he belongs.

See *The Purple Rose of Cairo*

SHEPARD, KRISTIN

Femme fatale. This scheming, vampy sister of **Sue Ellen Ewing** comes to town to seduce **J.R.** Her schemes don't work and she ends up pregnant and discarded by ruthless J.R. Not one to be double-crossed, Kristen makes him pay. With guts and true grit she attempts to murder J.R. with a shot heard round the world. Her penalty: get out of town!

See *Dallas*

SHERMAN, RICHARD

Your basic, everyday, uptight, neurotic New Yorker, Sherman has a hyperactive imagination and a wife and son who are away for the sweltering summer. He lives in an air-conditioned apartment and works for Brady and Company Publishing, developing Pocket Edition books. He's been married for seven years to Helen and they have "a towheaded, freckle-faced, little space cadet named Ricky." He promises Helen that he won't smoke or drink while she's away, but gets so nervous wrestling with temptation that he does anyway. The source of temptation: **The Girl** who's subletting the apartment upstairs, a gorgeous, sexy blonde. He is constantly fantasizing situations where he debonairly sweeps her off her feet and into bed, and that he is irresistible to women. "I arouse them, it's kind of an animal thing." He always wears a suit, even at home, likes classical music, and is clumsy. "Not me, not me, and I'm not gonna smoke, either."

See *The Seven Year Itch*

SHERWOOD FORREST, CORKY

Perky, cute feature reporter for Washington, D.C., newsmagazine show, *FYI*. A former Miss America (she took over when the winner was forced out), Corky covers the show's softer stories. Her proper southern upbringing and chirpy manner often irritate her idol, veteran newswoman **Murphy Brown**. Now single, Corky married and divorced writer Will Forrest.

See *Murphy Brown*

SHIMERDA, ANTONIA

An Eastern European immigrant who ends up in a frontier prairie town. There she faces many hardships: her father kills himself; she must work herself to the bone to survive; a lover leaves her with an illegitimate child. She still manages to maintain her optimism and personal dignity. Loves dancing.

See *My Antonia*, Willa Cather

SHIRLEY, ANNE

A young orphan whose sweetness is tempered by an indomitable spirit and a resourceful imagination. She does her best to be good and helpful, but sometimes her schemes get away from her. She's a good student and loves school; in fact, her ambition is to become a teacher. Anne likes to think big and gets a kick out of using big words.

See, e.g., *Anne of Green Gables*, L. M. Montgomery

SHIVELY, MARY JO

Cute, sardonically witty divorcée. Her petite frame and youthful appearance are in sharp contrast to a jaded view of life. She's the mother of Claudia and Quinton and works for Sugarbakers design firm, trading quips with **Julia** and **Suzanne Sugarbaker** and **Charlene Frazier Stillfield**. Mary Jo struggles with moral issues and believes in liberal causes. Tries to raise her children right. Has no patience for bigotry.

See *Designing Women*

SHREVIE

The only married guy in a small group of Baltimore buddies, Shrevie has started to ignore his wife because he fears that they have nothing to talk about. He is obsessive about his carefully filed record collection and loves to "bullshit the night away" with friends at the diner, over plates of french fries and gravy.

See *Diner*

SIEGFRIED, CONRAD

The head of a dastardly enemy intelligence agency, KAOS. The temperamental Siegfried seeks to do harm in the world, wherever he can. He loves to best CONTROL agent **Maxwell Smart** and would actually like to have him work for KAOS. Siegfried is very attracted to **Agent 99**. A primary reason he doesn't wreak more havoc is his dependence on bumbling agent **Starker** to carry out his evil plans. Wears black and speaks in clipped German accent.

See *Get Smart*

SIFUENTES, VICTOR

He is a young, dedicated Hispanic lawyer, sensitive to having been hired as token minority figure in the mostly white law firm of McKenzie, Brackman, Chaney and Kuzak. He sets out to show his skills nonetheless and proves to be invaluable to the firm. Victor likes to take on cases that help minorities but can handle anything the partners throw his way. He's the good friend of **Mike Kuzak** and eventual lover of **Grace Van Owen**.

See *L.A. Law*

SILVER, DAVID

Insecure and needy, David tries desperately to fit in with a slightly older crowd at West Beverly Hills High. Eventually comes into his own as a D.J. He at one point dates lovely **Donna Martin**. Into the music scene, he becomes a bit too cool for his own good and gets hooked on crystal meth.

See *Beverly Hills 90210*

SILVER, "LONG" JOHN

Nicknamed Barbecue for his cooking ability, the respected and feared Silver is a seaman who has a parrot named Cap'n Flint and uses a crutch to make up for his missing leg. On an adventure to

The Simpsons™ and ©Twentieth Century Fox Film Corporation. All Rights Reserved

The Simpsons

Skeleton Island, he escapes hanging for mutiny only through the intervention of his young friend **Jim Hawkins**.

See *Treasure Island,* Robert Louis Stevenson

THE SILVER SURFER

Sentinel of the Spaceways. As the noble and unselfish Norrin Radd, he volunteers to work for the terrifying and god-like Galactus in order to save his own people. In a final rebellion against Galactus, the Surfer becomes a hero in his own right. A tragic figure, prone to self-sacrifice.

See *The Silver Surfer*

SILVERBERG, MILES

Uptight television wunderkind, the executive producer of a newsmagazine show, *FYI*. Miles landed the post when he was around twenty-five. Committed but neurotic, Silverberg has his hands full managing a staff of star reporters, who, while pros at their trade, are mostly older than he is, given to bickering and infighting, and frequently (in the case of **Murphy Brown** especially) a thorn in the side of network brass.

See *Murphy Brown*

SIMMS, CHARLIE

A working-class scholarship student at a snooty New England prep school filled with privileged youths. He has a mischievous streak but adheres to his principles, even when it would be politic to do otherwise. Something of a loner because of consciousness of his lower-class upbringing, Simms is susceptible to outside influences and is often at the mercy of stronger-willed individuals.

See *Scent of a Woman*

SIMONE, BOBBY

He's a hunky, young detective for the New York City police force. Bobby comes over to the 15th Precinct after spending some time away from the streets after the death of his wife. He partners up with **Andy Sipowicz**, a veteran detective on the squad. Simone also keeps racing pigeons in a coop on the roof above his apartment.

See *NYPD Blue*

THE SIMPSON FAMILY

Just your average, everyday American family of five.

Yeah, right. Homer Simpson is the none-too-bright patriarch of the clan. He's balding, tubby, and constantly hungry. He works at Springfield's nuclear power plant, where he naps and consumes donuts. "Hmm…donuts." Marge is the family's moral compass. Possessor of the world's tallest blue beehive hairdo, she spends most of her time trying to raise her three children (and Homer). While Marge is usually straight as an arrow, she occasionally loses her grip on reality. She has two sisters, Selma and Patty. Bart is the oldest child, a sociopathic treasure-trove of catch phrases, a kind of Tom Sawyer on a skateboard, who spends a lot of his time in school detention. Bart is an underachiever, but is nevertheless smart and sarcastic. He idolizes TV kids' show host Krusty the Clown. "I'm Bart Simpson, who the hell are you?" Lisa, the middle child, is the family genius and plays a mean saxophone. While Lisa excels at anything she does, no one seems to notice. She fights with Bart but adores him. Maggie is the youngest child. She is the most normal member of the family, possibly because she's still a baby. Maggie never goes anywhere without her pacifier. All the children watch the exceedingly violent *Itchy & Scratchy Show*. Abraham Simpson is Homer's elderly father, who loves complaining, pining for the old days, and *Matlock*.

See *The Simpsons*

SIMPSON, HOMER

This simple, earnest fellow from Wayneville, Iowa, worked there as a bookkeeper. After losing that job, Homer moves, on a whim, to Southern California. He meets **Faye Greener** and becomes one of her many admirers. Simpson rues the day, however, when Faye comes to live with him after her father dies.

See *The Day of the Locust,* Nathanael West

SINAI, SALEEM

One of 1,001 children born in the first hour of India's independence—"Midnight's Children." "Cucumber-nosed" Saleem was born to a street singer but swapped at birth for Shiva, the child of an aristocratic family. All Midnight's Children have special gifts; Saleem's is telepathy, by which he communicates with the other children and plans a "midnight parliament."

See *Midnight's Children,* Salman Rushdie

SINCLAIR, HELEN

Faded Broadway actress of the 1920s, looking for a shot at a triumphant comeback. Dresses elegantly and carries herself with grace, acts at least as well offstage as on. Despite Prohibition, maintains a steady flow of alcohol. Interested in the work of up-and-coming playwright **David Shayne**. Has a million variations on the phrase "Don't speak."

See *Bullets over Broadway*

SINCLAIR, RAY

White-bread 1980s New York investment banker who meets a mysterious, sexy downtown girl, **Audrey Henkel**, and is lured by her into playing hooky from his sheltered existence and taking a trip with her to the wild side of life. On the way, Ray experiences a freedom and openness he's been lacking in his corporate life, and finds that there is more to existence than debentures and arbitrage.

See *Something Wild*

SINGER, ALVY

Neurotic New Yorker. Professional comic who scorns simplistic morals, the anti-Semites he sees under every rock, missing opening credits of movies, and anything associated with Los Angeles. Huge Knicks fan; one of the few regulars at screenings of Nazi documentary *The Sorrow and the Pity*. Involved in on-again, off-again relationship with **Annie Hall**. "Why don't you take sodium pentothal? Then you could sleep through the whole thing."

See *Annie Hall*

SIPOWICZ, ANDY

This veteran New York City police detective works at the 15th Precinct with his new partner, **Bobby Simone**. He was previously teamed with **Detective John Kelly**, with whom he had developed a close relationship. A recovering alcoholic who stayed drunk during much of his early career (drinking caused the breakup of his marriage), he manages to get sober with the help of Alcoholics Anonymous. A born and bred New Yorker, Sipowicz is a graduate of the school of hard knocks. But underneath his growl is a man with a good heart. He gets involved with **Sylvia Costas**, a lovely D.A. who provides Andy with more incentive to stay on the wagon. He also has a son from his marriage, Andy Jr., whom he hadn't seen for years. Now he's trying to build a better relationship with the young man. Andy's great strengths as a detective are a highly tuned gut instinct and an ability to get criminals to confess their crimes. He also has a bad temper when it comes to dealing with "scumbags" and has difficulty accepting the politics that are part and parcel of the police department. He's no fashion plate, with his collection of short-sleeve shirts in a variety of outdated plaids. He is passionate about his tropical fish.

See *NYPD Blue*

SIR

Aging stage actor-manager in the grand old style, totally dependent on his dresser **Norman**. He is a Shakespearean performer of note, who rules despotically over his touring theatrical company. Though self-absorbed and egotistical, Sir has undeniable talent and a voice that demands respect. "Stop the train!"

See *The Dresser*

SISSY

Asking men "Are you a real cowboy?" at Gilley's roadhouse gets Sissy in trouble. She meets **Bud Davis** that way, and they marry. When Bud beats her, she sinks into the arms of Wes, a paroled bank robber. Her attempts at building self-esteem are destroyed by the men in her life.

See *Urban Cowboy*

SIX

Best friend to **Blossom Russo**, Six has a wardrobe as eccentric as her personality; she isn't always as levelheaded as Blossom is. She is the sixth child in her family, hence her name. Has a crush on Blossom's brother **Joey Russo**.

See *Blossom*

SKYWALKER, LUKE

This fair-haired, idealistic, parentless young man knows that there must be more to life than the dreary routine he follows with his foster parents on a faraway planet. Eventually, with the help and teaching of an elderly neighbor, **Ben Kenobi**, Luke achieves the realization of his true end in life: to become a member of the revered and powerful order of Jedi Knights and to fight against the

Sissy

Catherine Sloper

Empire that rules over the galaxy with a cruel and oppressive hand. Kenobi teaches him the Way of the Jedi, including mastery of the Force, whereby an adept can focus his untapped inner power in such a way as to perform astonishing feats. He ultimately joins forces with the raffish **Han Solo**, a nomadic spaceship pilot, **Princess Leia Organa**, a scion of an ancient noble family and symbol of resistance to imperial authority. Their main antagonist is **Darth Vader**, the emperor's most trusted and potent minion and himself a Jedi Knight who has gone over to the Dark Side. Luke goes through a series of adventures and battles on various worlds, usually aided by both his human allies and some nonhumans as well: Chewbacca, a giant, hairy creature called a Wookie, and two remarkably human robots, Artoo Deetoo and Ceethreepio, among others. He and his fellow rebels must battle monstrous combat machines, equally monstrous and outlandish creatures from many planets, and, ultimately, a colossal Ultimate Weapon devised by the forces of the Empire: the Death Star.

See *Star Wars*

SLADE, LIEUTENANT COLONEL FRANK

He is a blind, bitter, alcoholic, potentially suicidal retired marine who lost his sight while juggling hand grenades. Despite his lack of vision, he does have an acute sense of the world around him, particularly its young, feminine elements, and knows instantly when someone attempts to water his drinks. While he has the capacity to be charming with strangers, he tends more often to be harsh, rude, and hurtful, especially with the members of his own family. Over time, he's alienated all of his friends as a result of guilt over the accident that took his sight and the life of a fellow serviceman. Nonetheless, he retains a taste for the good things in life, including good food and lots of drink and expensive call girls. At times, Slade seems bent on ignoring his handicap to a suicidal extent. He becomes a mentor to **Charlie Simms**. Pet expression of satisfaction: "Hoo-aaah!"

See *Scent of a Woman*

SLAUGHTER, MURRAY

Murray is a sweet-natured newswriter for WJM-TV in Minneapolis. He is happily married to wife Marie and the father of Bonnie, Ellen, and Laurie Slaughter. He's always throwing zingers at the station's egotistical, incompetent anchorman, **Ted Baxter**, which usually go right over Ted's head. Murray is a positive thinker, a good friend, and a little sweet on his deskmate, associate producer of the news **Mary Richards**.

See *The Mary Tyler Moore Show*

SLOCUM, BOB

A miserable, low-ranking corporate executive obsessed with detailing the reasons for everyone's unhappiness, his own included. He thinks something specific must have happened to create such pervasive malaise, but overlooks the importance of his environment: a sterile, suburban neighborhood, and the corporate monolith for which he works. He loathes his boss, resents his wife, and can't even find pleasure in his many affairs. Slocum's rage is vented only in dreams of violent revenge. He feels little affection for two of his three children, and accidentally kills the one (and the only thing or person) he cares for.

See *Something Happened,* Joseph Heller

SLOPER, CATHERINE

Painfully shy, hopelessly simple daughter of a wealthy, domineering father. With her low self-esteem and submissive nature, she is no match for her powerful papa. She is a social cypher, who can't seem to snag a beau, for all her family wealth. Even though she tries to be fashionable, her clothes are always ill-fitting and slightly out of style. She feels guilt for having disappointed her father, who she believes deserves a more beautiful and clever child. But deep down inside, there's a core of strength that even she's unaware of, until faced with a crisis.

See *Washington Square,* Henry James

SLOPER, DR. AUSTIN

This stiff, bullying physician unfairly blames his daughter, **Catherine Sloper**, for her mother's death during childbirth. His cold, calculating manner frightens people, including the shy Catherine. He's resigned to the idea that his daughter will never live up to his expectations, but it still rankles. His cruelly honest judgments of Catherine devastate her, but, as he is ruled by reason rather than feelings of the heart, he isn't too concerned. He feels he must be protective of his daughter, believing that she could be an attractive prey to fortune hunters.

See *Washington Square,* Henry James

SLOTHROP, TYRONE

This American naïf is set loose in Europe during World War II. As a child, he was the unwitting subject of behavior-control experiments; now he finds himself on a quest to find the A4 rocket, a secret, experimental German weapon with devastating potential, without knowing why he's seeking it. In bomb-besieged London, in Switzerland and the French Riviera, he slowly learns bits and pieces of what's happening to him—but never enough to draw firm conclusions. He becomes ultra-paranoid, believing everyone knows the truth about him except Tyrone himself. Everyone—friends like Captain Prentice, lovers like Katje—seems plugged into a conspiracy to make him fail in his quest. He crosses paths with historical figures, like Malcolm X, in his Boston shoeshine days. He's last sighted in postwar Germany, in the chaotic interval between the fighting and the institution of new government.

See *Gravity's Rainbow,* Thomas Pynchon

SMALL, LENNIE

Goliath with the soul and mind of a child. All he wants to do is be with his best buddy, ranch hand **George Milton,** and pet soft, furry animals. A "huge man, shapeless of face, with large, pale eyes," he has trouble remembering anything except what's to eat, but memorizes George's litany of how they're going to get a place of their own, "an' live off the fatta the lan', an' have rabbits." He carries a dead mouse in his pocket that he stroked to death. "I like to pet nice things with my fingers, sof' things." Strong as a bull, but unaware of it, he crushes the hand of **Curley,** the boss's son, with his bare hand. Lennie's an excellent worker as long as he doesn't have to think. He does whatever George tells him, even if it means jumping in the river, though he can't swim a stroke. People confide in him because he forgets everything he hears. He doesn't have a mean bone in his body, and is bewildered when he accidentally kills Curley's wife **Mae.** "I done a bad thing. I done another bad thing."

See *Of Mice and Men,* John Steinbeck

SMART, JANE

She's a prissy, raven-haired witch-cellist residing in Eastwick, Rhode Island. Her specialty is potions, into which she pours just a dash of her ex-husband, Sam, who hangs in the cellar among the herbs. Hell hath no fury like a witch scorned, and she rallies sister sorceresses **Alexandra Medford** and **Sukie Ridgemont** to avenge their betrayal by Darryl Van Horne.

See *The Witches of Eastwick,* John Updike

SMART, MAXWELL

Bumbling secret agent who is nevertheless the top spy for Washington-based intelligence agency CONTROL. Smart, or Agent 86, works directly for **the Chief** on top-secret missions, often paired with **Agent 99.** He has in-depth knowledge of the enemy intelligence agency KAOS, and so is often charged with foiling their dastardly plans which seek to imperil U.S. intelligence operations. As an ace spy, Max is surprised by nothing, and is always prepared for every possibility. His arsenal of espionage gear includes myriad disguises, alibis, and gadgets to catch the bad guys off guard. Among his technological tools is a telephone built into the sole of his shoe. For secret conferences with the Chief, they retreat under the "cone of silence" that envelops the Chief's desk. Information he needs to help on a case is elicited from Hymie, a computer disguised as a human. Unfortunately, Smart's bark is worse than his bite, and he is often tricked and even duped by KAOS's **Siegfried.** Often, it is Agent 99 who bails Max out and saves the day for CONTROL. Max stays cool in those anxious moments before 99 rescues him from a tough spot, and usually insists to her that he was just about to save himself and certainly could have and would have. He loves 99 but is jealous of her skills as an agent. "Would you believe…?"

See *Get Smart*

SMILEY, GEORGE

He may be the star of the British Secret Service, but he's no James Bond. Smiley is short, bespectacled, and shaped like an English muffin. After studying 17th-century German literature at Oxford, he was recruited by the Crown in 1928, and served brilliantly in Germany during World War II. Later, he settled down in England with his beautiful wife and conducted ingenious schemes of counter espionage. Smiley is at his best in the interrogation room: polite, overly formal, ever patient, yet relentlessly skeptical. Yet Smiley views his greatest triumphs of spy-catching with ambiguous feelings, alternating between a devotion to country and feeling sorry for those he destroys in the line of duty.

See *Tinker, Tailor, Soldier, Spy,* John LeCarré

MR. SMITH

Lecherous old man who visits **Dante Hicks**'s convenience store when **Randal** is working behind the counter. He first demands softer, more expensive bathroom tissue—because of his hemorrhoids—then convinces Randal to lend him some reading material, a porn magazine. His chance to experience a genuine sexual male fantasy—when a pretty girl comes into the bathroom, mistakes him for her ex-boyfriend Dante, and uses his body to pleasure herself—doesn't come to fruition, because he's been dead for hours, the victim of a heart attack while "reading" the porn magazine.

See *Clerks*

SMITH, BURL "GOPHER"

Gopher's a goofball crewman on the cruise ship *Love Boat.* His position as yeoman-purser gives him a certain cachet, which he uses to attract beautiful guests of the female persuasion. But his boyish good looks and silly antics seem to captivate mostly airheads. Occasionally, he finds temporary true love with gorgeous, intelligent women. Gopher often violates ship's protocol to help a passenger or fellow crew member and risks the wrath of **Captain Stubing**. Best friends with **Isaac Washington**, **Julie McCoy**, and **Adam Bricker**.

See *The Love Boat*

SMITH, CORA

Archetypical innocent-on-the-outside, fiery-on-the-inside woman. The pretty blond wife of **Nick Smith**, whom she helps run the family restaurant. She seems calm and conservative. But beneath that facade there's a wild woman, sick of dull old Nick, waiting to break loose. When **Frank Chambers**, a charming drifter, comes by, there's an instant attraction—the wild woman is finally about to be set free. Cora makes love to Frank with a passionate abandon that gives a simple kitchen table a whole new lease on life as a sex device. Once she has had a taste of Frank, she abandons every inhibition and moral restraint, and is ready for *anything*...not excluding murder.

See *The Postman Always Rings Twice,* James M. Cain

SMITH, ESTHER

She's a typical American teen who enjoys tennis and going to dances and parties with her friends. She's in love with the boy next door, John Truitt, to whom she becomes engaged in her senior year in high school. A St. Louis resident, she's eagerly anticipating the opening of the 1904 World's Fair there.

See *Meet Me in St. Louis*

SMITH, JEFFERSON

He is an idealistic rural naïf who's abruptly thrown into the snakepit of Washington politics as a junior senator when his predecessor dies. He's thrilled to be named to the seat by his idol, senior senator **Joseph Paine**. Previously, he'd been head of the Boy Rangers in his state and editor of *Boy's Stuff*, a tiny newspaper. His father, Clayton Smith, was a champion of lost causes, killed by a bullet in the back. Smith is young and earnest, and his enthusiasm is contagious. A patriot to his soul, Jeff recites Lincoln and Jefferson, believes in the goodness of mankind, and spends his free time gazing into Honest Abe's eyes at the Lincoln Memorial. He admires his cynical secretary, **Clarissa Saunders**, and tells her to "always try to see life around you as if you just came out of a tunnel." Smith authors a bill to start a national boys' camp, but his purity doesn't sit well with the corrupt leaders of the elite men's club that is the Senate. He's staggered to learn that Paine is no better than the worst of them and had chosen Jeff because he thought the young man could be easily manipulated. Then he decides to fight the evil, come what may. "Lost causes are the only causes worth fighting for."

See *Mr. Smith Goes to Washington*

SMITH, NICK

A big, dull Greek American who runs a roadside restaurant with his wife, **Cora Smith**. Nick doesn't suspect a thing when Cora begins a torrid affair with **Frank Chambers**, a charming drifter—in fact, he continues to see Frank as his friend. This, it turns out, is a big mistake.

See *The Postman Always Rings Twice,* James M. Cain

SMITH, RENO

He puts on a friendly face, but Smith controls an entire town through the fear that their terrible secret will be discovered. He tries to convince **John J. MacReedy** to go away, first through hints and then through threats. Like most bigots, Smith is a man whose ignorance and insecurity fuel his beliefs.

See *Bad Day at Black Rock*

SMITH, VALENTINE MICHAEL

Michael's not your ordinary immigrant. The product of an extramarital affair between two scientists on Earth's first manned trip to Mars, he was raised by Martians and sent back to Earth as an unwitting spy for the Old Ones…what we would call ghosts. He's rich beyond imagination, having inherited from all the geniuses who made up the original mission. He's a genius in his own right by any Earthly standard and, in fact, a Martian in a human body, with an absolute innocence of all aspects of life on Earth. Michael's a quick study, however, and with the disciplines and mental tools given him by his foster parents, he begins to "grok" what being human really means.

See *Stranger in a Strange Land,* Robert A. Heinlein

SMITH, WEB

He's the Los Angeles Police Department's Special Liaison Officer to work with Japanese big shots visiting his town; currently, he's attempting to solve a politically sensitive murder in the highest boardroom of the Japanese corporate business community in L.A. His suspicion and bitterness rise to the surface when he's teamed up by department brass with his predecessor as Liaison Officer, **John Connor.** He knows the Japanese language and some nasty martial arts moves, but he really doesn't understand the culture of deceit he's up against.

See *Rising Sun,* Michael Crichton

SMITH, WINSTON

A middle-aged man who rebels against "Big Brother"—the symbol of his futuristic, repressive society—first by keeping an illegal diary, then by having an illicit love affair and allying himself with enemies of the state. He's drawn to **Julia,** an earthy young woman, because, unlike his wife, whom he divorced for failing to produce offspring, she's capable of desire (labeled a Thoughtcrime) and enjoys sex. Smith feels contempt for his middle-class neighbors for their sheeplike conformity to the dictates of the state and is both resentful and envious of the lower classes for their mindless, physical natures. Captured and tortured by authorities, Smith confesses to everything they charge him with but remains inwardly defiant.

See *1984,* George Orwell

SMITH, DR. ZACHARY

He is an evil, untrustworthy traitor whose character is underlined by his pinched face and skinny body. It was his act of sabotage aboard the *Jupiter II* that caused it to go irreparably off course, which has never been forgotten by **Don West** or the **Robinsons.** He is always treated with an element of mistrust, though he and the others need each other for various reasons. Often scheming with aliens to get away, he's always running back to the ship in the end.

See *Lost in Space*

SNAP, CRACKLE, POP

Forerunners of the very successful Cap'n Crunch, these three brothers created the first breakfast cereal that made recognizable sounds when milk was added. Best known for their sartorial splendor, later adopted by the Cat in the Hat.

See *Rice Krispies Cereal*

SNOW, CHRISSY

A blonde with a heart of gold and a head full of (mostly) air. She shares a place with **Jack Tripper,** who lusts after her—something she's too dim to realize—and with **Janet Wood,** who protects her from Jack and all other men.

See *Three's Company*

SOLO, HAN

He's a dashing, passionate, star-traveling ne'er-do-well. Han enjoys a cynical but loving relationship with Chewbacca, a huge, hairy Wookie, with whom he roves around the galaxy, making money where he can and however he can. Though a mercenary on the surface, Solo turns out to have deeper inner qualities, which lead him to join forces

Dr. Zachary Smith
Photo courtesy of CBS

with **Luke Skywalker**, **Princess Leia Organa**, and **Obi-Wan Kenobi** in an epic battle against the tyrannical Empire and its villainous military leader, **Darth Vader**. Just because he's serious about bringing liberty, however, doesn't mean that he won't toss around a lot of wisecracks or make a lot of moves on Princess Leia. A hotshot pilot and skilled spaceship mechanic, Han can tweak his rusted old ship into true hot-rod performance and dodge enemy ships, meteors, and disintegrator rays with poise and coolness. A good man to have on your side in a fight, but a bad man to lend money to.

See *Star Wars*

SOLO, NAPOLEON

The suave, urbane American superagent who worked for UNCLE (the United Network Command for Law Enforcement). Working from the secret American headquarters in New York, he teamed with **Illya Kuryakin** to fight the international crime syndicate THRUSH.

See *The Man from UNCLE*

SOMMERS, JAIME

She's a onetime pro tennis player and **Steve Austin's** high school sweetheart. Jaime was injured in a parachuting accident, after which Steve got the government to save her through the use of bionic technology. Two arms, a leg, and a bionic ear later, Jaime is a cyborg, and can crush a tennis ball in one hand. Her cover is as a teacher in tiny Ojai, California, but she fits in assignments for the OSI.

See *The Bionic Woman* and *The Six Million Dollar Man*

SONIA

This pretty blond widow with a great set of pipes hails from the small central European country of Warshovia. She's mega-rich—she owns 52% of the country. When she meets dashing **Count Danilo**, she falls for him (like most women, apparently), but convinces herself she doesn't love him. So off she goes to Paris to find a husband. After a series of comic misadventures, she ends up with Danilo after all, who leaves behind his womanizing ways to marry her.

See *The Merry Widow*

SONNY

He's a foulmouthed Italian American Vietnam veteran in an unhappy marriage and desperate for money. In addition to his heterosexual marriage, he has been unofficially married to his neurotic homosexual partner, **Leon**, a preoperative transsexual. Sonny's attempting to turn his life around by robbing a Brooklyn bank with **Sal**. Is constantly running into Murphy's law in everything he undertakes. An unlikely media darling, whose mind is always racing, plotting, planning. "Attica! Attica!"

See *Dog Day Afternoon*

SORRELL, FIONA "PICKLES"

This bubbleheaded blonde is the wife of jokester **Buddy Sorrell**. She's rarely seen, but we know that she apparently can't cook or keep house, and there is a possibility that she's been unfaithful. She was once married to Floyd B. Bariscale. Why is she called Pickles? Because all the Fionas in her neighborhood were called Pickles. Were there many? "No, just me."

See *The Dick Van Dyke Show*

SORRELL, MAURICE "BUDDY"

A human joke machine. A writer for *The Alan Brady Show,* Buddy gets along well with cowriters **Sally Rogers** and **Rob Petrie**, but can't stand producer **Mel Cooley**, on whom he practices insulting jokes. Buddy likes to perform stand-up routines at parties. He was bar mitzvahed in his midforties. He spends as little time as possible with wife **Fiona "Pickles" Sorrell**. Likes to eat prune Danish. Always ready with a throwaway line.

See *The Dick Van Dyke Show*

SOUSÉ, EGBERT

It's pronounced soo-ZAY ("Accent graahve over the *e*"). The ultimate henpecked husband, harassed by wife, mother-in-law, children, and life in general. Takes refuge in adult beverage consumption at friendly tavern. Every branch of his family tree has it in for him. Knows many useless facts on which he'll expound to anyone within earshot. Easily exasperated; often makes sarcastic cracks only he can hear. "Has Michael Finn been in here today?"

See *The Bank Dick*

SPACELY, COSMO G.

The mean-spirited, not-too-bright CEO of Spacely Sprockets. Spacely constantly battles his archcompetitor, Cogswell Cogs. His small body houses a very loud voice. Mr. Spacely has a pronounced Napoleon complex and is very demanding of his employees. One harassed employee is nice guy **George Jetson**, of whom Cosmo constantly takes advantage, often nagging him on his way home via TV phone.

See *The Jetsons*

SPADE, JACK

When brother Junebug O.G.'s (over-golds) on gold chains, and Mr. Big's henchmen come to collect on Junebug's debts and leave him much the worse for wear, Spade vows revenge. He seeks help from 1970s neighborhood heroes: John Slade, Hammer and Slammer, and Flyguy. Slammer: "What makes you think you can be a black hero?" Spade: "I'm an ex–football player."

See *I'm Gonna Git You Sucka*

SPADE, SAM

The original tough guy in a cruel world, Sam Spade knows that when the chips are down, we all stand alone. By turns seething with righteous anger or coolly calculating, Sam is a steely-eyed private investigator in San Francisco in the 1920s. Caught in a web of intrigue following the murder of his partner, Miles Archer, Sam ultimately reveals a practical code of justice that underlies his bitter cynicism about human nature. The trouble begins when a beautiful young woman calling herself Miss Wonderly hires the partners to follow a man named Floyd Thursby. Miles accepts the job and is found murdered later that night in Chinatown; Thursby's body is discovered half an hour later. Sam becomes the prime suspect when the police find out that he not only loathed his late partner but was having an affair with Archer's wife, Iva. Soon, Miss Wonderly reappears, reveals herself as Brigid O'Shaughnessy and begs Sam to help her. Even though Sam knows Brigid is full of lies, he agrees to work for her and ultimately begins a romantic involvement with her as well. The plot thickens with unseemly characters all in pursuit of a mysterious statuette of a falcon, and Sam expertly plays them off against each other until he is the only one left standing or not in jail. Even his beloved Brigid is left to dangle in the breeze when he learns that she killed his partner. After all, what does love mean in a world of lies?

See *The Maltese Falcon,* **Dashiell Hammett**

SPAULDING, CAPTAIN JEFFREY T.

Mustachioed African explorer, usually wears jodhpurs, pith helmet, glasses, smokes an ever-present cigar. Prone to strange interludes. Spaulding has eyes for wealthy Mrs. Rittenhouse, though is not averse to looking elsewhere for a little fling. A moral man, he never takes a drink (unless someone else buys). "I once shot an elephant in my pajamas. How he got into my pajamas, I have no idea."

See *Animal Crackers*

SPAULDING, EDNA

Edna has heart and guts. Well-meaning people try to shelter her from the harsh realities of life, but those realities make themselves felt. She somehow gets up on her feet and fights off the ones who would foreclose on her family farm. This woman's got moxie.

See *Places in the Heart*

THE SPECTRE

He was Detective Jim Carrigan until he was murdered. But the grave wasn't the resting place for this dude; he was turned into the Spectre, who pursues and catches murderers, even though he's deceased. After all, what has he got to be afraid of now?

See *The Spectre*

SPENCER, HENRY

Electric-haired denizen of anonymous city where he lives in a run-down apartment building. Fleetingly involved with **Mary X** but is also attracted to sultry neighbor who lives across the hall. Has hidden parenting instincts when it becomes necessary. His head isn't attached to his neck very tightly, though it makes a great pencil eraser.

See *Eraserhead*

SPENCER, JEFF

One-half of the glamorous P.I. firm housed at 77 Sunset Strip in Hollywood, Jeff is a former government agent with a law degree and a talent for judo. With his partner, **Stu Bailey**, and their young charge, **Gerald "Kookie" Kookson**, he fights crime in all the most exotic hot spots.

See *77 Sunset Strip*

SPENCER, LAURA VINING

Lovely Laura is giving and smart, but attracted to

"dangerous" men; maybe it all goes back to her illegitimate birth. She marries Scotty Baldwin and then begins a tempestuous affair with **Luke Spencer**; after he rapes her, he becomes the love of her life. Once kidnapped by a man named Stavros Cassadine, she also married him. Back with Luke, the two have a son, Lucky.

See *General Hospital*

SPENCER, LUKE

Roguish, wry, bad boy Luke doesn't have the looks of a matinee idol, but he does have the charm and the swagger, and so he gets away with murder—or close to it. After raping **Laura Vining**, he ends up marrying her, and theirs is a romance for the ages. Never one to walk the straight and narrow, Luke's owned a nightclub, gotten messed up with the mob, and still managed to become Mayor of Port Charles. His sister is Bobbie. When Laura disappeared for a while, he romanced Holly Sutton. He and Laura have a son, Lucky.

See *General Hospital*

SPENGLER, DR. EGON

A bespectacled technician, studious and serious about his ability to use scanners and other hi-tech doodads to find and contain spooks, phantasms, and specters. Joins up with **Raymond Stantz** and **Peter Venkman** to establish the Ghostbusters business. He's full of practical advice his partners cheerfully ignore. His partners use backpacks carrying unlicensed nuclear accelerators of his design and manufacture. Hobby: collecting spores, molds, and fungus.

See *Ghostbusters* and *Ghostbusters II*

SPENSER

The thinking man's private eye. You want him to help you out in a jam, whether it's finding a lost loved one or finishing the *New York Times* crossword puzzle. Spenser is a tough customer, but he's smart, literate, and compassionate, as interested in books as he is in crooks. (Although his wardrobe betrays his working-class bent: usually black jeans and a T-shirt, topped off with a shoulder holster.) A former boxer and cop, Boston-based Spenser relies on skills of both occupations to solve cases—occasionally punching his way out of trouble, occasionally turning to his two police contacts, Lieutenant

Quirk and Sergeant Belson, for help. The other big asset Spenser has is his old friend **Hawk**, who's even tougher and street savvier than he is. Spenser's soft side comes out with his girlfriend, Susan Silverman, a psychologist.

See *Spenser*

SPICOLI, JEFF

Way cool surfin' dude and perennial student at Ridgemont High School, where he's known to have pizzas delivered to the classroom. His dreams are often about getting national media recognition by riding the perfect wave on his surfboard. Wears his hair shoulder length and clothes distinctively casual. Jeff's brain is usually tuned into an alternative outlet from those surrounding him, which doesn't seem to bother him in the least. All in all, a totally awesome guy. "Whoa!"

See *Fast Times at Ridgemont High*

SPIDER-MAN

A wisecracking wallcrawler. Bitten by a radioactive spider in a lab experiment gone wrong, teenaged **Peter Parker** is given superhuman strength, the ability to climb walls, and a special "spider sense." People often refer to him as "your friendly neighborhood Spider-Man." With the aid of his own web-shooter invention, Spider-Man "catches crooks just like flies—Look out!"

See *Spider-Man*

THE SPIDER WOMAN

A "strange woman" who lives far away on a tropical island. She wears a long gown of silver lamé that "fits her like a glove." Alone on her island, she's caught in a giant spider web that grows out of her own body. When a shipwrecked man is washed up on the beach, she nourishes him back to health. She cries diamond teardrops.

See *Kiss of the Spider Woman,* Manuel Puig

MR. SPOCK

Half human, half Vulcan, the first officer of the starship *Enterprise,* Spock is a man at war with himself: his Vulcan side is emotionless, brilliant, and ruled by logic; his human side gives him compassion and a real affection for his captain, **James T. Kirk**, to whom he is fiercely loyal. (He did get the Vulcan pointy eyebrows and ears, though.) Spock's father, Ambassador Sarek, married Spock's human mother, Amanda, because it seemed like a good idea at the time, but Spock has no such long-lasting love affairs, although he returns to Vulcan every seven years for a violent mating ritual called the Pon farr (it almost kills him); once he falls in love with a prehistoric woman when he's thrown back in time (his modern Vulcan brain—purged of emotion—hasn't evolved yet) and is also tempted by a blonde after being sprayed by a spore. His other Vulcan traits include the ability to "mind meld" with someone by laying his hand on his or her face and a handy "Vulcan nerve pinch" which instantly disables a combatant with a few well-placed fingers on the neck. Spock is ultimately a man of science, and as such finds deadly situations "fascinating" or "most illogical," a detachment that drives the *Enterprise*'s doctor, **Bones McCoy**, nuts. Spock will do anything for his captain, though, idolizes his father, and rises through the ranks at the Federation to become an admiral. Spock's blood is green, someone once stole his brain, and as for his first name—"you couldn't pronounce it."

See *Star Trek*

SPOON, JAKE

Jake is a happy-go-lucky sort of feller who once served as a Texas Ranger under the command of **Woodrow Call**. But he's hardly a law-and-order fanatic, and he's not much good at anything except getting himself into trouble of one kind or another. He can shoot a gun, but you'd probably be safer if you were the one he was shooting at. He's willing to work on either side of the law, if the pay is right.

See *Lonesome Dove*, **Larry McMurtry**

SPRAGUE, HOWARD

He's a square. Insecure and uncomfortable with himself, county clerk Howard lives with his mother, wears dark suits, and has trouble dating. He spends his free time bowling, and exchanging gossip with Goober and **Floyd Lawson** at the barbershop. Howard once ran against **Bee Taylor** for the Mayberry Town Council. In search of a new image, Howard moves to a groovy bachelor pad and sports love beads. He wonders if Millie might be the woman for him.

See *The Andy Griffith Show*

SPRINGER, JANICE

She is the emotionally frail girlfriend of **Harry "Rabbit" Angstrom**, ex–high school basketball star, who's ambivalent about commitment. But when he gets her pregnant, he does what is considered the right thing, and marries her. The pressures of life with Harry and her deep insecurities make her turn to the bottle, and she's drunk when she accidentally drowns their baby daughter. The marriage, never ideal, deteriorates, and there are long periods of separation, most (but not all) initiated by him. Eventually, she and Rabbit settle down together, as much from fatigue and familiarity as anything else.

See *Rabbit Run*, John Updike

SQUIER, ALAN

A writer who is in search of something worth living or dying for. He roams the country in his search and never finds much. When he arrives at a little cafe in the Arizona desert, he is drawn to aesthetically inclined waitress-painter **Gabrielle Maple**. He says, "I belong to a vanishing race—I'm one of the intellectuals." He signs his five-thousand-dollar life insurance policy over to her and persuades hardened murderer **Duke Mantee**—who's also dropped by the cafe—to kill him. This way, she can use the insurance money to go to France and study painting. He feels that at least his death will have made some kind of difference.

See *The Petrified Forest*, Robert E. Sherwood

SQUIGGMAN, ANDREW "SQUIGGY"

This slick-haired, girl-crazy, 1950s truck driver works for the Shotz Brewery in Milwaukee with best friend Lenny Kosnowski. Short, greasy-haired, and funny-looking, with a screechy voice, Squiggy often strikes out with the ladies. He's very fond of "pals" **Laverne De Fazio**

Spider-Man
© & ™ 1996
Marvel

and **Shirley Feeney** and spends free time with them, bowling and eating pizza. Uneducated and unsophisticated, Squiggy has no goals in life.
See *Laverne and Shirley*

ST. HUBBINS, DAVID
He's the lead singer of Spinal Täp, an art-metal band whose popularity has skidded to the point of being reduced to gigs at air force bases and curtain-raisers for puppet shows. He's the composer of overblown rockers like "Big Bottom." Almost lets his girlfriend's hunger for power destroy the band, a la Yoko Ono.
See *This Is Spinal Täp*

THE STAGE MANAGER
He oversees and narrates the story of a small New Hampshire town, Grover's Corners. Not unlike God, the Stage Manager sees all and tells all. He focuses on two young people of the town, **Emily Webb** and George Gibbs: their families, lives, dreams…and fates. His story is a trip back to a time when small towns were really different from urban America.
See *Our Town,* Thornton Wilder

STAN
Beer-bellied, small-town buddy of **Mike**, **Steven**, and **Nick**. Tries to hide sensitivity through foul-mouthed boozing and partying with his pals. Enjoys pool, singing off-key, and hunting deer. "Fucking A!"
See *The Deer Hunter*

STANDISH, CLAIRE
Born to shop, even when she should be in school. Consequently, she's ended up in Saturday detention hall with **Andrew Clark**, **John Bender**, **Brian Johnson**, and **Alison Reynolds**. Prim, well-mannered rich girl, very society-conscious; she knows whom to hang out with and whom not to acknowledge. A classic high-class high school snob.
See *The Breakfast Club*

STANTZ, DR. RAYMOND
He is a goofy, enthusiastic seeker of apparitions, a Peter Pan type who's afraid to leave the university atmosphere. "I've worked in the private sector," he cries. "They expect results!" He takes out a third

mortgage on his home to establish Ghostbusters with partners **Egon Spengler** and **Peter Venkman**.
See *Ghostbusters* and *Ghostbusters II*

STARK, VERA
She is a pragmatic, liberal, white lawyer in present-day South Africa who devotes her practice to the causes of the oppressed black majority.
See *None to Accompany Me,* Nadine Gordimer

STARKER
This much-abused, incompetent secret agent conspires with boss **Conrad Siegfried** to bring the villainous agency KAOS espionage victories over U.S. counterpart agency CONTROL. He's frequently thwarted by equally inept Agent 86, **Maxwell Smart.** Often, Starker resorts to physical violence in attempt to "get Smart." Must endure the wrath of Siegfried when KAOS loses to CONTROL.
See *Get Smart*

STARKWELL, VIRGIL
A frail, bumbling nebbish of a thief. Despite being wanted in six states for armed robbery and the illegal possession of a wart, he's a hopeless failure at his chosen profession. For example, bad handwriting undermines one bank stickup attempt—one clerk reads "I have a gun" as "I have a *gub*."
See *Take the Money and Run*

STARLING, CLARICE
Clarice, an attractive female FBI agent, retains her professionalism in the midst of a sexist world. She fends off the advances of smarmy **Dr. Frederick Chilton**; she's used by her boss as bait to enlist serial killer **Hannibal Lecter**'s help in tracking down another serial killer, known as **Buffalo Bill.** Professional though she is, however, she's awed by Lecter's piercing intensity, charm, and remarkable intelligence—he can use the smallest details to piece together extraordinary deductions. Special agent Starling is frightened to the core by Lecter's evil but is so dedicated to her job that she won't show it. Over time, her loathing for Lecter's twisted sensibilities is mixed with grudging respect for his mental endowments. In the end, she finds that she is able to communicate with him where others—psychiatrists and veteran investigators—have failed. She also gains hard-won acknowledgment

that she is a peer within the male-dominated FBI hierarchy.

See *The Silence of the Lambs*

STARR, BRENDA

A globe-trotting ace reporter, Brenda Starr is made up of equal parts glamour and toughness. She divides her time between breaking sensational news stories and pursuing a seemingly doomed love affair with the dashing and mysterious Basil St. John, who must raise and consume black orchids in order to stave off a deadly malady.

See *Brenda Starr*

STARSKY, DAVE

A rough-and-tumble cop, Starsky wears jeans and sneakers and tries to blend in on the streets. He has a very close relationship with his partner, **Ken "Hutch" Hutchinson**. Starsky—a bachelor—roars around Southern California in his jacked-up, red 1974 Ford Torino.

See *Starsky and Hutch*

STEADMAN, HOPE MURDOCH

A conflicted, thirty-something, career woman/ stay-at-home mom. She is smart, attractive, idealistic, and passionate in her beliefs. She's given to constant instrospection and self-assessment and is never sure she's doing the right thing. On the one hand, she loves being a mom, but, on the other, she doesn't want to sacrifice a good career. She also worries about selling out. She's married to advertising man **Michael Steadman** and surrounded by supportive friends. She certainly needs them.

See *Thirtysomething*

STEADMAN, MICHAEL

This smart, ambitious advertising executive constantly struggles with Big Life Questions. It sometimes makes him whiny. He's the kind of person who, no matter how well things are going, will always find something to worry about. Is he selling out? Can he support his family? Is he a good husband? Is he a good father? Has he lost his ideals? Should he raise his kids as Jews? Is there a God? Why can't they make an easy-opening sardine can? The fun never ends for Michael.

See *Thirtysomething*

STEED, JONATHAN

He's a debonair British secret agent working for an unnamed intelligence service. Nothing shakes the equanimity of proper and suave ace spy Jonathan Steed. He's always coolly ready to deal with whatever evildoer seeks to harm the British Empire or the world at large. Steed is equipped with every modern technological trinket known to mankind. But it is his mind that is of the most value to home office chief "Mother," and the greatest threat to enemies as well. In his proper British coat and weskit and outfitted with the de rigueur umbrella and bowler, Steed could be any banker off to work. But he is a potent force against insidious evil, especially when teamed up with his partner, the lovely agent **Mrs. Peel**.

See *The Avengers*

STEELE, REMINGTON

Suave, sophisticated, and handsome, this Irishman runs his eponymous detective agency with **Laura Holt**, whom he occasionally romances. Laura named the agency, though, and Remington is just a poseur, whose real name and background remain obscure. However, his skills gained as a (now reformed) jewel thief and con artist serve him in good stead as a sleuth, to say nothing of what he's learned from watching movies. His checkered past includes a stint as a boxer. He loves *The Honeymooners*.

See *Remington Steele*

STEIN

Head of Stein and Company, Stein is a wealthy, honest, and respected merchant. An Anglophile, thanks to a Scotsman's generosity, Stein gives **Lord Jim** a chance to redeem himself after his disgrace in the *Patna* affair. Stein is a kindly and perceptive man, who sees that Jim is tortured by an extremely sensitive and romantic sensibility.

See *Lord Jim,* **Joseph Conrad**

STEINBERG, BERNIE

Young, honest, and handsome, Bernie is an aspiring writer making his living driving Cab Number 12 around New York City when he meets and marries **Bridget**. Problem is, he's Jewish and she's Catholic. Bernie's parents are Sam and Sophie, who own the deli that Bridget and Bernie live above.

See *Bridget Loves Bernie*

NIGHT OF THE LADIES OF THE EVENING!

Vivian Ward
Tralala
Gloria Wandrous
Irma La Douce
Lana
Bree Daniels
"Pretty Baby" Violet

STEINBERG, BRIDGET FITZGERALD

Raised in wealth by her Irish Catholic parents, blond, lovely Bridget teaches elementary school at Immaculate Heart Academy. Although it's hard on her parents, Walter (owner of a company called Global Investments) and Amy, Bridget loves and marries Jewish cabdriver **Bernie Steinberg**.

See *Bridget Loves Bernie*

STEMPLE, LISA

She's the younger sister of **Jamie Buchman**, and her sister's absolute antithesis: single, flaky, and totally irresponsible. Lisa has a knack for putting her foot in her mouth and wreaking havoc with a single action. Though she loves Jamie, she can't help being a little jealous of her "perfect life." Her mother, Theresa, and father, Gus, worry that Lisa will never get married.

See *Mad About You*

STEPHENS, SAMANTHA

A beautiful blond witch, she marries the very conservative and mortal adman Darrin Stephens against her family's wishes and becomes a suburban housewife on Morning Glory Circle in Westport, Connecticut. Promises Darrin she'll never use her powers, but somehow all the witches in her orbit manage to cause enough trouble that she has to, just to bring order back from chaos. Accesses her powers by wiggling her nose. Often comes up with better ad campaigns than Darrin does. Has two children, **Tabitha** and Adam. Pronounces "Well…" with two syllables.

See *Bewitched*

STEPHENS, TABITHA

The daughter of witch **Samantha Stephens** and mortal ad executive Darrin Stephens, young Tabitha is definitely part witch. From her crib, begins using her powers (she has to use her finger to wiggle her nose) to make her toys come to life. Once she conjured up Prince Charming. Is generally not encouraged to use her witchly abilities, but what kid could resist trying them now and then? Grows up to work as a production assistant on local California station KLXA.

See *Bewitched* and *Tabitha*

STEPHENSON, AL

A successful bank vice-president who returns from World War II filled with painful memories of battle. He has a loving wife and children but is still wracked with doubts about himself. Although he gets his old job back, he is a different person. The war has changed him and he isn't sure how to resolve the conflict between who he was and who he is now.

See *The Best Years of Our Lives*

STERN, CLIFF

Documentary-film maker of little renown. Currently trying to get funding for cinematic portrait of respected psychiatrist, he's settled for what he can get: making a PBS documentary about his despised but successful brother-in-law **Lester**. Has an obsessive sense of personal morality but is a fatalist at heart. A huge fan of old movies and Chinese food.

See *Crimes and Misdemeanors*

STERN, SANDY

Magical defense attorney who's got "three of the jurors thinking about inviting him for dinner." Dignified. Reasonable. Judicious. Born Alejandro Stern, he speaks with an elegant, soft Spanish accent. Indulges in a cigar only in his office. He uses an intricate network of information—cops, reporters, clients—to defend accused murderer and colleague **Rusty Sabich**, and wins the case. "Observing Stern work is like tracking smoke, watching a shadow lengthen."

See *Presumed Innocent*, Scott Turow

STERNIN, DR. LILITH

A tightly wound psychiatrist, with horn-rims and hair so mercilessly pulled back it must hurt her scalp. She marries fellow psychiatrist **Dr. Frasier Crane**, a regular at the Boston bar Cheers. She's frosty on the outside, but once those glasses come off, and the hair is let down, she becomes a tigress—for a while, anyway.

See *Cheers*

STETSON, LEE

An operative with the covert U.S. government organization known only as the Agency, Lee is one of the good guys. He enlists the help of a naive housewife, **Amanda King**, who eventually becomes his partner and later his wife. Lee lives and works in

Washington, D.C., and his code name is Scarecrow.

See *Scarecrow and Mrs. King*

STEVEN

Married friend of **Mike**, **Stan**, and **Nick**, Russian Orthodox by faith. Vietnam POW, he lost both legs and use of one arm while trying to escape. Trying to forget his pain while recuperating in a V.A. hospital. Recipient of unusual overseas gifts, all kept hidden in his sock drawer.

See *The Deer Hunter*

STEVENS, CHRIS

The local deejay for station KBRH in tiny Cicely, Alaska. A native of Wheeling, West Virginia, this self-educated intellectual picked up his smarts on the streets and during a stretch in prison. He's very eclectic on his radio show (which seems to run for about eighteen hours a day, every day), plays all kinds of music, and has been known to quote Walt Whitman and many others. One of the town's spiritual leaders, he got a mail-order theology degree obtained from the back pages of *Rolling Stone* magazine.

See *Northern Exposure*

STEVENSON, LEONA

A wealthy, bedridden hypochondriac and telephone fanatic. She's beautiful, shrewd, and determined to have her own way at all times. After being a spoiled daddy's girl during her childhood, she's now a spoiled, demanding wife to an employee of Daddy's. She's horrified to pick up a phone one day and, because of crossed wires, hear two men planning a murder.

See *Sorry, Wrong Number*

STILES, TOD

Left unexpectedly penniless when his wealthy father dies, Tod decides to put what money he has into a Corvette and go "on the road" with his friend **Buz Murdock**. His road-tripping lifestyle centers mostly on famed Route 66, where Tod finds the adventures he's seeking. He eventually settles down and marries a woman named Mona.

See *Route 66*

STILLFIELD, CHARLENE FRAZIER

A down-to-earth "just folks" kind of girl who hails from Poplar Bluff, Arkansas. She once worked as a secretary in the capitol at Little Rock and now works at Sugarbakers design firm with the **Sugarbaker** sisters and **Mary Jo Shively**. Married to air force captain Bill Stillfield. She has a daughter, Olivia. She's a *National Enquirer* reader and a TV trivia buff. Her attention span is short, and she'll believe almost anything.

See *Designing Women*

STINGO

This sensitive, idealistic young man leaves the South for New York City to become a writer. There, he becomes involved in the lives of his neighbor **Sophie Zawistowska**, with whom he is helplessly in love, and her lover, **Nathan Landau**. He's baffled by the dark side of human nature which they represent, and stunned by the aspects of life they've experienced, things that he has hardly dreamed of.

See *Sophie's Choice*, William Styron

STIVIC, GLORIA

Liberal, feminist daughter and newlywed. Cute, vivacious, and curvaceous Gloria inherited her mother **Edith's** good heart and willingness to please and rebelled against her father's racist view of life. The result is a somewhat confused but loving individual whose mission it is to show her father the error in his bigotry. Tie-dyed, unshaven husband **Mike Stivic** provides her with the encouragement she needs to fulfill her potential and shows her the folly of her parents' ways. Gloria is often in the middle of fights between Mike and **Archie** and, like her mother, goes to pieces when it comes to playing referee. She sweetly encourages her mother to become "liberated" and wants the world to know she is a modern woman. It's obvious she and Mike have a healthy sex life, despite living with her parents. She longs for the day when Mike gets his degree and a job, and they can have their own home.

See *All in the Family*

STIVIC, MIKE

Egghead liberal, pseudo-intellectual, son-in-law. Married to **Gloria Bunker**, daughter of **Archie** and **Edith**. Lives with his wife at her parents' house, 704 Houser Street, Corona, Queens. Studies sociology

and has no job. Must live with having his unemployed status thrown in his face daily by his racist,
bigoted father-in-law, who calls him Meathead.
Tries to show Archie how ridiculous and groundless
many of his beliefs are, but usually ends up in a bellowing match. Best friend is black next-door neighbor Lionel Jefferson, who often appears to pull
Archie's leg. Has to deal with a very emotional and
unpredictable wife who is trying to find herself.
Gets along well with mother-in-law Edith and tries
to teach her to stand up to Archie. Has an obvi-
ously good sex life with Gloria. Has aspirations to
be a professor and to move out of Archie's house.
Not without a tendency to patronize his wife,
which sometimes leads to tension between them.
See *All in the Family*

STOCKTON, JO
She's a small-town girl with uncommon looks who
dreams of making it big as a fashion model. The
protégée of famed photographer **Dick Avery**.
Though shy and awkward at moments, Jo has the
capability for growth and the inner beauty one
needs to compete on the runways of Paris.
See *Funny Face*

STODDARD, RANSOM
Ransom Stoddard is a young, idealistic lawyer from
the East. He's unprepared for the pragmatic flexibility of old-time western law, which allows for a
fair gunfight, among other things. The fact that he's
a greenhorn doesn't mean he's weak. He bolsters his
courage with his lawbooks and convictions and
does what he feels is right.
See *The Man Who Shot Liberty Valance*

THE STONE FAMILY
The perfect, wholesome suburban clan. Alex, the
father, is a handsome pediatrician who works out of
an office connected to their house; Donna, the
mother, is lovely, helpful, and the provider of all
things Mom-like. (They met when Donna was
working as a nurse.) Living in a nicely appointed
home in Hilldale, Alex and Donna have two kids,
Mary and Jeff. Mary is a pretty, popular teenager
who goes to Hilldale High, then to a nearby college. She hangs out at Kelzey's Malt Shop. Her
younger brother is Jeff, who also hangs out at
Kelzey's, but squeezes in Hotenmeyer's for burgers.

He plays football and dates a girl named Bebe.
When Mary moves out, the Stones adopt Trisha, a
young orphan who'd been living with her uncle.
See *The Donna Reed Show*

STONE, BARBARA
Overweight, abrasive millionaire heiress. She'll try
anything, including urine injections, to lose extra
pounds. Her French poodle, Muffy, delights in pee-
ing on husband **Sam Stone**'s Oriental rug. After
she's kidnapped, she turns into an exercise freak and
loses twenty pounds: "All my life I've wanted a
slinky little figure." Big hair; fond of blood-red nail
polish. Her shopping list includes Lancome Throat
and Firming Massage Cream, Royal Queen Bee
Jelly, and Sperm Whale Oil. When she learns her
ransom has been cut from $500,000 to $10,000,
she shrieks, "I've been kidnapped by K-Mart!"
See *Ruthless People*

STONE, BENJY
A hapless junior writer on *King Kaiser's Comedy
Hour,* the top-rated TV comedy show in 1954. He
is assigned to babysit the swashbuckling movie
actor—and notorious drunk and womanizer—
Alan Swann the week he's guesting on the show.
"Mr. Swann, I think I'm going to be unwell."
See *My Favorite Year*

STONE, JABEZ
Impoverished New Hampshire farmer of the
1840s. Amazingly naive in the art of the deal.
Despite inherently bad business sense, he has a
knack for making connections. Also very good
when it comes to picking out attorneys.
See *The Devil and Daniel Webster*

STONE, MIKE
A lieutenant with the San Francisco Police
Department, Mike is a veteran of the force with
more than two decades of police work under his belt.
He's paternal and compassionate but also believes in
the system as the way to get things done and is very
tough on criminals. A widower, he has a college-age
daughter and is partnered with **Steve Keller**.
See *The Streets of San Francisco*

STONE, SAM
This thieving millionaire passionately hates every-

thing about his wife—even "the way she licks stamps." He married the boss's daughter to get her money. Crude and oversexed, he keeps a hot, red-headed mistress. He's known as the "Spandex Mini-Skirt King," a fashion design he ripped off from one of his employees. Sam lives in posh Bel Air, gulps champagne like water, and lives for money. When kidnappers steal his shrill wife, **Barbara**, he is ecstatic and dares them to kill her. His advice: "Never let the seller know you're hot to trot."

See *Ruthless People*

STONER, HARRY

Harried, middle-aged, Beverly Hills resident and owner of Capri Casuals, a 1970s L.A. clothing manufacturer. Sick of the rat race, he daydreams of the great baseball teams he followed as a child, trying to recapture a simpler, happier time. But he's stuck in his actual present, and, feeling forced into an unethical choice to save his livelihood, he hires an arsonist to torch a factory, hoping the insurance money will be enough to keep him in business.

See *Save the Tiger*

DR. STRANGE

This "Master of the Mystic Arts" uses his powers of conjuring to save the universe from supernatural evildoers. Stephen Strange was originally an arrogant, selfish, and very successful surgeon, until a car accident caused severe nerve damage that ended his career. To escape his misery, he traveled to the Himalayas and sought out the mystical Ancient One, who taught him not only the secrets of white magic but also the value of generosity. The newly incarnated Dr. Strange went on to battle the forces of the netherworld, often by invoking the "the all-seeing eye of Agamotto" or "the hoary hosts of Hoggoth."

See *Dr. Strange*

DR. STRANGELOVE

Wheelchair-bound scientist of German origin working for U.S. government. He participated in the creation of the top-secret Doomsday machine and is intrigued by the possibilities that could arise from a nuclear holocaust and the consequential breeding of a new society. His right arm has a mind of its own. Wears dark glasses and smokes. Has a

devilish smile. "Mein Führer, I can walk!"

See *Dr. Strangelove: or, How I Learned to Stop Worrying and Love the Bomb*

STRAUSS, MARGARET

Hollywood socialite and star of the 1940s, married to celebrated conductor **Roman Strauss**. She was involved with a mysterious and scandalous murder, though her status in the case is not as clear as it seems. Appears quite often in dreams of others years after her own death.

See *Dead Again*

STRAUSS, ROMAN

Bearded orchestra conductor, married to **Margaret Strauss**. A popular bon vivant around Hollywood, though he carries a dark secret with him. Has an aversion to mirrors and unusual future kinship with **Grace** and **Mike Church**.

See *Dead Again*

STREET, DELLA

She is the consummate career secretary. She dresses immaculately, never has a hair out of place, and never touches a typewriter (but takes perfect short-hand). She's totally devoted to her job and has no life outside the office...except when she dons her fur coat to go to dinner or the theater with her boss, **Perry Mason**. But their relationship is purely professional. He has no private life, either.

See *Perry Mason*

STRIKER, TED

Former pilot, scarred by post-traumatic stress resulting from wartime action. He remains a determined individual and a romantic. When the going gets tough, he takes control of a commercial jetliner. Manages to rise above mechanical failures, the presence of lunatics and incompetents all around him, a steady stream of bad puns, and a truly horrendous perspiration problem.

See *Airplane!*

STROHEM, SABINE

The mysterious Sabine is a postage stamp designer and wildlife artist living in a small Pacific island nation. She discovers that she sees **Griffin Moss**'s artworks in her mind's eye as he creates them, and starts a passionate correspondence with him. Is she his Muse? What's their link? Their efforts to meet in the flesh seem doomed to frustrating failure.

See *Griffin and Sabine,* Nick Bantock

STRONG, KAY LEILAND

A theater major at Vassar, where she bloomed as the de facto leader of her clique of girlfriends, Kay nonetheless has to settle for sales jobs at department stores. Despite her aspirations to become a director she comes no closer to the theater than marriage to an unsuccessful playwright.

See *The Group,* Mary McCarthy

STUBING, CAPTAIN MERRILL

The captain of the *Love Boat* guides its guests and crew through calm or stormy seas, not to mention the problems and joys of romance. He is the widowed father of **Vicki**, who lives on the ship. While a nice guy, he's serious and dedicated to his job, chastising unprofessional behavior on the part of crew members, but also full of fatherly advice. He occasionally has short-term romances and dares to hope that love will find him again.

See *The Love Boat*

STUBING, VICKI

Vicki, the lonely, illegitimate daughter of *Love Boat* captain **Merrill Stubing**, presents herself to the astonished captain, who hadn't dreamed of her existence, and then comes aboard to live. The love-starved Vicki and her father develop warm and affectionate bonds. But the *Love Boat* is hardly a conventional place to grow up; coming of age there means that sex and romance are even more a part of daily life than they would be on dry land. But she does find a "big sister" in **Julie McCoy**.

See *The Love Boat*

STULWICZ, BENNIE

A mentally challenged adult office worker. Good-natured, trusting, and loving Bennie lights up the hallways of McKenzie, Brackman, Chaney and Kuzak as he delivers mail, makes photocopies, and carries messages. Hired through the uncharacteristic kindness of **Arnie Becker**, Bennie gets to prove that retarded adults can be productive members of

Superman

society. His ongoing courtship with a mentally challenged woman shows that he has the same feelings and desires as the next man. Occasionally, Bennie gets into trouble through misunderstandings, but his friends at McKenzie, Brackman are there to look out for him.

See *L.A. Law*

STYLES, FURIOUS

Divorced father of **Tre Styles**, he lives in South-Central Los Angeles despite crime and gangs that infest the neighborhood. Furious tries his best to be a role model to his son, avoiding drink, drugs, and other vices that have ruined many of his peers. He's willing to wield a gun, if necessary, to defend his home.

See *Boyz 'n the Hood*

STYLES, TRE

High school senior, son of **Furious Styles**. Trying to make the best of daily life in a South-Central Los Angeles neighborhood torn by gangs and violence. Though Tre has gang member friends, including **Doughboy**, he's thus far managed to avoid being recruited into their fold. Has his sights set on a college education at Howard University.

See *Boyz 'n the Hood*

SUGARBAKER, JULIA

This classy, witty southern lady runs Sugarbakers design firm with sister **Suzanne Sugarbaker**, **Mary Jo Shively**, and **Charlene Frazier Stillfield**. Julia dates courtly Reese Watson. Politically active and a believer in liberal causes and women's rights, she tries to keep Suzanne in line and change her bigoted ways. Stands up for herself. *"Su-zanne!"*

See *Designing Women*

SUGARBAKER, SUZANNE

Sexy, bubbleheaded former beauty queen. Runs interior design firm with sister **Julia Sugarbaker**, **Mary Jo Shively**, and **Charlene Frazier Stillfield**. Outspoken opinions demonstrate both bigotry and lack of intellect. Deep down she has a good heart and is easily hurt. Collects alimony from three ex-husbands and is always on the lookout for number four. She likes them old and rich. Brunette, buxom, and proud of it, she reeks of money. Adopts a pet pig. Won't listen to the advice of her sister. Comes

to value opinions of **Anthony Bouvier**.
See *Designing Women*

SULLIVAN, DONALD "SULLY"

A hard-living, strong-willed, eternally broke blue-collar worker in upstate New York. You could think of him as Peter Pan if he weren't so crusty, old, and fond of alcohol. Sully has spent his whole life running from his painful childhood memories, shirking all family responsibilities along the way. When his son, whom he deserted many years before, returns to town with Sully's grandson, suddenly Sully is confronted with all the mistakes he's made. But he's not sure what to do about it, or what he *can* do.
See *Nobody's Fool*, Richard Russo

SULU

The chief navigator on the starship *Enterprise,* Sulu is a key component of **Captain Kirk**'s bridge crew. Sulu is competent and bright, but beneath a cool exterior beats the heart of a Japanese warrior. Sulu eventually becomes a captain, and his daughter joins the Federation.
See *Star Trek*

SUMMERS, MARY ANN

This innocent farmgirl is a castaway on a desert island with other passengers of the SS *Minnow*. She has pigtails and freckles and wears gingham. Makes coconut cream pies and daydreams about the fun she used to have on the farm. At present, she's getting an education from **Ginger**.
See *Gilligan's Island*

SUMNER, ABBY CUNNINGHAM EWING

A vicious vixen, Abby constantly schemes to get her way, and her plans often include someone else's husband. She is a dishonest but successful business-woman. With her wavy blond hair, enormous blue eyes, and very short skirts, she easily reels in her male victims. Abby loves her two children, but she's not much of a role model.
See *Knots Landing*

SUMNER, GREGORY

Ex–United States senator turned extremely prosperous businessman. He knows power is an aphro-disiac and uses it accordingly. A smooth talker in expensive suits, Sumner can be ruthless if someone gets in his way. But he's met his match in **Paige Matheson**, the strong and much younger daughter of his friend Mac MacKenzie.
See *Knots Landing*

SUPERGIRL

Her birth name was Kara, and she is the younger cousin of **Superman**. After her home planet, Krypton, was destroyed, she lived in Argo City, a clear-domed community of former Kryptonians. But then the dome was punctured during a meteor storm, and the resultant release of Kryptonite radiation propelled her to the planet Earth, where she lives as **Linda Lee**. Of course, Superman wound up here, too.
See *Supergirl*, Mort Weisinger and Otto Binder

SUPERMAN

The Man of Steel has it all: awesome strength, the ability to fly, bullet-resistant skin, and x-ray vision. A native of the planet Krypton, Superman was sent to Earth by his scientist father when his home planet was about to explode. On his new home planet, Superman developed a secret identity as a journalist. Is in love with girl reporter and mortal **Lois Lane**. His younger cousin follows in his do-gooder footsteps. No matter what peril faces Metropolis or even the whole world, Superman is there to handle it. Can often be seen flying through the air. "This is a job for Superman!"
See *Superman*

SUSAN

Free-spirited, proto–Generation X vagabond on the run in New York from Atlantic City gangsters. Has a penchant for unusual Egyptian jewelry and midriff-exposing wardrobe. She is the subject of several personal ads in the New York newspapers. When it comes to public grooming, she can be very resourceful with limited means and in confining circumstances.
See *Desperately Seeking Susan*

SUTPHIN, BEVERLY

This Baltimore housewife looks like a Betty Crocker ad; she makes a cool meat loaf, dotes on her kids, Misty and Chip, and believes deeply in recycling, which she does while dancing to Barry Manilow's "Daybreak." Her only little flaw is intolerance for other people's peccadilloes—neglecting to rewind videotapes, flouting seat belt laws, wearing white shoes after Labor Day, or not recycling. Such individuals, in her opinion, don't deserve to live. And she takes it upon herself to see that they don't.

See *Serial Mom,* John Waters

SWALE, MIKE

This small-town boy thinks he's been around the block after living for a time in Buffalo. He even has a deep, dark secret. But bitchy New Yorker **Bridget Gregory** proves to be totally outside his experience and takes him way out of his depth. By the time she's done with him, he's reduced to a sex addict, with no moral compass, who'll stop at nothing, not even murder, to get his regular sexual fix.

See *The Last Seduction*

THE SWAMP THING

In his pre-mutant life, he was scientist Dr. Alex Holland. But his lab was attacked by mercenaries hired by his archenemy, Arcane. In the ensuing bedlam, he spilled an unstable experimental mixture, containing vegetable cells with animal nuclei, all over himself. The result: a smelly, ugly, deformed, but sensitive creature, known as Swamp Thing, who now makes his home in the swamps (hence the name), because the mutation process that vegetablized him can't be reversed. But he may be able to photosynthesize, which would cut his grocery bills considerably.

See *Swamp Thing,* Len Wein and Bernie Wrightson, and *Swamp Thing,* Wes Craven

SWANN, ALAN

Alan's the star of countless swashbuckling epics, what we used to call a "matinee idol." After 30 years of boozing and carousing his way through endless Hollywood parties, he's pickled, unpredictable, and given to antics. He drinks and parties to forget he's not the star he once was and so he won't be reminded of his secret past. He's been everywhere, done every single thing in this life…except one. He's never done this newfangled thing, television. That's okay; he'll do it anyway. What's that? It's before a live audience? Swann erupts, "Live? I can't go on live!! I'm a movie star—I'm not an actor!"

See *My Favorite Year*

SWAY, MARK

A tough eleven-year-old living in a trailer park with his young mother and little brother, Mark is thrust into adult responsibility and danger when he and his brother witness the suicide of a gangster's lawyer. He's on his own, but he's smart enough to know he needs a good attorney, which he finds in the tough but motherly **Reggie Love**.

See *The Client,* John Grisham

SWIFT, TOM

A peerless inventor, fearless adventurer, and all-around superteen. Blessed with the most ingenious mind in the world, Tom foils crime by creating technological marvels, including a lightning-fast motorcycle, a phototelephone, a submarine, and a giant cannon to protect the Panama Canal from gangsters.

See *Tom Swift and His Motor Cycle,* Edward L. Stratemeyer ("Victor Appleton")

SYLVIE

Her fellow townspeople think she's mad, while her nieces, whom she cares for after their mother commits suicide, differ over whether she's crazy or an eccentric saint. Sylvie likes the dusk so much she refuses to turn on the lights, obsessively collects newspapers and tin cans, and creates a dream world so amusing she doesn't need the outside world for entertainment.

See *Housekeeping,* Marilyn Robinson

SZALINSKI, WAYNE

Szalinski is a failure as an inventor-scientist and as a father until one day when things go both right and wrong: his shrinking machine works, but it inadvertently shrinks his kids to miniscule size. This makes him realize what disruptions his obsessions have caused to family life. He is a weak, meek man with a tremendous enthusiasm for science.

See *Honey I Shrunk the Kids*

SZELL, CHRISTIAN

Aka the White Angel, due to his hair color. This brilliant Nazi Auschwitz research doctor and dentist experimented on prisoners, stripped them of their valuables, and, at the end of World War II, fled with his ill-gotten gains to Argentina, then Paraguay. A ruthless, dangerous man, even though no longer young, he carries a razor-sharp knife strapped to his right forearm. His unlikely nemesis is graduate student **Thomas Babington Levy**.

See *Marathon Man*

TABER, ROSLYN
Roslyn is a sad golden girl who knows how to make a man feel happy, but not herself. She's freshly divorced, an ex–dance instructor who never finished high school. Aimless and going nowhere, she rents a station wagon and follows cowboy **Gay Langland** to the Nevada countryside. She's sensitive enough to cry when rodeo rider **Perce Howland** is thrown from his horse. Decides to stay with Gay and have a "brave child." "Oh, Gay, what is there? Do you know? What is there that stays?"

See *The Misfits*, Arthur Miller

TAGGART, DAGNY
She's an ice princess with a heart of fire, but it seems that her only passion is running the Taggart Transcontinental Railroad. Capitalistic to the core, she believes the herd mentality will ruin the country. Dagny does everything in her considerable power to promote individual creativity. Dagny has a brilliant mind. She commands respect of her all-male peers. Her brother, **James Taggart**, is president of the railroad and Dagny's ideological opposite. Her search for a real man, a man who can help her mold a promising future, finally ends when she answers the question "Who is John Galt?"

See *Atlas Shrugged*, Ayn Rand

TAGGART, JAMES
He's weak and wishy-washy and he presides over the Taggart Transcontinental Railroad—in name only. He inherited the business when his father died. But James prefers hobnobbing with Washington bigwigs to hands-on management of the railroad, which he leaves to his exceptionally dynamic, capable sister, **Dagny**. He's unhappy, tends toward petulance, and is losing his hair. His workers refer to him as "the hobo on the gravy train."

See *Atlas Shrugged*, Ayn Rand

TAGGART, SERGEANT
Long-suffering Beverly Hills police officer. A believer in law and order. Realizes police work is difficult but is aghast when unorthodox behavior appears under his command. Begrudgingly puts up with antics of out-of-town detective **Axel Foley**.

See *Beverly Hills Cop*

TALBOT, ANN
Talbot is a top criminal defense lawyer, with great determination and resourcefulness. Whether as a mother, daughter, or sister, Ann is devoted to family. She maintains close contact with all of her relatives, and keeps traditions of the old country in her own home. Her son, Mikey, is named after her father, **Mike Laszlo**. Although divorced, Ann is on good terms with her lawyer ex-husband and her ex-father-in-law, the head of a prestigious law firm.

See *The Music Box*

TAMARA
This Holocaust survivor has long been thought dead by her husband, **Herman Broder**. But she recently turned up in New York, where she is trying to rebuild her life. A realist who understands the complexities and ironies that are so much a part of human existence.

See *Enemies: A Love Story*

TAMBO, SHELLY
Young, pretty, former Miss Northwest Passage. Shelly originally came to little Cicely, Alaska, through the instigation of **Maurice Minnifield**, who was a judge at the pageant. Now she is married to **Holling Vincoeur**, who is three times her age. (Her first husband was hockey player Wayne Jones of the Saskatoon Seals.) Works at the Brick, the local tavern, with owner Holling. She recently gave birth to a little girl, Miranda. Known for using throw-back phrases like "totally bitchin'."

See *Northern Exposure*

TANNEN, BIFF
This big burly bully type is the perennial nemesis of **George McFly** from school days into adulthood. Lives to torture the hapless nerd. Fond of bullying weaker beings and other inferiors. Not terribly bright, but genuinely nasty.

See *Back to the Future*

NEW YORKERS
Peter Parker
Detective Andy Sipowicz
Alvy Singer
Kramer
Rhoda Morgenstern
Detective Phil Fish
Eustace Tilley
Egon Spengler, Peter Venkman, and Raymond Stantz
Allen Bauer

Andy and Opie Taylor

TARLEK, HERB

Mr. Polyester. A would-be "swinger," Herb seems completely unaware of the fact that he's a loser. He acts like he's the ultimate in hipness as well as the ultimate ladies' man. He is a minority of one in believing himself a classy dresser, in his mismatched outfits and white belt. He works as the advertising director for WKRP, a not-too-successful radio station in Cincinnati. He isn't a creative genius and comes up with a lot of harebrained ad ideas. Though he pals around with newsman **Les Nesman**, it's not clear that they like each other that much. He indulges in futile fantasies about a relationship with WKRP's receptionist, **Jennifer Marlowe**.

See *WKRP in Cincinnati*

TARZAN

An English lord raised by apes in the African jungle, Tarzan embodies the poise and dignity of a nobleman and the courage and fortitude of a man of nature. He may swing through trees like a wild thing, but Tarzan must struggle with a heart that is English at its core. When Tarzan's parents, John and Alice Clayton, Lord and Lady Greystoke, are marooned by mutineers on a steaming African coast, they have little chance of survival. Still less has their infant son who is born in their lonely jungle cabin. When little Lord Greystoke is a year old, both of his parents die. Miraculously, the baby is seized by an ape, Kala, who, crazed with grief at the death of her own offspring, immediately adopts him. She calls him Tarzan, which means, in her language, "white skin." Under the care and guidance of the motherly Kala, Tarzan grows into an equal member of a roving band of apes, led by the fierce Kerchak. Tarzan takes longer to learn the skills of jungle survival than do his ape brothers, but he becomes inhumanly strong and exceptionally ingenious. He feels irresistibly drawn to the deserted Greystoke cabin, where he teaches himself to read. After years in the jungle, Tarzan comes into contact with a marooned American professor and his daughter **Jane Porter**. Feeling an inexplicable kinship with the white strangers, Tarzan becomes their protector, saving the professor and Jane from numerous brushes with death. Ultimately, he must choose between following Jane into civilization and remaining a wild and free man of the jungle.

See *Tarzan of the Apes,* **Edgar Rice Burroughs**

TATE, CHESTER

The arrogant, wealthy, philandering Chester is married to **Jessica Tate**, who is clearly too good for him. He's forever trying to convince her he's changed, for instance, after he's served time for murder. A bout with amnesia consigns him to menial labor, for a time. He and Jessica have two more or less adult daughters, Corrine and Eunice.

See *Soap*

TATE, FRED

A young boy with an over-the-top I.Q. whose intelligence and interests lie beyond the grasp of his waitress mother. Fred is quiet, well-behaved, and remarkably well-adjusted for a boy whose overwhelming mental faculties propel him beyond his humble surroundings. He is a combination of adult intelligence and youthful interests: although he can understand complex mathematical problems and complicated methodologies, he still wants a birthday party and to be accepted by his peers. Fred wants to please both his working-class mother, who wants him to remain a normal little boy, and his teacher, who encourages his intellectual interests. He's caught in a struggle between these two women who recognize his exceptional gifts, but have different ideas about how to raise him.

See *Little Man Tate*

TATE, JESSICA

This warmhearted, lovely, ditzy lady is the wealthy wife of unfaithful husband **Chester Tate**. She also has some affairs of her own. For some reason, Jessica keeps a soft spot for her errant husband, even after they divorce. The mother of two girls, Corrine and Eunice, Jessica's best friend is her sister, **Mary Campbell**.

See *Soap*

TATE, LARRY

A partner in the advertising firm of McMann and Tate, white-haired Larry is boss to Darrin Stephens, whose wife's witchly powers often end up messing with his mind. A true sycophant, he says whatever he thinks the client wants to hear, no matter what. Fires Darrin—and rehires him—on a regular basis. Married to **Louise**. "You son of a gun!"

See *Bewitched*

TATE, LOUISE

Married to **Larry Tate**, she's as calm and lovely as Larry is neurotic and ambitious. Puts up with all his shenanigans, seeing less of the supernatural phenomena than he does. Quite likes **Samantha Stephens**, Darrin Stephens's wife. A housewife, she often entertains for her husband's clients.

See *Bewitched*

TATTOO

He is a heavily accented, lisping little person and the right-hand man to **Mr. Roarke** in the running of dream resort Fantasy Island. His job seems to consist mainly of asking questions with highly obvious answers. "Zee plane! Zee plane!"

See *Fantasy Island*

TAYLOR, SHERIFF ANDY

Sheriff Taylor is the stable guiding hand for his family and the townfolk of Mayberry, North Carolina. He lives with maiden **Aunt Bee Taylor** and young son **Opie**. Andy's calm, nonviolent approach to law and order earns him the town's respect and a Hollywood script, *Sheriff without a Gun*. He is the cousin, boss, best friend, and protector of ineffectual deputy **Barney Fife**. Though he dates schoolteacher Helen Crump, their relationship is very chaste. Likes to sing ballads, play the guitar, and fish with Opie at Myer's Lake.

See *The Andy Griffith Show*

TAYLOR, AUNT BEE

The warmhearted old maid and substitute mother for **Opie Taylor** and his father, **Andy**. Aunt Bee has blue hair and is given to calico dresses and aprons. She dotes on the "Mayberry After Midnight" gossip column in the *Mayberry Gazette*. Aunt Bea is a keen rival of spinster and town opinion leader Clara Edwards, with whom she competes in rose gardening, pickling, preserves, and pies. Though a proper southern lady, she occasionally duels with Clara over the affections of a gentleman. She frets some about Andy and Opie. "Now, Andy, Opie's just a boy!"

See *The Andy Griffith Show*

TAYLOR, GEORGE

Solid in both body and mind, he's an astronaut whose ship crash-lands on a planet where the roles of apes and men are reversed. After taking a mute but cute human female as his mate, he manages to escape from ape scientists before they dissect his brain—only to learn that he's time-traveled to Earth's post-apocalyptic future.

See *Planet of the Apes*

TAYLOR, JALEESA VINSON

Wisecracking, no-frills, college student at mostly black Hillman College, starting as a twenty-six-year-old freshman. Previously divorced. She has no time for schoolgirl silliness. She's the sage of the dorm, solving problems for **Whitley**, **Dwayne**, and others.

See *A Different World*

TAYLOR, JILL

Good-humored wife of Tim Taylor, puts up with her husband's constant, and disastrous, attempts to work on projects around the house. Always prepared with a sarcastic retort. Tries vainly to get Tim to really talk to her. Only woman in a house of four males, she rules the roost.

See *Home Improvement*

Mr. Rourke and Tattoo
©1996 Capital Cities/ABC, Inc.

TAYLOR, KELLY

The perfect blonde, Kelly knows the ins and outs of the social landscape like only a Beverly Hills native could. Shows the ropes to newcomer **Brenda Walsh**, her best friend in high school until Kelly starts dating Brenda's ex-beau, **Dylan McKay**. Eventually settles on the more commonsense choice when she

begins a relationship with **Brandon Walsh**. Her parents are divorced, her mother—a model—is an alcoholic. Attends California University; plans to pursue modeling.
See *Beverly Hills 90210*

TAYLOR, OPIE

Norman Rockwell's American boy come to life, Opie has freckles, red hair, and an occasional cowlick. He hates to dress up or go to parties with girls. When he tugs at his collar in church on Sunday, he's admonished by **Aunt Bee**, the closest thing he has to a mother. Opie idolizes his dad, **Sheriff Andy Taylor**, and stops by the courthouse after school to share his day's happenings and problems with his "paw" and **Barney Fife**. Opie loves his teacher, Miss Crump, as does his father. His best friend is Johnny Paul Jason, who once ate tar. When he wrote an essay divulging the less-than-glamorous truth about the Civil War "Battle of Mayberry," he created a furor among townfolk. Opie looks to his father for answers to all of life's questions and usually finds them. "Golly, Paw, you know just about everything, don't you?"
See *The Andy Griffith Show*

TAYLOR, TIM

The amiable host of handyman cable-television show, *Tool Time,* Tim is nonetheless incapable of fixing anything in his own house. He's upstaged often on his own show by his cohost, Al. Tim's ineptitude often extends to his parenting and husbanding skills, but he tries hard. A traditional male trying to cope with a strong wife and three kids in the 1990s, he loves his wife, **Jill**, but has trouble communicating with her. Tim thinks that because he's married, he doesn't have to try very hard anymore. Likes gadgets, sports, and cars. Frequently relies on his neighbor **Wilson** to give him advice about how to deal with his wife, kids, and job.
See *Home Improvement*

MRS. TEASDALE

Buxom grande dame of the country of Freedonia and principal sponsor behind the appointment of its new leader, **Rufus T. Firefly**. A widow whose husband has left her a great fortune, she's intensely loyal to her country and upset over the thought of impending war with neighboring Sylvania. "Hail, hail, Freedonia, land of the brave and free!"
See *Duck Soup*

TEMPLAR, SIMON

Known as "the Saint," he is audacious, debonair, and impossibly savvy. Think of him as **James Bond**'s spiritual father. Though he lives outside the law, he's basically a Good Guy. He is a cheerful, amorous buccaneer with tony tastes. "Everything, you understand, quietly but unmistakably of the very best, and worn with that unique air of careless elegance…which only the Saint could achieve in all its glory."
See, e.g., *Enter the Saint,* Leslie Charteris

TEMPLE, NORA

A slender, spirited blond World War II widow. Temple's husband, George, was killed in the Italian theater during World War II. A strongly moral woman, Temple believes in fighting for her beliefs, even if her physical strength is not sufficient to back up her natural spunk. She works and lives in Key Largo with her late husband's father, James Temple. Her wedding ring has the inscription "evermore" engraved in it. She had an involvement with **Frank McCloud**.
See *Key Largo*

THE TERMINATOR

An unstoppable killing machine sent to the present from the future to terminate **Sarah Connor**, who will give birth to future human leader **John Connor** if she's not done away with. Possessed of an artificial intelligence beyond anything currently conceivable, the Terminator is not just ruthless but also cunning, versatile, and meticulous. Real live tissue covers his almost indestructible mechanisms and skeletal framework. He has an Austrian accent, but it just adds to his charm. "I'll be back."
See *The Terminator*

TEVYE

Resident milkman in the small Russian village of Anatevka. He is married to Golde and the father of five daughters. Tevye is proud of his Jewish heritage, though often subjects God to a grilling in private dialogues. Can be impossibly stubborn at times, particularly in dealing with his family. Given to occasional but hearty singing and dancing when the moment is right. "Would it have spoiled some vast eternal plan if I was a wealthy man?"

See *Fiddler on the Roof*

THADDEUS, "THE CHIEF"

Serious Washington bureaucrat. He heads U.S. intelligence agency CONTROL, and is constantly at odds with evil rival intelligence agency KAOS. The Chief works from his Washington office, dispatching secret agents on missions of national security. His top agents include Agent 86 (**Maxwell Smart**), **Agent 99**, and the ubiquitous Agent 13. He's often exasperated by the antics of Maxwell Smart but knows Max is often the only man for the job.

See *Get Smart*

THATCHER, CHARLES "CORKY"

A Down's syndrome teenager, smiling, good-natured Corky is mentally challenged but gifted with humor and genuine goodness. His clear view of a mixed-up world helps his family and those he meets to better understand the meaning of life. Corky is "mainstreamed" at the local public school and is thrown together with sister Becca and her friends, posing a challenge during her painful teenage years. Constantly demonstrates to all that most of our problems are trivial.

See *Life Goes On*

THATCHER, REBECCA "BECCA"

She is an insecure, uncomfortable young teenager. Her glasses and straight hair are only two of the impediments to popularity and success for Becca as she enters high school. A perfectionist and worrier, she's always agonizing over something. She loves her mentally challenged brother, **Corky**, but wishes he were less of a responsibility and not her classmate. Often, though, it is he who shows her what's important and helps her to grow and become a good person.

See *Life Goes On*

THAYER, ETHEL

Spry, cheerful septuagenarian New Englander married to crotchety husband **Norman Thayer, Jr.**, whom she tries to buoy with optimism. She acts as mediator between her husband and daughter, who have never gotten along. As both her husband's

protector and his partner, her energy and diplomatic skills come in handy.

See *On Golden Pond*

THAYER, NORMAN, JR.

This ill-tempered 80-year-old former teacher works hard at his rudeness. His bitterness stems from a growing sense of mortality and fear of death. He maintains a shaky, arm's-length relationship with his daughter and is reluctant to make the first move at reconciliation. Although he loves his family, he finds intimacy difficult and shakes it off uncomfortably.

See *On Golden Pond*

THE THING

Brooklyn native Ben Grimm reluctantly helps his three friends steal a rocket and fly to the moon, but on the way they are belted by cosmic radiation and turned into superpowered freaks. Grimm perhaps gets the worst of it, being turned into an orange, stone-skinned brute. Now renamed the Thing, he is the most cantankerous and quarrelsome member of a team of superheroes known as the Fantastic Four. For all his nasty temper and ugly complexion, he has a tender heart, and is tormented by his impossible love for the blind and gentle Alicia Masters.

See *The Fantastic Four*

THOMAS, BIGGER

The quintessential frustrated and angry young black man; precursor to the violent homeboys who now populate gangsta rap songs. He grows up to hate whites and sees them as responsible for his not having a chance at success. The eldest son in a fatherless welfare family, he despises his mother's futile hope of becoming assimilated into mainstream American society. Bigger works as a chauffeur for the rich Dalton family and becomes friendly with young Mary Dalton, a naive white liberal. He hates himself for the erotic attraction he feels toward her, and his powerfully conflicted emotions have fatal consequences. He seems to feel empowered only when acting violently. Pushed into a career of violence, he is caught and tried. But he's still exploited, this time by Marxist ideologues, who use him to decry the racial and economic injustices perpetrated by capitalism. A man who never had a

©1996 Capital Cities/ABC, Inc.

Tonto

chance, Thomas is at least allowed to have a final sense of what he is and how he got there.

See *Native Son,* Richard Wright

THOMPSON, SADIE

Sadie is a prostitute. A good-hearted and witty woman on the lam from prison, she's stranded on the island of Pago Pago with militant missionaries, soldiers, and thieves.

See *Rain,* John Colton and Clemence Randolph

THORNDYKE, DR. RICHARD H.

This phobia-plagued, charming, renowned Harvard psychology professor replaces the murdered Dr. Ashley as chief of psychiatry at the Psychoneurotic Institute for the Very, Very Nervous. He is framed for murder by his colleagues, but with the help of his girlfriend (Victoria Brisbane), limo driver (Brophy), and mentor (Dr. Lilloman), proves his innocence and causes the downfall of the true murderers: **Dr. Charles Montague** and his sidekick, **Nurse Diesel**.

See *High Anxiety,* Mel Brooks

THORNHILL, ROGER

He's handsome, he's urbane, he's an advertising executive who stumbles into a deadly case of mistaken identity. After that, he finds himself arrested for drunk driving, wanted for murder, and the intended prey of a deadly team of espionage agents, led by nasty **Philip Vandamm**. The upside is that he meets and is smitten by lovely, if mysterious, **Eve Kendall**. The downside (other than the fact that people want to kill or arrest him) is that he doesn't know whether she's a friend pretending to be an enemy, or vice versa. He's definitely out of his usual Madison Avenue territory. While desperately running for his life, he encounters a whole series of bizarre adventures and hairbreadth escapes. Between being arrested for murder and being killed by spies, what's the more desirable choice? Flip a coin.

See *North by Northwest*

THORNTON, JOHN

A trail-hardened, good-hearted man who travels to the Northwest Territory of Canada to search for gold. Meets Buck, a sled-dog originally kidnapped from Southern California, when Buck is nearly dead from exhaustion and abuse. The two develop a deep love for one another, but it is brought to an unfortunate and unexpected end.

See *The Call of the Wild*

THORNTON, SEAN

"Trooper Thornton" returns to the town of Innisfree in his native Ireland to settle and marry, but mainly to get away from boxing; in his last bout he killed a man. He courts beautiful **Mary Kate Danaher**, but must overcome the constant bullying and threats of her big brother, whom he'd rather not fight. Eventually, they do come to blows.

See *The Quiet Man*

THREADGOODE, IDGIE

She's an untamed, freckle-faced "bee charmer" from Alabama and a teller of tall tales. At ten, she announces, "I'm never gonna wear another dress as long as I live!" and she doesn't. Shattered when her beloved brother, Buddy, is killed by a train, she's "too hurt to cry." Idgie takes up with her brother's old mistress for a time. Then she falls in love with preacher's daughter **Ruth Jamison**, rescuing her from an abusive husband. She can't cook worth a damn, but, together with Ruth, opens the Whistle Stop Cafe. She raises Ruth's son, Buddy, Jr., as her own, and holds a funeral for his severed arm after it is run over by a train. Idgie is rumored to have murdered a man. A friend to hobos, blacks, and drunks, she believes "there are magnificent beings on this earth that are walking around posing as humans."

See *Fried Green Tomatoes at the Whistle Stop Cafe,* Fannie Flagg

TIBBS, VIRGIL

A shrewd and sophisticated police detective from the North who gets embroiled in a murder case while passing through a dirt-road Mississippi town. The main problem: he's black and therefore immediately accused of the unexplained death of a rich white man. Tibbs's anger won't subside after he is cleared of suspicion and recruited to help solve the crime by the arrogant and unsurprisingly bigoted local sheriff. To get to the bottom of the case, Tibbs has to run a virtual gauntlet of violent rednecks who want him out of town or dead. "They call me Mister Tibbs!"

See *In the Heat of the Night* and *They Call Me Mister Tibbs!*

TIBIDEAUX, ELVIN

A hesitant, soft-spoken, deferential Princeton student, polite Elvin is sure of one thing: his love for **Sondra Huxtable**. Her tolerance of him eventually grows into love, and he feels he has all he needs. Since he's totally uninterested in the corporate world, Elvin tries various career paths before settling on med school. Becomes father of twins shortly after marriage to Sondra.

See *The Cosby Show*

TIBIDEAUX, SONDRA HUXTABLE

Sondra is gentle and quite smart, the eldest daughter of the Huxtable clan. Usually a "good girl," Sondra studies at Princeton and follows a predictable track toward success until she meets and marries somewhat goofy Elvin. Shortly thereafter, she becomes the mother of twins. Even after marriage and motherhood, she often visits parents **Cliff** and **Clair Huxtable** for advice and comfort.

See *The Cosby Show*

TILDEN

A high school football star who seems to have hit the line too often without his helmet; Tilden works on his family's decaying farm, finding bountiful harvests where no seeds were planted, and the keys to the future buried in the secrets of the past.

See *Buried Child,* Sam Shepard

TIPTON, JOHN BERESFORD

This mysterious, retired financier anonymously gives away a million tax-free dollars to a different stranger every week. Not really a philanthropist, he's a "student of human nature," interested in observing how money changes people. His executive secretary, **Michael Anthony**, delivers the cashier's checks to stunned recipients, who must give the money back if they ever disclose its source.

See *The Millionaire*

TITA

Passionate and sensual Tita is tormented with love for her beloved Pedro. She is nonetheless forced to remain single and devote her life to her selfish mother's care. Practically raised in the kitchen, she pours her suppressed feelings into her cooking, and the food she cooks affects in unusual ways those who eat it.

See *Like Water for Chocolate,* Laura Esquivel

TOBIAS, SARAH

Sarah is a foulmouthed, hard-drinking blue-collar worker living in a small, close-knit community. She enjoys partying with male buddies, but she doesn't always sense when those parties start to get beyond her control. Single-minded about justice when wronged. "I drink to take off the rough edges."

See *The Accused*

TODD, SWEENEY

An infamous barber and serial killer of Victorian London, Todd was born Benjamin Barker. He kills his tonsorial patrons indiscriminately, as practice for revenge upon the man who had him imprisoned and who made off with his wife and daughter. Because meat is scarce, he gives the bodies to his landlady, **Mrs. Lovett**, who uses them as filling for her celebrated meat pies.

See *Sweeney Todd,* Stephen Sondheim and James Lapine

TOM THE PRIEST

A defrocked priest whose fall is linked to his love for drugs, Tom is now living in a run-down Portland hotel. Despite his down-and-out living conditions, he still dresses with a dapper sense of fashion. An expert on the subject of narcotics use who has been around and tried everything at least once, he refuses to touch anything but the highest-quality abusable substances. An old friend of **Bob**. "I predict that in the near future, right-wingers will use drug hysteria as a pretext to set up an international police apparatus."

See *Drugstore Cowboy*

TONTO

The **Lone Ranger**'s loyal and stoic Indian sidekick. Like his more high-profile partner, Tonto is an expert gunslinger and horseman. With his headband and fringed buckskin suit, Tonto is always there to bail out his "kemosabe" when it looks like the guys in black hats will finally prevail.

See *The Lone Ranger*

TONY

Tony is a little boy with "the Shine"—psychic ability—who's not happy to be stuck in a remote Colorado hotel for the winter with his mom and writer father, **Jack Torrance**. His psychic powers soon provide him with more and more reasons to be dissatisfied with the hotel. Not even his beloved Big Wheels proves to be much of a consolation for him. "Redrum!"

See *The Shining*, Stephen King

TONY

Teenager Tony is a leader of a gang, the Jets, but he's more open to the possibilities of the world than his cronies. He falls in love with a pretty Latina, **Maria**, sister of the leader of a Puerto Rican gang, the Sharks, and the end results are tragic. "Maria! I just met a girl named Maria!"

See *West Side Story*, Arthur Laurents, Stephen Sondheim, and Leonard Bernstein

TORANAGA

One of the highest-ranked samurai in a war-torn Japan, he has the ambition and the smarts to defeat his opponents and become Shogun, the military ruler of Japan. Enlists the help of **John Blackthorne** and his knowlege of guns to give himself an edge. Intelligent and ruthless, he is not given to feelings of sentimentality; he is a "big-picture" kind of guy.

See *Shogun*

TORRANCE, JACK

Struggling with writer's block, on the edge of nervous crisis because of guilt and the tension of trying to stay on the wagon, he's a recovering alcoholic who takes a job as caretaker of a remote Colorado hotel for the winter, hoping that the isolation will force him to get some work done. He ignores the misgivings of his wife and kid, **Tony**, that the place is too creepy. The bracing atmosphere and old-time elegance of the hotel have a pronounced effect on Jack, which is heightened when the place is definitively snowed in by winter blizzards. He continues to labor at his typewriter, but the work he produces is of very doubtful salability. Isolation and evil associations also make Jack a less-than-ideal husband and father, and it soon becomes clear that Jack's idea of a perfect writer's getaway leaves just about everything to be desired. "He-e-e-ere's Johnny!"

See *The Shining*, Stephen King

TORTELLI LeBEC, CARLA

This diminutive, feisty, tart-tongued waitress has an unkind word for everyone where she works (the Boston bar Cheers). Customers and fellow employees alike are victimized by her verbal abuse, but the particular target of her zingers is fellow waitress **Diane Chambers**. The fact that Diane is involved with her idolized boss, **Sam Malone**, makes Carla all the more anxious to plague Diane. Carla has children from several relationships and eventually takes on yet another husband, hockey player turned Ice Capades penguin Eddie LeBec.

See *Cheers*

TRACY, DICK

An incorruptible plainclothes police detective dedicated to the eradication of crime in his city. To cleanse society of its filth, Tracy employs his cunning street smarts and a host of high-tech gadgets, including 2-Way Wrist Radio, the Atom Light, and the Teleguard Camera. His enemies all possess faces as repulsive as their rotten criminal souls: the gruesome Mrs. Pruneface; the revoltingly skin-blemished Wormy; and Flyface, so putridly filthy that insects swarm around him wherever he walks. But Tracy is as pure of heart as his opponents are foul. He is just as devoted to the good citizens of the metropolis as he is to his devoted wife, Tess Trueheart.

See *Dick Tracy*

TRACY, DR. MARSH

The Great White Vet. Handsome, virile, and single American veterinarian Dr. Tracy—known as "Daktari" to the locals—heals sick animals in Africa with help from his daughter Paula. His pets are Clarence, a cross-eyed lion, and Judy, a mischievous chimpanzee.

See *Daktari*

TRAHERNE, JUDITH

A fun-loving socialite with a zest for life, now she faces the ultimate challenge—she's been diagnosed as having a malignant brain tumor. Married to Dr. Frederick Steele, Judith's true love is her prized racehorse, Challenger. When the pressures of her illness mount, Judith is capable of revealing previously untapped qualities of sheer courage while looking death in the face.

See *Dark Victory*

TRAINER, JACK

A high-power but nice-guy executive who meets

the lovely and ambitious **Tess McGill** at a power dinner, never guessing that she's only a lowly secretary in the office of his lover, **Katherine Parker**. He helps Tess work on a deal she originally proposed but Katherine tried to steal. He's just your basic Wall Street insider with a heart of gold.

See *Working Girl*

TRALALA

This young, Brooklyn-warehouse-district hooker, despite the abuse she takes, and the cynicism she's acquired as a result, still somehow retains an element of innocence and hope. But she's doomed to her station in life; when she has the chance to escape it and move to Manhattan and a real, loving relationship, she feels so out of place that she's compelled to return to the mean streets she calls home.

See *Last Exit to Brooklyn,* Hubert Selby

TRAVEN, LIEUTENANT JACK

Can a Special Weapons and Tactics explosives expert find love on a city bus hurtling down the Los Angeles freeway at over fifty miles per hour? Well, first, there's a little issue of this bomb to locate and disarm. Jack Traven is a cop who doesn't play by the rules, perhaps because he has one of the toughest jobs in law enforcement: stopping criminals who use bombs as their weapons. He's relentless in his attempts to save innocent bystanders from dying, whether it involves leaping between speeding vehicles or hurtling through the subway tubes atop a runaway train.

See *Speed*

TRAVIS, ANDY

Andy's the competent, calm, sharp program director of Cincinnati radio station WKRP. He's the closest thing to a normal person to be found there and has made some partially effective efforts to give the station life and better revenues. He's also a natural mediator, which comes in handy in controlling the frequent staff disagreements and meddlesome input from his boss, **Arthur Carlson**.

See *WKRP in Cincinnati*

TREAT AND PHILIP

They're orphans living in a beat-up, unbelievably sloppy old house on the outskirts of Newark, New Jersey. Treat is an angry young street punk, who makes their meager living by a life of petty crime. He bullies his hyperactive little brother, Philip—a young adult, Philip's not little anymore—and scares him into staying inside the house by retelling the story of Philip's childhood allergic reactions to the outdoors. Philip instinctively wants to better his lot and teaches himself to read, a fact he hides from Treat, because it means that Treat has lost power over an aspect of Philip's life, which Treat would see as a threat. One night, Treat gets drunk with **Harold**, a well-dressed man he takes for a traveling salesman. But when he tries to rob Harold, he finds that the man is actually a world-wise gangster from Chicago, who foils Treat's plot. Luckily for the orphans, Harold takes a liking to them, and, with his suitcase full of cash, cleans up both the boys and their house, making the three of them into a tight little family. Philip, especially, is pleased with this turn of events; finally, with Harold's help, he has the courage to venture out into the world. Though Treat dislikes the way Harold has usurped his power over Philip and the way Harold forces him to try to control his rage, he's happy with the responsibilities entrusted to him by the older man. Though the time Harold can remain with the youngsters is limited by circumstances beyond their control, he leaves them with a legacy of life skills to make it in the world.

See *Orphans*

TREMAIN, JOHNNY

A spunky orphan working as an apprentice to a Boston silversmith, young Johnny joins the Sons of Liberty and suddenly finds himself in the middle of the American Revolution. Bright, brave, and full of patriotic vigor, he is a welcome recruit for the rebelling colonists. When he's not riding with Paul Revere, hobnobbing with Samuel Adams, or marching on his Tory-held hometown, Johnny muses on the meaning of freedom for himself and his emerging country. His only other passion is for the young and pretty Cilla Lapham, a fellow junior revolutionary.

See *Johnny Tremain,* Esther Forbes

TRIMBLE, COLEY

Jeering, perspiring, trigger-happy follower of **Reno Smith**, who would like to get rid of **John J. MacReedy** as soon as possible. He's a slow-witted thug who's good for the heavy work but not much else.

See *Bad Day at Black Rock*

TRIPPER, JACK
He's a bit of a bumbler, but he's basically an all-right guy. He has stumbled into what many young men might consider the fulfillment of a dream: to share an apartment with two good-looking young women, **Chrissy Snow** and **Janet Wood**. But Chrissy's too dumb and naive to realize when Jack's coming on to her, and Janet's too smart and tough to ever let him get anywhere with either of them. To be allowed to share the place with the girls, he tells the landlord he's gay.

See *Three's Company*

TROI, DEANNA
Half Betazoid, half human, Deanna uses her Betazoid powers of telepathy in her position as ship's counselor aboard the starship *Enterprise;* a degree in psychology also helps. Deanna is incredibly intuitive, beautiful, and once had an affair with **Will Riker**. She loves chocolate and has a sometimes fractious relationship with her eccentric mother, Lwaxana, who calls her "little one."

See *Star Trek: The Next Generation*

TROUT, KILGORE
A lonely science fiction writer, Kilgore Trout remains unknown because he submits his stories without a return address. Trout's pessimism is finally broken when a millionaire discovers him and asks him to speak at a conference. During Trout's cross-country journey to the conference, he hitches a ride on an olive truck and has his feet encased in industrial waste while crossing a creek.

See *Breakfast of Champions,* **Kurt Vonnegut Jr.**

TROUT, PARIS
He's racist and paranoid but is still a respected businessman in a small southern town. He abuses his wife and exploits members of the black community by lending them money at extortionate rates. He feels no remorse after killing a young black woman.

See *Paris Trout,* **Pete Dexter**

TROY
Handsome, goateed, shaggy-haired slacker; proto-typical Generation Xer. Well read in bohemian classics. Dismays **Lelaina** with his lack of ambition but finally wins her with his pure ideals and emotional honesty.

See *Reality Bites*

TRUESMITH, WOODROW LAFAYETTE
As the son of a World War I hero, this shy young man is expected to perform heroically in World War II—but chronic hayfever relegates him to a stateside job in a shipyard. Afraid to face his hometown, especially his mother and sweetheart, he arranges to have letters mailed from the front, showing that he's living out the townspeople's expectations. Then he meets a group of marine veterans, led by a crusty sergeant who knew his dad. They decide to bring him home as the hero he has claimed to be, even though he no longer wants any part of the deception.

See *Hail the Conquering Hero*

TRUMAN, SHERIFF HARRY S.
He is a dark-haired hunk of a lawman in the little Pacific Northwest town of Twin Peaks. He seems to be one of the few morally and spiritually "clean" persons in the whole place. He has to put up with a deputy who faints at the sight of blood and an office secretary who often appears to be only a few I.Q. points better off than a house plant. But he helps FBI agent **Dale Cooper** investigate the death of **Laura Palmer**. Harry's in love with a gorgeous Chinese woman, but she's up to no good.

See *Twin Peaks*

TUBBS, DETECTIVE RICARDO
This smooth-mannered Miami cop wears a designer wardrobe and a big gun, despite the chance that it'll spoil the fit of his jacket. He's the devoted partner of **Sonny Crockett** and goes out of his way to be there for his partner, as they fight to rid Miami of the scourge of illegal drugs and the criminals who sell them.

See *Miami Vice*

TUCO
An untrustworthy Mexican bandit, Tuco forms an uneasy alliance with Blondie, aka **Joe**, alias (for some reason) the Man with No Name, to hunt for a Confederate government treasure chest. His neck

ends up in a noose far too often for his taste, even though he usually extricates himself before the noose tightens. "When you have to shoot, shoot. Don't talk."

See *The Good, the Bad, and the Ugly*

TUFNEL, NIGEL

Dim-witted but lovable killer lead guitarist extraordinaire for Spinal Täp. Known for his amps, because their control knobs go up to 11, "one more than 10." When someone criticizes the cover of the band's next album, *Smell the Glove,* for being sexist, responds, "What's wrong with sexy?"

See *This Is Spinal Täp*

TULL, RICHARD

Failed novelist and alcoholic going through a massive midlife crisis. He's tortured by the success of his untalented friend, Gwyn Barry, who writes inane, implausible novels. Tull, on the other hand, writes grand, experimental fiction. Barry's novels sell by the millions. Tull's sell an average of two copies (when they get published) and give people migraines by page nine. Tull wants more from life. He wants to be famous. He wants someone to read his books. He wants to be able to have sex again. And, more than anything else, he wants to hurt his successful friend.

See *The Information,* Martin Amis

TULLY, LOUIS

Though short and slight, Louis tries to be a health and fitness nut to impress the babes. He likes to play exercise tapes at high speed to get a great workout in half the time. An obsessive, nerdy accountant, he invites clients to his parties in order to write the parties off. Hobbies: playing Twister, break dancing, being possessed by evil demons.

See *Ghostbusters* and *Ghostbusters II*

TURGIDSON, GENERAL BUCK

Fun-loving satyr and high-ranking general in the United States military. He loves war, both on the battlefield and in the bedroom. While not especially bright, he's extremely enthusiastic about his work and enjoys crisis situations. "I'm not saying we won't get our hair mussed, I'm saying ten to twenty million people killed—tops—depending on the breaks."

See *Dr. Strangelove: or, How I Learned to Stop Worrying and Love the Bomb*

TURNBLAD, EDNA

The grossly obese, whiny mother of **Tracy Turnblad**, would-be teen queen. Edna spends her days ironing their matching mother-daughter outfits and clucking over her daughter's adolescent excesses: two-tone bouffant hair and dancing on *The Corny Collins Show.* "You're just a teenage Jezebel."

See *Hairspray*

TURNBLAD, TRACY

Tracy is a plump but agile teenager obsessed with being on *The Corny Collins Show,* a TV dance program in 1962 Baltimore. Unfortunately for her, she's hated by bitchy blonde Amber von Tussle, a senator's daughter and a member of the Corny Collins Council; the council decides who gets to dance on the show. Tracy is a better dancer than Amber, but her weight is held against her. Tracy perseveres and fights the forces of ignorance, bigotry, and uncoolness along the way.

See *Hairspray*

TURNER, DALE

This world-weary, gravelly-voiced, African American jazz musician is an expatriate living in Paris. He's recognized as one of the great jazz saxophonists of all time, but substance abuse and racism have hurt him professionally and personally. Now he plays mostly at a smoky little Paris club, the Blue Note. His wisdom and dignity sometimes shine through an alcohol- and drug induced haze, but he often has difficulty staying straight enough to play. Despite his problems, Dale has many admirable qualities. He's patient with those who have seen less and thus understand less about life than he does. Many of those close to him, including his fans and landlady, try to help him stay sober, but he keeps falling off the wagon. Nearing sixty years of age, he feels himself near death and is, in fact, amazed to have made it this long. His music has a soul-stirring quality, poignant and filled with regret, yet never completely defeated. His greatest influences are Monk and Bird as well as Gershwin and Cole Porter.

See *Round Midnight*

TY D BOWL MAN

Destined to spend his life floating around the toilet tank in a small rowboat. Doesn't seem to mind.

UNLIKELY *JEOPARDY!* FINALISTS

Boo Radley
Lennie Small
Woody Boyd
Chrissy Snow
Latka Gravas

Felix Unger

Assures you that your toilet is clean.
See *Ty D Bowl*

TYLER, BLANCHE

She's a phony fortune-teller romantically involved with seedy cabdriver **George Lumley**. Blanche takes pleasure in fleecing clients out of their money. Now engaged in looking for a missing boy as part of a get-rich-quick scheme and also inadvertently involved with diamond theft, international kidnapping, and possibly murder.
See *Family Plot*

TYLER, BLUE

This tough little child actress is no Shirley Temple. Blue becomes a star by conveying a taboo adult sexuality. When barely past puberty, she shacks up with a Las Vegas gangster. After his murder, Blue disappears into oblivion, only to be discovered forty years later living in a Michigan trailer park.
See *Playland,* John Gregory Dunne

TYLER, ROLLIE

A movie special-effects wizard, capable of creating the most incredible illusions using makeup, latex, explosives, and other tools of the trade. Now way over his head in trouble and on the run from feds and felons alike. A quick thinker and very creative in emergency situations. A friend of **Leo McCarthy**.
See *F/X*

THE TYRONE FAMILY

A tormented Connecticut family, trying to maintain a thin cloak of unity, all the while veiled in a thick fog of deceit. Patriarch James is an actor whose great success has come at the expense of his wife, Mary, and two sons, James Jr. and Edmund. James is a cold and unforgiving man. Mary is the emotional hub around which the entire Tyrone family turns. She has a fatal addiction to morphine, having been given a great deal of the drug to ease her agony attendant on the birth of her younger son. Her addiction, though, is only one of several issues which the members of the family refuse to acknowledge. James Jr. the drunk, prodigal, and dissolute elder son, has a gift for talk and an exceptional capacity for drink. Apparently possessed of a death wish, but unable to end his life by the short-est means, Jamie is killing himself in the slowest possible way—by constant heavy drinking. He tortures himself with guilt for what he does and doesn't do. (On the train ride home with his mother's coffin, he occupied himself with a whore, and then was too drunk to attend the funeral.) Younger son Edmund's gentle poetic spirit and writing is being snuffed out by a "cold" that is really consumption. Like Mary's addiction, Edmund's battle with consumption is ignored by the family. Edmund's bookshelves are filled with "decadent" and "gloomy" writers his father deplores: Freud, Nietzsche, and Sola, to name a few. Of his life he says "The fog is where I wanted to be."
See *Long Day's Journey Into Night,* Eugene O'Neill

LIEUTENANT UHURA

The lovely black communications officer on board the starship *Enterprise,* she's forever receiving and sending messages via hailing frequencies all over the cosmos. Clearly, she and **Captain Kirk** have a mutual admiration society, but they only get romantic once, when under the control of some nasty aliens.
See *Star Trek*

UNCLE MARTIN

He's not really anybody's uncle—not on this planet, at any rate. He hails from Mars and crash-landed his spaceship near Los Angeles (his Martian name is Exagitious $12\frac{1}{2}$). On Mars he was a professor of anthropology who specialized in the primitive planet Earth. Once on Earth, he's befriended by **Tim O'Hara**, a newspaper reporter who witnessed the spacecraft's landing. In order to keep his identity a secret, he poses as Tim's Uncle Martin. He has antennae at the back of his head that raise and lower. He can read minds, levitate, and disappear at will.
See *My Favorite Martian*

UNGER, FELIX

For neat-freak Felix, cleanliness is not only next to godliness, it ranks higher in importance. He would find dust in a hospital operating room and endear himself to you by flicking lint off your clothes while chatting. By trade, he's a portrait photographer who owns his own business. He's an art aficionado and a lover of opera and thinks of himself as a great chcf (*spécialité de la maison:* meat loaf a la Unger). He's allergic to almost all substances and must frequently clear his sinuses by honking like a rutting goose. Unaccountably, his wife, Gloria, found life with him intolerable and divorced him. He has since moved in with old friend **Oscar Madison**, also divorced. Familiarity soon breeds exasperation, since Oscar is the exact opposite of Felix in terms of lifestyle, preferring to live in squalor. Felix dates Miriam Welby but still loves Gloria and cherishes dreams of getting back together with her. He's also a doting father to his adolescent daughter. He manages to coexist with Oscar, even though Oscar's sloppiness would drive him up the wall, except that that would leave unsightly marks. "Oscar, Oscar, Oscar."

See *The Odd Couple*

URKEL, STEVE

The nerdiest of the nerds; high-waters, big glasses, nasal voice, annoying demeanor. He's a neighbor of the Winslows, has got a major crush on their daughter, Laura (who rightly can't stand him), and comes over to bother the whole family constantly. Apparently once ate a mouse and likes to snack on dog biscuits with anchovy paste. Not unintelligent, he once constructed a robot that looked just like him.

See *Family Matters*

UTLEY, GEORGE

Crusty old handyman who helps out **Dick** and **Joanna Louden** at the Stratford Inn in Norwich, Vermont. (His family had been caretakers there for over two hundred years.) Member of the Beaver Lodge who enjoys bird-watching. Invented a board game called Handyman: The Feel Good Game. Calls his trusty hammer Old Blue.

See *Newhart*

VADER, DARTH

A futuristic embodiment of Evil; a bad-guy-in-a-black-helmet for the interstellar age. A fallen Jedi Knight, Darth Vader has given himself to the Dark Side and works for the Empire, overseeing evil deeds throughout the galaxy. Dressed imposingly in black robes and a metallic black mask, he commands extensive interstellar military forces from his post in the Death Star, an astoundingly immense space station. He's a demanding leader, known for punishing his underlings with random acts of lethal violence. Vader is made even more frightening by the mask covering his face, a powerful, portentous voice, and a whole lot of heavy breathing. The flies in his galactic ointment, who fight for liberty and freedom for all creatures under the Empire's yoke, include **Luke Skywalker**, **Princess Leia Organa**, and **Han Solo**, among many, many others. But he is a worthy and tough opponent to anyone who dares to oppose him. He has a particularly strong interest in Luke Skywalker, whom he recognizes as an especially serious threat to the Dark Side.

See *Star Wars*

VAIDEN, KATE

A middle-aged woman who stops to look back at her life, unconventional by the standards of her time and place. Orphaned at eleven, stripped of her innocence too early, she bears a child at seventeen and abandons it. Intelligent, resilient, and courageous, Kate has, for better or worse, made her own life. Her wish to locate her son sends her searching back through her life.

See *Kate Vaiden,* Reynolds Price

VALANCE, LIBERTY

A sociopath with no concept of right or wrong…except insofar as it applies to himself. If he wants it, or does it, it's right. He's a bully who kills without compunction, robbing the local folks at will and forcing them to accept it.

See *The Man Who Shot Liberty Valance*

VALE, CHARLOTTE

She was an ugly duckling, raised by a domineering and controlling mother. Charlotte was the youngest child, and only daughter, of four children. Lonely and introverted in youth, she grows into a fat, frumpy, neurotic young woman on an apparent beeline toward spinsterhood. En route, she takes a detour into nervous breakdown, driven there by the total domination of her dragon of a mother, who insisted on controlling every aspect of Charlotte's life. She's helped enormously by her therapist, Dr. Jaquith, and is transformed into a lovely, poised woman who can take charge of her life. On an ocean voyage, she meets and falls in love with married architect **Jerry Dorrance**, and, though Jerry won't break with his wife, Charlotte insists on wearing the camellias he sends her as a token of their love. She is so much in love with Jerry that she takes the responsibility of raising **Tina**, his daughter. She says it is the first time in her life that she has been needed by somebody. "Jerry, don't let's ask for the moon, we have the stars."

See *Now, Voyager*

VALE, MRS. HENRY WINDLE

Mrs. V—Leeza—is the loving sister-in-law of **Charlotte Vale**. Supportive and warm-hearted, she goes to great lengths to help Charlotte blossom. Leeza, a self-assured, sophisticated Bostonian, is fashionable and always socially correct. She's one of the few people in the known world who's not afraid of her domineering mother-in-law.

See *Now, Voyager*

VALE, SUZANNE

She's the daughter of a famous mother—musical star **Doris Mann**—and she's having a rough time with her own acting career. Her wit is sharp, but her self-esteem is low, a problem for which she turns to drugs and booze. When that doesn't work, she goes in for rehab and struggles to remain clean and sober. Meanwhile, Doris, who wants to help, never seems able to do the right thing, from Suzanne's viewpoint. Her latest plan is to break into the music business, toward which end she has shot a video. She's also considering dating the doctor who pumped her stomach when she was last zonked out on pills.

See *Postcards from the Edge*, Carrie **Fisher**

VALENS, DOROTHY

Troubled, self-loathing nightclub singer. Expresses love and anger through sex. A physical masochist who allows herself to be used as a toy in violent carnal psychodramas, particularly with **Frank Booth**. Also involved in unique personal situation with **Jeffery Beaumont**. Performs as featured chanteuse in a run-down roadhouse, where she specializes in Bobby Vinton tunes. Not only sings "Blue Velvet," also likes to wear it. Lives alone since beloved husband and son disappeared under mysterious circumstances. Liable to show up sans wardrobe at the least convenient times imaginable. "Hit me!"

See *Blue Velvet*

VALENTINE, BILLY RAY

Philadelphia con man who specializes in posing as a blind, legless veteran who demands handouts from passersby. What keeps him going is his quick wit and ability to weave yards of meaningless patter into the kind of bluff that allows him to make a getaway. He may be living on the streets, but he's working hard at getting ahead. These are just the sort of skills that the wealthy **Mortimer Duke** thinks will make Billy Ray a successful commodities broker. Most winning quality: his easy smile and infectious laugh put people at ease. Least desirable trait: well, he's dishonest. He *does* sound like a successful broker!

See *Trading Places*

VALIANT, EDDIE

A down-on-his-luck detective hired by Roger Rabbit, Maroon Cartoon's biggest star who is accused of killing R. K. Maroon, the studio chief. Originally reluctant to take the case because his brother was killed by a "Toon," he and Roger become close friends and discover the mystery of Toontown, battling the sinister Judge Doom in the process.

See *Who Framed Roger Rabbit?*

VAN DAM, ASSISTANT COACH LUTHER

Befuddled sidekick and best buddy. As assistant coach for the Minnesota State University Screaming Eagles, Luther is the confidant and adviser to coach **Hayden Fox**. Unfortunately, he has little intellect and still less common sense. But he means well and is a true friend. What he lacks in tact he makes up for in cheer and goodwill.

See *Coach*

VAN MEER

He is an honest and eminent Dutch diplomat, one of only two signers of the Dutch treaty with Belgium. Van Meer memorizes the top-secret clause #27 in the treaty, knowledge of which must not get to the Other Side. But the Other Side, in the form of a villainous spy ring, kidnaps him for this information. When tortured to give up his secret, he bravely and stubbornly refuses to talk. "You can do what you want with me, but you'll never conquer them. The little people

everywhere who give crumbs to the birds."
See *Foreign Correspondent*

VAN OWEN, GRACE
An idealistic, sometimes emotionally troubled lawyer. Directed by a passion to work for the cause of justice, Ms. Van Owen goes from being a top prosecutor, to a judge, to a defense lawyer—all with the same levels of zeal and proficiency. Her love life is equally jumbled as she goes from a politician to **Michael Kuzak** and eventually to **Victor Sifuentes**. Grace has an easy physical grace and a model's face.
See *L.A. Law*

VAN PELT, LINUS
Soft-spoken, intelligent, sensitive little boy. He fears he'd be helpless without constant contact with his security blanket, but he's probably the most mature member of his gang. Linus stoically puts up with his sister **Lucy Van Pelt**'s mocking. He also lends support and encouragement to hapless **Charlie Brown**, helping his friend get up when he's been knocked down.
See *Peanuts*, Charles Schultz

VAN PELT, LUCY
This sassy, manipulative brunette girl just loves making a fool of poor **Charlie Brown** by playing pranks on him, such as pulling away a football just as he's about to kick it. She's the big sister of **Linus**, whom she teases mercilessly; she also has a huge crush on Beethoven fanatic Schroeder, who's too into his music to notice her.
See *Peanuts*, Charles Schultz

VANCE, CARLOTTA
She was a society *grande dame*, but her position and looks have long been in decline. Although her social power is fading, she still wants to know all the gossip and likes directing soirees. Carlotta maneuvers like a battleship, has a sharp eye, a sharp tongue, and a shrewd sense of humor, which she aims at herself as well as others.
See *Dinner at Eight*

VANCE, SUSAN
Wealthy eccentric socialite with definite ideas on just about any and everything. Has little regard for social conventions. Adores her beloved feline Baby, a well-trained leopard that scares the bejesus out of everyone else. Has her sights set on **David Huxley**.
See *Bringing Up Baby*

VANDAMM, PHILLIP
This evil, cosmopolitan foreign agent works for enemies of the U.S. and seeks to destroy a man he believes to be a threat to him: one George Kaplan. He comes to believe that Kaplan is masquerading as adman **Roger Thornhill**—or is it the other way around? Anyway, he attempts to lure Kaplan-Thornhill to his destruction by using beautiful **Eve Kendall** as bait, which shows the kind of scum he is. Kendall has been his lover, after all, but he'll use whatever and whomever he has to, to achieve his immoral ends.
See *North by Northwest*

VANDERGELDER, HORACE
An elderly, wealthy merchant who holds the dubious distinction of being the most influential man in a city where nothing happens—Yonkers, New York. Called Wolf-Trap by his employees, he's President of the Hudson River Provision Dealers' Recreational, Musical, and Burial Society. He's also an irritable and vain old curmudgeon just softhearted enough to facilitate three marriages, including his own.
See *Hello, Dolly* and *The Matchmaker*, Thornton Wilder

VANDERHOF, GRANDPA MARTIN
He could be the spokesperson for contentment. Martin Vanderhof is a man who chose, one busy day, to retire from the rat race and be happy. He's reached his goal and currently presides over a clan of bizarre but exceptionally cheerful eccentrics. Under his roof, and with his blessing, this extended family does everything from ballet and playwriting to making fireworks in the basement. The U.S. government has declared him dead.
See *You Can't Take It with You*, George S. Kaufman and Moss Hart

VANDERKELLEN, STEPHANIE
Haughty maid who worked for **Dick Louden** at the Stratford Inn in Norwich, Vermont. Comes from a wealthy family and took the job so she could experience "real life." Dated, broke up with, and finally

married Michael Harris, a young producer at the local television station, who calls her "cupcake." After a long honeymoon, returned to live at the Stratford Inn, soon giving birth to a girl named Baby Stephanie.

See *Newhart*

VARGAS, RAMON MIGUEL "MIKE"

This handsome, morally upright, Mexican narcotics officer is honeymooning with his new wife, Susan, in a U.S. border town when he stumbles into a complicated and ugly situation. Even though he's out of his jurisdiction, when a rich man is murdered and a guy named Sanchez is arrested for the crime, Vargas can't help but do a little investigating on his own—he smells the stink of corruption coming from the American detective on the case, one **Harry Quinlan**. As he gets drawn deeper into the sticky mess, his wife also becomes involved—much against her will. Vargas emerges with the knowledge that he has vindicated his suspicions—but also knowing that in the process he has taken a small but significant first step toward ethical compromise.

See *Touch of Evil*

VARJAK, PAUL

An unpublished writer. The first place of his very own is a one-room apartment in a brownstone in the East Seventies in Manhattan. "My books were there, and jars of pencils to sharpen, everything I needed to become the writer I wanted to be." Paul drinks bourbon nightcaps, is a lousy horseback rider, and loves fellow tenant **Holly Golightly** the way he'd "once been in love with my mother's elderly cook and a postman who let me follow him on his rounds."

See *Breakfast at Tiffany's,* Truman Capote

VEGA, VINCENT

Perpetually dour enforcer for West Coast crime boss **Marsellus Wallace**. Sports shoulder-length, greasy hair and a gold hoop earring in his right ear. He's a heroin user and doesn't respond well to being given orders. He's had opportunities to travel but has limited appreciation of the finer qualities foreign culture offers. He can dance a dynamite twist.

See *Pulp Fiction*

VELASCO, VICTOR

A romantic Bohemian who must pass through **Paul and Corrie Bratter**'s apartment to reach his top-floor space. He's charming and energetic, with a crazy lifestyle that he doesn't hide from his neighbors. He woos and wins **Mrs. Ethel Banks**, in spite of herself.

See *Barefoot in the Park*

VENKMAN, DR. PETER

Sly con artist using his scientific training to get babes and avoid working in the real world. Breezy, smooth, wisecracking. Talks partners **Raymond Stantz** and **Egon Spengler** into establishing Ghostbusters because "the franchise rights alone will make us rich beyond our wildest dreams!"

See *Ghostbusters* and *Ghostbusters II*

VERNA

This tough-talking grifter will do anything to help chiseling brother **Bernie Bernbaum** stay alive. Verna keeps besotted crime boss **Leo** on a string, while spending the night with his cynical, tough second-in-command, **Tom Regan**. She tells Tom: "The two of us, we're about bad enough to deserve each other."

See *Miller's Crossing*

VICKIE

Vickie is a chubby, wisecracking Generation Xer. She's overqualified for her job at the Gap. She deals with the uncertainties of her future with sardonic wit—which doesn't eliminate the real angst she feels.

See *Reality Bites*

CAPTAIN VIDEO

Brilliant, handsome, and heroic—and self-appointed champion of freedom and justice throughout the universe circa 2254. He battles evil everywhere, aided by his futuristic inventions: his sidekick, the Ranger, and his legion of Video Rangers. "The Guardian of the Safety of the World," he works from a mountaintop hideaway and battles enemies like Dr. Pauli and the lovely villainess Atar.

See *Captain Video and His Video Rangers*

VIN

A happy-go-lucky gunman with lousy taste in

clothing. Vin is the slob among a group of seven men hired to protect a Mexican village from **Calvera** and his banditos. He has lately been plagued by a noisy conscience and questioning his goals and chosen way of life. He has a good heart and a terrible gambler's instinct.

See *The Magnificent Seven*

VINCOEUR, HOLLING

A sixty-something naturalist and adventurer who lives in tiny Cicely, Alaska, Holling owns the town's local tavern, the Brick. He's best friends with **Maurice Minnifield**, who introduced Holling to his very young wife, **Shelly Tambo**. The couple recently had a baby daughter, Miranda. Holling's family is known for its extremely long life expectancy and an occasional indulgence in cannibalism. An avid bird-watcher.

See *Northern Exposure*

VIOLET

A beautiful twelve-year-old girl living in a New Orleans brothel in 1917. She loves ragtime music and riding her pony. Her mother, **Hattie**, a prostitute, wants to leave the life and shows her maternal side by auctioning Violet off to the highest bidder, who will then have the privilege of deflowering her.

See *Pretty Baby*

VITALE, TINA

Gum-cracking, dissatisfied Italian American mistress of singer **Lou Canova**. Eyes perennially obscured by garish sunglasses, huge hair done up with half a ton of spray. Self-centered, a glutton for punishment, she's from a New Jersey mob family. Tina has firm belief in the miraculous visions of her neighborhood medium. Not as tough as she thinks she is.

See *Broadway Danny Rose*

VLADIMIR "DIDI"

An archetypal tramp. Vladimir tends to think and worry too much, as he waits interminably with his companion, **Estragon**, for the long-delayed but ever-anticipated arrival of Godot, who's due to meet them anytime now. Until he does, they pass the time in conversation.

See *Waiting for Godot,* Samuel Beckett

VON ASCHENBACH, GUSTAVE

This fifty-something writer is proud of his self-discipline and the orderliness of his life—until he suddenly finds himself yearning for freedom and release from his self-imposed burdens of work and duty. Although he's had fantasies about life in a tropical, primeval wilderness, he settles on Venice. Ignoring the dangers of the cholera epidemic sweeping the city, he stays, discovering unplumbed depths of passion through succumbing—in more ways than one—to a consuming passion for Tadzio, a beautiful Polish boy. Von Aschenbach eventually dies of cholera.

See *Death in Venice,* Thomas Mann

VON GAIGERN, BARON FELIX

Elegant but down-at-the-heels aristocrat who has taken to stealing jewels to support his lifestyle. His movie-star looks, charm, and exquisite tailoring are an attractive combination that fools his victims. Although he's a thief, he adheres to his own nobleman's code of honor and will not lower himself to petty crime. He only robs from people who he believes can afford to suffer the losses without financial harm. He rather regrets what he does but believes that a job must be done well if it is to be done at all.

See *Grand Hotel,* Vicki Baum

VON SHTUPP, LILI

Fraulein Von Shtupp is a jaded Germanic nightclub singer with an act and dialect reminiscent of Marlene Dietrich in *The Blue Angel*. Capable of both cutting derision and high passion. Signature song is "I'm Tired." Willing to use her considerable seductiveness as an espionage tool. Won over by **Sheriff Black Bart** in his attempt to preserve the town of Rock Ridge.

See *Blazing Saddles*

WACO KID

Aka Jim. Despite mellow disposition, the Kid's the fastest gun in the West. Retired from gunslinging when he discovered that one of his challengers for the title was six years old. Despite severe drinking problem, he retains incredible hand speed. Teamed up with **Sheriff Black Bart** to help the town of Rock Ridge while serving time in Rock Ridge jail.

See *Blazing Saddles*

SEEING TWO PSYCHIATRISTS

Bruce Wayne
Dorothy Michaels
Mrs. Edwina Doubtfire
Clark Kent
Norman Bates

WADE, JENNA

Pretty, shapely, waiting-in-the-wings girlfriend. On-again, off-again lover of fickle **Bobby Ewing**. Old girlfriend from "years back," Jenna reappears when Bobby has hit a snag with **Pamela**. Interested in having a husband and father for her daughter, she finds what she's looking for in Dallas. Marries Bobby in one of his off times with Pam, but it isn't to last. She later finds happiness with Ray Krebs.

See *Dallas*

WAGGONER, SUZI "PEPPER"

The energetic and optimistic Pepper has been a housewife, a call girl, and an employee of Burger World on the Florida coast. Her onetime husband is dangerous killer **Junior Frenger**, and she is in possession of a $10,000 C.D., which will be her passport, she hopes, to a new and successful life. Her goal is to open her own Burger World franchise. And she wants to marry a steady type and raise a family.

See *Miami Blues*

WALES, JOSEY

A loner, a man of acts and few words, who turns his back on civilization and lights out for Indian territory. Josey Wales is an unrepentant Confederate who became a fugitive when he took a Gatling gun to a band of Yankee troops who had killed his comrades in cold blood. On the road West, he runs across a number of interesting characters, including an old Indian who claims that his horse, not he, surrendered to the white man, the survivors of an ill-fated family of adventurers, and a young Indian girl. Suddenly, this ragtag band of homesteaders becomes a community, with the outlaw Wales as its leader and father figure.

See *The Outlaw Josey Wales*

WALESKA, VALENE EWING GIBSON

A neurotic, naive, sweet woman, easily manipulated. Valene is loyal and trusting, often to her detriment. Frequently a victim, she suffers from depression. Relies heavily on best friend **Karen MacKenzie**. Looks like a fragile blonde. Still loves her first husband, **Gary Ewing**, despite his betrayal.

See *Knots Landing*

WALKER, COALHOUSE, JR.

He's a successful ragtime piano player in New York during the time between the turn of the century and World War I. Self-confident and proud, he refuses to act deferential to the whites around him, as is expected of African Americans in that era.

See *Ragtime*, E. L. Doctorow

WALKER, DORIS

Starched, professional executive at Macy's who does not believe in Santa Claus but is in charge of the department store's Christmas displays. She has taught daughter **Susan** that Santa Claus isn't real, but then she hires a man calling himself **Kris Kringle** to be her store Santa, and she suddenly gets a strong dose of Christmas fever and faith.

See *Miracle on 34th Street*

WALKER, DR. RICHARD

He is an American doctor whose Paris vacation is rudely interrupted when his wife disappears. At present, he's searching for her, showing determination and surprising bravado in the face of deadly secrets. Reluctant to trust strangers due to his current predicament, though willing to take a few risks with some people. Dislikes rooftops.

See *Frantic*

WALKER, IRENE

Beautiful hitwoman-housewife, as well as a liar and thief. Irene is a "specialist" at the top of her field. She loves money and what it can buy, like her red convertible Excalibur. As a cover, she claims she is a tax consultant. When she finds herself falling for Prizzi family hitman **Charley Partanna**, she hesitates: "I've always had to protect myself." After she marries Charley, she insists on continuing to work, and feels uncomfortable as a Pole amongst a clan of Italians. She's rarely unemployed. Irene: "I've been doing three, four hits a year for the last four years." Charley: "That many?" Irene: "Well, it's not many if you consider the size of the population." When she thinks she's the Prizzis's next intended hit, she decides that either she or Charley has to go…permanently.

See *Prizzi's Honor*

WALKER, KIT

An alias used by **the Phantom** after he became a naturalized citizen of the United States. After coming to America, he created the Jungle Patrol, a crime-fighting organization that he leads. Before living in the States, he was a citizen of Great Britain and used the alias Sir Christopher Standish. Kit's fiancée is Diane Palmer.

See *The Phantom*, Ray Moore

WALKER, MATTY

Smoky socialite trapped in an unbearable marriage. Looking after detested niece and currently having a passionate affair with nickel-and-dime lawyer **Ned Racine**. Despite oppressive heat of Florida summer, Matty's body temperature constantly runs a few degrees higher than normal. She is also a dead ringer for her best friend, an old high school chum.

See *Body Heat*

WALKER, SUSAN

Physically, she's a little girl, but emotionally and mentally, she's something of an old lady. She has been taught by her mother, **Doris**, that Santa Claus is pure fantasy and scorns those children who believe in him. She also adores young Fred Gailey and shares his hopes that he might marry Doris. Department store Santa **Kris Kringle** makes her see the light and brings out the child in her that had been there all the time, under the prematurely old surface.

See *Miracle on 34th Street*

WALKER, TOMMY

This kid sure plays a mean pinball. His abuse on the part of those around him, including his alcoholic redheaded mom, his oily dad, and his perverted uncle, drives him to cut himself off from the world by becoming deaf, dumb, and blind. He takes refuge in playing pinball games and becomes a super expert at the game, one of the tops in all the land, who always gets the replay. Tommy faces all kinds of obstacles in his quest for excellence, including the Acid Queen, before finally defeating the reigning Pinball Wizard, an outrageously garbed and bespectacled man. In the process, he becomes a kind of messiah figure.

See *Tommy*, the Who

WALLACE, MARSELLUS

A wealthy California underworld kingpin, newly married to **Mia**. He wears a gold hoop earring in each ear and speaks in a soft, understated tone laced with menace. He traffics in illicit merchandise and fight fixing and retains a contingent of enforcers, including **Vincent Vega** and **Jules Winnfield**.

See *Pulp Fiction*

WALLACE, MIA

This beautiful young wife of California underworld kingpin **Marsellus Wallace** has a taste for kitsch, soulful ballads, and cocaine. Mia is a high-cheekboned, manipulative tease. She has good physical coordination and enjoys dancing, smoking, and most forms of indulgence. An elegant dresser.

See *Pulp Fiction*

WALLY

An aspiring actor and playwright, pudgy, balding Wally seems to live life vicariously through the adventurous tales told by his mysterious friend **Andre**, who roams the world as a "spiritual seeker." As a child, Wally had a wealthy family and thought only about art. But, ironically, now that he's become an actor, he's forever broke and always thinking about money. Among Wally's favorite pastimes are cuddling under electric blankets and eating the delicious dinners his girlfriend Debbie cooks for him. Wally is subject to intense bouts of nostalgia, remembering with vivid clarity the taxi rides he took as a child, the store where his father bought him a pair of shoes, and the place where he shared ice cream with a childhood sweetheart. Although he is anxious to learn about spiritual matters from Andre, his pragmatic nature keeps Wally rooted in the material world.

See *My Dinner with Andre*

WALSH, BRANDON

Twin of **Brenda**, he is perfect at everything he does: school, friends, jobs, parents—whatever it is, Brandon handles it with a maturity well beyond his years. Indeed, once romances a much older woman. Best friends with **Dylan McKay**, a relationship that gets rocky when Brandon starts dating Dylan's ex-girlfriend, **Kelly Taylor**. Brandon is a real politician.

See *Beverly Hills 90210*

WALSH, BRENDA

Pretty and popular, Brenda moves with her family, including twin brother **Brandon**, from

My name is Inigo Montoya. You killed my father. Prepare to die.— Inigo Montoya

Minneapolis to Beverly Hills, where fitting in with the cool crowd at Beverly Hills High is a full-time occupation. Becomes best friends with **Kelly Taylor**, who shows her the ropes of Southern California life. Brenda dates—and loses her virginity to—bad boy **Dylan McKay**, who then comes between her and Kelly. Leaves California to study drama in London. She's so perfect, some people hate Brenda.

See *Beverly Hills 90210*

WALSH, JACK

A former Chicago cop run out of town for not taking a bribe, the bad-tempered, foulmouthed Walsh now works as a bounty hunter. He dreams of making enough money to open a coffee shop. "If you don't cooperate, you're gonna suffer from fistophobia."

See *Midnight Run*

WALTER, PRIOR

The thirty-third—thirty-fourth if you count the bastards—in a long line of Prior Walters. Afflicted with AIDS and recipient of visits from a prophesying angel. Occasionally works as a club designer or caterer but mostly just lives "very modestly but with great style off a small trust fund." Is abandoned by his boyfriend, **Louis Ironson**, when he becomes ill.

See *Angels in America,* Tony Kushner

THE WALTON FAMILY

A large Virginia mountain family that sticks together through the great events of the 20th century. The household includes John and Olivia Walton, their seven children, and John's parents, Zeb and Esther. John is the head of the financially poor but emotionally rich clan. Gruff, stoical, and a little rough around the edges, he works hard to keep food on the family's table during the Great Depression. Moral but not a churchgoer, John doesn't accept handouts. Olivia is the caring but weary matriarch. She's a no-nonsense type, but never raises her voice. Religious and calm in a crisis, she holds her family together. Zeb Walton is mischievous and a tad less responsible than his son. Esther is feisty, ramrod straight and has unwavering faith in God and her family. John Boy is the eldest son. Revered by his siblings, he's reflective, romantic and responsible.

While John Boy does not want to disappoint his father, he yearns to leave Walton's Mountain, and spends much of his free time writing in his journal, leading to a career as a screenwriter. Jason is sensitive and musical, playing piano and the church organ. Like JohnBoy, Ben is responsible, but more of a realist. He takes over his father's lumber mill. JimBob is overshadowed by, and somewhat less responsible than, his older brothers. He becomes a race car driver. Mary Ellen, serious and somewhat rebellious, becomes a medical doctor. There are also quiet but fun-loving Erin and cute, pig-tailed Elizabeth, the youngest Walton and the apple of her daddy's eye.

See *The Waltons*

WAMBAUGH, DOUGLAS

An elderly but energetic lawyer in Rome, Wisconsin. In his eighties, Wambaugh is still active, despite the fact that he suffers from a mild form of multiple sclerosis. He champions underdogs and realizes a lifelong dream by arguing a case before the Supreme Court. Wambaugh's penchant for courtroom theatrics makes him a thorn in the side of Judge **Henry Bone**.

See *Picket Fences*

WANDA

She's an American living in London with boyfriend **Otto**. Wanda is trying to con **Archie Leech** in order to pull off a major robbery. She enjoys playing psychological games with others, though she is frustrated by incompetence, of which she sees a good deal. Despite her criminal activities, Wanda has a good heart and a tongue-in-cheek sense of humor. She is a sucker for a man who can speak in another language.

See *A Fish Called Wanda*

WANDROUS, GLORIA

A voluptuous good-time girl, Gloria calls herself a model but gets paid for other services rendered. Perhaps because of her career, Gloria has trouble staying with one man, except for a platonic relationship she maintains with her songwriting neighbor. She loves wealthy, handsome **Weston Liggett**, but he's married and she feels guilty about keeping him from his family. Gloria gets good money for what she does but makes it clear to her customers that they aren't buying her. Her independence and headstrong opinions aren't always popular, but she'd rather play by her own rules than someone else's.

See *Butterfield 8,* John O'Hara

WAPSHOT, HONORA

Crusty, eccentric, and self-assured, Honora commands the wealthy Wapshot family of St. Botolphs, Massachusetts. She lives alone, doling out money to support her cousin, **Leander Wapshot**, and his two spoiled sons. Proud of the family heritage, she makes sure to let her donees know there are plenty of moral strings attached to her money.

See *The Wapshot Chronicle,* John Cheever

WAPSHOT, LEANDER T.

The ne'er-do-well scion of a distinguished New England family, Leander holds a romantic attachment to tradition, which he calls the excellence and continuousness of things. He lives for life's simple pleasures, above all sailing in his boat, and regaling his sons with stories about the golden days of his youth. He and his boys live off the largesse of his wealthy cousin, **Honora Wapshot**.

See *The Wapshot Chronicle,* John Cheever

WARD, ALAN

An enthusiastic young FBI agent, bent on bringing the bad guys to justice, but only by staying strictly within the law, and with a strict adherence to the FBI's code of ethics as he understands it. He's intuitive, idealistic, intelligent, and brave of heart, all the features an FBI agent should have. But, initially, he's short on field experience.

See *Mississippi Burning*

WARD, VIVIAN

She's the fulfillment of most male fantasies, and will satisfy men's needs if the price is right. Vivian's from a disadvantaged background and is impressed by luxuries. She's lucky to meet and be hired by heavy-duty business shark **Edward Lewis**, because all he wants is decorative companionship for a week while he's in Los Angeles to work. Vivian's generous to a fault and hasn't yet developed the cynicism typical of ladies for hire. Oh, yes, she also knows a lot about cars.

See *Pretty Woman*

WARDEN, SERGEANT MILTON

An imposing, vigorous sergeant at a Hawaiian army base whose qualities of leadership and authority make up for the total lack of same in his commander, **Captain Dana Holmes**. Warden is tough but fair, and the troops respect him. Warden dislikes Holmes but masks his feelings, because he also feels guilty about the affair he's having with **Karen Holmes**, his commander's wife. Because he doesn't want to risk ruining what he has with Karen, he tends to disregard the captain's misuse of authority.

See *From Here to Eternity,* James Jones

WARNE, PETER

Warne is an out-of-work newspaperman who sees a chance meeting with runaway heiress **Ellie Andrews** on a bus as a potential means to get his job back. As they travel from Miami to New York, he gradually gets to know her, in the process breaking down the cultural and physical "Walls of Jericho" that separate them. In this instance, familiarity breeds attraction. Warne's initial interest in a story evolves into a strong romantic interest in the beautiful young woman.

See *It Happened One Night*

WARNER, BLAIR

With a flip of her blond hair, beautiful and sophisticated Blair openly shows her distaste for all things blue collar while at prestigious Eastland School for Girls. However, she goes on to Langley College, and then Langley's law school, outgrowing her spoiled-rich-kid attitude and assuming the position of headmistress at Eastland, which, incidentally, she has now bought, and plans to make coed.

See *The Facts of Life*

WARSHAWSKI, V. I. "VIC"

As a champion of Chicago's underdogs, nothing pleases this tough lady private eye more than "a lucky shot to the groin" of an abusive husband or corporate exploiter. Even though she takes on rich and powerful crooks with a feminist vengeance, Vic is more sensitive than the typical gumshoe; she bruises when punched and misses her mother.

See, e.g., *Tunnel Vision,* Sara Paretsky

WASHINGTON, ISAAC

A dedicated friend. His skills as good listener and patient counselor are needed in his job as bartender aboard the *Love Boat,* of which he is the sole African American crew member. Confidant and friend of **Gopher Smith**, **Julie McCoy**, and **Adam Bricker**. Flirts with women passengers. Helps male passengers with romantic problems.

See *The Love Boat*

WATSON, DR. JOHN H.

The faithful recorder of the cases taken by his close friend, London consulting detective Sherlock Holmes. After serving as a medic in the Second Afghan War, in which he was wounded, Watson earned his M.D. and set up a practice in London. Watson first meets Holmes through an advertisement to share digs at 221B Baker Street in west London and goes on to share many of his friend's most interesting and harrowing adventures. In awe of his friend's powers of observation and reasoning, Watson is in his own right doggedly loyal, resourceful, and steady under fire. Although he lives and works in his friend's shadow, Holmes knows that Watson is an important asset to his work. Watson meets his first wife, Mary, during the case titled *A Study in Scarlet.* She presumably dies an untimely death, because Watson eventually rejoins his friend at Baker Street.

See *The Adventures of Sherlock Holmes, A Study in Scarlet, The Hound of the Baskervilles,* et al., **Arthur Conan Doyle**

MRS. WATTS

A little old lady with more than a touch of vinegar in her, Mrs. Watts is also a little girl, or at least she wants to be a little girl again. To do this, she sneaks away from her family's apartment in the choking confines of the city to make one last visit to her childhood home in the country.

See *The Trip to Bountiful,* Horton Foote

WAYNE, BRUCE

Extremely wealthy and well-known social figure throughout Gotham City, though somewhat boyish and shy around women. He lives on the fortune he inherited years ago when his parents were murdered. Wayne's best friend and closest confidant is his butler, Alfred. Keeps private life deliberately secretive; has unknown dark psychological side. Abhors crime and wrongdoing. His alter ego is the flamboyant crime-fighting figure **Batman**; his great wealth has funded all of the crime-fighter's myriad special devices.

See *Batman*

WAYNE, DWAYNE

Kind of nerdy, with short hair and trademark round glasses with flip shades, a student at mostly black Hillman College. Attracted to **Whitley Gilbert**. Roommate and best friend of **Ron Johnson**. Likes school and does well, especially math. Cocky, but solid moral character underneath. Has big aspirations.

See *A Different World*

WEBB, EMILY

She is a simple, small-town girl from Grover's Corners, New Hampshire. Sweet and innocent, Emily is in love with her neighbor George Gibbs. She dreams that they will marry and raise a family as happily as her parents did. "Do human beings ever realize life while they live it?—every, every minute?"

See *Our Town,* Thornton Wilder

WEBBER, GEORGE

When the aunt that raised him dies, this talented young writer becomes a perpetual outsider. George moves from his southern hometown to New York City and achieves a measure of fame, but his dismay with the viciousness and banality of the United States during the Depression compels him to flee to Europe, knowing he can never really go home again.

See *You Can't Go Home Again,* Thomas Wolfe

WEBER, WARREN "POTSIE"

A slightly awkward but nice teenage guy. He's cute but a little geeky, although once called by his friend **Richie Cunningham**'s sister, **Joanie**, a dren—the opposite of a nerd. Polite. Potsie will never be supremely confident. He loves music. He was once forced to do "lip-ups" by cool guy **Fonzie** to get in shape for kissing.

See *Happy Days*

WEBSTER, NORMA RAE

She's poor, she's a single mother, and she's trapped

in a dead-end job, but the plain-spoken Norma Rae is one underdog who makes the best out of daunting circumstances. Like everyone in her town, she works in the textile mill, which has no union, pays minimum wages, has few benefits, and does little or nothing about brown lung disease. Then a union organizer from New York turns up in town. After a while, the organizer begins to make a little sense to her. She grows less blind to the conditions at the mill. Norma Rae becomes an organizer herself, and slowly her eyes are opened to her world and her potential to have power over it.

See *Norma Rae*

WEISS, JANET

An innocent, milk-fed, all-American girl. Janet is affianced to equally wimpy **Brad Majors**. Though she has carefully guarded her virginity since she learned what the word meant, she's never come into contact with anyone quite like **Dr. Frank N. Furter** or his androgynous creation, **Rocky Horror**.

See *The Rocky Horror Picture Show*

WELBY, DR. MARCUS

A kindly, wise, family medical practitioner with a wonderful bedside manner. He lives and works in Santa Monica, California, where he has a private practice and employs a young associate, **Dr. Steven Kiley**. He also relies a great deal on his nurse and receptionist, Consuelo Lopez. Often, Dr. Welby will apply a psychiatric approach to medicine. He has a daughter, Sandy, and a grandson, Phil.

See *Marcus Welby, M.D.*

WELLS, KIMBERLY

Television news reporter with a sixth sense for good stories, eager to move up from "human interest" fluff pieces to hard news. Ready to ask the right questions and get to the heart of the matter in order to get her job done. Something of a crusader, she unashamedly wears her feelings on her sleeve. Works regularly with camera operator **Richard Adams**.

See *The China Syndrome*

WELLS, RUDY

This brilliant surgeon working for the U.S. government invented the nuclear-powered electro-mechanical devices, labeled "bionics," that give

Steve Austin and Jaime Sommers superhuman powers. He continues as their doctor. He had one of his biggest hurdles when Jaime initially "rejected" her bionics. Also "bionicized" sixteen-year-old Andy Sheffield, Steve Austin's son, Michael, and a German shepherd named Max.

See *The Six Million Dollar Man* and *The Bionic Woman*

WENDICE, MARGOT

Wealthy heiress rolling in family money, married to poor, spendthrift tennis player **Tony Wendice**. Is an extremely close friend of writer **Mark Halliday**. Though demure, she can still hold her own in life-and-death situations.

See *Dial M for Murder*

WENDICE, TONY

He's a luckless tennis pro, hard up for cash. Married to wealthy heiress **Margot Wendice**. Not at all sporting when it comes to using murder, blackmail, and other forms of deceit to raise his economic status when circumstances become difficult. Believes his wife is having an affair with **Mark Halliday**.

See *Dial M for Murder*

WERTHAN, MISS DAISY

Elderly Jewish woman of rural Georgia and very stubborn in her ways. Her proper demeanor reflects Miss Daisy's background as a schoolteacher. At the insistence of her son, she reluctantly employs **Hoke Colburn** as her chauffeur, though she tries to keep Hoke at an emotional arm's length.

See *Driving Miss Daisy*

WEST, MAJOR DONALD

A handsome, young spaceship pilot who has been frustrated by **Dr. Zachary Smith**'s traitorous actions, Don West is on a continuing quest for a way back to Earth. Instead, he succeeds only in leading the *Jupiter II* from planet to planet, getting no closer to home. Luckily for Don, the **Robinsons** are terribly friendly and nice, especially daughter **Judy**, who seems to mature before his lonely eyes.

See *Lost in Space*

WEST, JAMES T.

He is a United States Secret Service agent during the administration of Ulysses S. Grant. West is devoted to his country, and all the women that live in it, probably in that order. Regardless of whether he's in the midst of a fight or saving the world, he always has time to scope out and, with luck, learn the address of any nubile woman in the vicinity, even if she's a villainess. The only thing that he may love more than picking up women is fighting. If there's a possibility of fisticuffs within a hundred miles, he'll be there. He doesn't worry if he loses and gets captured, because he knows that **Artemus Gordon**, his fellow agent, will eventually show up in a cunning disguise and free him. He loves to wear a Spanish-cut jacket and pants that ought by rights to cut off all circulation to his legs. But the ladies seem to love it, so what is the risk of gangrene weighed against that?

See *The Wild, Wild West*

WESTLAKE, PEYTON

Criminal boss with a sadistic streak few thugs can match. Likes to keep a cigar box full of the rotting, dismembered fingers of his victims. He is a figure of menace to many in the big city, particularly **Darkman**.

See *Darkman*

WESTON, ELLIOT

A quirky, creative, offbeat advertising artist. He would just as soon not grow all the way up and become totally responsible, even though he's married with two children. Elliot tends to be restless and can't stay serious for long. He's a good father and a loving husband to his sweet wife, **Nancy**, even though he cheats on her. The success of his friend **Michael Steadman** makes him jealous. Despite his flaws, there's substance here, and it comes to the fore when his wife is diagnosed with cancer.

See *Thirtysomething*

WESTON, NANCY

The long-suffering wife of **Elliot Weston**, she's nice to a fault and a bit of a martyr. Nancy is the parent with her feet on the ground. She's also a talented artist. A dedicated mom, she dotes on her two children but wouldn't mind more excitement in her life and more attention from her spouse. Then she gets cancer, and she finds strength, not only within herself but from the increased support and comfort of her reawakened husband.

See *Thirtysomething*

WESTRUM, GIL

One-half of a team of leathery old cowboys, Westrum combines a wry sense of humor with spur-sharp prairie wisdom. He and his partner Steve Judd are symbols of the Old West, but when they're hired to protect a shipment of gold, the two Plains veterans clash over the meaning of right and wrong in a changing world.

See *Ride the High Country*

THE WHAMMER

Large, nasty, womanizing baseball star—a Babe Ruth–like superslugger, without Ruth's winning personality. He goes in on a bet pitting him against **Roy Hobbs**, a hot young pitcher from the sticks. To his amazement and chagrin, he strikes out on three straight pitches. The resulting sports-pages cartoon gives Hobbs his very first taste of fame.

See *The Natural*, Bernard Malamud

WHEAT, SAM

Kind, gentle, hunky yuppie. He loves his girl, **Molly Jensen**, but never tells her so before he's killed by the guy he thought was his best friend, who wants Molly. Sam comes back on the scene as the nicest dead person since Casper the Friendly Ghost, helping to solve the mystery of his death (with psychic **Oda Mae Brown**'s help) and finally getting the chance to tell Molly what she wants to hear: "I love you."

See *Ghost*

WHEELER, BOBBY

He has matinee-idol looks; small wonder that he aspires for stardom. But bills must be paid, and so he works as a driver for the Sunshine Cab Company in Manhattan. He feels he has what it takes to become a great actor someday, even though his boss, **Louie De Palma**, feels that he's seen radial tires with more talent.

See *Taxi*

WHEELER, JOE

Wrongly accused of murder, now he is on the run from an enraged lynch mob. He proves resourceful under extreme pressure, with a knack for making clever end runs around his enemies. Joe's a quick learner who can adapt to his situation and keep one step ahead of trouble. However, he does have some difficulties with his love life thanks to his current scrape.

See *Fury*

WHEELER, ZOYD

This weathered old hippie regularly dives through a plate-glass window to prove he's insane, to keep getting disability checks from the government. He lives up in northernmost California and bemoans the failed promise of peace and love of the sixties, and more specifically, the transformation from radical filmmaker to FBI informant of his ex-lover, Frenesi Gates. But he still keeps the faith.

See *Vineland,* Thomas Pynchon

MR. WHIPPLE

Vigilant store clerk whose big thrill in life is to catch people squeezing toilet paper. Watches too many detective movies. Still lives at home. "Please don't squeeze the Charmin!"

See *Charmin toilet paper*

WHIRLWIND, MARILYN

This quiet, sage Native American is the assistant of Dr. Joel Fleischman, a job she applied for and accepted even though no job opening actually existed. She is a native of Cicely, Alaska, where she is wise in the ways of nature and Eskimo tradition. Wonderful dancer.

See *Northern Exposure*

WHITE, CARRIE

A pathologically shy, emotionally sheltered, and physically immature high school senior who sits at the bottom of the social pecking order. Her pale complexion, stringy hair, and dowdy clothes also set her apart. Singled out by a popular clique of girls, Carrie becomes the object of their petty spite. Shielded as she is from the world by her fanatically religious mother, the innocent Carrie is ill-equipped to understand the motives of her classmates. However, Carrie's outwardly harmless demeanor masks a frightening inner power of which she is unaware, until a cruel trick is played on her by classmates on prom night. Then her psy-

chokinetic strength is suddenly and fearsomely displayed.

See *Carrie,* Stephen King

WHITEMAN, DAVE

This uptight, status-conscious Beverly Hills businessman hasn't been able to get his wife to sleep with him for years, so he's been having an affair with the Latina housekeeper. He befriends **Jerry Baskin**, a free-spirited homeless type, who helps him and his family work on their dysfunctional relationships.

See *Down and Out in Beverly Hills*

WHITESIDE, SHERIDAN

He's acid-tongued, Falstaffian, and snobbish and is famed as a "critic, lecturer, radio orator, intimate friend of the great and near great." Temporarily trapped by circumstances in hopelessly bourgeois Middle America, Whiteside strives to make everyone around him aware of the fact that nothing is good enough, no food tasty enough, and no person interesting enough to please him.

See *The Man Who Came to Dinner,* George S. Kaufman and Moss Hart

WHITNEY, WHITEY

Average boy, and a good friend of **Beaver Cleaver**. He plays baseball, roughhouses, and goes to the matinee with Beaver, Larry, and Gilbert. Teases girls. Follows **Wally Cleaver** and **Eddie Haskell** around, conspiring to ruin their plans. Sometimes sides against Beaver on moral issues, succumbing to peer pressure. "Aww, Beave, come on, let's do it!"

See *Leave It to Beaver*

WHITTIER, POLLYANNA

For Pollyanna, a pretty, perfectly mannered and intelligent orphan, the sky is either blue or full of silver linings. Her natural kindliness and optimism overcome the grouchy ingratitude and soured worldview of the adults into whose lives she breezes. Spreading sunshine by the sheer force of her charm and personality, she wins the hearts and affection of almost everyone she comes into contact with. Her favorite pastime is the "Glad Game," in which she attempts to find happy aspects in any situation. Though just as naive as every other preteen, Pollyanna has a peculiar talent for discerning the

"EARTH TO..."

Howard Beale
Blanche DuBois
Walter Mitty
Jim Ignatowski
Elwood P. Dowd

troubles of the adults around her. After she loses her parents, she comes to live with her mother's sister, Aunt Polly, the richest and most powerful lady in the quaint, picturesque little town of Harrington. As soon as she arrives, the "Glad Girl" proves to be an accidental godsend for several members of the town. Her indirect but luminous hints about the ways of life light the way for the timorous preacher, get the hypochondriac Mrs. Snow out of bed, aid the romance of Nancy, the maid, and make that curmudgeonly recluse, Mr. Pendergast, come out from behind the shutters of his old mansion and help that endearing, orphaned tyke, Jimmy Bean. Finally, when Harrington holds an old-fashioned outdoor bazaar, the townspeople give Pollyanna a collective thanks for her warmth and perpetual positive outlook on life.
See *Pollyanna,* Eleanor H. Porter

WHURLIZER, AMANDA

Foulmouthed, strong-armed pitcher for Little League team. Wears team name "Bears" on front of her uniform, team sponsor "Chico's Bail Bonds" on the back. She throws hard and is willing to hit batters when necessary—or even when not. A pioneer for women's rights in her own way, proving her talent to the boys and disbelieving **Coach Buttermaker** with every ball pitched.
See *The Bad News Bears*

WIATT, J. C.

She's a fast-rising advertising executive whose yuppie eyes are set on a corner office with its breathtaking view of Manhattan. Constantly on the go, must schedule everything down to the minute, including lovemaking sessions with boyfriend. Not remotely the maternal type, though amazingly adaptable to personal and diaper changes when duty calls unexpectedly.
See *Baby Boom*

WICKED WITCH OF THE WEST

This creepy, malevolent, gnarly-faced witch gets angry at **Dorothy Gale** for killing her partner in evil, the Wicked Witch of the East. Her voice is a cackling shriek, which rises to a laugh of glass-breaking intensity. She does have great fashion sense: she wears all black to accent her charms and dresses her army of flying monkeys in what are

either fezzes or bellhop's caps. The witch pulls out all the stops in trying to get Dorothy: sedative poppies, flying monkeys, the works. But Evil can never defeat true Good, and even the wickedest witch has an Achilles' heel. In the end, this witch turns out to be all wet. "I'll get you, my pretty—and your little dog, too."
See *The Wizard of Oz,* L. Frank Baum

WILDER, JOAN

A quiet romance novelist whose life is nothing at all like her steamy, exotic prose—until she gets caught up in a plot that she would have hesitated to use in one of her books. It starts when an urgent telegram from her sister sends Joan off to Colombia, bringing with her what is supposed to be a treasure map. But a not-so-funny thing happens on the way to Cartagena, and she finds herself stranded in the jungle, where American bad-boy bush pilot **Jack Colton** comes to her aid and reluctantly teams up with her to find the sister and check out the map. The twosome fight a running battle with various thugs, and Joan discovers that living an adventure such as the ones she writes serves to bring out previously untapped veins of sensuality, of which Jack is the happy beneficiary.
See *Romancing the Stone*

WILHELM, TOMMY

This Upper West Side Jewish New Yorker is in a real slump. Jobless and unable to keep up support payments to his wife, who's left him, he struggles to keep his head abovewater. In a fit of foolish optimism, he tries to "seize the day," giving all his money to a con man to invest in a "sure thing" in the commodities market. The results are about what one would expect, and Tommy is left to the dubious comfort and support of his father and wife.
See *Seize the Day,* Saul Bellow

WILKE, MARY

Radcliffe grad in her thirties, from Philadelphia where "We believe in God." Mary is the coinventor of the Academy of the Overrated, a means through which she can indulge herself in putting down every writer and artist beloved by **Isaac Davis,** whom she infuriates with her smugness. Still, she is not without endearing qualities. She calls her dog

Waffles and her analyst Donny. Her ex-husband was her professor, with whom she was having an affair. "I was sleeping with him and he had the nerve to give me an F." "No kidding," Isaac says. "Not even an Incomplete?" Now she's involved with a married man, but she is increasingly attracted to Isaac.

See *Manhattan*

WILKES, ANNIE

Dumpy and plain, Annie Wilkes is a former R.N. with extensive medical training and experience who now lives on a remote farm in Colorado. She's an obsessive fan of romance novels, especially the ones about Misery Chastain. These books are her substitute for a life, and she vicariously projects herself into the exciting and turbulent existence of the gorgeous Misery. She idolizes the author of the books, **Paul Sheldon**, and knows every detail about the famous writer. In addition, Annie was abused as a child by a psychotic mother. Skills: farm work, nursing, setting and breaking bones, mercy killing.

See *Misery*, Stephen King

WILKES, ASHLEY

The sensitive, thoughtful, delicate son of a wealthy Georgia plantation owner. He marries his cousin **Melanie Wilkes**, bitterly disappointing beautiful, headstrong **Scarlett O'Hara**, who has adored him since they were children. He loves Scarlett's intensity and vitality, but Melanie is his strength and soulmate. Although a loyal southern gentleman, he goes off to war reluctantly; he recognizes its folly but does nothing to protest it. After the war, he's ashamed to need Scarlett to support his family by providing him with a job. A compassionate person, he planned to free his slaves and now dislikes driving the convict labor at Scarlett's lumber mill. He is painfully aware of his shortcomings and understands that when the Old South was destroyed, so was his way of life.

See *Gone with the Wind,* Margaret Mitchell

WILKES, MELANIE

Frail in body but strong in spirit, young Melanie marries her cousin **Ashley Wilkes**, thereby earning the envy of **Scarlett O'Hara**, who has been carrying a torch for him since they were children. Everyone loves Melanie except Scarlett, but still, she reluc-tantly promises Ashley that she'll look after her while he is away at war. Melanie is so good and free from malice that she can't imagine that Scarlett harbors bad feelings toward her. She feels forever in Scarlett's debt after Scarlett saves her and her son. Soft-spoken, empathetic, and kind, Melanie is nonetheless a perceptive woman, who can see and appreciate the raffish **Rhett Butler**'s good qualities (which Scarlett ignores) and understand the danger he undergoes to rescue Ashley when her husband is wounded. It's Melanie's unselfish and unreserved love for Scarlett that ultimately proves to be her downfall.

See *Gone with the Wind,* Margaret Mitchell

WILLARD, CAPTAIN BENJAMIN

Taciturn, morose army intelligence officer. Field officer in military-sponsored assassination operations, primarily active in Vietnam War era. Divorced from wife due to strains career put on marriage. Smoker with alcoholic tendencies. Encountered **Lieutenant Colonel Kilgore** while on mission to assassinate **Colonel Walter E. Kurtz**.

See *Apocalypse Now*

WILLARD, GEORGE

Naive and inexperienced in life, George works as a reporter for the *Winesburg Eagle,* a position that gives him the perfect position from which to view the citizens of this small northern Ohio town. The son of a widow who runs a boardinghouse, George is well known and popular in the community. The observant and nonjudgmental George learns about life from his fellow citizens, to whom he is always willing to lend an ear. His natural compassion and understanding eventually make George privy to the secret griefs of many of Winesburg's citizens, although he does not always understand or sympathize with them. Restless and claustrophobic in his stifling hometown, George leaves Winesburg and disappears into the night to seek his fortune in an unnamed big city.

See *Winesburg, Ohio,* Sherwood Anderson

THE WILLIAMS FAMILY

With New York City–based nightclub entertainer-comedian Danny Williams as its patriarch, life for the Williamses is generally fun; even though Dad can at times be a bit of a crank and he's on the road a lot, deep down he's got a heart of gold. His lovable kids are Terry, who goes to West Side High before attending college (she pledges a sorority) and getting married, and Rusty, a champion speller whose heroes are Elvis Presley and Wyatt Earp. When he grows up, Rusty marries a woman named Susan. The kids' mom is understanding Margaret, who passes away. Later, Danny woos and marries Kathy (he calls her Clancey), a nurse with a young daughter of her own. Danny's Uncle Tonoose brings Danny's Lebanese background into their Manhattan apartment; he loves goat cheese and grape leaves and talks of family ancestors like King Achmed the Unwashed. The Williamses' dog is named Laddie.

See *The Danny Thomas Show, Make Room for Daddy*

WILLIAMS, DANNY "DAN-O"

A clean-cut, conservative cop. Dan-O is the right-hand man to superdetective **Steve McGarrett**, head honcho of Honolulu P.D.'s elite Five-O unit. He treats McGarrett with a mixture of awe, respect, and adulation, with a dash of admiration thrown in.

See *Hawaii Five-O*

WILLOUGHBY, "LONG" JOHN (JOHN DOE)

A former bush league baseball pitcher, he rides the rails and plays the harmonica while down and out and looking for a job. He's hired to portray "John Doe," a prototypical out-of-work American distraught enough to decide to jump off a building on Christmas Eve. "John Doe" becomes a popular and inspirational figure, inspiring people to band together and help their fellow humans. He becomes a believer in the essential truth behind the fictional facade, recognizing that he has become a sort of modern-day Christ figure, in that he was willing to kill himself and sacrifice his life for the people. "I know how they feel, I've been lonely and hungry for something practically all my life."

See *Meet John Doe*

WILSON

Wise and perceptive next-door neighbor of **Tim** and **Jill Taylor**. Wilson dispenses advice from behind his tall fence and is literally the voice of reason. Knows the solution to every problem. Never seems pompous or overbearing. Calls Tim "neighbor" and gets him out of trouble with Jill.

See *Home Improvement*

WILSON, GRADY

Buddy and occasional target of **Fred Sanford**, Grady is as long-suffering as any best friend can be. He eventually marries a woman named Dolly.

See *Sanford and Son*

WILSON, KIP "BUFFY"

Moves with best friend **Henry Desmond** into the Susan B. Anthony Hotel—a women-only residence—for the cheap rent; dresses up as his "sister" Buffy to pull it off. In art direction at an ad firm, he dreams of being a painter. Madly in love with another resident of the hotel, **Sonny Lumet**.

See *Bosom Buddies*

WILSON, MYRTLE

Earthy mistress of **Tom Buchanan**. She's trapped in a loveless marriage. Because she's always been poor, she is easily impressed by Buchanan's money and his promises that he'll one day divorce his wife, **Daisy Buchanan**, in order to marry her. She despises her husband, a garage owner and mechanic who misrepresented himself before their marriage as someone who had a higher station in life.

See *The Great Gatsby*, F. Scott Fitzgerald

WILSON, STEVE

As editor of the *Illustrated Press*, the "paper of record" in Big Town, Steve knows it's his job to track down corruption and expose crime. His star reporter is **Lorelei Kilbourne**, with whom he has a flourishing romance, for a time. When she moves on, he romances Diane Walker, a commercial artist.

See *Big Town*

WIND IN HIS HAIR

Elderly Sioux chief who befriends white army official **John W. Dunbar**. Respected by members of his tribe for his wisdom, ability as a warrior, and other leadership qualities. Knows that the encroachment of the whites on Sioux lands will lead to the end of his nation.

See *Dances with Wolves*

WING, BENNETT

Respected psychoanalyst and patient, long-suffering husband of **Isadora Wing**, Wing's cool and distant Oriental manner frustrates his more emotional Jewish wife. He raises no objections when Isadora runs off to have a fling with **Adrian Goodlove**, a fellow psychoanalyst.

See *Fear of Flying,* Erica Jong

WING, ISADORA

A tortured and neurotic poet, Isadora Wing was born into an artistic upper-class New York Jewish family and immerses herself in psychoanalysis in hopes of answering the life questions that torment her. She is sassy, irreverent, and scathingly honest in her quest for truth and knowledge. Unhappy in love, her tepid marriage to **Bennett Wing** does not fuel her yearning for a passionate life to match her creative fires, so Isadora indulges in a rich sexual fantasy life whose ultimate experience would be the "zipless fuck," a brief, torrid, anonymous, and purely sexual escapade after which the lovers would part company, hopefully forever. Her affair with another psychoanalyst, **Adrian Goodlove**, is part of her quest.

See *Fear of Flying,* Erica Jong

THE WINGFIELD FAMILY

The Wingfields live in a dingy St. Louis apartment. Since Amanda's husband left her, she's been eking out a living selling magazine subscriptions by phone. Daughter Laura is frail and shy. She's twenty-three, didn't finish high school, and dropped out of business school. Laura was crippled by a childhood disease which left one leg shorter than the others. Her mother is obsessed with having "gentlemen callers" come courting Laura, but Laura lives in a small world, the center of which is her collection of little glass animals. Her favorite is the unicorn. Tom, now the man of the household, feels he must always protect his sister. He's a writer, dreamer, and warehouse clerk. When life gets too heavy, he goes to the movies. Tom plans to join the merchant marines.

See *The Glass Menagerie,* Tennessee Williams

WINGO, TOM

Tough on the outside, hurting on the inside, this irreverent househusband comes from a family of emotional cripples. His marriage is crumbling; he embarrasses his kids. The poor white trash son of a shrimper-with-a-temper and a Lady Macbeth–like mother, he "hates women because he was raised by a woman, and hates men because he was raised by a man." He's an English teacher and high school football coach, now unemployed in both capacities, and also a lover of language "with the ability to lie without remorse." He has an attraction for failure, and, though something of a feminist, remains in chauvinistic South Carolina in a futile attempt to "fix my childhood by making my adult life wonderful." When his twin sister, Savannah, attempts suicide, he travels to New York to battle and then fall in love with her psychiatrist, **Susan Lowenstein**. After his own sessions with Lowenstein, he reveals a horrific family secret and finally makes peace with his past. "I am a teacher, a coach, and a well-loved man."

See *The Prince of Tides,* Pat Conroy

WINNFIELD, JULES

A hit man and enforcer, based in Inglewood, California. His boss is California crime magnate **Marsellus Wallace**. Jules has a penchant for citing the text of Ezekiel 25:17 before executing a victim. Despite his bloody calling and temper, he actually has a longing for higher things: spiritual enlightenment and a sense of greater purpose to his existence. He is absolutely without fear.

See *Pulp Fiction*

WINSTON, DALLAS

Arrested for the first time at age ten, "Dally" is the one hardened thug in a gang of teenage "greasers." He helps **Johnny Cade** and **Ponyboy Curtis** when they need to hide from the law after an accidental killing. "His eyes were blue, blazing ice, cold with a hatred of the world."

See *The Outsiders,* S. E. Hinton

WINTER, HENRY

He's got the mind of an austere English gentleman, trapped in the hulking body of an American college student. A classics major, Henry remains aloof from the petty antics of the general student body at Hampden College. Even within his closed circle of intellectual friends, he has a threatening mysteriousness about him, particularly to the loose-lipped **Edmund "Bunny" Corcoran**.

See *The Secret History,* Donna Tartt

WINTHORPE, LOUIS, III

This Philadelphia blue-blood snob works as an investment banker for **Randolph** and **Mortimer Duke**. His employers put him through hell in order to satisfy their curiosity and see which of them will win a one-dollar bet. Louis sinks quickly to the bottom of the social barrel, where he is found and rescued by kindly hooker **Ophelia**. His previous, privileged life irreparably destroyed by the Dukes's callous game, Louis learns a few truths about the important things in life, and emerges from his ordeal a stronger and better person. Richer, too.

See *Trading Places*

THE WIZARD

The ruler of Oz, he's seemingly very imposing and powerful. But seeing isn't always believing, and you can't always judge a book by its cover. Moreover, an empty can makes the loudest noise. Get the idea? **Dorothy Gale** and her dog, Toto, eventually do. But he means well.

See *The Wizard of Oz*, L. Frank Baum

WOJOHOWICZ, STANLEY

"Wojo" to his friends, this detective at New York's 12th Precinct looks like a Teamster, but he's a real softie at heart, even if he's not too bright. Constantly aggravated by people's reaction to his surname ("Just like it sounds. Wojohowicz."), he's still generally of good humor—although he can get riled. A hunt-and-peck typist.

See *Barney Miller*

WOLFE, NERO

As well known for his corpulence as he is for his brilliance at solving crimes, private detective Wolfe loves gourmet food and his greenhouse full of orchids as much as he detests exercise. Fortunately he has his assistant Archie Goodwin, a sprightly, young man-about-town, to run his errands for him.

See *The Rubber Band*, Rex Stout

WONKA, WILLY

The quirky owner of a renowned candy factory, which contains fabulous features like a chocolate river and a psychedelic train ride. The work force is made up of strange-hued dwarfs called Oompah-loompahs. After he conducts a contest in which several children are given the opportunity to tour his factory, Willie chooses **Charlie Bucket** to take part in his candy empire.

See *Charlie and the Chocolate Factory*, Roald Dahl

WOO, JING-MEI "JUNE"

June, whose parents left China bent on finding a new life in America, has spent her life in an effort at total assimilation—turning her back on her heritage and becoming more American than any fifth-generation San Franciscan. But she finally learns about her mother's painful life in China and, with this knowledge, seeks a new balance between her family's past and her own present and comes to accept what and whom she comes from.

See *The Joy Luck Club*, Amy Tan

WOOD, JANET

This smart, tough-as-nails brunette lives with **Chrissy Snow**, a vacuous blonde whom she envies for her ability to attract men, and **Jack Tripper**, who lusts after Chrissy—and from whom she must protect Chrissy.

See *Three's Company*

WOOD, LORENA

Lorena is a right pretty young woman, and about all the little village of Lonesome Dove has in the way of scenery. She's a lady of easy virtue, and despite the fact that she has no competition whatever in Lonesome Dove, she wants out in the worst way. Her dream is to go to San Francisco, where the action and money are. If her choices in men weren't so bad, she'd be there already.

See *Lonesome Dove*, Larry McMurtry

WOODHOUSE, ROSEMARY

This shy, pretty, young housewife has just moved into a Manhattan apartment with her husband, an aspiring actor. The couple is befriended by **Minnie Castavet** and her husband, their nosy neighbors. The Castavets become a fixture in their lives, indeed to a much greater extent than she would like...but it's hard to dislike the Castavets, who try so hard to please. And Rosemary is too kind to be rude to them, or anybody else. More than anything, she is a woman with a very strong maternal instinct.

See *Rosemary's Baby*, Ira Levin

WOODRUFF, SARAH

Nicknamed "Tragedy," and thought by locals to have been driven mad by an unfaithful lover, she captures the heart of a young, free-thinking aristocrat in 1867 Dorset. "(Her) clothes were black. The wind moved them, but the figure stood motionless, staring, staring out to sea...."

See *The French Lieutenant's Woman*, John Fowles

WOOSTER, BERTRAM "BERTIE"

The sincere and well-intentioned but hopelessly dimwitted scion of an upper-class English family, Wooster lives the bachelor life in his tony W1 London flat with **Jeeves**, his gentleman's personal gentleman, or valet. Wooster's view of his world is often a far cry from reality. When he is not being harangued by his harridan Aunt Agatha, Wooster often finds himself in the cross fire of friends' romantic and get-rich-quick schemes, not to mention his own occasional itch for matrimony. He is invariably rescued from these misadventures by the ever-resourceful Jeeves. Wooster is a member of the aptly named Drones Club, where he often takes lunch and hobnobs with friends and fellow members, such as Gussie Finknottle, Tuppy Glossop, Bingo Little, and Sippy Sipperly.

See *The World of Jeeves*, P. G. Wodehouse

WORF

Passionate and complex, Worf is in many ways a classic Klingon warrior, but, as the first Klingon to serve aboard a Federation starship—the *Enterprise*—Worf has learned to mute his more bellicose instincts. Raised on Earth after his family was massacred, Worf knows humans but doesn't always understand them. He has a son, Alexander, and a romantic interest in **Deanna Troi**.

See *Star Trek: The Next Generation*

WORLEY, SID

Sid's an honorable southern boy, a straight arrow who's trying to fulfill the dreams abandoned at the death of his older brother. He's even engaged to his brother's girlfriend. He's determined to be a top-of-the-class naval officer, even if it kills him.

See *An Officer and a Gentleman*

WORRELL, ERNEST P.

Obnoxious, in-your-face personality, low, two-digit I.Q., but with oddly likable demeanor. Prone to a variety of troubles, which fall into his lap with great frequency and regularity. He's close personal friends with a guy named Vern. In the past he's been a summer camp counselor and saved Santa Claus but currently is in trouble because of a nefarious look-alike. "Know what I mean?"

See *Ernest Goes to Jail*

WORTH, MARY

A neighborly street peddler always into everybody's business. A bit plump, a bit gray, and every bit lovable, Mary is constantly arguing with cheapskates and fending off con men who try to weasel away her meager earnings. All the money from selling apples goes to making a better life for her disabled nephew Denny.

See *Mary Worth*

WOTTON, LORD HENRY

Erudite, cynically witty nineteenth-century-London libertine. With his worldly charm, he seduces **Dorian Gray** into following in his hedonistic, amoral footsteps. Seemingly desires Dorian in a more-than-friendly way and gets quite jealous when he takes up with a girlfriend.

See *The Picture of Dorian Gray*, Oscar Wilde

WYATT

Born-to-be-wild biker, traveling across country on his motorcycle with friend **Billy**. Loves his dope, his bike, and the open air. In search of the "real America" but thus far not too crazy about what he's found. He loves freedom, but there's a cynical shell there, too.

See *Easy Rider*

Rosemary Woodhouse

WEAK LOUD TYPES

Barney Fife
Major Frank Burns
Shaggy

WYETH, MARIA

The beautiful and talented Maria skyrockets to fame as an actress and just as quickly plummets into alcoholism and depression. After suffering through a rocky marriage, a botched abortion, and the decline of her career, she assists a friend's suicide and lands in a mental hospital. When asked why she goes on living, her best answer is, "Why not?"

See *Play It as It Lays,* Joan Didion

X, MARY

Reluctant girlfriend of **Henry Spencer**. He lives with eccentric family somewhere in a gloomy, unreal, nameless city. She's the mother of a monstrous baby, probably fathered by Henry. Prone to tears and disappearances.

See *Eraserhead*

YADWIGA

Gentile Polish woman, living in Brooklyn, New York, with her husband, **Herman Broder**, whom she saved from the Nazis during World War II. She doesn't speak much English, leaving her somewhat isolated and unable to do much about Herman's neglectful ways toward her. She is still entirely devoted to her husband despite his tyranny and philandering.

See *Enemies: A Love Story*

YAKUSHOVA, LENA "NINOTCHKA"

This grim, strait-laced Communist envoy is captivated and seduced by Paris. Her staunch mistrust of perfume, gowns, flowers, and delicious food is worn down by the city of light and the efforts of a charming playboy. At first, she's immune to the delights of the French capital, insisting on eating dull food and visiting landmarks of academic interest only. But as the atmosphere warms her chilly Russian demeanor, she loses her hard edges and softens. Her once-steadfast commitment to the Communist cause becomes fuzzy, and she finds herself making compromises that she never would have before.

See *Ninotchka*

YATES, ROWDY

As second-in-command to trail boss **Gil Favor**, Yates is a tried-and-true assistant on their cattle drives across the West; he eventually takes over as trail boss and organizes his own drive.

See *Rawhide*

YENTL

She's a young Jewish girl who wants to be a scholar. But Orthodox Jewish girls are not permitted to study books, so she disguises herself as a boy and is accepted by a community of scholars. To complicate matters, Yentl falls in love with one of them, Avigdor, who thinks she's a boy and is himself in love with another girl, Hadass. Hadass's father will not let Avigdor marry her, so the boy convinces Yentl to marry his girlfriend, hoping that at least he can visit the two people he cares for most deeply. Yentl and Hadass are wed, but ultimately the truth must be told.

See *Yentl*

YOSEMITE SAM

A pint-sized sharpshooter with a cowboy hat as big as he is, and an attitude for tough-talking that often gets him in trouble. He's from Yosemite in California, but he talks like a Texan. Wears a black mask across his eyes. Sam once nearly married the same rabbit that he's always trying—in vain—to shoot. When he's not a cowboy, he spends time chasing his nemesis disguised as a pirate, a knight, or a gladiator.

See *Merrie Melodies*

CAPTAIN YOSSARIAN

Not-crazy-enough bombardier of the 256th Squadron, stationed in Italy during World War II. He doesn't want to fly any more combat missions because "it's too dangerous." Yossarian implores everyone who'll listen to ground him. Frantic because thousands of people he's never met are "trying to kill me," he'll do anything to get out of the war. He invents a nonexistent liver condition to spend time in the hospital and conveniently runs a low-grade fever of 101 degrees. He won't eat fruit and refuses to follow orders because "it doesn't make a damned bit of difference who wins the war to someone who's dead." Yossarian delights in giving pompous **Colonel Cathcart** a hard time. He calls God a "bumbling country bumpkin." Though he's cynical and callous, he does care deeply about his fellow soldiers. When a young radio gunner loses his guts, Yossarian loses his nerve and stops

wearing clothes. He receives a medal for heroism stark naked. He also claims there is a dead man in his tent. He's caught in a "Catch-22"—anyone sane enough to want to get out of combat duty isn't really crazy—and decides to desert and flee to Sweden. "I'm not running away from my responsibilities. I'm running to them."
See *Catch-22* and *Closing Time,* Joseph Heller

YOUNGER, LENA "MAMA"

A mother and a maid. Born the daughter of sharecroppers, Lena has become the matriarch in an apartment in which live three generations of Youngers. The moral center of their world, she unequivocally demands they respect each other, God, and God's name. She has two children: a daughter, Beneatha, who dreams of becoming a doctor, and a married son, **Walter Lee**, who chafes at the fact that his dreams are out of synch with his circumstances. Lena dreams of a garden. While not an activist, she speaks her mind and follows her conscience, no matter the tide of opinion. She is recently widowed and must now decide what is best to do with the insurance money. "Seems like God didn't see fit to give the black man nothing but dreams—but He did give us children to make them dreams seem worth while."
See *A Raisin in the Sun,* Lorraine Hansberry

YOUNGER, WALTER LEE "BROTHER"

A chauffeur by trade and a dreamer by nature, Walter Lee lives in frustrating awareness of the gap between what he feels is his due and the actuality of the world and its limitations. He lives with his wife and son in his mother's apartment. As an African American, he does not have the same access to the American Dream as the people for whom he works. Brother dreams of making deals, of gaining material wealth, and thereby getting respect. He desperately wants to give to the people he loves all that they deserve; and he is terribly frustrated by his inability to do it. "And you—ain't you bitter, man? Don't you see no stars gleaming that you can't reach up and grab? You happy? Bitter? Man, I'm a volcano. Bitter? Here I am a giant—surrounded by ants! Ants who can't even understand what I'm talking about."
See *A Raisin in the Sun,* Lorraine Hansberry

ZACH

Award-winning director of Broadway musicals, currently casting his new show. Likes to remain unseen while auditioning dancers. He prefers to know something personal about his performers, feels it gives him some insight when making final choices. Formerly involved with **Cassie**.
See *A Chorus Line*

DR. ZARKOV

Scientific genius whose knowledge often proves useful to his courageous friend **Flash Gordon**.
See *Flash Gordon*

ZAWISTOWSKA, SOPHIE

She is a shy Polish Catholic beauty with a mysterious past, who lives with **Nathan Landau**, a charming but hot-tempered Jew. In the same Brooklyn building lives **Stingo**, a young southern WASP and aspiring writer who, over time, becomes her confidant. She allows Stingo to fall in love with her and become enraged at Nathan's abuse of her, before finally revealing the truth about her life as a Catholic survivor of the Nazi takeover of Poland. Her staying with Nathan has much to do with her own past, as both a victim of Nazi atrocity and the daughter of a Nazi sympathizer. She feels tremendous guilt at what happened to Jews in Europe, which has contributed to Nathan's mental disintegration. But her personal guilt, it turns out, has deeper and more horrible roots, as Stingo eventually learns.
See *Sophie's Choice,* William Styron

ZELIG, LEONARD

The Man Without a Personality. He suffers from an obscure condition called a Chameleon Complex. This makes him change his appearance to fit into any situation, because he feels safest when he's just like the rest of the crowd. So he becomes, by turns, obese, an African American jazz musician, a rabbi, a WASP, etc. He's also the subject of intense study and is analyzed by noted intellectuals like Saul Bellow and Susan Sontag. Treated by **Dr. Eudora Fletcher**.
See *Zelig*

MR. ZERO

The model corporate man, Mr. Zero has been a

bookkeeper in the same firm for twenty-five years. He has never made any trouble, neither at work nor at home. As a reward for his loyalty, he's sentenced to death and executed for killing his boss, when the latter plans to replace him with an adding machine.

See *The Adding Machine,* Elmer Rice

ZHIVAGO, YURII ANDREIEVICH

A man caught on the rocks of Mother Russia, battered by the tides of history. Orphaned at ten, Zhivago is sent to Moscow to study medicine. After attaining his degree, he marries Antonina Gromeko. Despite his marriage, his life is intertwined with that of **Lara Guishar**, the great love of his life. Zhivago, a dreamer and romantic, writes a series of poems about Lara, a work that takes a place in the higher works of Russian literature. He serves as a doctor in the Czar's army during World War I, and then for Communist partisans during the Russian Civil War. Zhivago has a son, Sashenka, and a daughter, Tania. Following Lara's departure to Vladivostok, Zhivago becomes depressed and dissolute. He dies in Moscow in 1929.

See *Doctor Zhivago,* Boris Pasternak

ZIFFEL, FRED

A humorless, hardworking farmer and the neighbor of the **Douglases**. He can't help but be suspicious of their foreign, cityfolk ways. Always walking in to find Oliver or Lisa doing something unusual. Thin, craggy-faced, and weatherworn, Fred Ziffel rarely smiles. But he's immensely proud of his genius, humanlike pig, Arnold.

See *Green Acres*

ZIGGY

Short, bald, and big-nosed, Ziggy goes through life with a smile on, his only companions a dog, a duck, a fish, and a plant. Ziggy wears a long shirt, with no pants. He is being treated by a psychiatrist for no reason in particular. Was once told by a wise man on a mountain top that the entire meaning of life is "if it itches, scratch it."

See *Ziggy,* Tom Wilson

ZIGGY STARDUST

Gender-bending rock star of the 1970s who bridged the gap between psychedelia and punk. A mean guitarist, Ziggy hit it big with his band, the Spiders from Mars. He was the biggest of the glam rockers, flamboyant and outrageous, wearing makeup and futuristic clothing. Increasingly captivated by his own myth, Ziggy finally became a parody of himself and self-destructed—just another rock 'n' roll suicide.

See *The Rise and Fall of Ziggy Stardust and the Spiders from Mars,* David Bowie

ZIPPY THE PINHEAD

Blithe, silly, and sweetly optimistic. This is the idiot as a savant of some kind. He's decidedly un-neurotic. With his sidekick Griffy, he explores the mad labyrinth of modern life, usually finding some unexpected, oddly skewed charm. "I'm dancing with Fred Astaire and I'm not even on drugs."

See *Zippy*

ZIZENDORF

Living in a German town after World War II, Zizendorf is a conniving megalomaniac who greatly resembles a certain notorious German dictator. He wants to return his people to what he believes to be their rightful place as world leaders, with himself at their head, naturally. Accordingly, he plots with a group of escapees from an insane asylum to kill an American soldier assigned to oversee the region.

See *The Cannibal,* John Hawkes

ZORBA, ALEXIS

An earthy, sixty-year-old Greek who, through the strength of his passionate personality, breathes new life into a younger, cerebral narrator, "the Boss." Living with unquenchable intensity, he turns what could have been a stale mining venture on Crete into Dionysian adventure. He takes an elderly courtesan as his mistress, and prods the Boss into an affair with the village widow. The Boss sees him at first as a lion or wolf, then as a primitive Greek demigod. Zorba knows that everything—wood, stones, wine, earth—has a soul. He dances whenever he needs an outlet for great emotions, revealing his deepest self. "He suddenly made tremendous bounds into the air, as if he wished to conquer the laws of nature and fly away. One felt that in this old body of his there was a soul struggling to carry away this flesh and cast itself like a meteor into the darkness."

See *Zorba the Greek*, Nikos Kazantzakis

ZORIN, MAX

A maniacal billionaire computer entrepreneur *not* from Redmond, Washington. As a child, he took part in some Nazi genetic engineering experiments, which have left him somewhat psychotic. He's intent on making his computer chip manufacturing company the largest in the world and will use both his brains and his maniacal tendencies to do it. Zorin owns a vast estate in England, where he races prize thoroughbreds.

See *A View to a Kill*

ZORRO, DON DIEGO DE LA VEGA

A Spanish nobleman and former fencing champion better known simply by his last name, Zorro is a masked renegade swordsman whose trademark is to slash a Z on the clothes of his enemies before stealing away into the night. He is always on the run from bounty hunters since a hefty price is on his head. With the aid of his mute but ingenious assistant Bernardo, Zorro usually manages to stay one step ahead of his pursuers. When all else fails he lets his sword do the talking, followed by a note written in verse: "My sword is a flame / to right every wrong / so heed my name."

See *Zorro*

ZUCCO, DANNY

A slick, singing 1950s greaser, Zucco is different from his fellow T-Birds at Rydell High because he is a dreamer. His summer romance with **Sandy** is strained upon returning to school by his image-conscious behavior. "You see Sandy, I got this image…"

See *Grease*

ZUCKERMAN, ANDREA

Brilliant, bespectacled Andrea always has her studies and future in mind, while her friends are more interested in parties and dating. Pretends to live with her grandmother to get into Beverly Hills High, although she's really from the Valley. Edits the school newspaper. Once in college, she gets pregnant and marries her boyfriend, a UCLA law student named Jesse.

See *Beverly Hills 90210*

ZUCKERMAN, NATHAN

A Jewish American novelist whose career begins with short stories which his family feels hold Jews up to ridicule, and proceeds to a best-seller that emphasizes its hero's unflagging lust. His father's dying comment to him is "Bastard!" and his dentist brother accuses him of causing both his parents' deaths. He tires of his notoriety, tries to escape to the anonymity of a "normal" calling, but realizes he needs to go on writing. "Hey, you do all that stuff in that book? With all those chicks? You are something else, man."

See *The Ghost Writer*, Philip Roth

INDEX

AUTHORS INDEX